TATTOO DELIRIUM

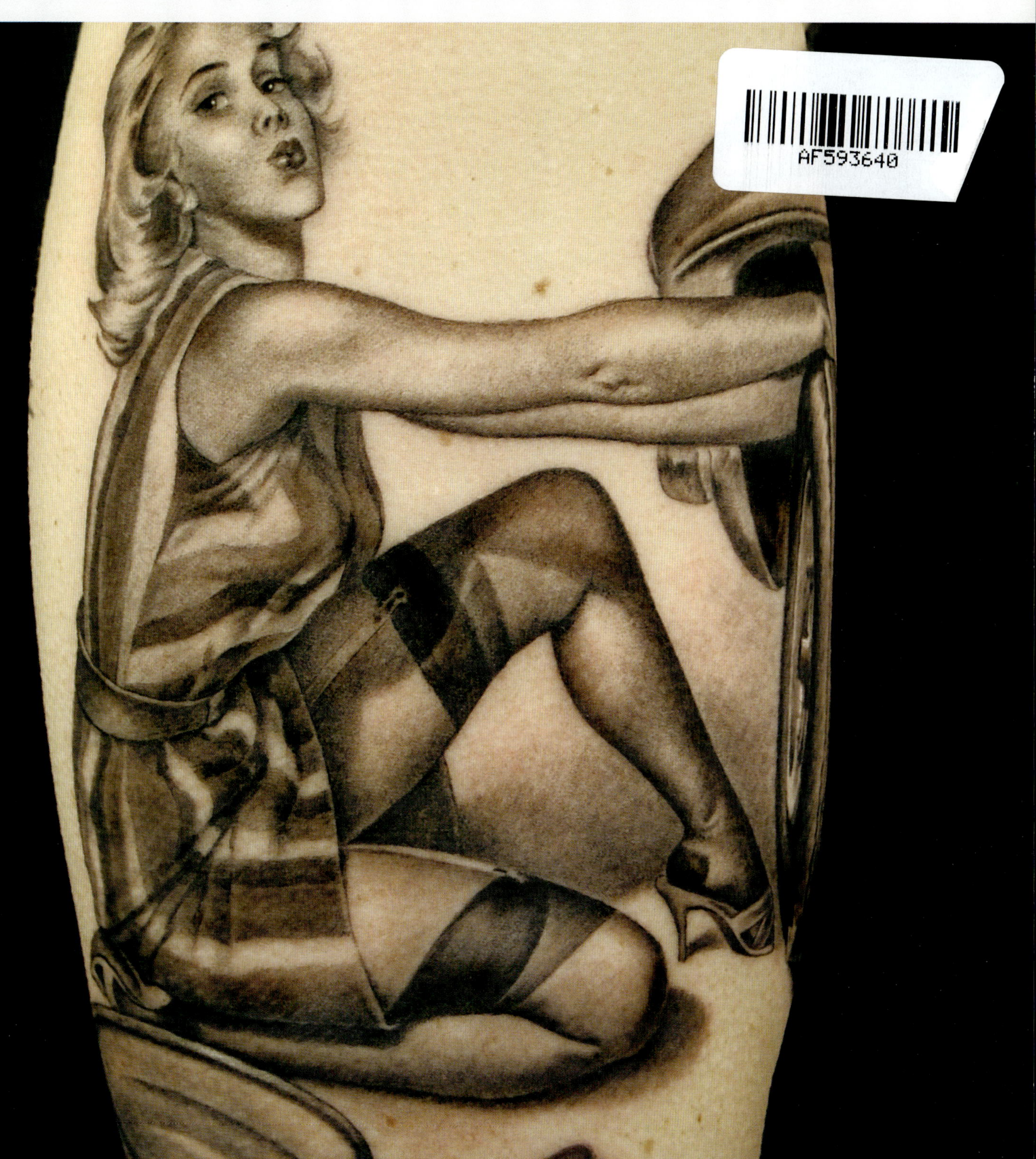

Tattoo Delirium

First published in 2009 by:
Collins Design
An Imprint of HarperCollins*Publishers*
10 East 53rd Street
New York, NY 10022
Tel: (212) 207-7000
Fax: (212) 207-7654
collinsdesign@harpercollins.com
www.harpercollins.com

Distributed throughout the world by
HarperCollins*Publishers*
10 East 53rd Street
New York, NY 10022
Fax: (212) 207-7654

Editor
Josep Mª Minguet

Author
Art direction, text, and layout
Eva Minguet

Translation
LocTeam

Library of Congress Control Number 2008943369

ISBN: 978-0-06-174032-9

Printed in Spain
First Printing, 2009

Cover artwork by Sunny Buick.
Page one artwork courtesy of Shane O'Neill.
Page three illustration courtesy of Sunny Buick.

TATTOO DELIRIUM

eva minguet

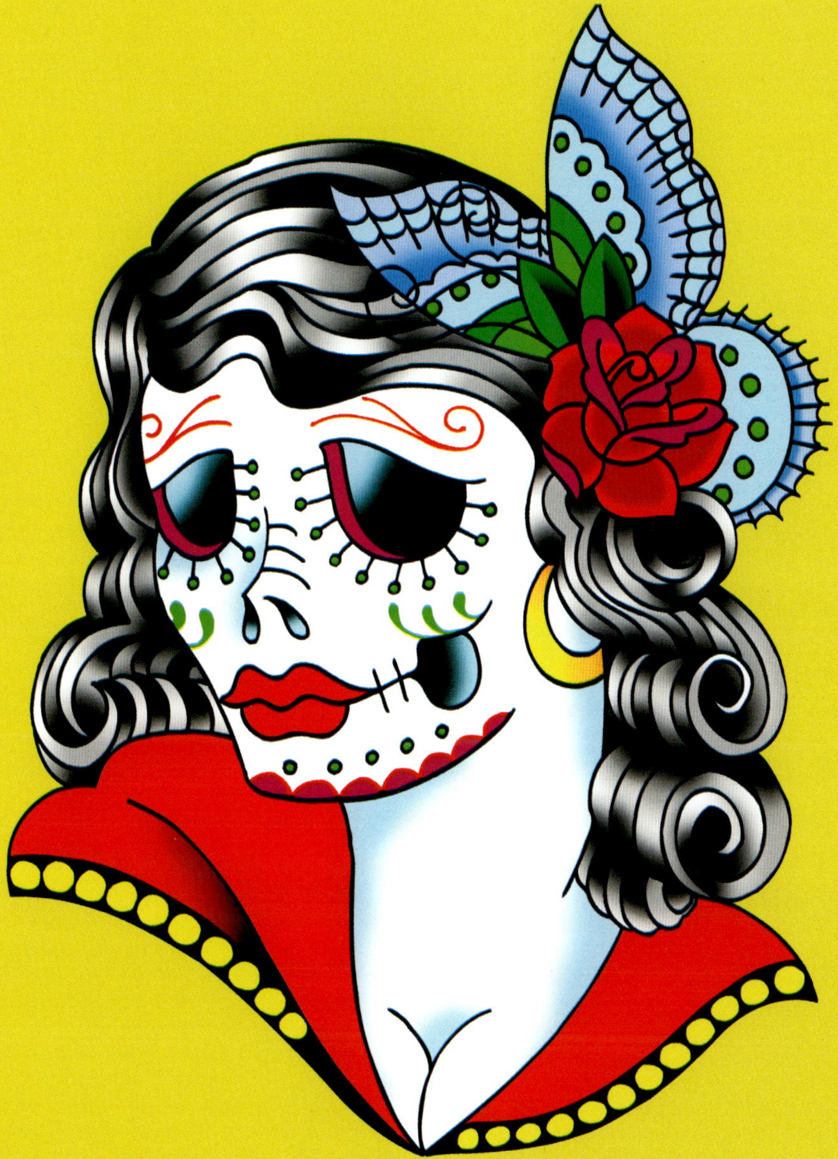

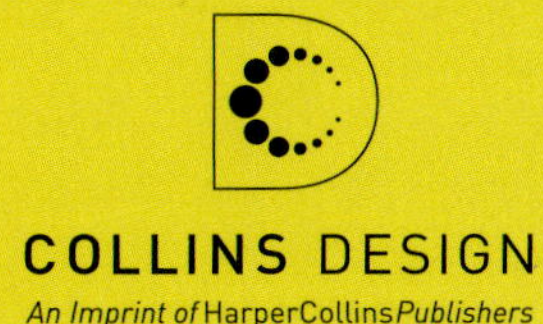

COLLINS DESIGN
An Imprint of HarperCollins*Publishers*

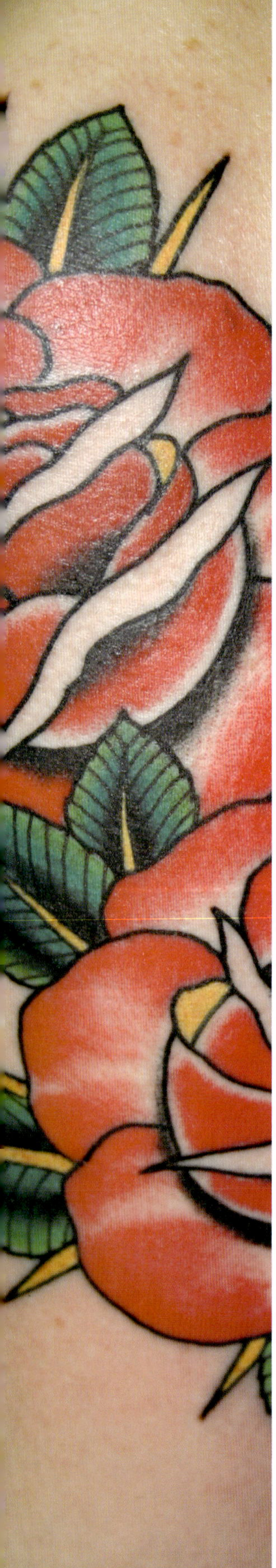

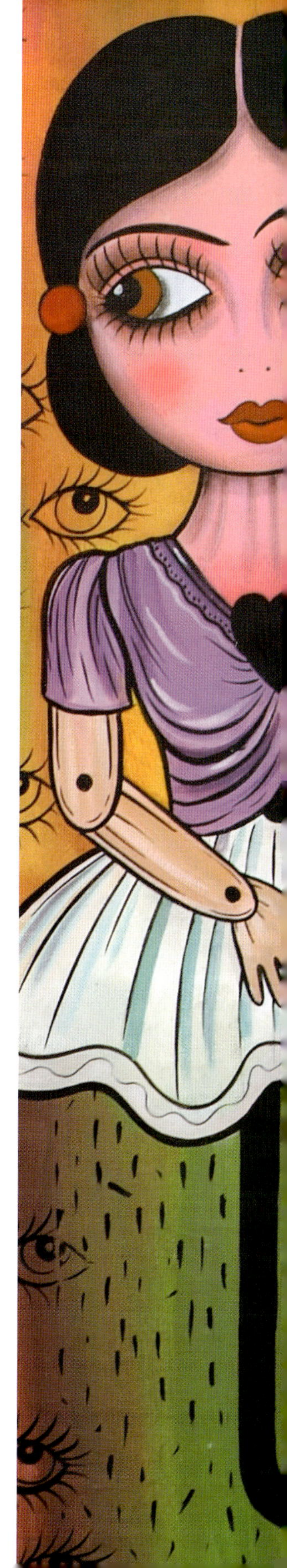

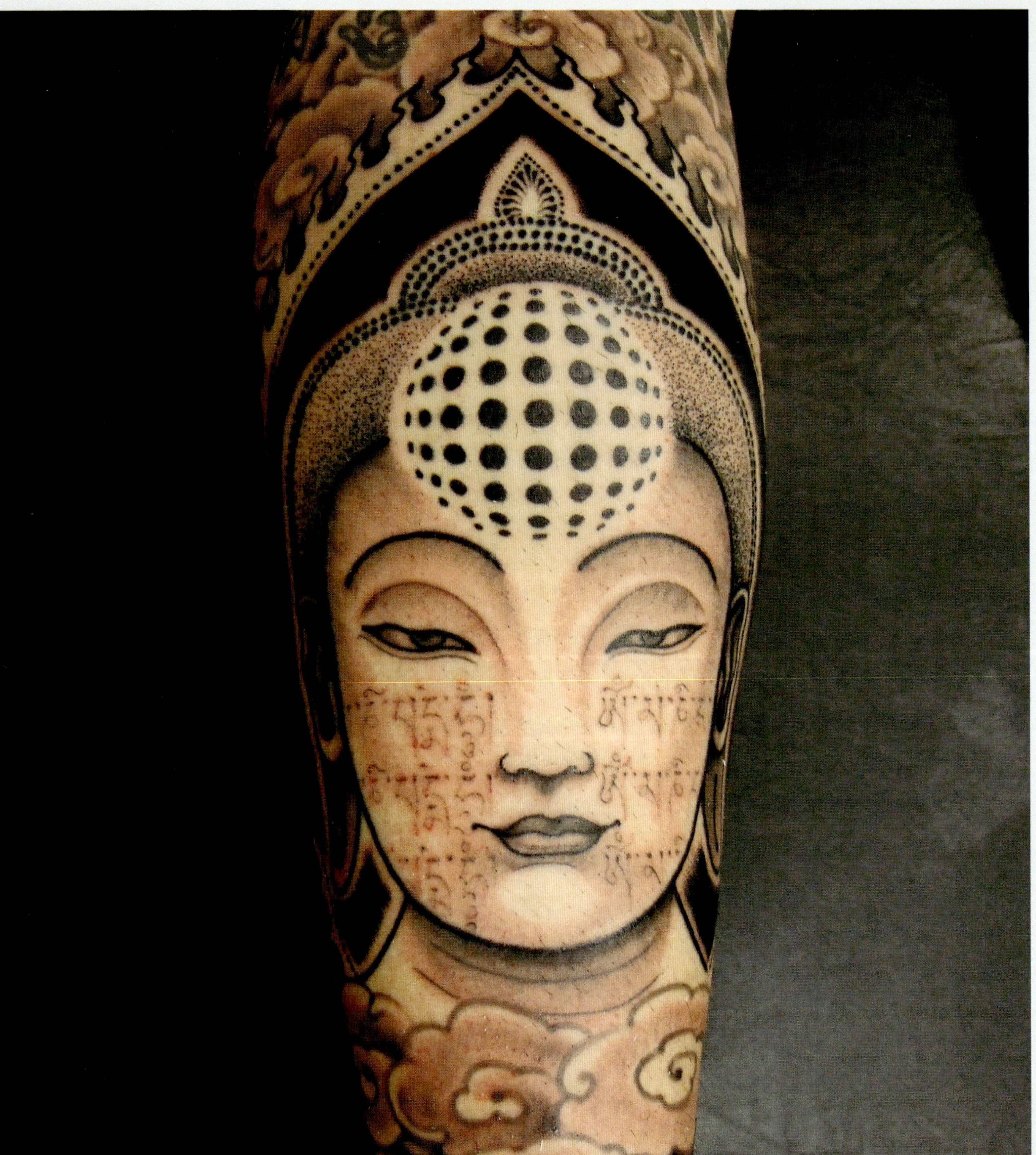

The world of tattoos is an unreal place. At one time, the tattoo was a symbol of rebellion and freedom for the counterculture, and currently it might be used as testament to a sense of personal change. Perhaps it is simply a reflection of popular trends.

We are, by default, part of a system of energies, and throughout our lives we feel the attraction of various influences. But there is no rule that explains why we mark our skin. In India, in acts of devotion to Lord Rama, the sadhus, or holy men, tattoo their bodies with the mantra, "Ram." This is an example of how we try to identify with our favorite characters. Each individual is quite different from everyone else, and we all have our own vision of our body and how we might change it. Fate will make each person find his or her own tattoo.

A tattoo can also be a catalyst for inner transformation. There are people who seek only the symbol, not the art, but ultimately everyone gets the tattoo he or she deserves. Some seek perfection, but others can't be bothered. Luck has a great deal to do with the end result.

I am familiar with the work of the other tattooists who appear in this book, and I think we all want to find a middle ground; a balance between technique and design, anatomy and legibility, beauty and tradition. Each of us, however, has a unique aesthetic vision of the style we portray: Japanese, old school, new school, tribal, neo-tribal, realistic, Chinese, and so on.

Despite everything we have learned, much more remains a mystery. Why do our clients get tattoos again and again despite the pain we inflict on them at each session? Might the power of art be stronger than the physical suffering that accompanies it? Could it be a sort of therapy? How can it be that human skin accepts the ink so well? How can it be that by making wounds with ink-filled needles we can achieve effects whose beauty would be impossible to attain through other means? Is it a miracle?

The following pages offer a chance to see some of these miracles on skin. I feel certain that many readers will change their perception of this art form, which is at once ages-old and forever young.

Jondix
STUDIO LTW, Barcelona

Left page artwork courtesy of Jondix.

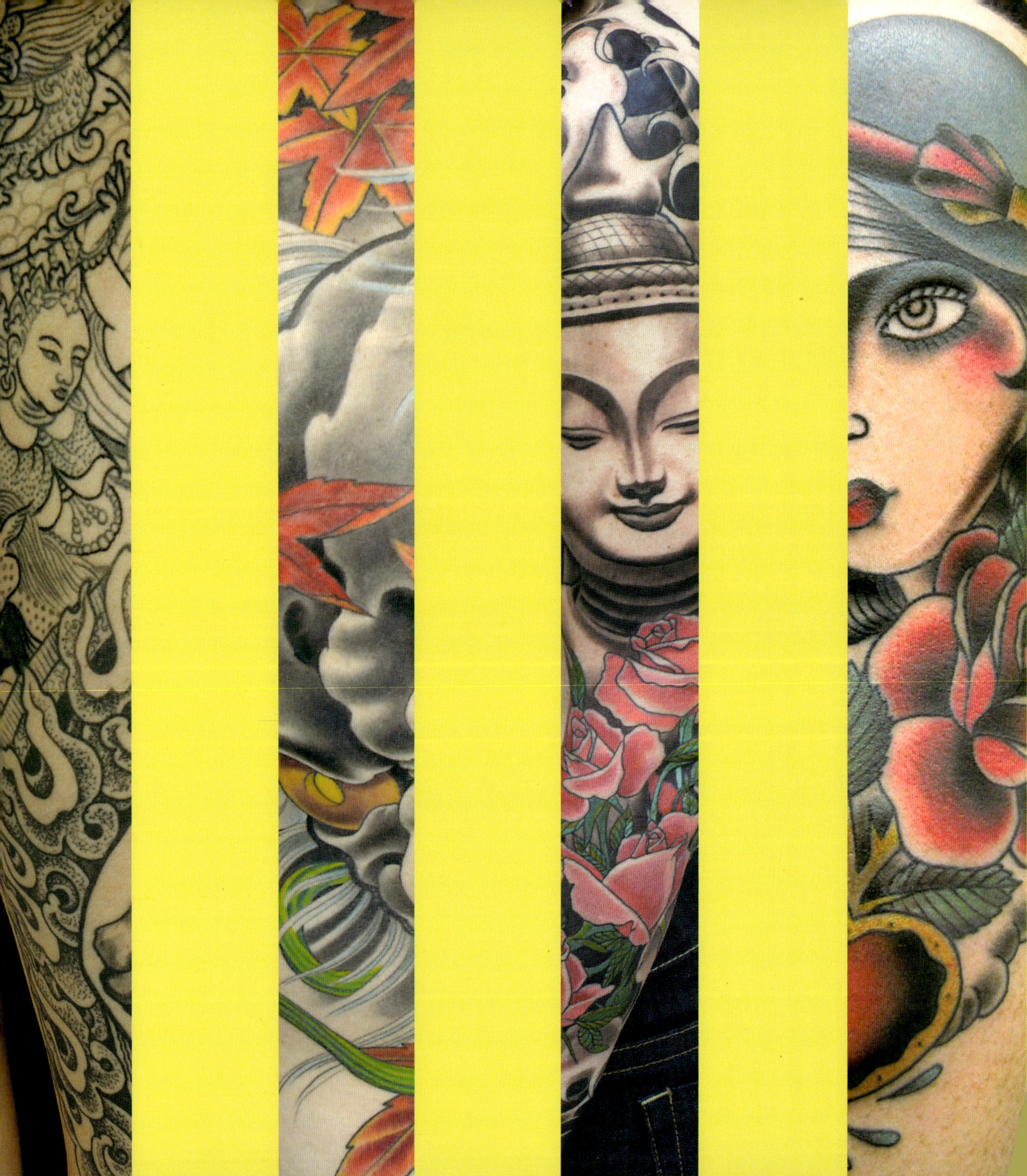

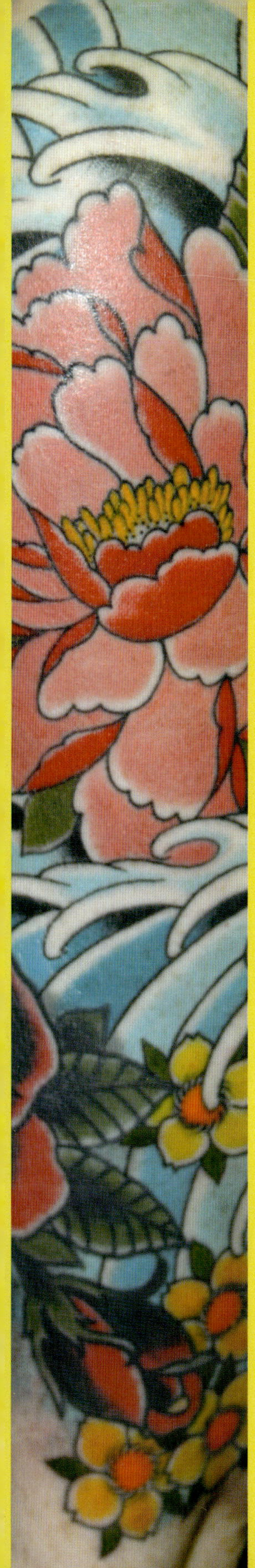

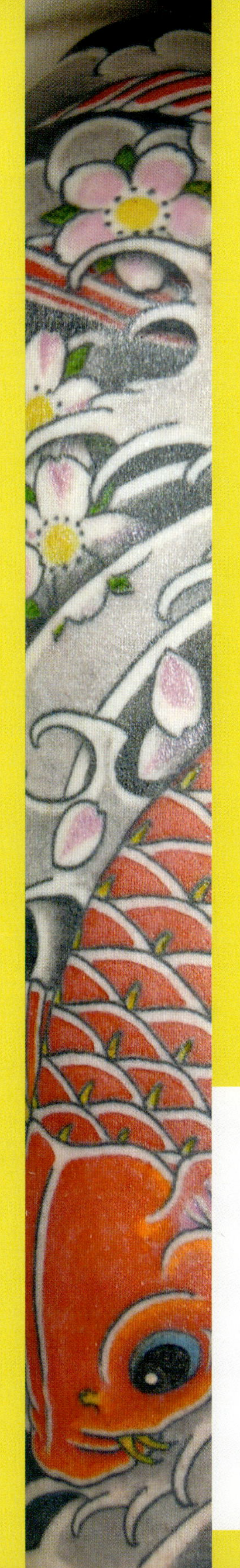

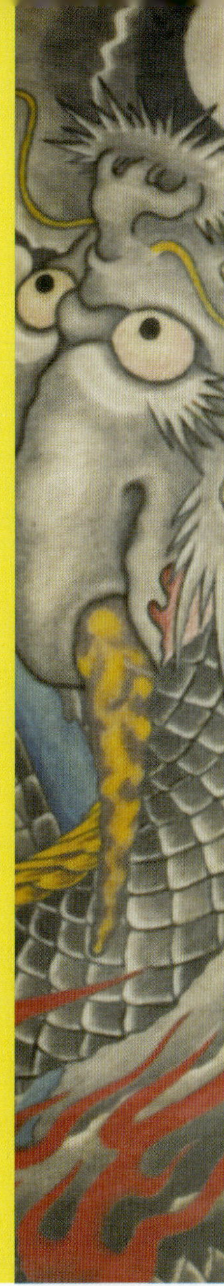

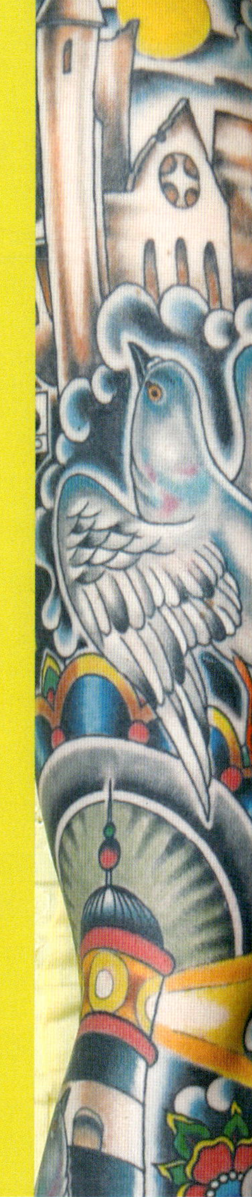

AN INTERVIEW WITH THE TATTOOERS

1. When did you start doing tattoo?
2. What is for you the tattoo world?
3. What is your tattoo style?
   (old school, Japanese, American, Celtic)
4. A little advice before you tattoo.
5. Where can we find you?

MISS ARIANNA

ITALY

1. I began as an apprentice. It was very hard! Then I worked and managed a tattoo shop not far my hometown before opening my first shop. During that time I never stopped learning, and even now I think there is always "room for improvement" in my art.

2. My passion, my work, my way of life!

3. My favorite tattoo style is traditional, maybe because it's like me: direct, clear and solid. It has a strength and stability not easy to find in other styles. It's a real tattoo! Without a doubt it is the style that satisfies me the most, both technically and graphically.

4. Remember, the tattooist is not merely a person who executes every customer's request, even the craziest ones!

5. My shop is called SKINWEAR—it is a big studio in the heart of downtown Rimini. I decided to open it in an apartment of an old palace from the 1700s. You can find me also at tattoo conventions all around the world.
   www.missarianna.com
   www.myspace.com/skinwear
   www.skinweartattooshop.com

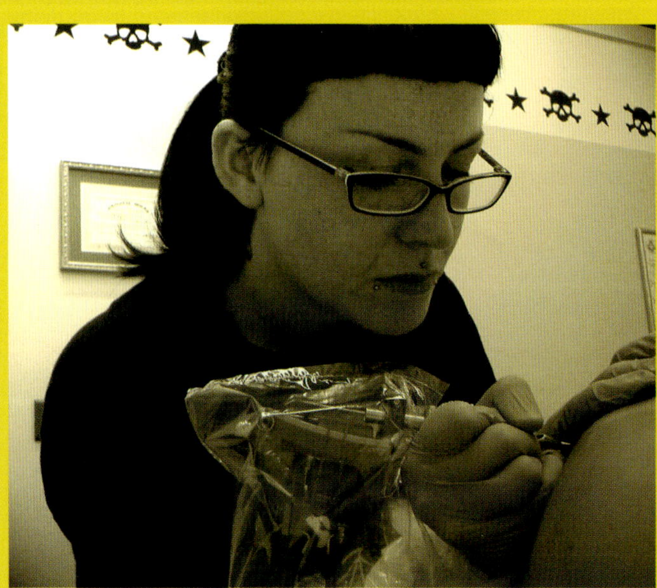

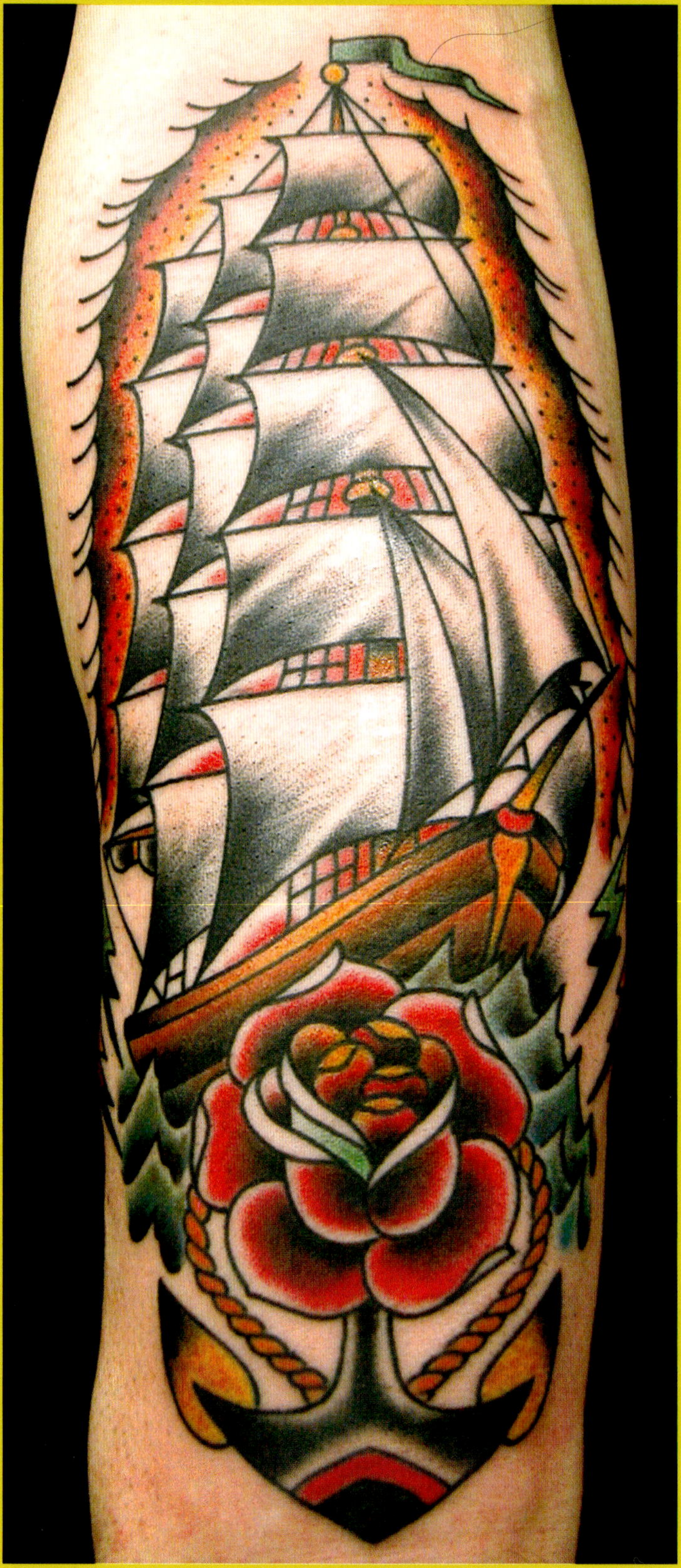

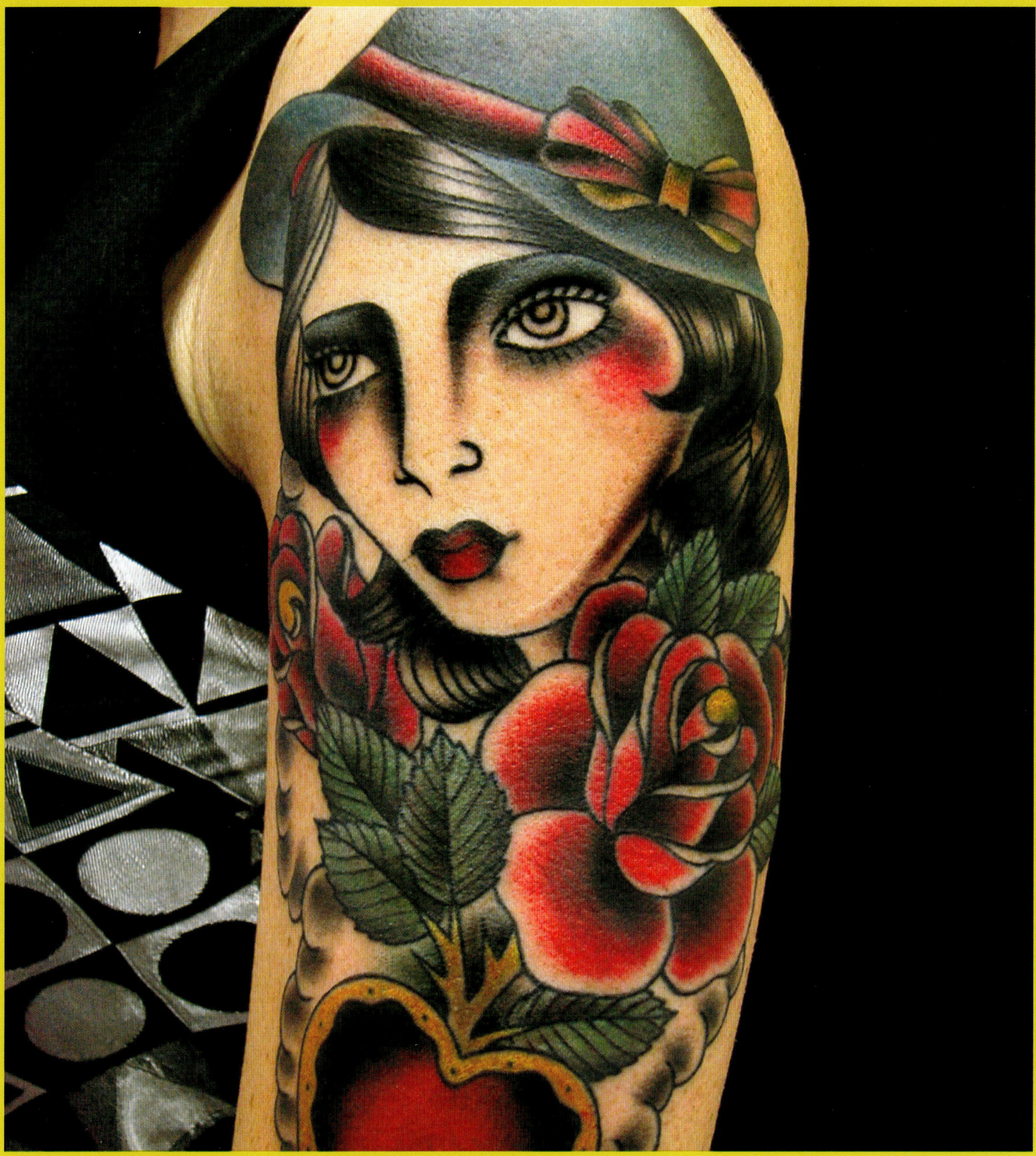

All images courtesy of Miss Arianna.

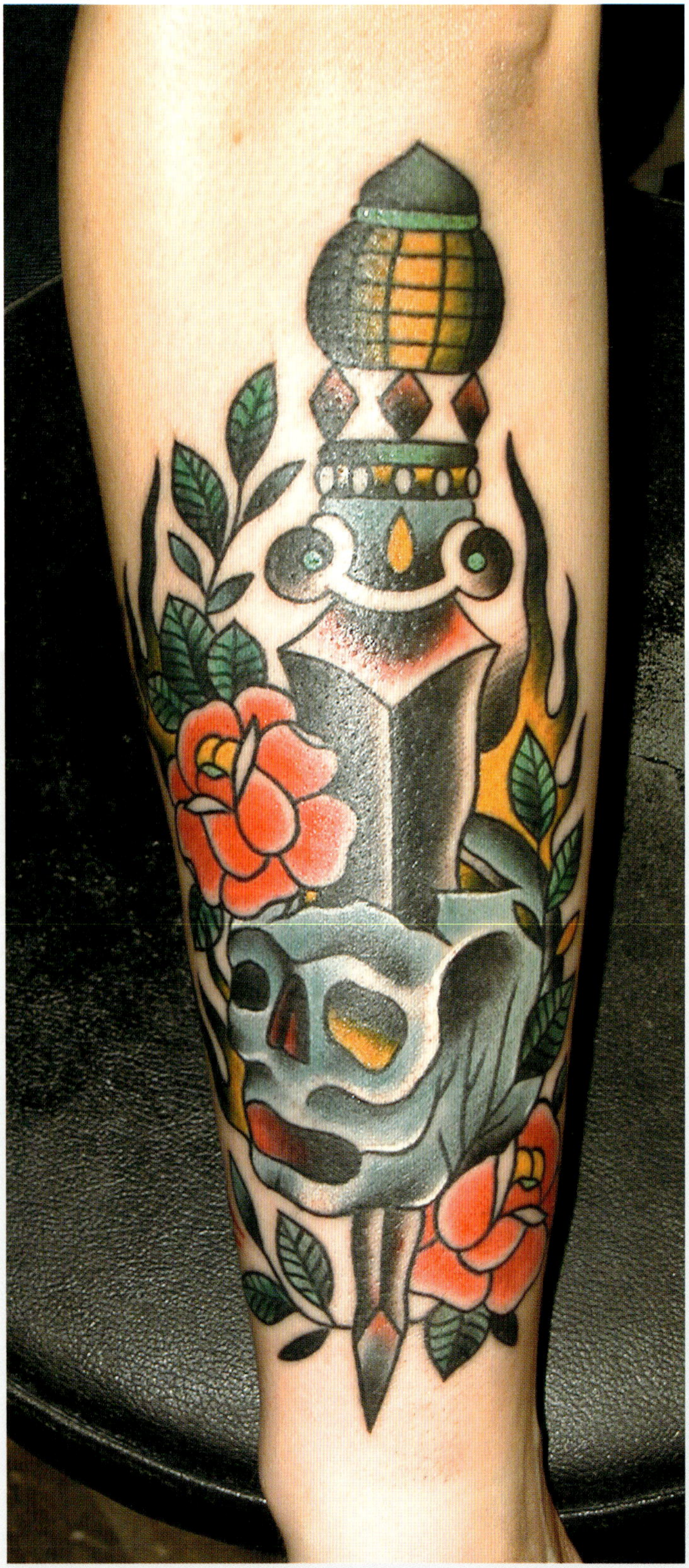

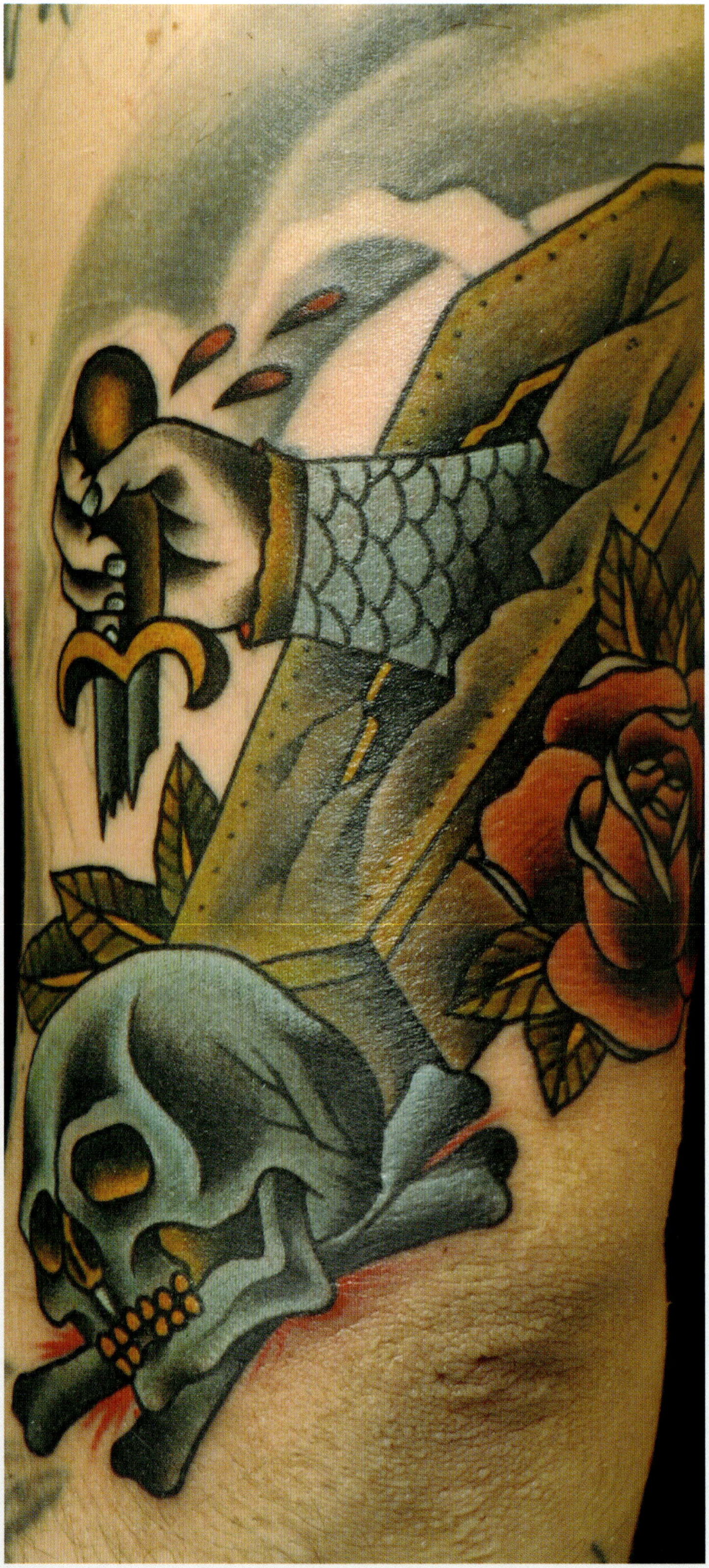

All designs on these pages by Miss Arianna.

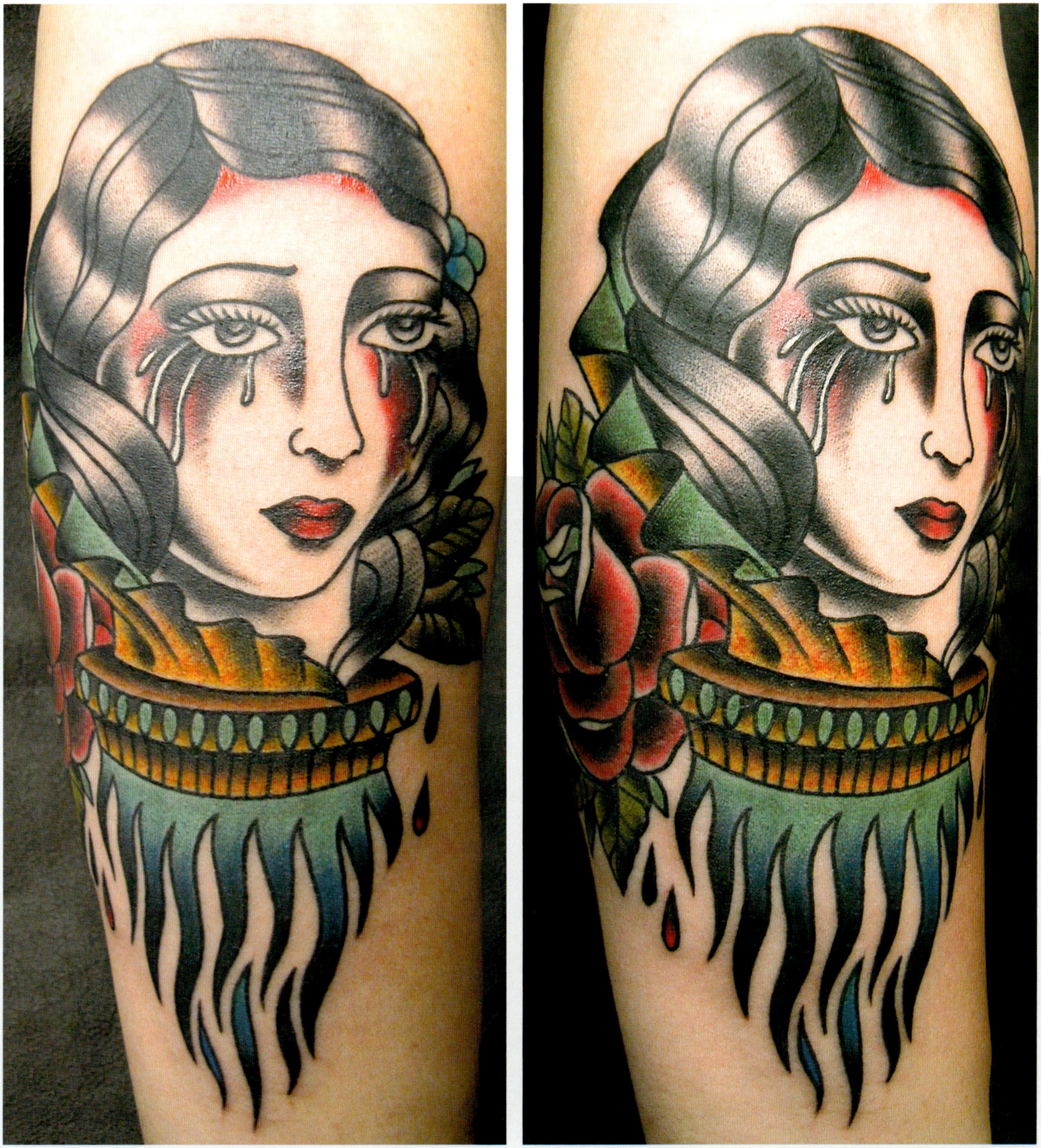

MISS ARIANNA

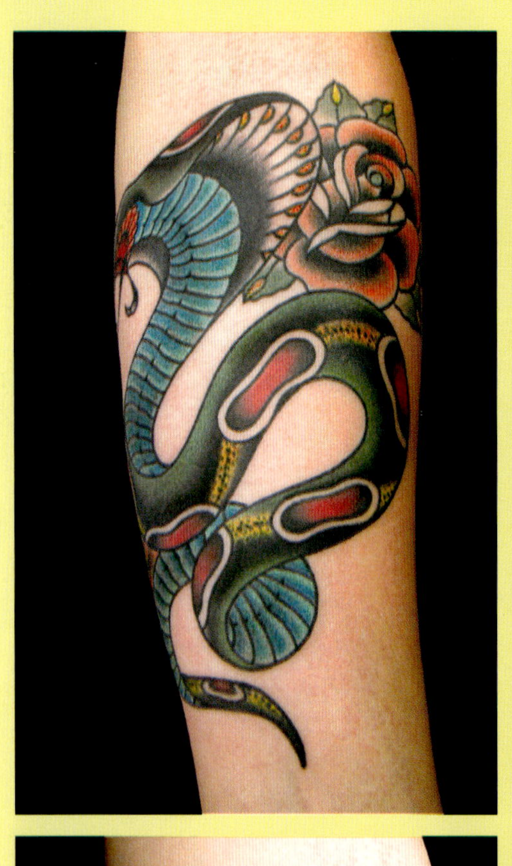

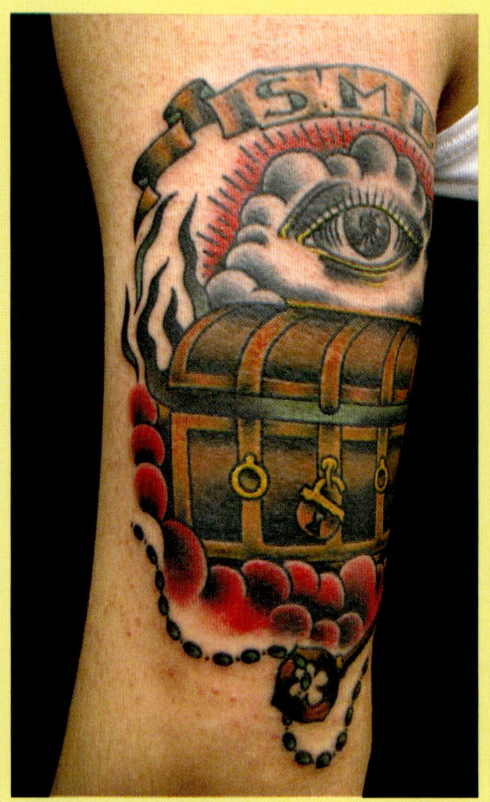

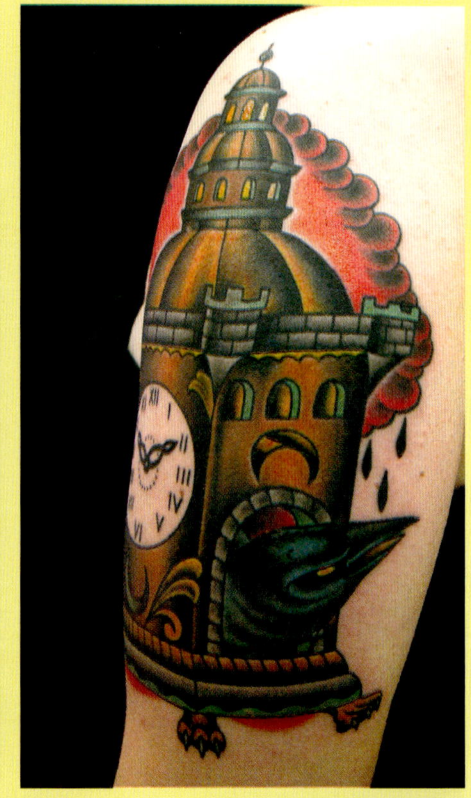

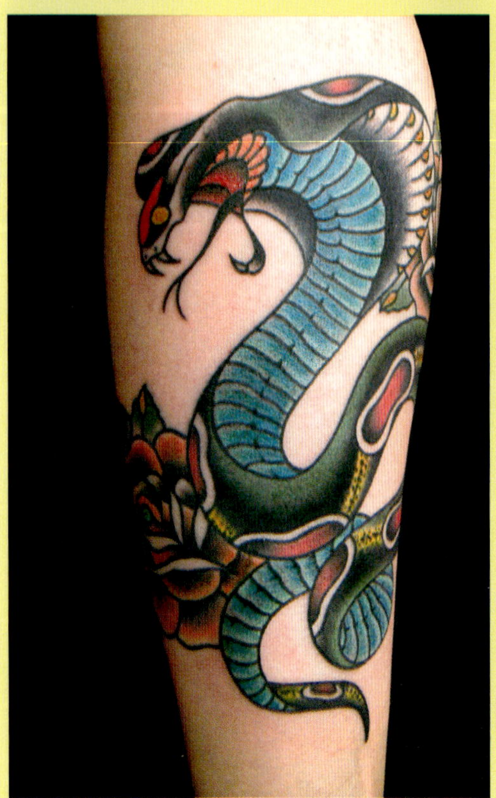

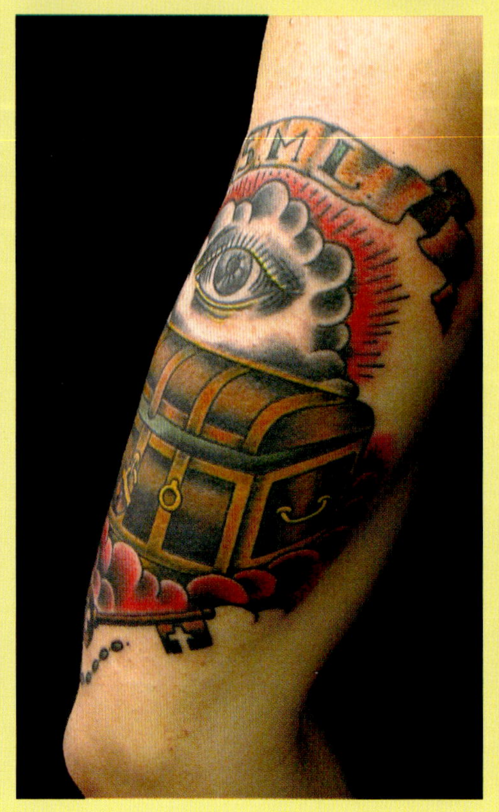

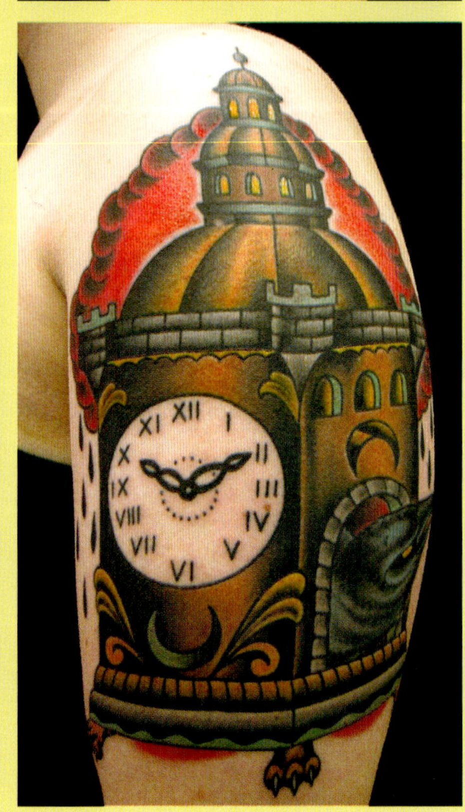

All images courtesy of Miss Arianna.

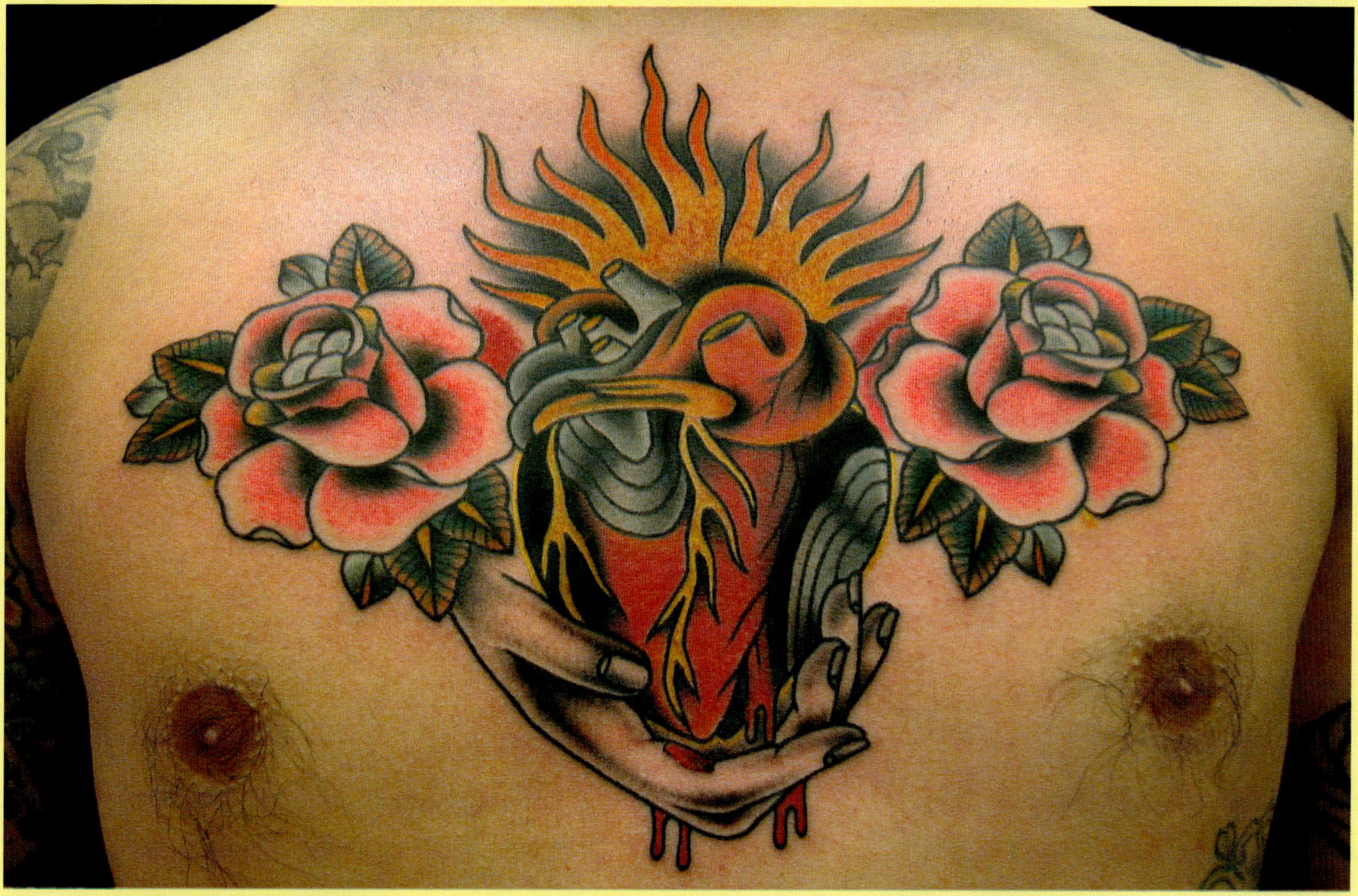

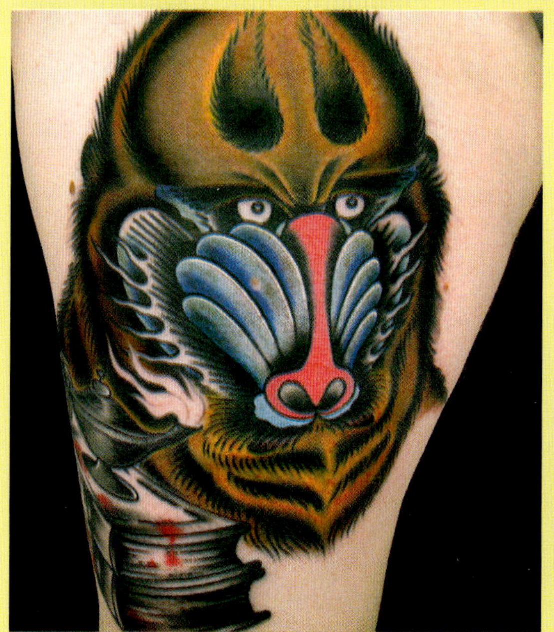

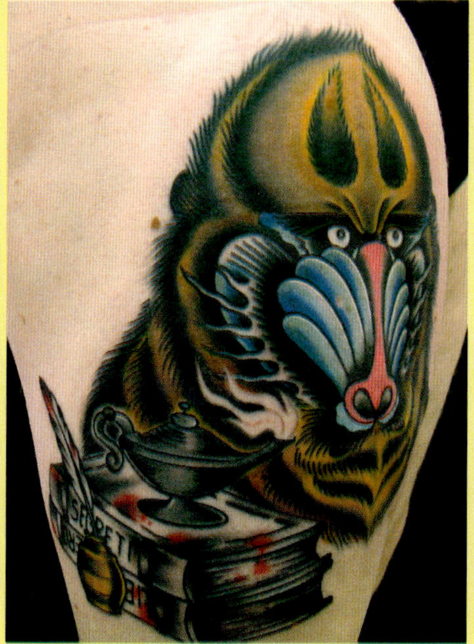

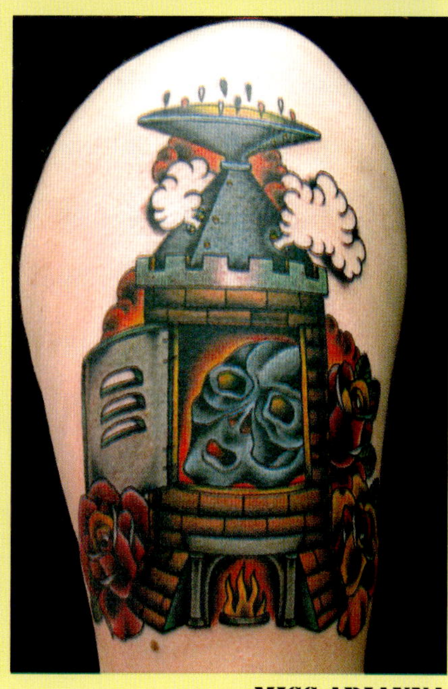

MISS ARIANNA

ALEX REINKE

AKA HORIKITSUNE

GERMANY

1. I started tattooing 13 years ago. I was 21 years old. Since the age of 14 I had had an interest in Japanese tattoos. I became a student of Horiyoshi III in 1999. Ever since then I've been on the long pathway to understanding what I'm really doing. In Japanese tattooing you need at least 30 years of studying on a daily basis, which makes me nothing more than a beginner right now.

2. It's kind of a lifestyle and quite a hard job. I am extremely thankful for the blessed life I can live because of tattooing, even though it does not leave a lot of space for anything else but tattooing. On the other hand, why would you want to do anything else?

3. Traditional Japanese tattooing.

4. Do your homework. Look closely at the artist's work. And ask yourself do I really want or need a tattoo? It lasts longer than you could imagine.

5. On the road!
   www.horikitsune.de
   holy-fox-tattoos@t-online.de

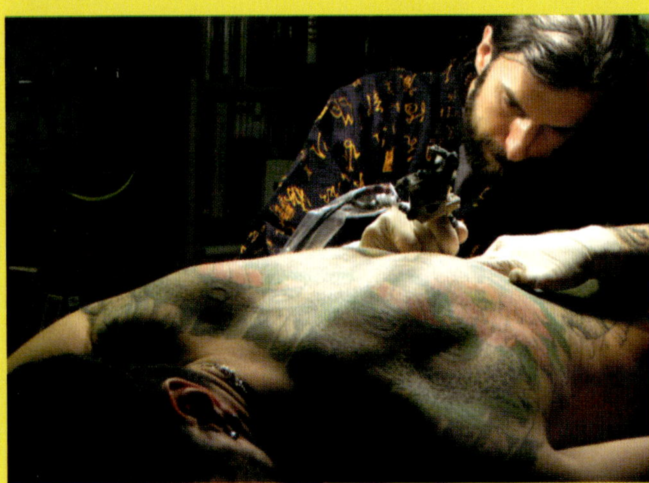

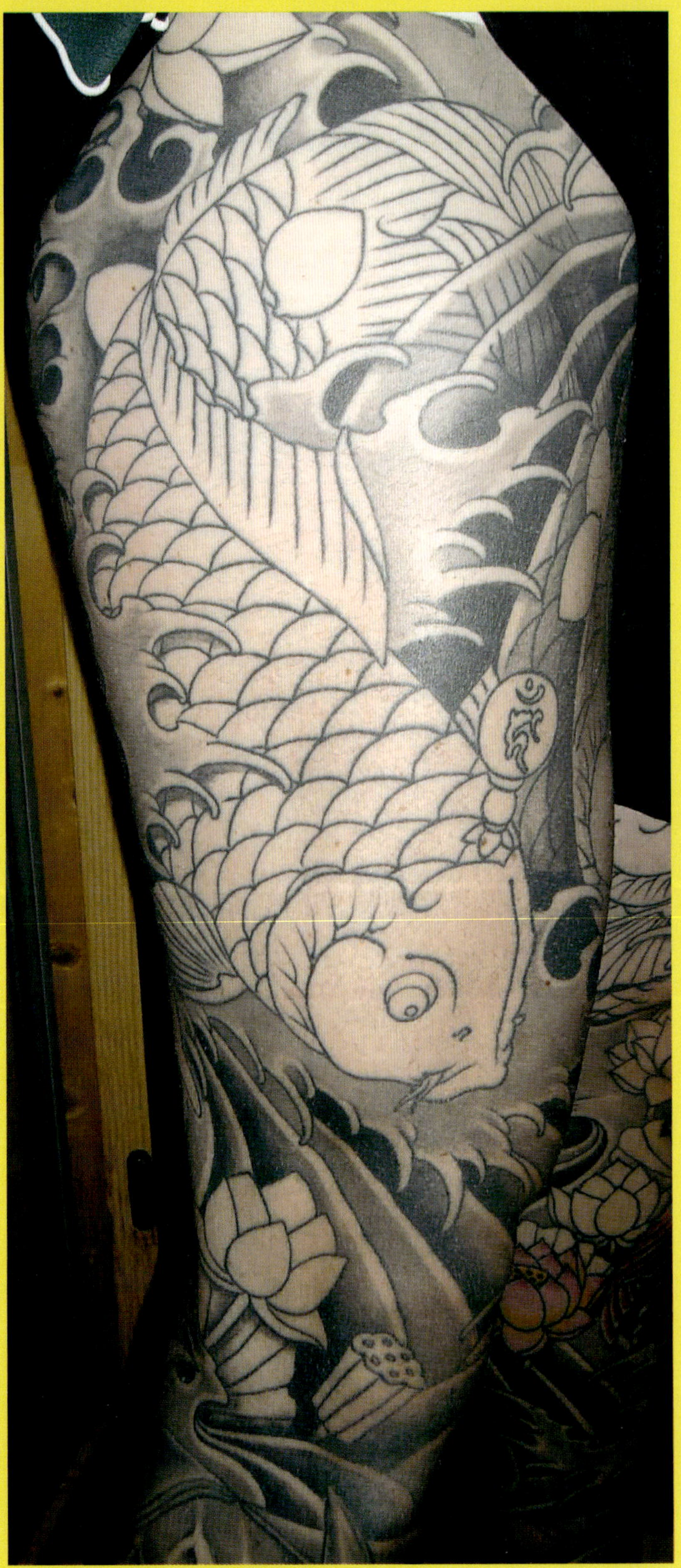

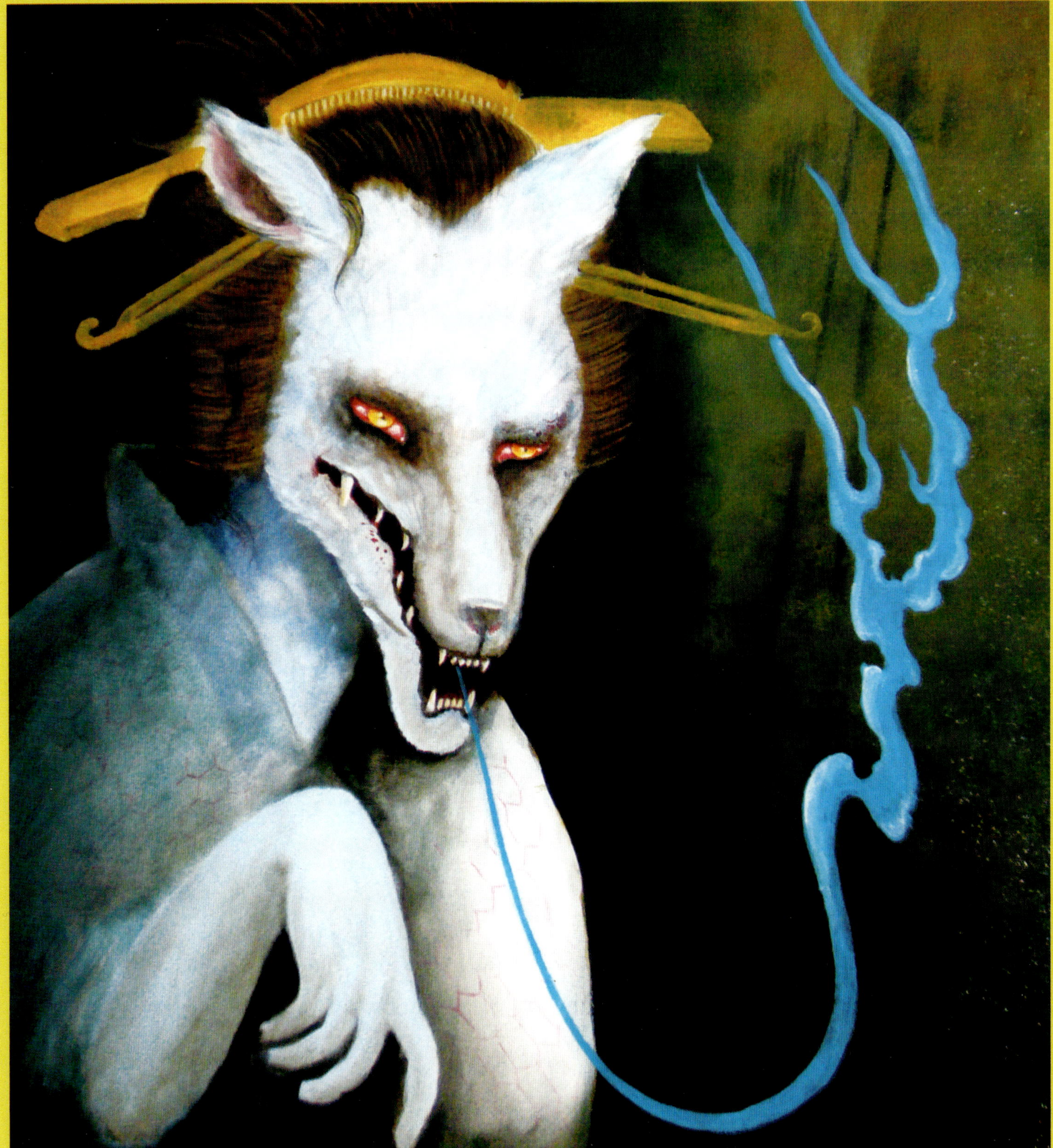

Oil painting made by Alex Reinke.

ALEX REINKE

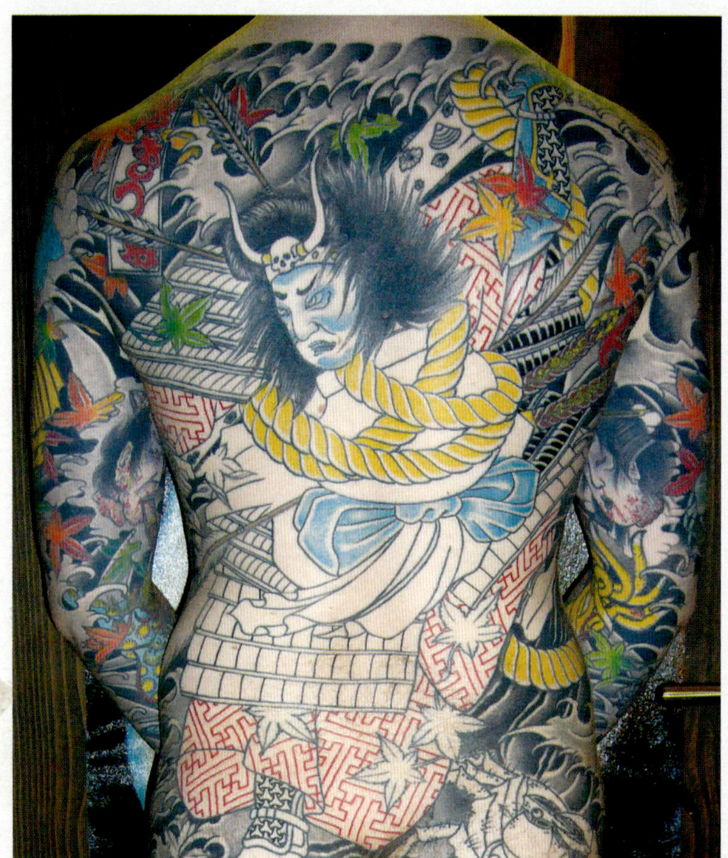
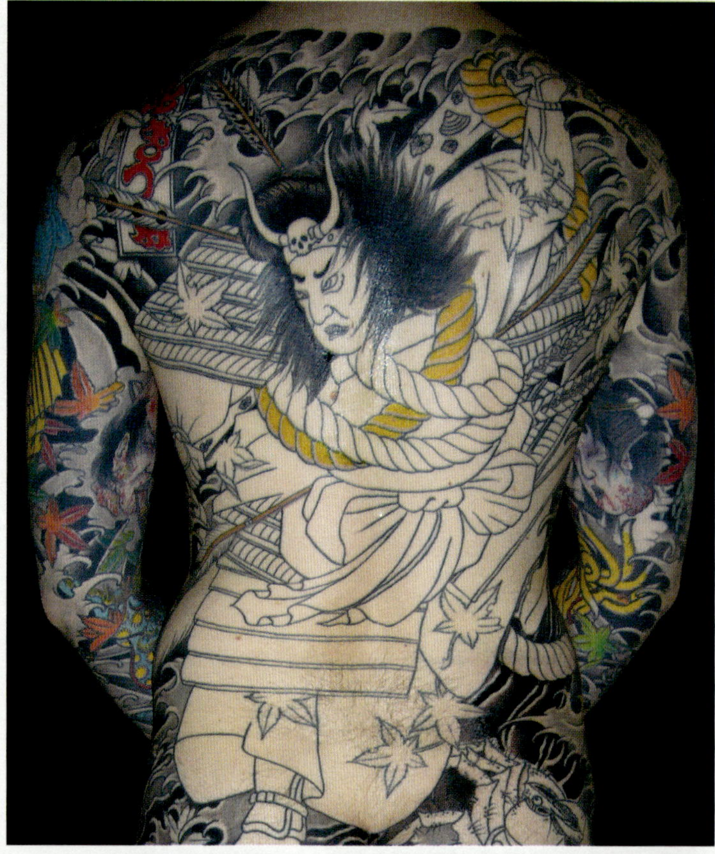
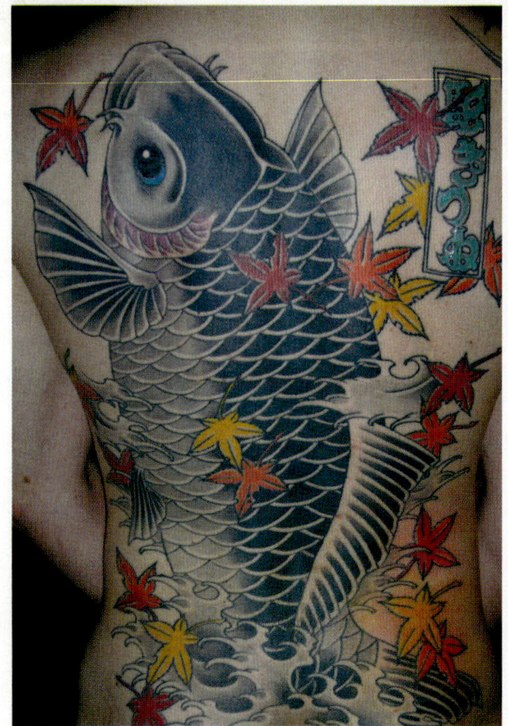
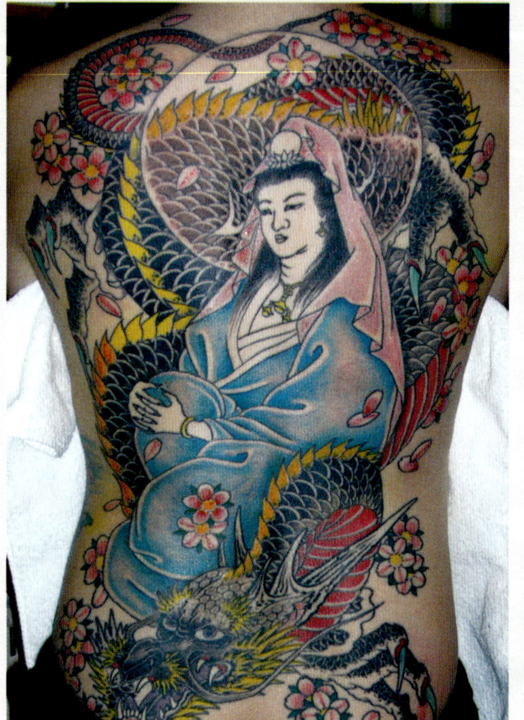
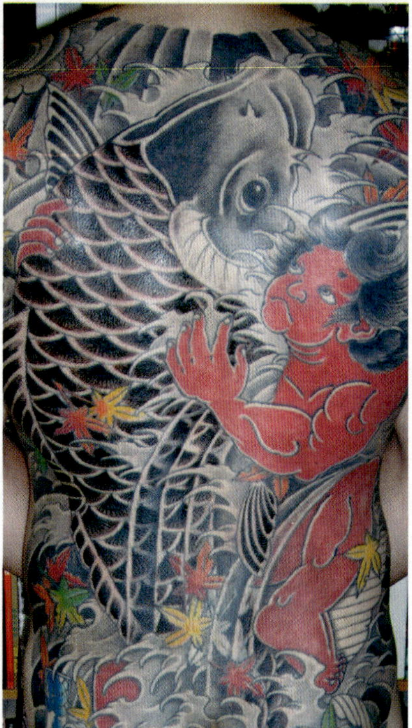

All images courtesy of Alex Reinke.

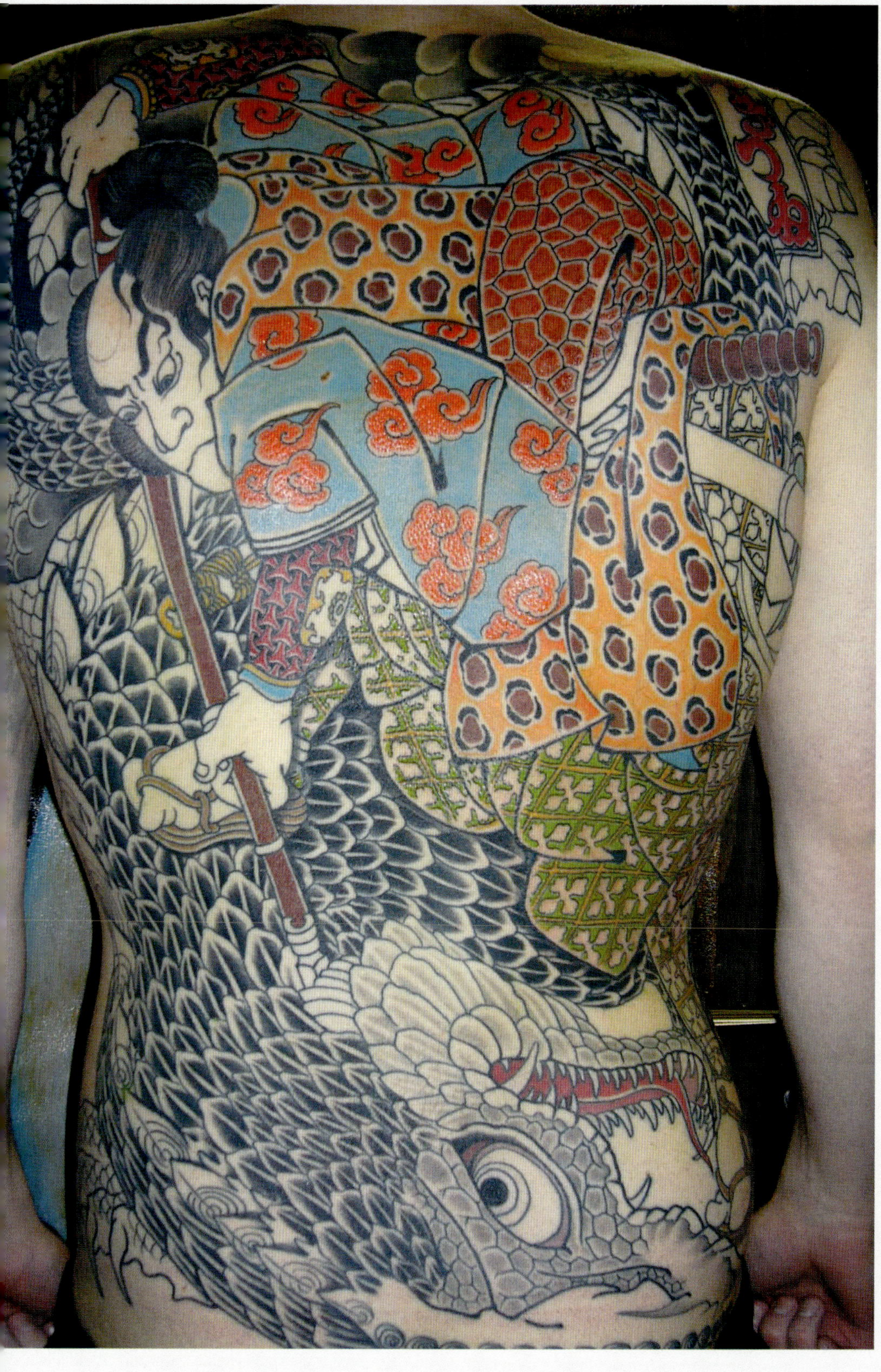

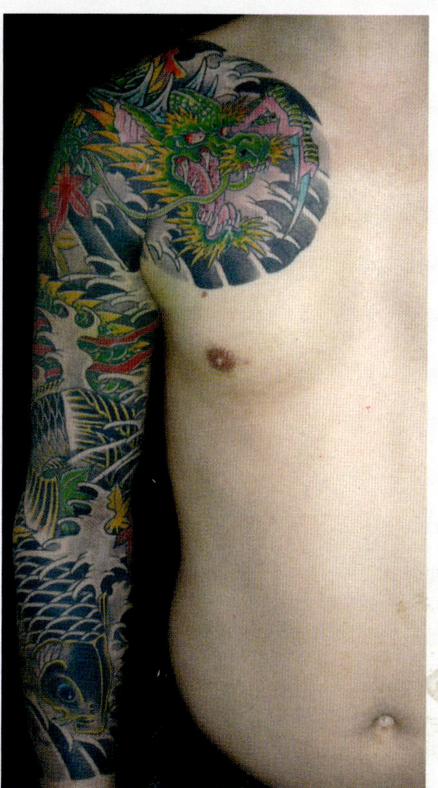

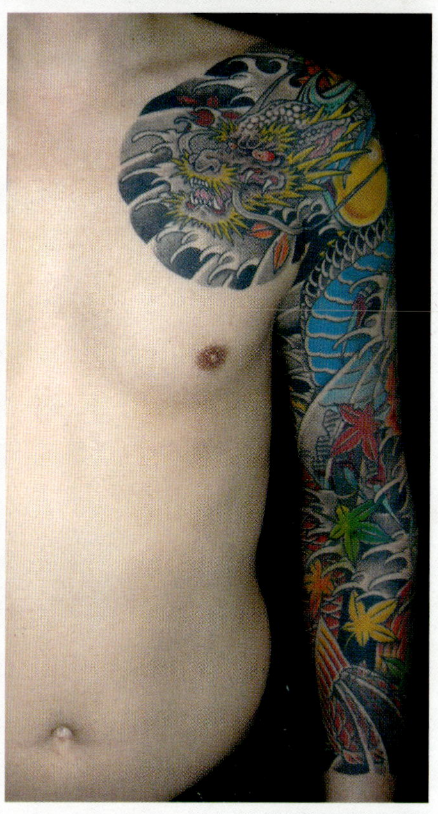

ALEX REINKE

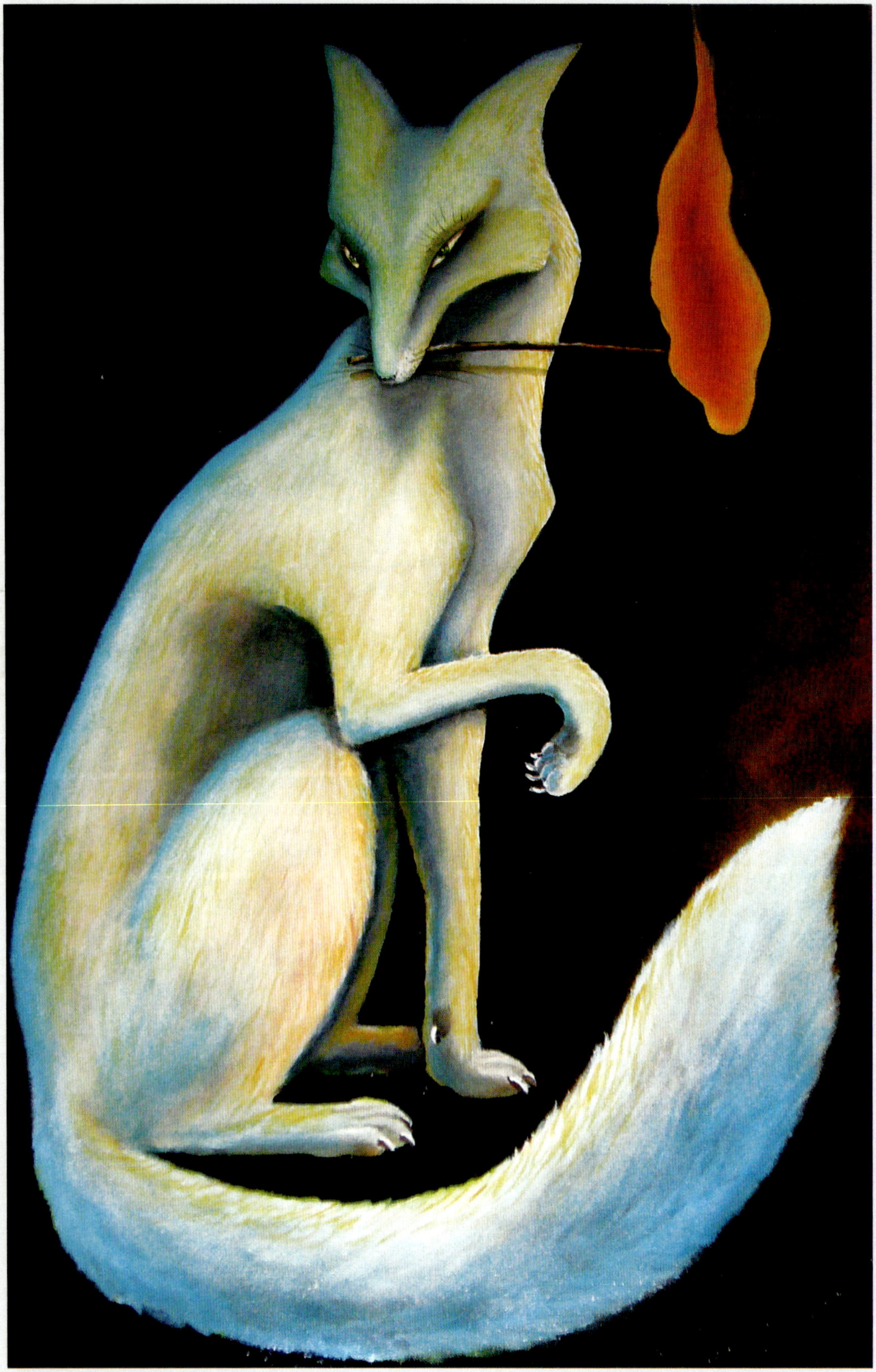

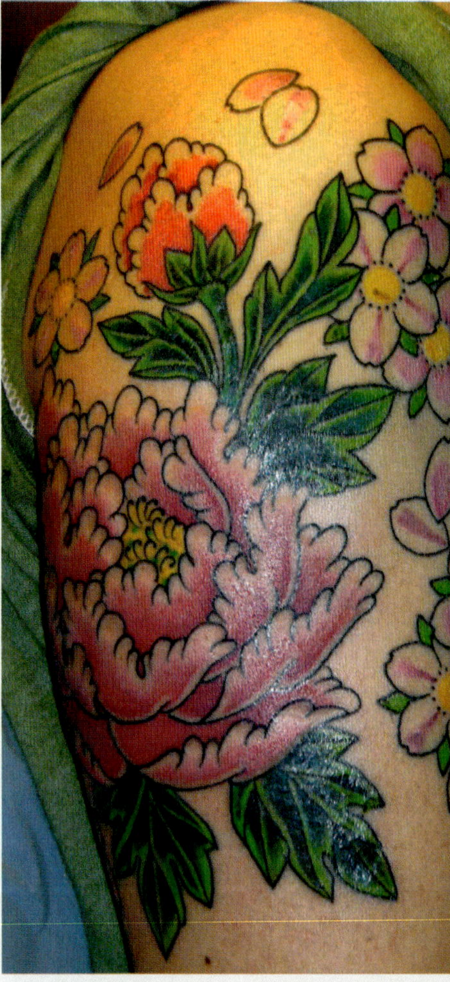

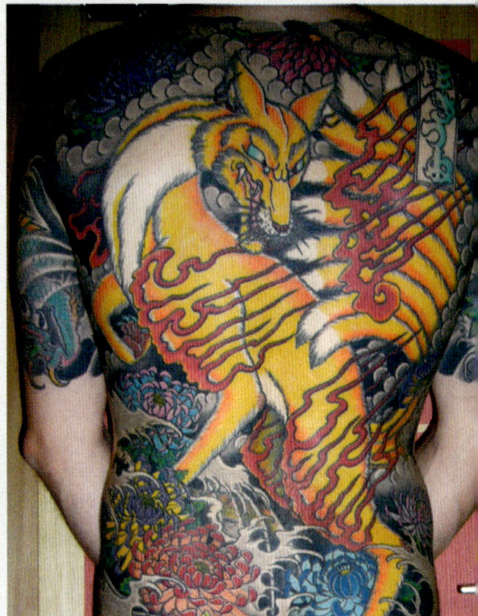

All designs on these pages by Alex Reinke.

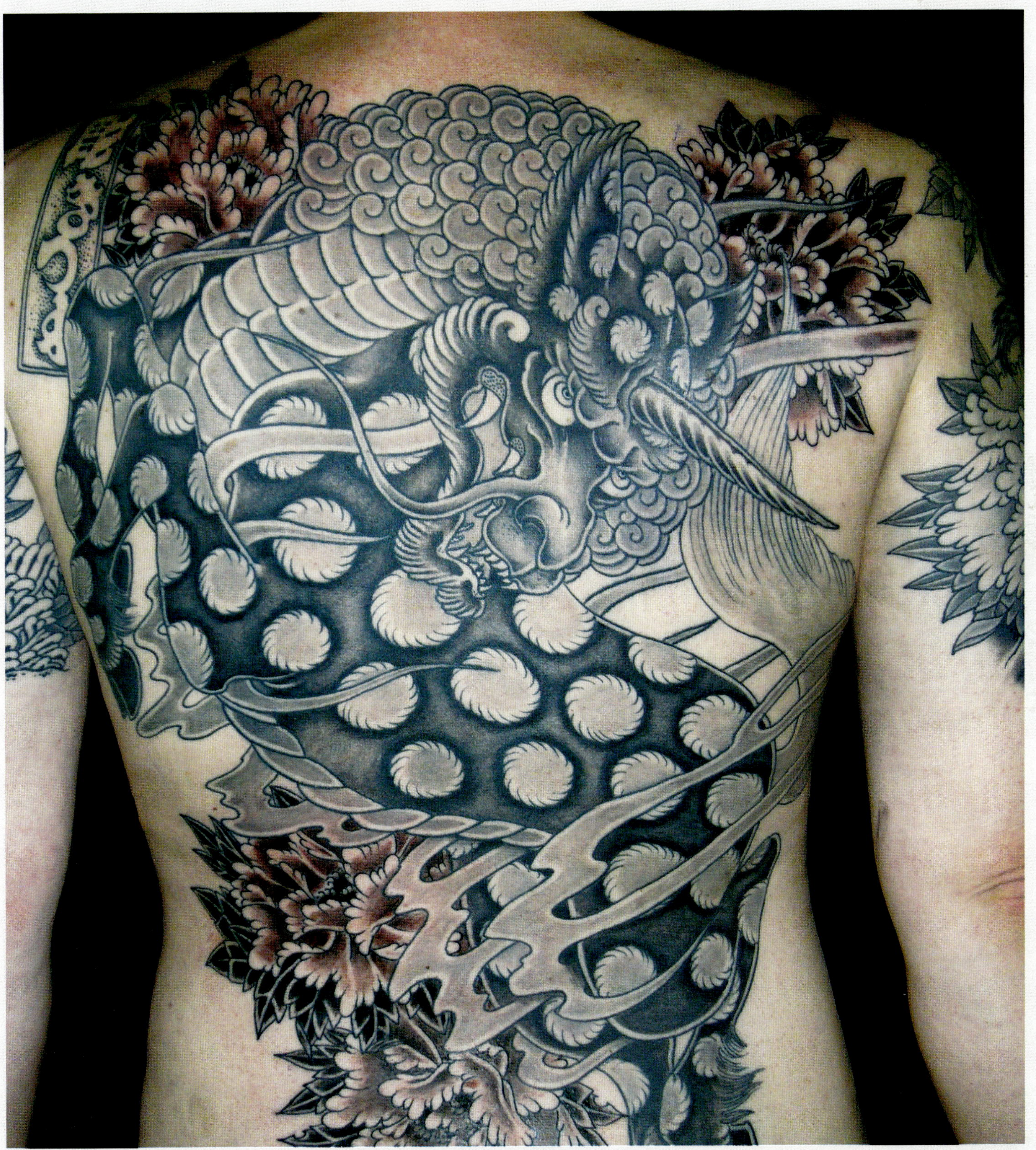

ALEX REINKE

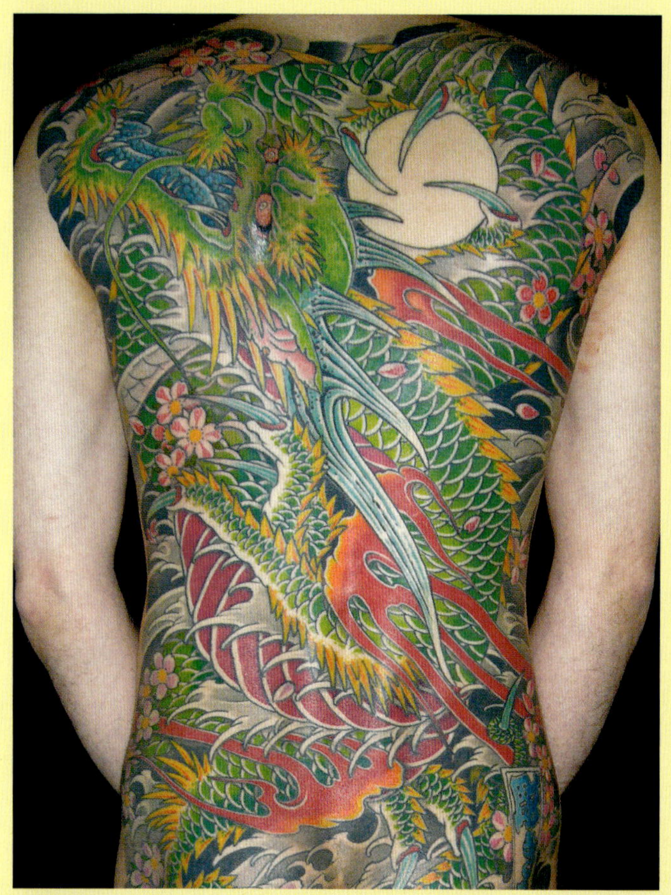
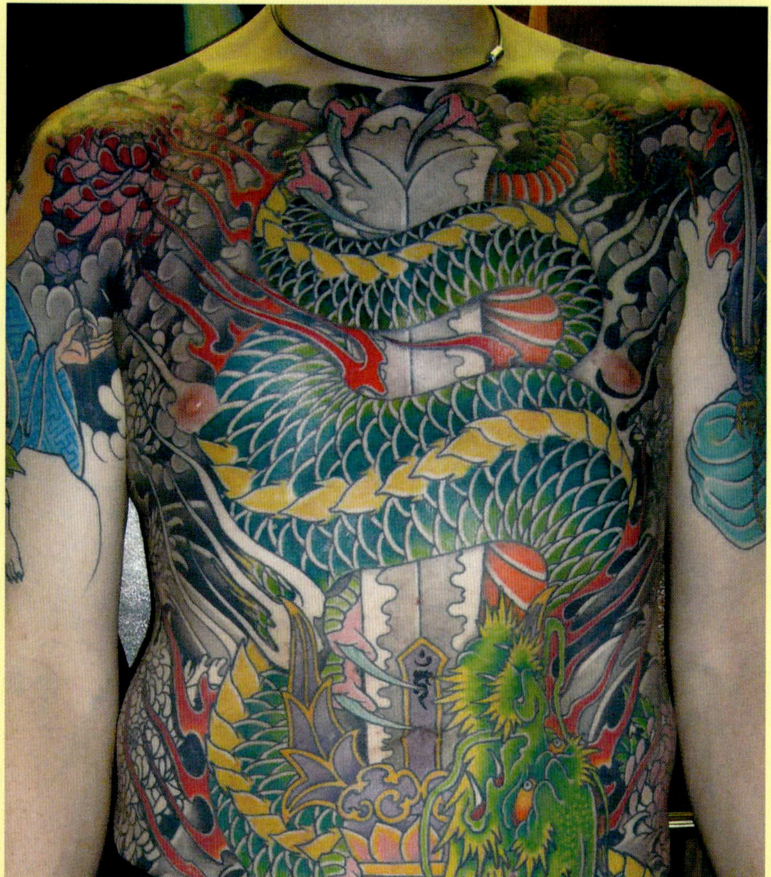
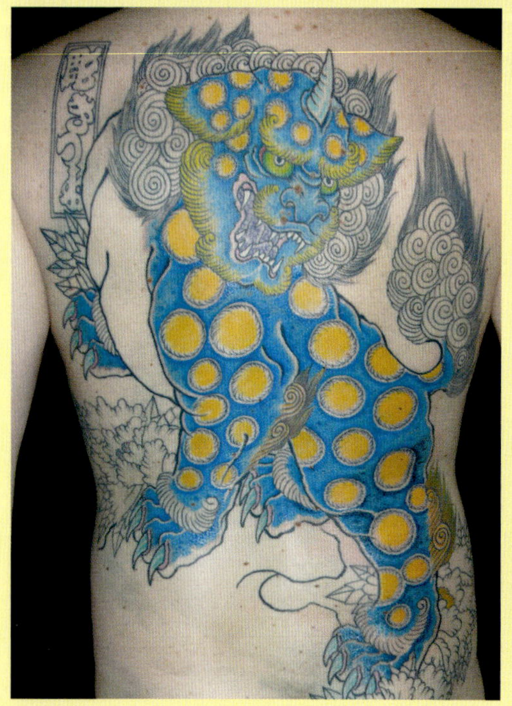
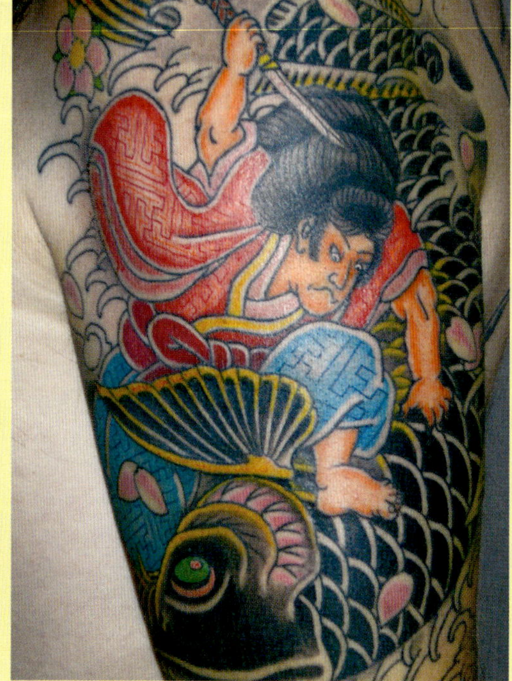
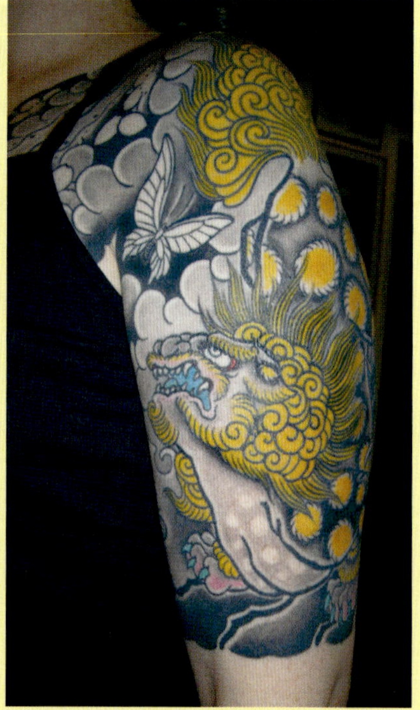

Images courtesy of Alex Reinke.

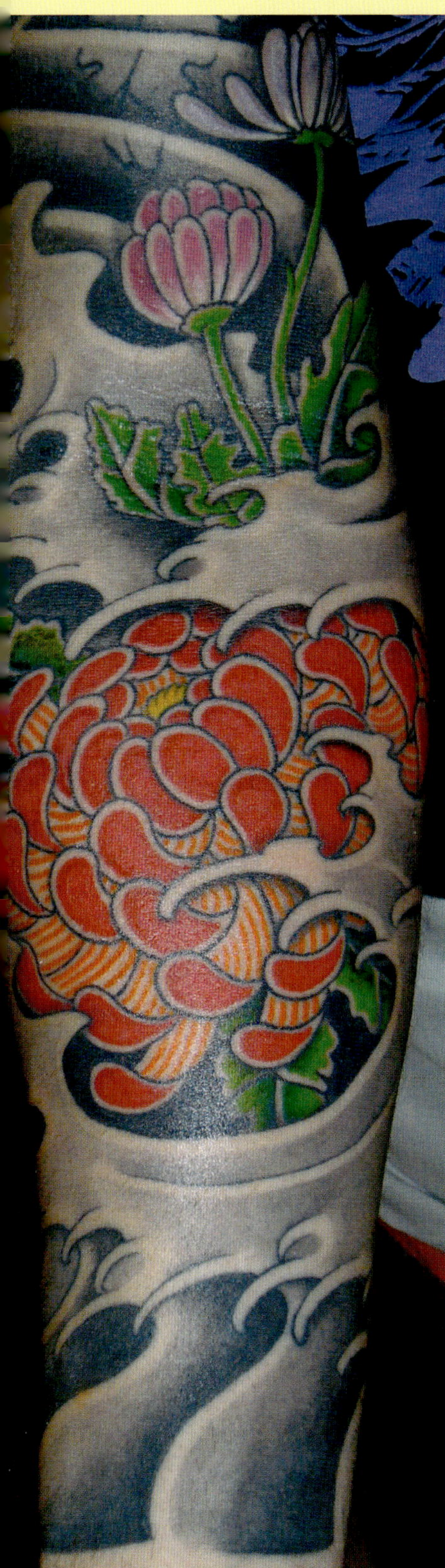

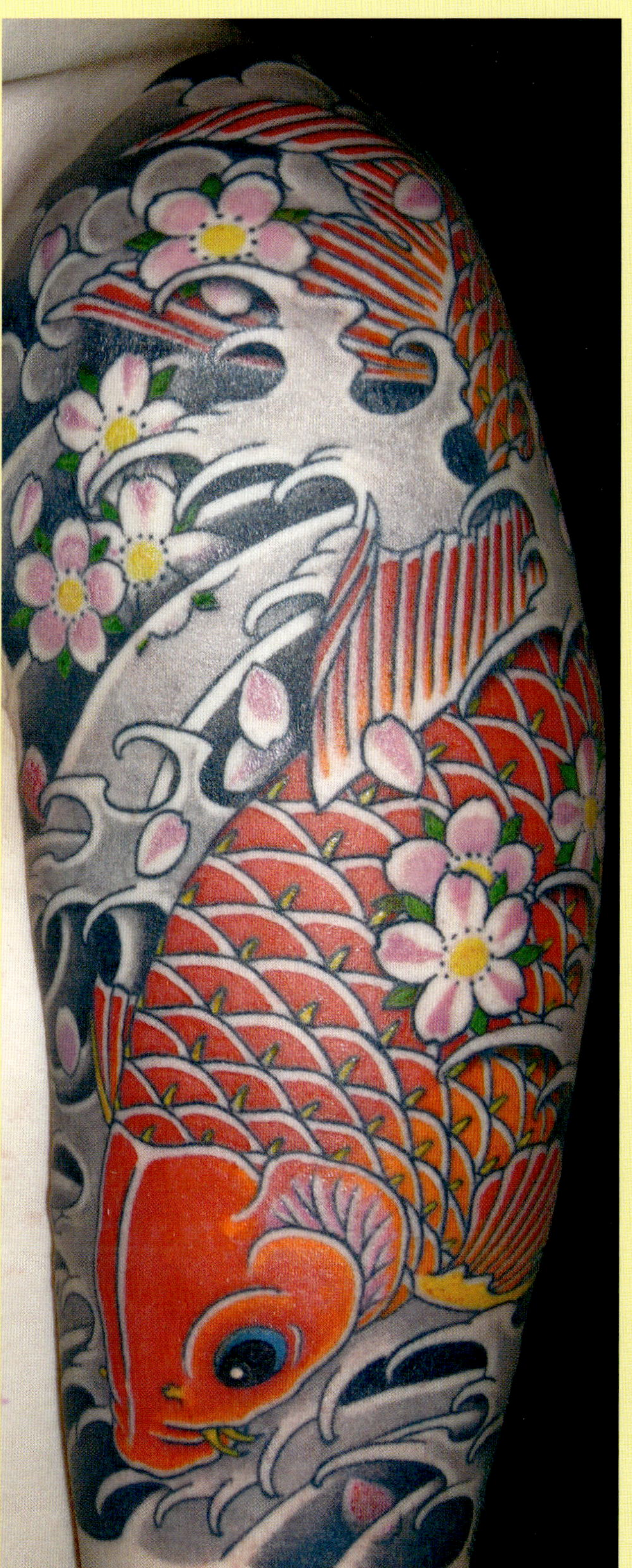

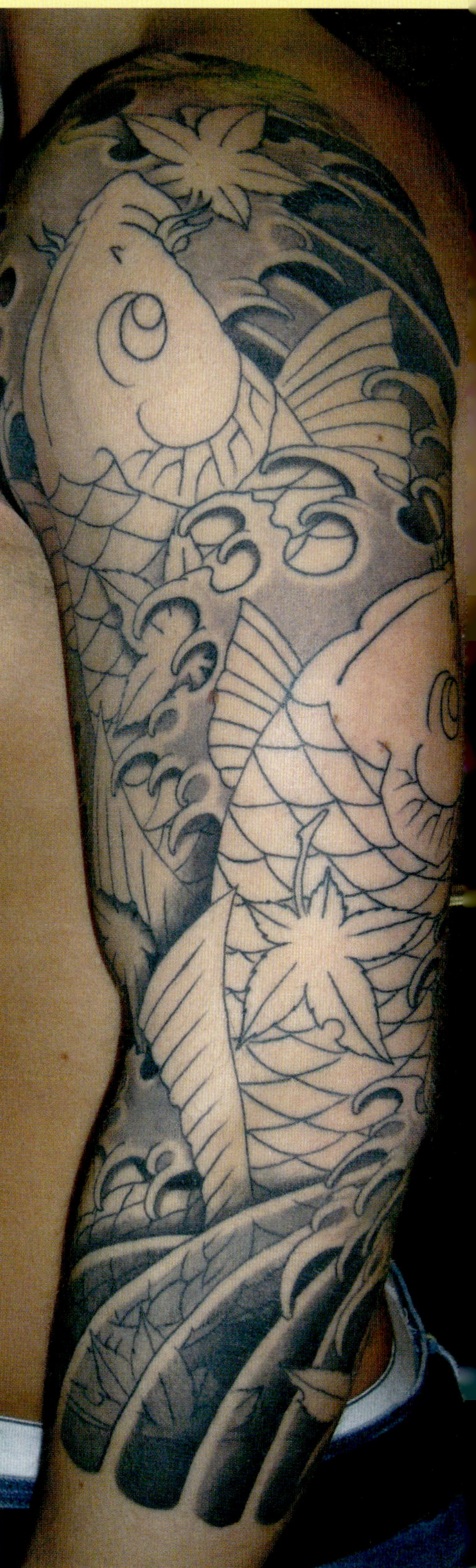

ALEX REINKE

EDU CERRO

USA

1. I first began to get into tattooing from being involved in the skinhead/punk rock scene of the late 1980s. Tattooing at the time was illegal in Oklahoma where I was living, so it was all underground with no street shops. Needless to say I started out doing homemade tattoos. After I got out of high school I moved to Kansas City, where I had made some friends who were tattooing at Grimm's Tattoo, and with their help I got in at a shop in New Jersey, which allowed me to get my foot in the door.

2. For me tattooing is everything that is exciting in art today. Tattooing has always had a tradition of drawing from all other art forms and fusing them together in new ways. In my opinion, the art of tattooing in the last 20 years has attracted some of the most talented people making art today in some way or another. If you look at some of the stuff tattooists are producing outside of their day-to-day tattoo work, you will find them involved in everything from painting and sculpture to machine building. While I dislike and feel quite disconnected from what the "tattoo industry" is like today, it can't be denied that we have been living through one of the most exiciting periods in its history.

3. I'm not sure that I have only one specific style that I work with, but if I have to guess I would say that it is somewhere between traditional and Japanese, with a dash of creepy thrown in.

4. When I decide to get a tattoo I view it the same as if I were buying a painting from someone whose work I like and admire. I think that if you approach getting tattooed this way you will never regret it.

5. www.laluzmala.com

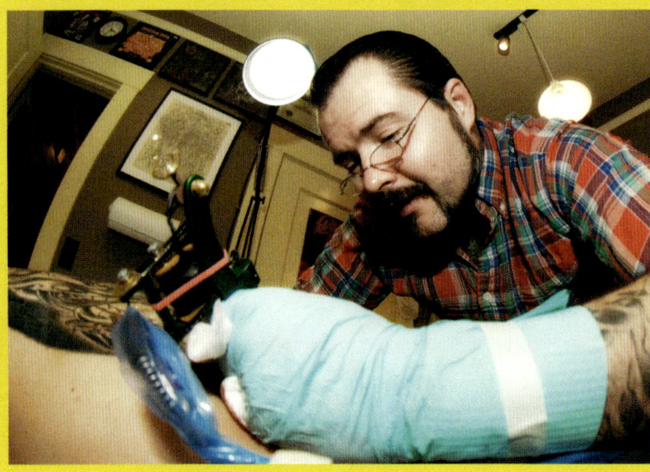

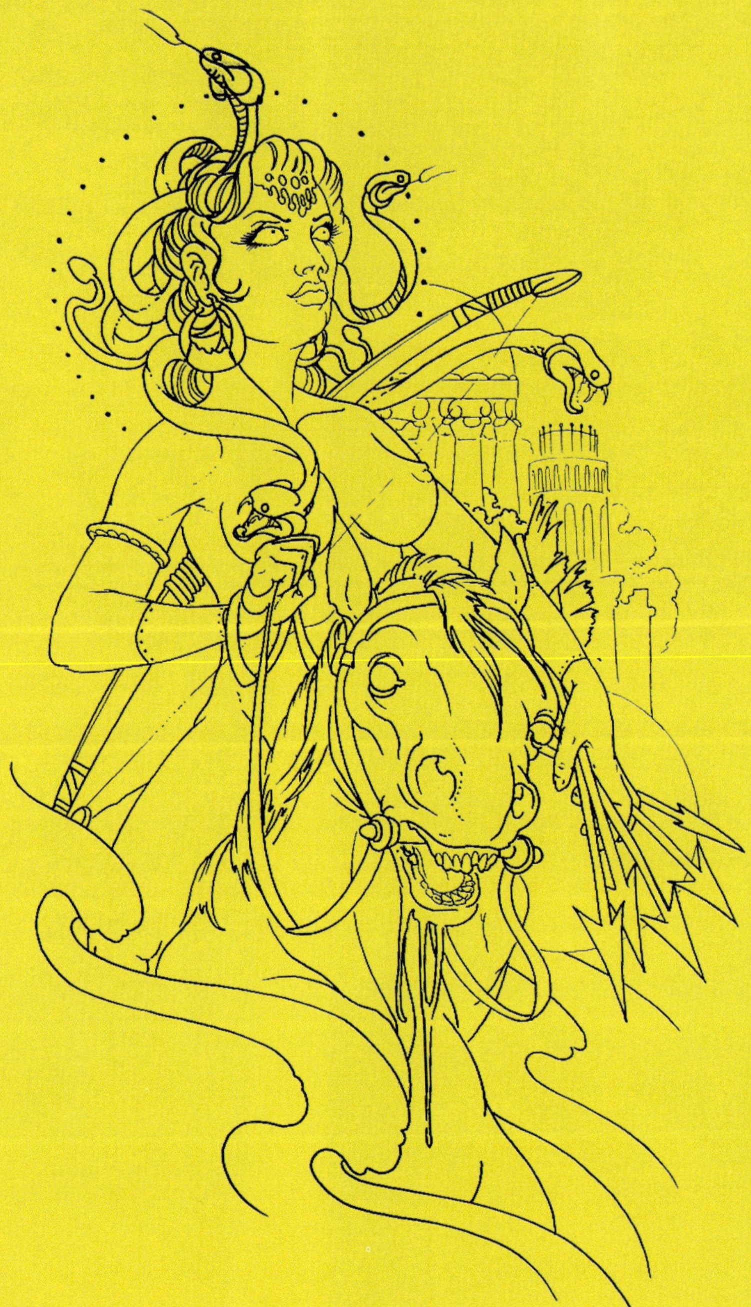

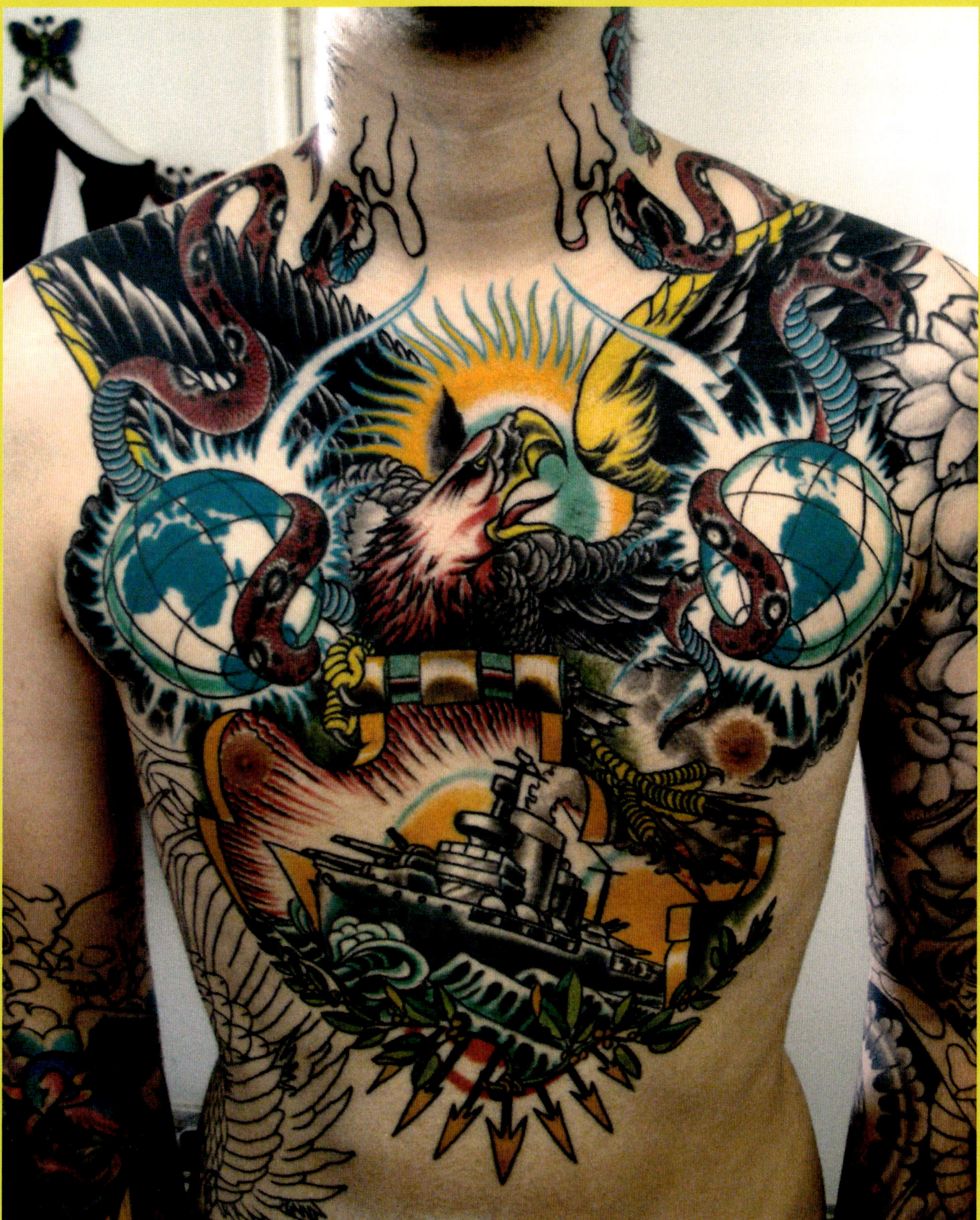

All images courtesy of Edu Cerro.

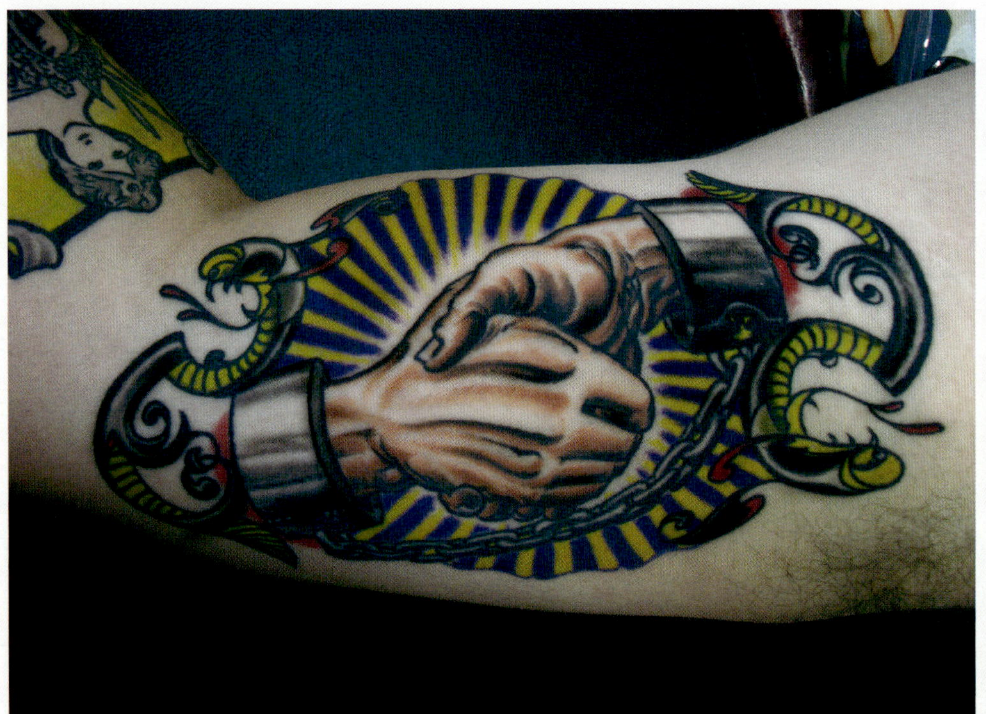
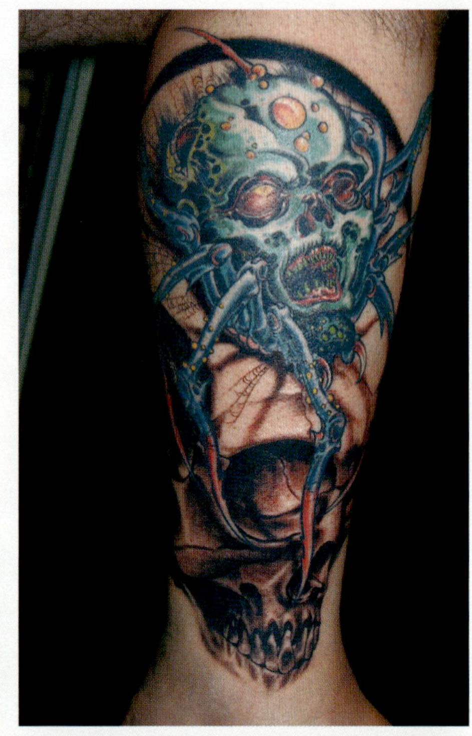
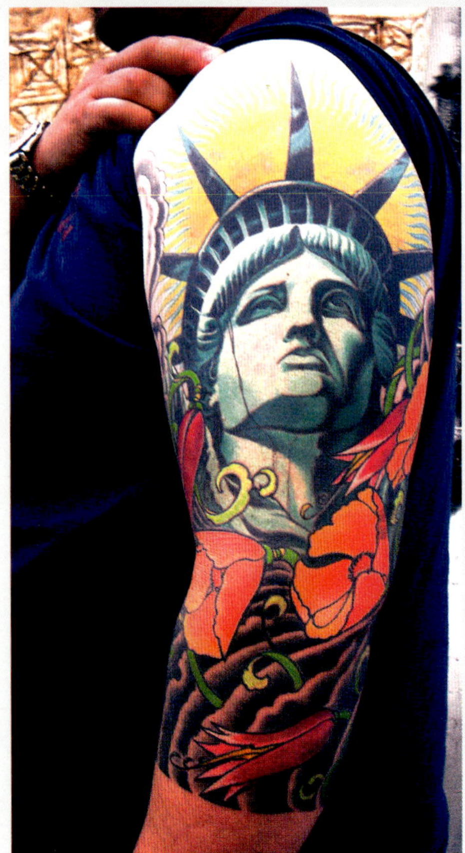
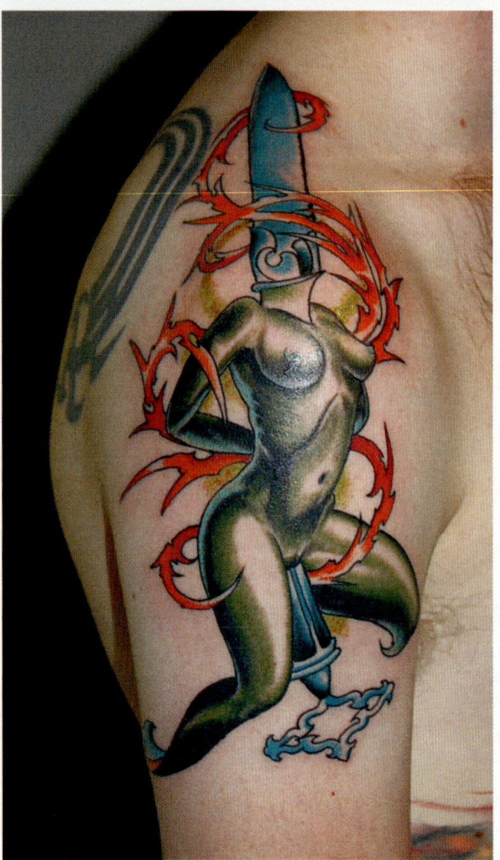
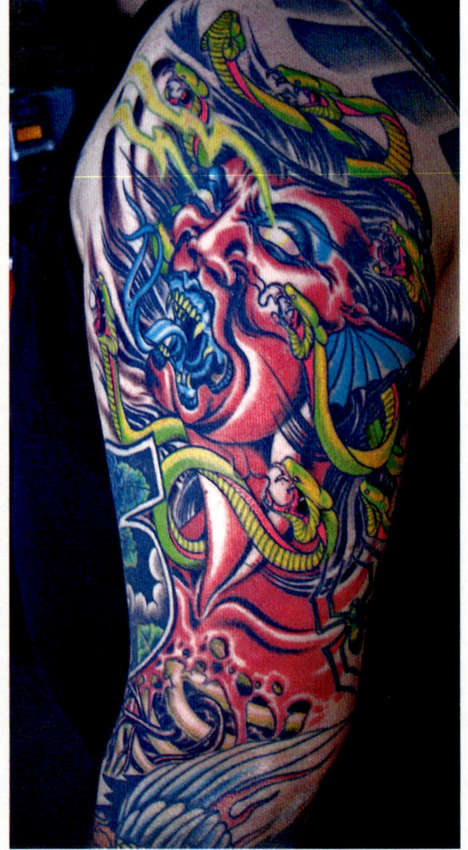

All designs on these pages by Edu Cerro.

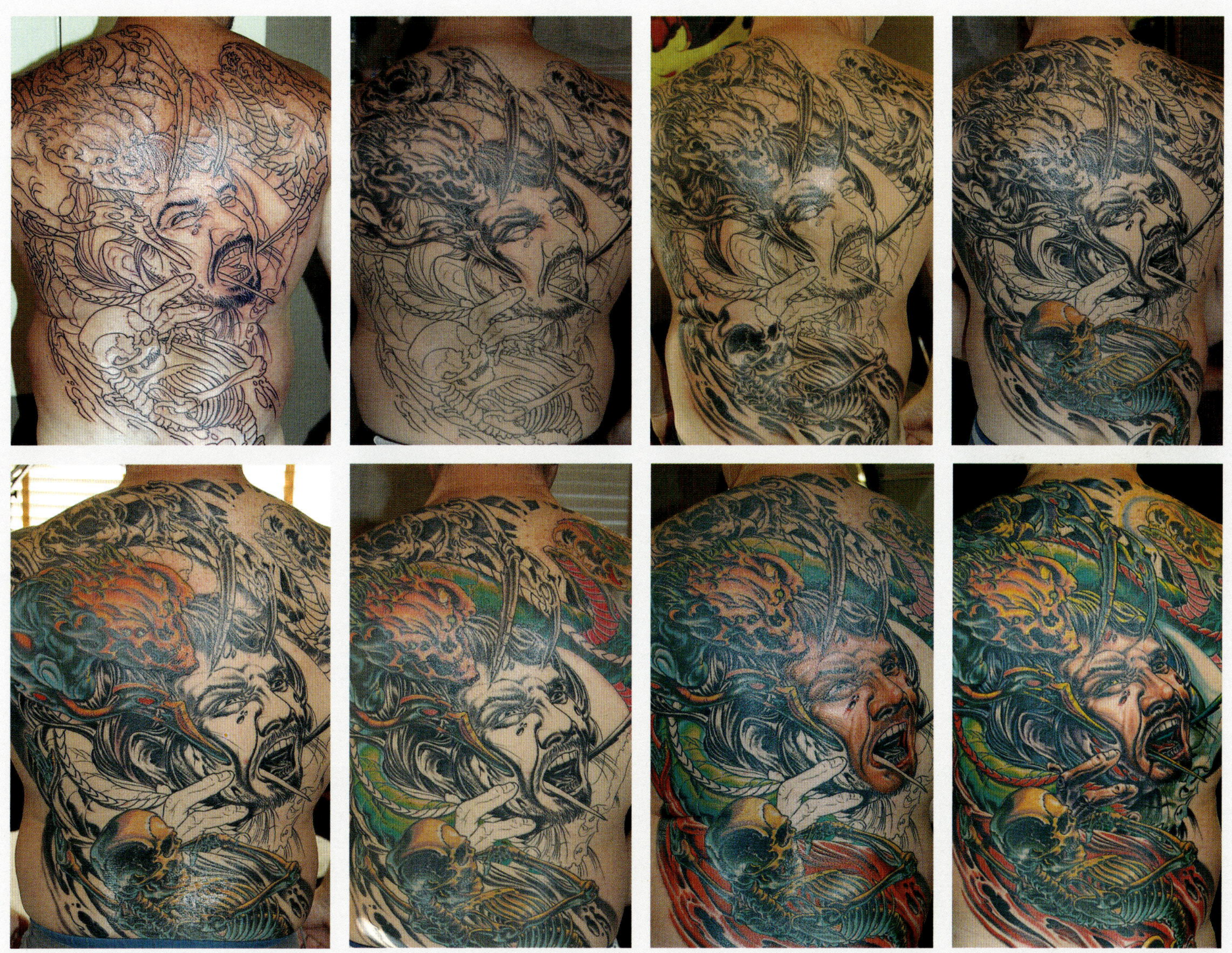

Step by step of a tattoo design by Edu Cerro.

ROB ADMIRAAL

HOLLAND

1. I began to work with a tattooist who offered me a job in exchange for teaching him about painting. He emphasized, however, that he could not "teach" me how to tattoo; I had to learn by myself.

2. For me tattooing taught me to create an image which had to go beyond taste, since taste is going to change within a couple of years while the tattoo will still be there. This led me to make very consistent images because the tattoo is also going to wear down over the years. So I stay away from light sources, surface matter, perspective, and all these reality-connected "outside" matters and instead show the more "inside" matters, hence making an image look more real than reality and opening doors to other dimensions since reality just doesn't offer that much. I will always look for the more archetypical ways an image is built.

3. My style is what the client wants, and it grows through communication with the client. People often choose what I make these days, which is a style leaning towards Japanese, whose only connection to reality is the suggestion of depth through the use of shadings.

4. We are not meant to get tattooed, so don't do it, love your body as it is. But on the other hand tattooing to me is a very striking way of showing that there is much more in this world than our often limited thinking assumes.

5. Rob Admiraal Tattoo Studio, Marnixstraat 151, 1015 VM Amsterdam, Holland.
www.admiraaltattoo.com

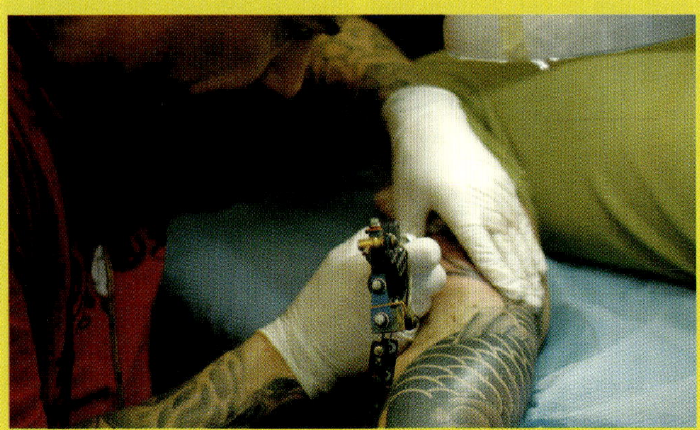

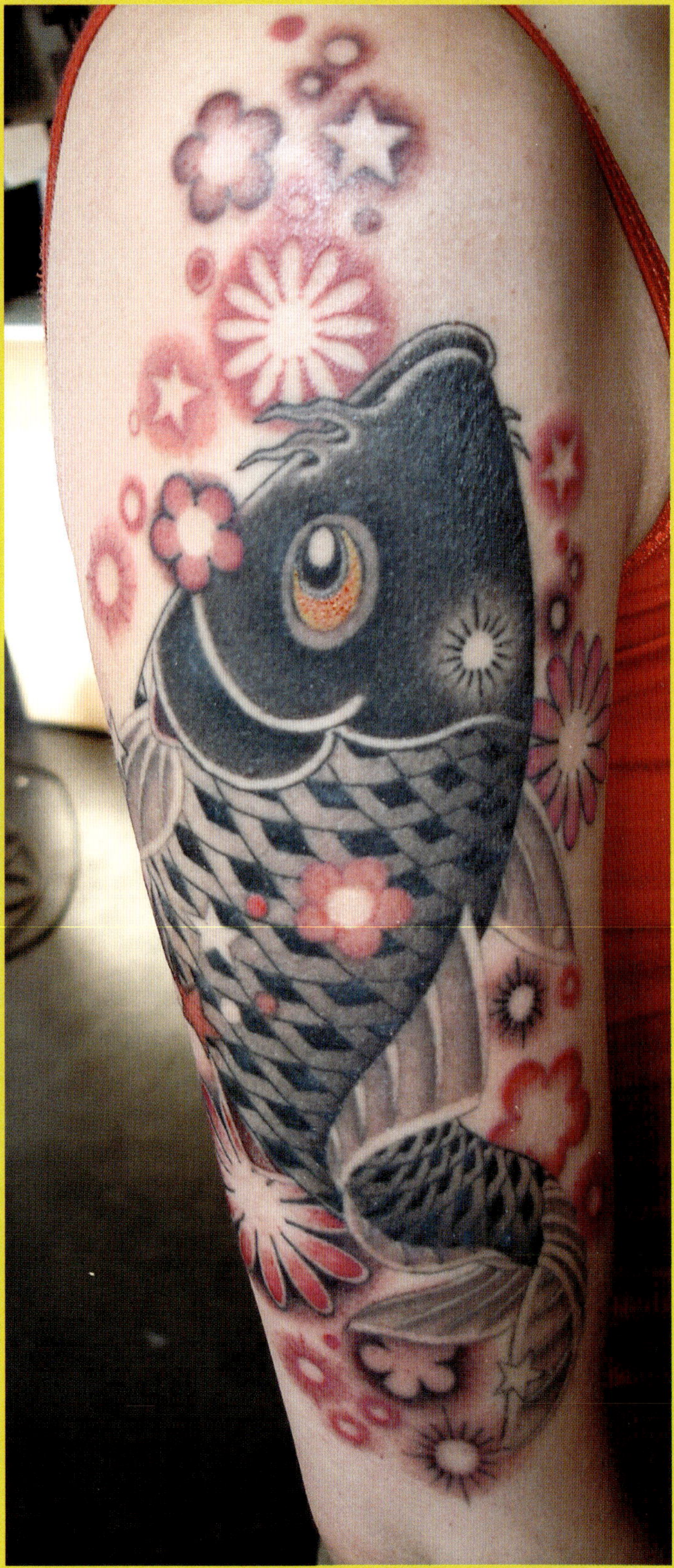

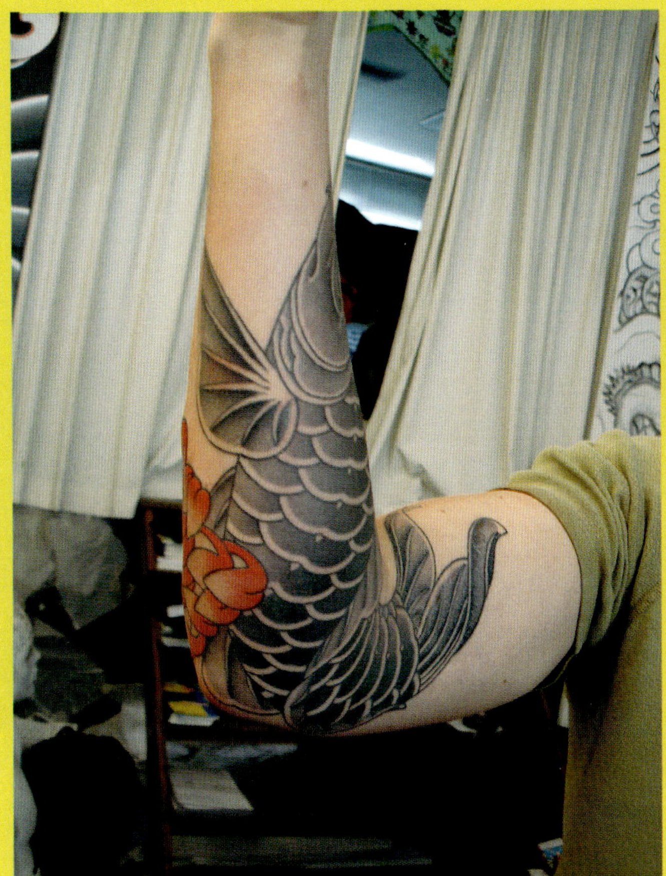

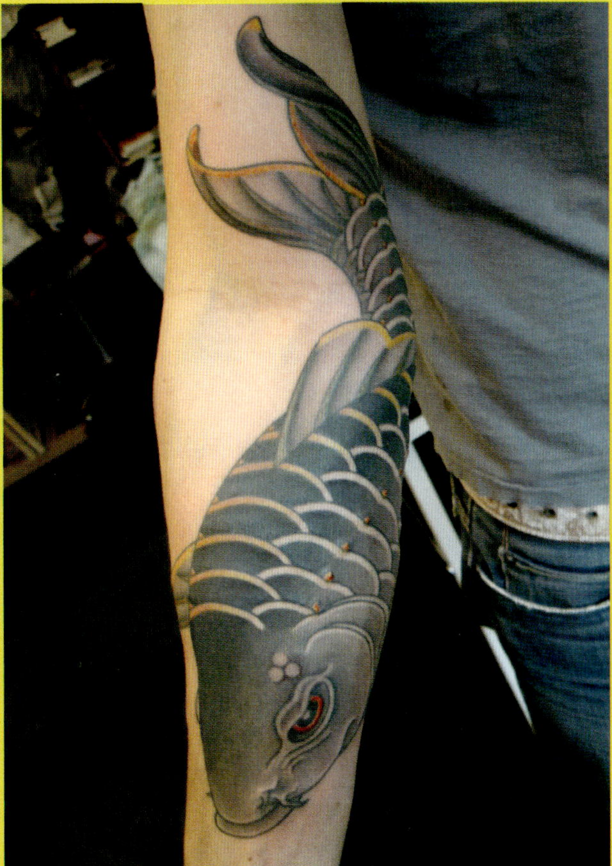

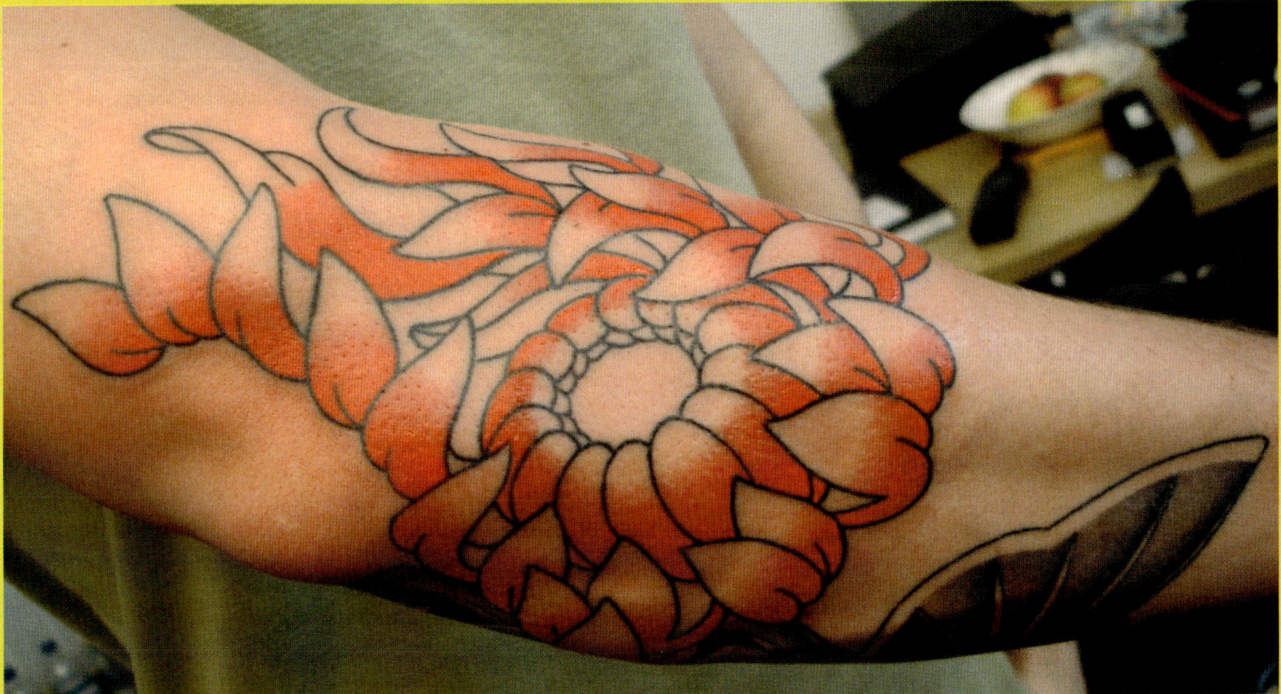

All designs on these pages by Rob Admiraal.

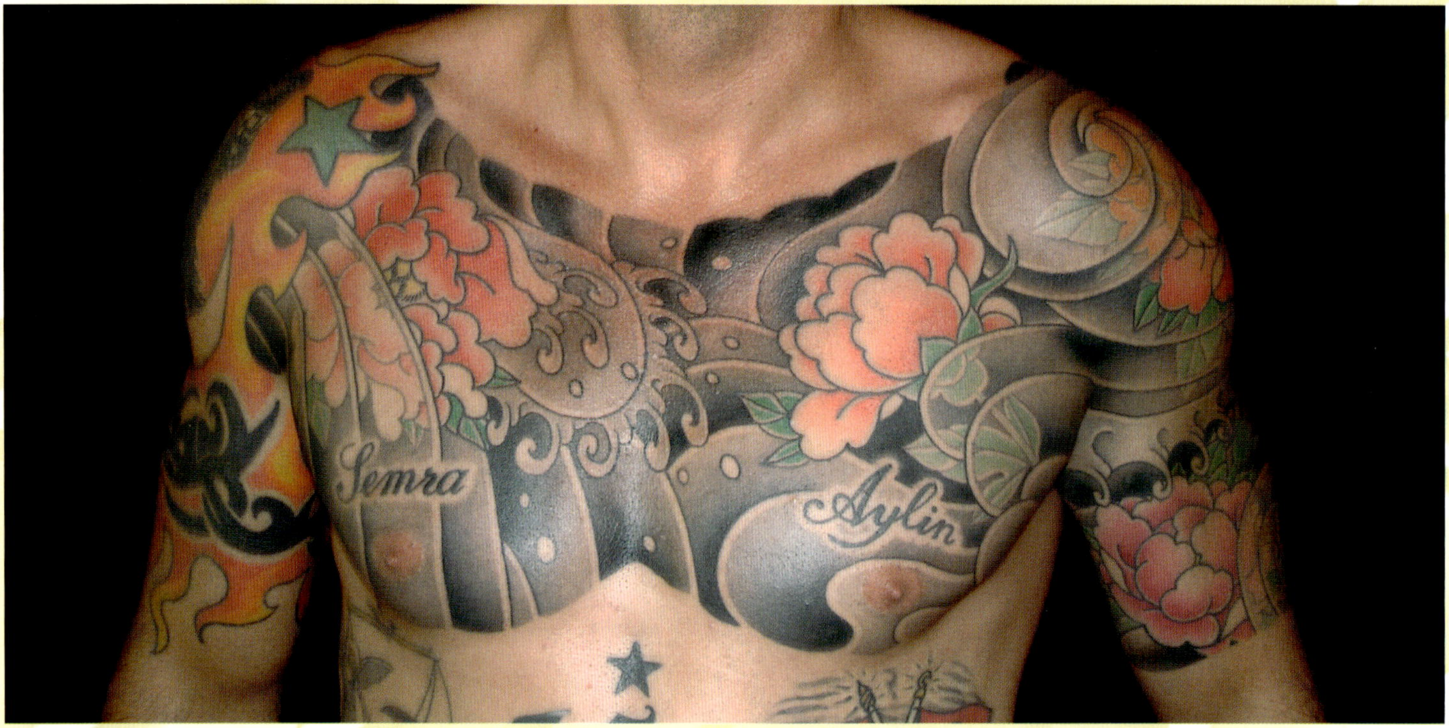

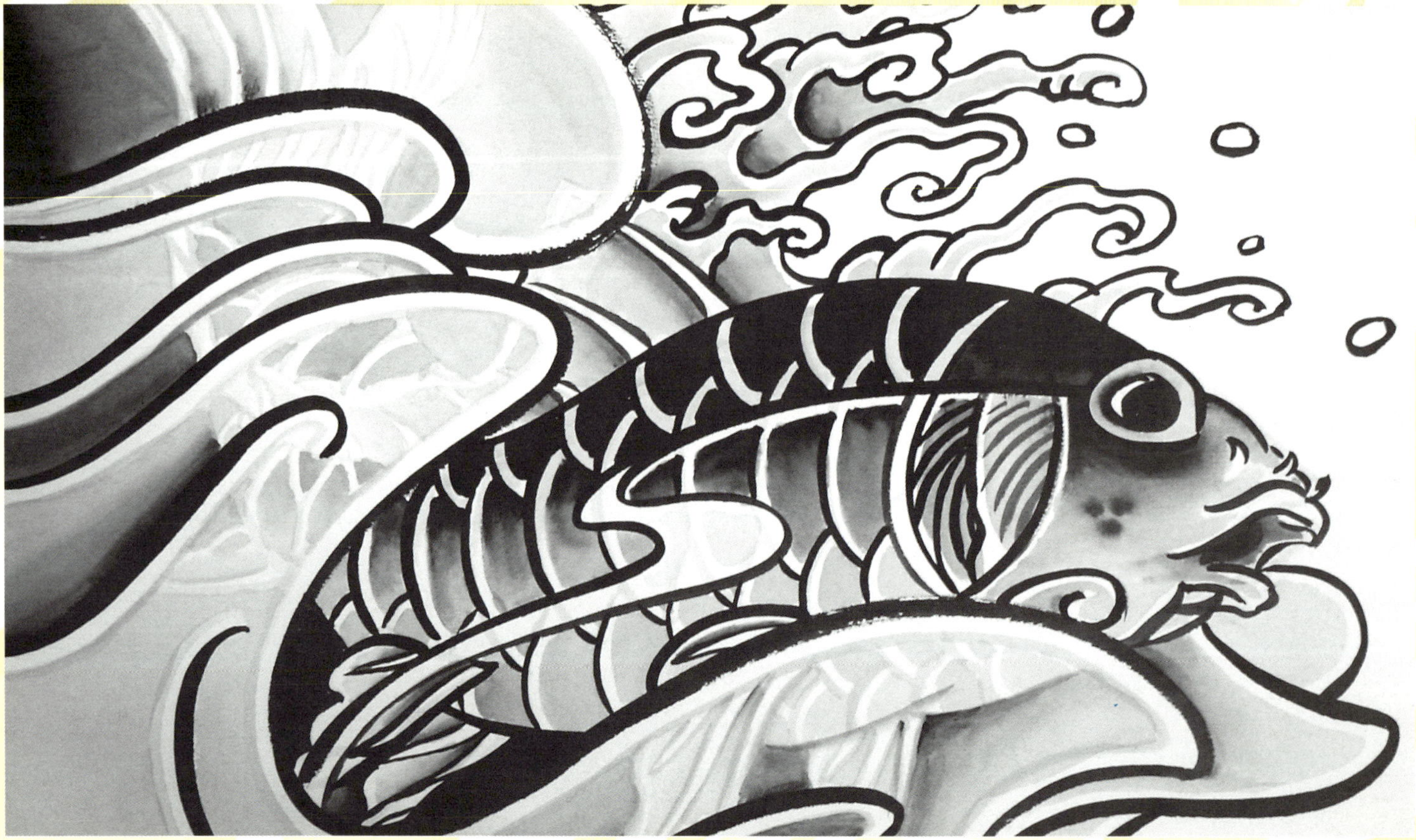

Images and illustrations courtesy of Rob Admiraal.

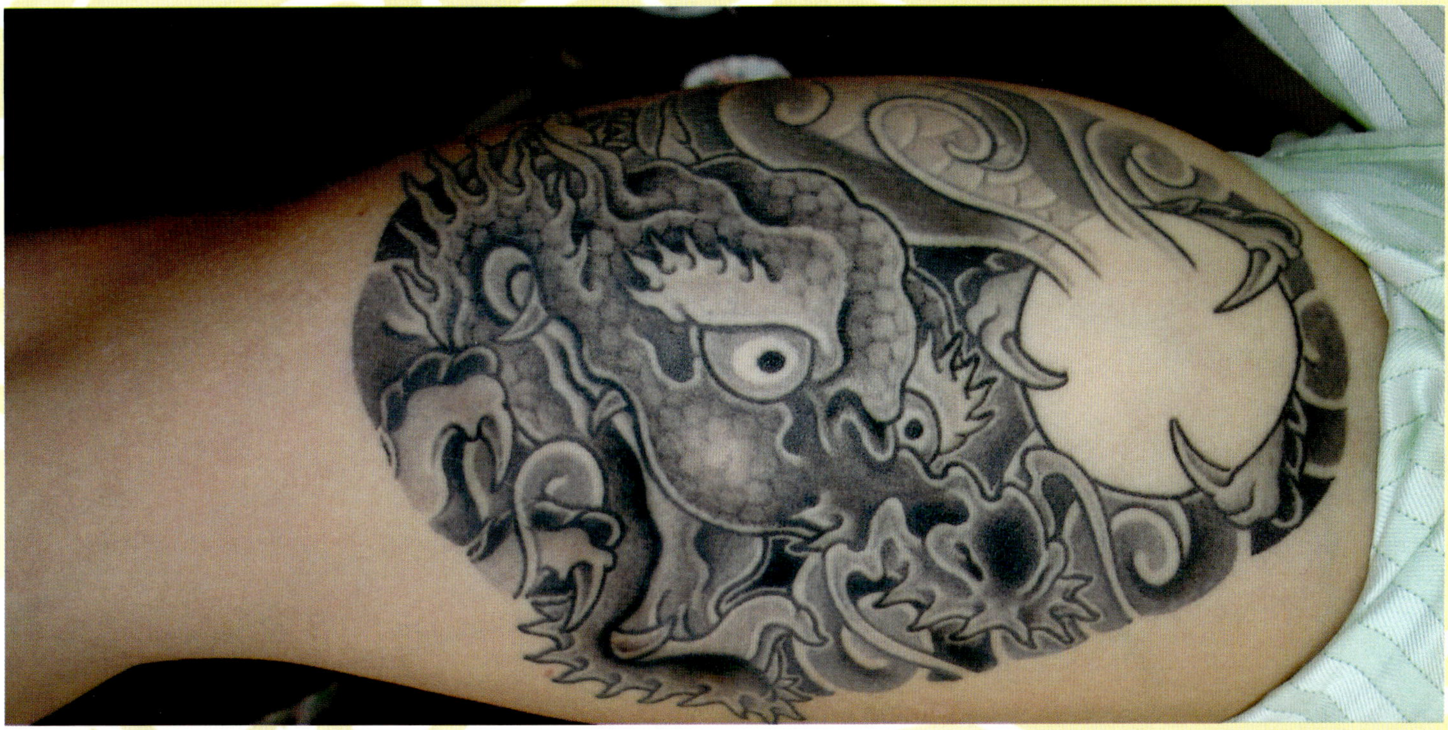

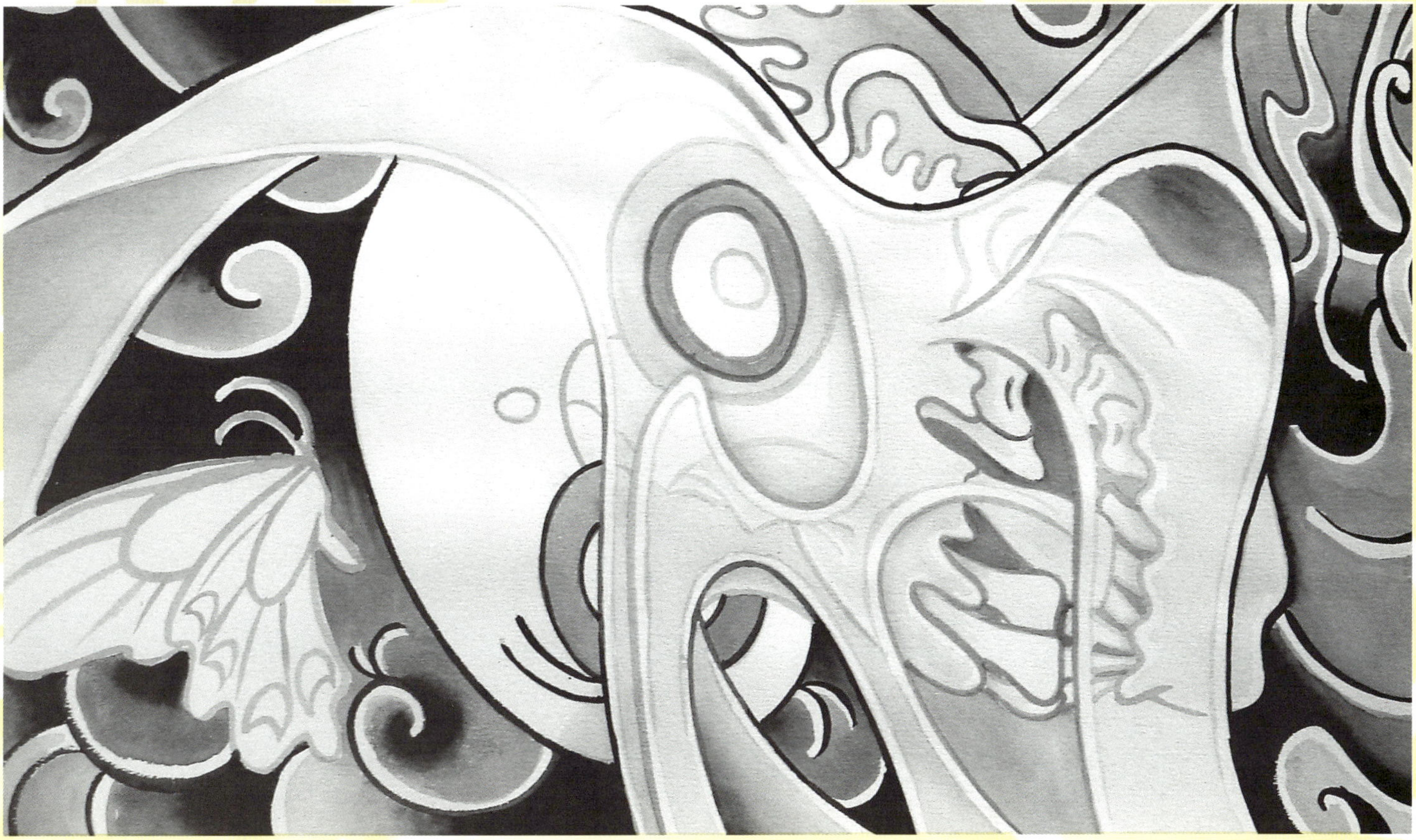

ROB ADMIRAAL

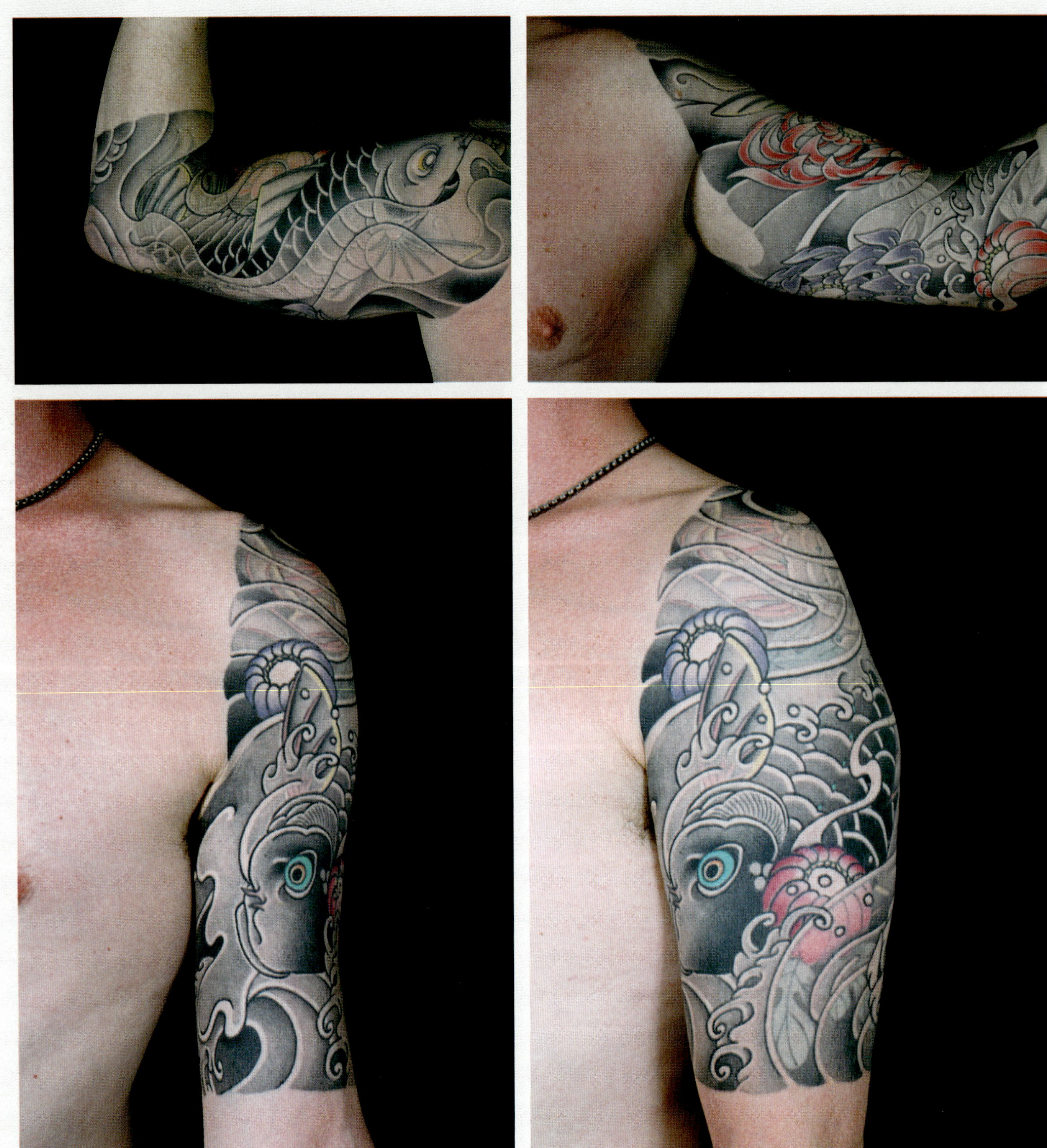

All designs on these pages by Rob Admiraal.

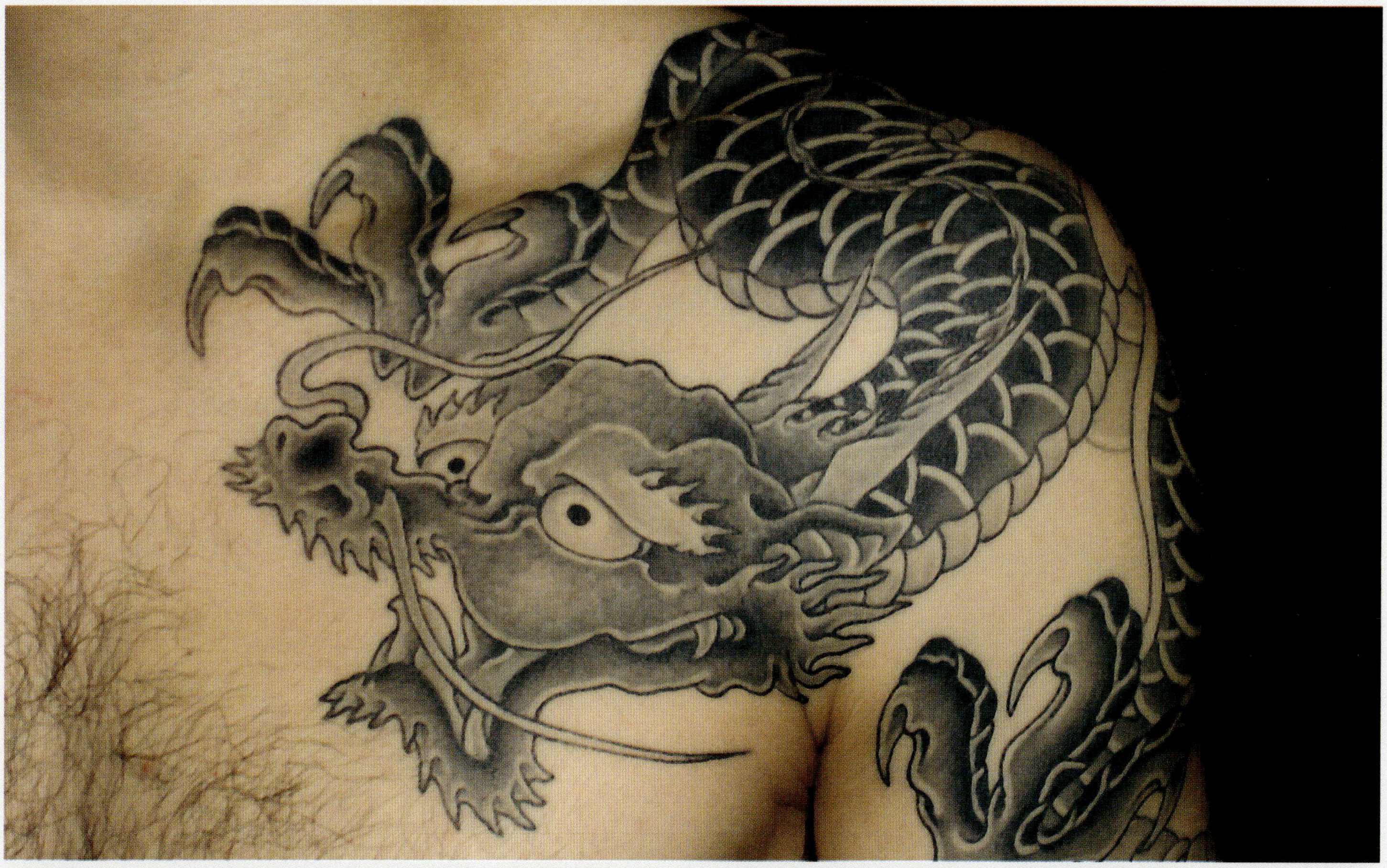

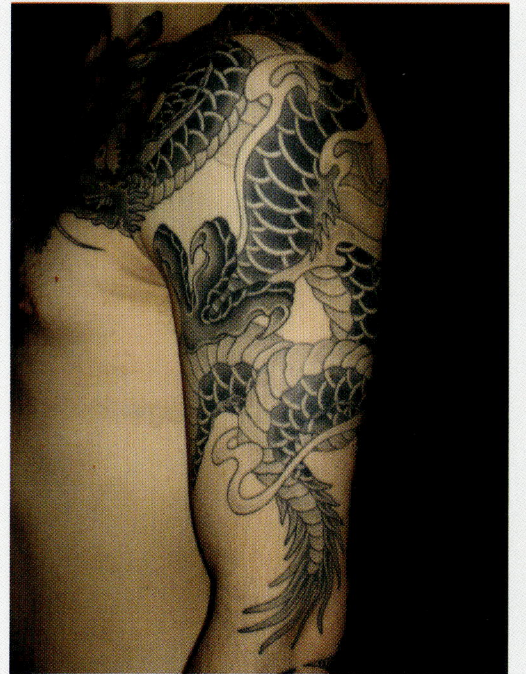

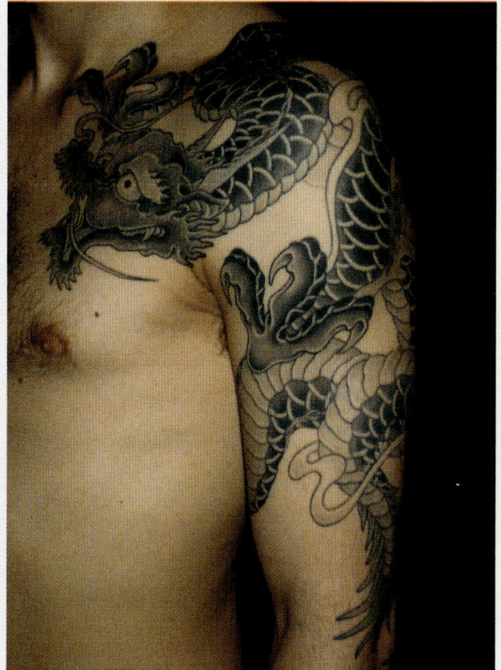

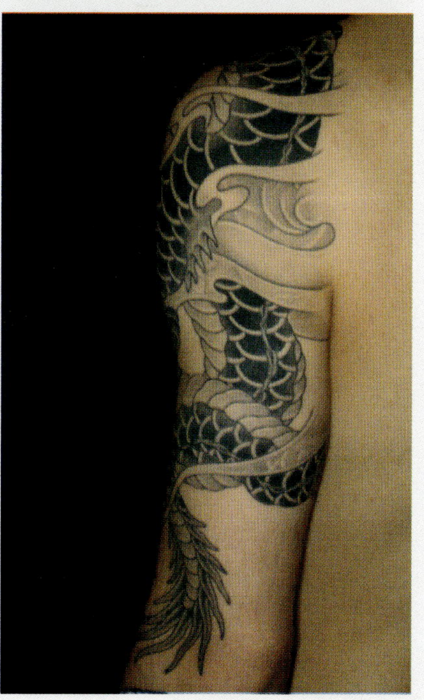

ROB ADMIRAAL

JONDIX

SPAIN

1. I had long been attracted to the mystical symbolism of Thailand, Tibet and other Eastern cultures—and particularly to Indian calligraphy. So, it was very fortunate that I crossed paths with the great Greek tattooist Tas, and later with Mike from Athens, without whom none of this would have been possible.

2. Tattooing is a kind of artistic or aesthetic expression, as well as a way of channeling sensations. There is something magical about the fact that the human skin can serve as a canvas for artistic creation. I often wonder what someone like Salvador Dalí would think about the art of tattooing if he were alive today.

3. My style could be defined as a mixture of Buddhist subjects and geometrical patterns, as well as ancestral decorations interspersed with futuristic motifs.

4. My advice for anyone who wants to begin tattooing is to be honest and sincere with your customers. Never deliberately copy or make tattoos that you are not fully satisfied with. It is essential for the person seeking a tattoo to carefully study the portfolio of local tattooists and choose an artist who specializes in the style they prefer.

5. My work can be seen at LTW, on Tallers Street in Barcelona, and at international conventions in London, Milan, Athens, New York and San José (California), etc. Moreover, once every year or so I do tattoos at the studios of friends, such as New York Adorned, Temple Oakland and others.
   www.holytrauma.com

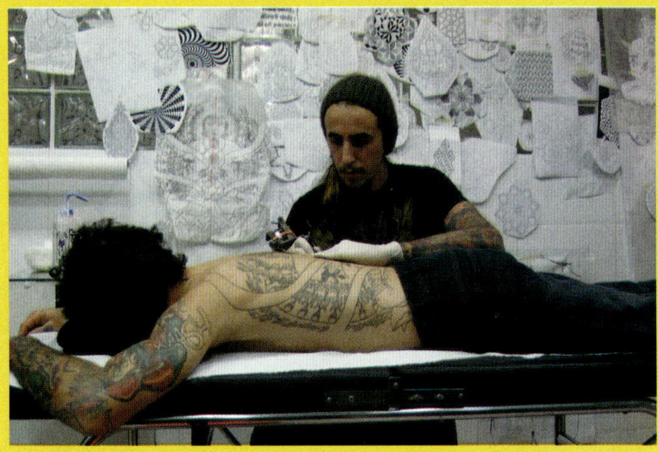

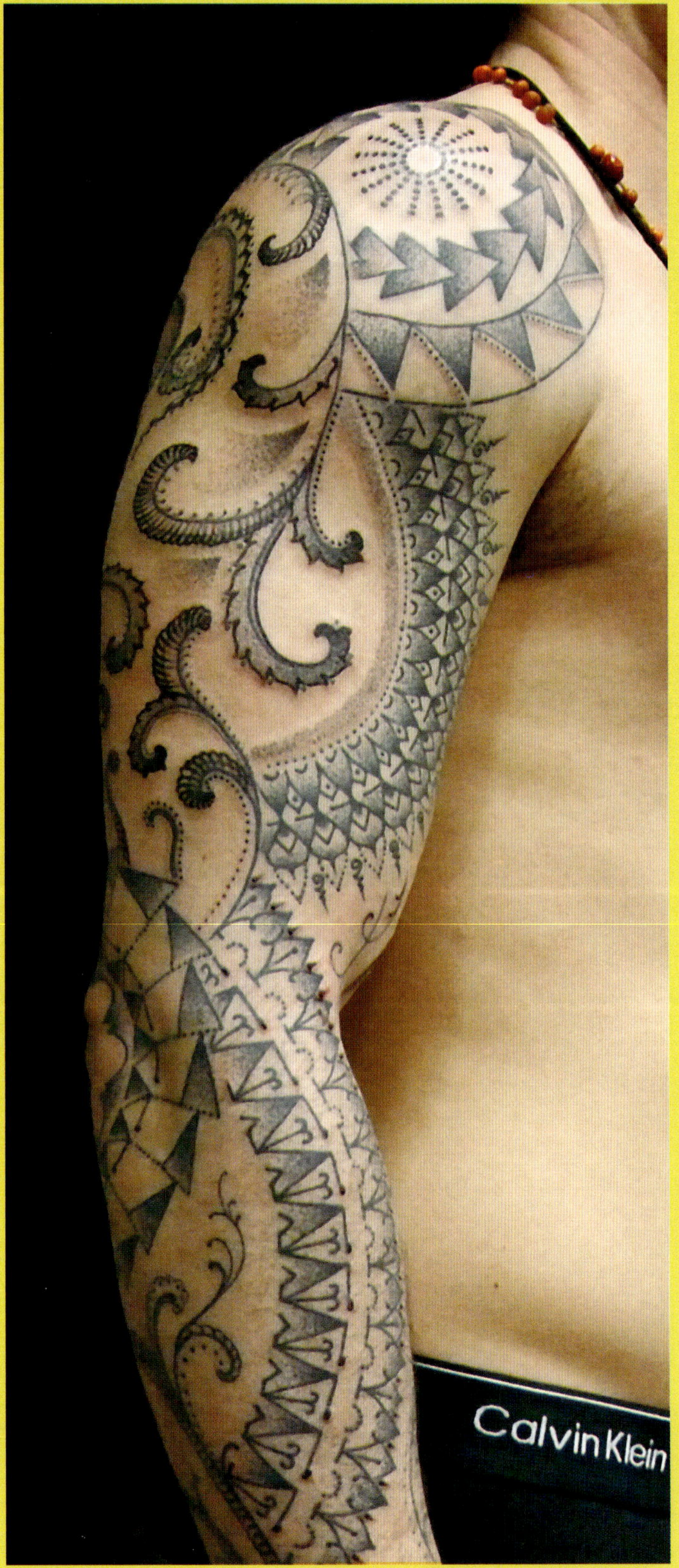

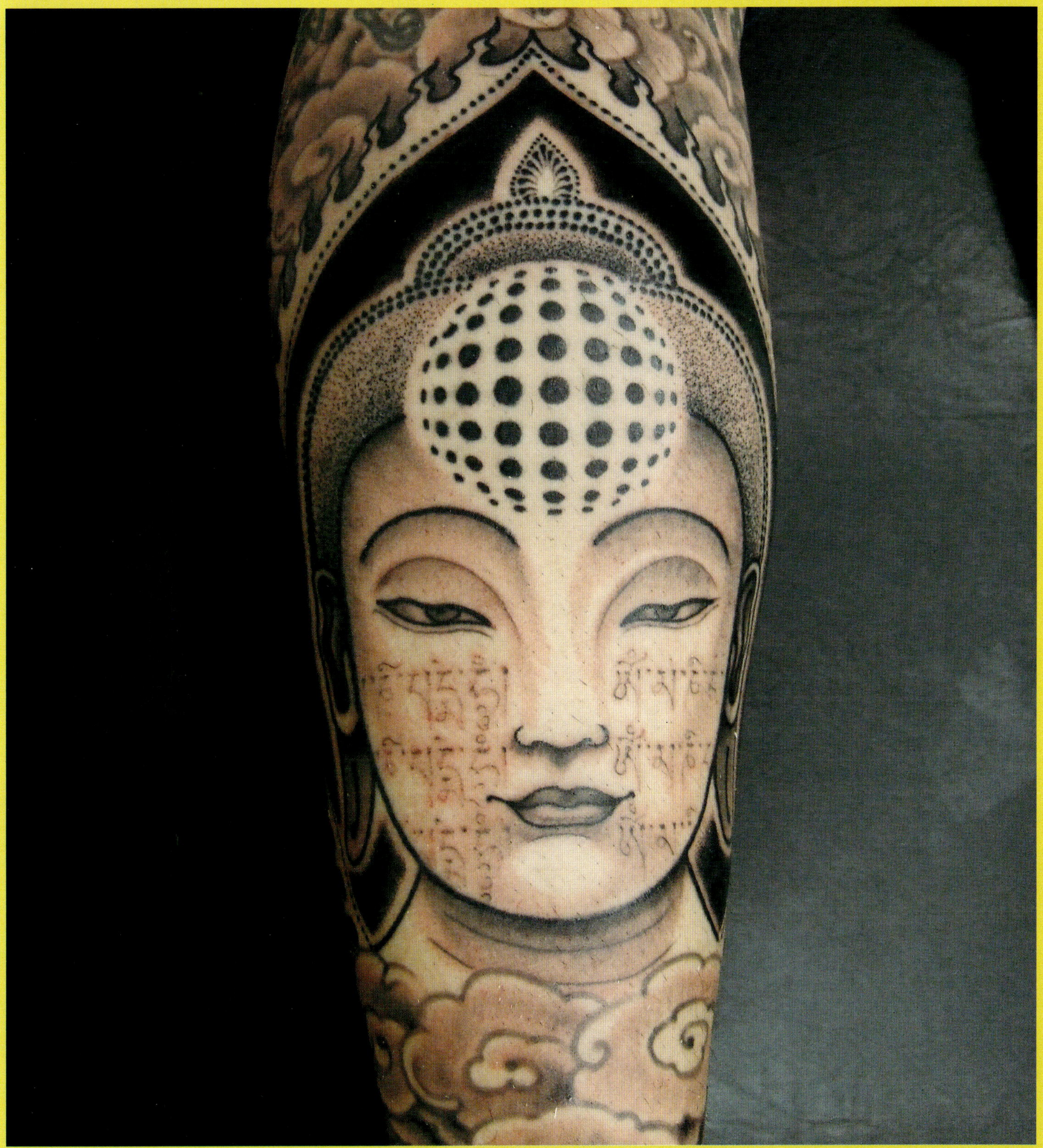

All these images courtesy of Jondix. On pages 36 and 37, illustration designed by Jondix.

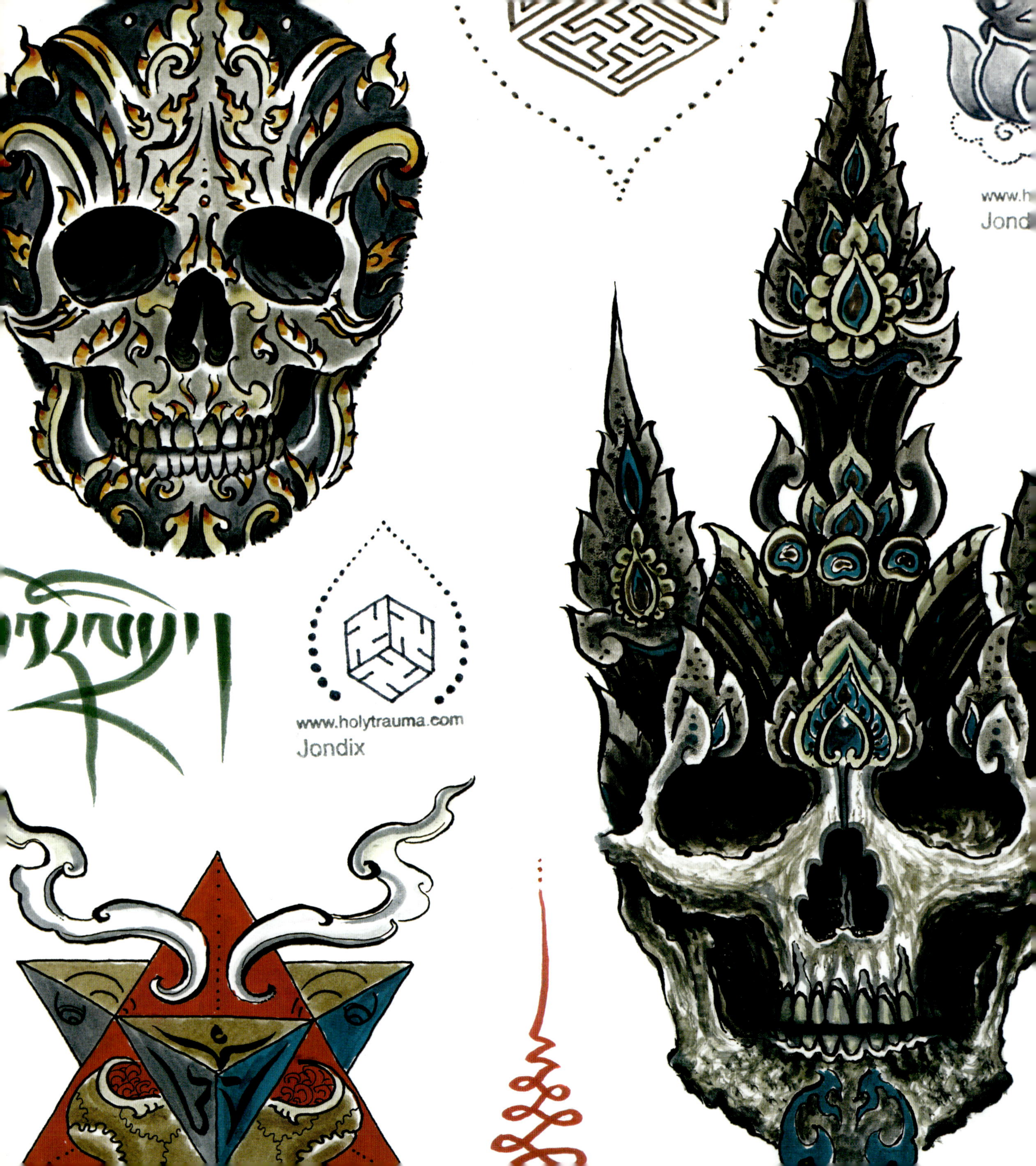
www.h
Jond
www.holytrauma.com
Jondix

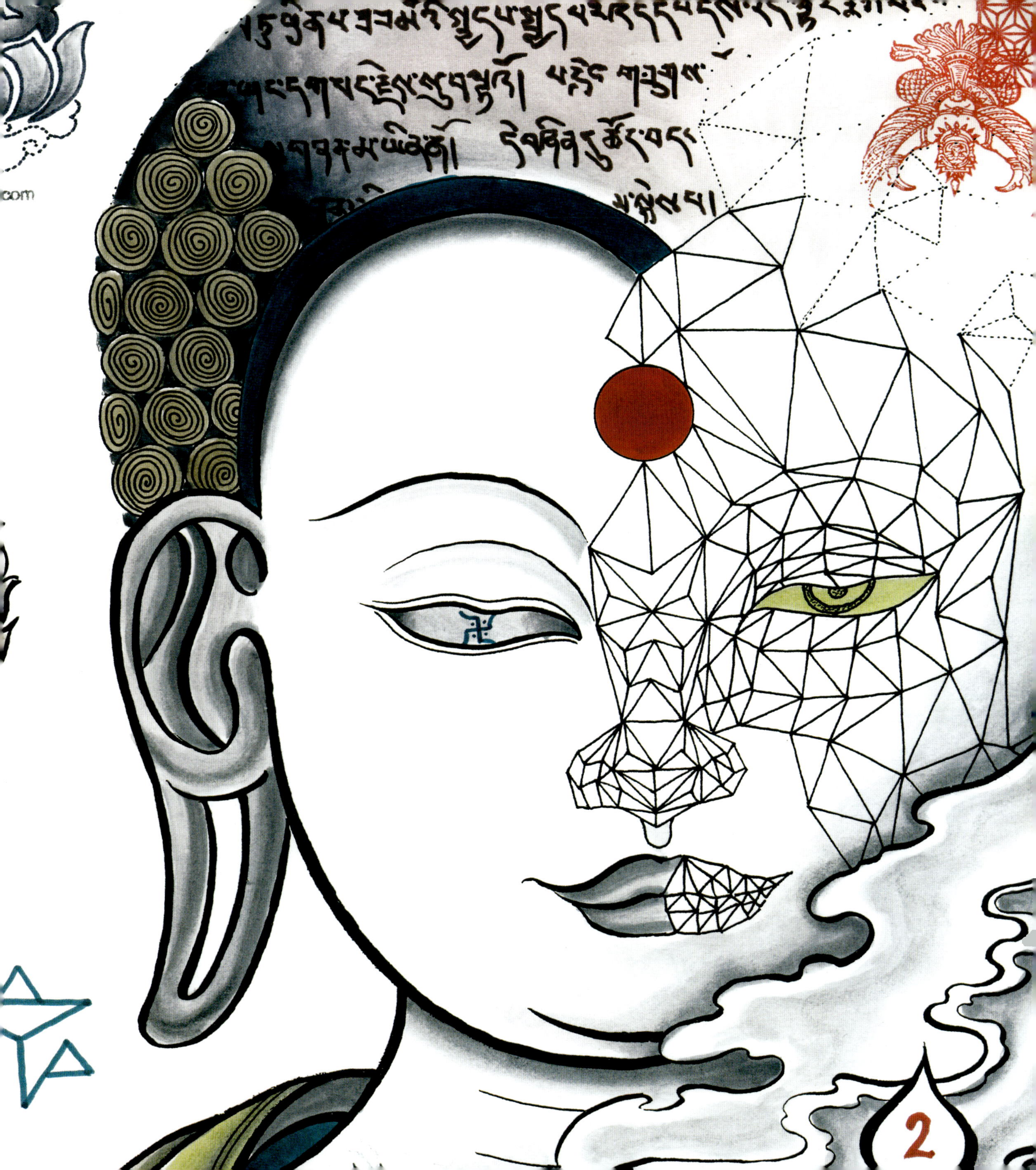

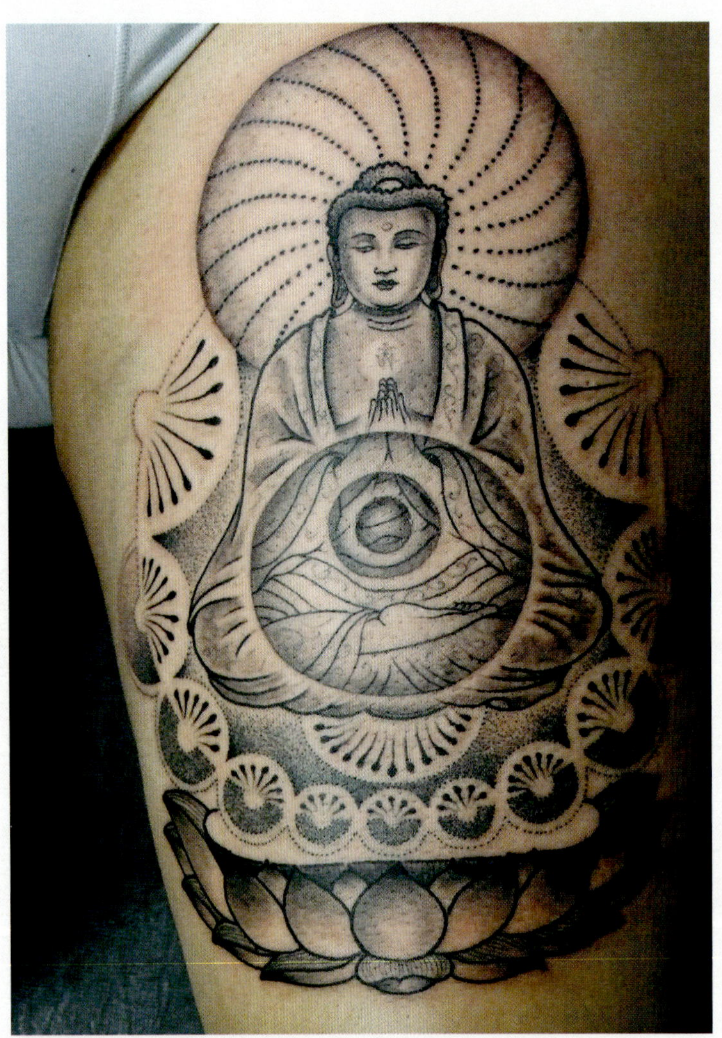

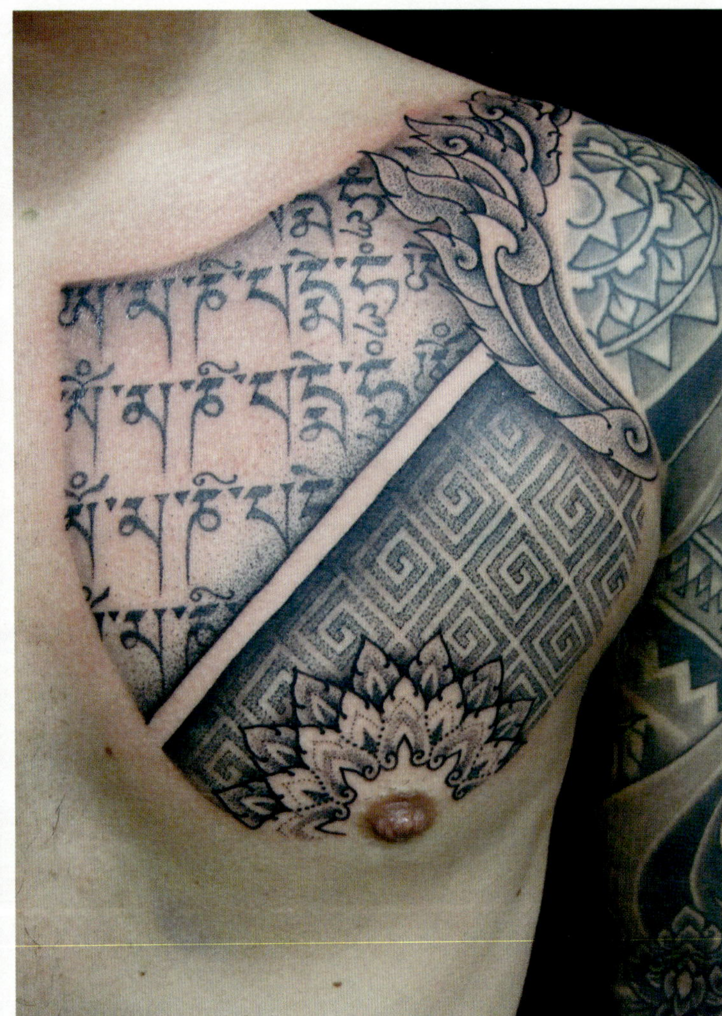

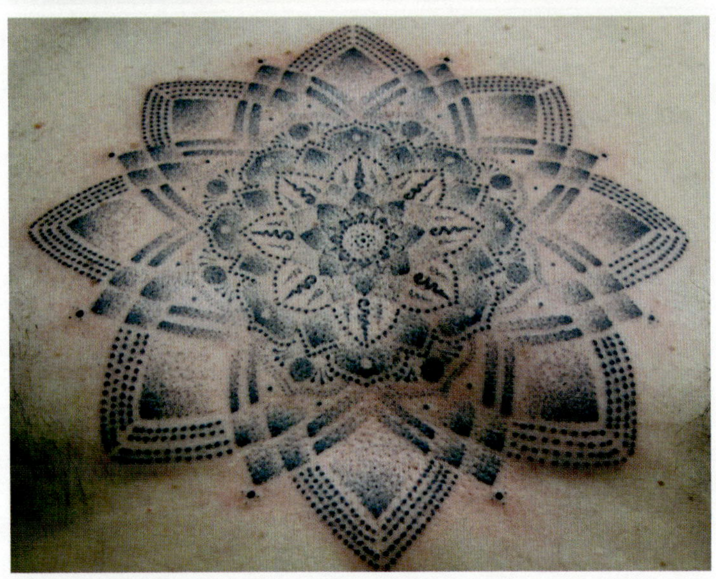

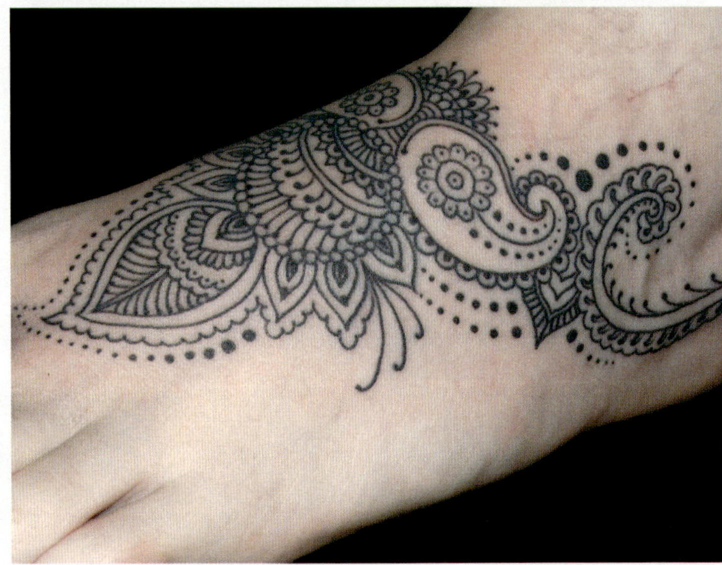

All designs on these pages by Jondix.

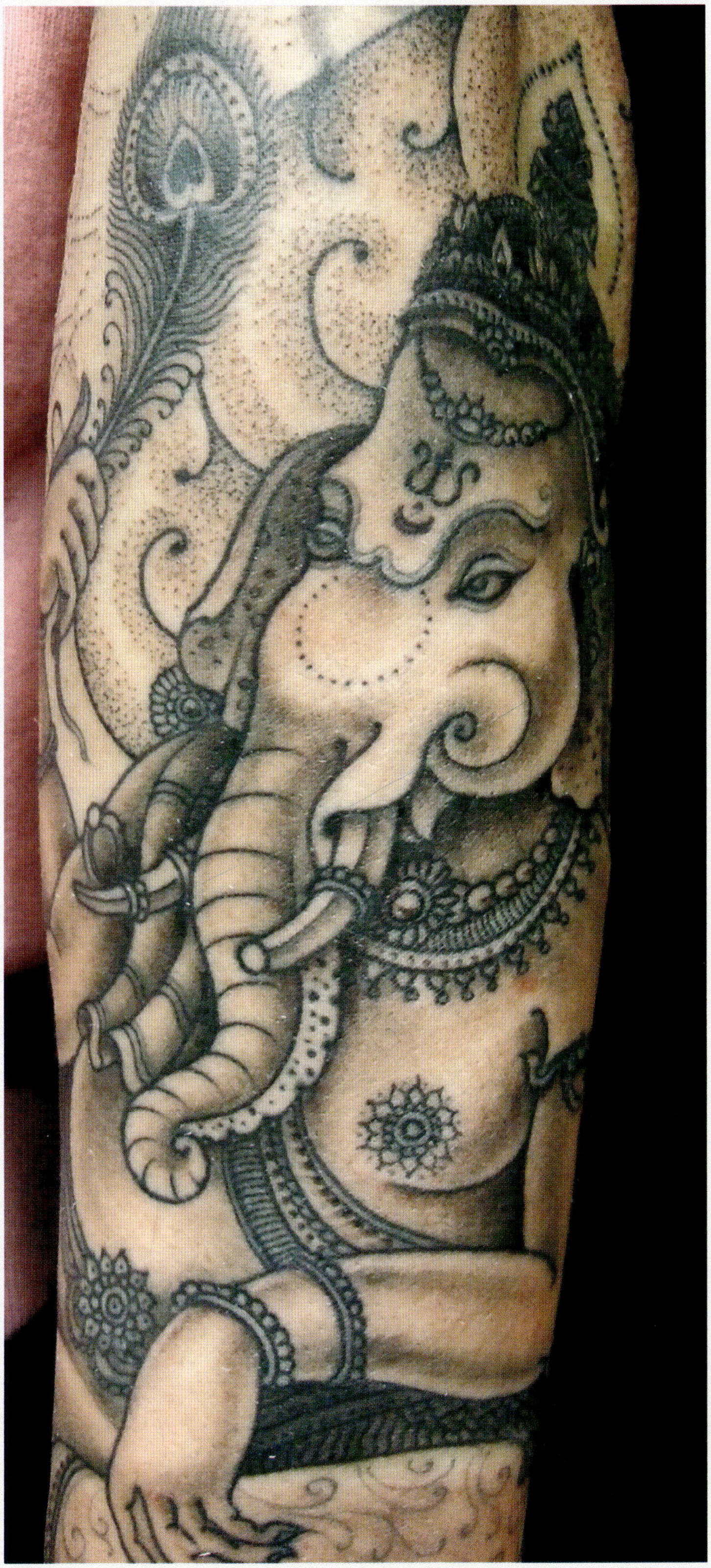

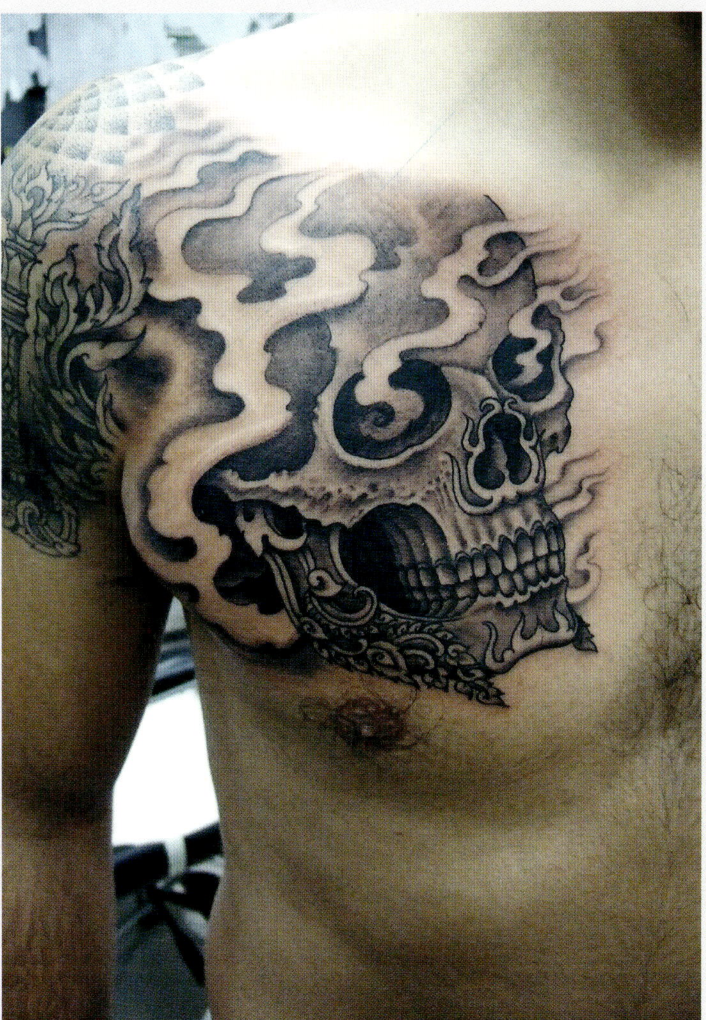

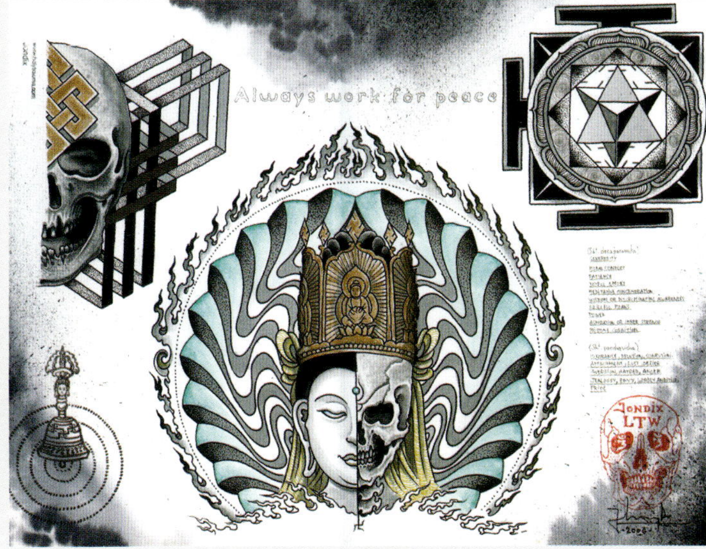
Always work for peace
Jondix
LTW

ALEX DE PASE

ITALY

1. I started tattooing at the age of 15. When I saw one of my friend's tattooed arms I was amazed. I started devising my first rough equipment using the plastic frame of Bic pens by melting their plastic and mounting the needles on it.

2. Tattooing is a real art form. Some artists paint on canvas, and others on skin. In the past, people used to buy paintings to make their houses prettier; now people are prepared to travel long distances in order to get an authored tattoo on their skin.

3. My style is color portraiture; it's what I know and I feel inside. Anything else bores me. In realism, on the contrary, the target is the everlasting quest for perfection and the perception of every single detail. It's a never-ending challenge which leaves room for improvement forever and ever. The use of colors is a further quest for difficulty, for the realism of pursuing naturalness. After all, we live in a world full of colors.

5. Alex De Pase Tattoo Studio.
www.alexdepasetattoo.com
www.myspace.com/alexdepase

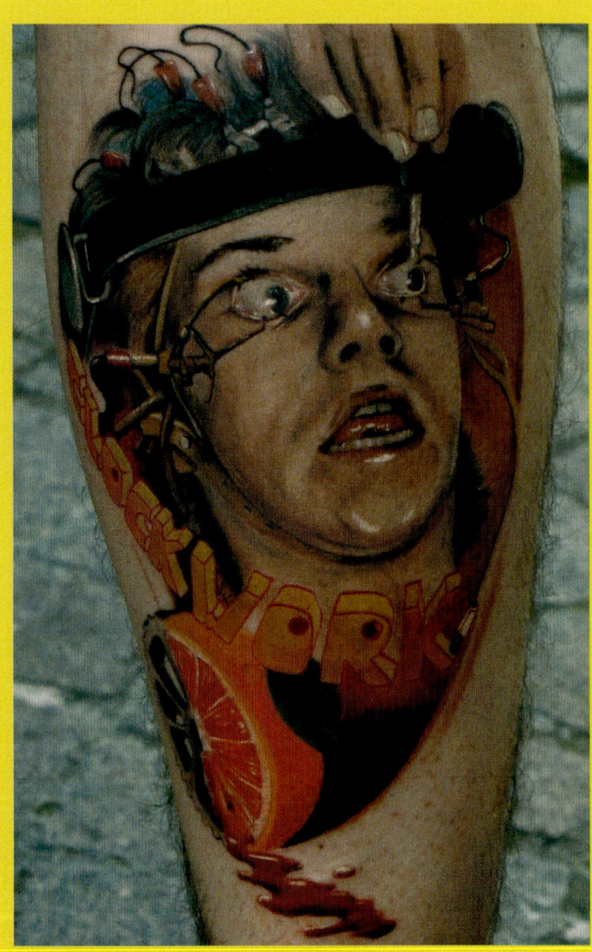

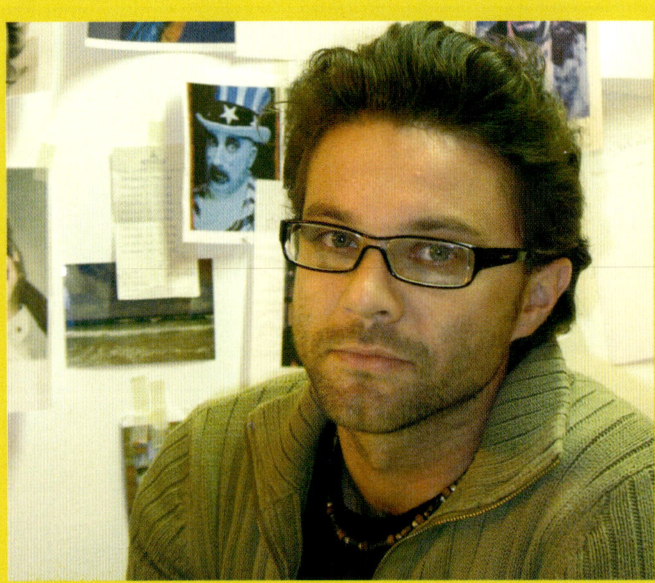

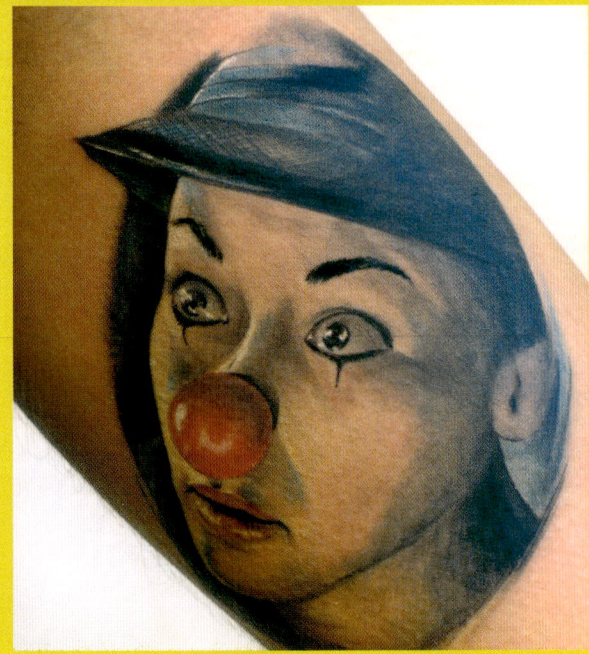

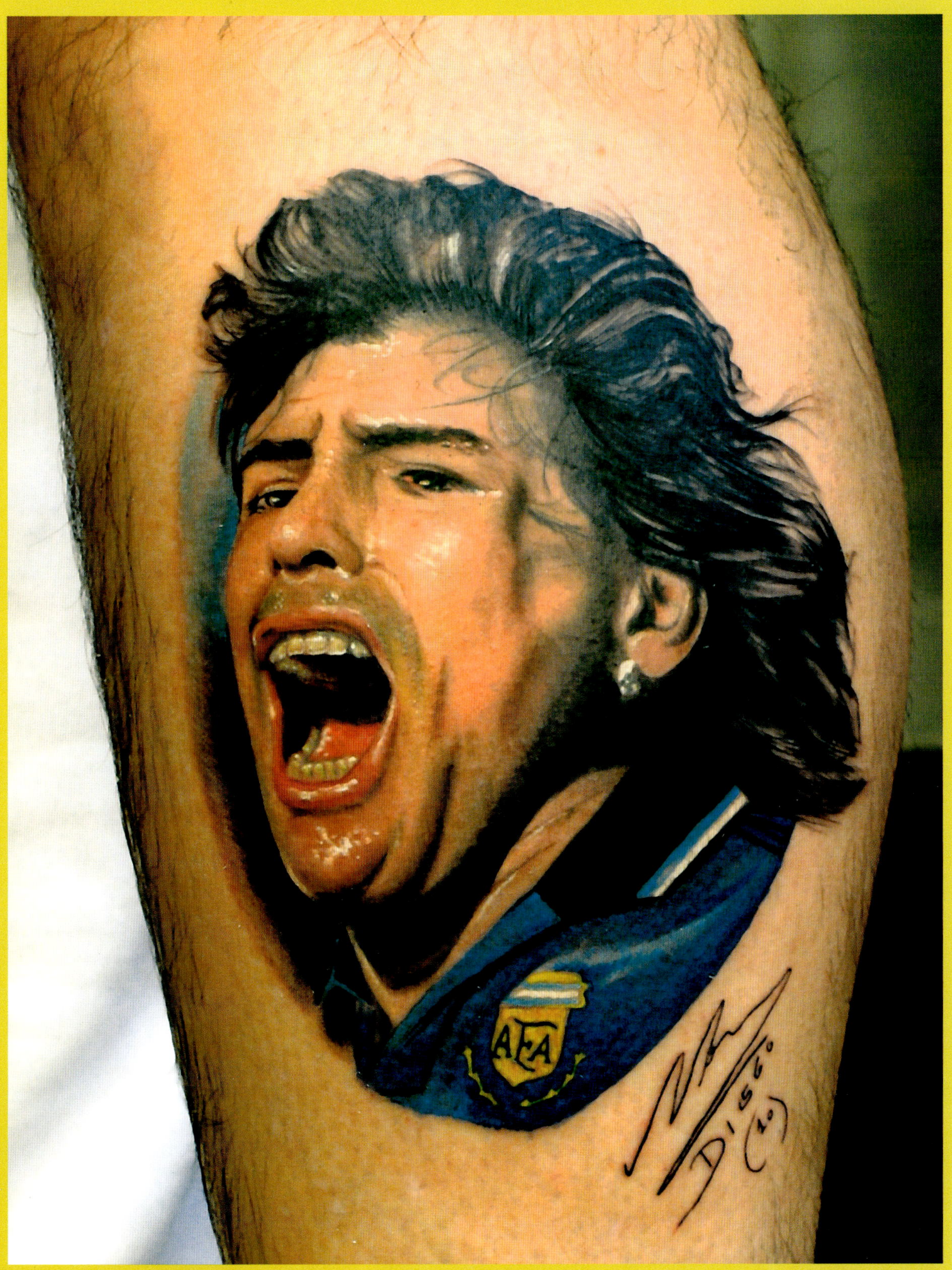

All designs on these pages by Alex De Pase.

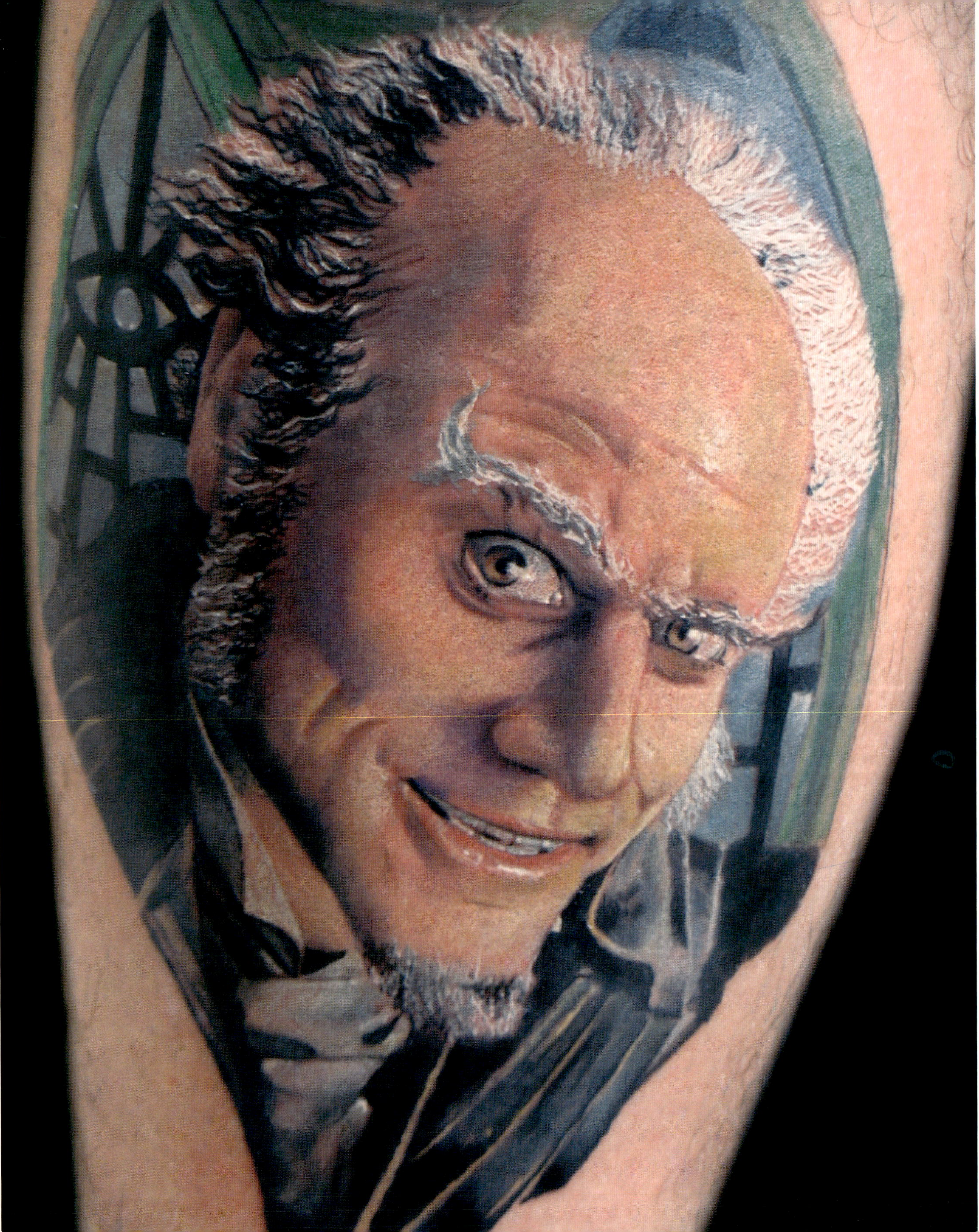

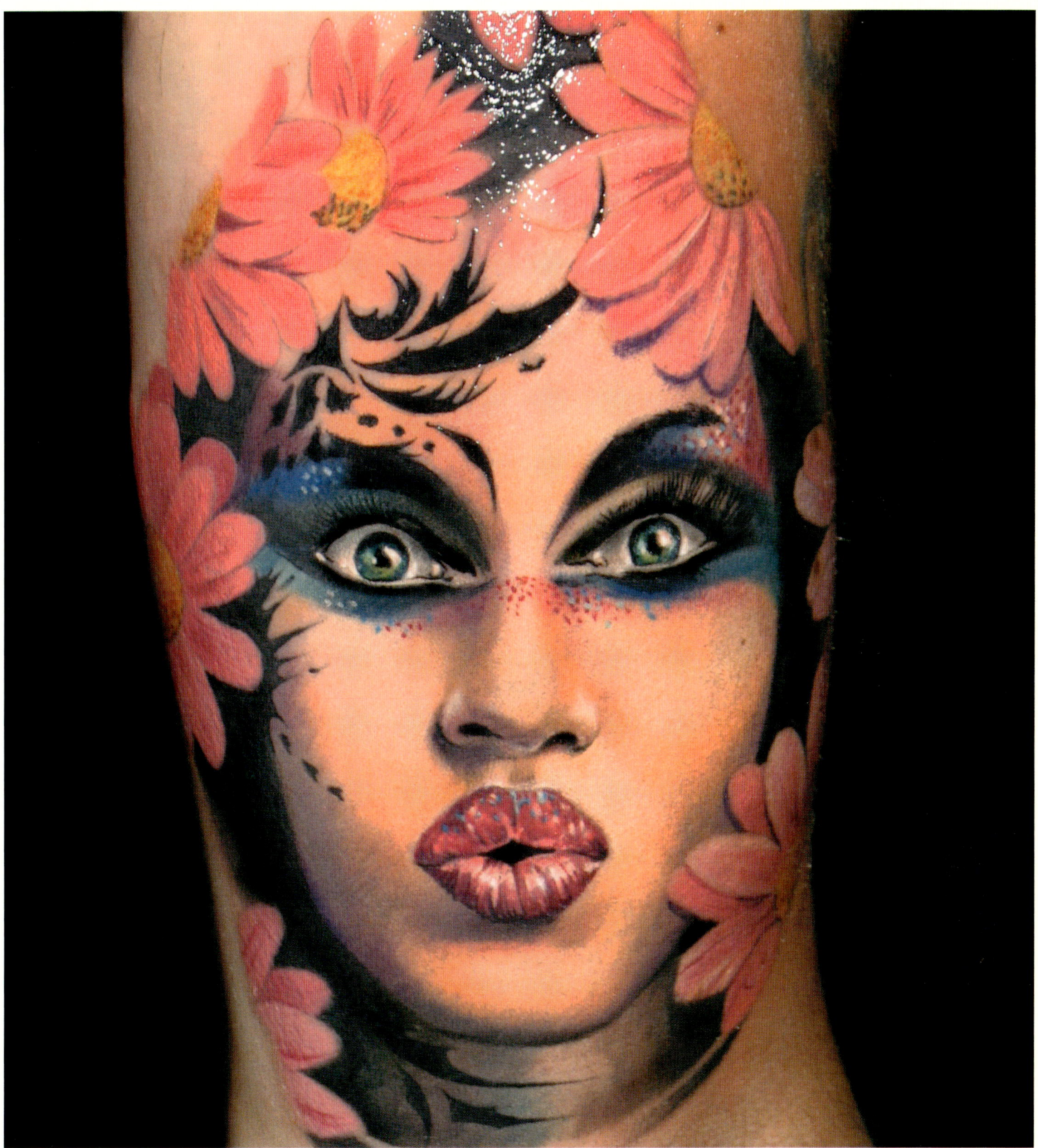

All images courtesy of Alex De Pase.

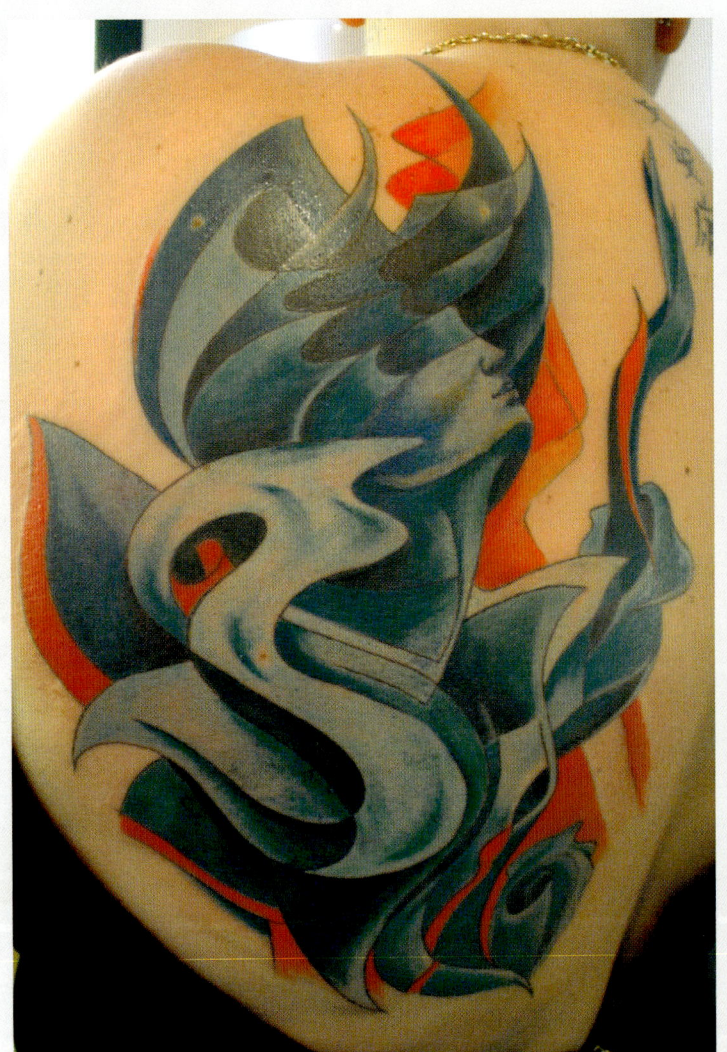

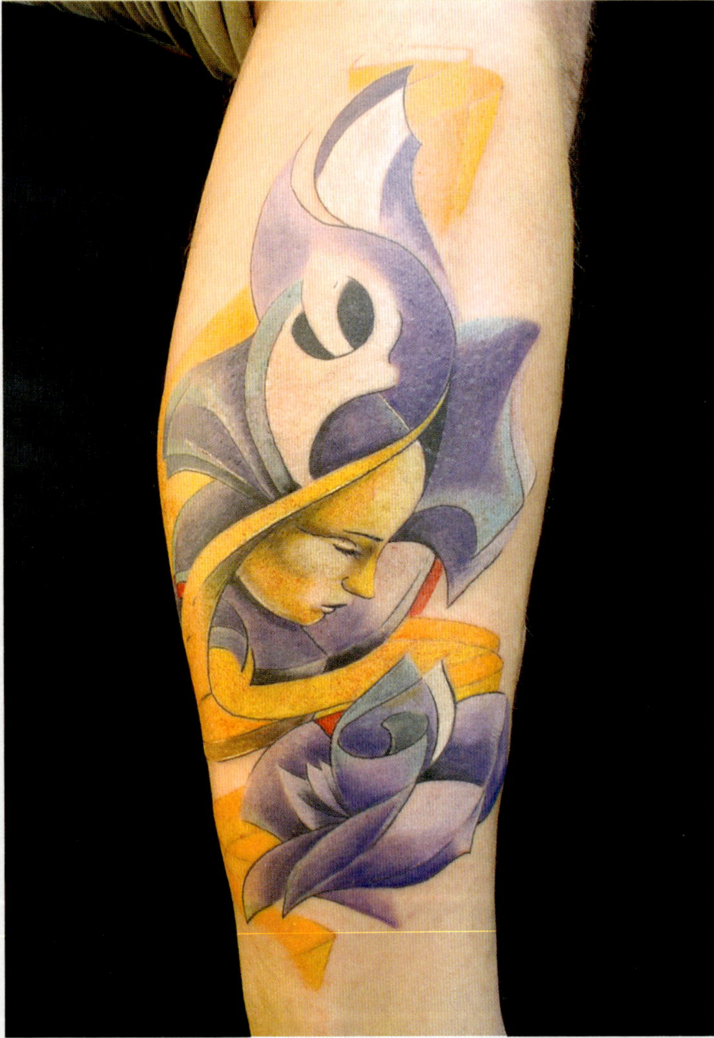

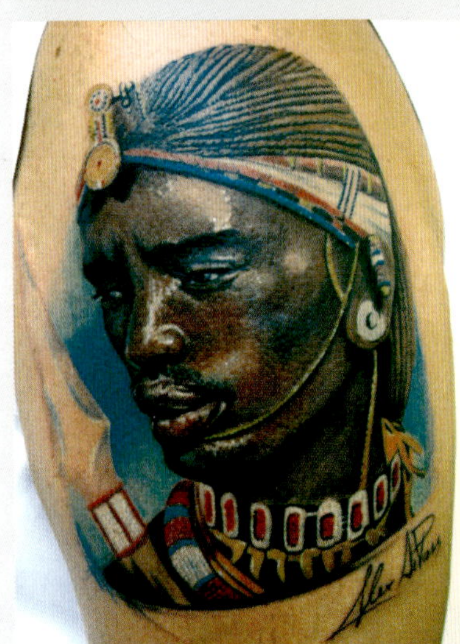

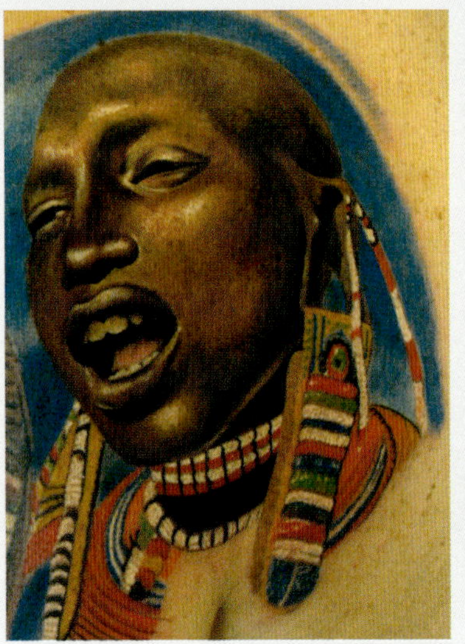

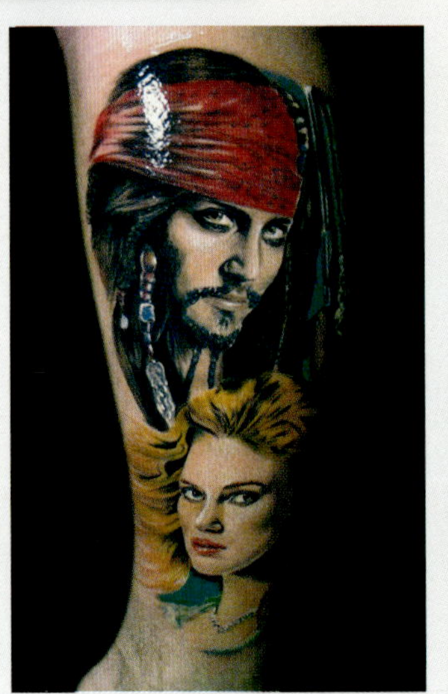

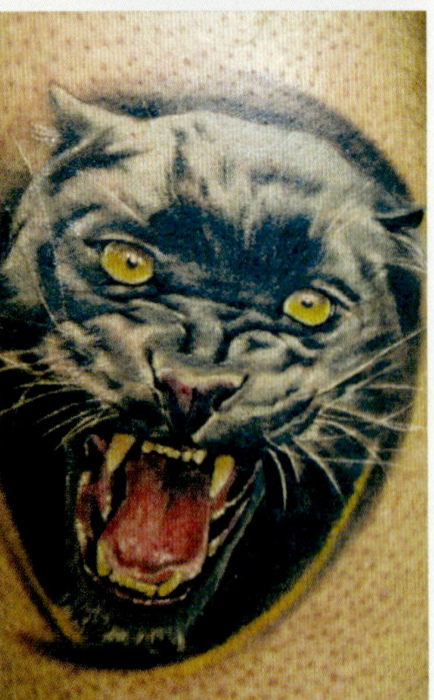

All images courtesy of Alex De Pase.

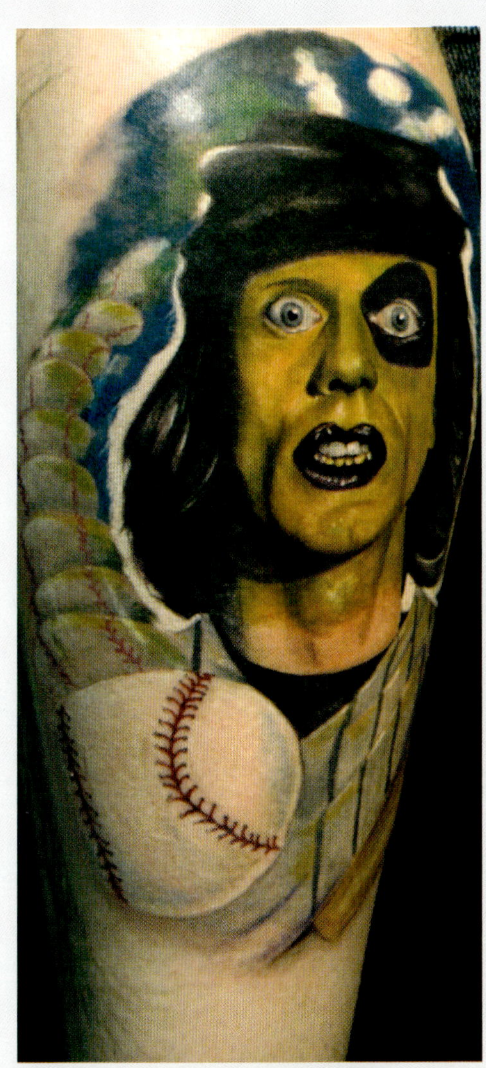
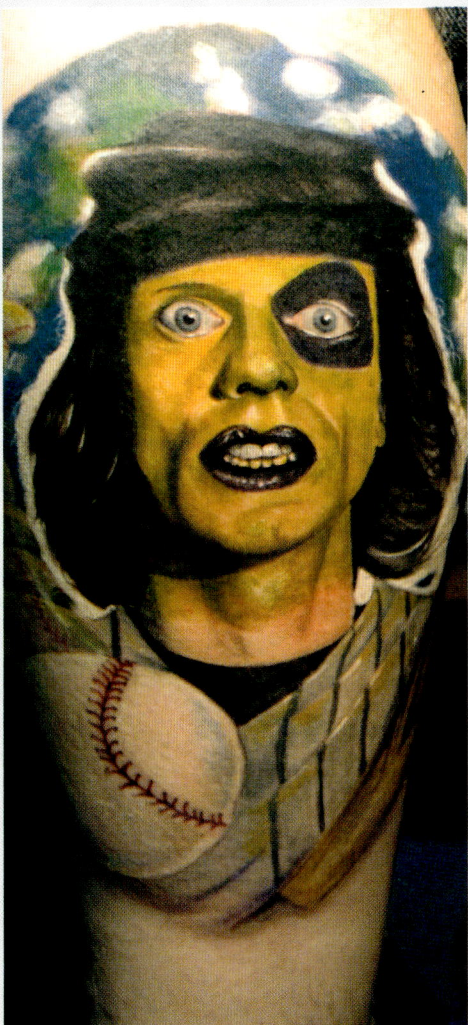
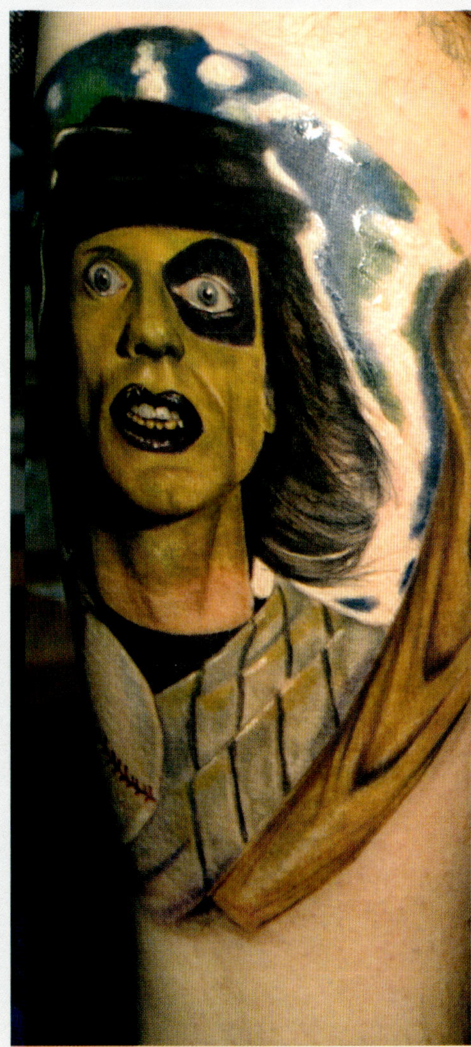
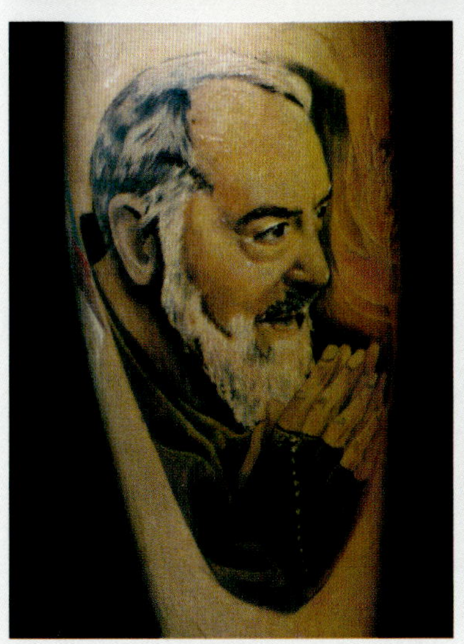
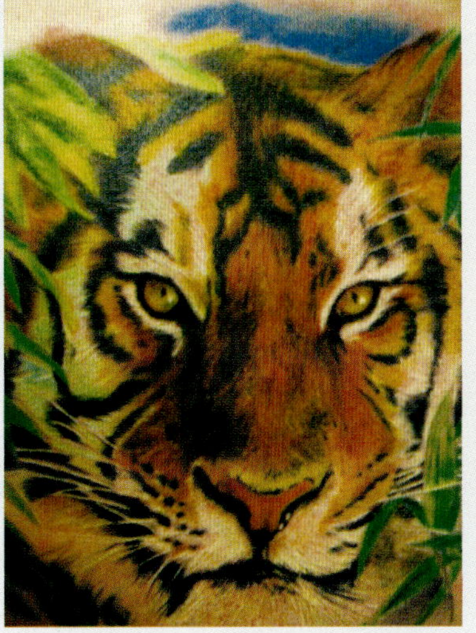
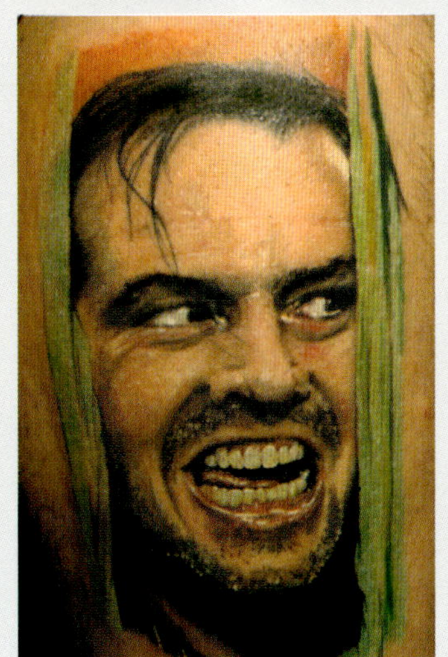
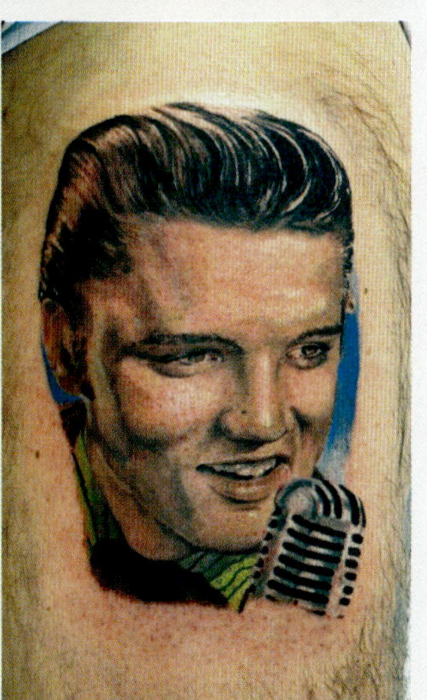

ALEX DE PASE

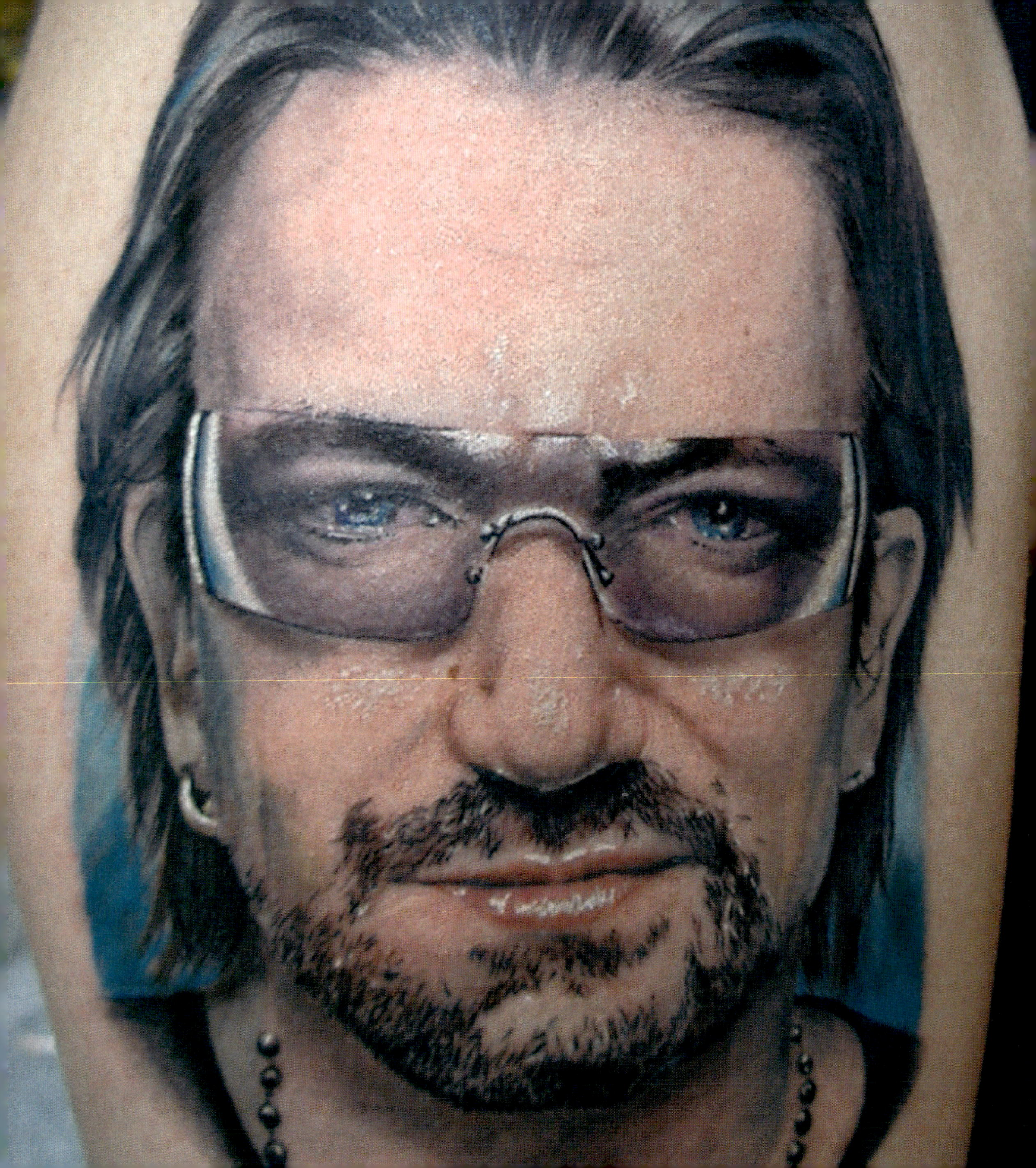

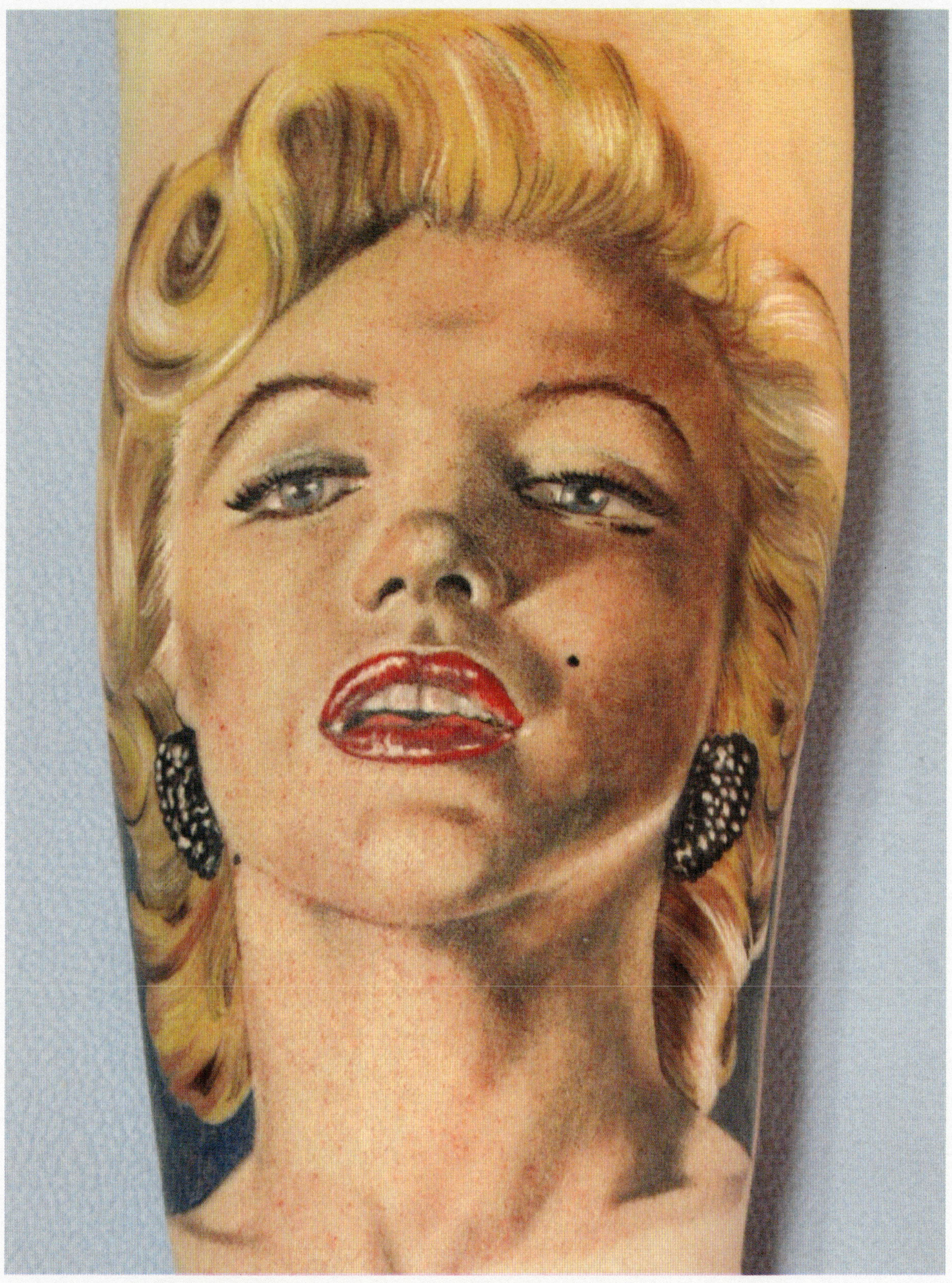

All images courtesy of Alex De Pase.

SUNNY BUICK

FRANCE

1. I decided at age 15 that I wanted to learn to tattoo. I met some people in San Francisco who were getting a lot of traditional tattoos and were going to learn to tattoo. I began to hang out at Lyle Tuttle's and stay there after hours. I helped to put together their magazine and I met Erno when he was opening his shop in the lower Haight. I asked many people for a job but no one took me seriously. Seven years later I bought some equipment and tattooed at the house of a friend who was also learning to tattoo. I tattooed alone in my house for four years before I got an apprenticeship with Henry Goldfield.

2. First, I think that tattoos are a part of fashion, a kind of decoration, just like hair or clothing. After that, there are deeper meanings and symbols and some very strong magic. I feel like the tattoo covers our nakedness and makes us more who we really are inside.

3. I tattoo in the simple and bold style of traditional American tattoos. I like to tattoo girls and sailor designs and also Mexican skulls. I'm also interested in circus imagery and science fiction, like robots and ray guns.

4. Never get a tattoo if you're thinking about having it lasered off later. Find the tattoo artist who has a style that matches your ideas. Take your time to save some money and do the project right. Get tattooed when you are in good physical health. Eat well and sleep well before the appointment.

5. www.sunnybuick.com
   www.myspace.com/sunnybuick
   www.sunnybuick.etsy.com

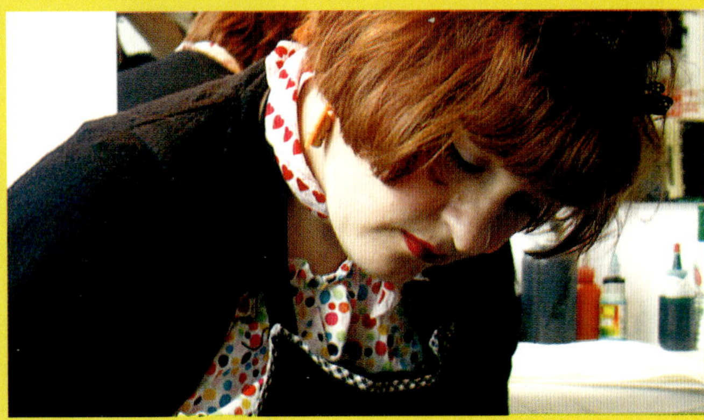

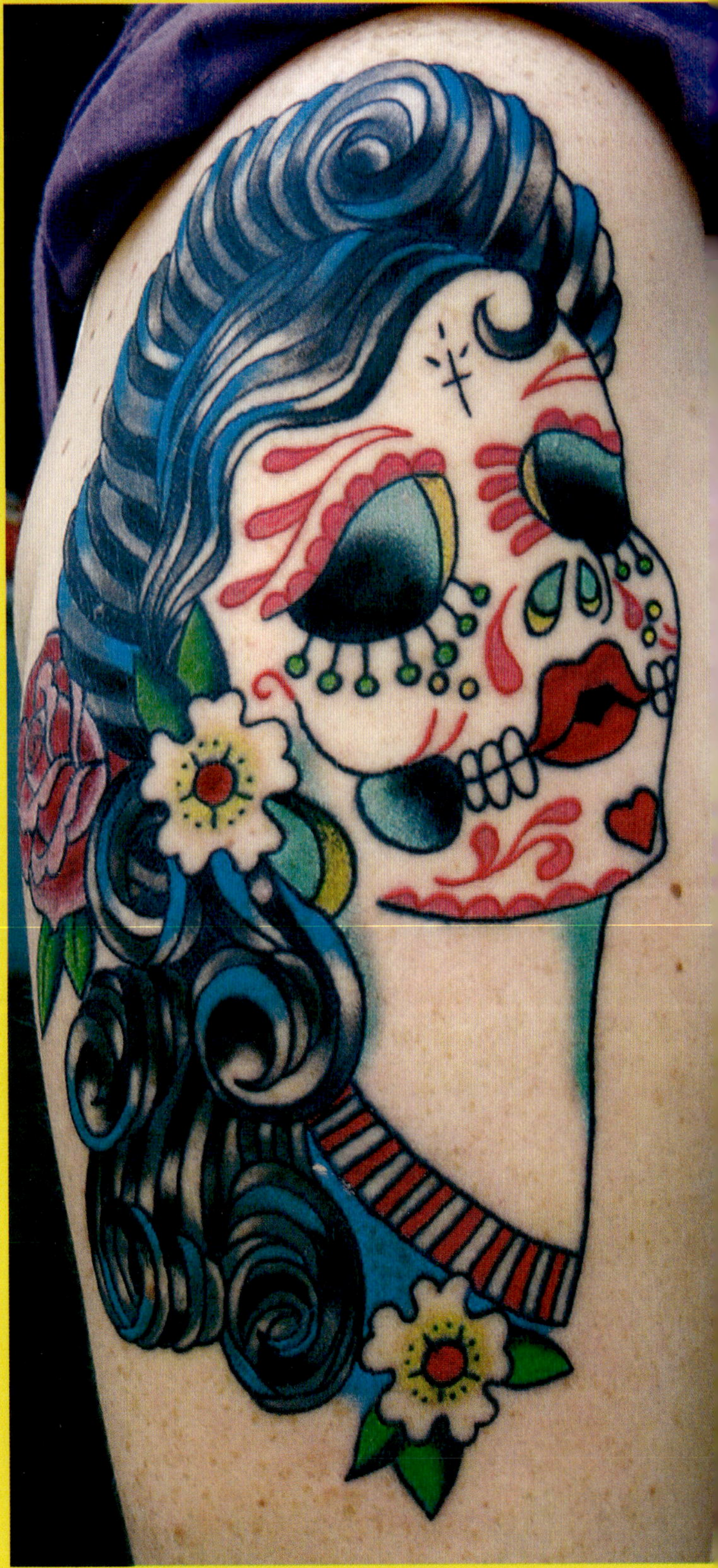

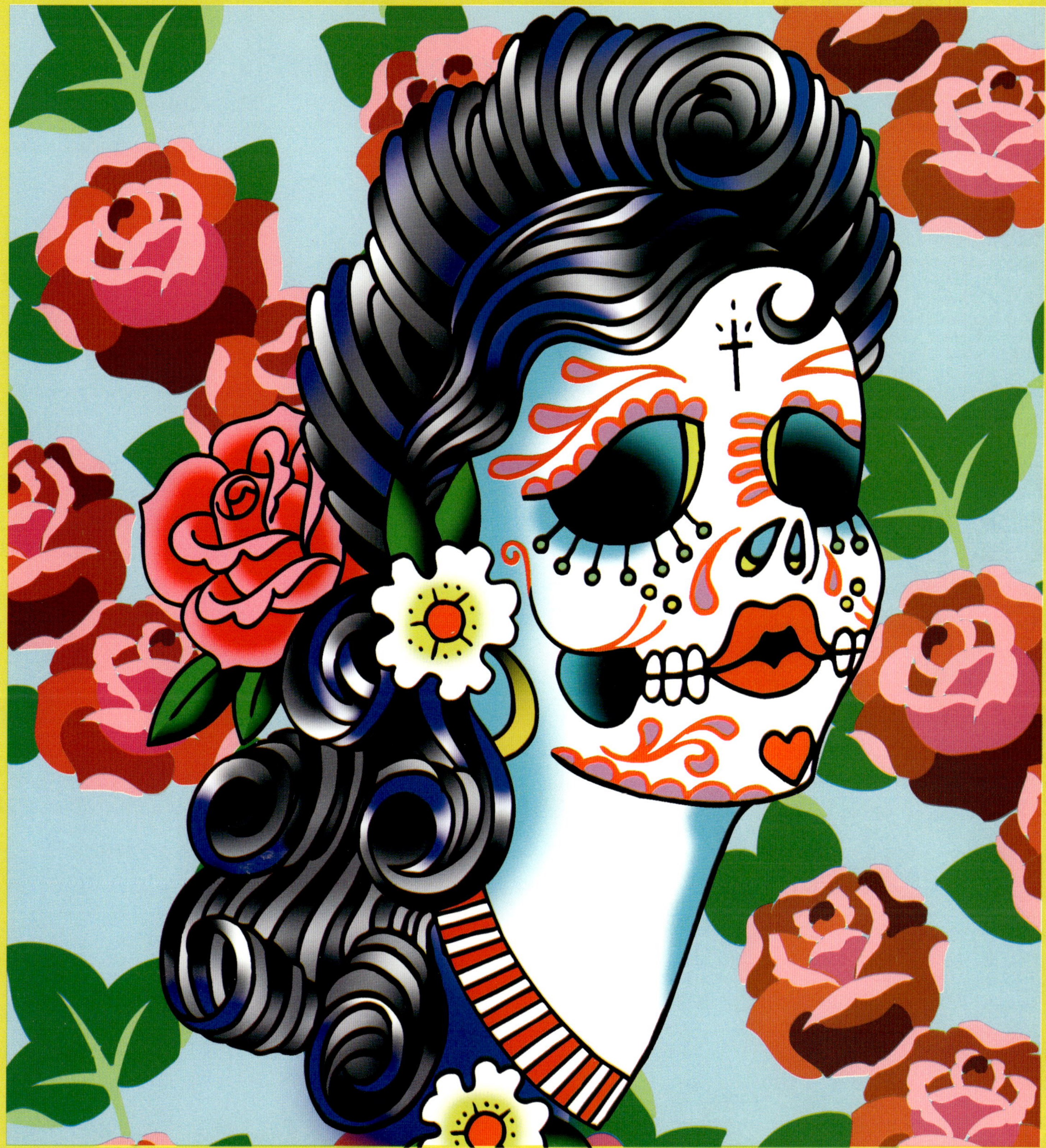

All designs on these pages and acrylic illustration made by Sunny Buick.

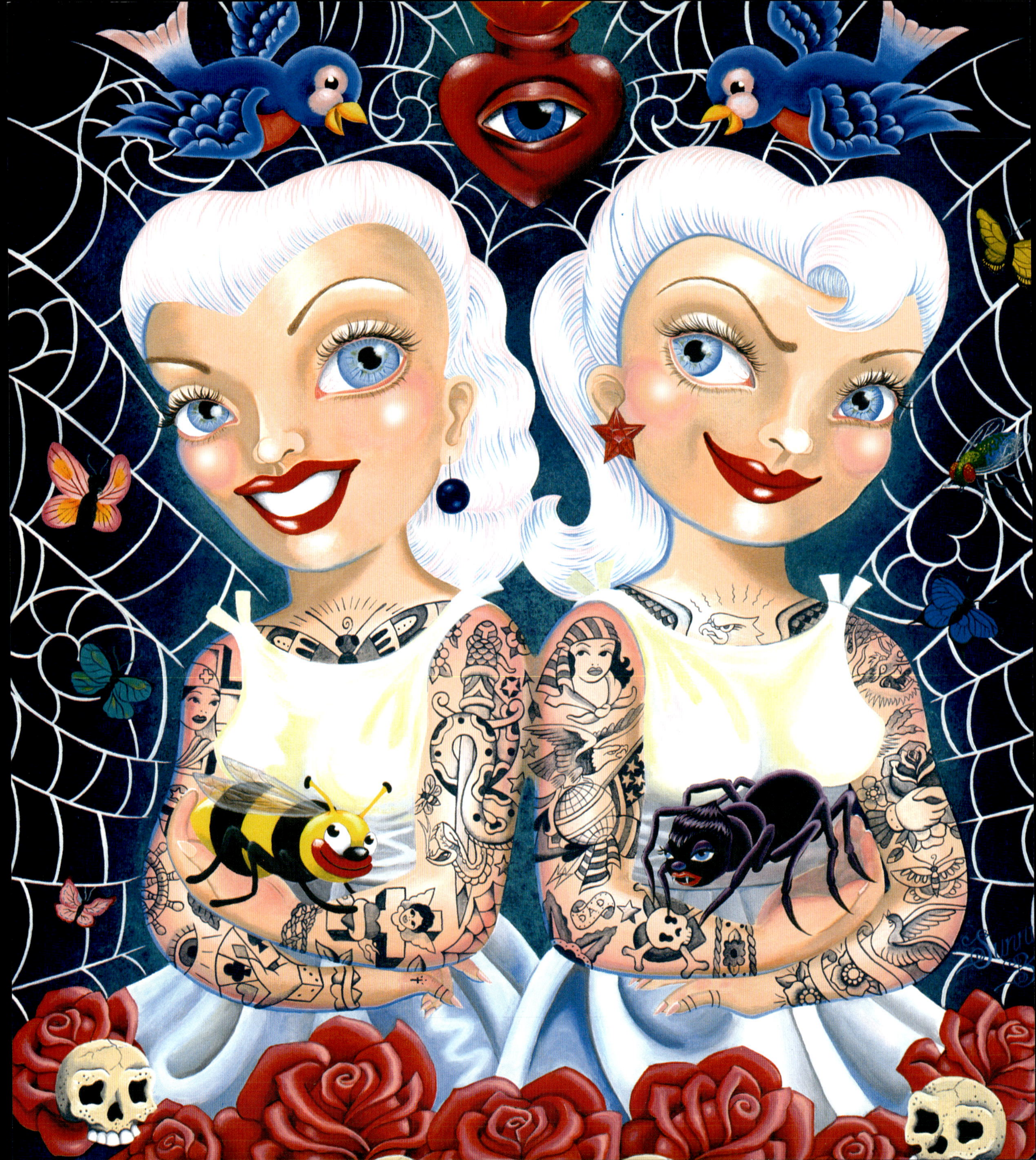
DAD

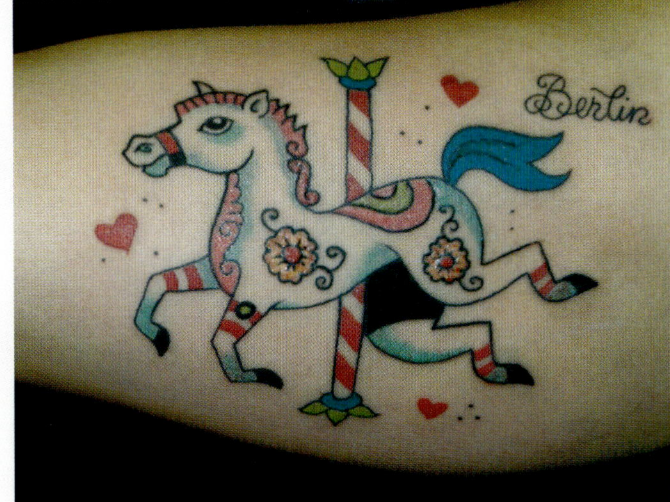

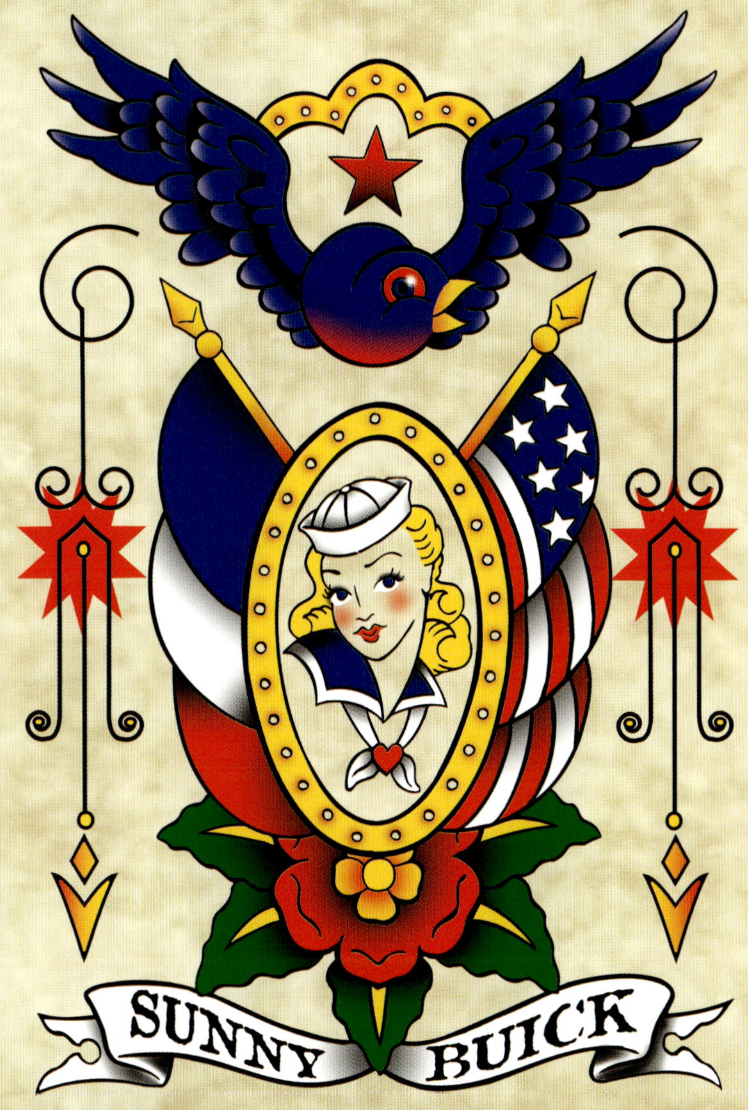

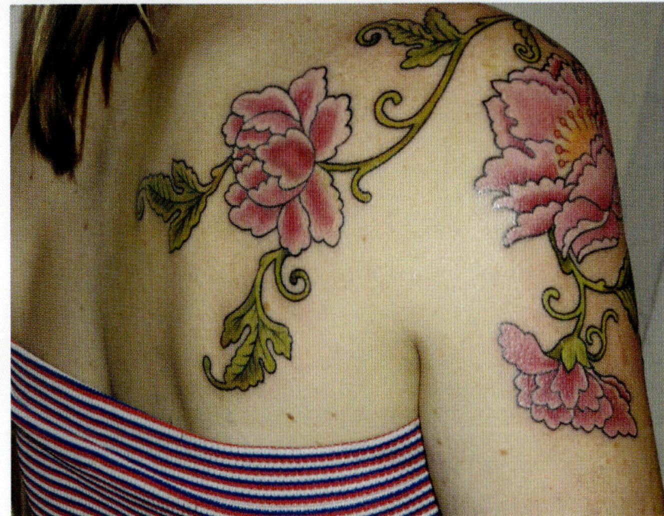

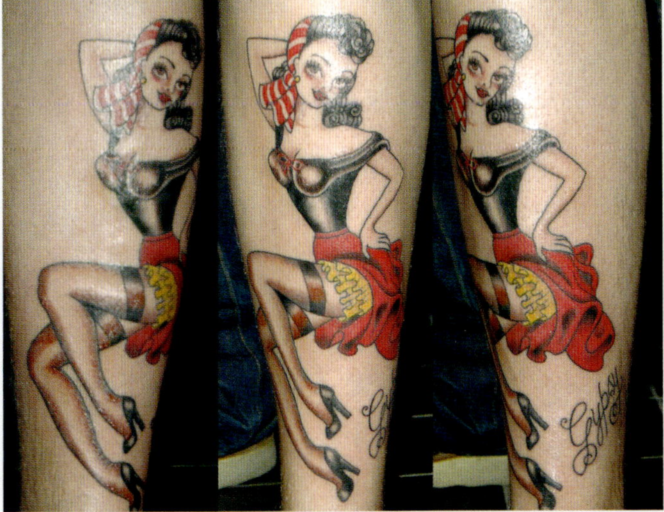

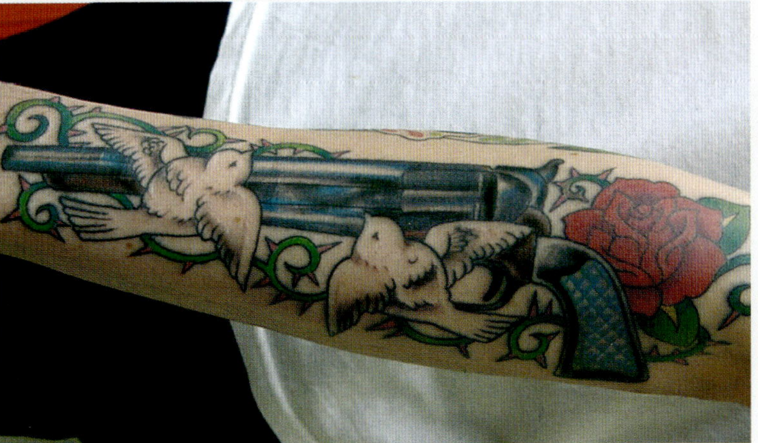

Left page acrylic painting and designs on this page by Sunny Buick. Image top right, Buick's business card.

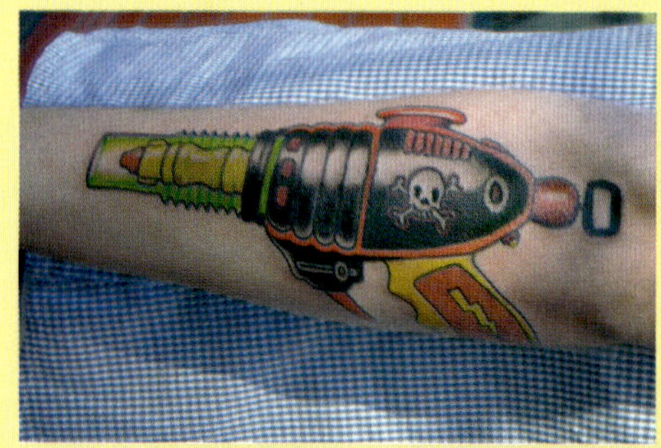

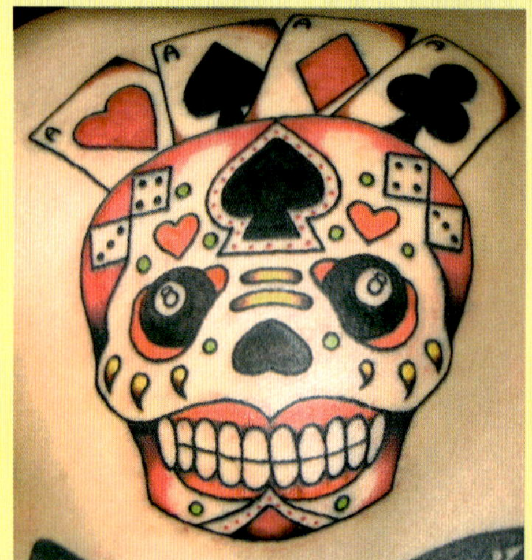

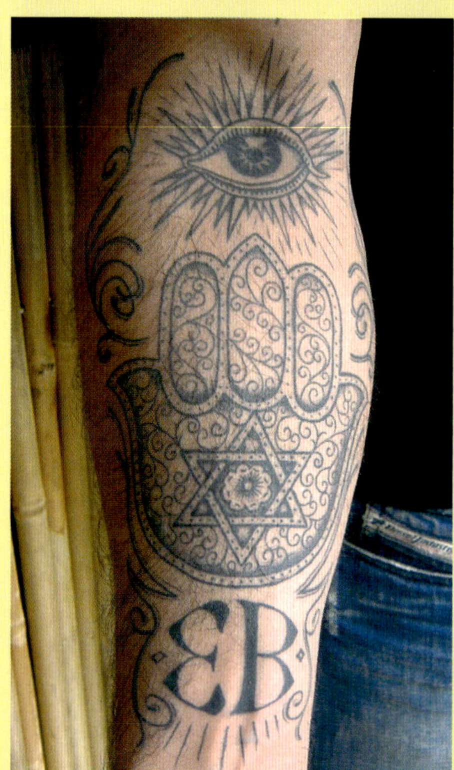

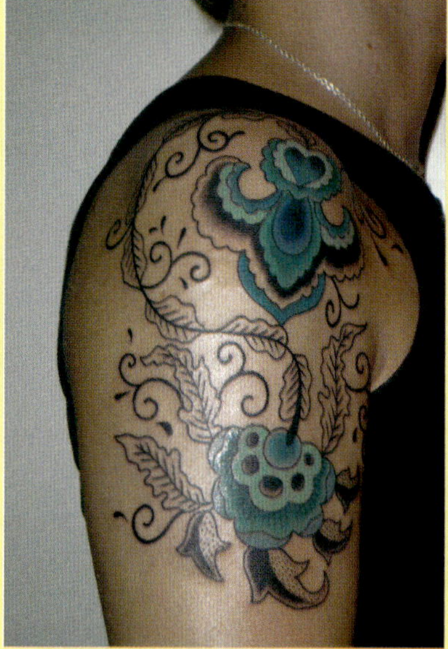

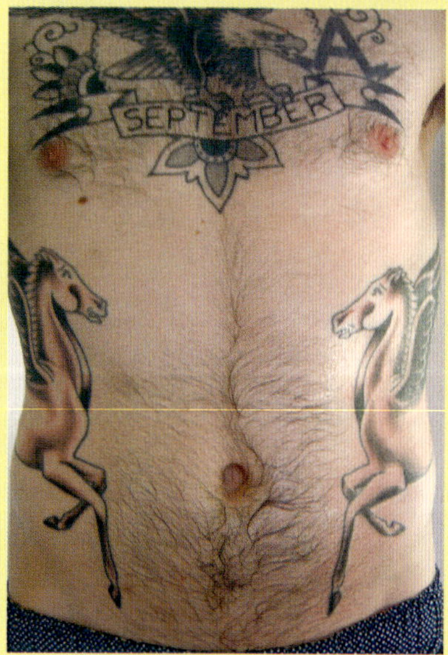

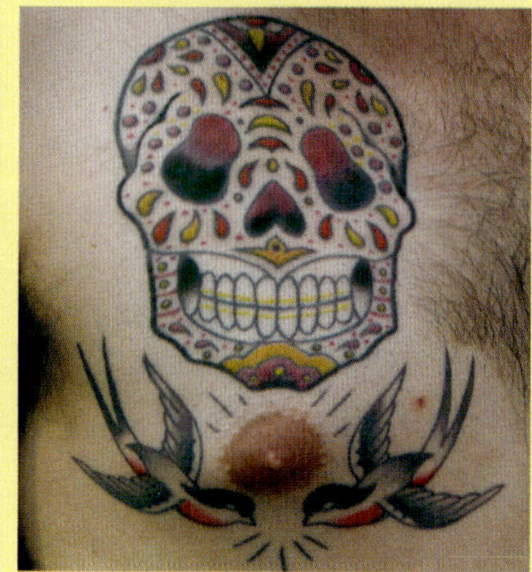

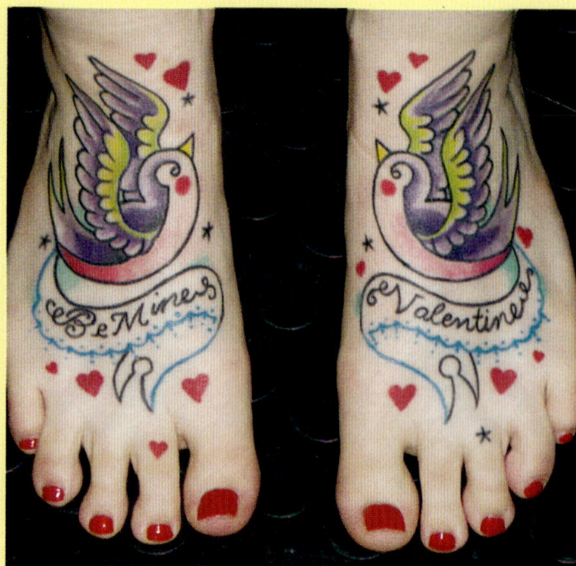

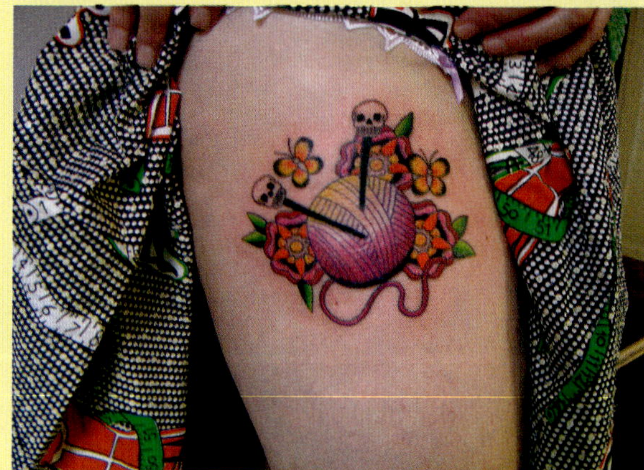

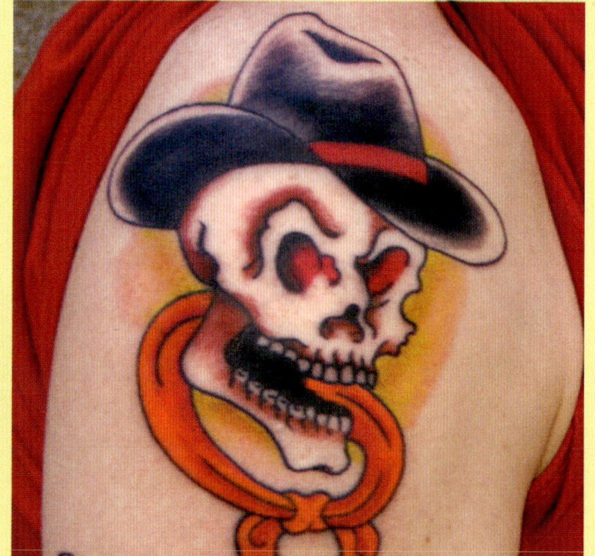

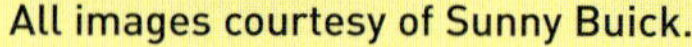
All images courtesy of Sunny Buick.

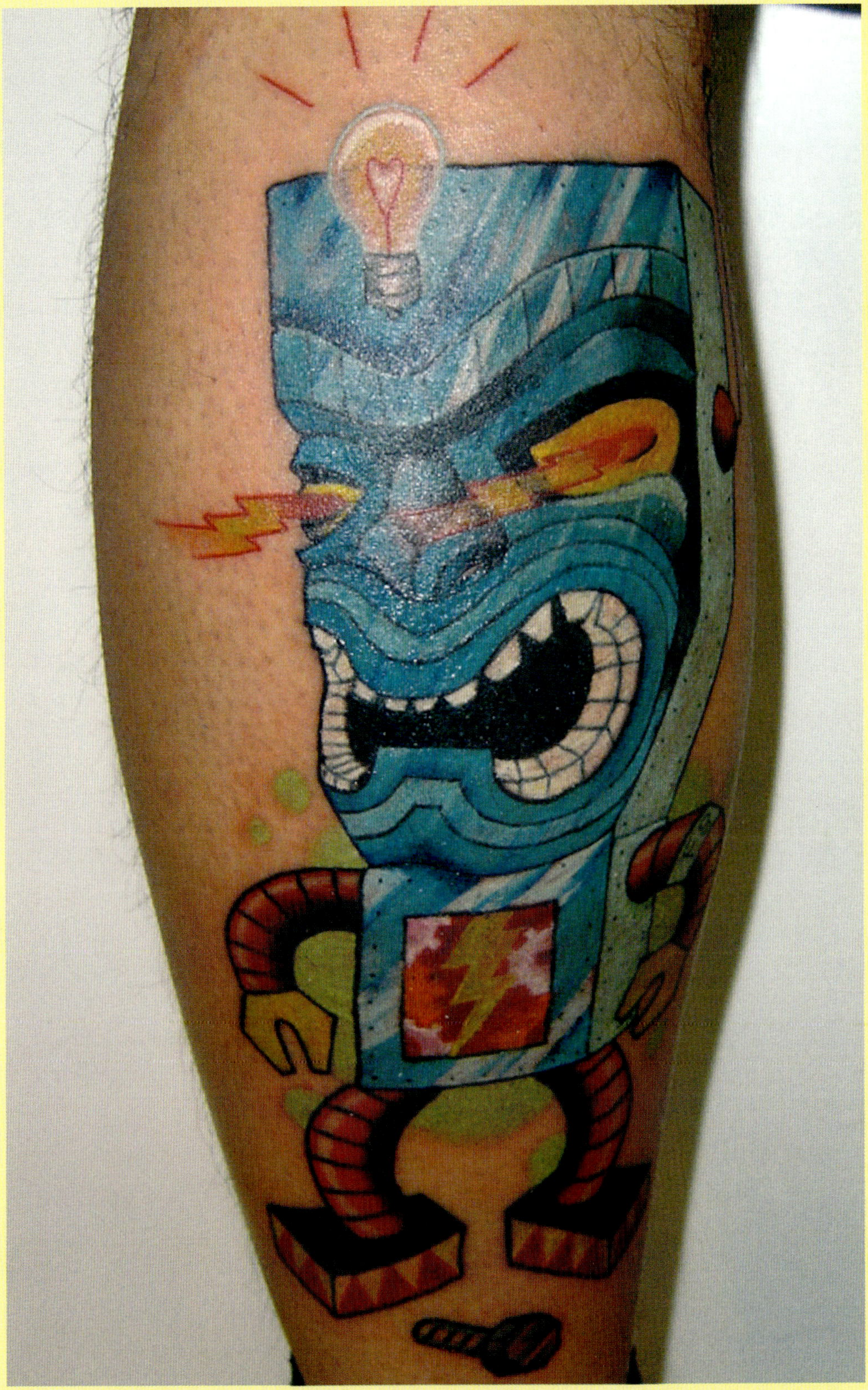

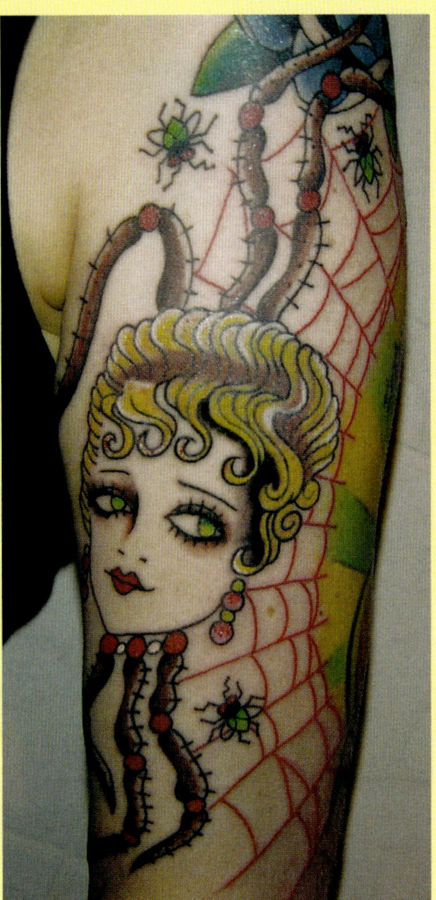

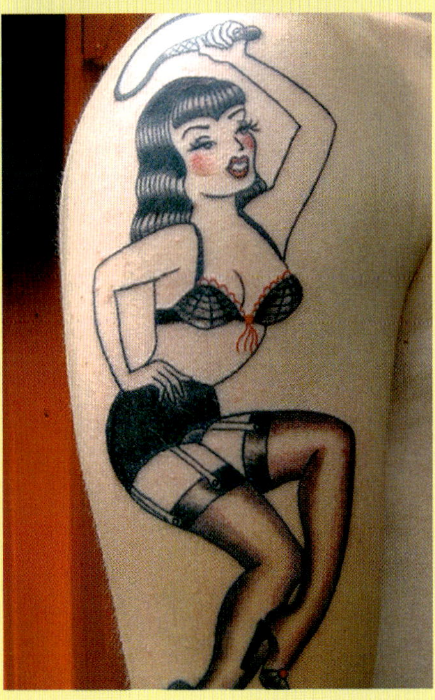

SUNNY BUICK

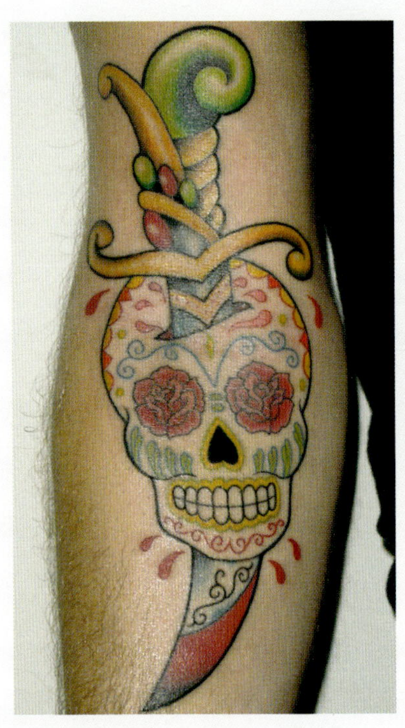
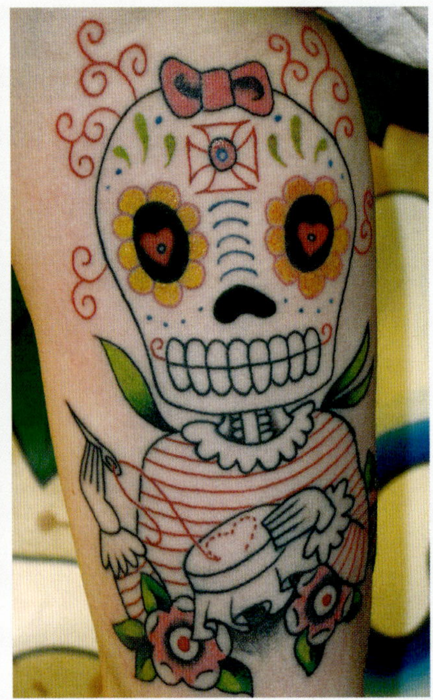
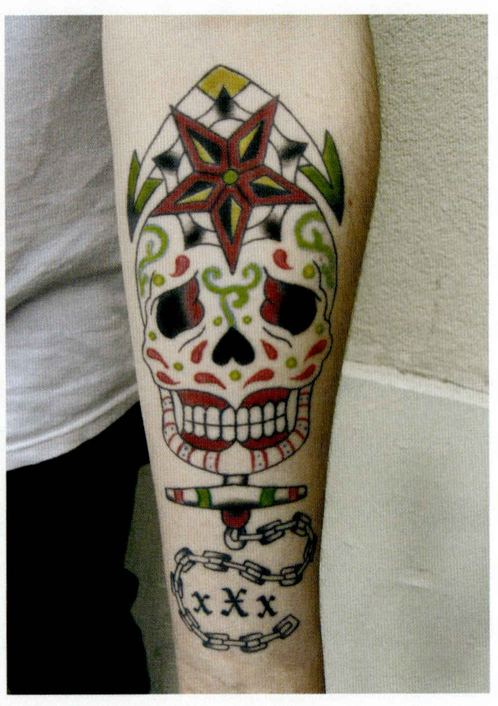

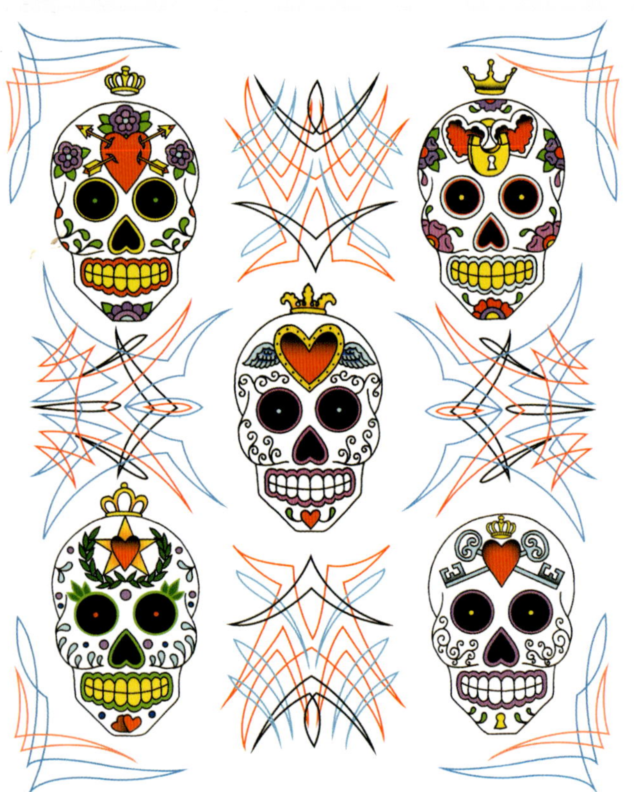
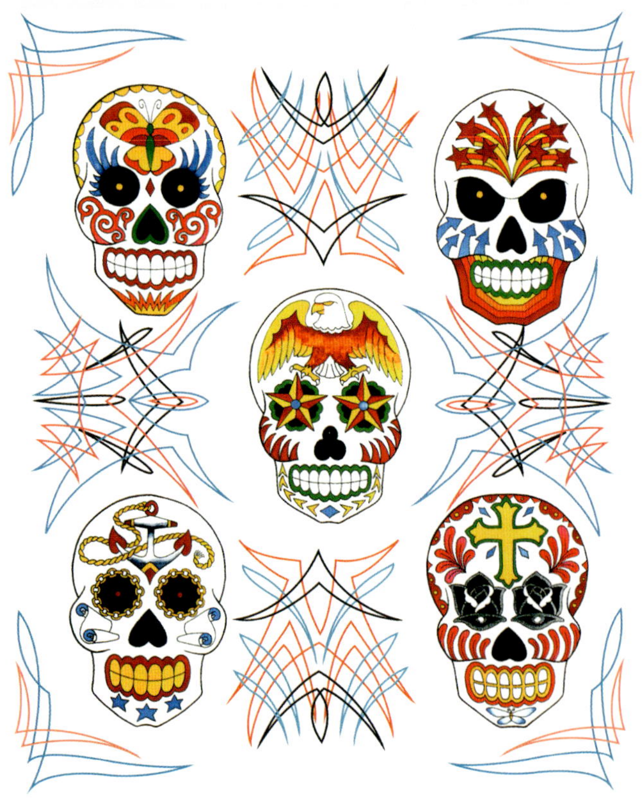

All designs on these pages by Sunny Buick.

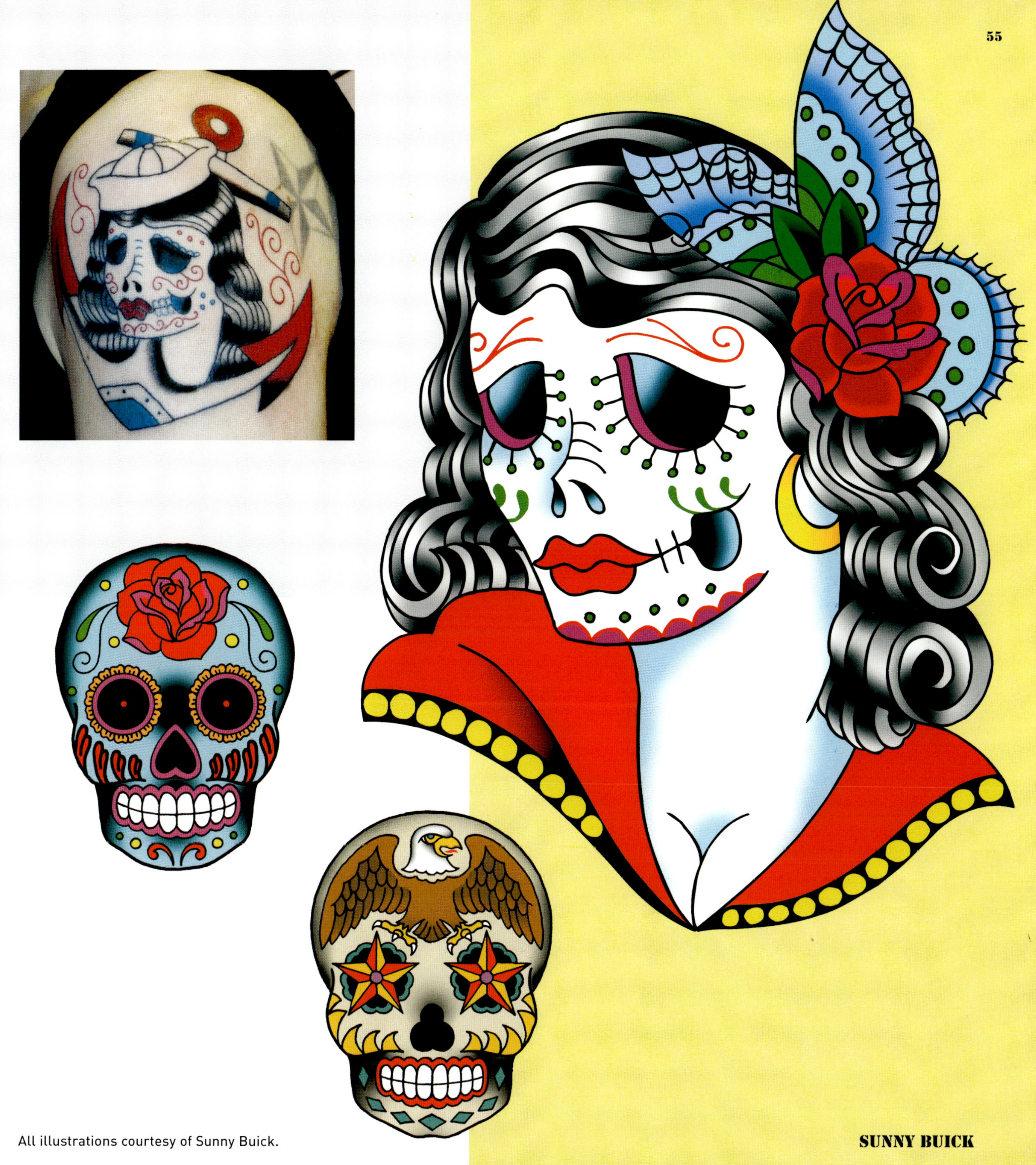

All illustrations courtesy of Sunny Buick.

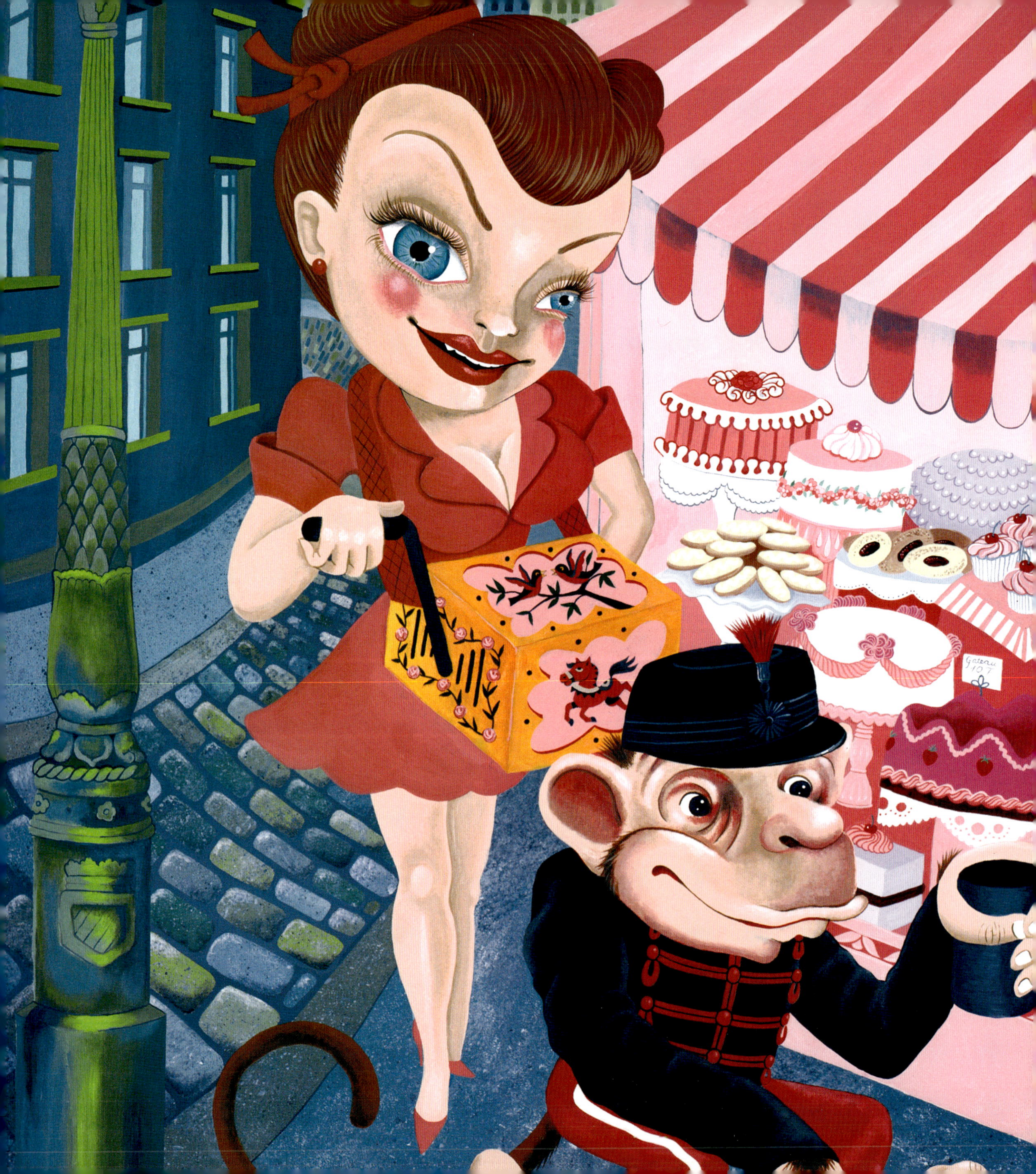
Gateau
107

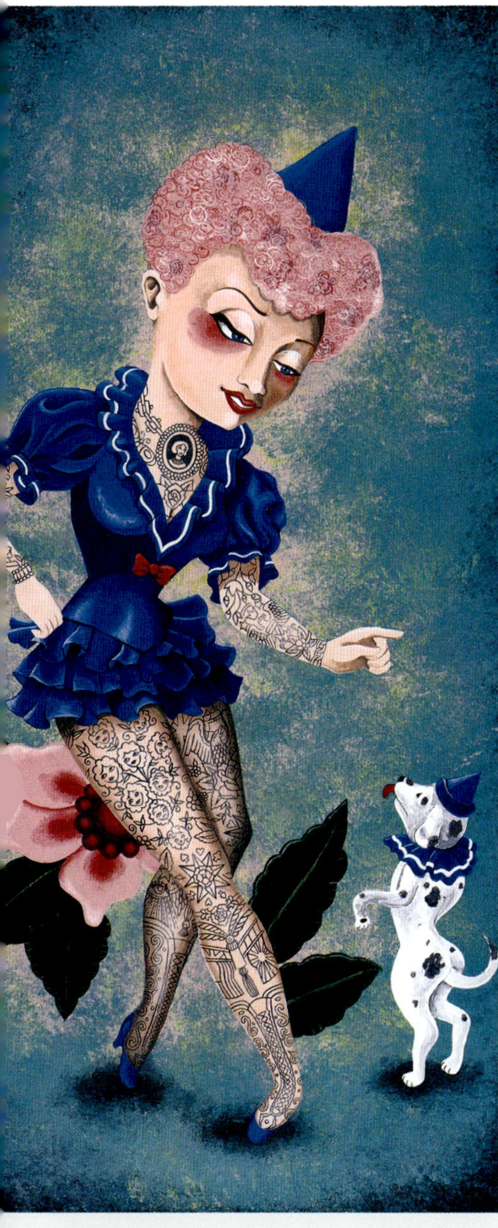

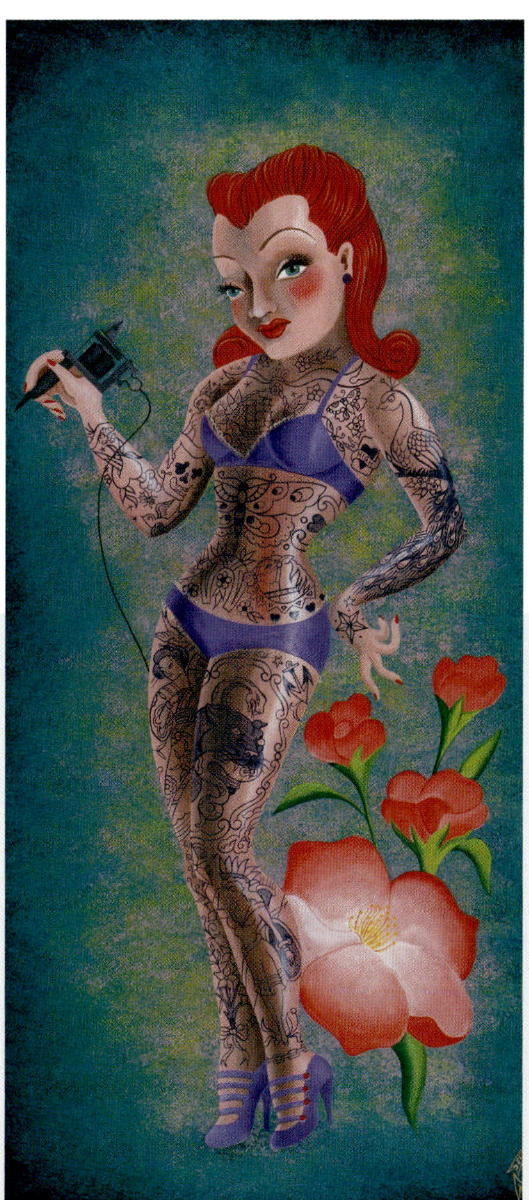

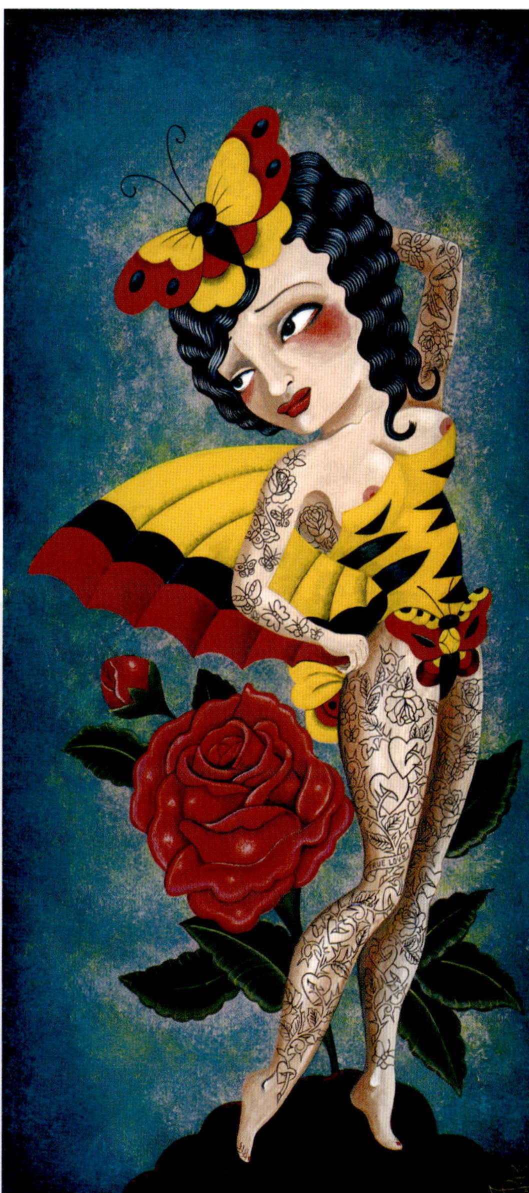

Acrylic illustrations on these pages made by Sunny Buick.

SHANE O'NEILL

USA

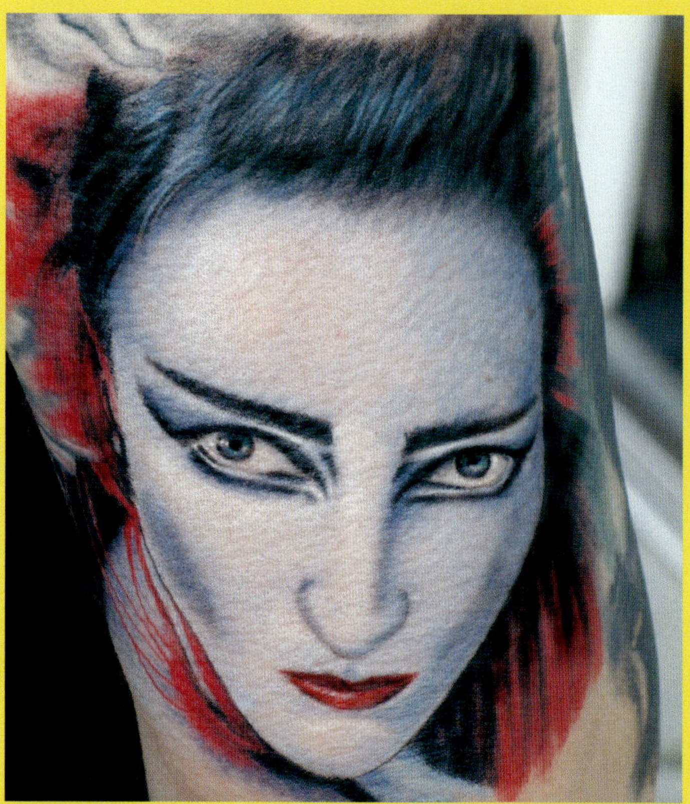

1. Before tattooing I was an illustrator, doing mostly product illustration, editorial and children's books. Through the encouragement of my brother I soon started to experiment with the tattoo machine as a medium. I quickly became consumed by the challenges that tattooing provides. Now, 11 years later, I still strive to become a better artist and to make my mark on tattoo history.

2. To me tattoos are a constant struggle, a challenge, a battle between me and the skin. Every new canvas reacts differently, and we as tattoo artists have to adjust and overcome the skin that wants to spew the ink back in our faces. It's a never-ending endeavor to attain the perfect tattoo which doesn't even exist!

3. Although I feel that I can produce a top-quality tattoo of any style, I mostly enjoy tattooing photo-realistic images on skin.

4. Respect the skin and always continue to learn more!

5. www.shaneoneilltattoos.com
   shanetattoo@yahoo.com

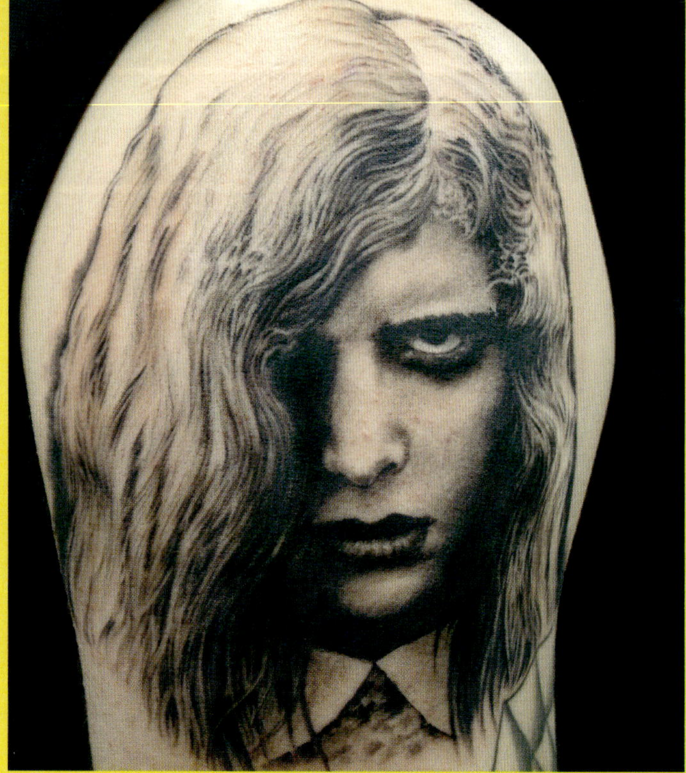

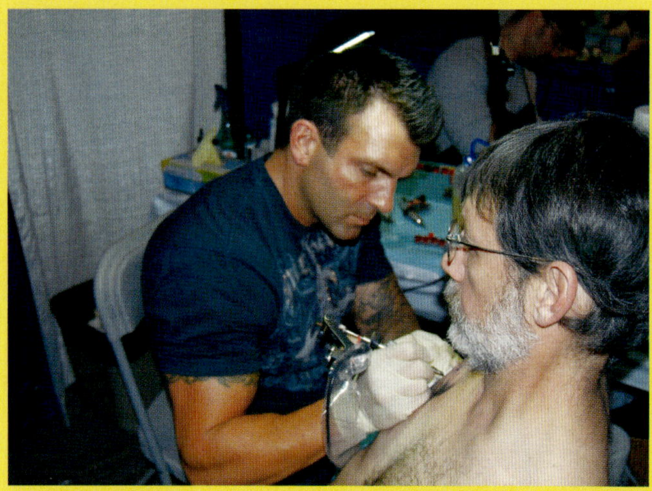

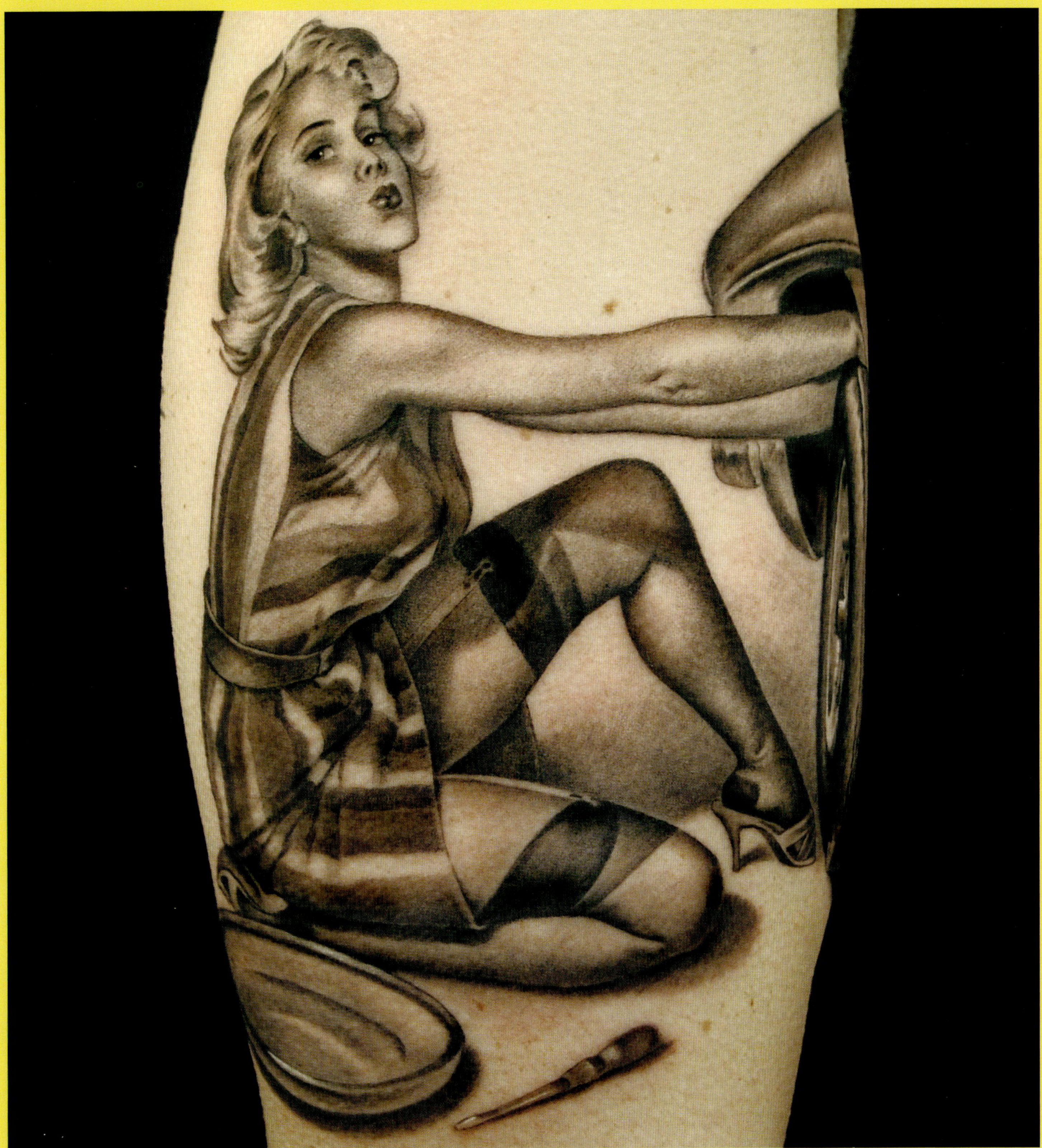

All images courtesy of Shane O'Neill.

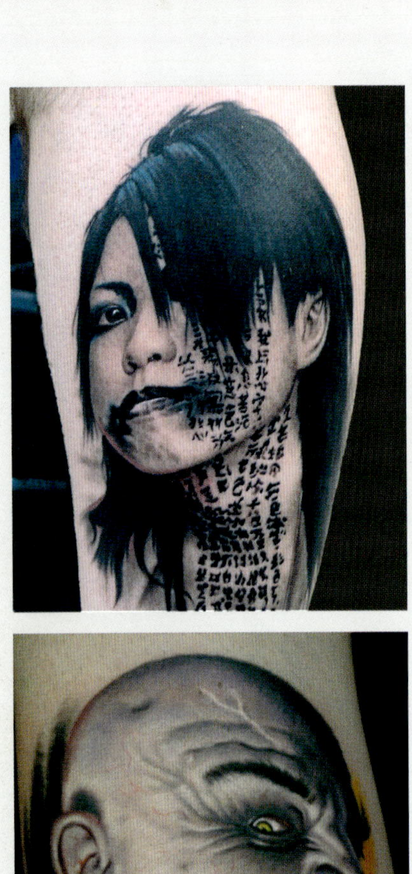

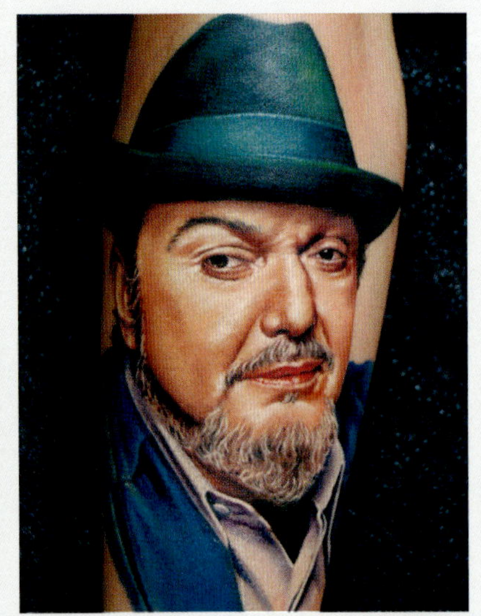

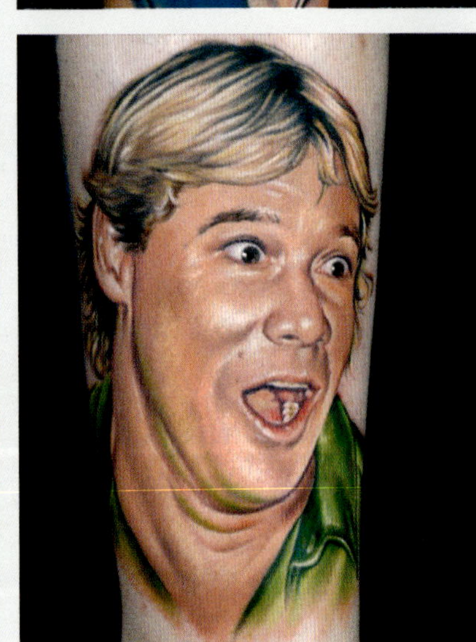

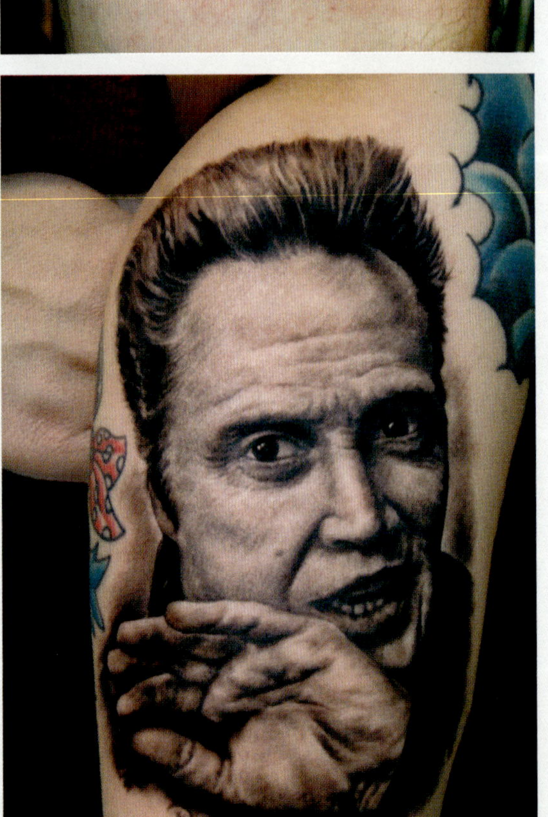

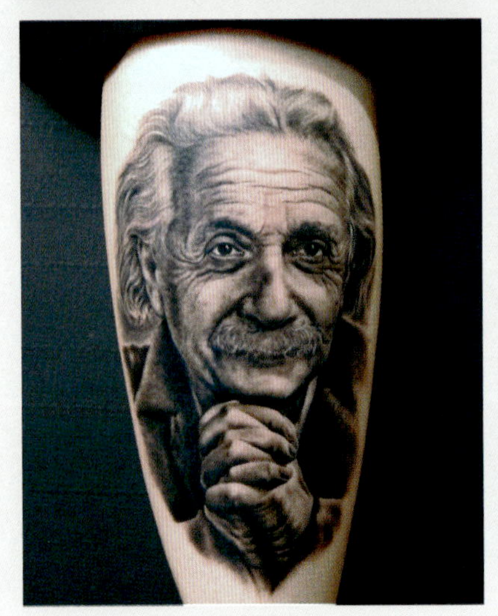

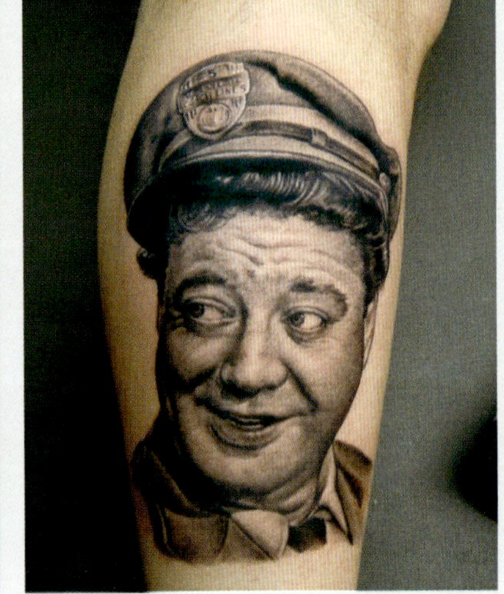

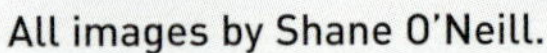

All images by Shane O'Neill.

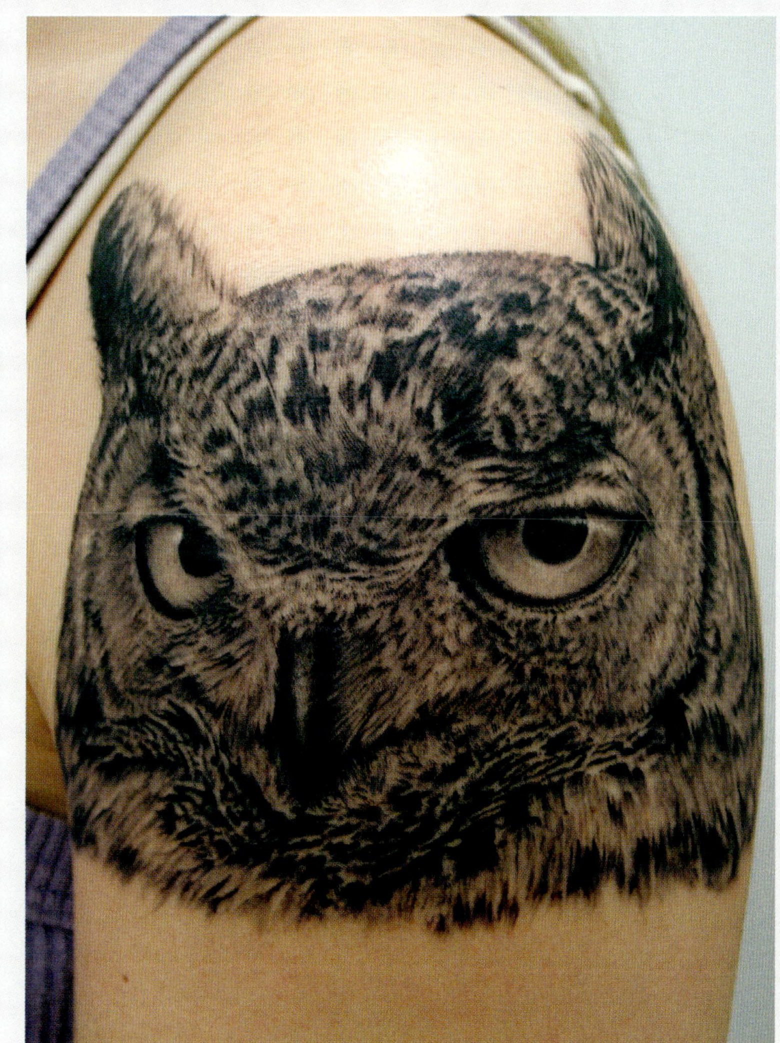

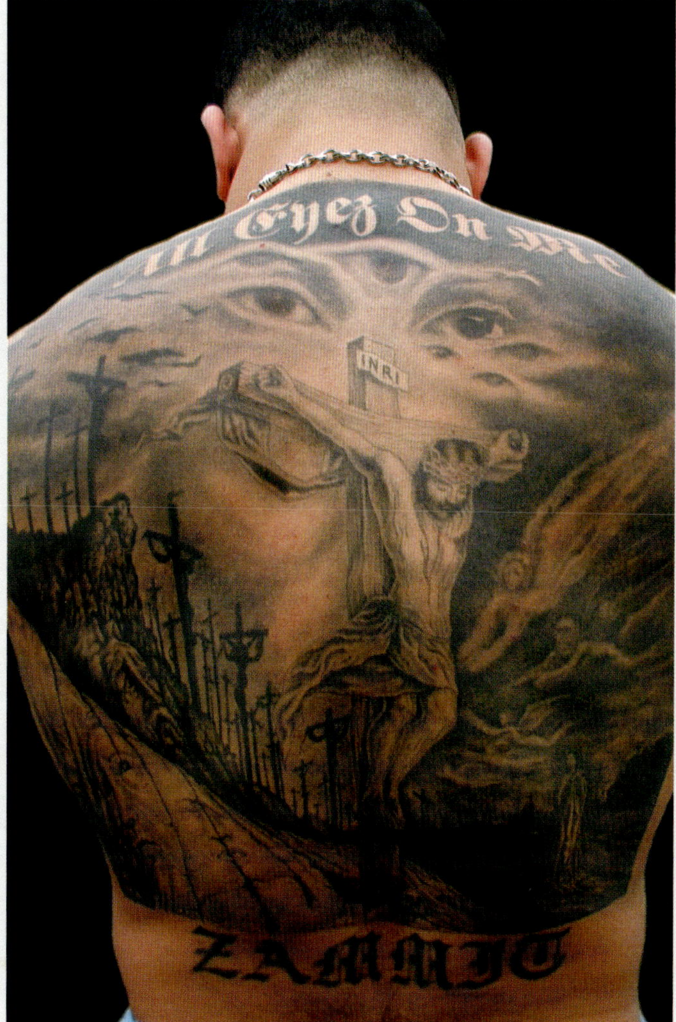

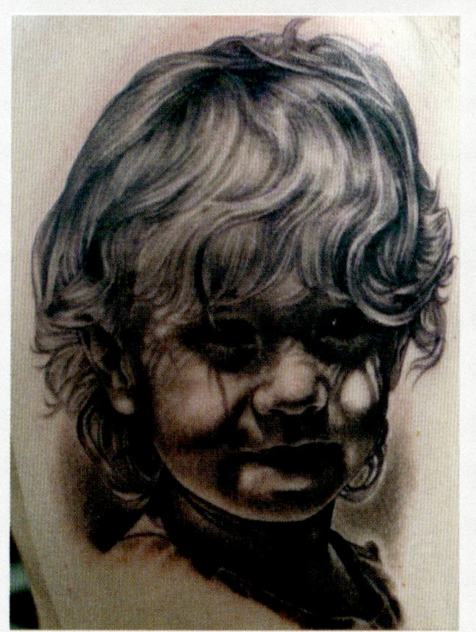

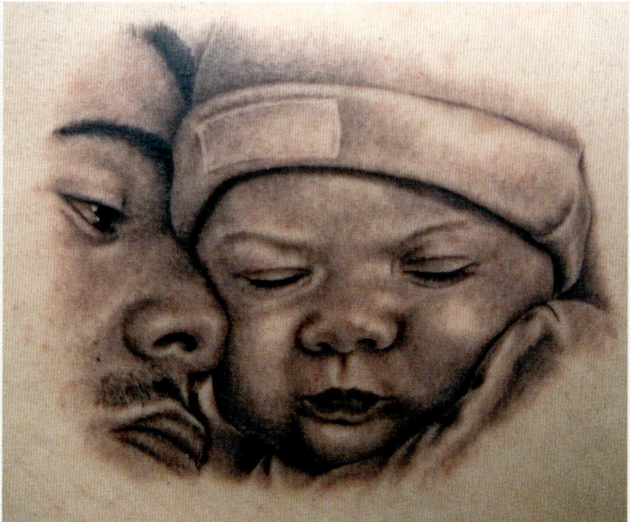

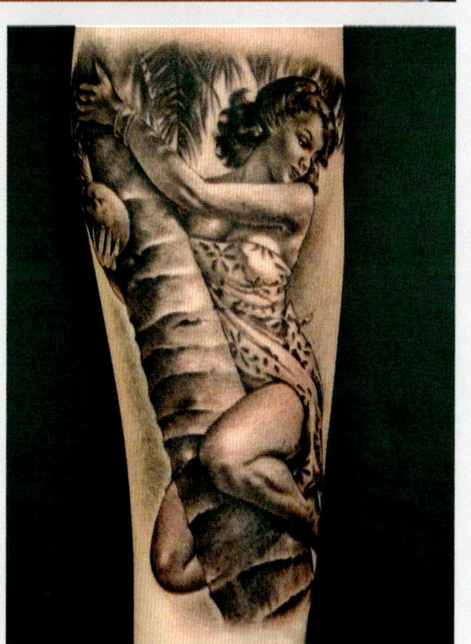

SHANE O'NEILL

STEVE BYRNE

UK

1. I did my first tattoo in 1997. I was 18 years old and worked in a street shop here in Leeds doing flash, walk-ins and eventually custom tattoos for the first five years. I consider myself self-taught.

2. Tattooing is the best job I could have ever asked for; it has provided me with some of the best life experience over the years. Aside from my family, it is the most important thing in my life.

3. I only do traditional Western and Japanese style tattoos these days. I'm not opposed to doing other styles, but I have a high demand from my customers for my own style and stick to what I can develop within as well as enjoy.

4. When you go into a tattoo shop, let the artist do their job. When people try to have too much control it can end up being detrimental to the finished piece.

5. My private tattoo studio, In Name And Blood, which is in Leeds, England. I travel a lot, but that's where I spend most of my time. Or on the internet.
www.myspace.com/innameandbloodtattoo

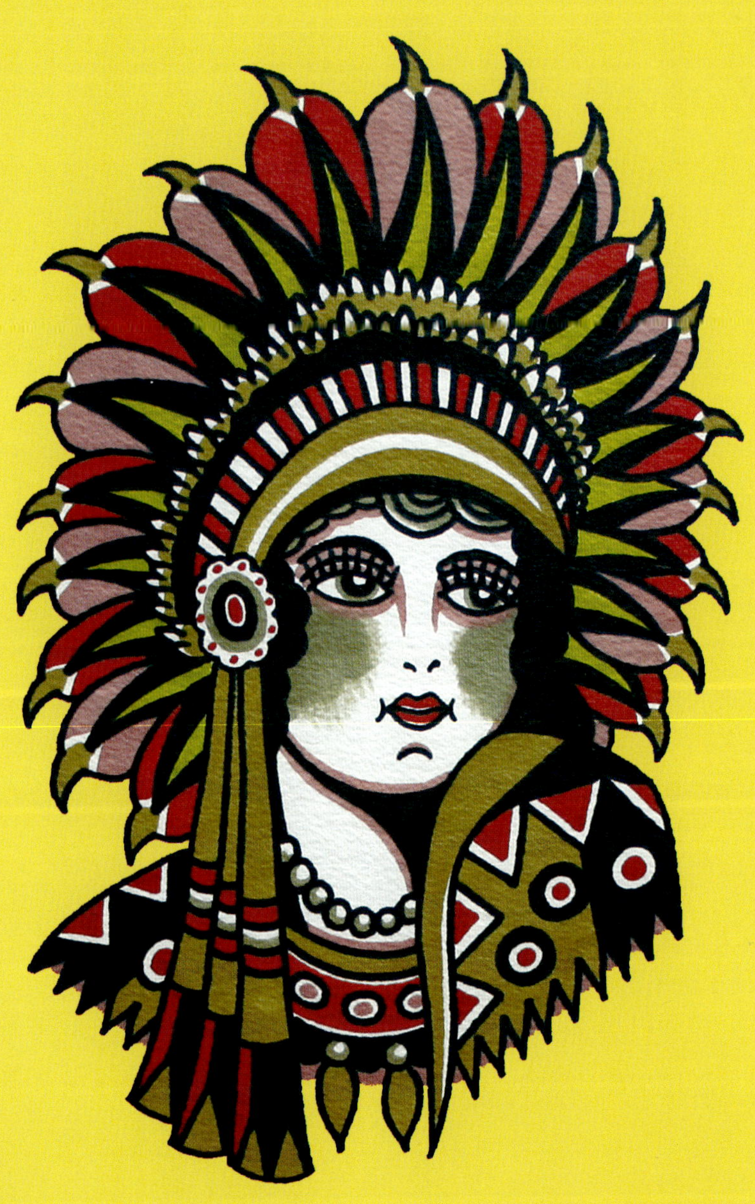

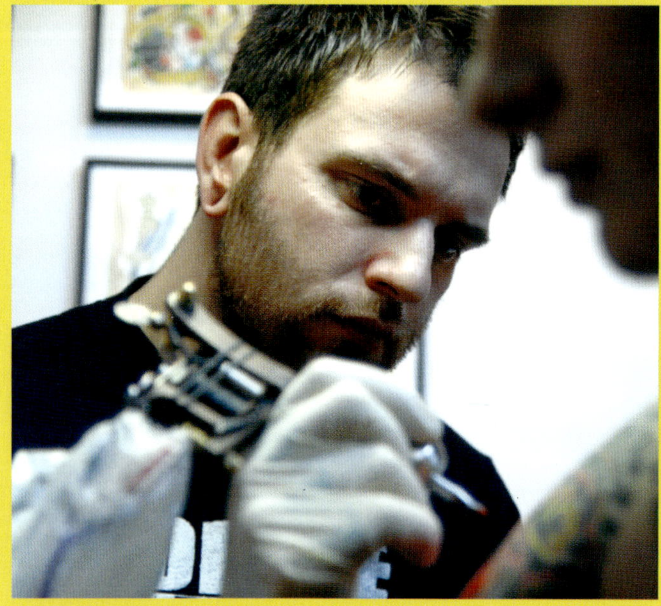

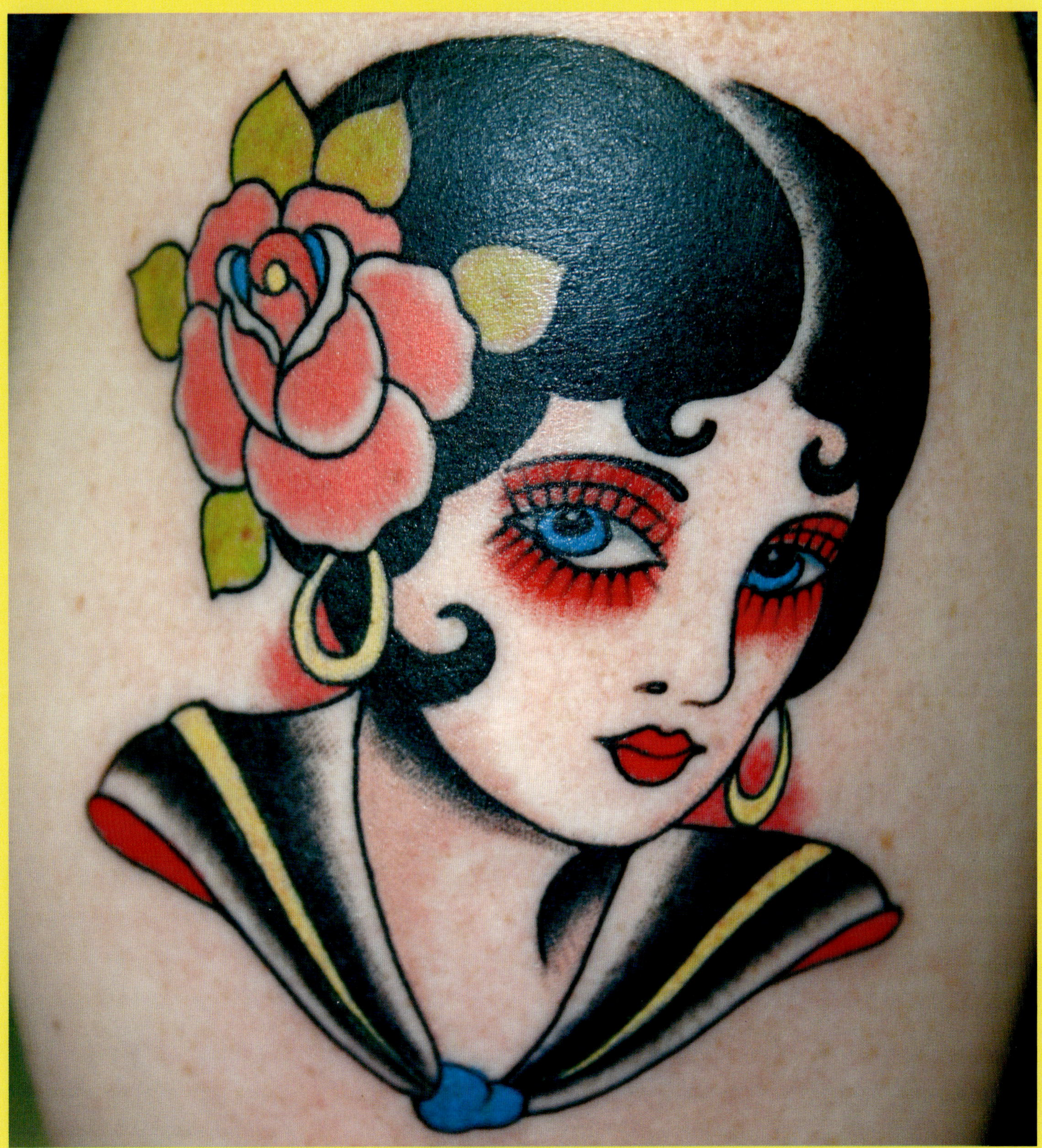

All designs on these pages by Steve Byrne.

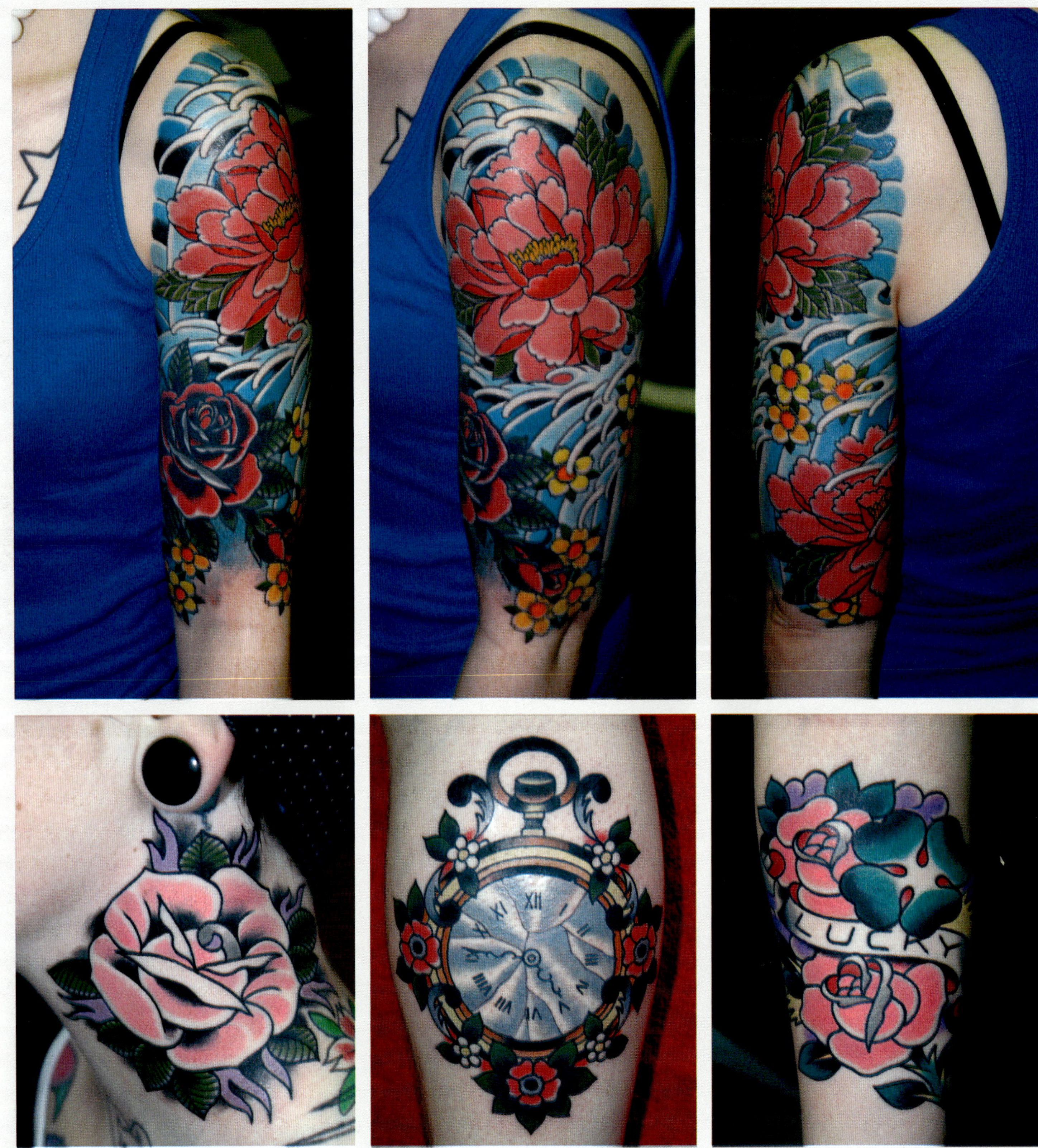

Images courtesy of Steve Byrne.

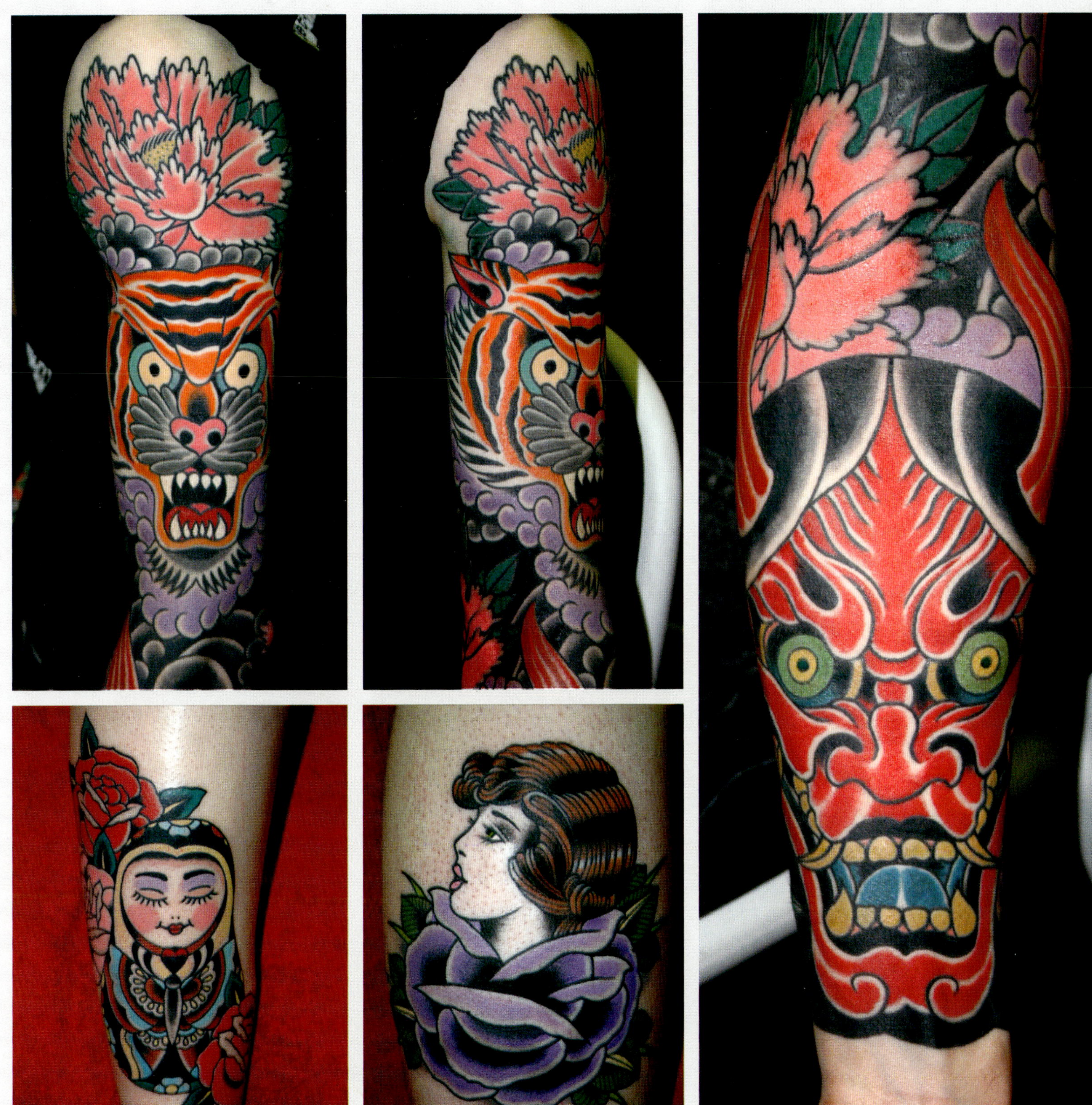

STEVE BYRNE

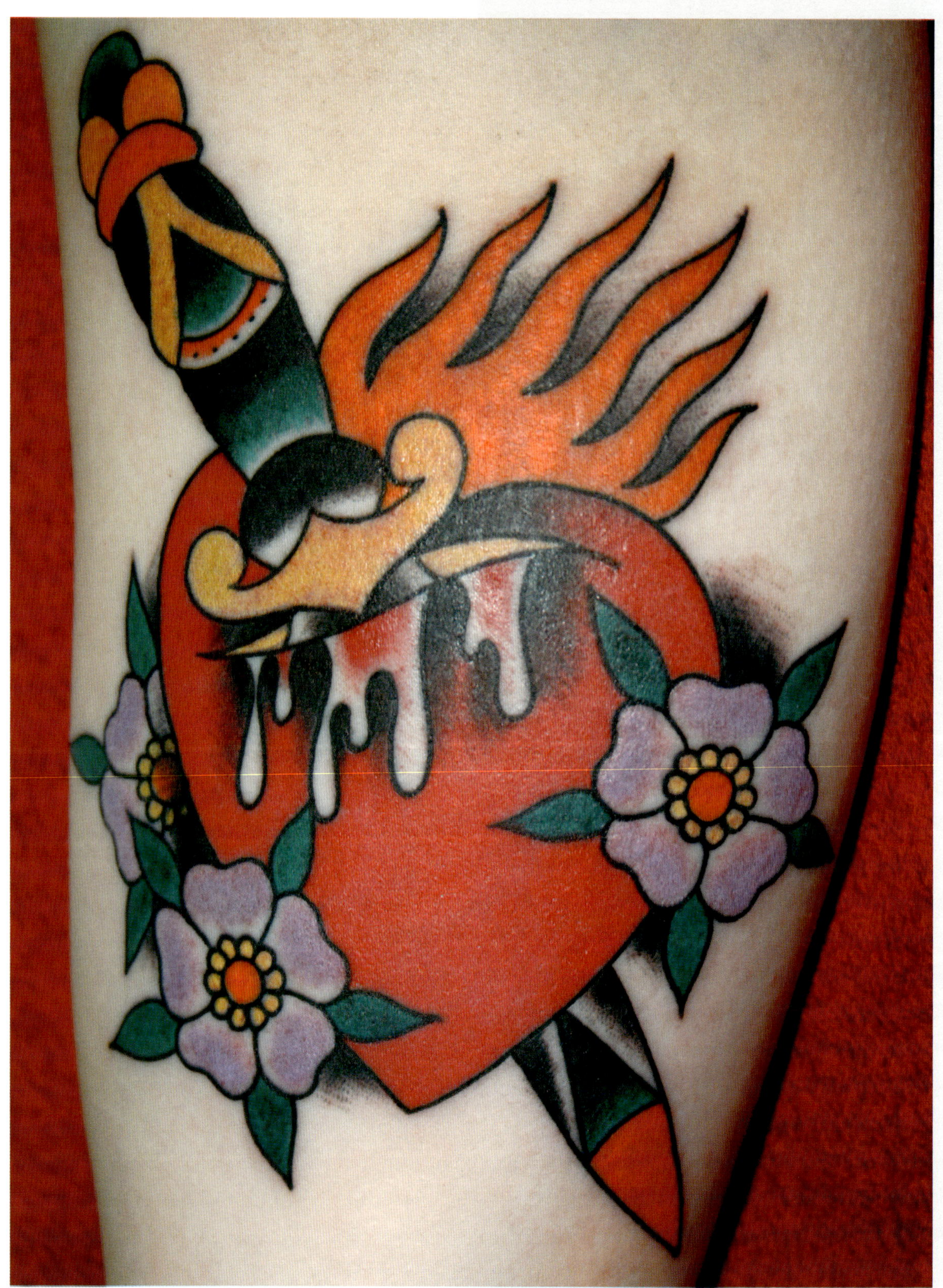

All artwork by Steve Byrne.

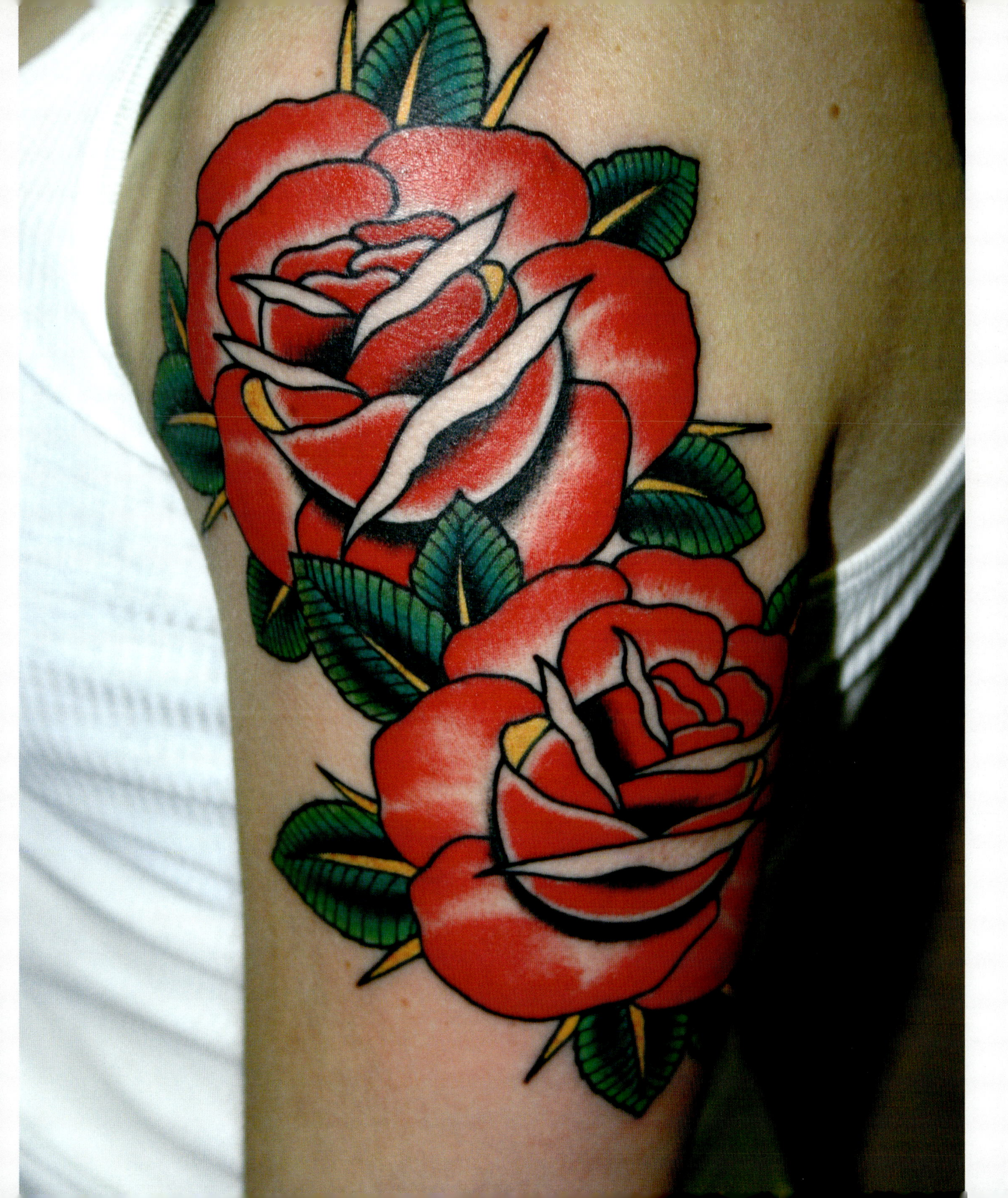

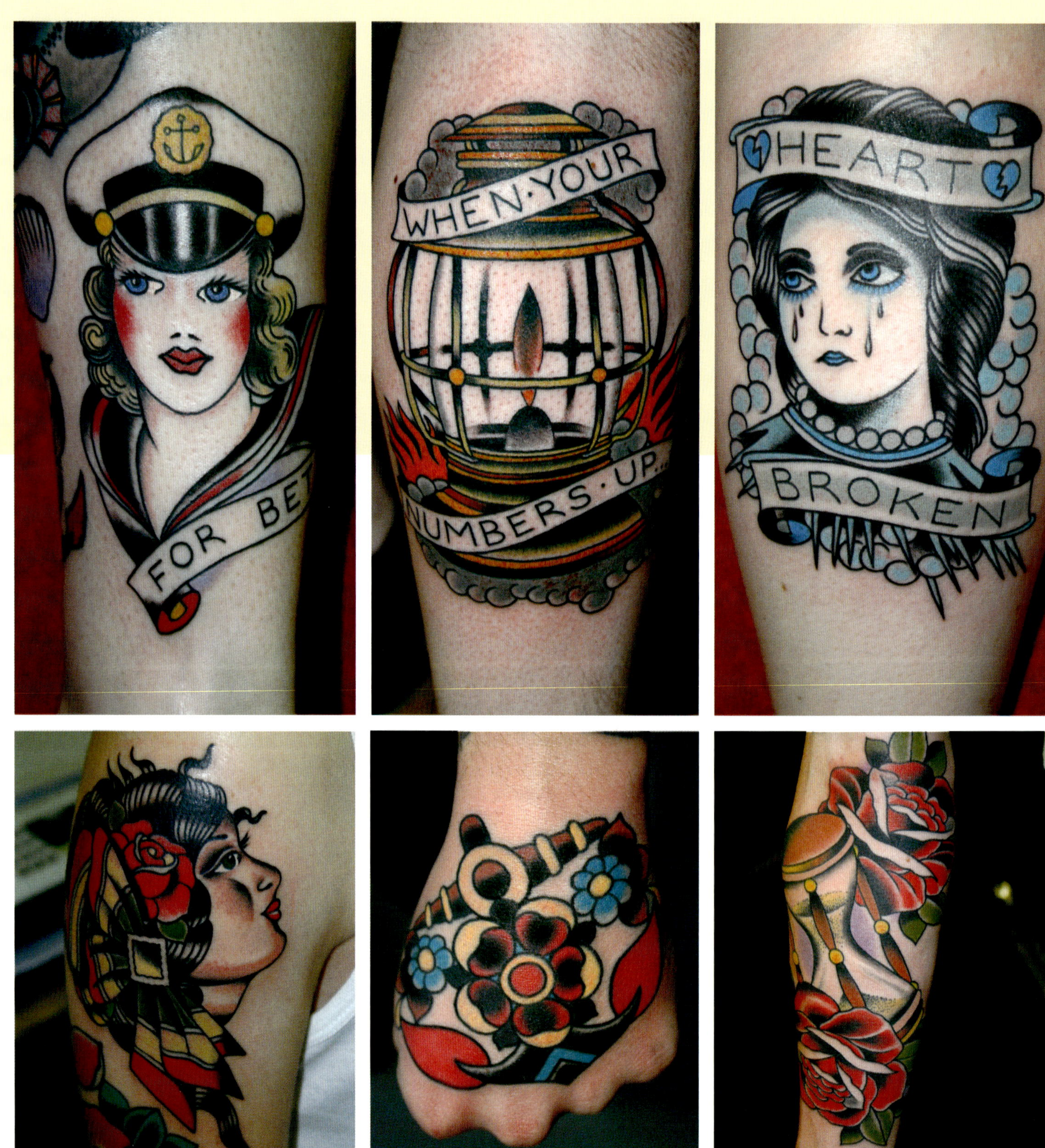

All images courtesy of Steve Byrne.

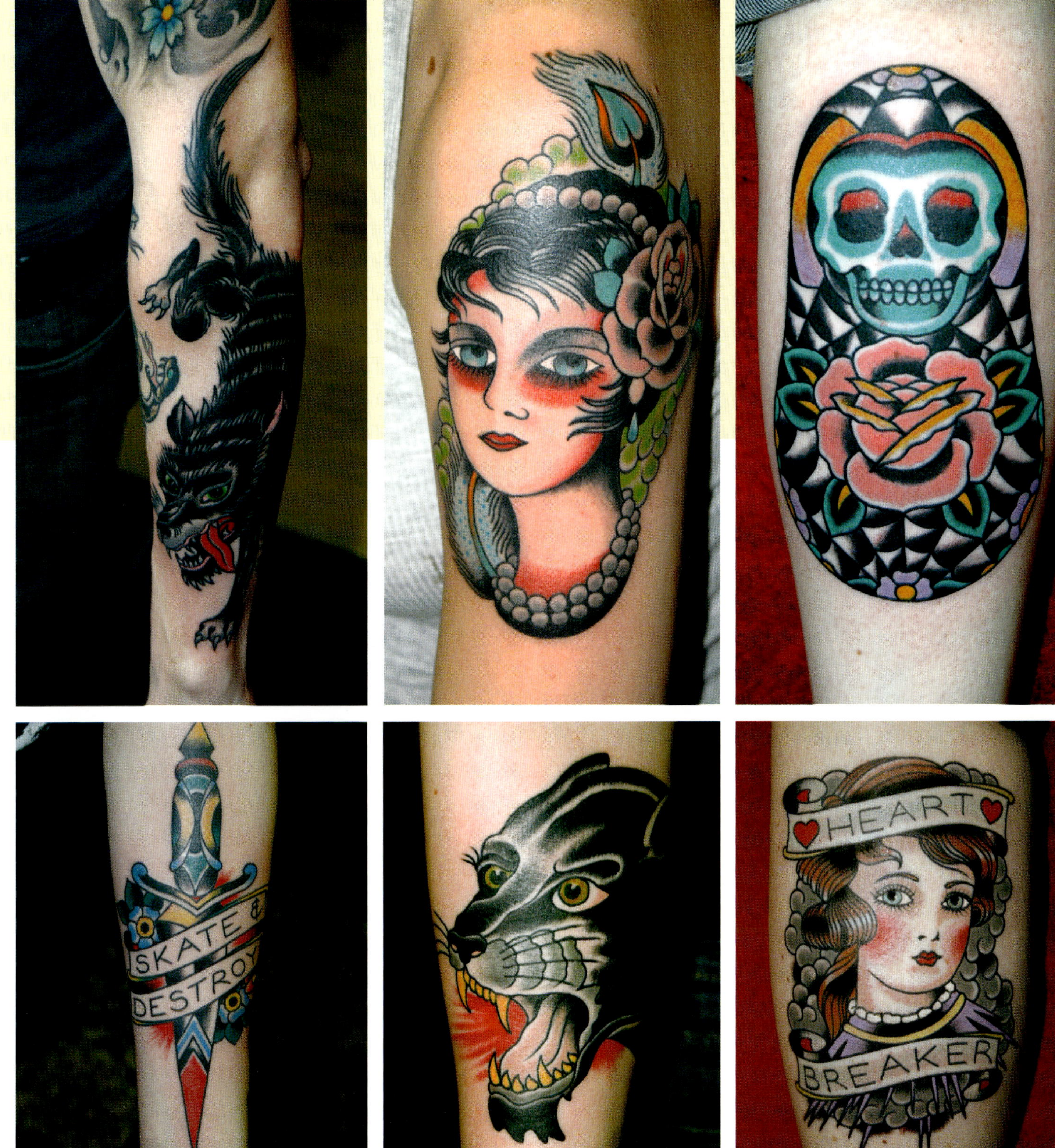

STEVE BYRNE

RINZING TATTOO

SWITZERLAND

1. I started tattooing and learning by myself, working in a factory during the day "to pay the bills," tattooing myself and my friends at night!

2. Tattooing means dedication, devotion and discipline. To be tattooed and wearing tattoos means accepting feeling pain to get something you believe in on yourself for the rest of your life.

3. We can say an Oriental, Tibetan style! I think we can say that because, during the past few years we (J. Dix and I) have been really pushing our drawings and tattoos to develop this style!

4. If you are into it, just think about it twice! After the first tattoo comes the second!

5. The Leu family's Family Iron street shop, Av. de France 36 1004 Lausanne, Switzerland 021/6248708. www.rinzing-tattoo.ch

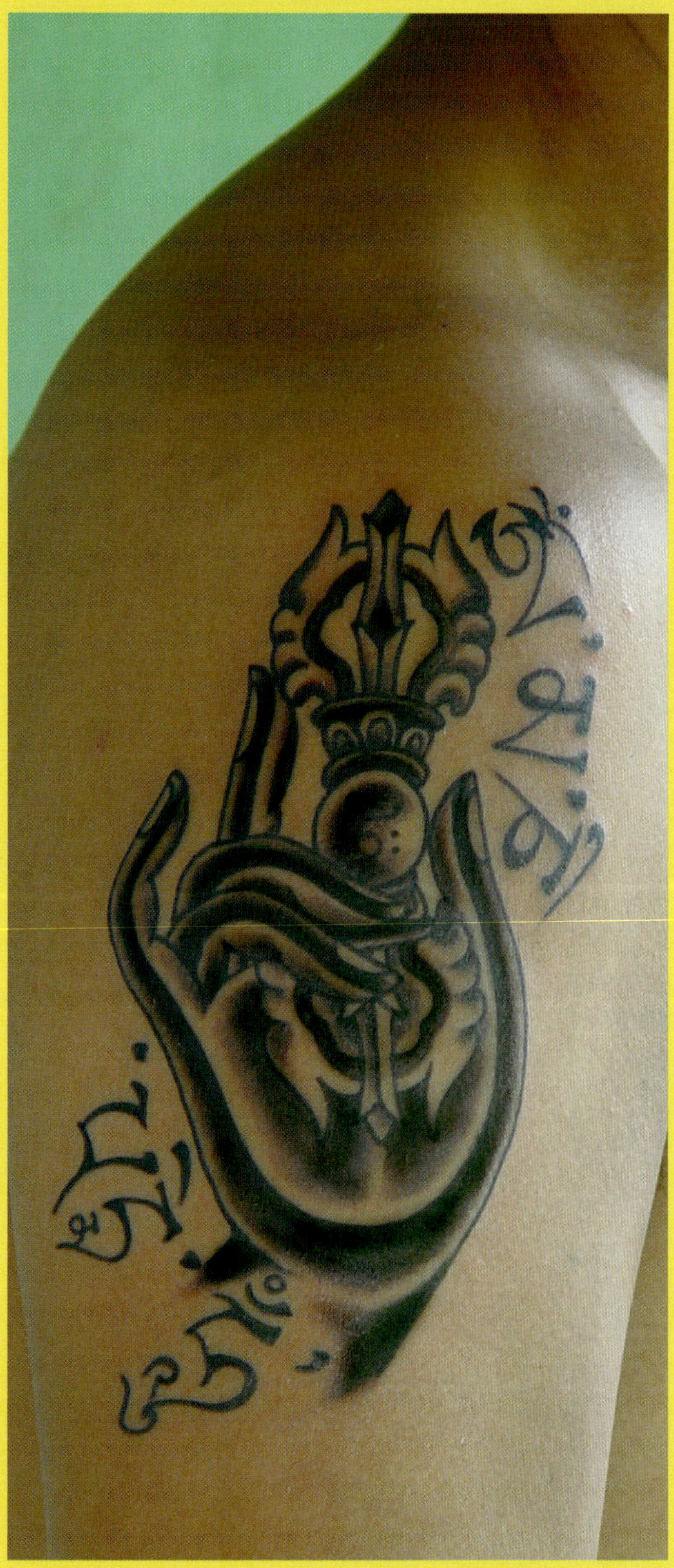

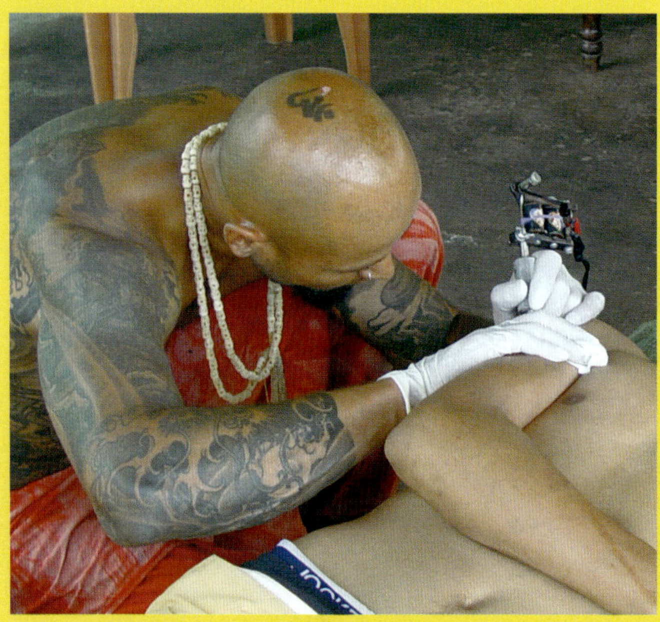

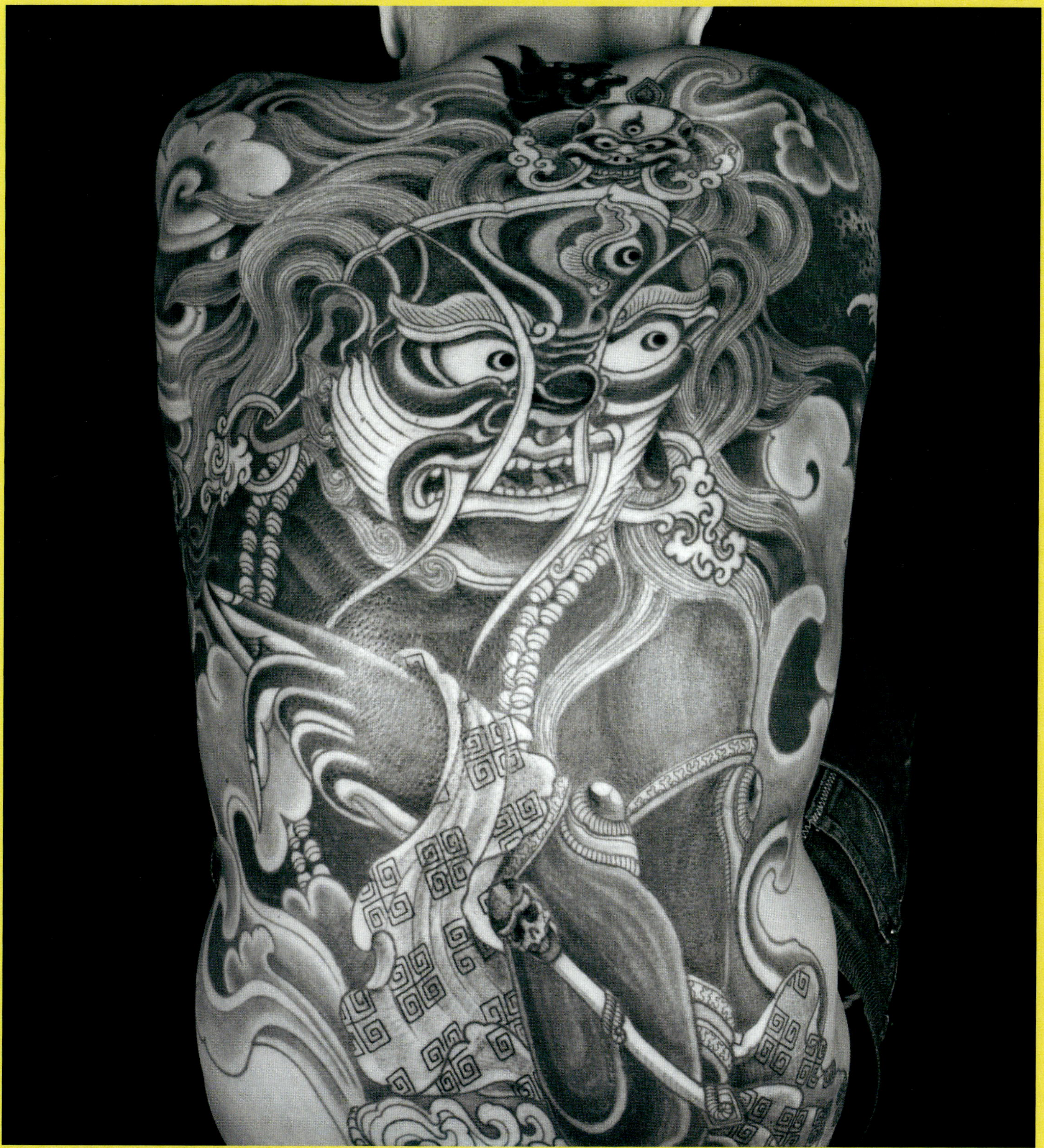

All images courtesy of Rinzing Tattoo.

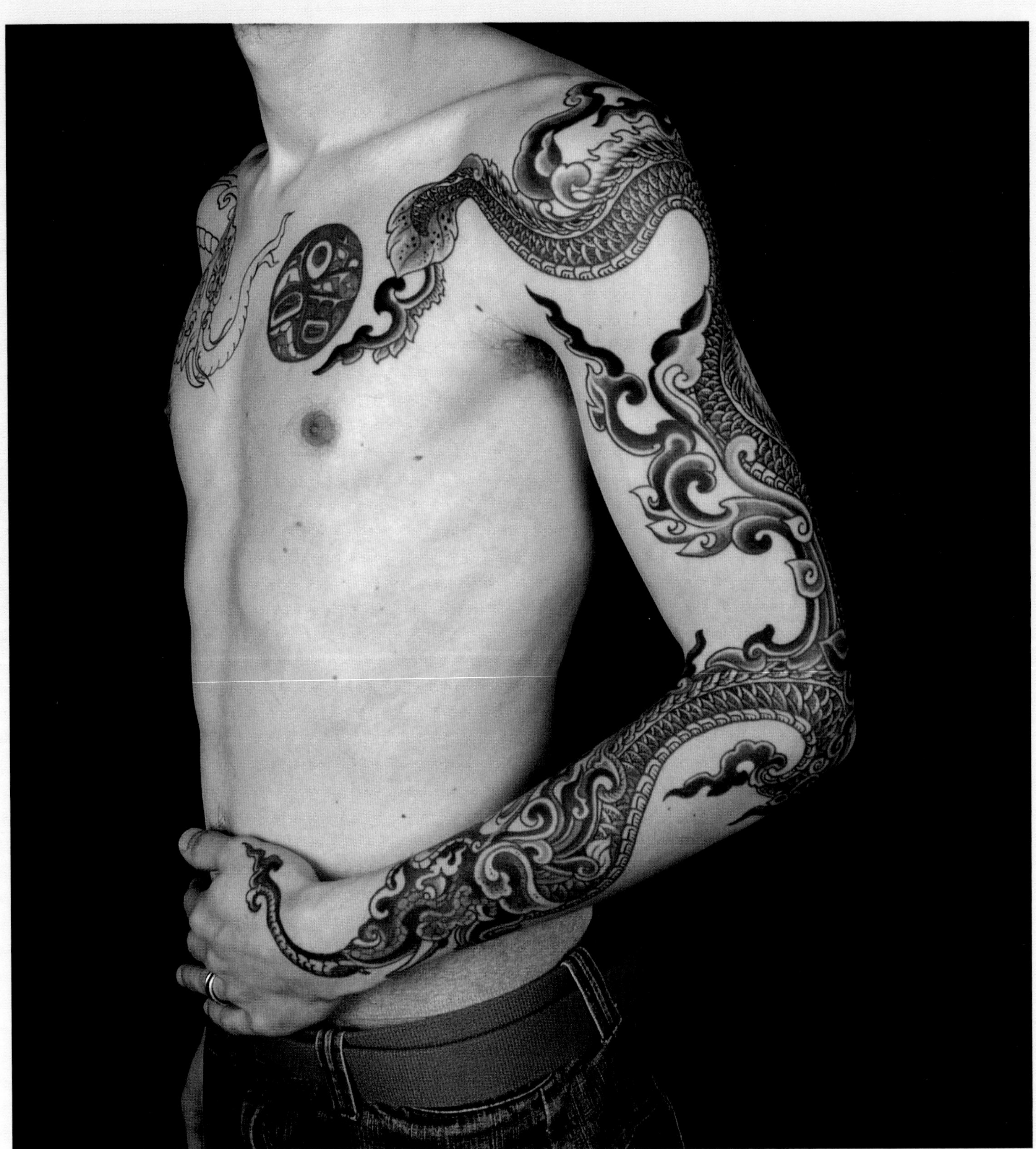

All artwork by Rinzing Tattoo.

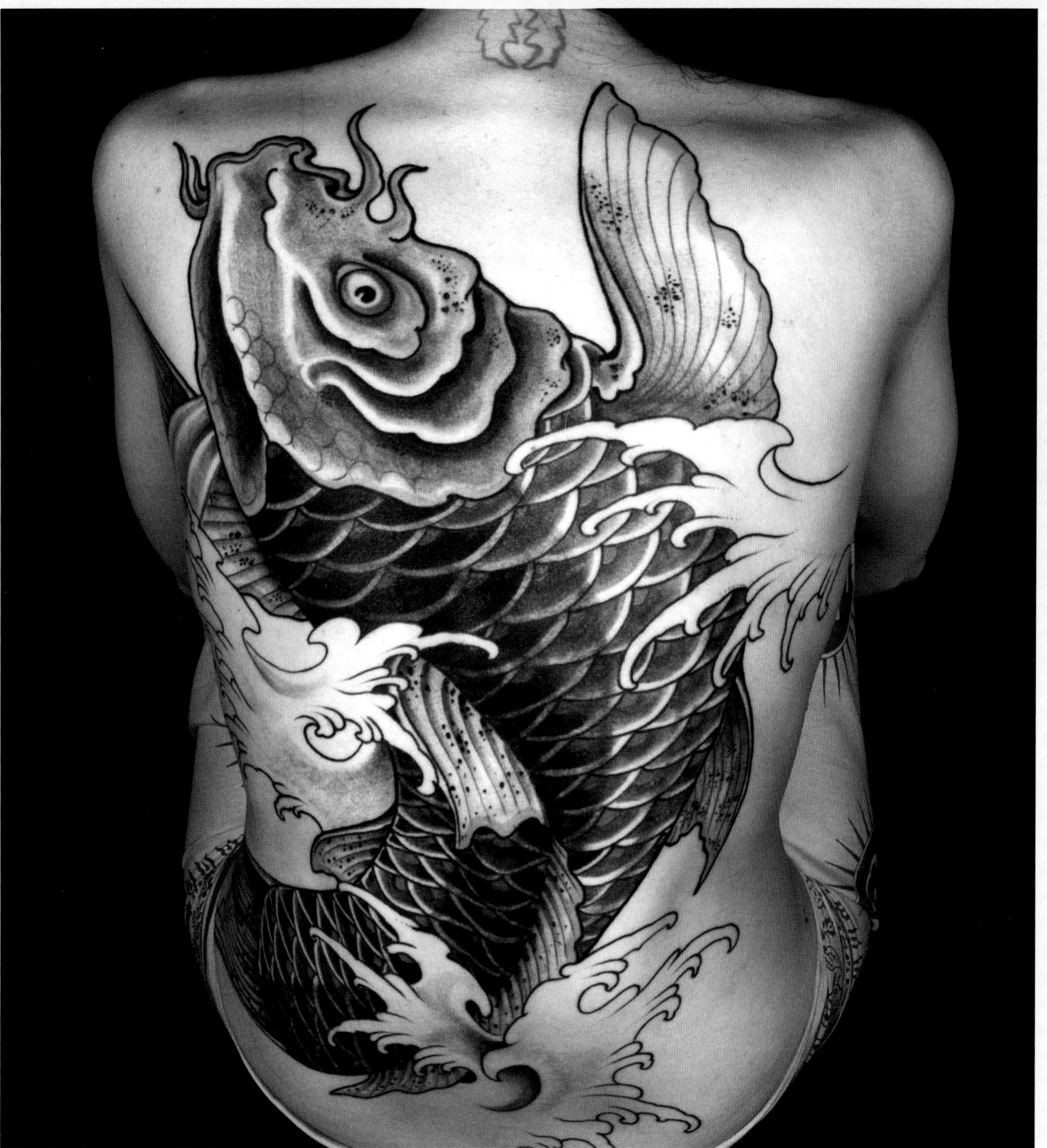

RINZING TATTOO

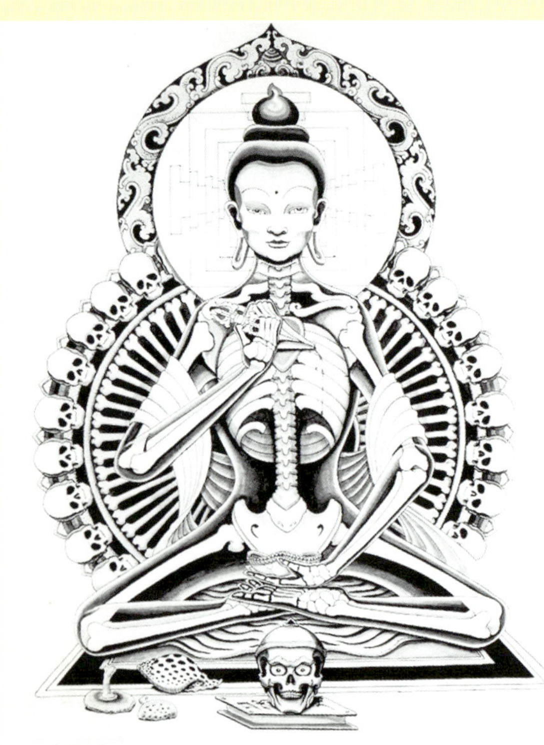

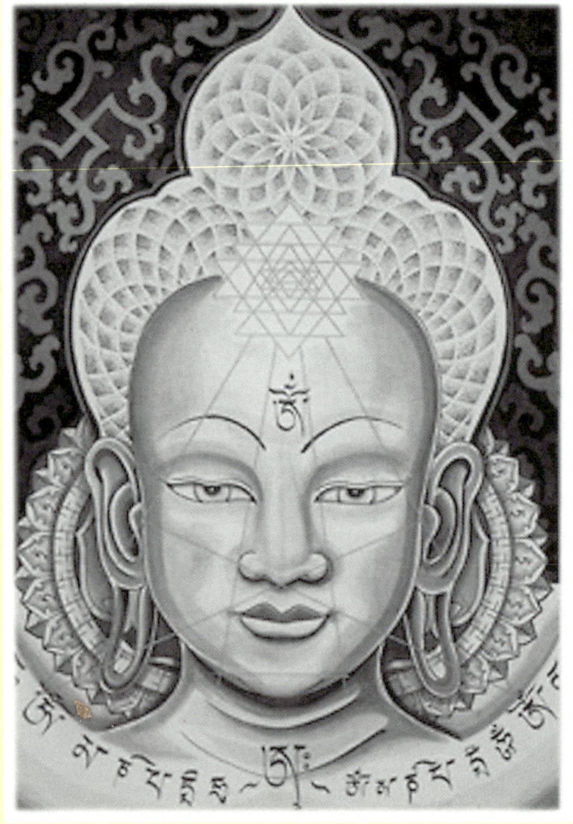

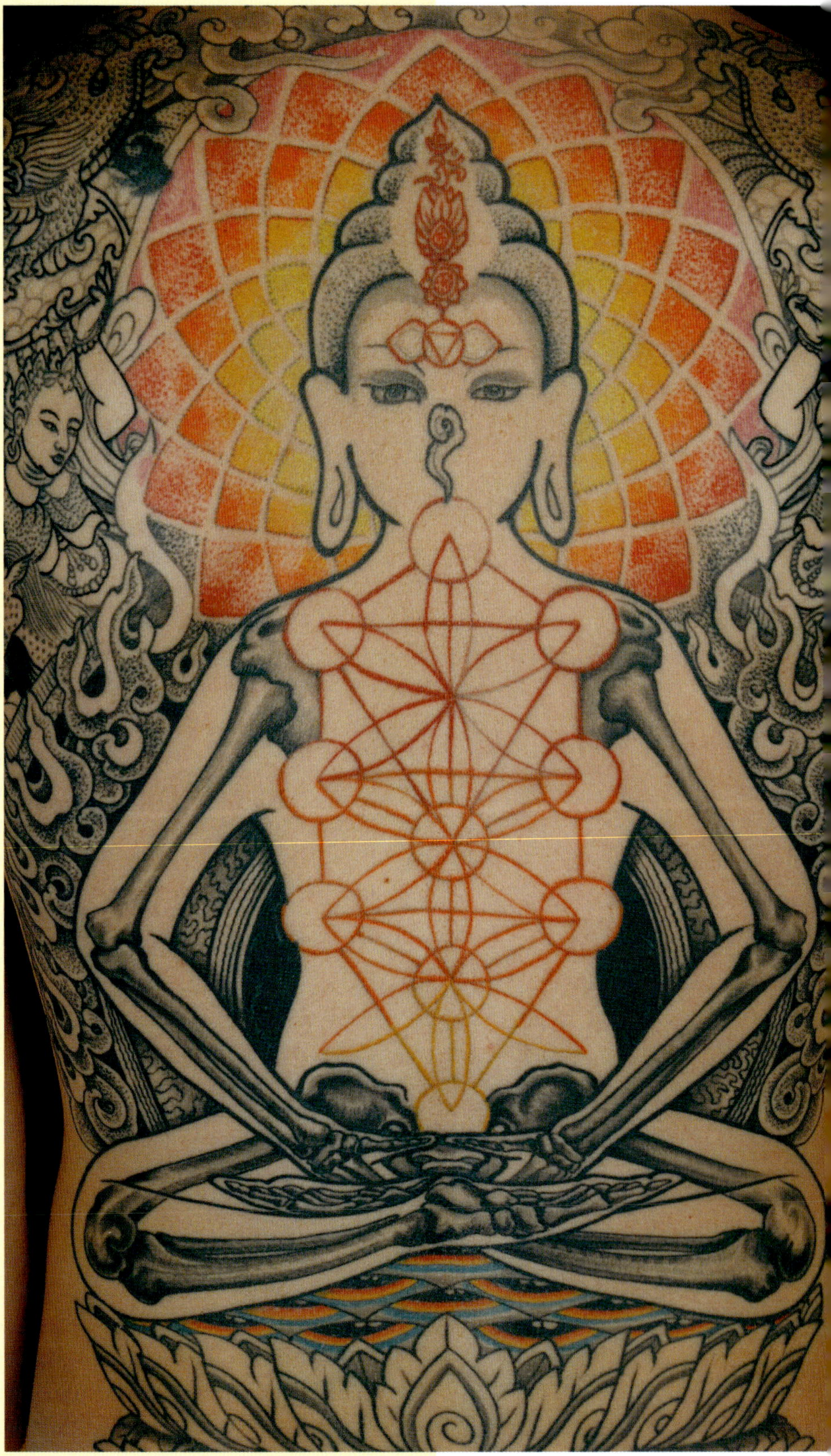

All designs on these pages by Rinzing Tattoo.

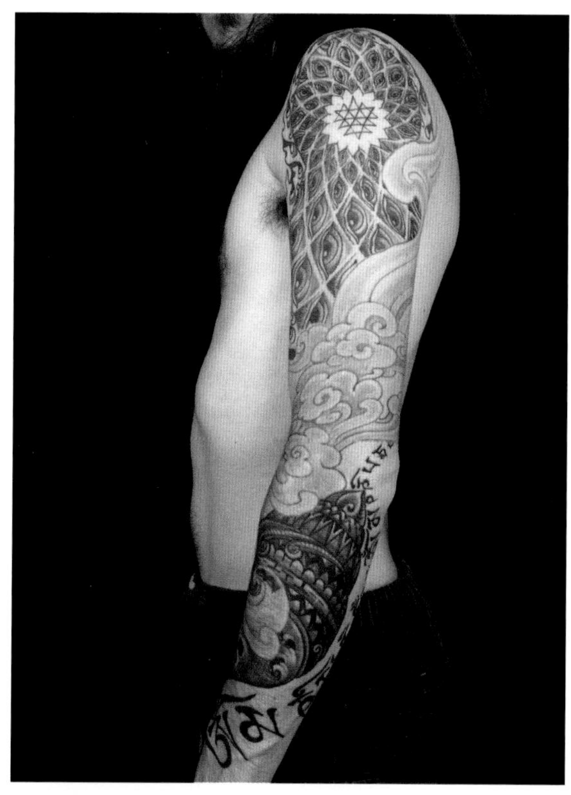

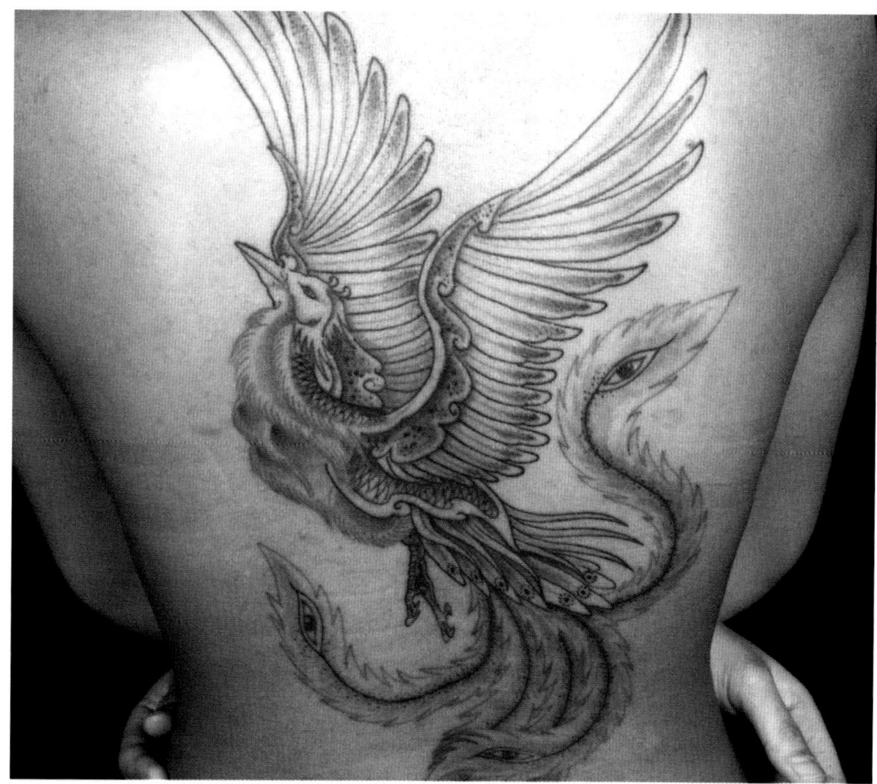

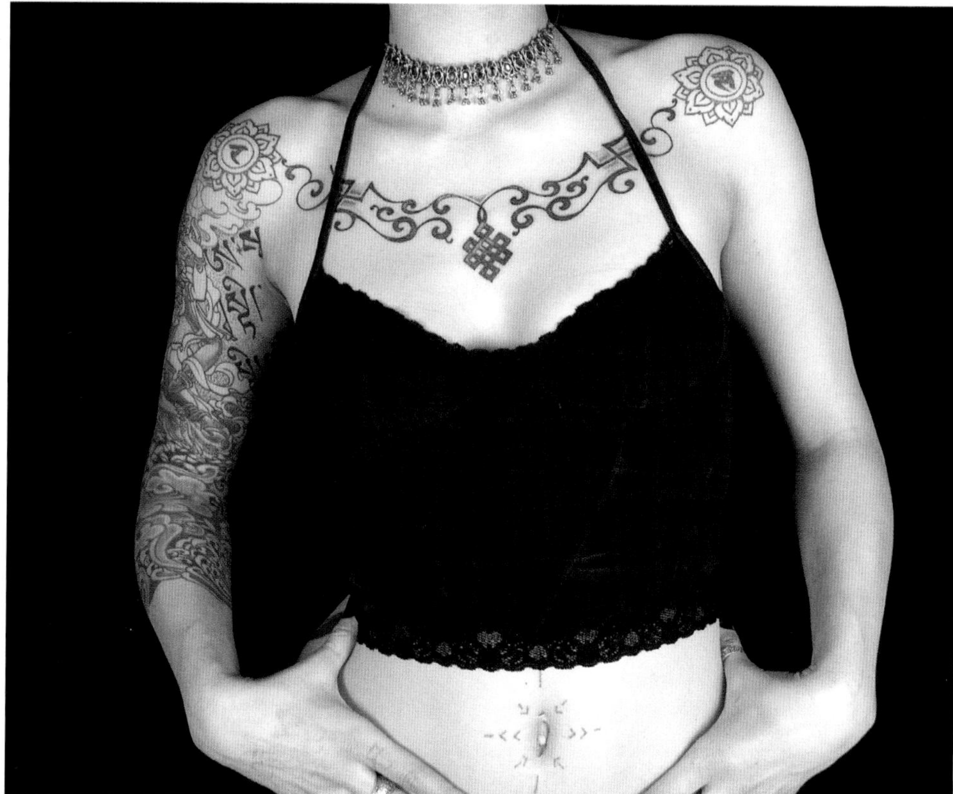

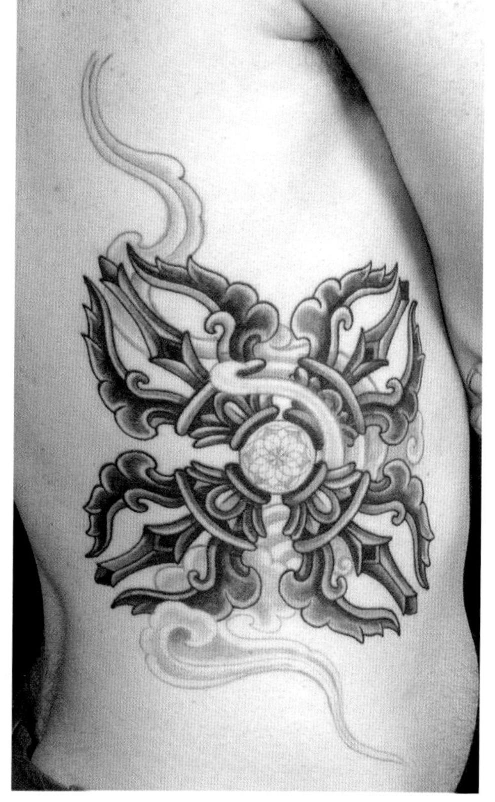

MOOREA TATTOO

TAHITI

1. It was a dare with my neighbor at the age of 12 that led to my first tattoo. I've been tattooing professionally since 1996. In addition to Moorea, I've tattooed in France, Spain, Switzerland, and the United States.

2. Tattooing is my culture. It connects me to my ancestry.

3. My style is traditional Polynesian tatau.

4. Take a shower and relax.

5. PK32, Haapiti Varari Moorea, French Polynesia.
   www.mooreatattoo.com

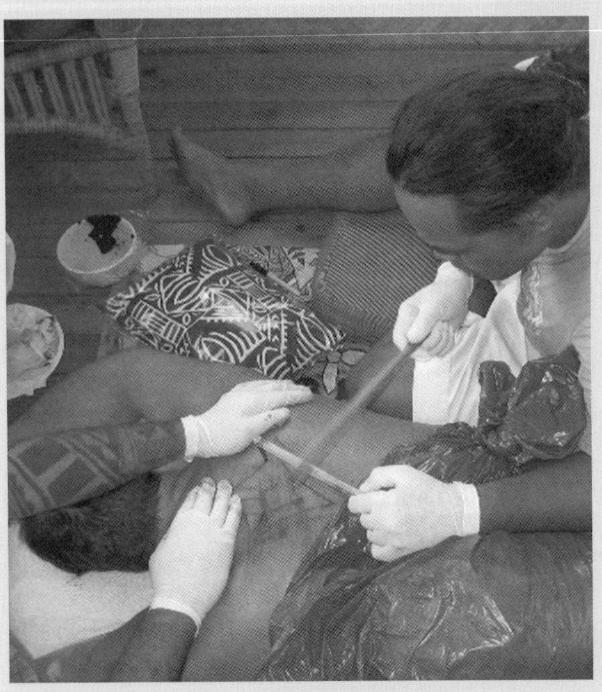

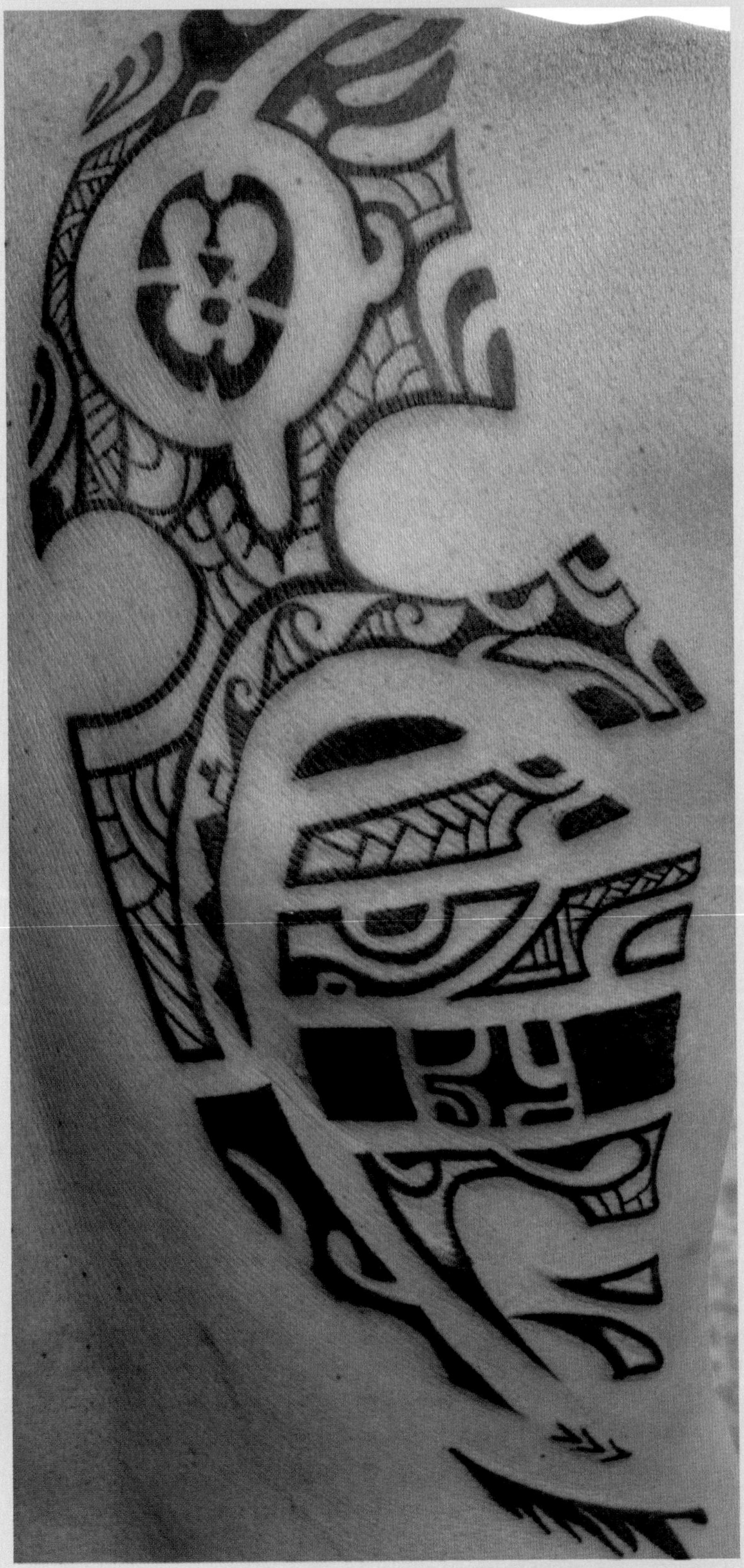

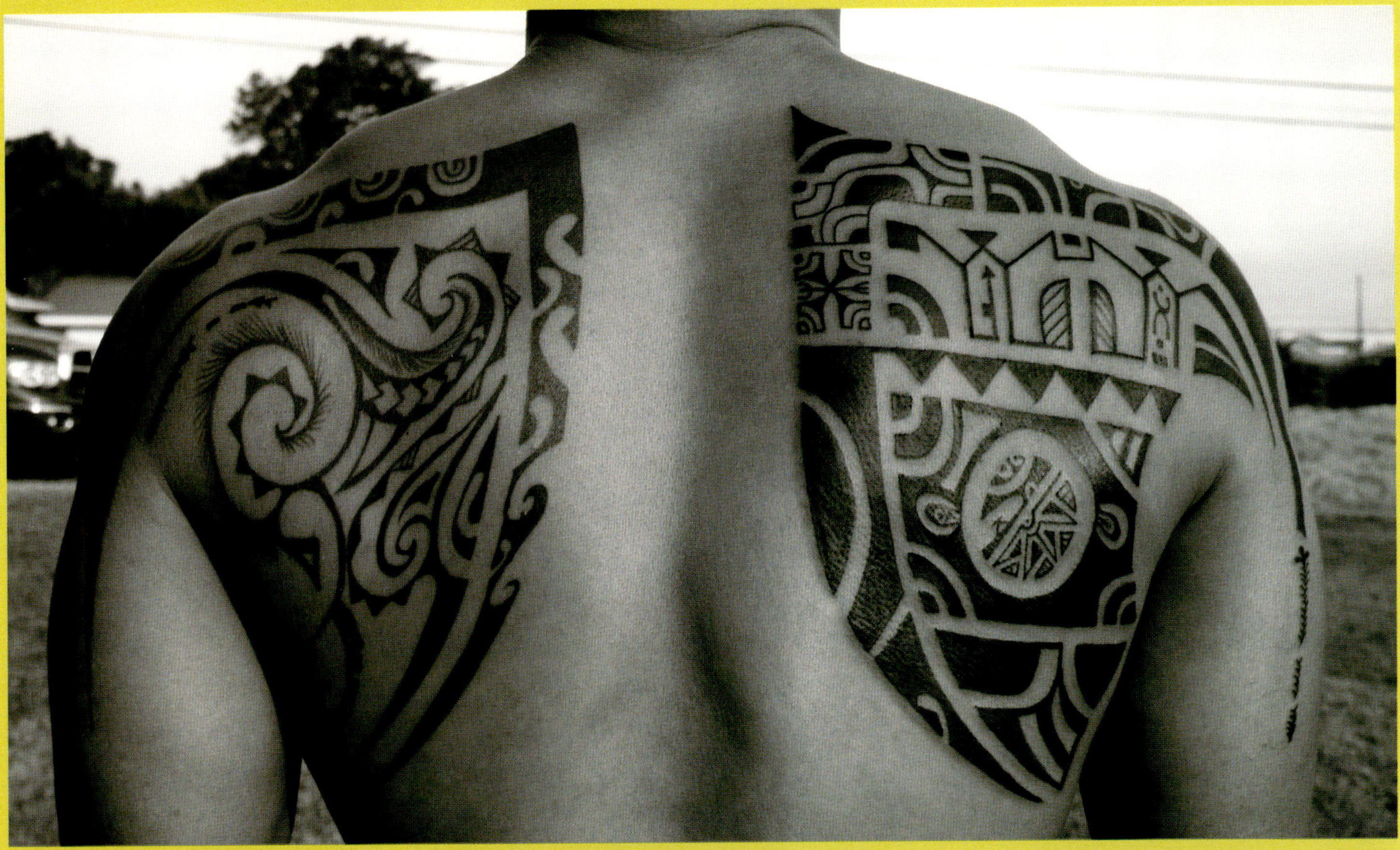

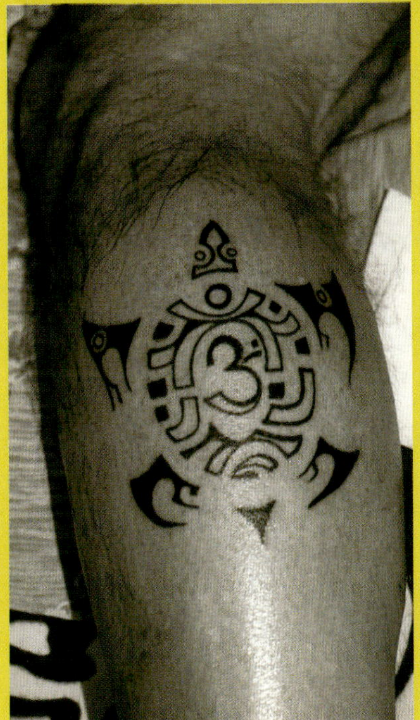

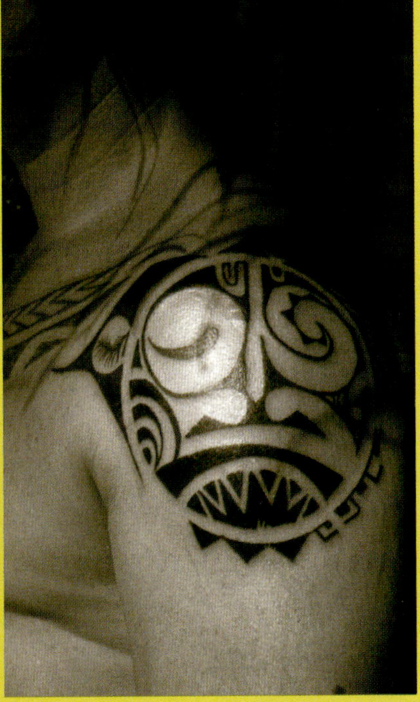

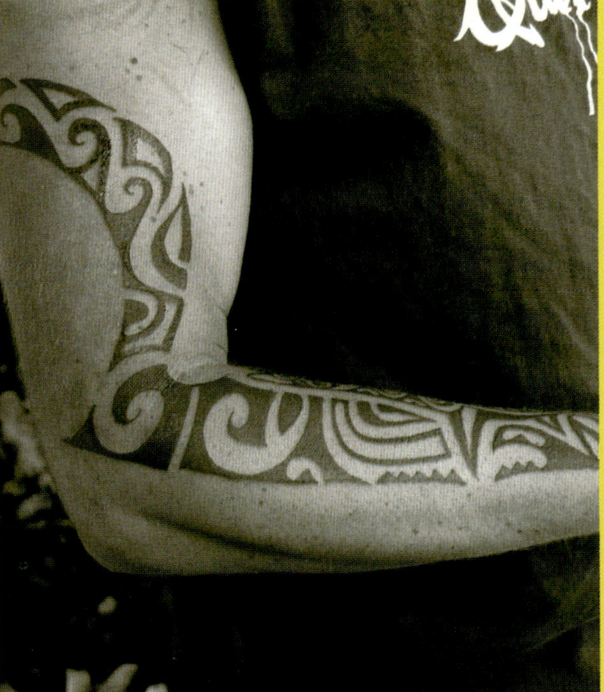

All images courtesy of Moorea Tattoo.

MARCUS KUHN

USA

1. I began tattooing in 1989 when I was working as a scenic artist in Los Angeles and was getting tattooed by Bob Roberts. I saw the power of tattoos and decided I could do it, so I began my journey. Back then it was harder as there were not so many people in the business. Eddie Deutsche and Guy Atchison helped me get some exposure and some names to travel and learn.

2. I love powerful tattoos: strong and clean and original.

3. I try to use traditional techniques from old American folk art and the Japanese Edo period aesthetics to make my own style. I hate that people have styles; a good tattooist can tattoo any style. For years I worked in street shops in Chicago and New York and Miami. There I became technically well-rounded, so now I try to always find my own way.

4. Find a good artist. That's all. Use your head; don't follow the herd.

5. At my shop Just Good Tattoos, 142 High Street, Portland, Maine. I travel a little, but mostly I stay at my shop, although now I spend a little time in London and Osaka.
www.marcuskuhn.com

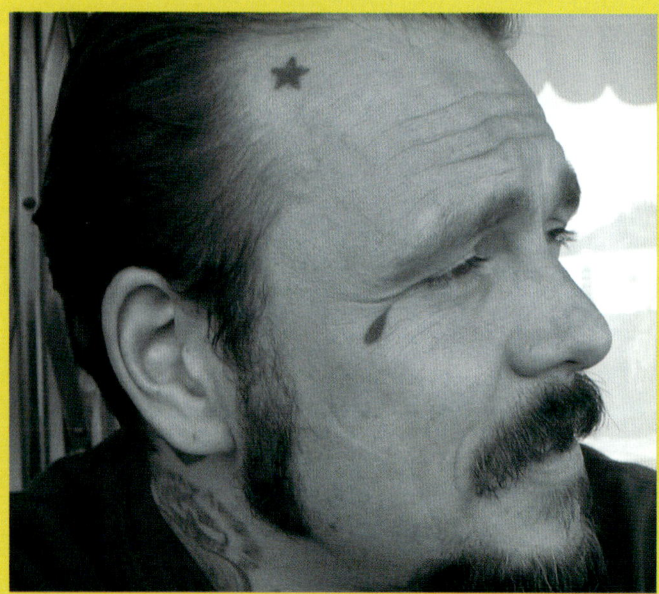

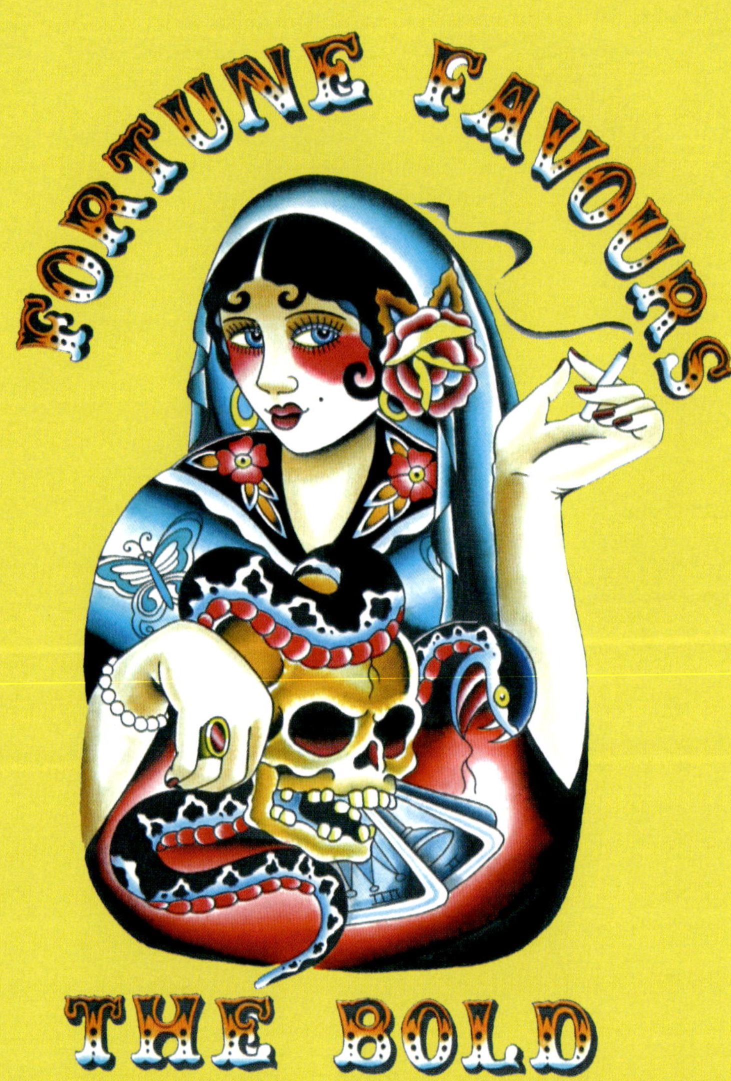

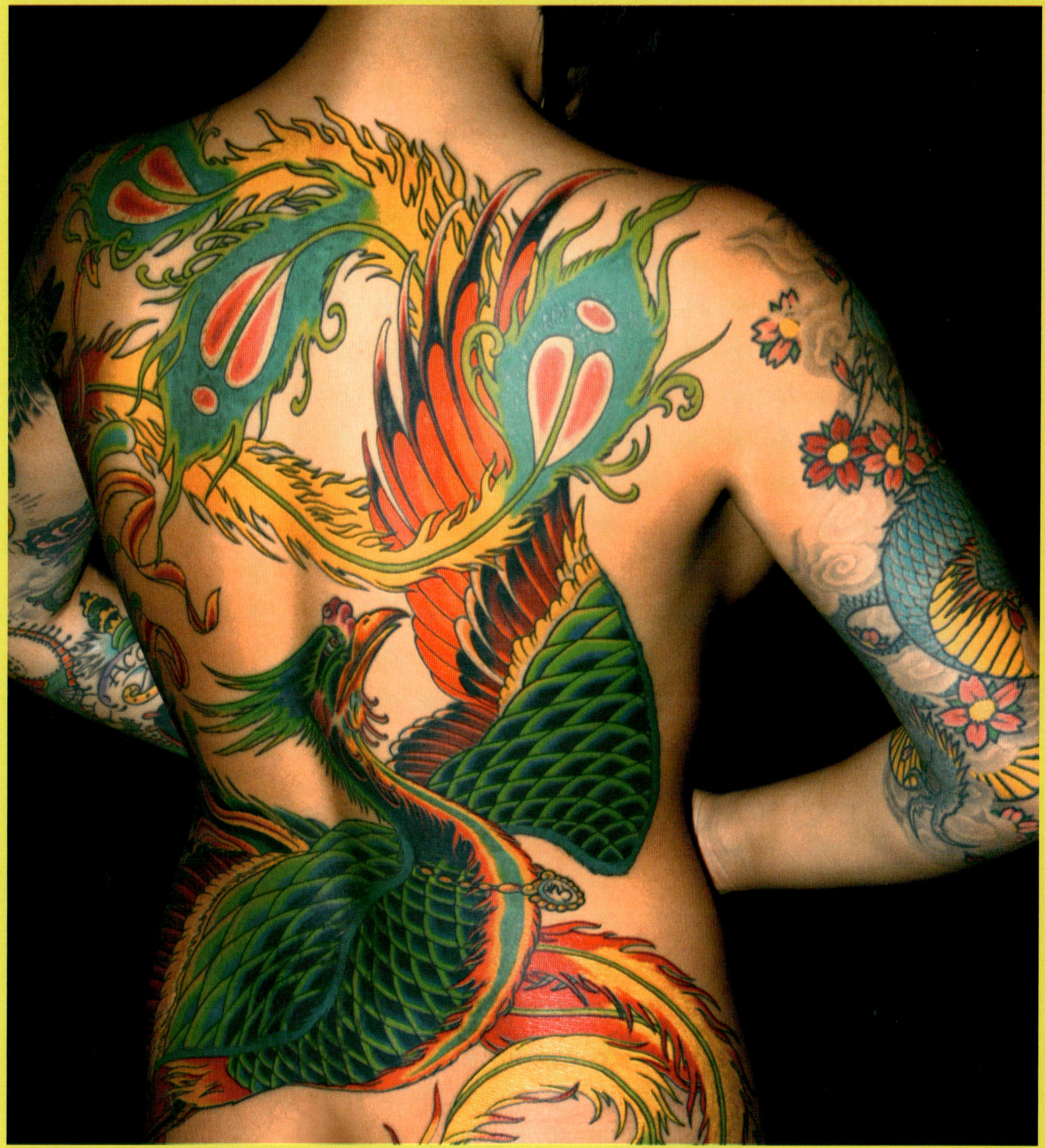

All images courtesy of Marcus Kuhn.

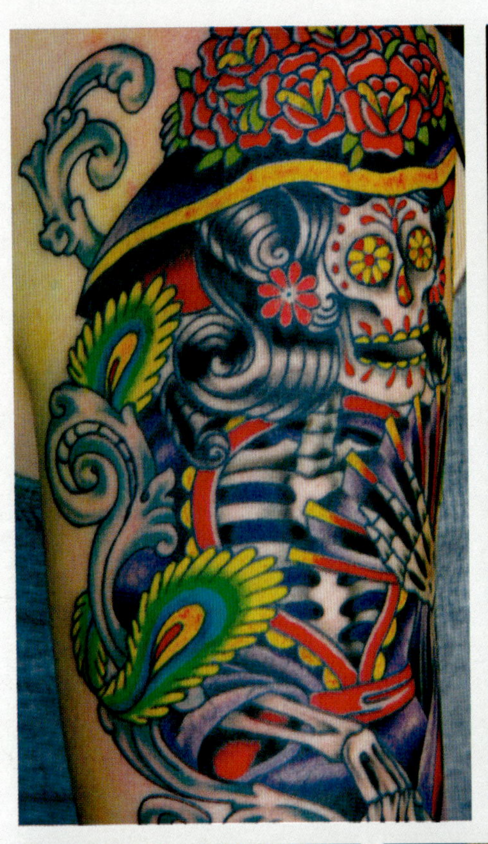
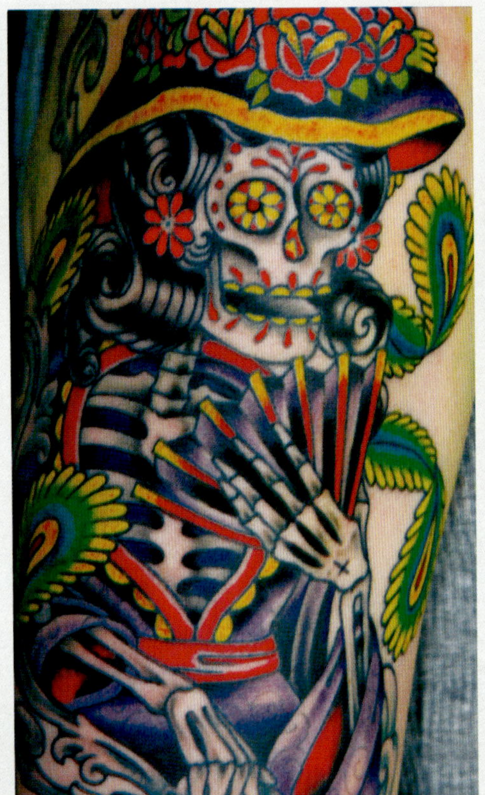
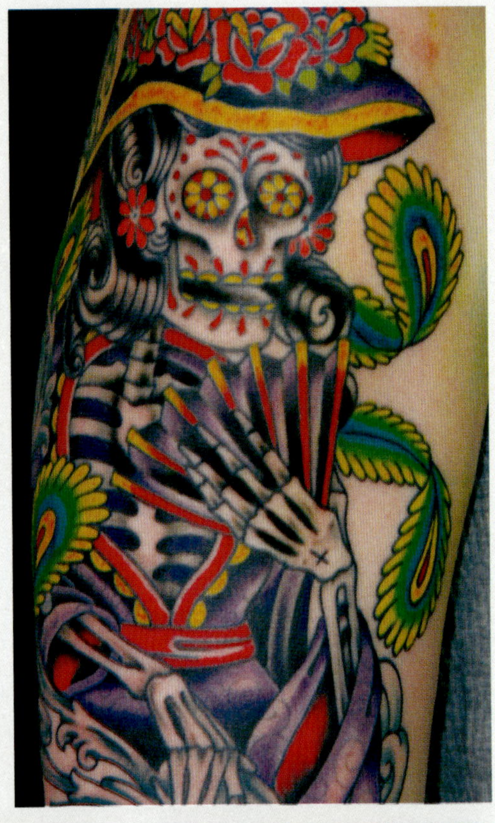
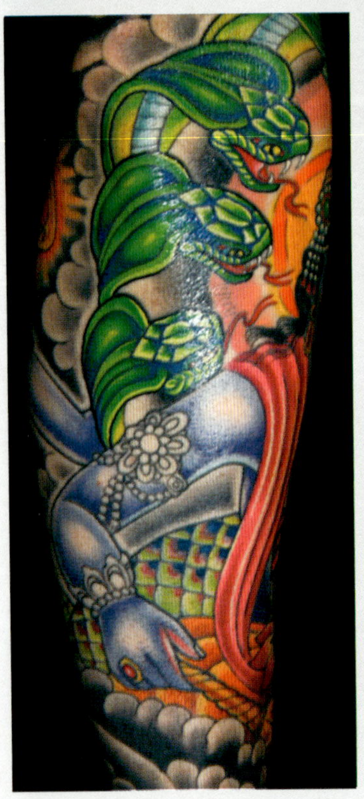
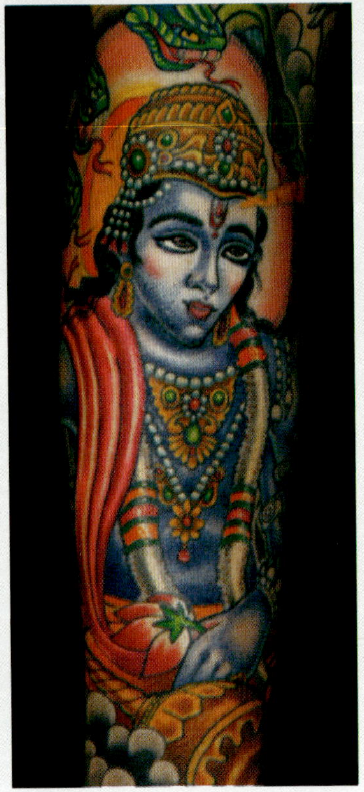
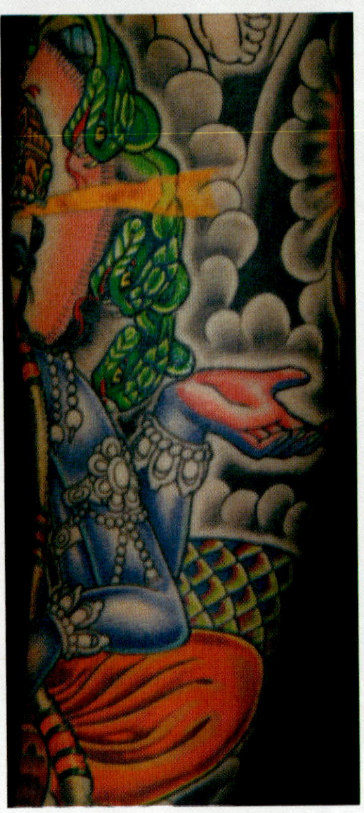
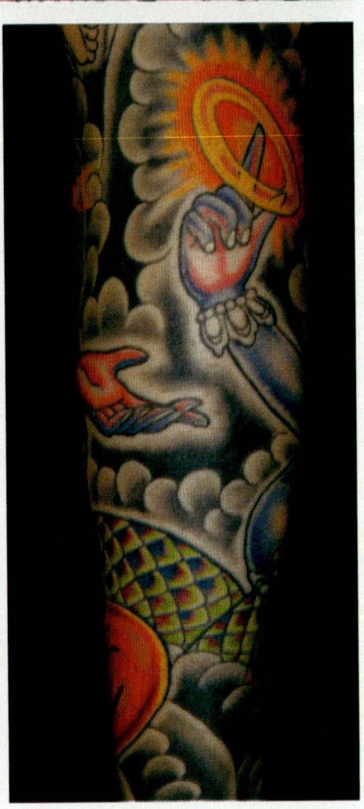

All artwork courtesy of Marcus Kuhn.

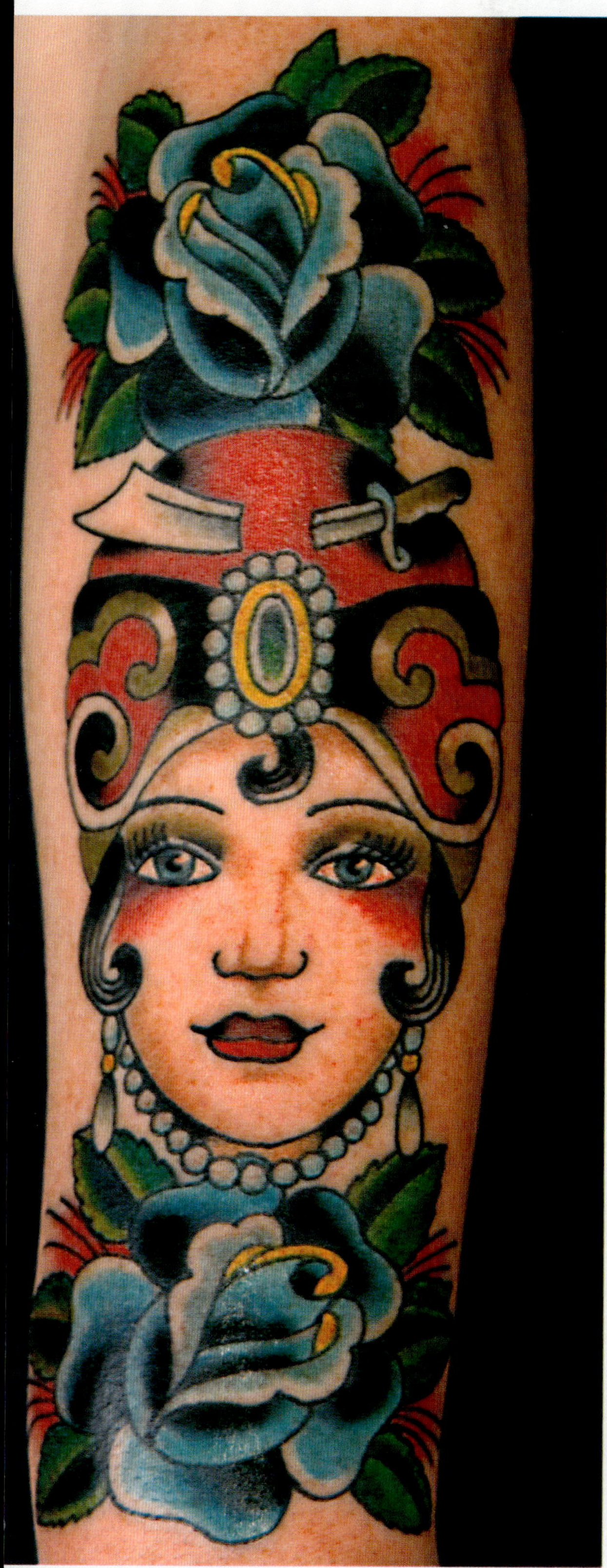

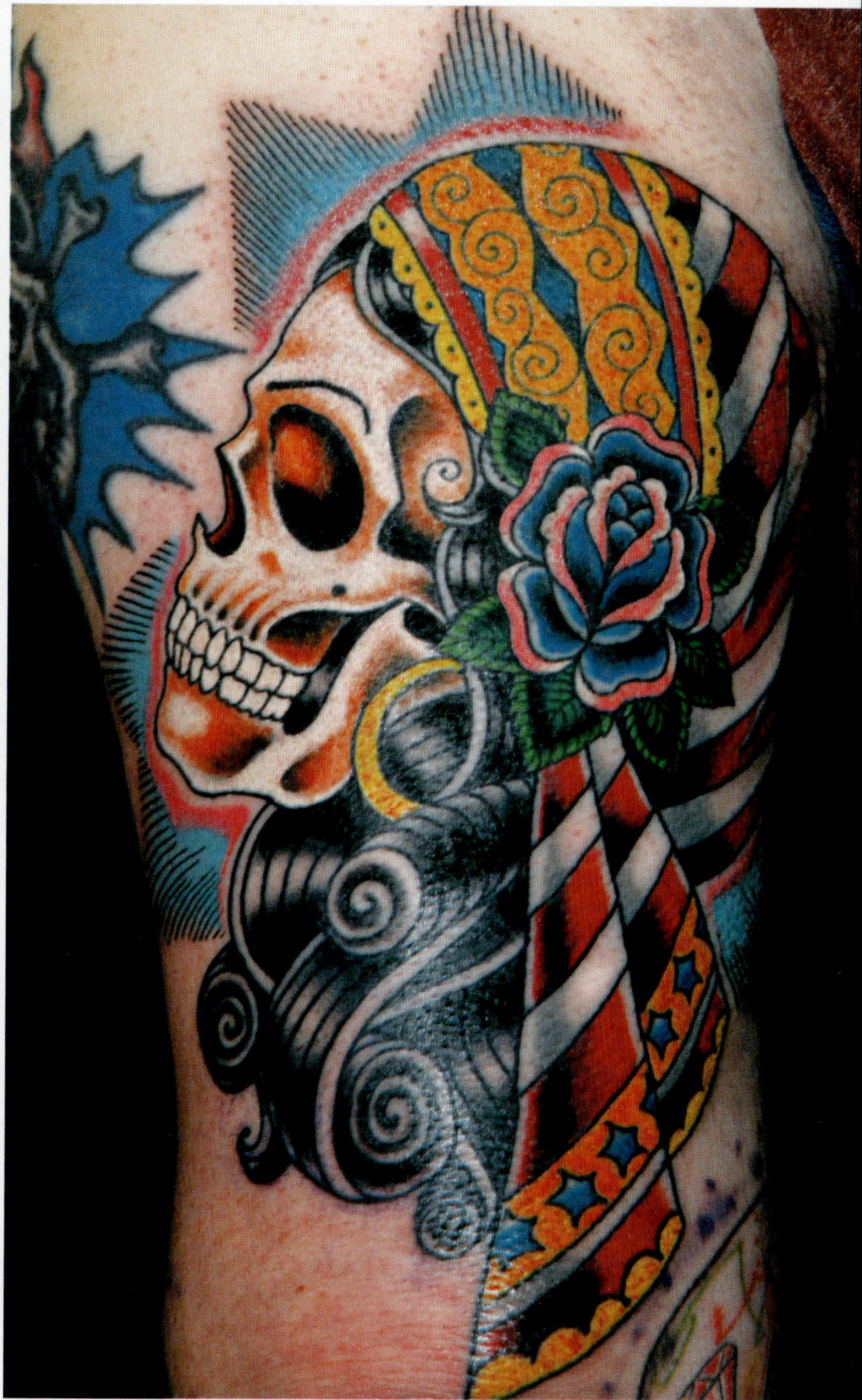

MARCUS KUHN

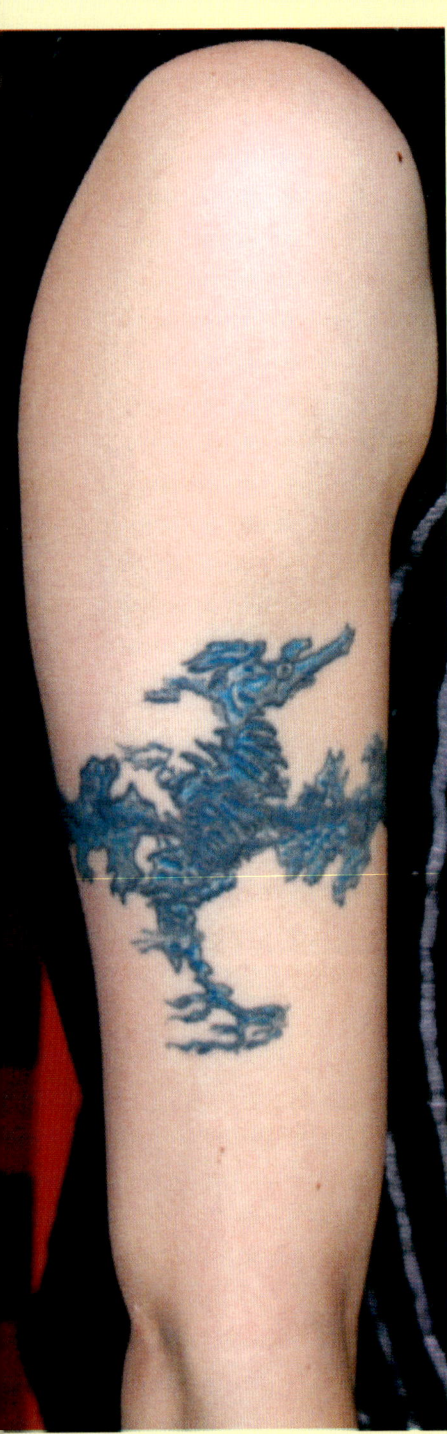

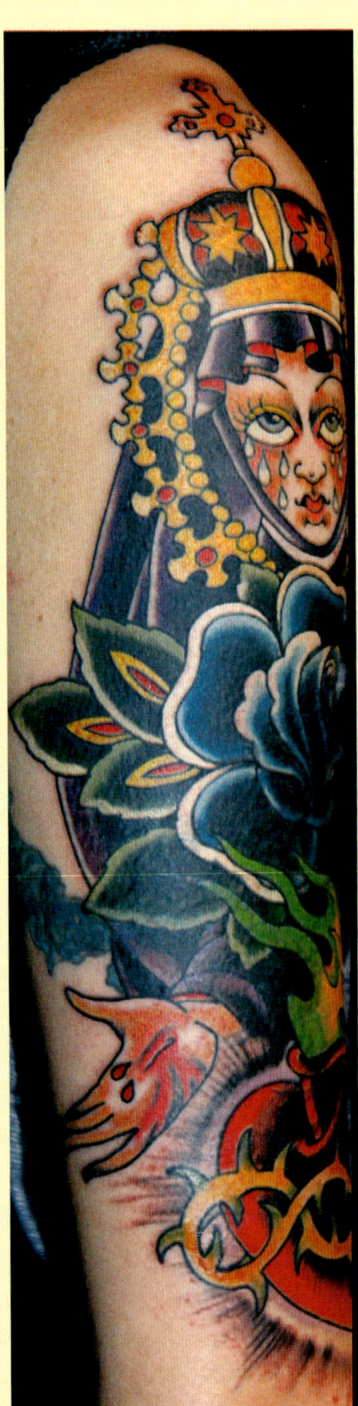

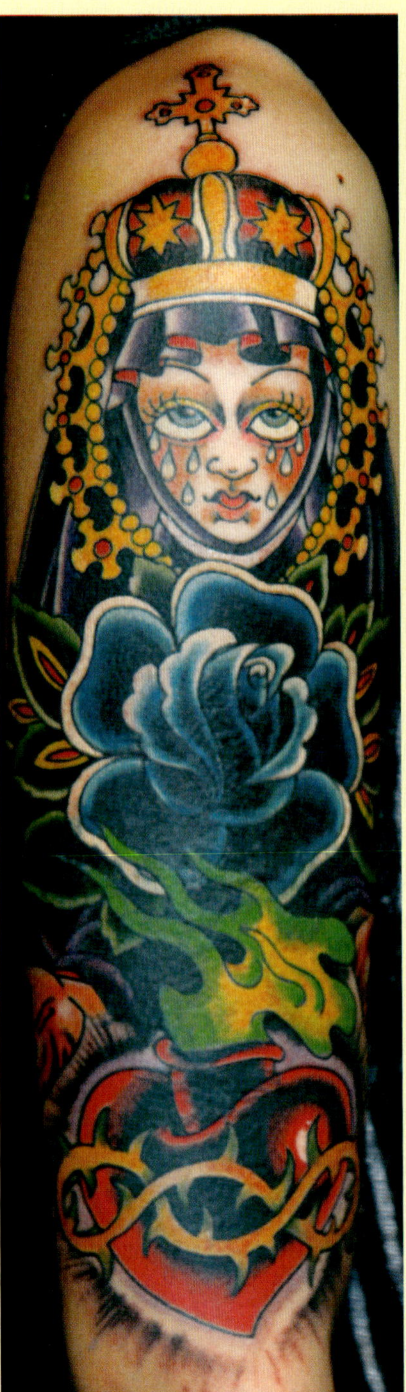

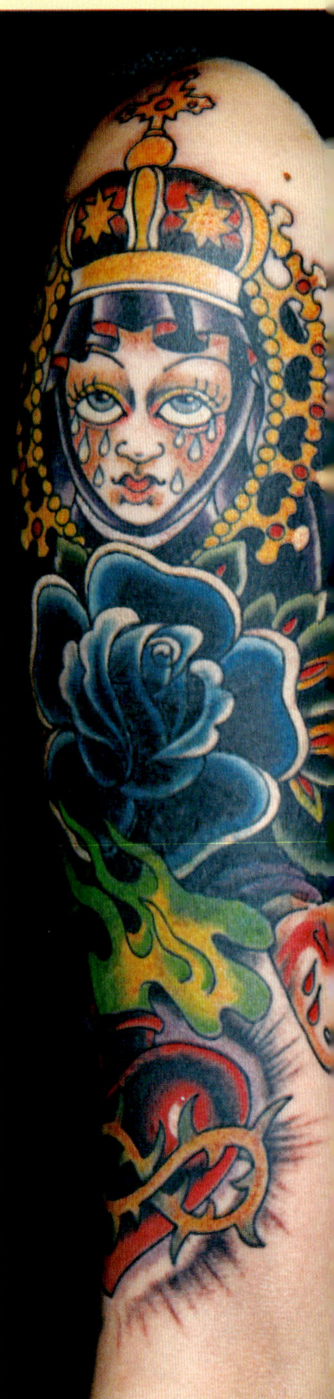

All artwork by Marcus Kuhn. Top left image: cover up by Marcus Kuhn.

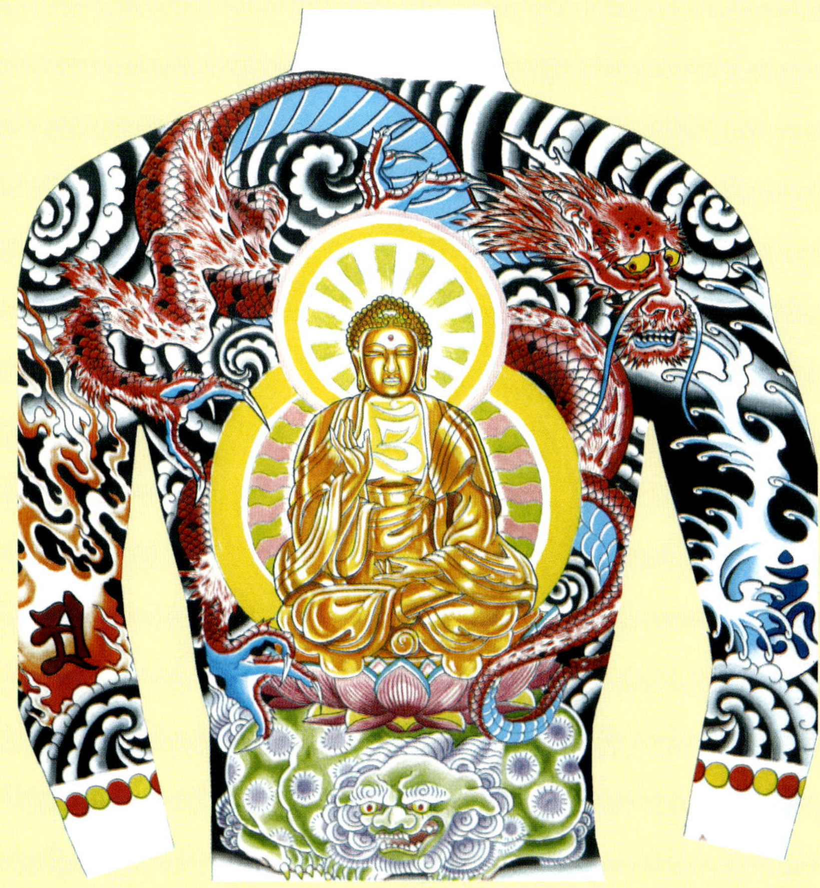

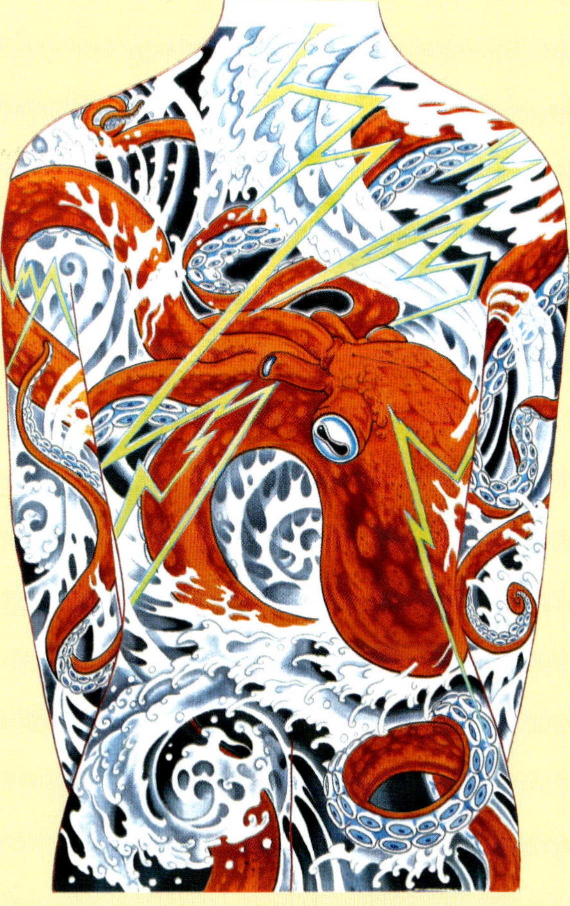

Tattoo designs by Marcus Kuhn.

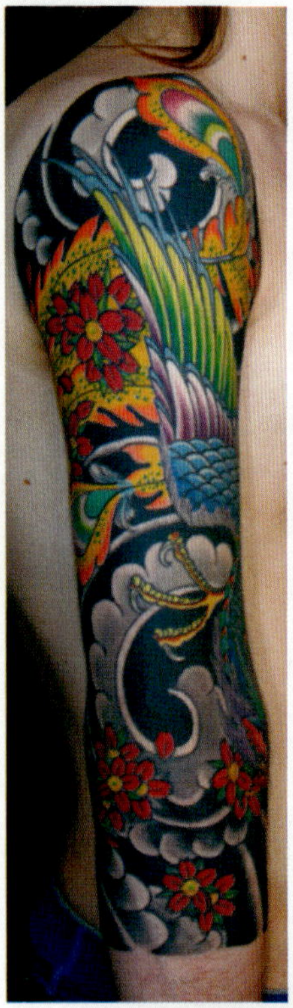

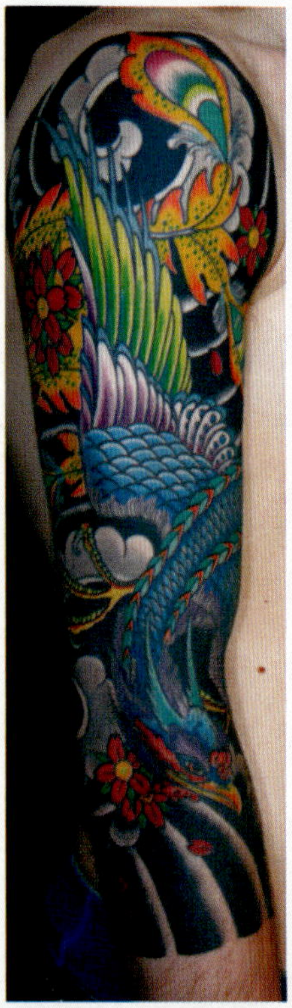

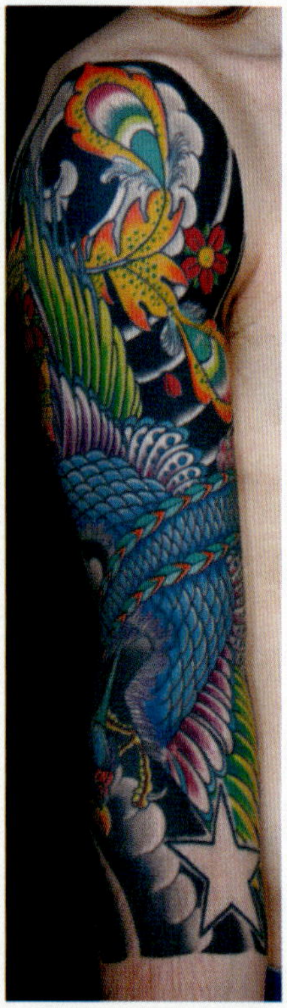

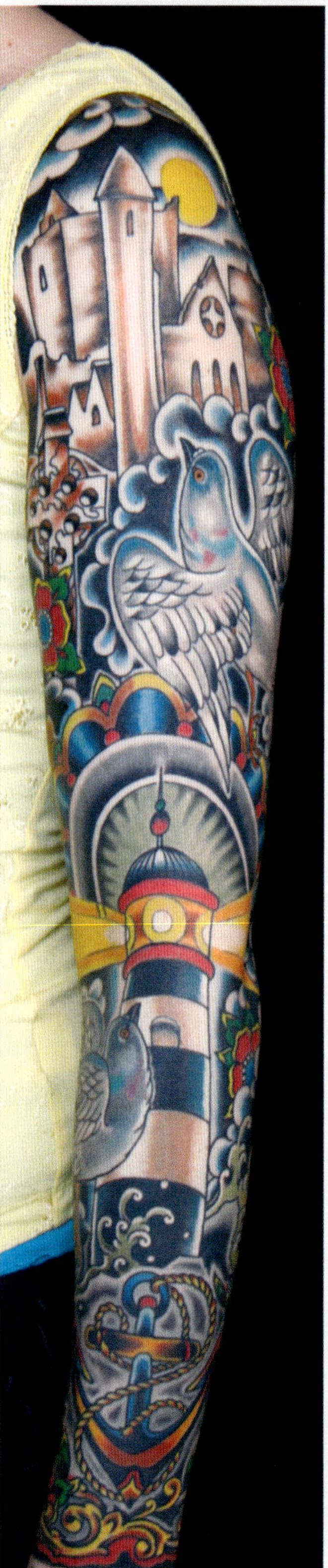

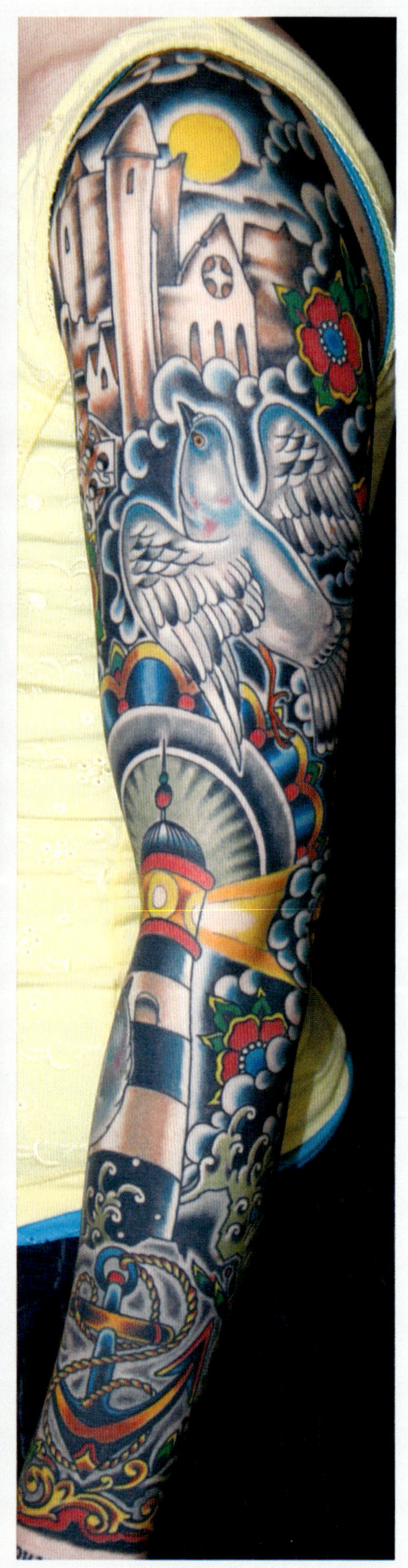

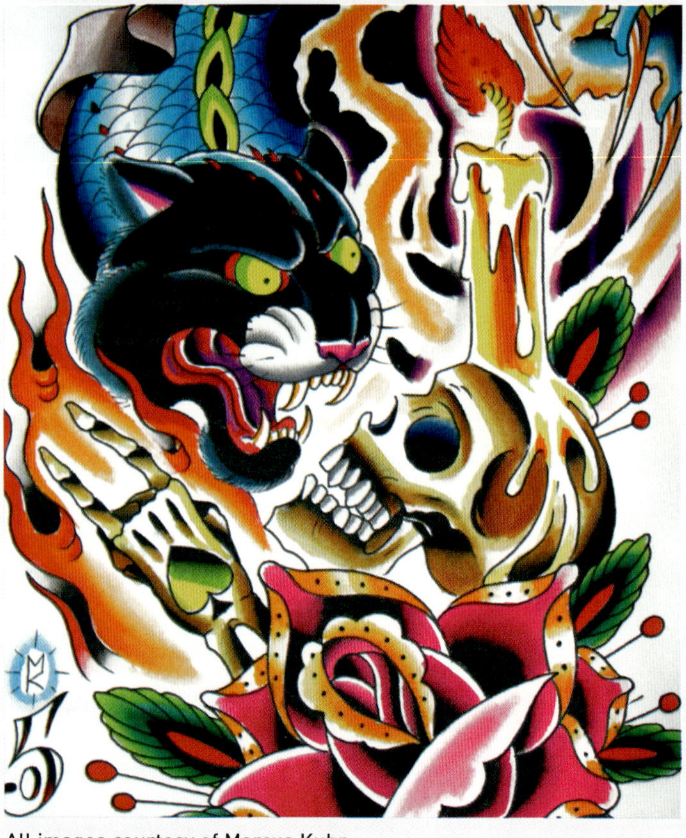

All images courtesy of Marcus Kuhn.

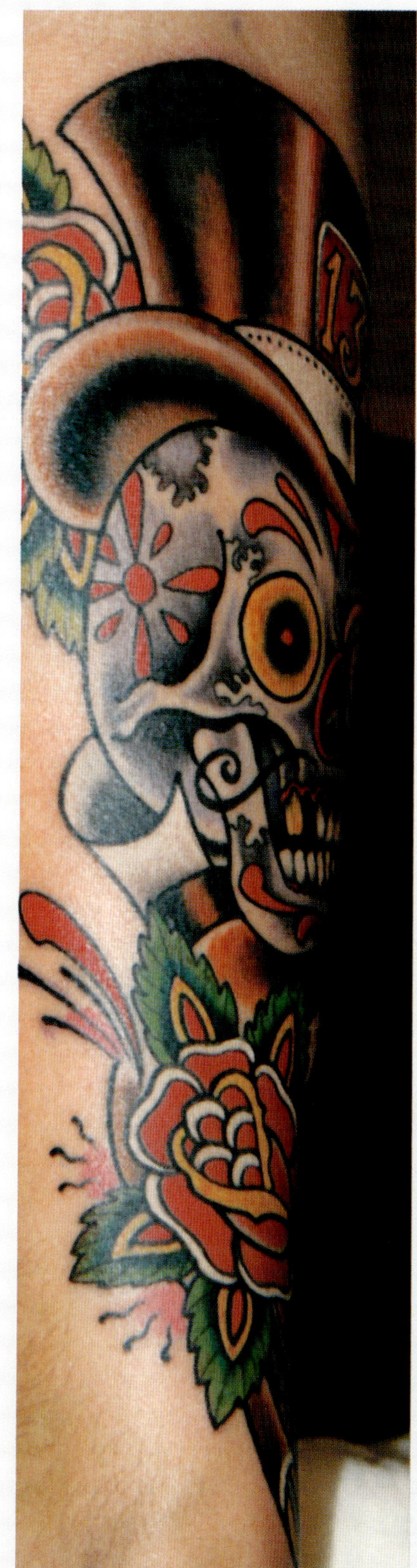

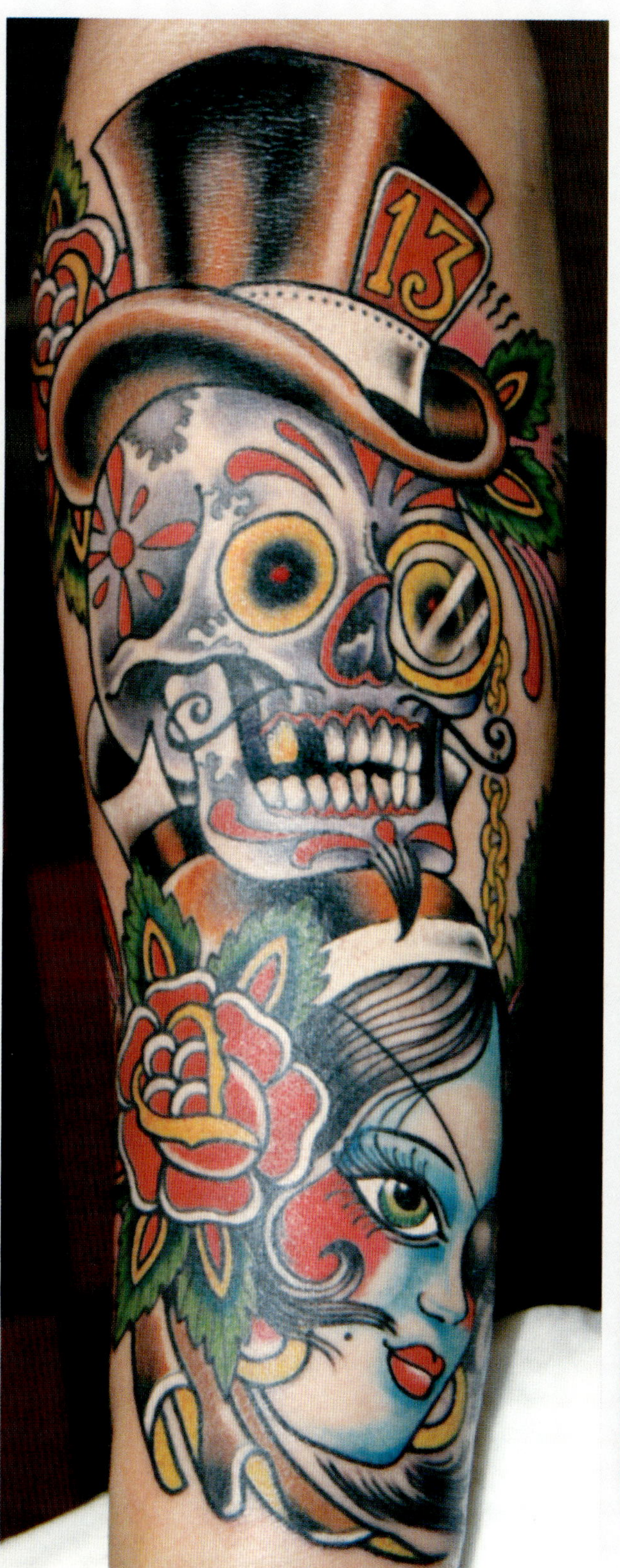

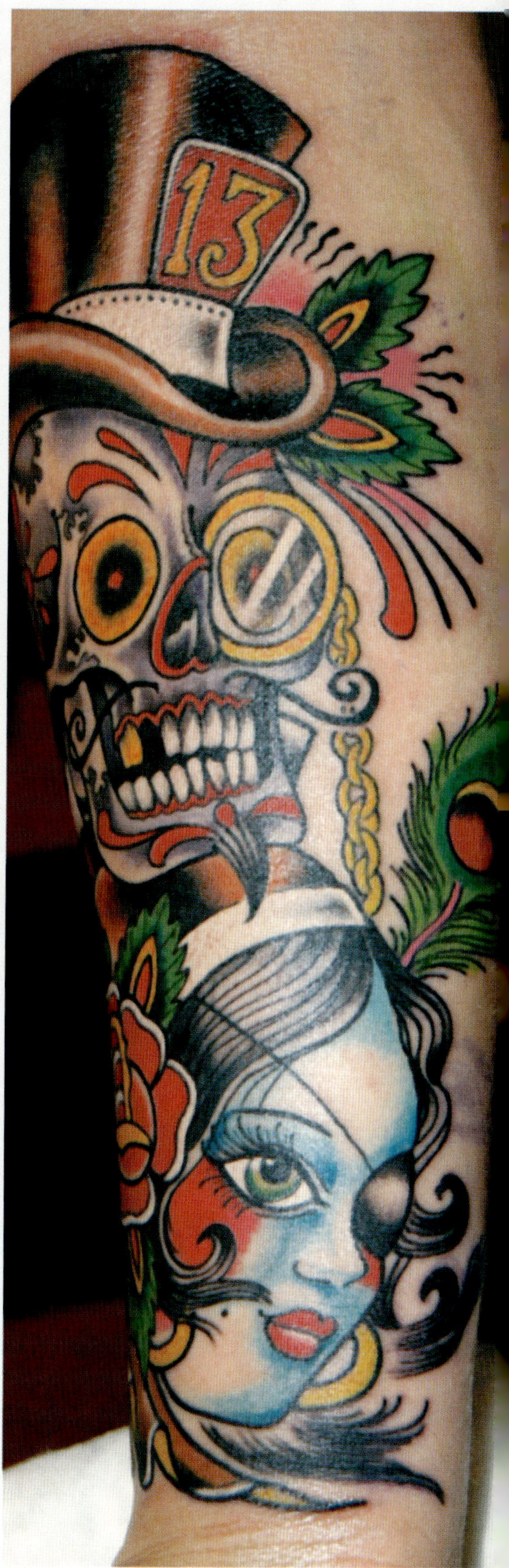

MARCUS KUHN

PLURABELLA

USA

1. I started tattooing in Hollywood, California in 1990 at Purple Panther Tattoo. I apprenticed there for a year with Rick Cosmo. In 1995, I moved to Ohio and worked with Mike Dorsey at Permanent Productions. About four years later, I opened my own private shop in Ohio called Plurabella.

2. Tattooing is basically everything to me. I suppose I should say some other things are more important, for instance, my feelings for my wife, but tattooing is right up there near the top. Tattooing itself is my inspiration. The more I do, the more I want to do.

3. I focus on creating large-format pieces that are custom fit to each client's unique form. Black-and-gray is my first love and I believe that is the foundation for good tattoo art. I like to juxtapose that element with a 10 to 30 percent ratio of color.

4. Measure twice, cut once.

5. I own a private, custom shop in Cincinnati, Ohio with my wife Brenda, who is also a tattoo artist. Though that is my home base, I travel regularly to Los Angeles, California to work with my clients on the West Coast. Every now and again I travel to European conventions.
www.plurabella.com

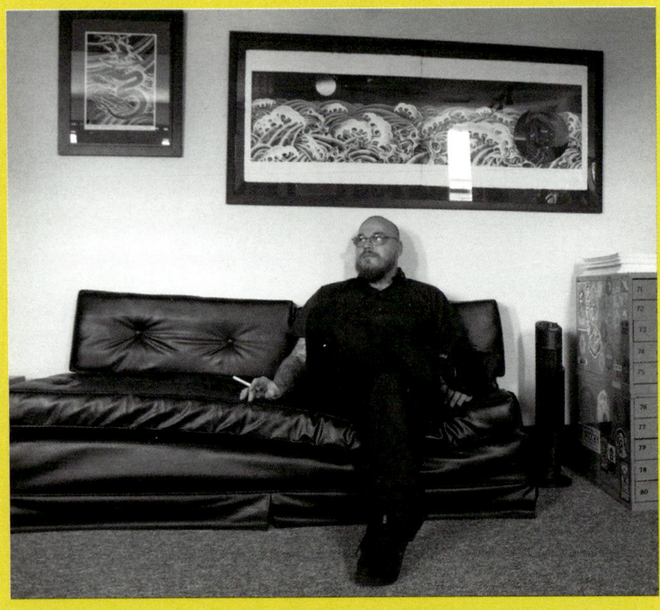

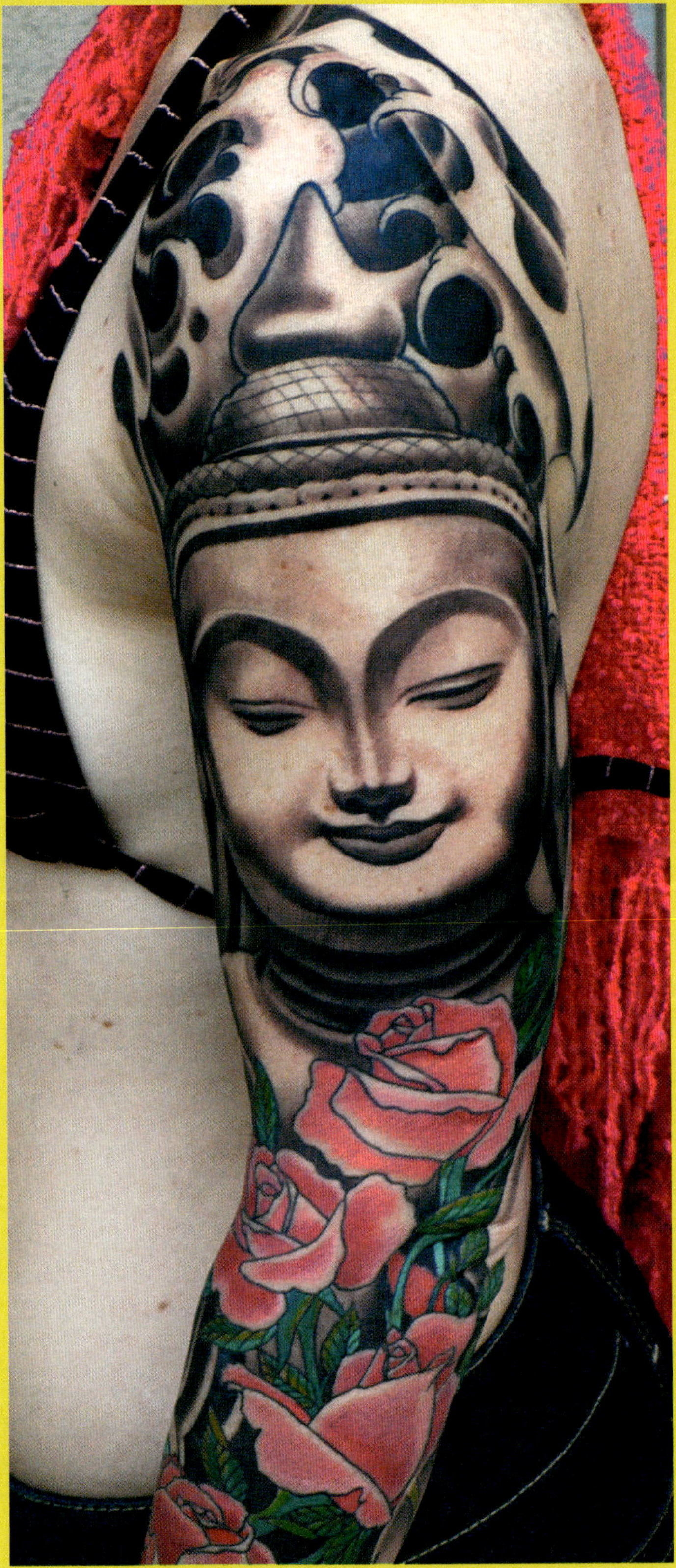

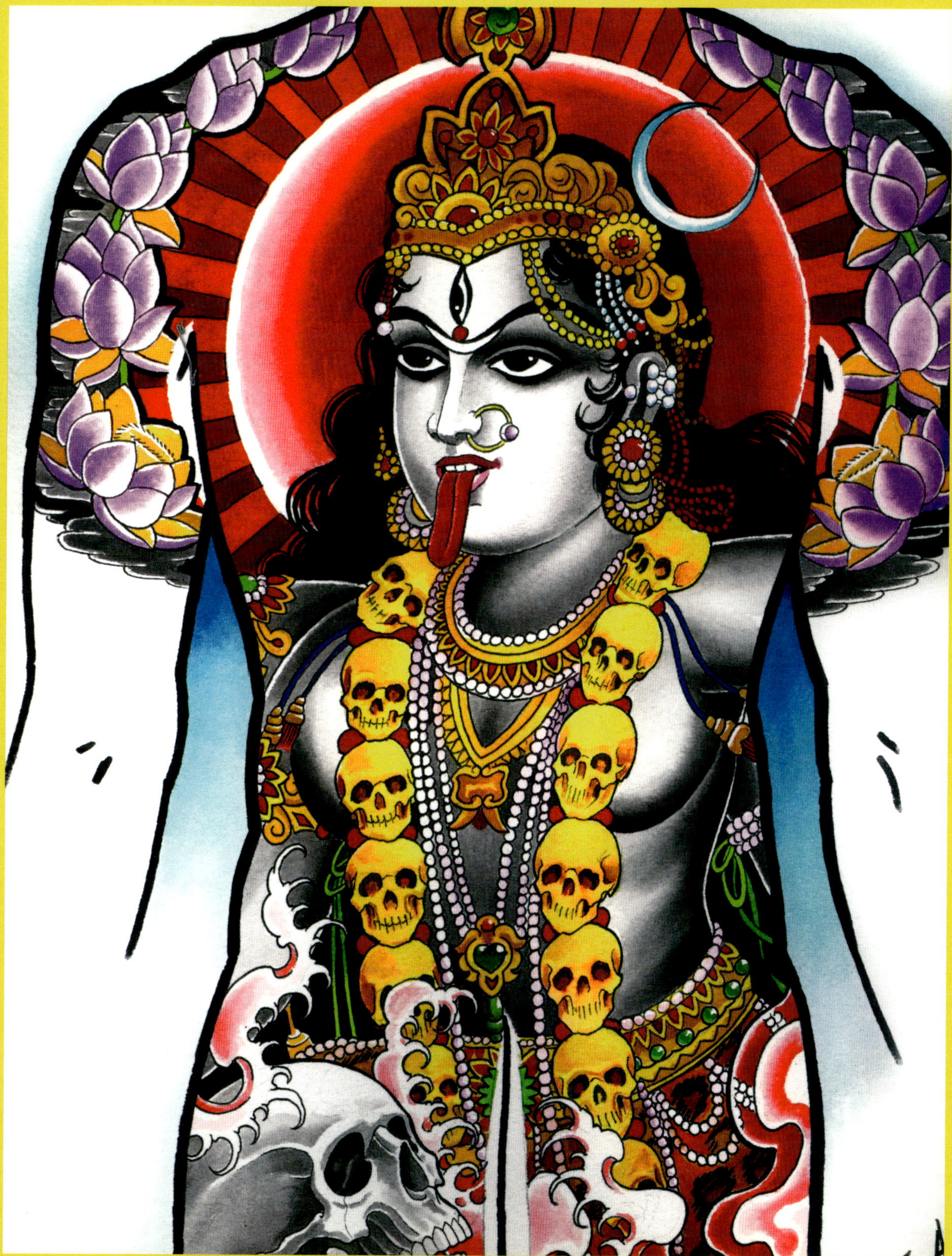

All artwork by Plurabella.

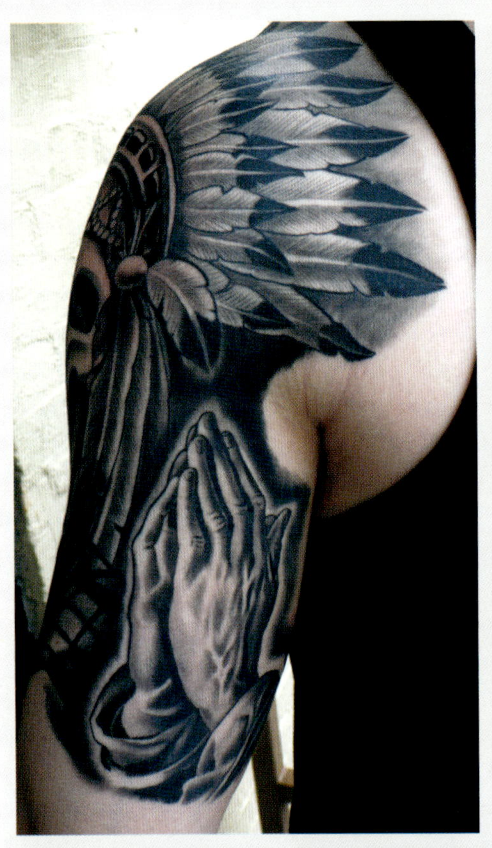

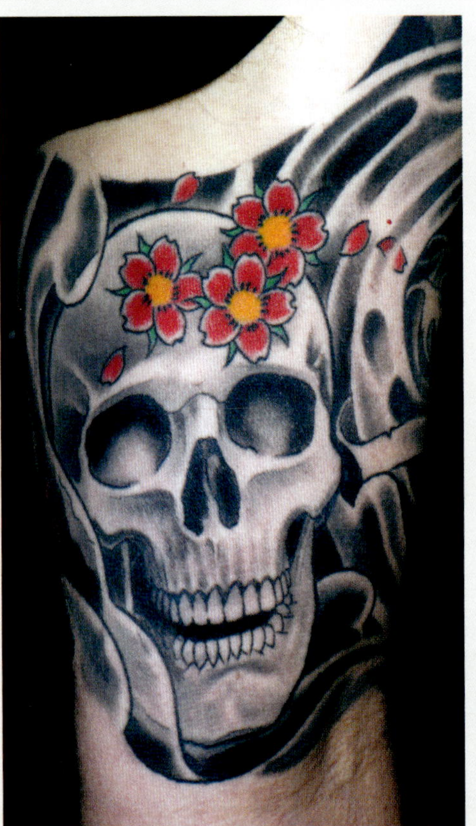

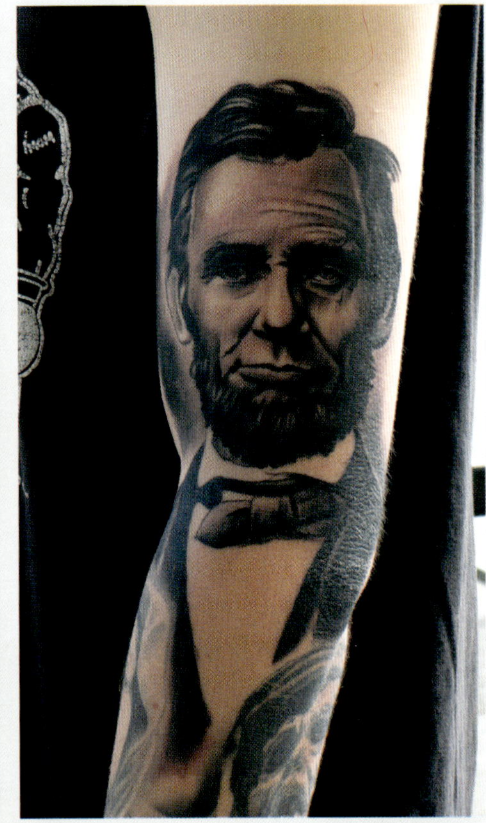

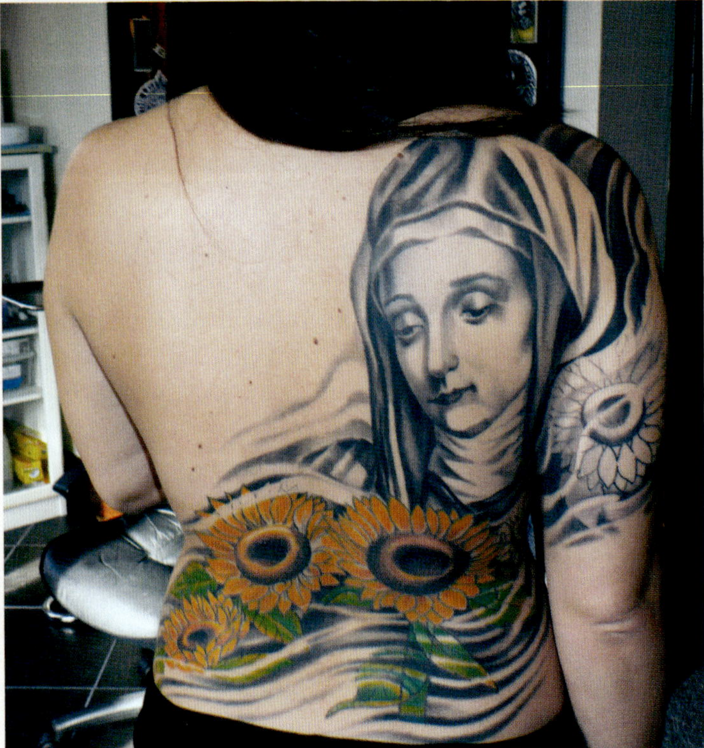

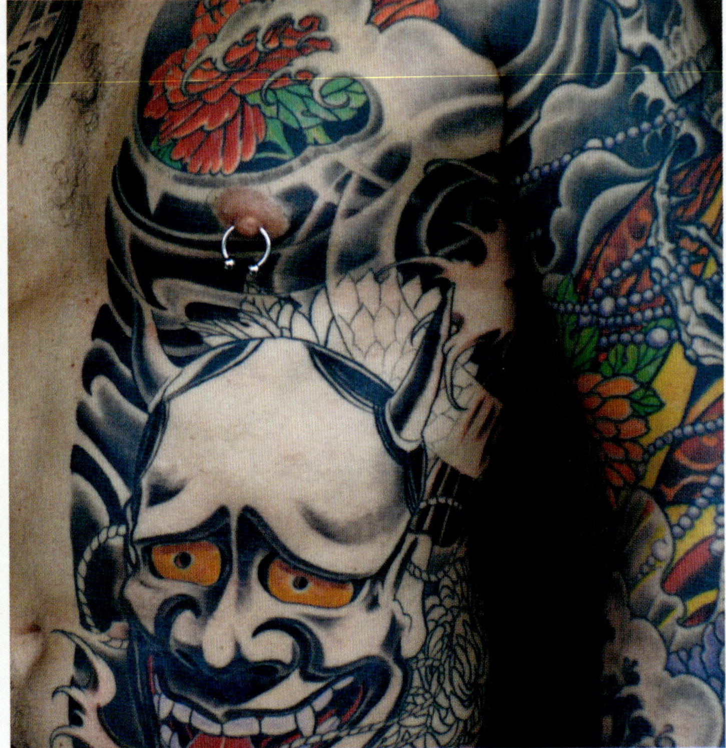

All images courtesy of Plurabella.

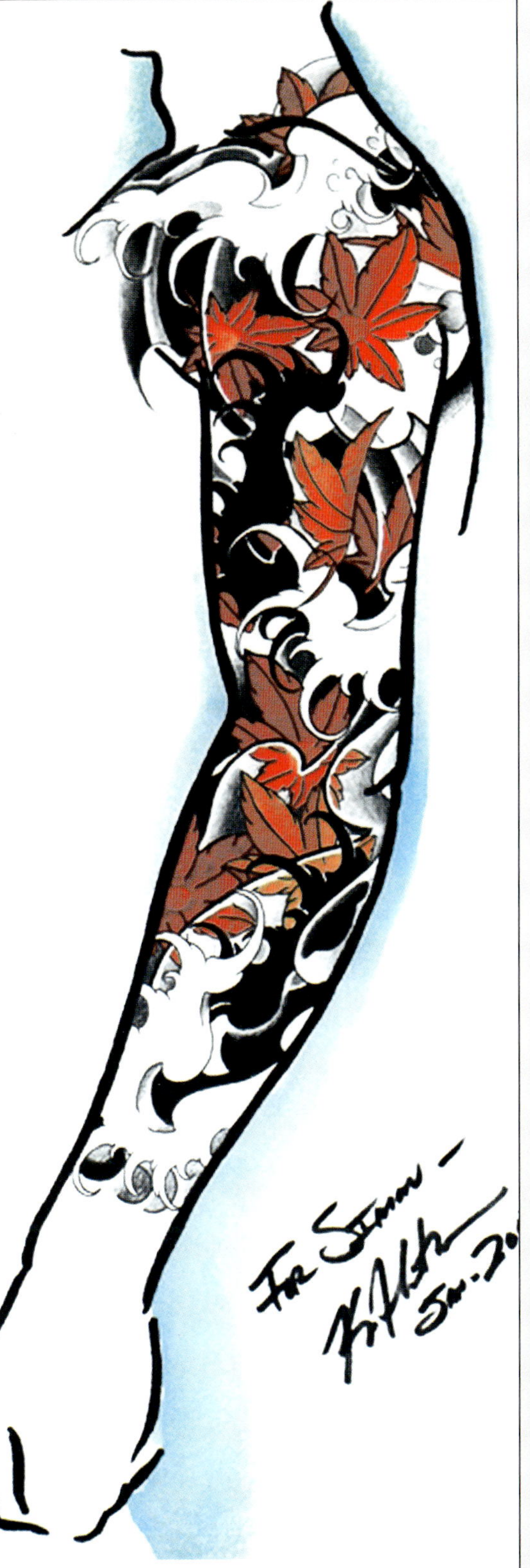

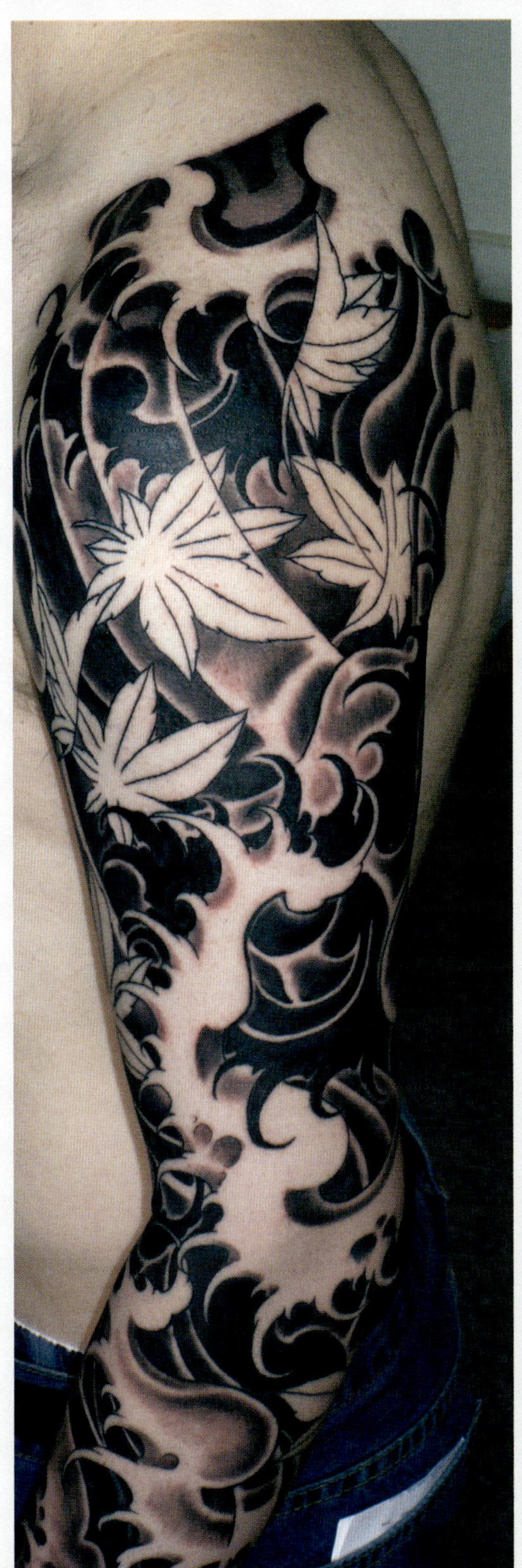

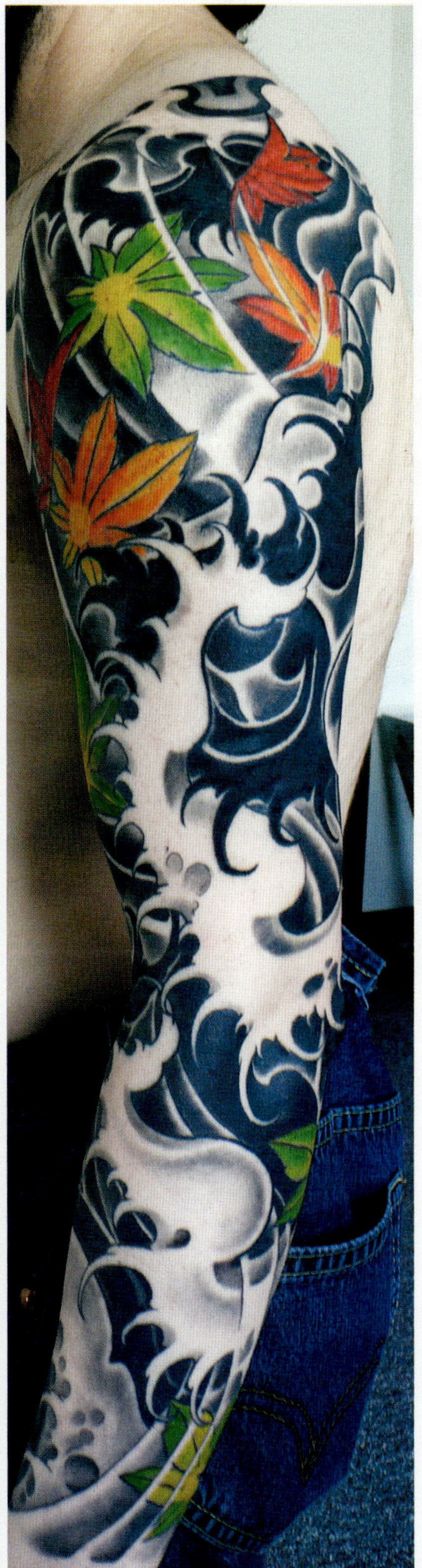

On this page: process of a tattoo by Plurabella.

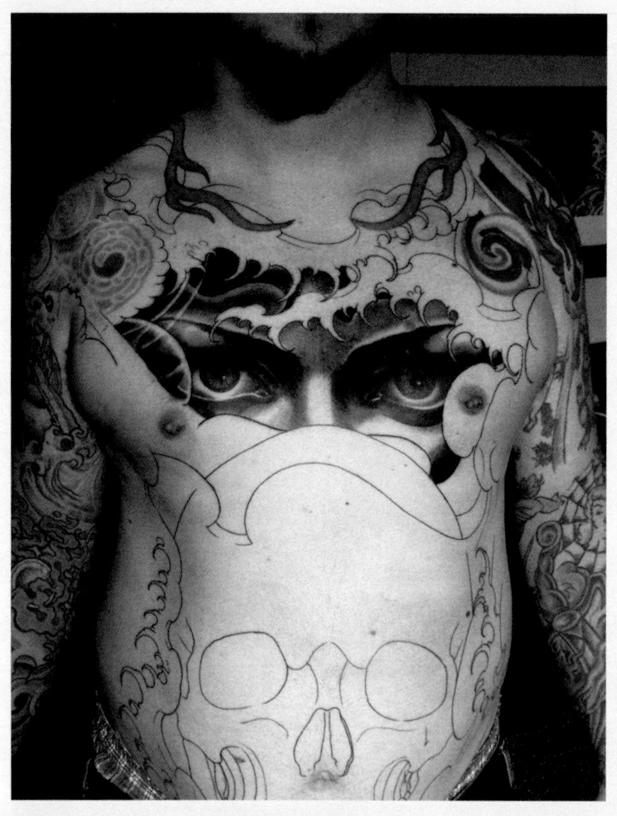

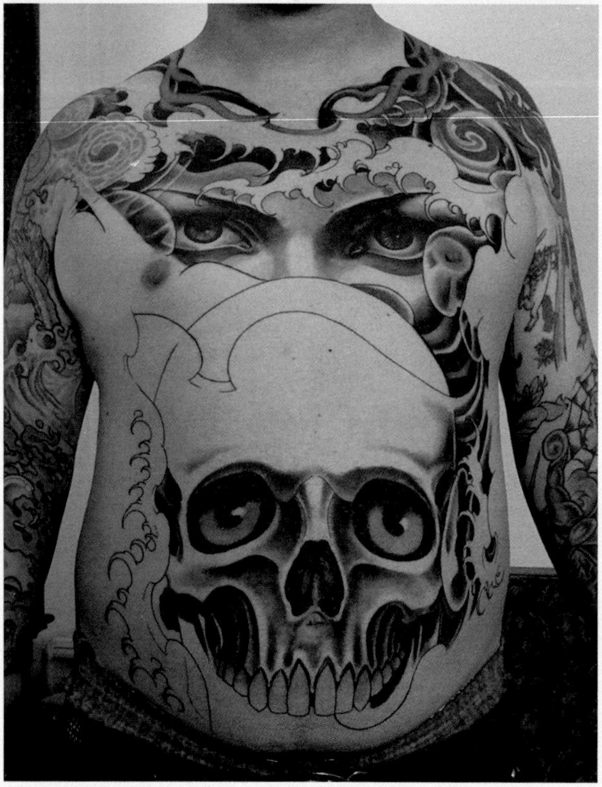

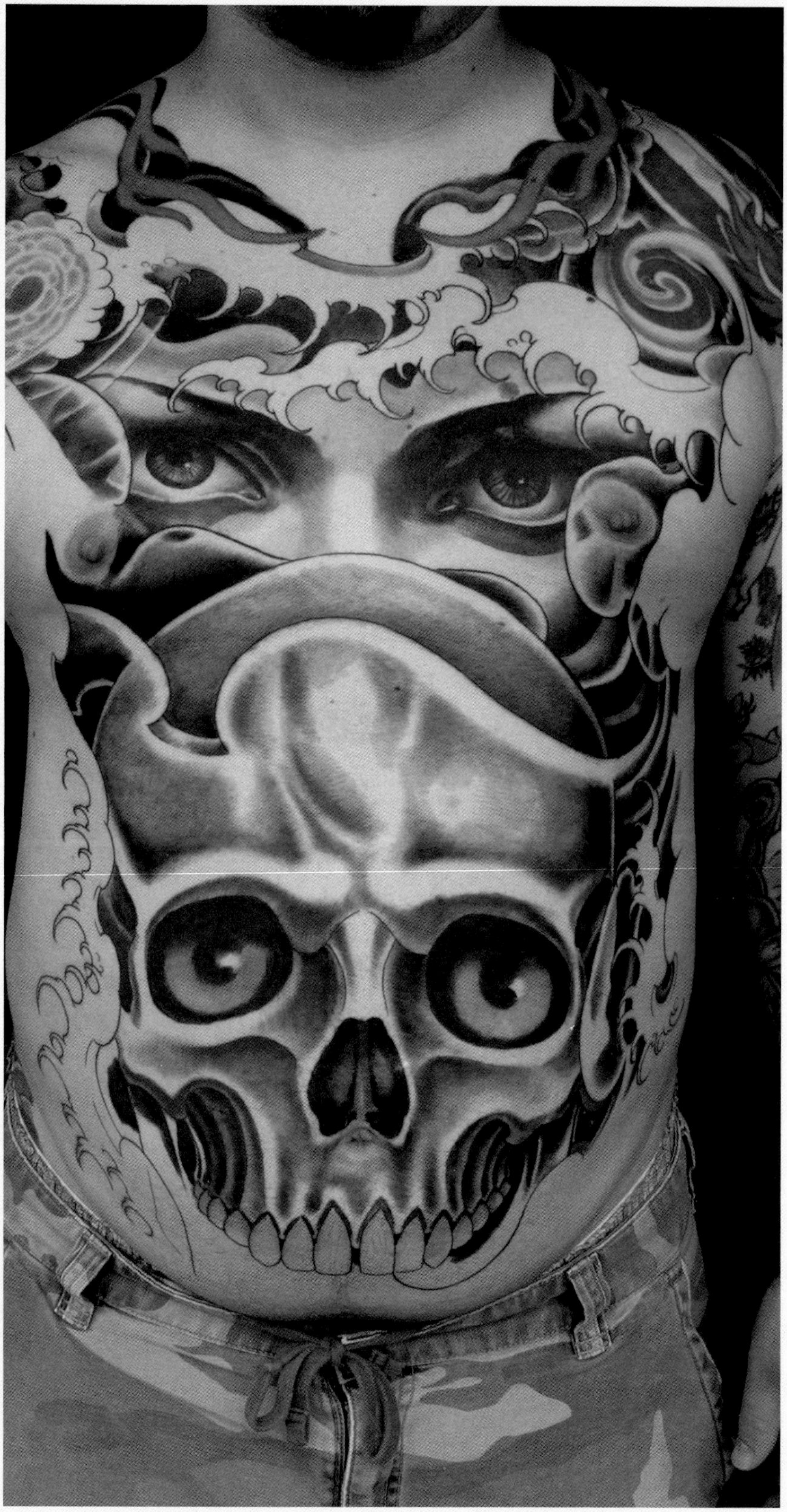

Step by step of a tattoo design by Plurabella.

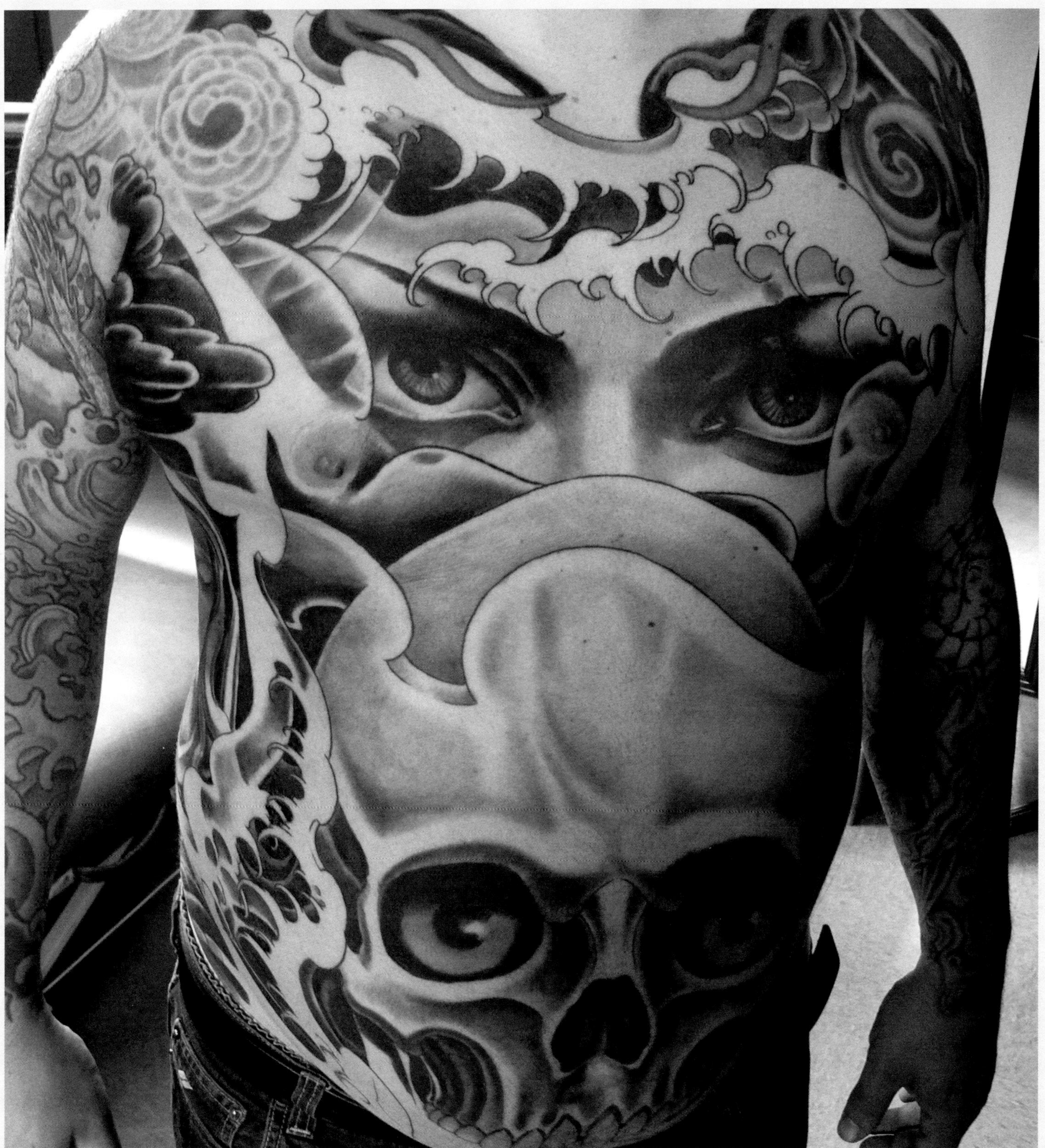

PLURABELLA

AMANDA TOY

ITALY

1. Torn apart by the spectres of my mind, I turned to a fantasy world coexisting alongside the hustle and bustle of reality. Tattooing was my therapy through which I managed to channel the excess energy that otherwise would have gone nowhere.

2. Tattooing for me is an extension of my being, of my naivety and of my sometimes childlike vision of the world.

3. The traditional American tattoo proved to be the start of my journey in which colors and shapes complementary to pop art have been my traveling companions, resulting in the incorporeal essence of my images.

4. In the maelstrom that my mind was, tattooing represented discipline and focusing on priorities. It might seem that these two quaint concepts are ill at ease with creativity; but it worked for me. I managed to improve my techniques. My piece of advice therefore is strength and passion.

5. I live and work in Trieste, Italy. I share the Original Classic Tattoo shop with the eclectic artist Rudy Fritsch. You can contact me at:
   info@amandatoy.it
   www.amandatoy.com
   www.originalclassictattoo.com

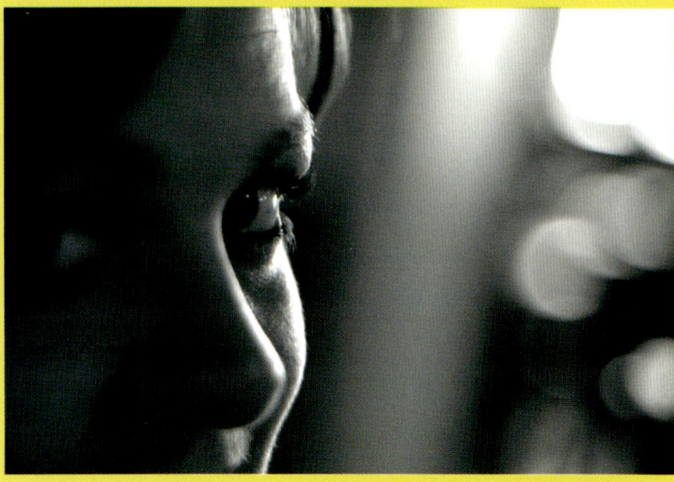

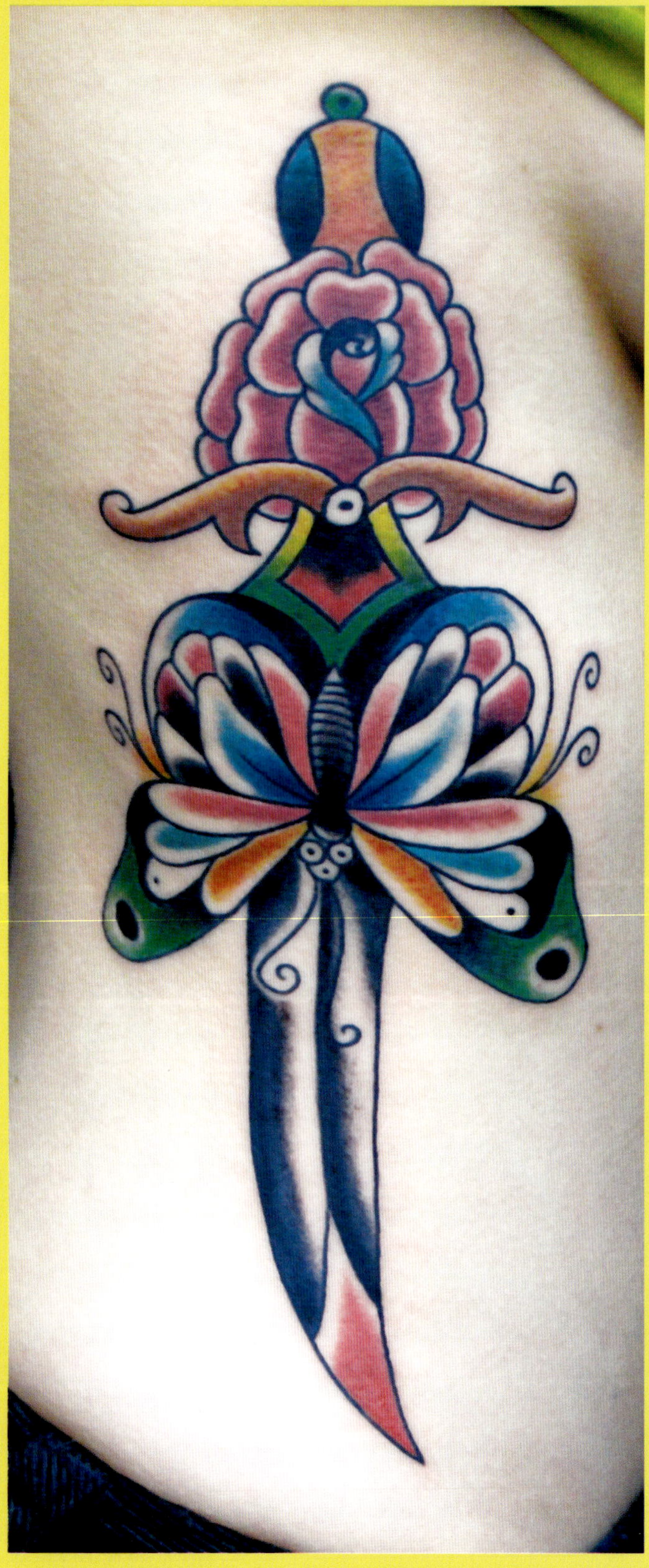

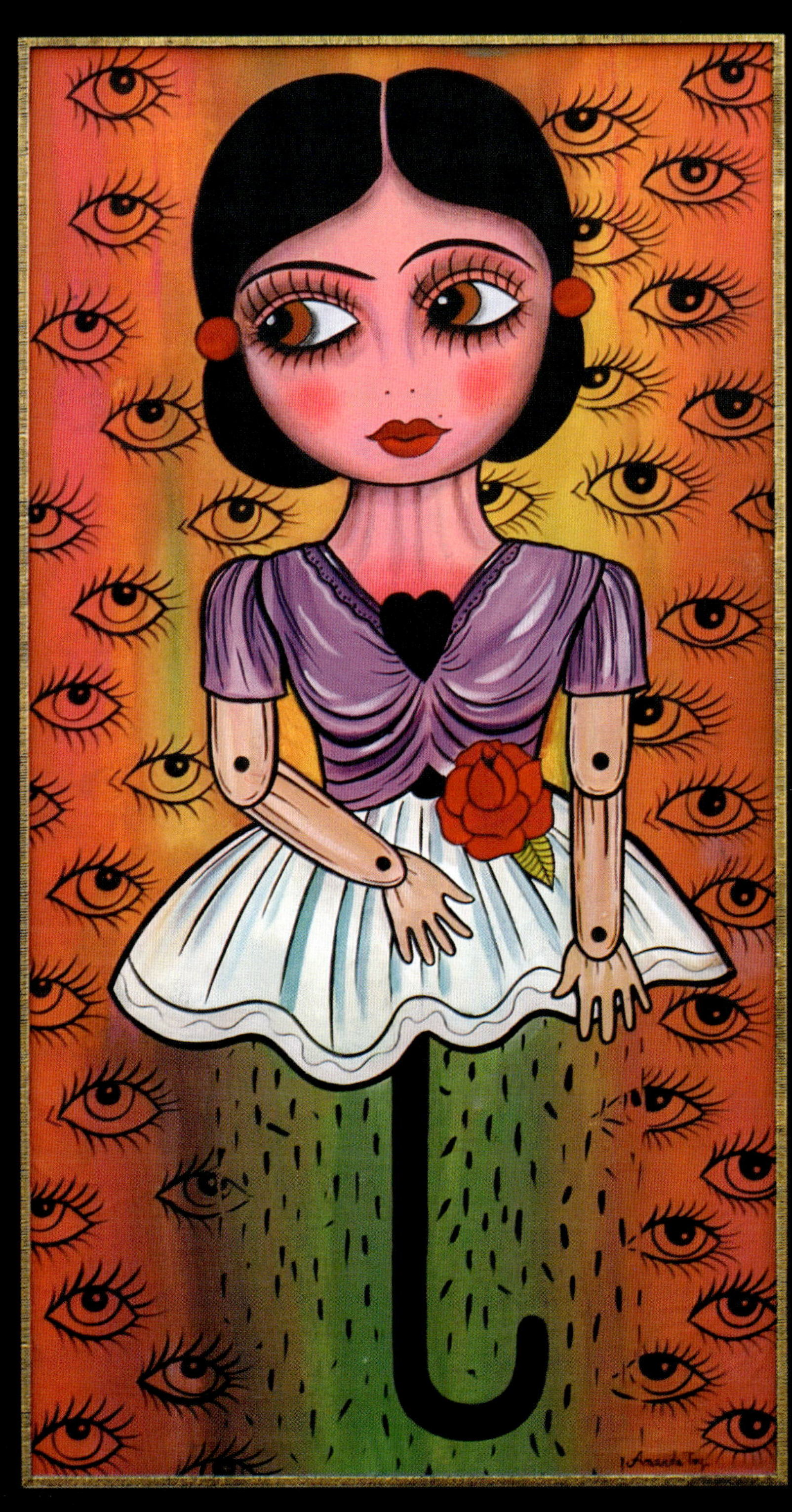

All images courtesy of Amanda Toy.

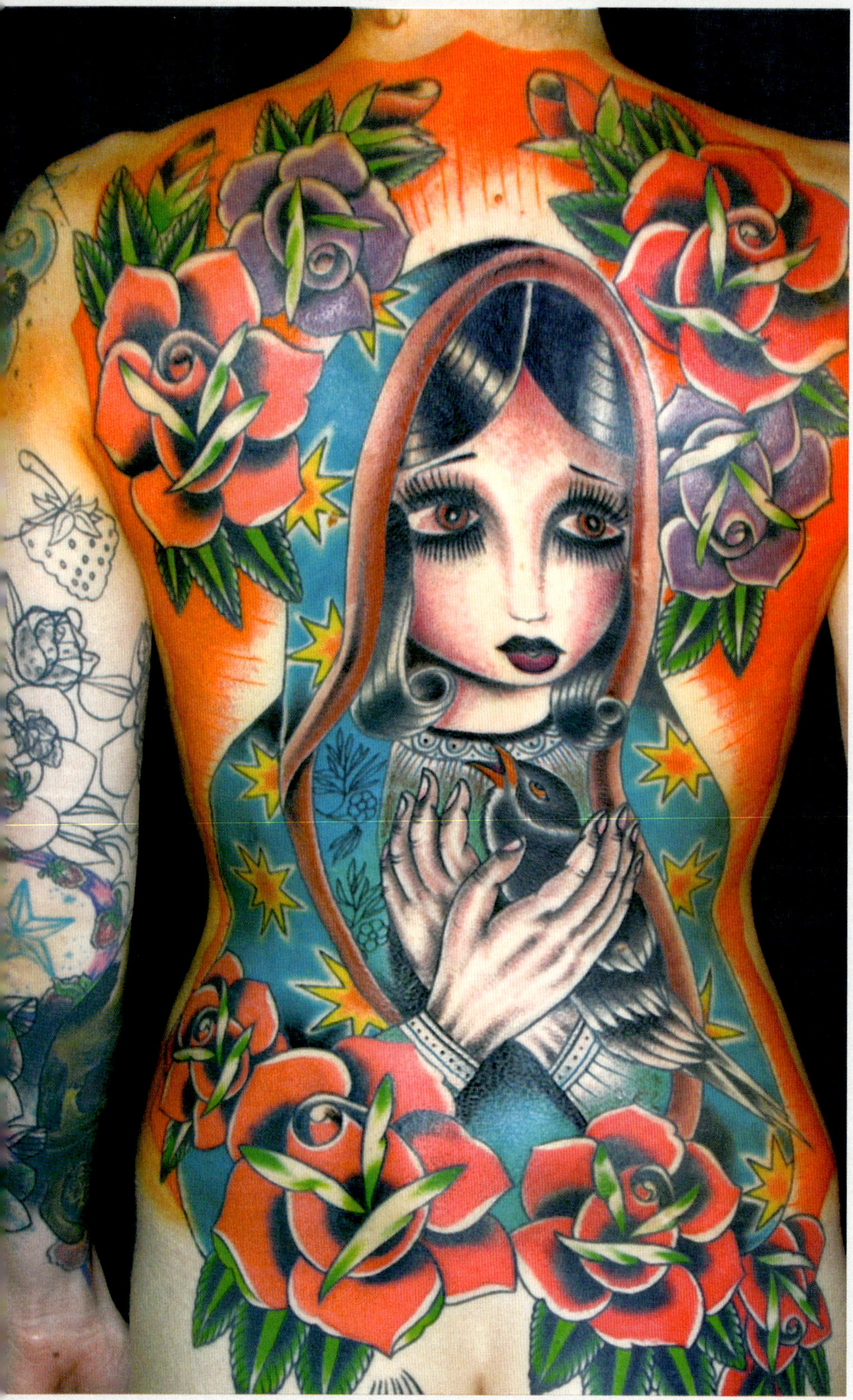

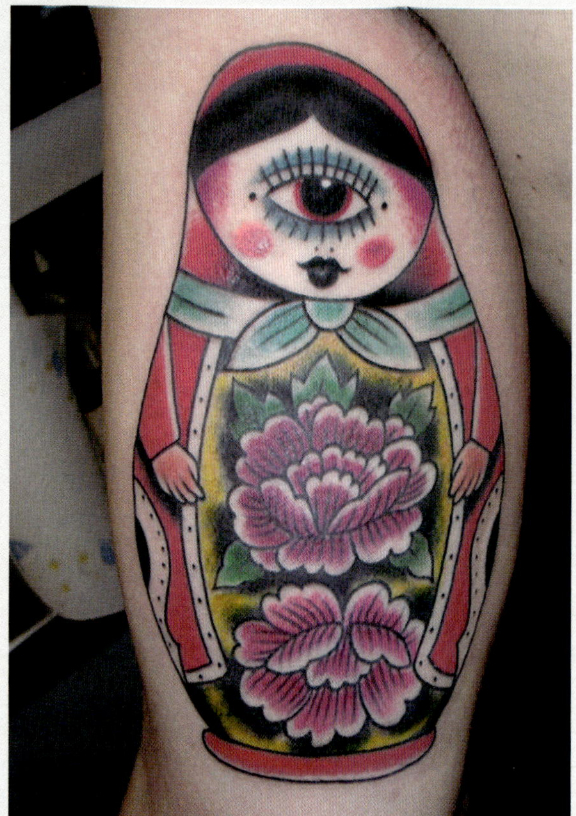

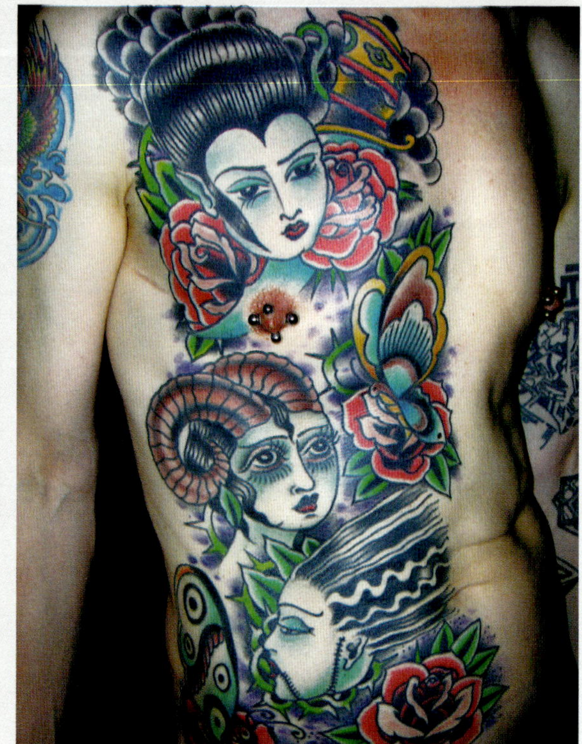

All designs on these pages by Amanda Toy.

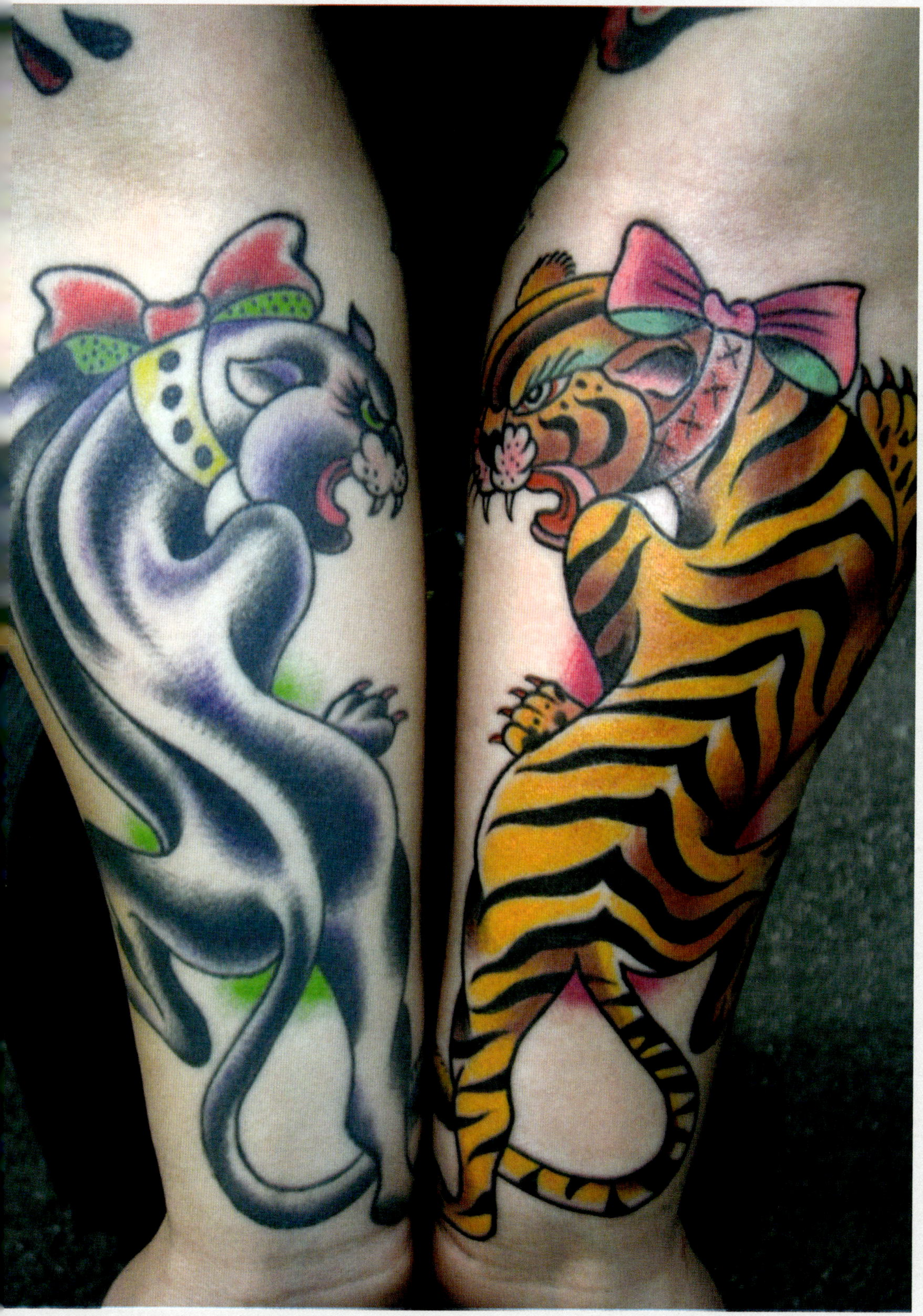

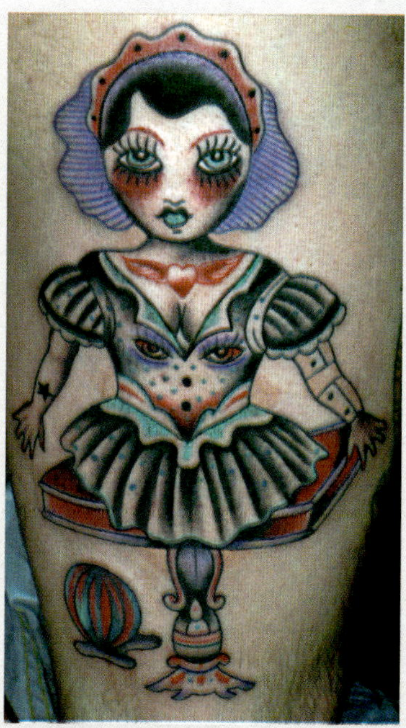

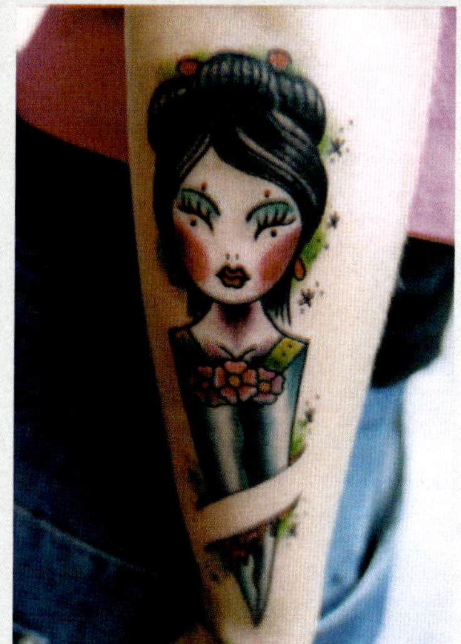

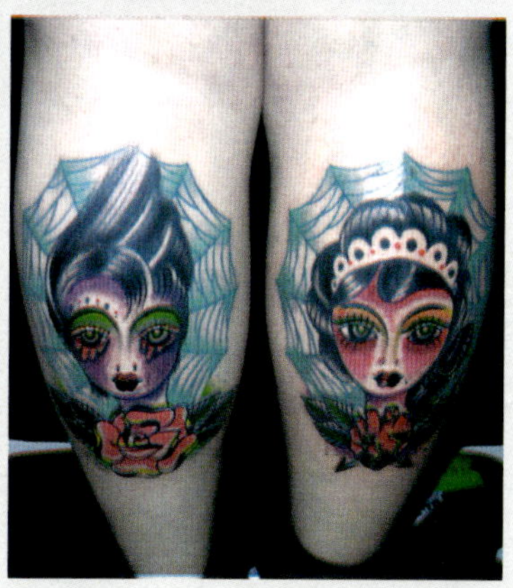

AMANDA TOY

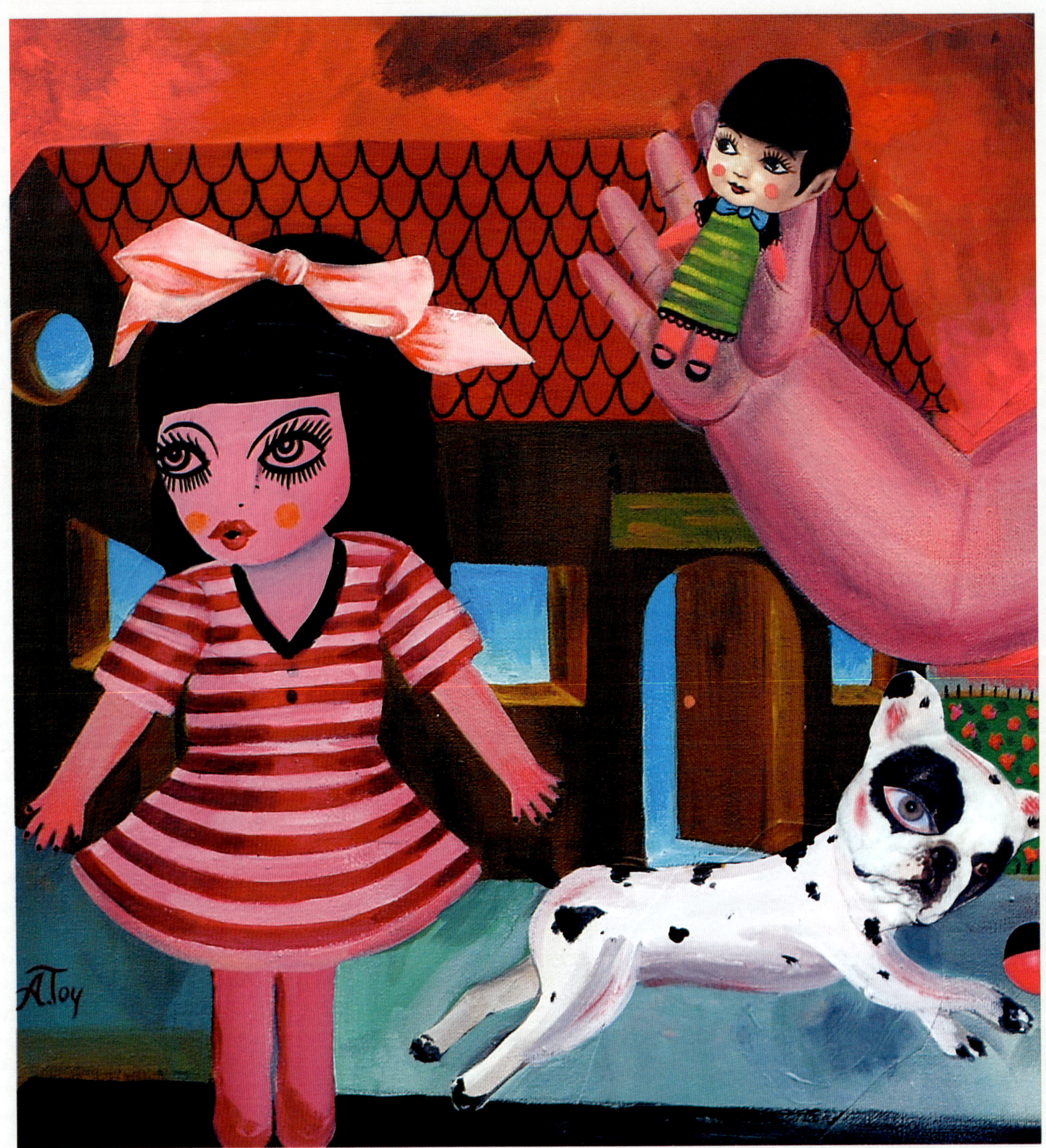

Oil on wood panel made by Amanda Toy.

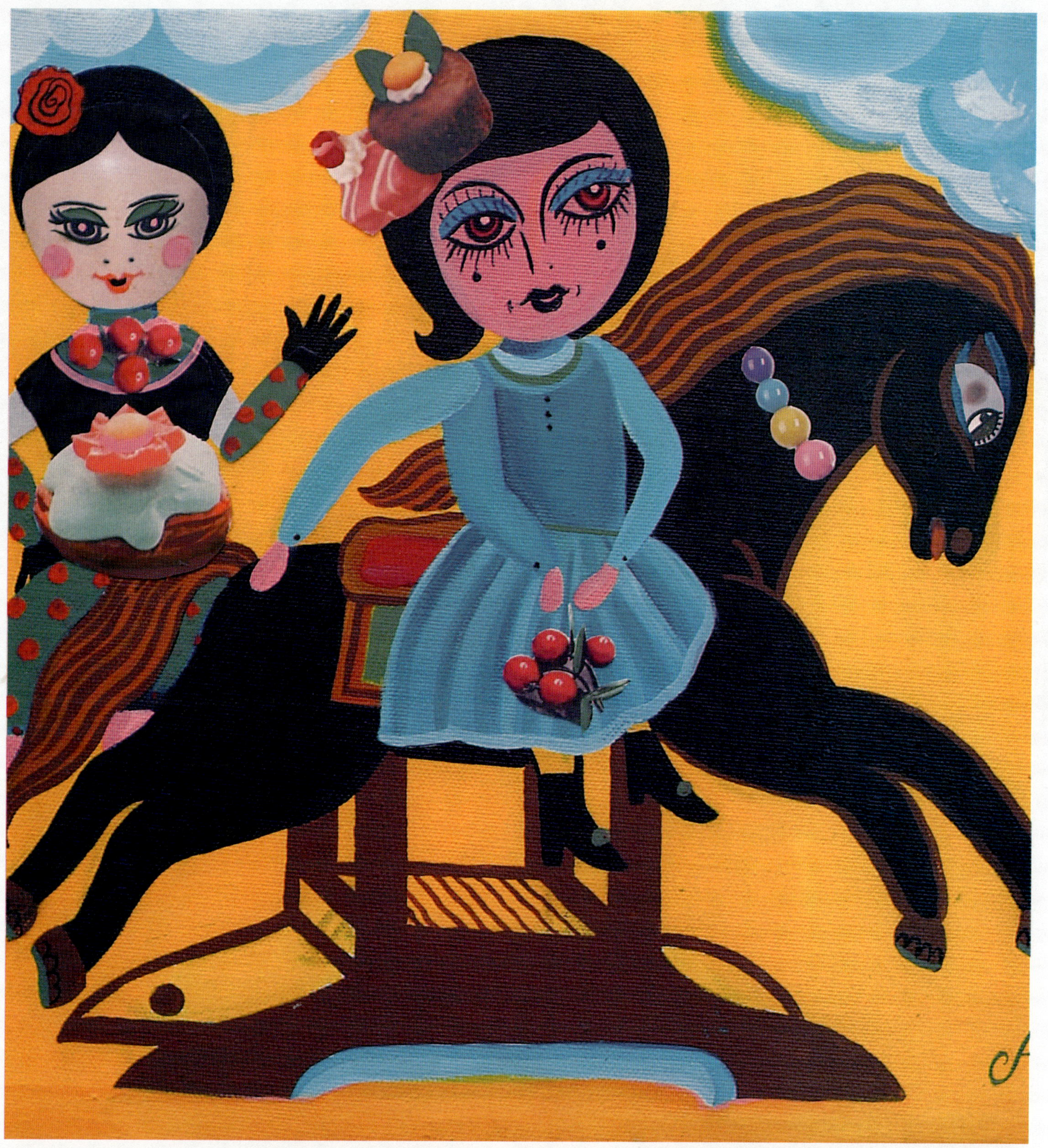

AMANDA TOY

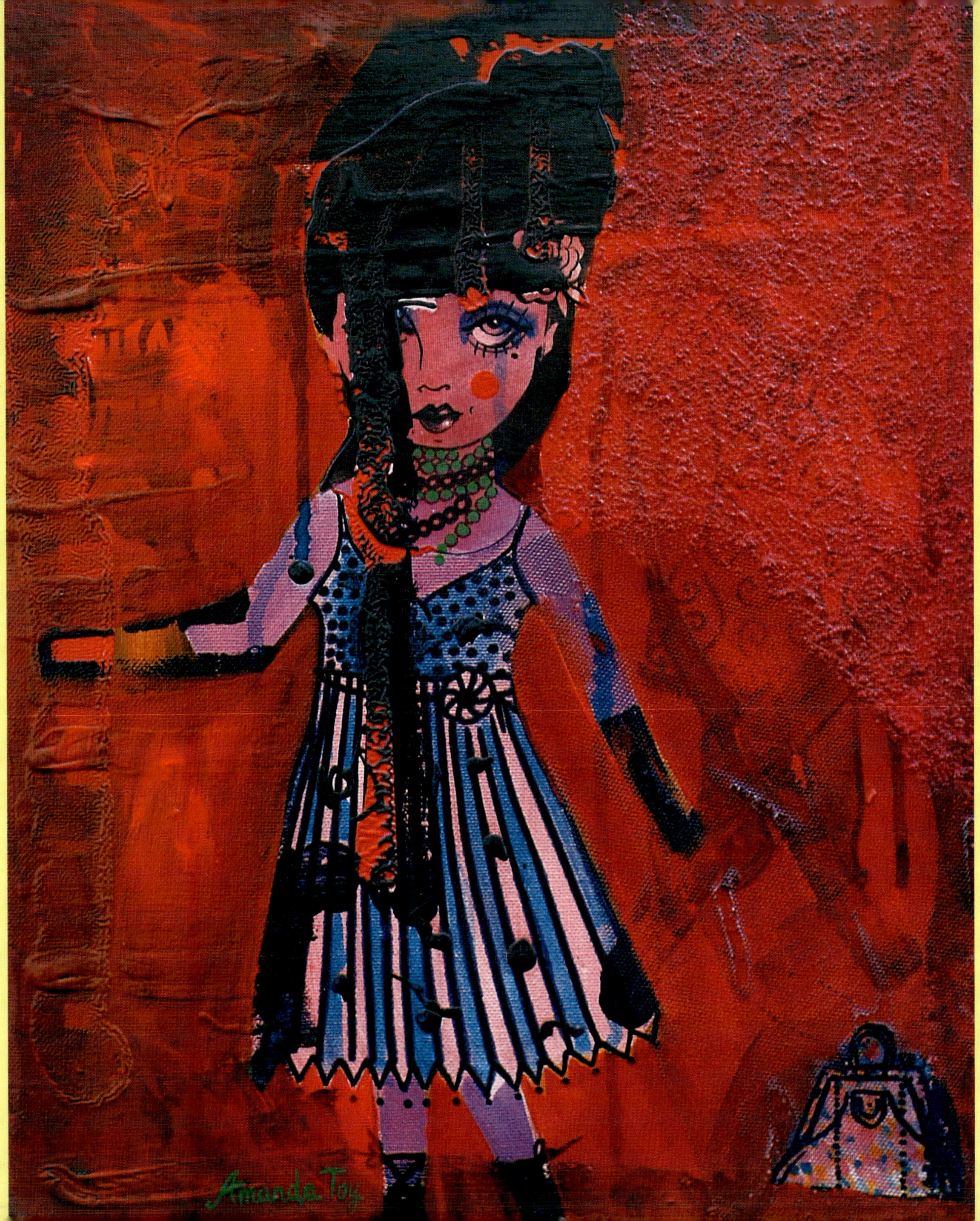
Amanda Toy

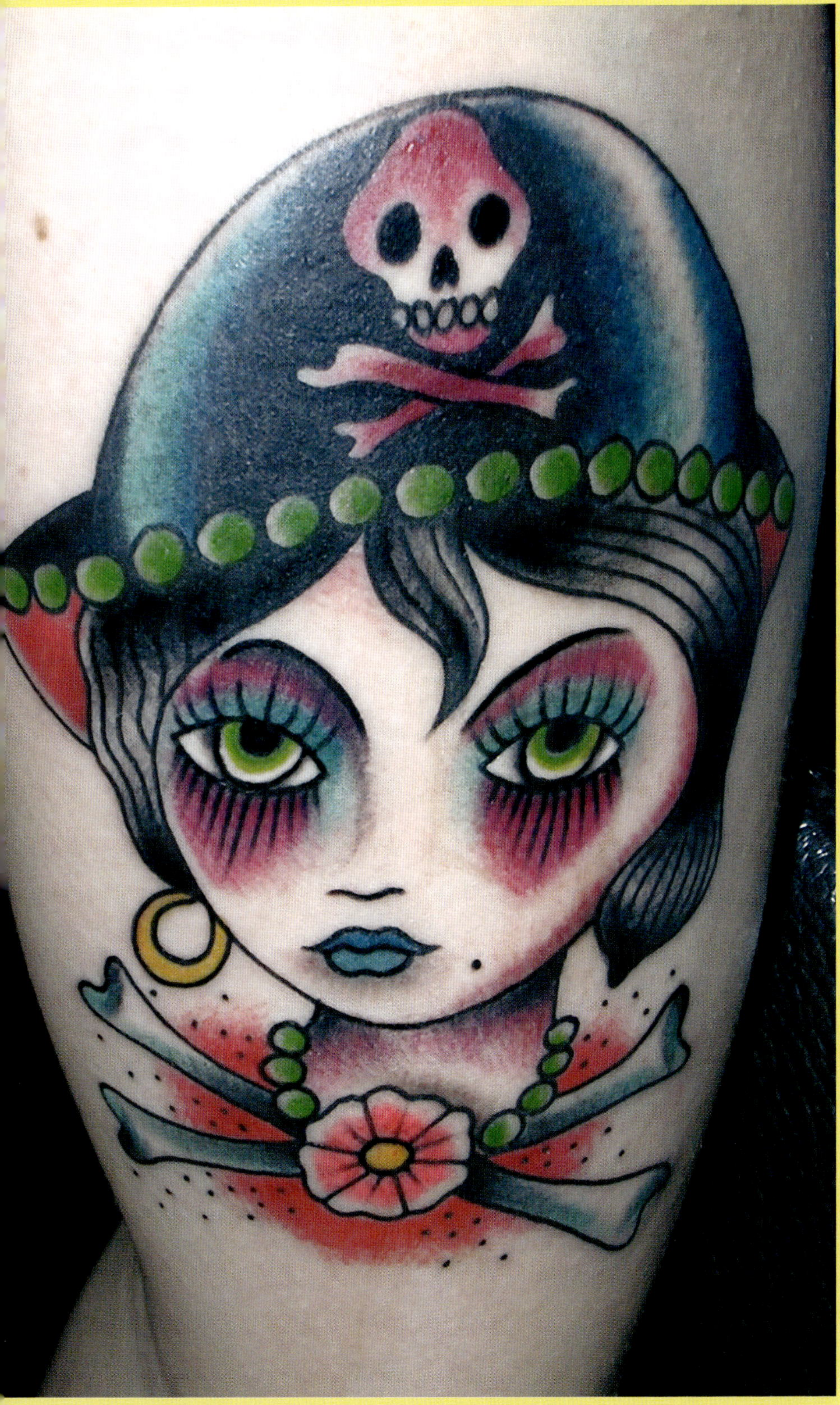

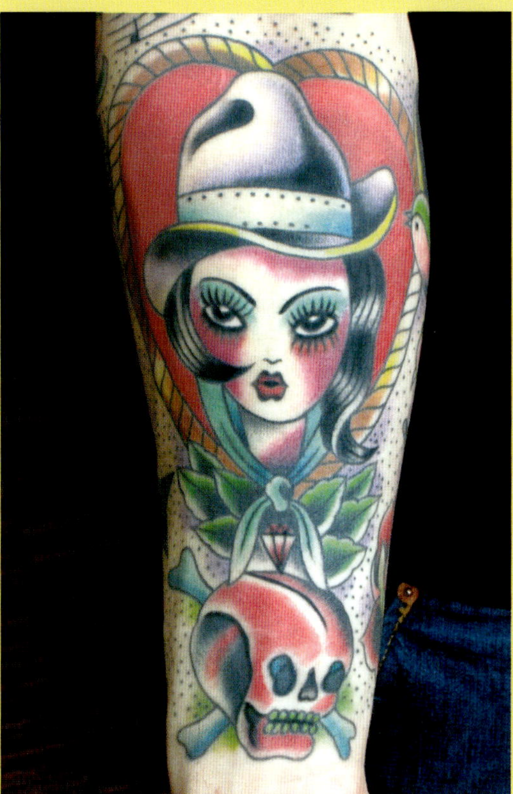

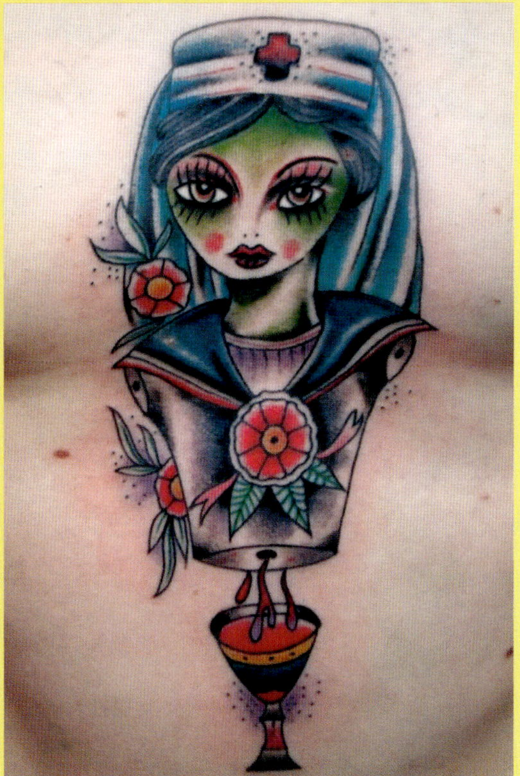

Left page oil painting and designs on this page by Amanda Toy.

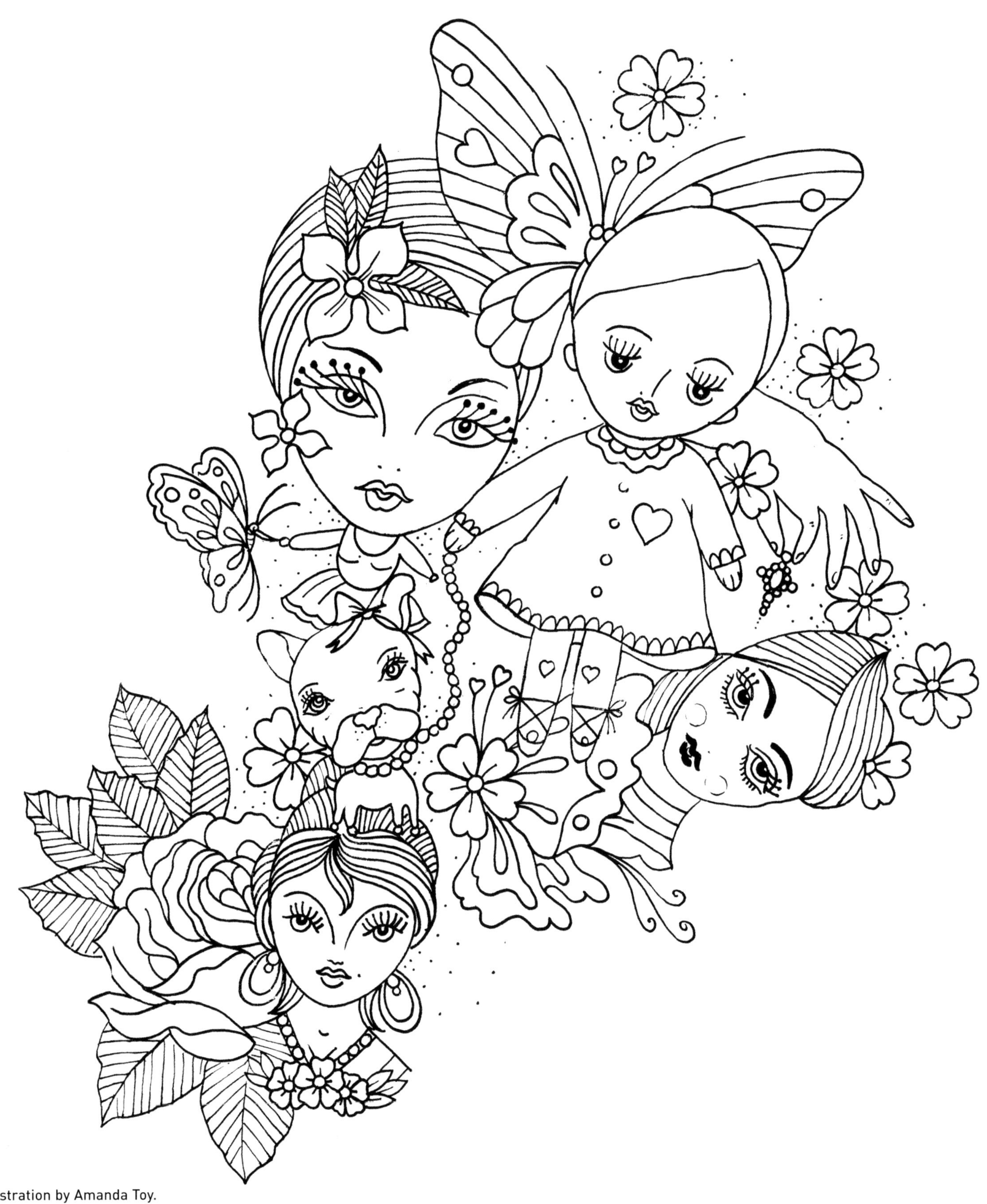

Illustration by Amanda Toy.

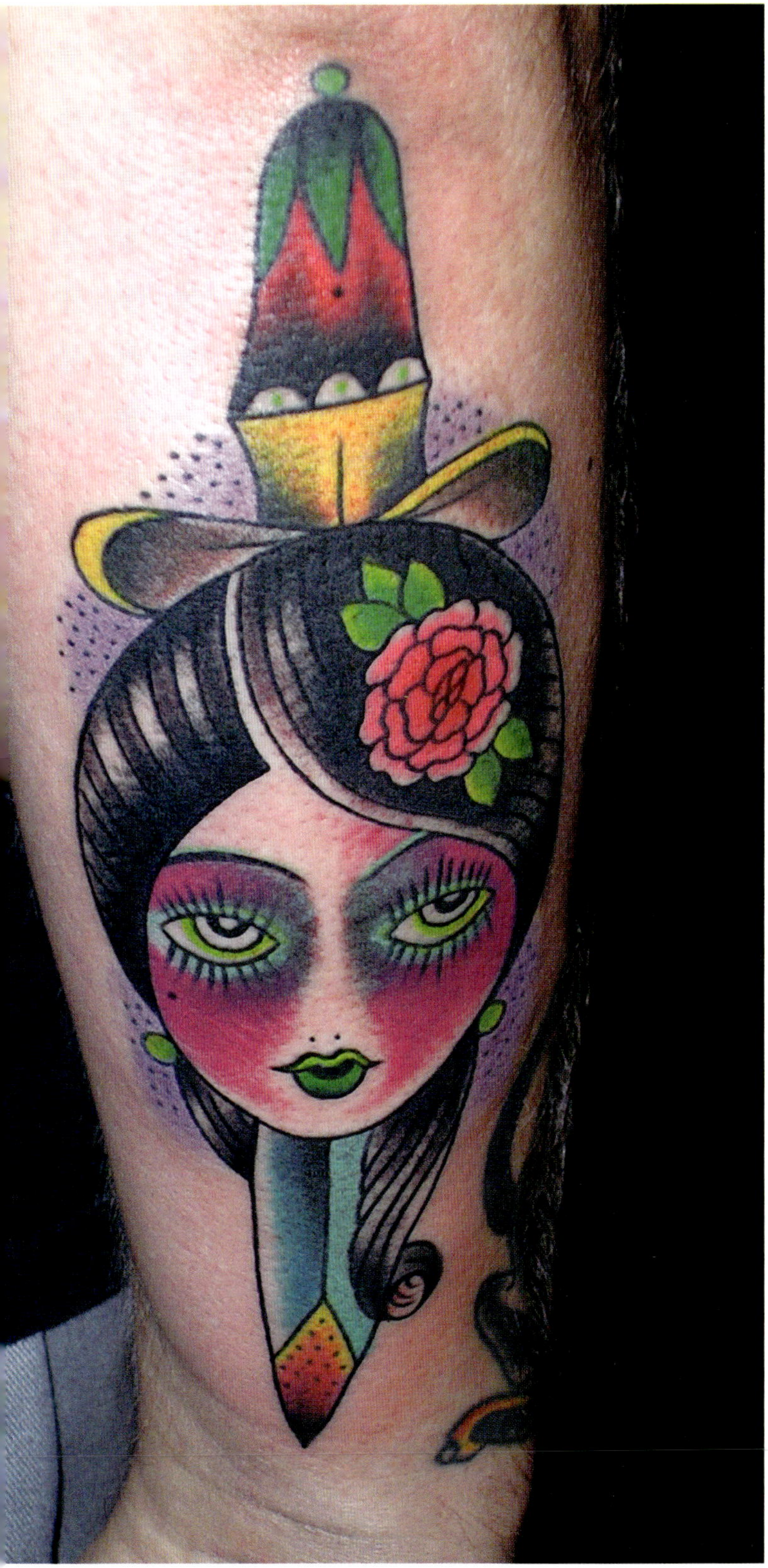

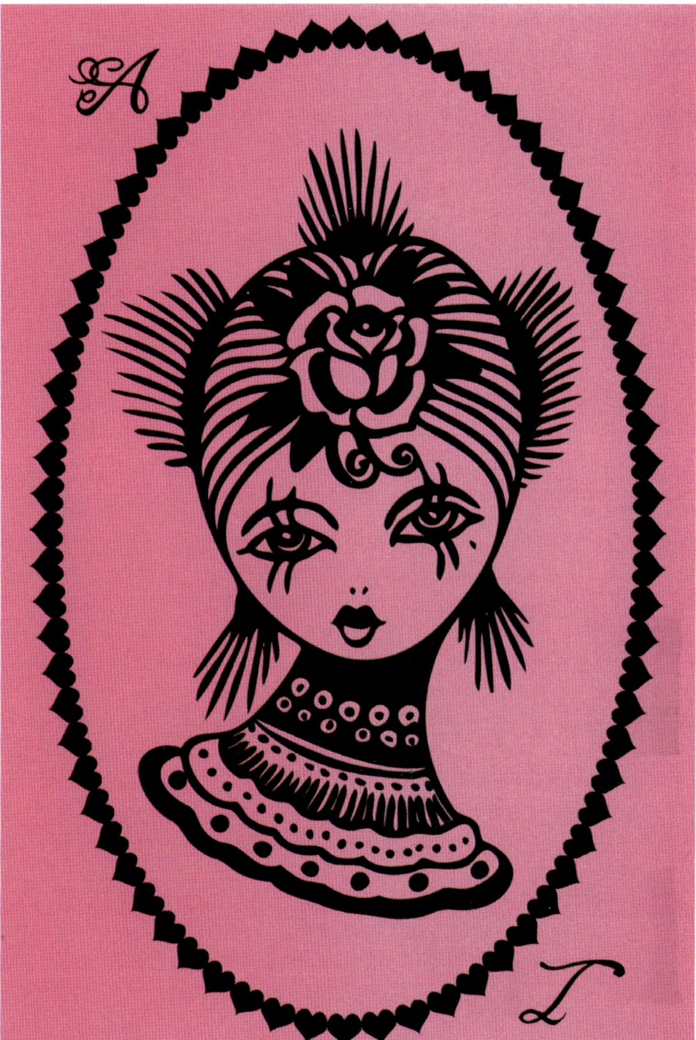

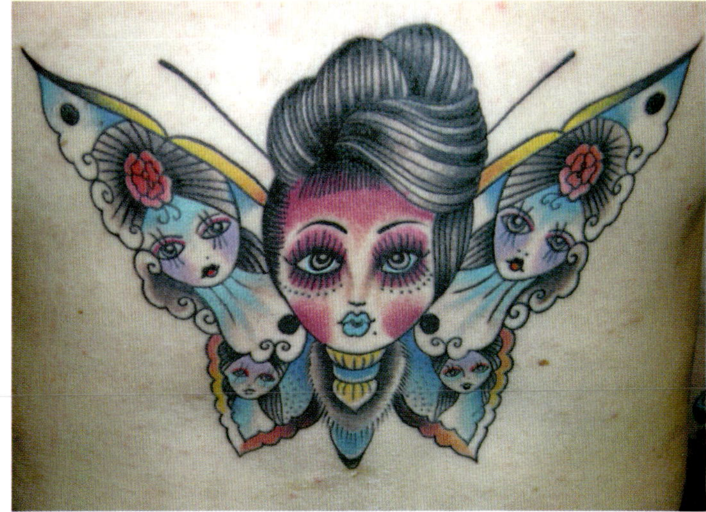

All artwork by Amanda Toy. Image top right, Amanda Toy's business card.

CALYPSO TATTOO

BELGIUM

1. I've been tattooing professionally for 16 years, specializing in blackwork. When I started, I looked around for an apprenticeship but couldn't find anyone to teach me, so I began on my own—a good experience for me because I was creating tattoos spontaneously, which helped develop my own style.

2. Tattoo for me is an evolving art that is in perpetual motion, always changing and based on communication.

3. My style is blackwork or tribal—a combination of multi-ethnic designs and geometric shapes created into a special work for the client, all in black ink.

4. Before getting a tattoo, get a good night's sleep, make sure you are feeling your best with full energy, and eat well.

5. My studio is Calypso Tattoo in Liege, Belgium. You can also find me at international tattoo conventions, and at guest spots, particularly at Tattoo Culture in Brooklyn, New York a few times a year.
   www.calypsotattoo.com

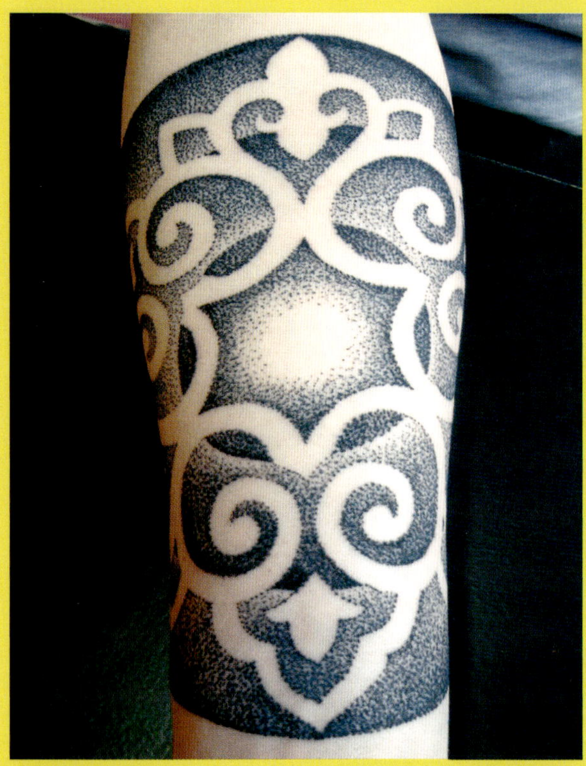

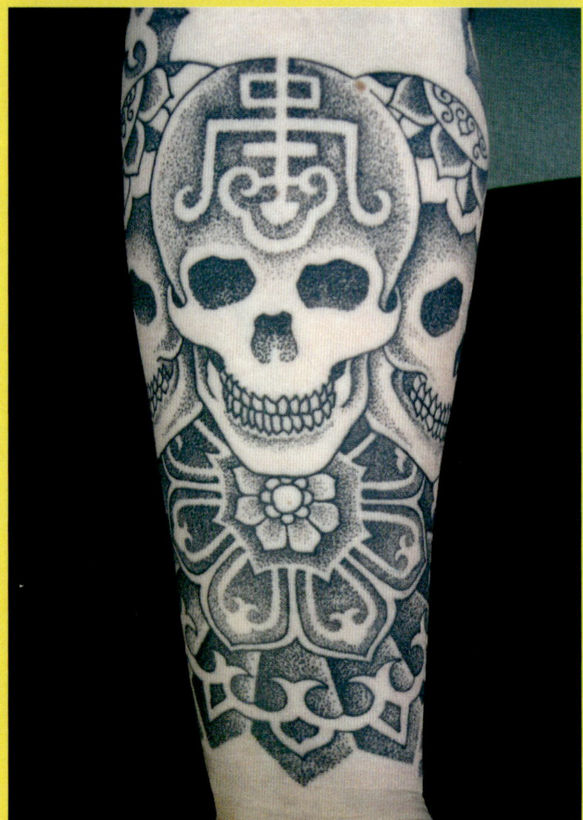

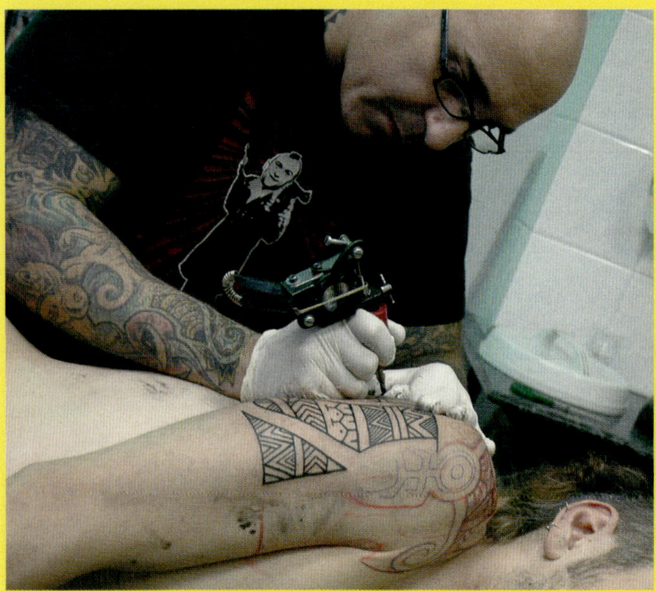

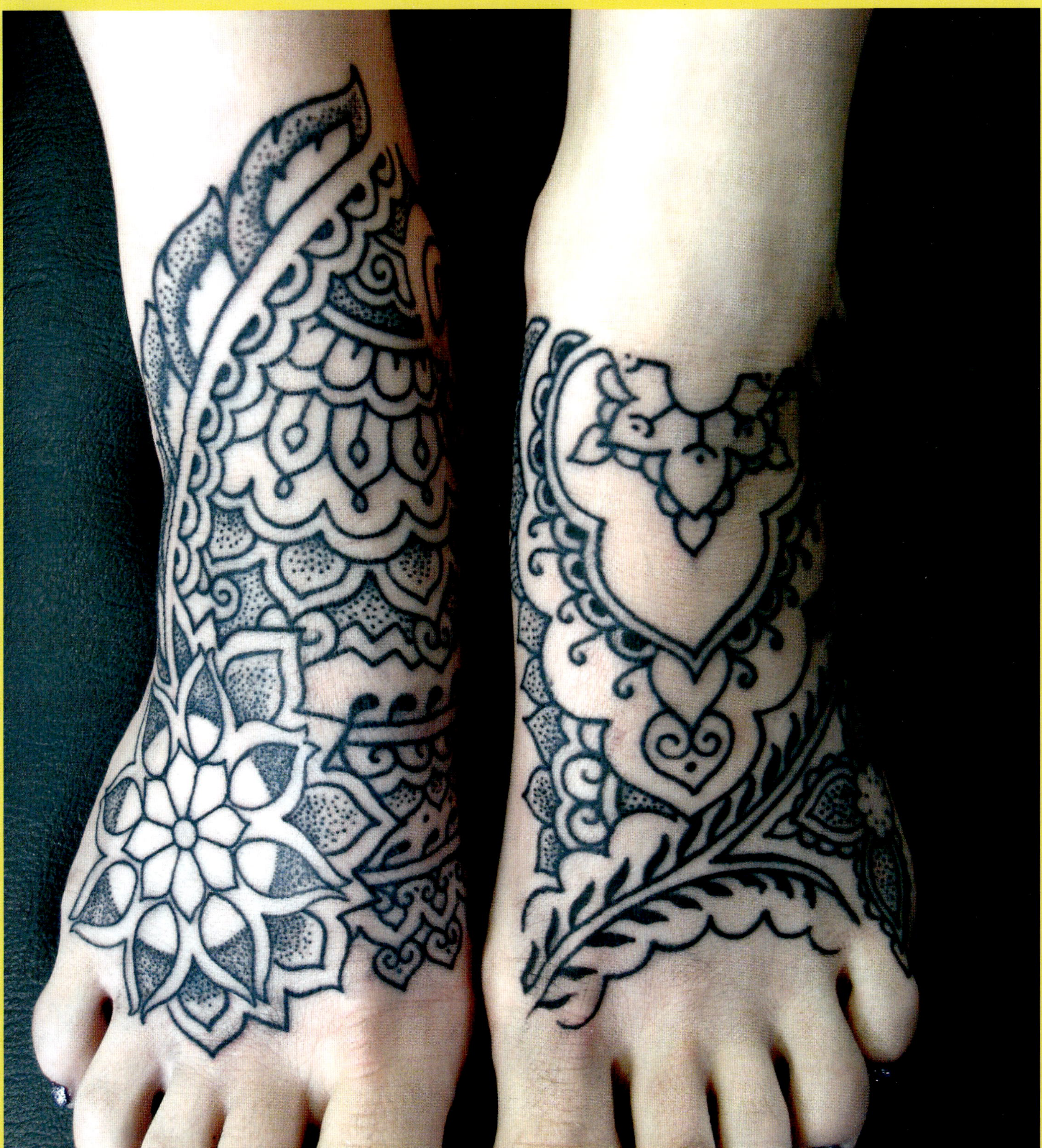

All artwork by Calypso Tattoo.

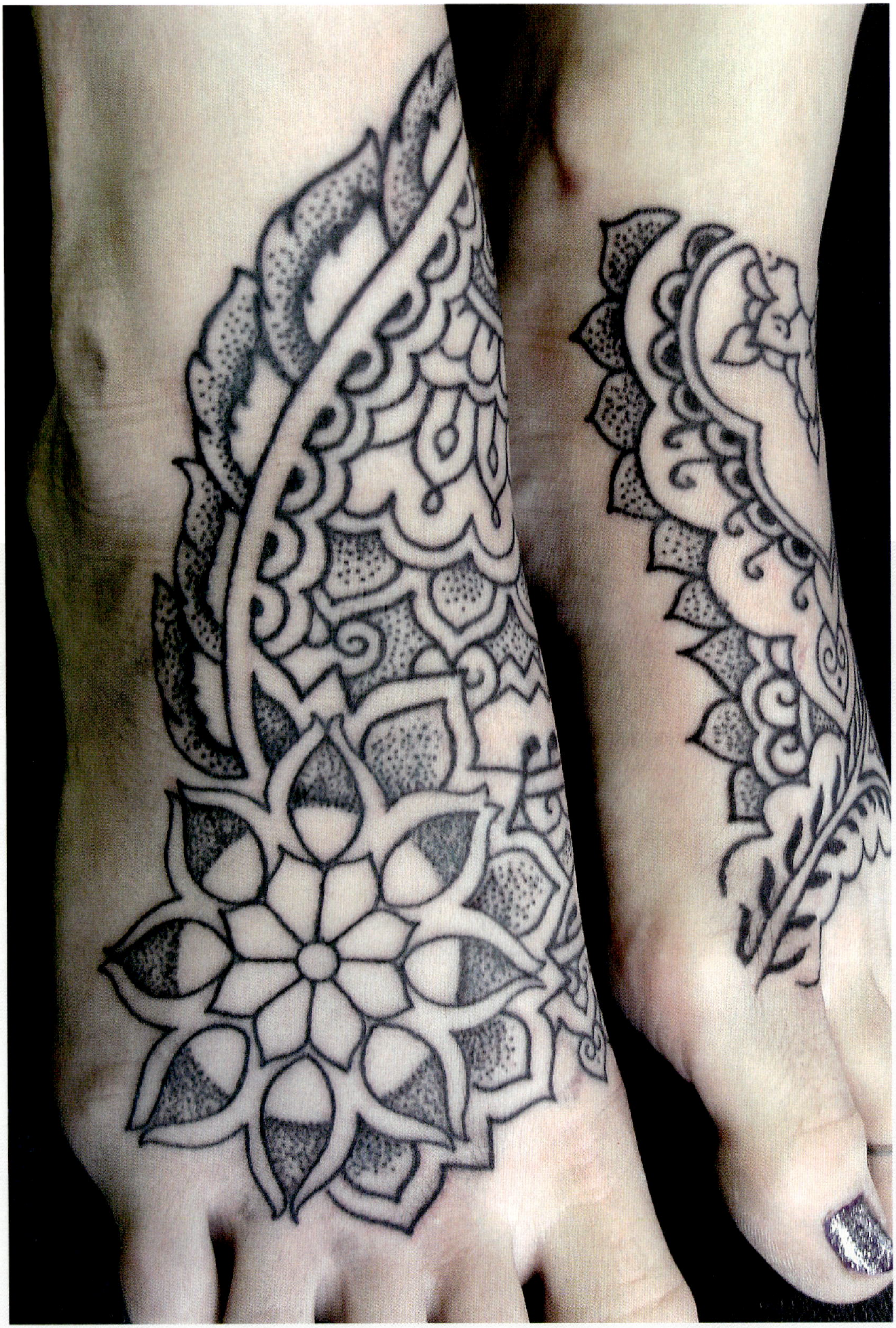

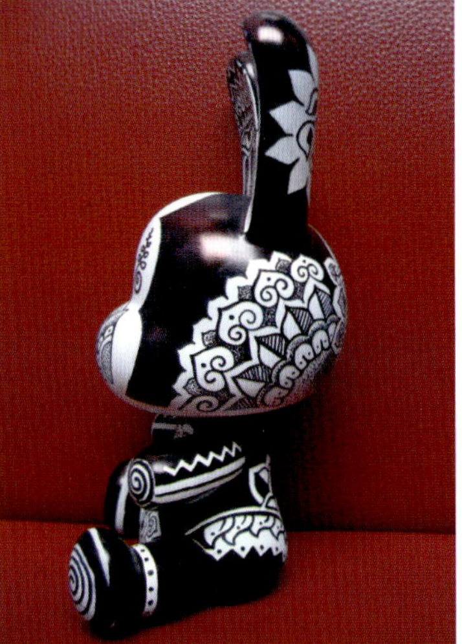

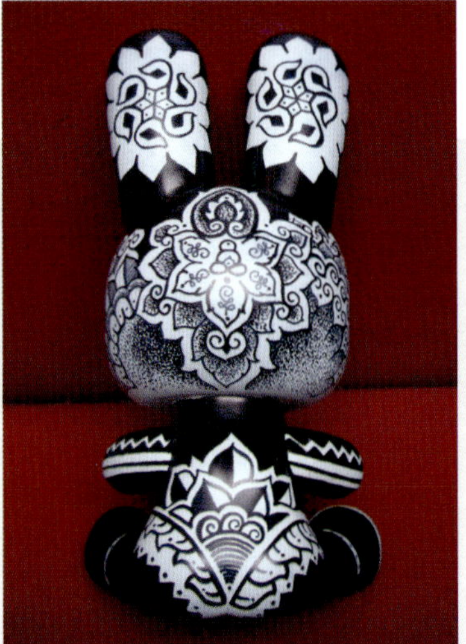

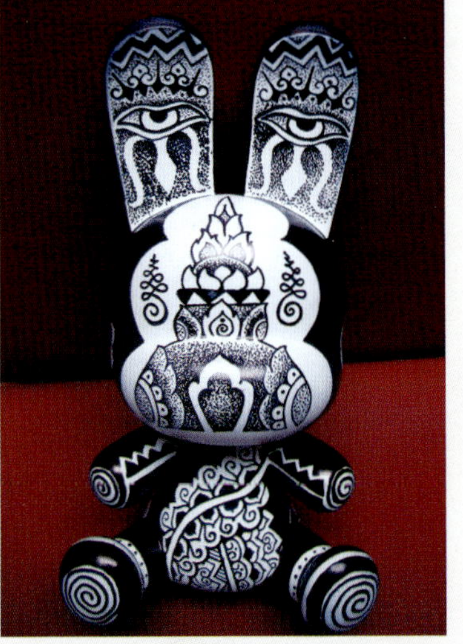

All designs on these pages by Calypso Tattoo.

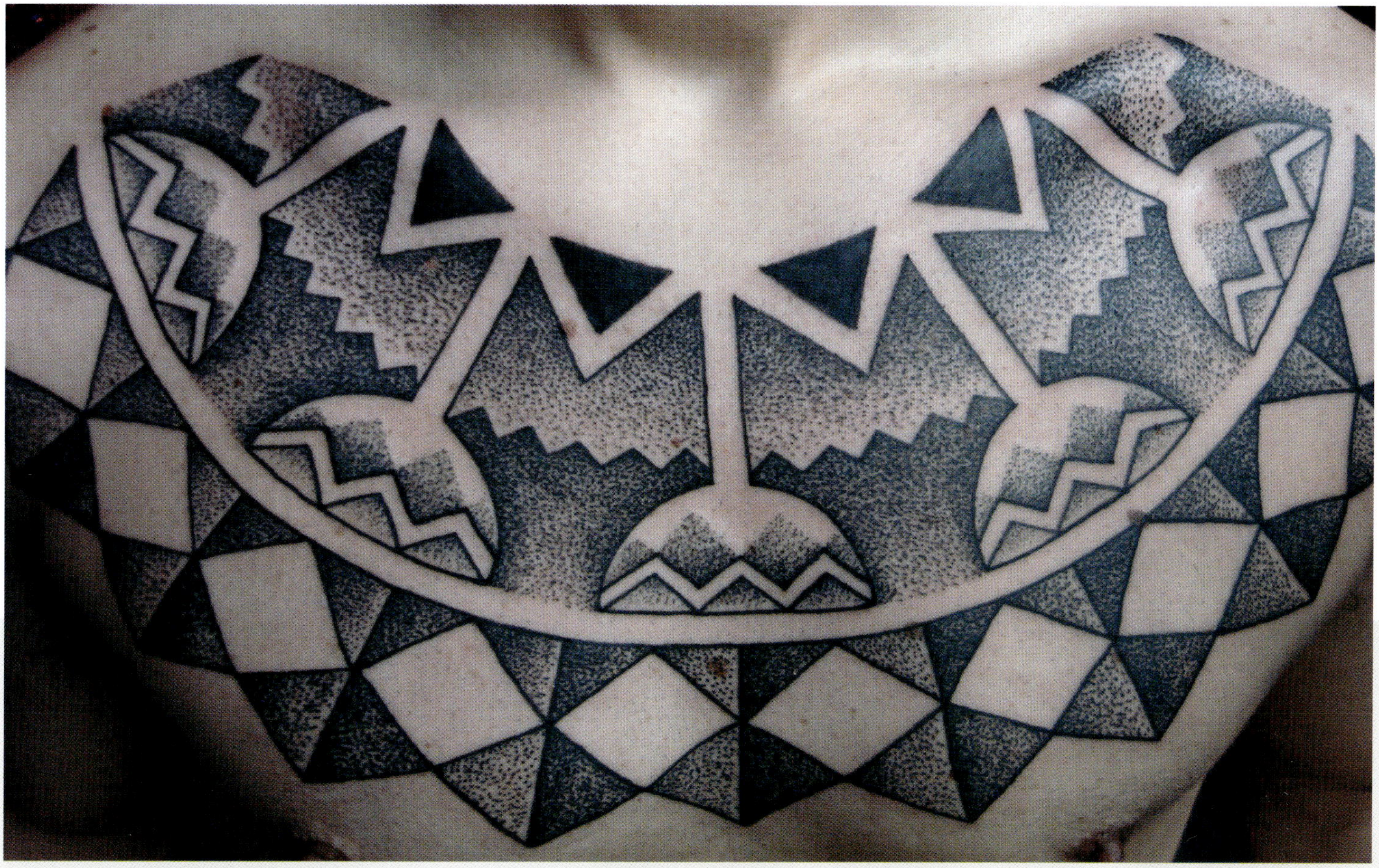

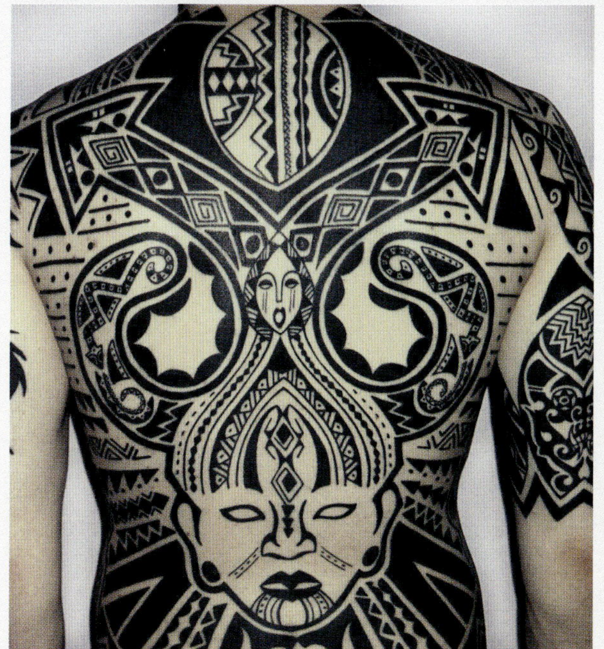

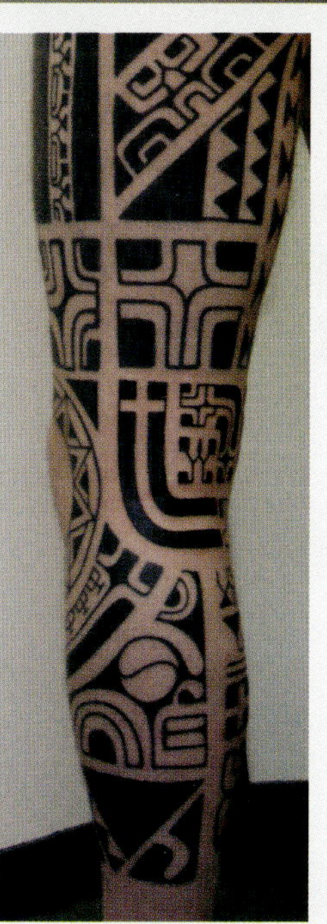

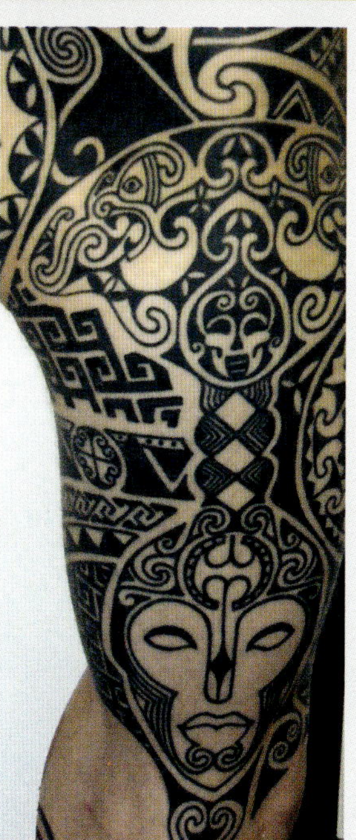

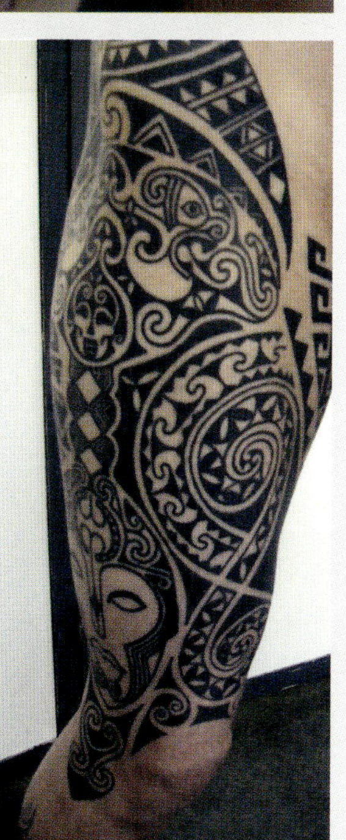

DAVID SENA

USA

1. In 1995 I was studying fine arts at The Cooper Union for the Advancement of Science and Art in New York City. That summer, I randomly found a job at Kaleidoscope Tattoo, one of the few tattoo studios in NYC back when tattooing was "illegal."

2. Tattoos are a very special means of self expression and recognition of your physical self in the world. I feel like I provide an honest service to society which essentially makes people happy to be alive.

3. I primarily do Japanese and blackwork/tribal, but I like doing any design/project that I think is cool and would feel inspired to work on.

4. Have confidence and patience.

5. I have been living in New York City for fifteen years and tattooing for eleven. Recently I opened a new studio in the East Village with my good friend Rodrigo Melo. www.northstartattoo.com

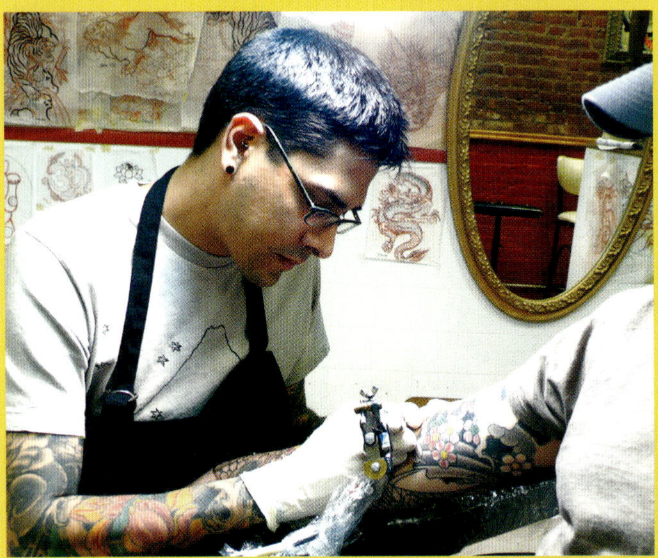

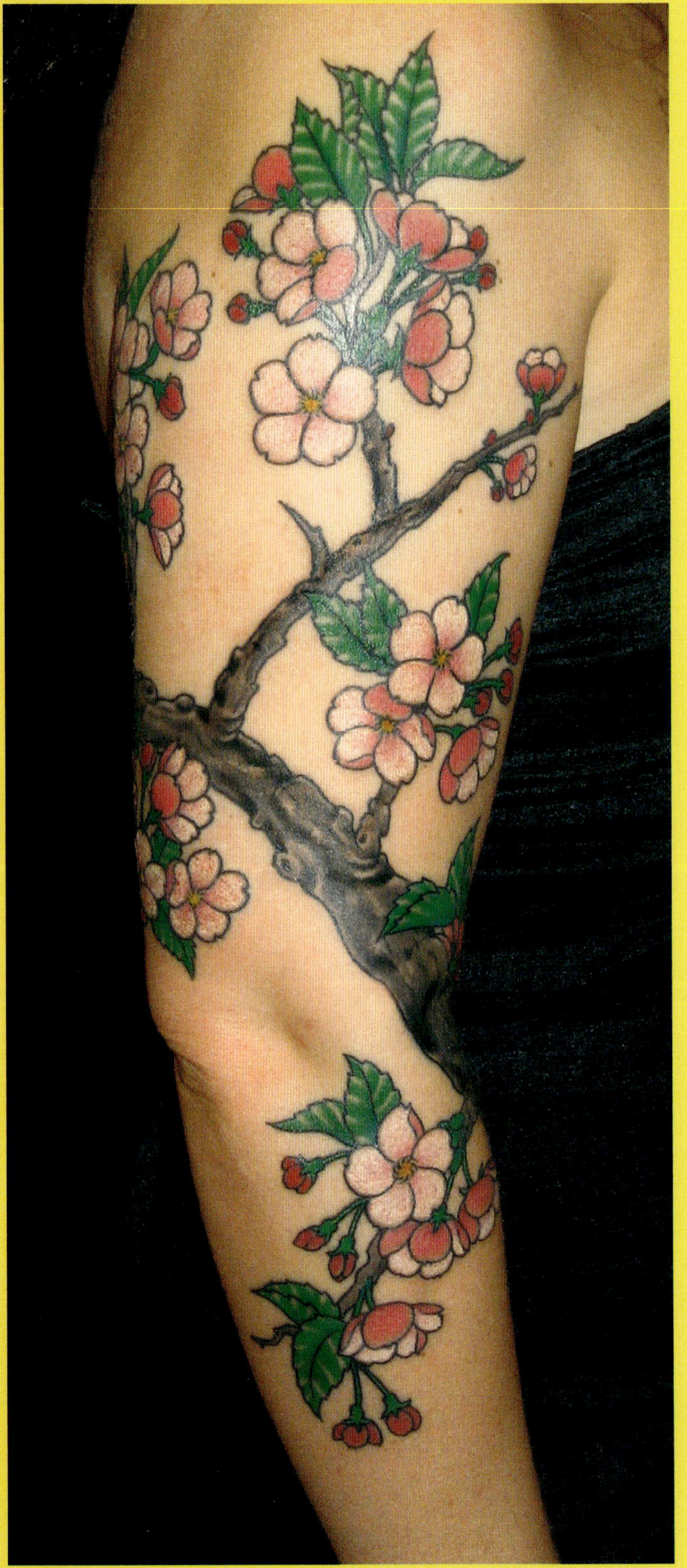

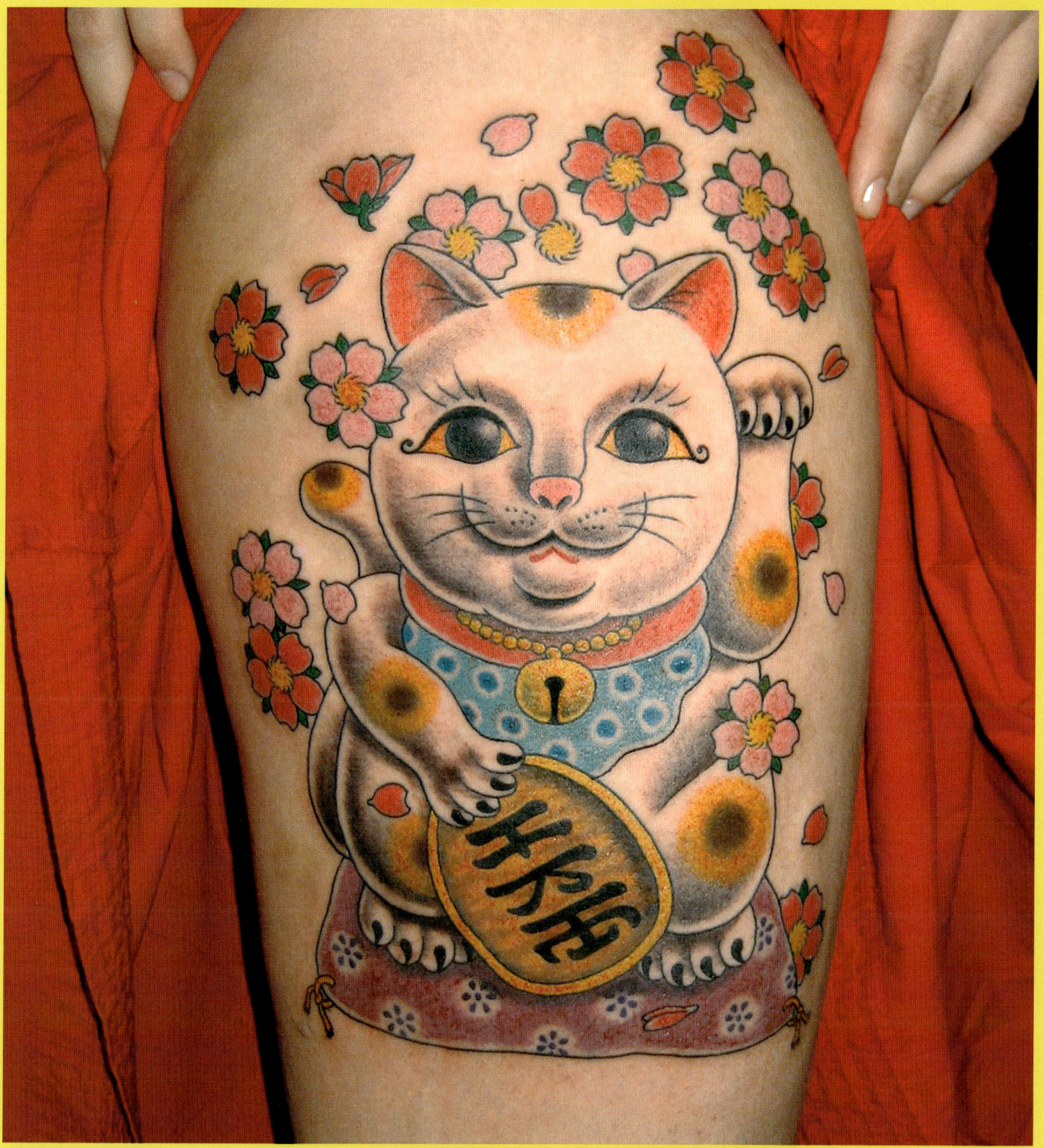

All artwork by David Sena.

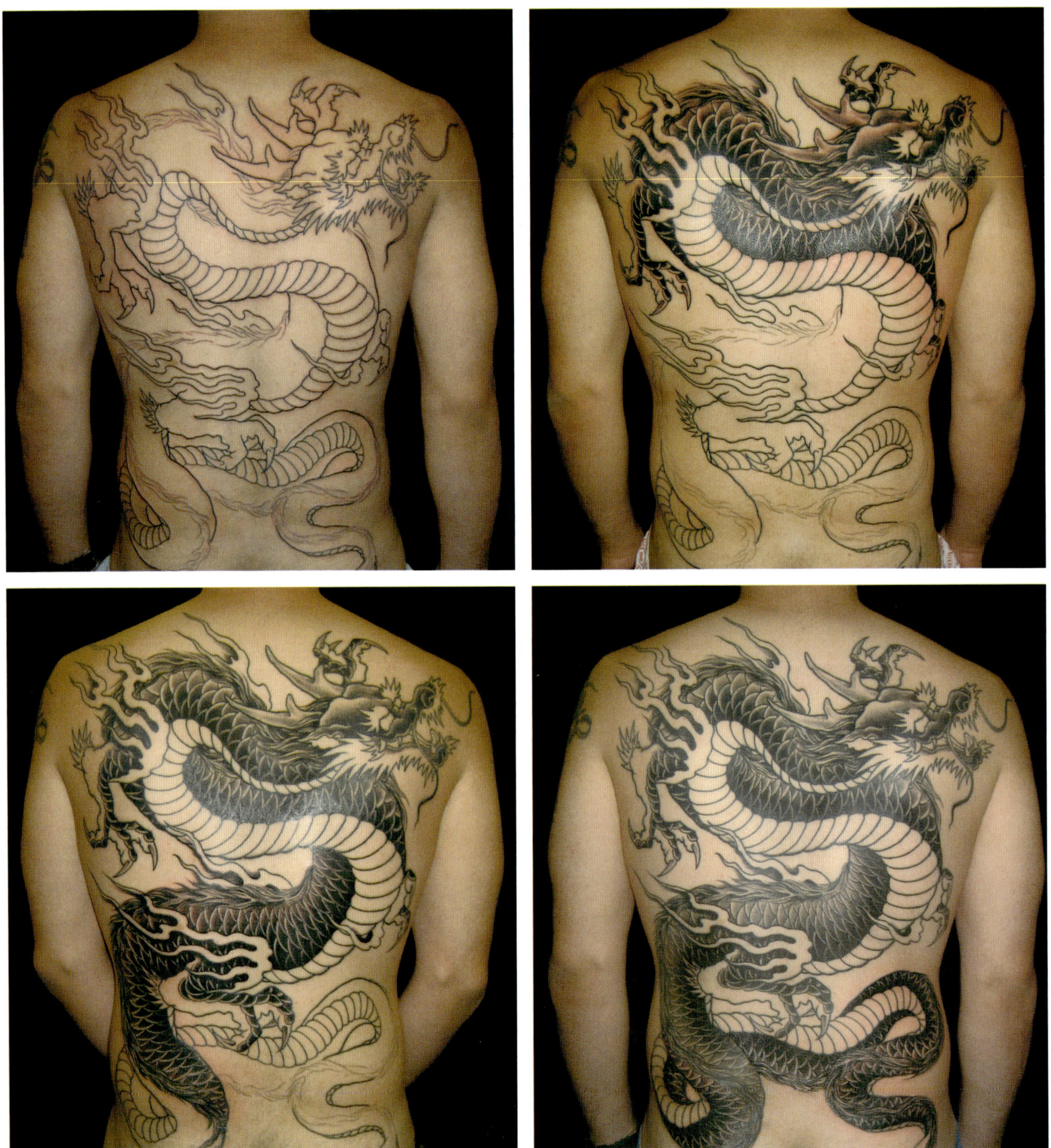

Step by step of a tattoo design by David Sena.

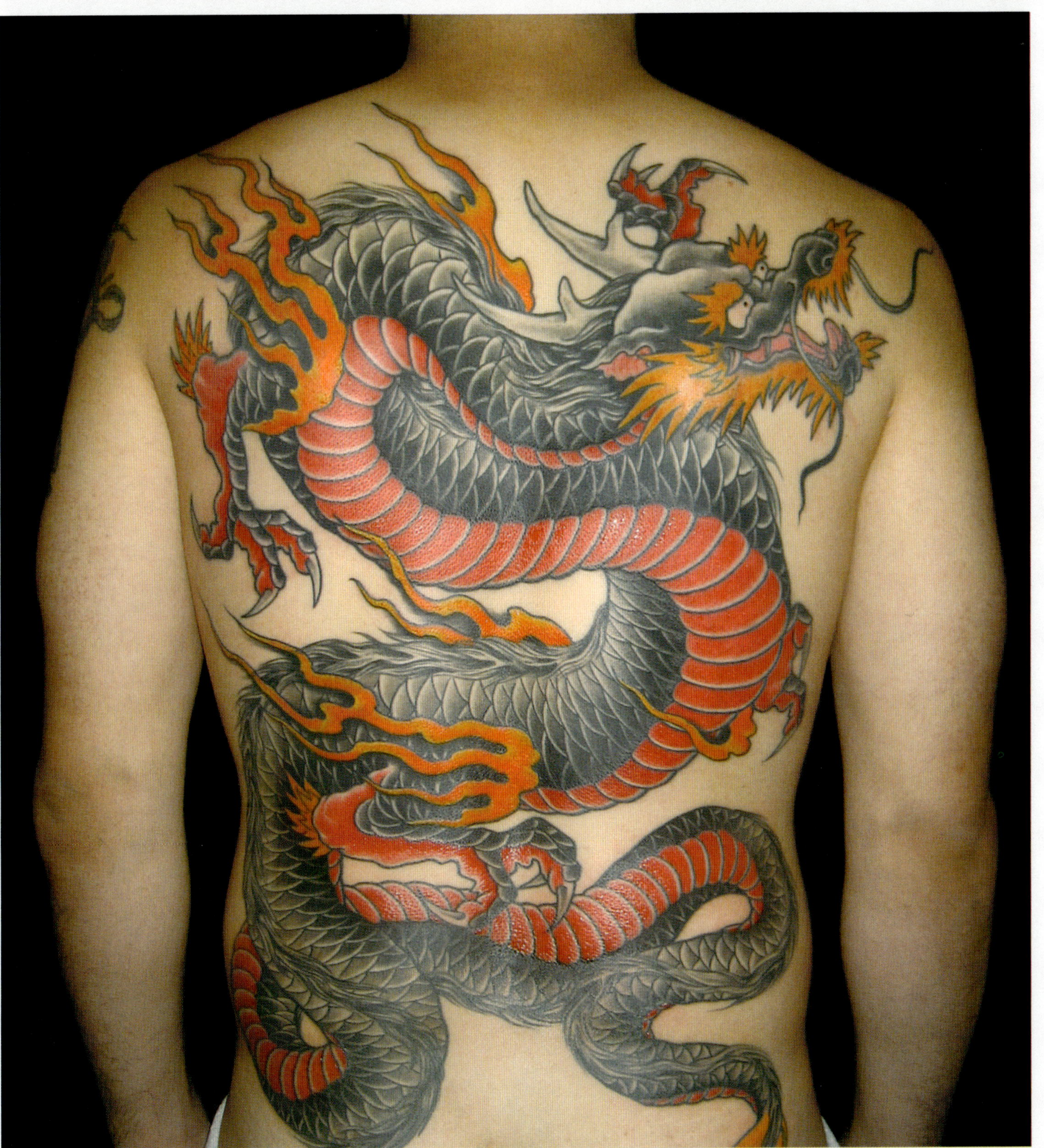

DAVID SENA

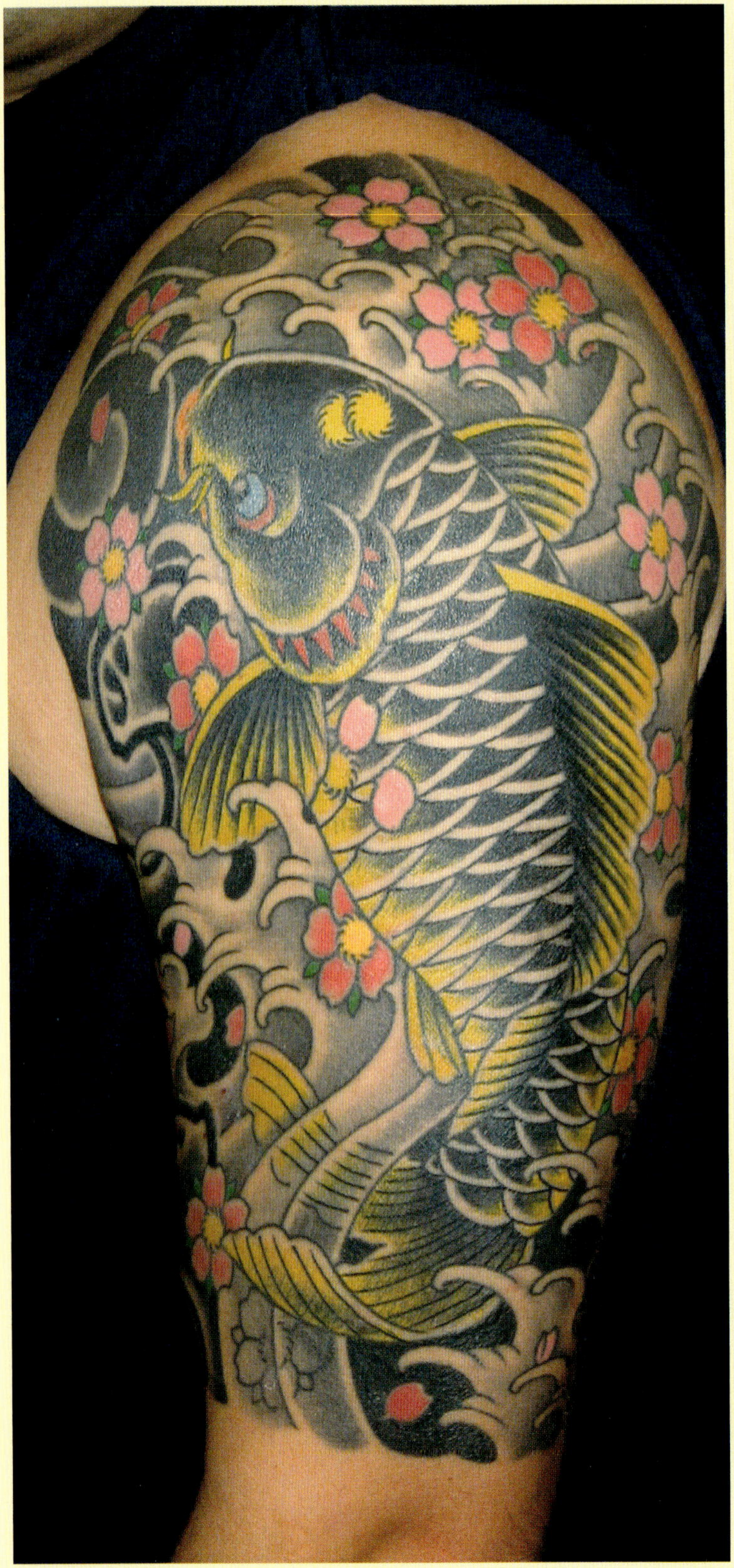

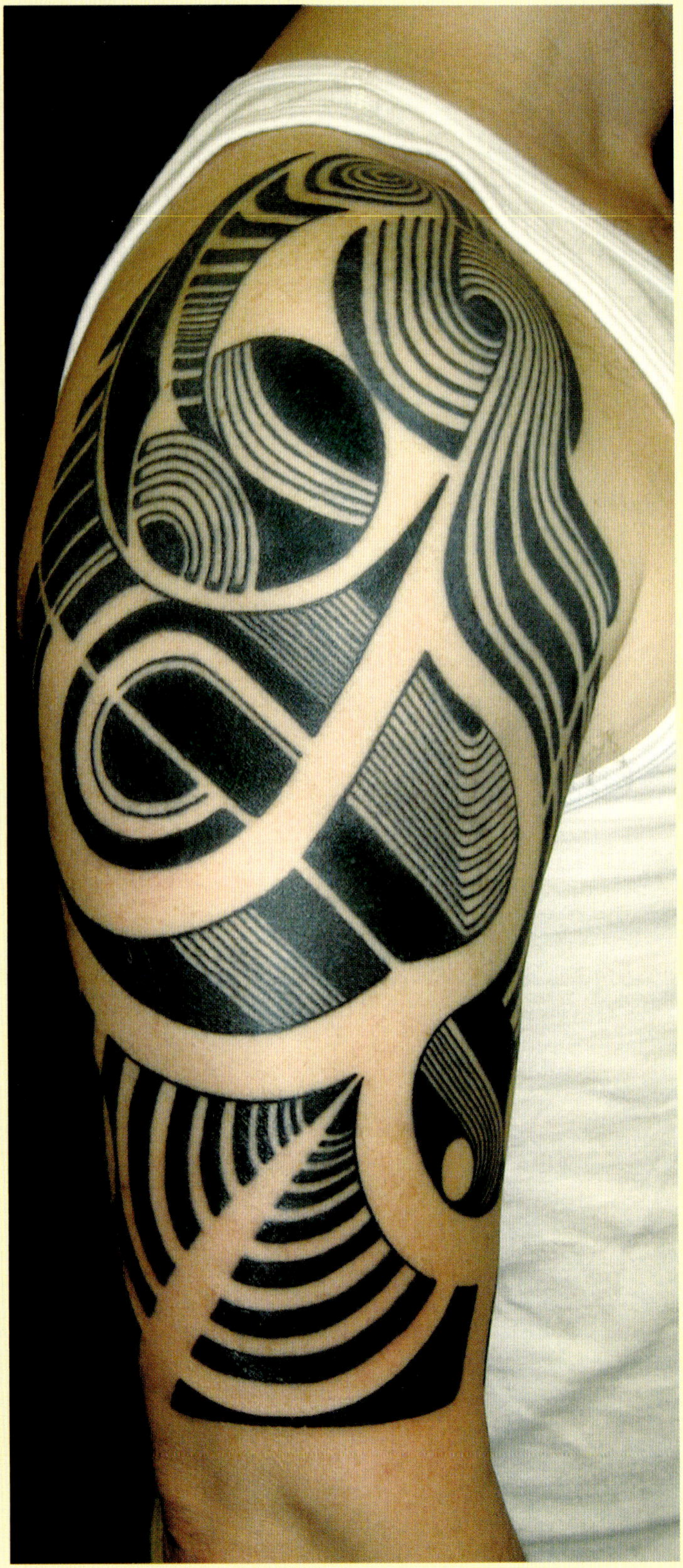

All designs on these pages by David Sena.

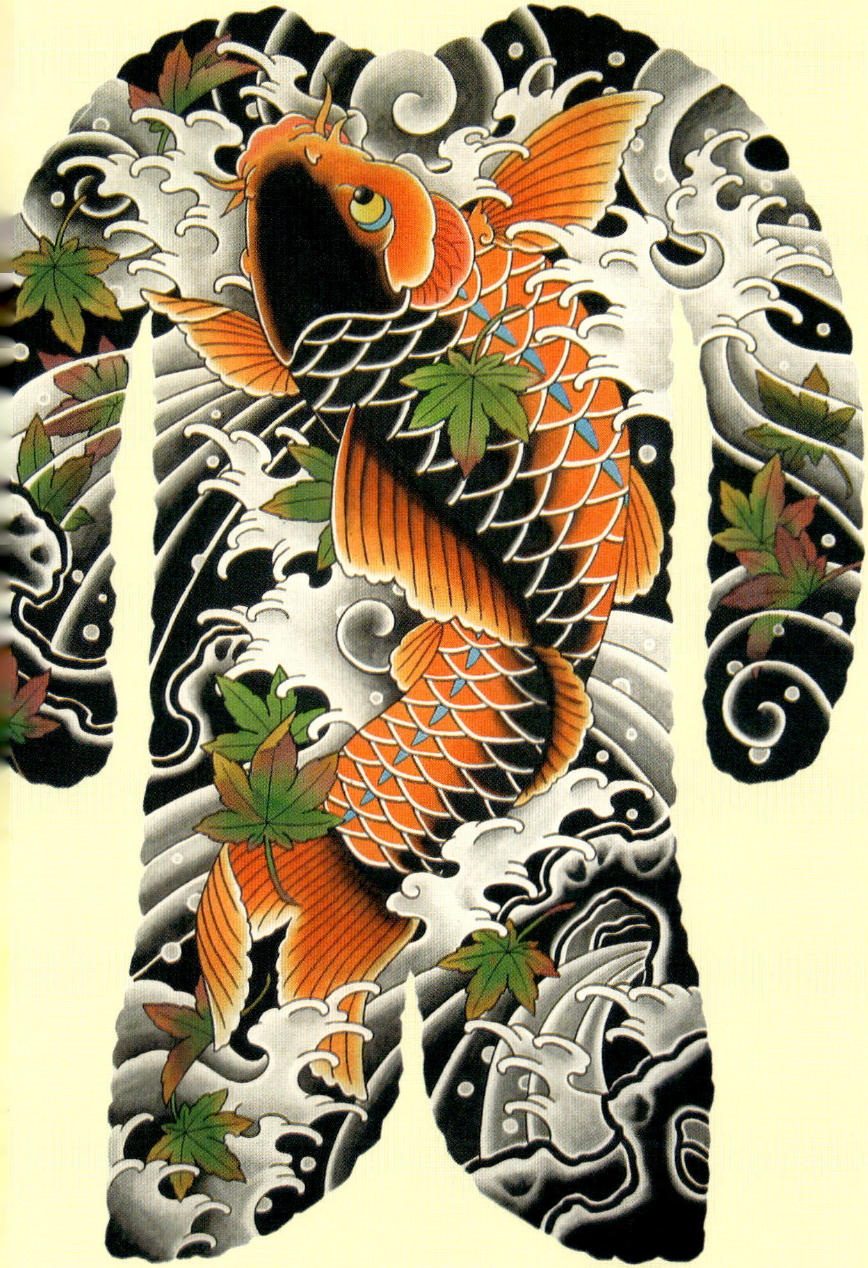

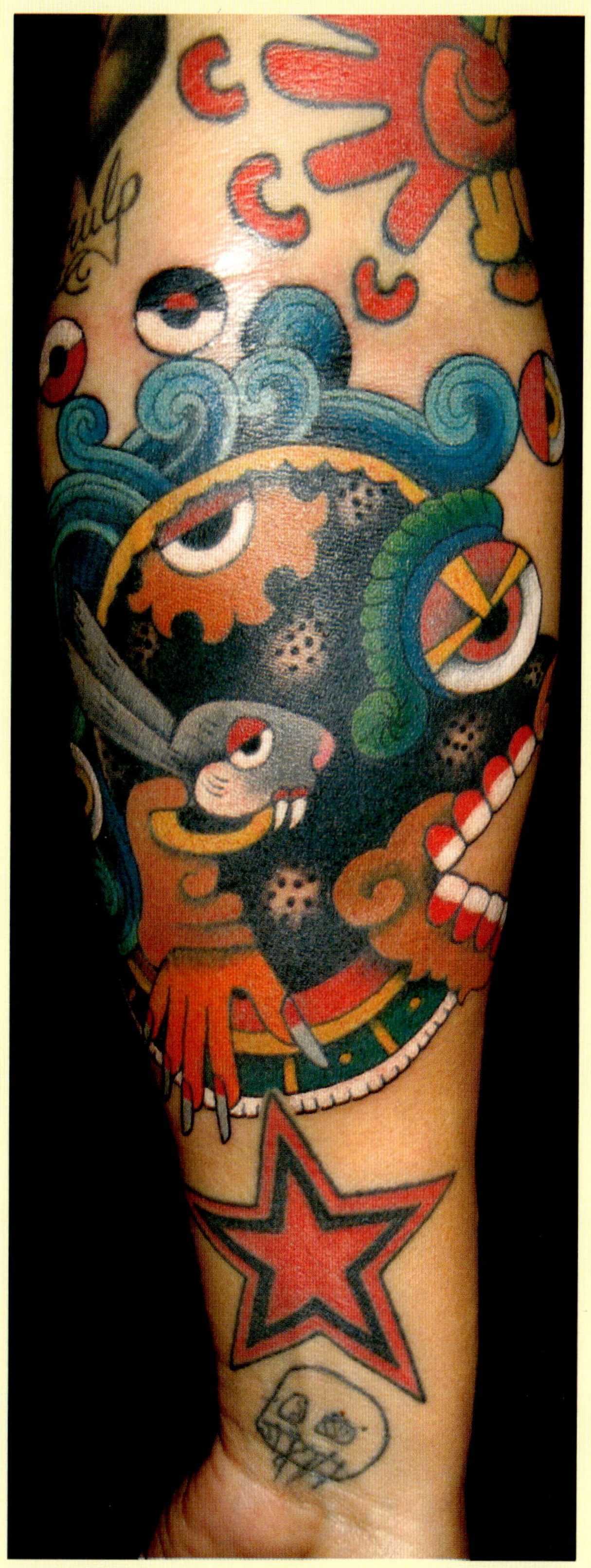

DAVID SENA

AARON DELLA VEDOVA

GURU TATTOO

USA

1. After serving in the U.S. Coast Guard for five years I was very focused on going to art school. Having drawn my whole life and knowing that being an artist was in my heart, I found an apprenticeship at a small tattoo shop in Las Vegas and thought tattooing would be a good way to work and pay my way through art school. After only a short while, I realized that I had stumbled across my dream. I quickly fell in love with the art and the job of tattooing and never made it to art school. That was 15 years ago now and I couldn't be happier.

2. I love the art of tattooing. I especially enjoy working on a craft or art that has such a profound connection to the collector. I paint as well, but I have never felt someone become as moved as when I finish a tattoo. I love being a part of that process. Plus I love the people. Through this profession I have been privileged to meet so many interesting people, many of whom have become lifelong friends.

3. I really enjoy jumping around to many different styles. Japanese, American, and so on. Really I just look for projects that inspire me artistically, so I am open to almost any style. I like doing large tattoos that cover significant areas of the body. I really enjoy doing tattoos that flow with the human form instead of just being in one particular spot.

4. To anyone who is looking into getting a tattoo done, do your research. Usually an artist's portfolio tells their story. In the end, people usually get the tattoo they deserve.

5. www.gurutattoo.com

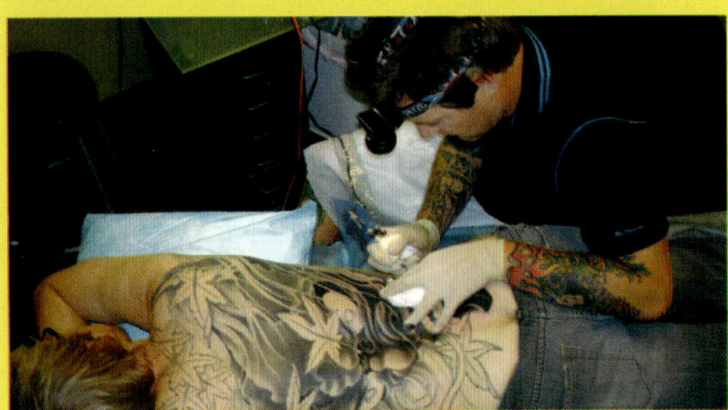

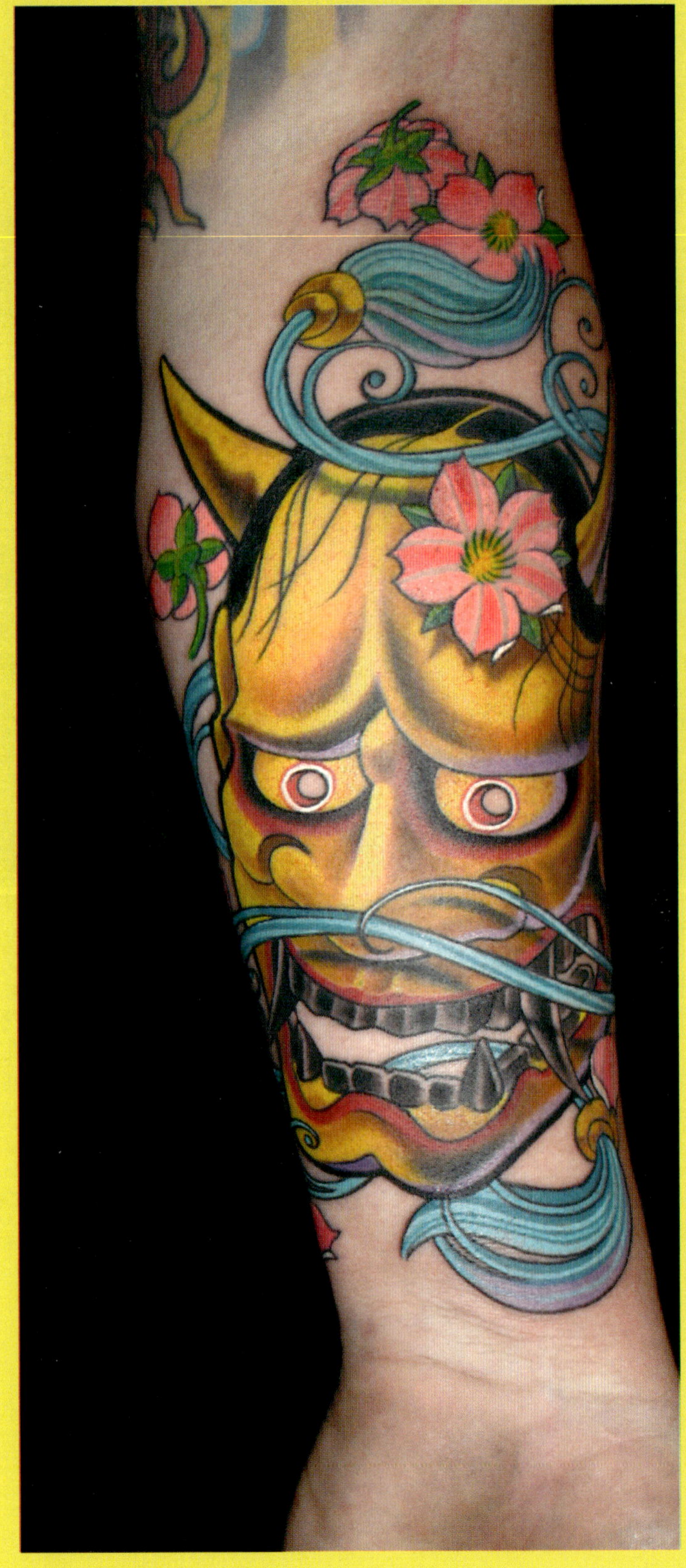

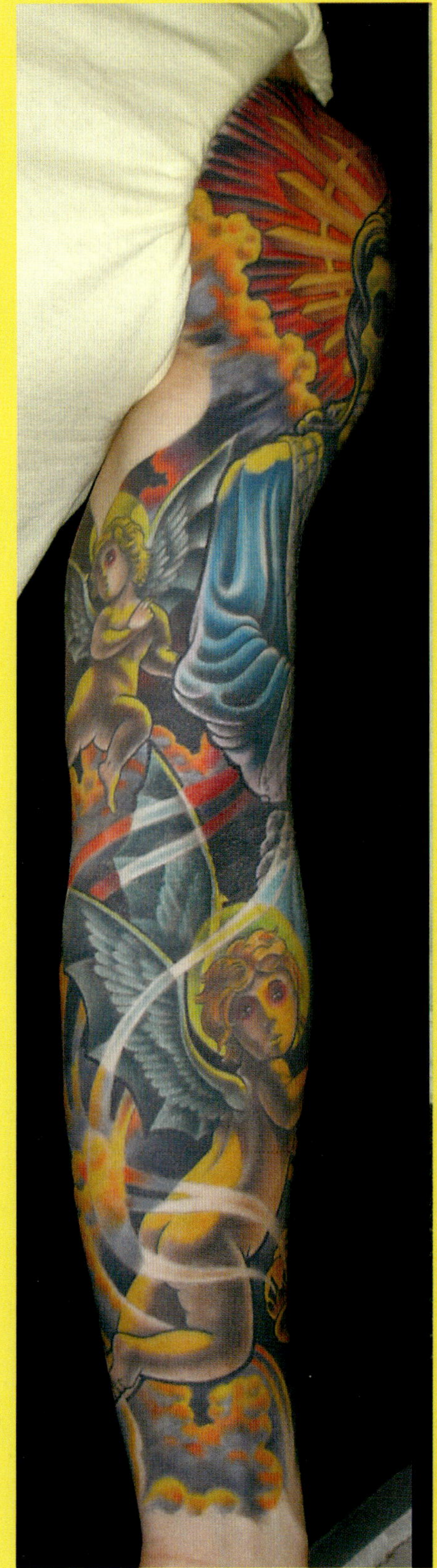

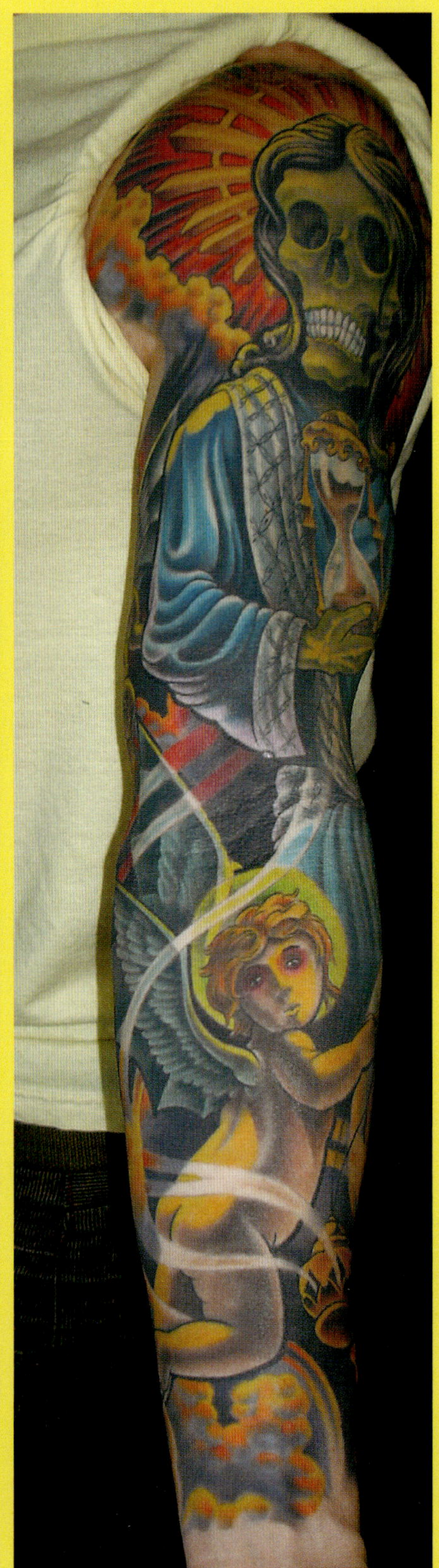

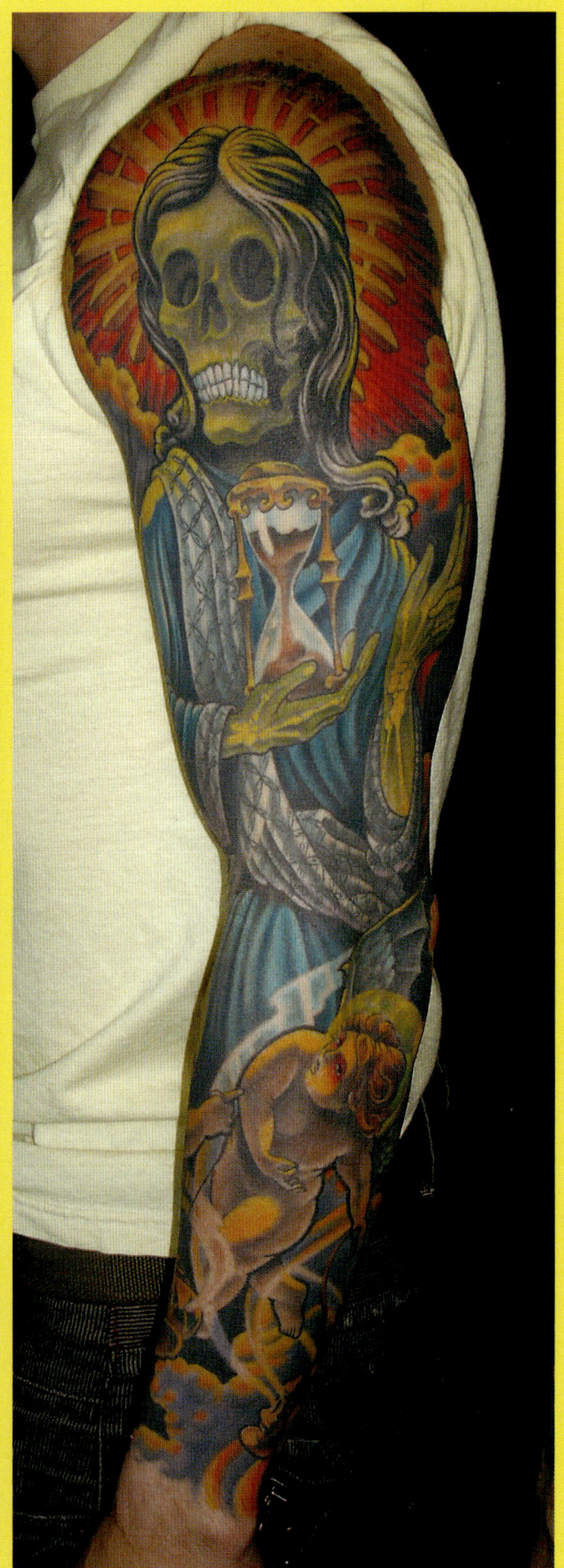

Images courtesy of Aaron Della Vedova at Guru Tattoo.

AARON DELLA VEDOVA

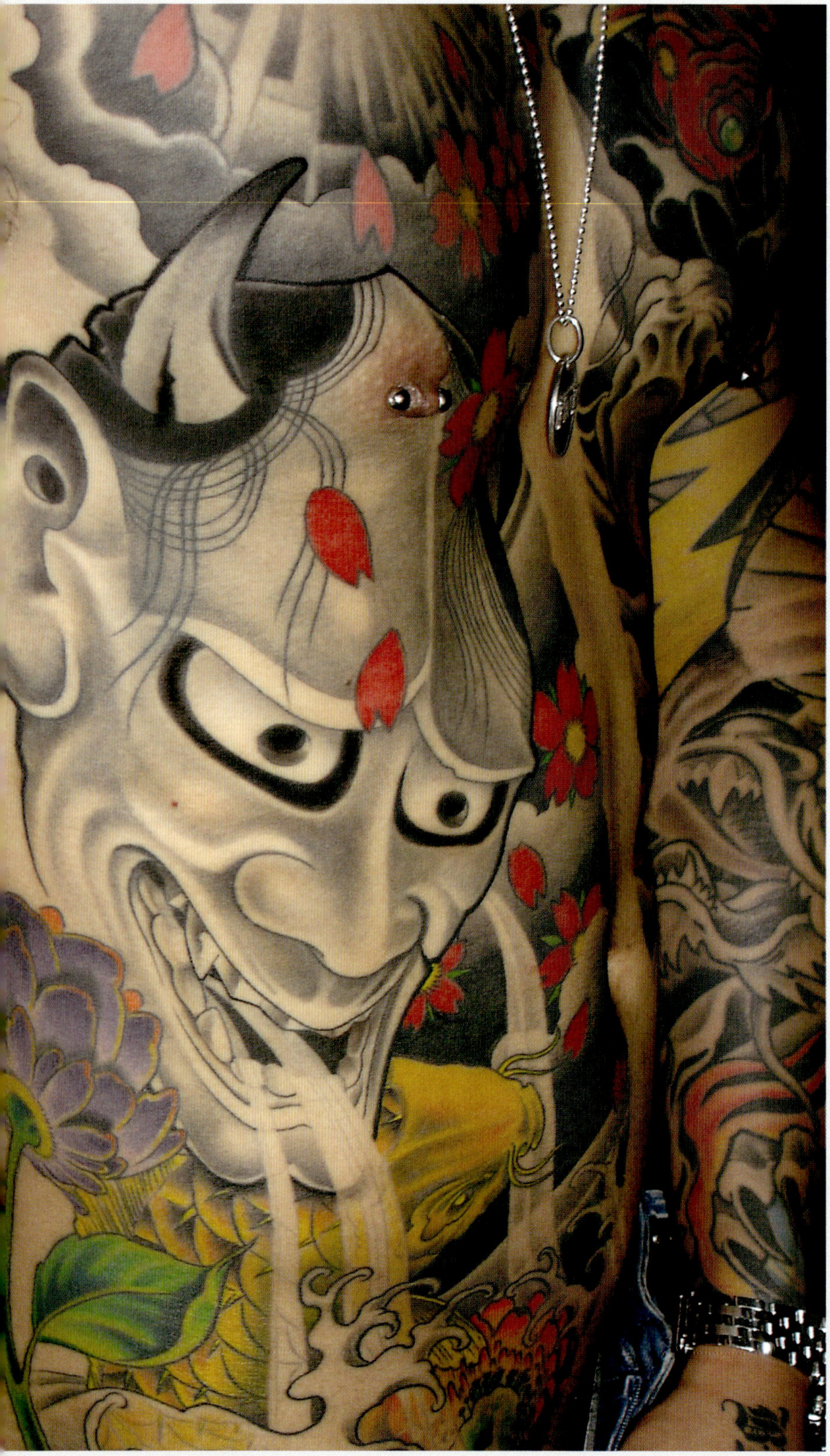

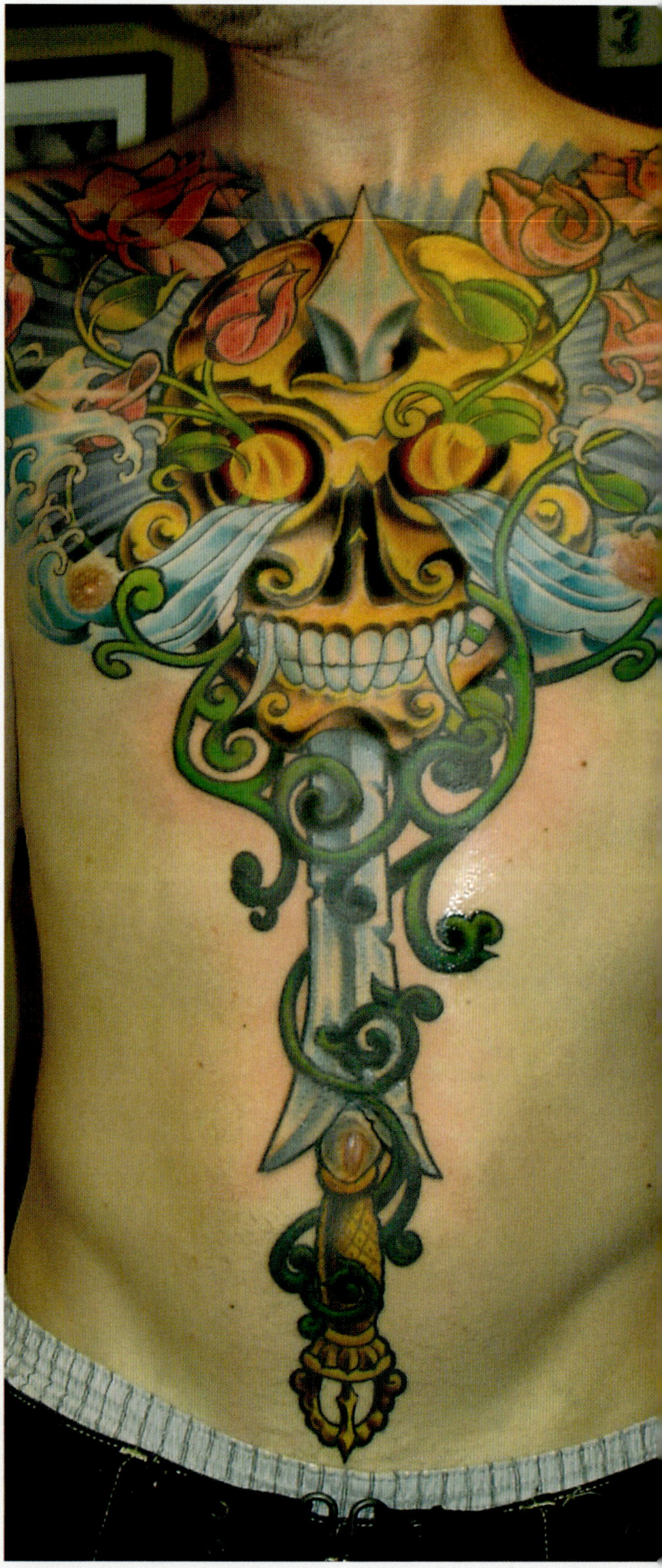

All images courtesy of Aaron Della Vedova at Guru Tattoo.

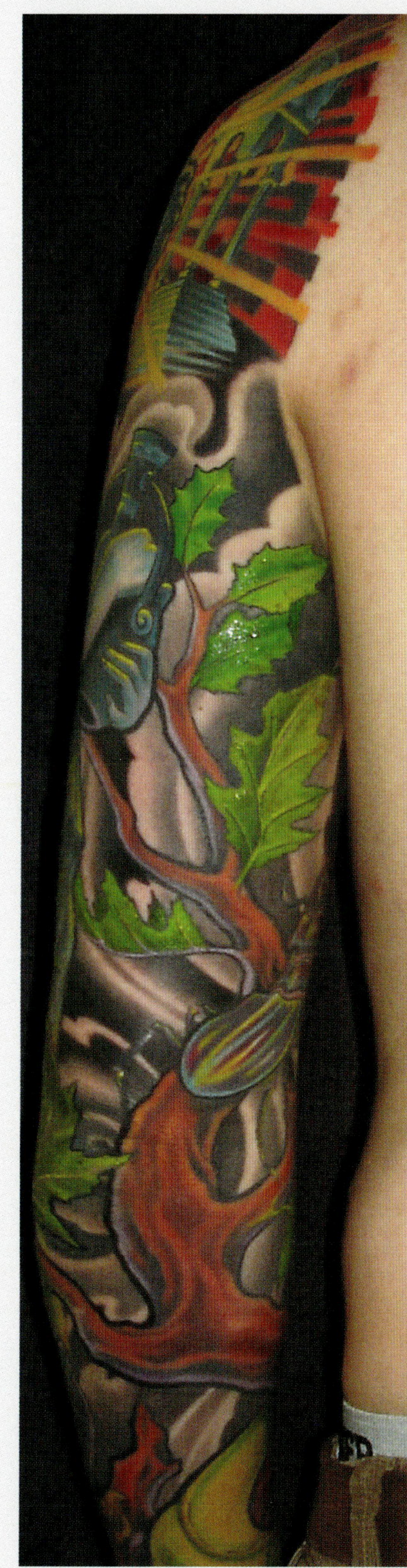

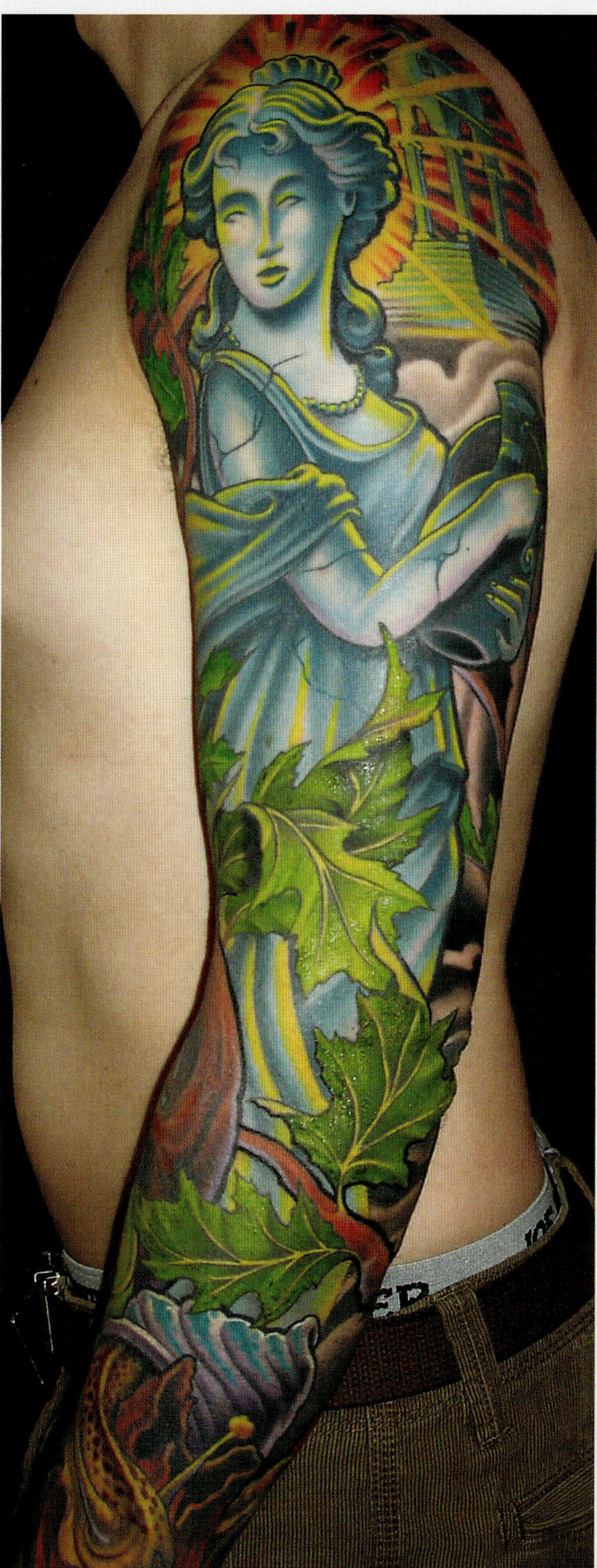

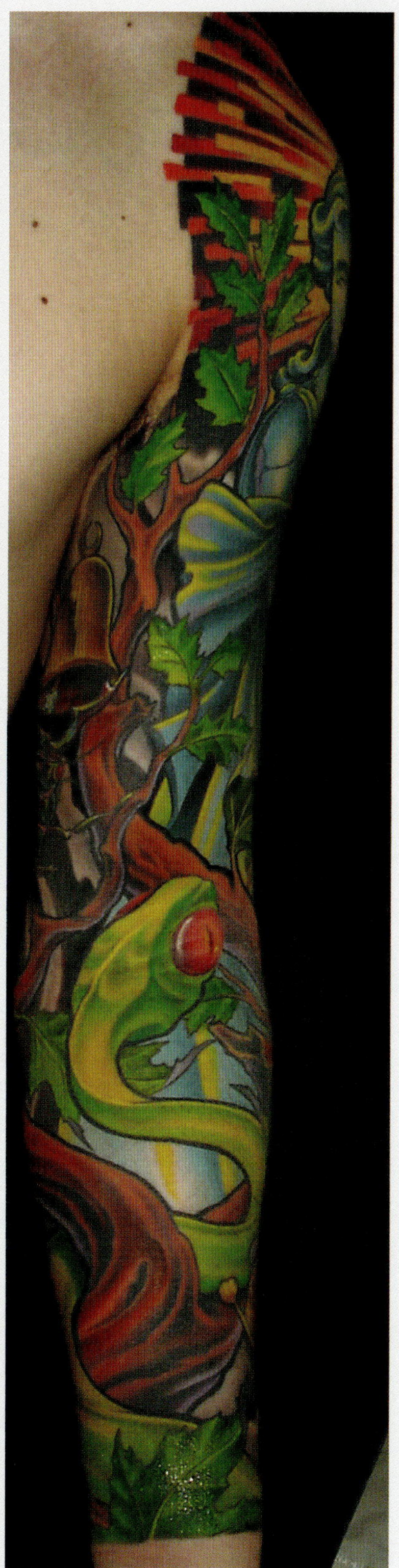

AARON DELLA VEDOVA

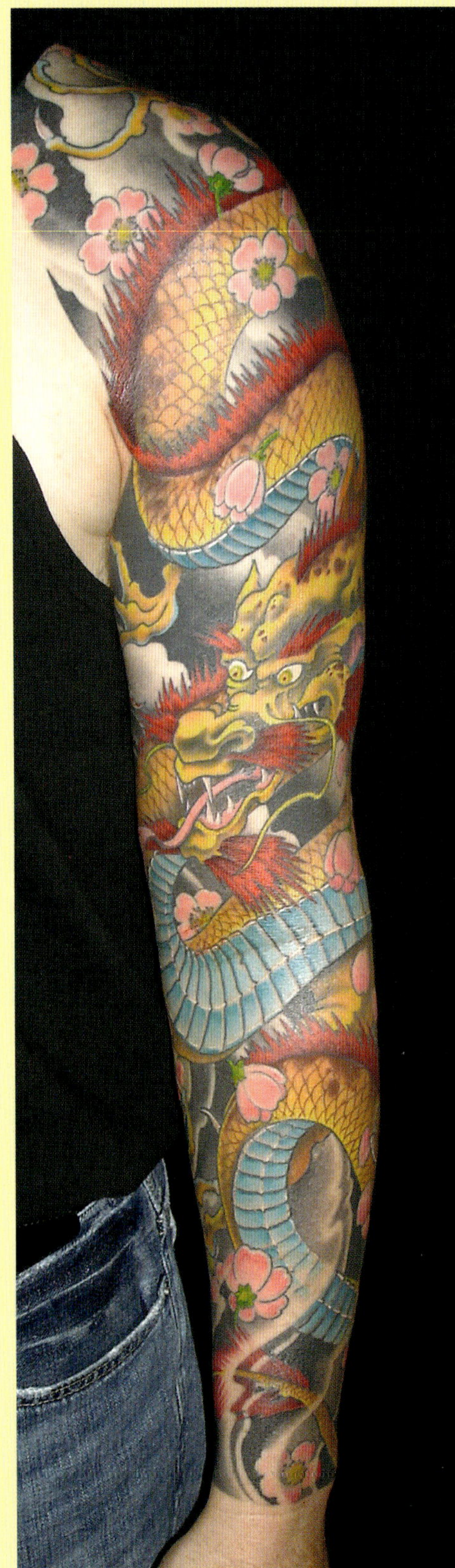

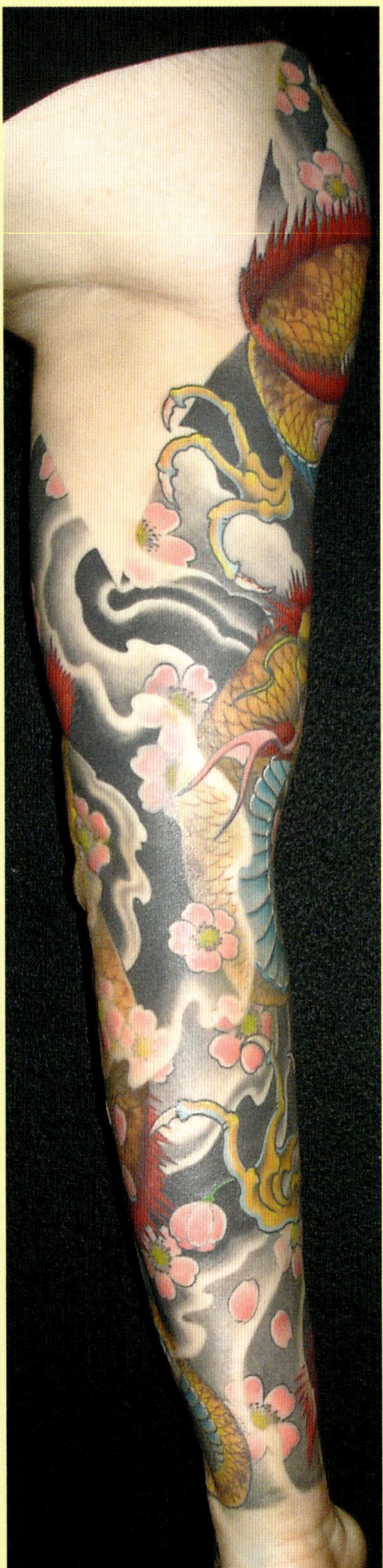

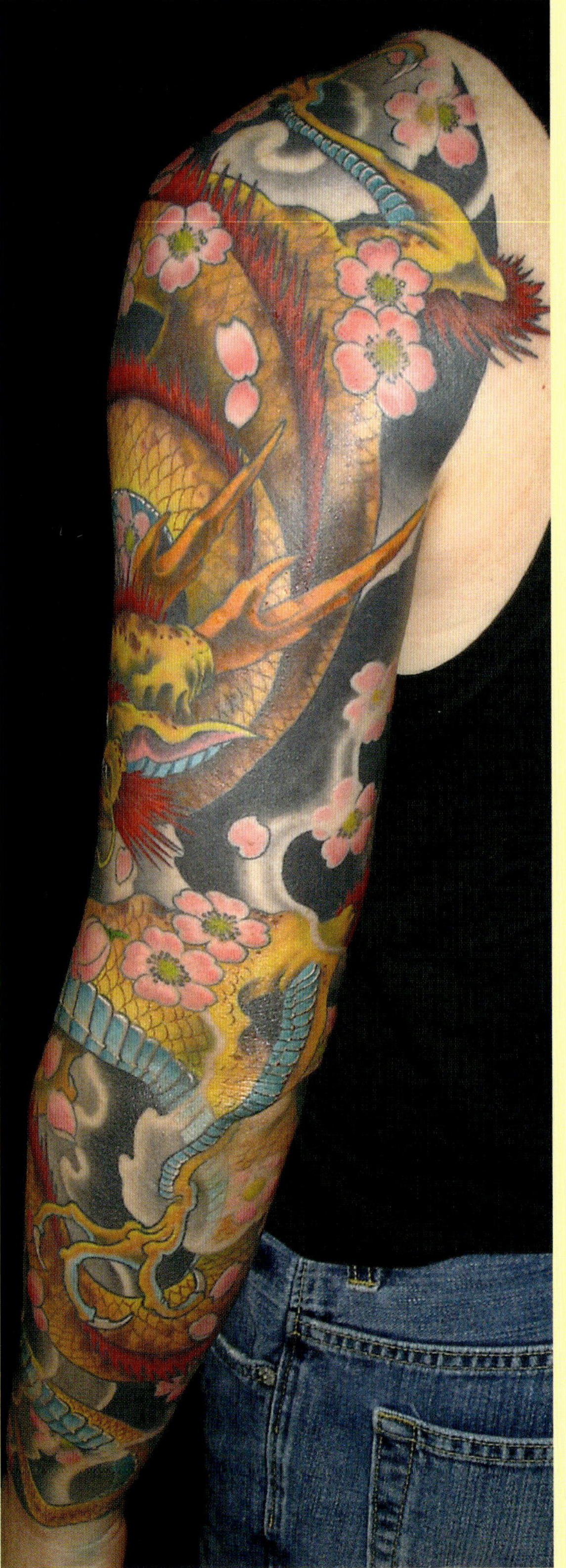

All designs on these pages by Aaron Della Vedova at Guru Tattoo.

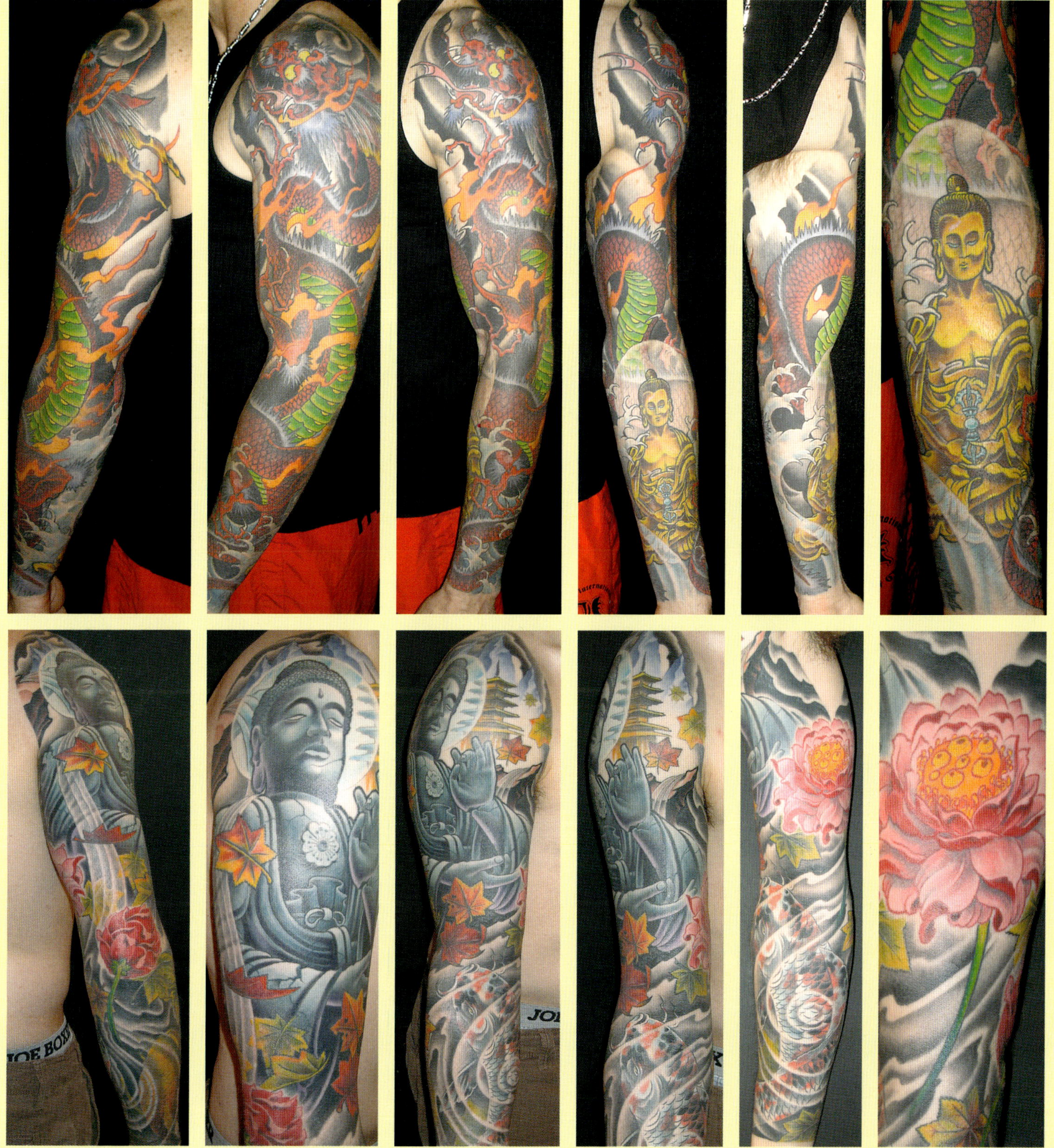

AARON DELLA VEDOVA

ADAM FORMAN

USA

1. I started as a self-taught tattoo artist in 1994. I was an art student trying to find my way and discover who I was as an artist. I am still on that path of self-discovery, but tattooing has been a wonderful vehicle of exploration both artistically and spiritually. I owe a great deal of who I am today to tattooing.

2. Tattooing is in a process of redefining itself in our contemporary society. It's amazing how the context of the tattoo, meaning the person wearing it, has as much influence as the artist who produces it. I guess tattooing to me is as much psychology as it is artistic expression. That's what can make it so beautiful.

3. I love European classicism and Japanese-style tattooing. I am doing my best to find their common ground.

4. Research your artist and get something beautiful. Sincerity counts.

5. I am currently working at High Voltage tattoo in Hollywood, California. You can always find me at www.dutchrubb.com

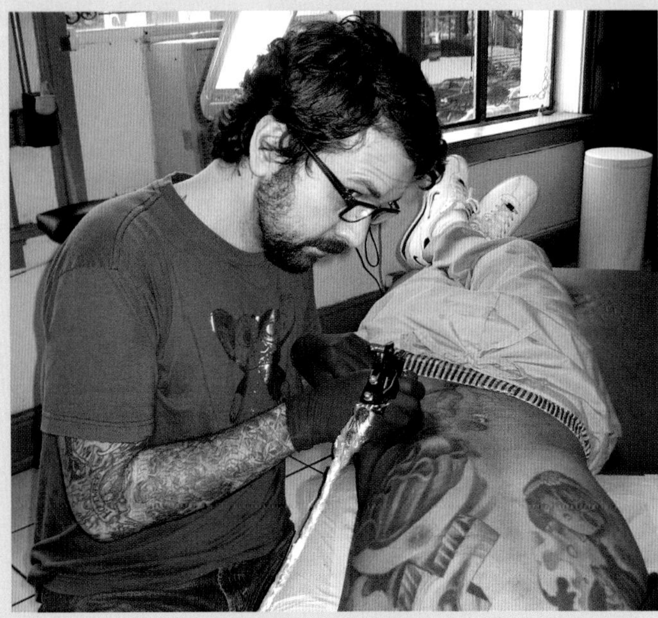

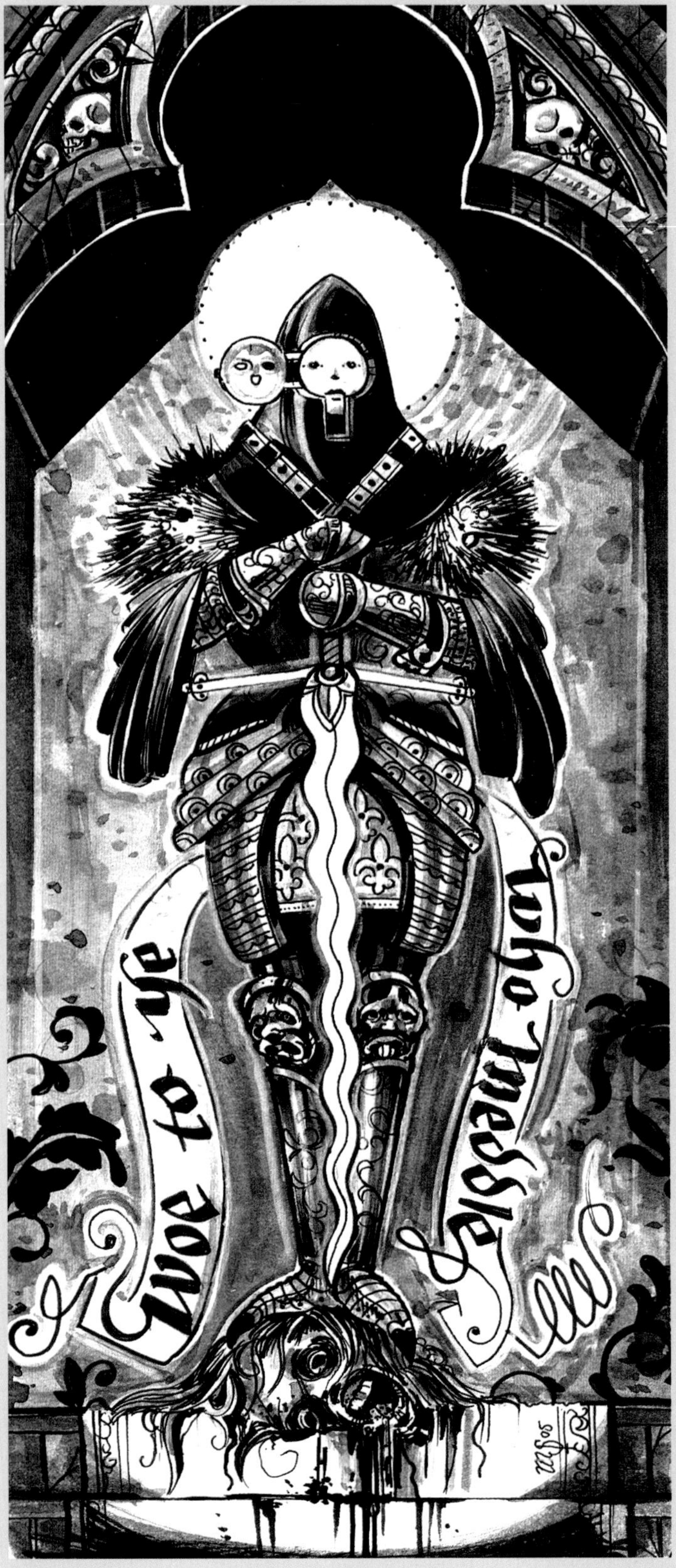

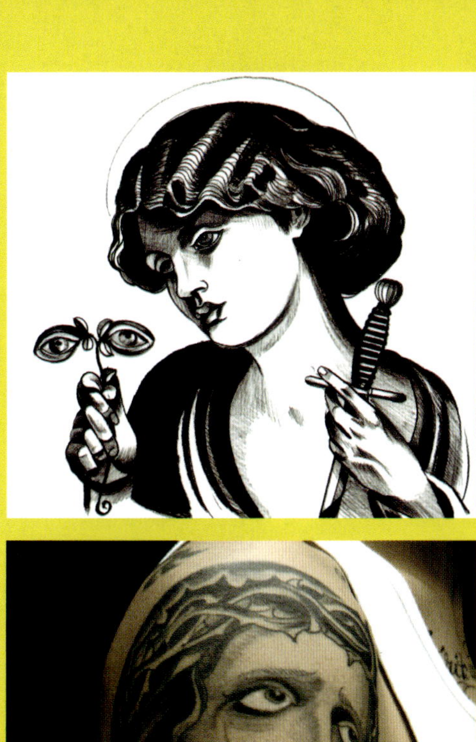

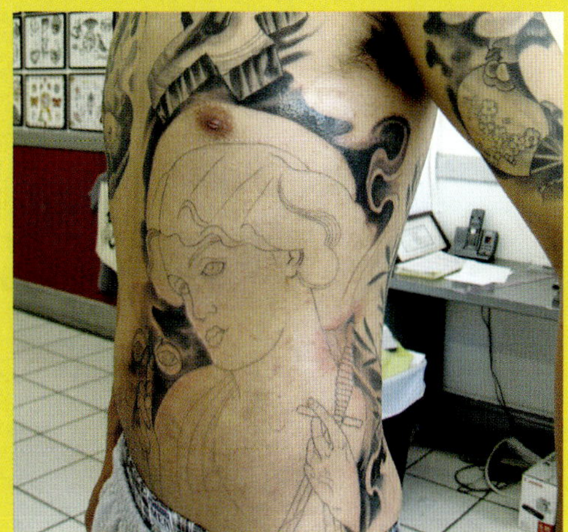

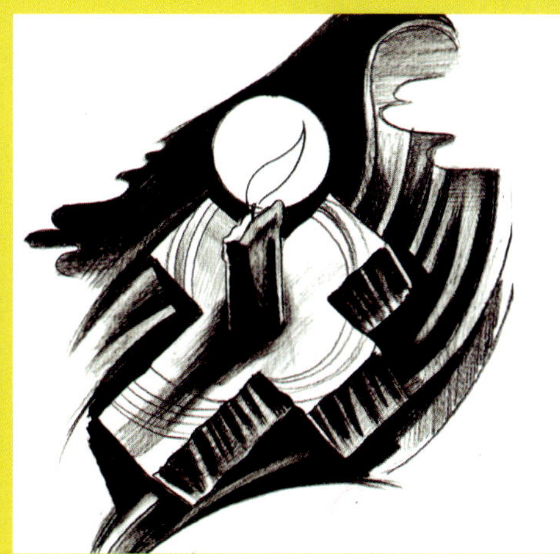

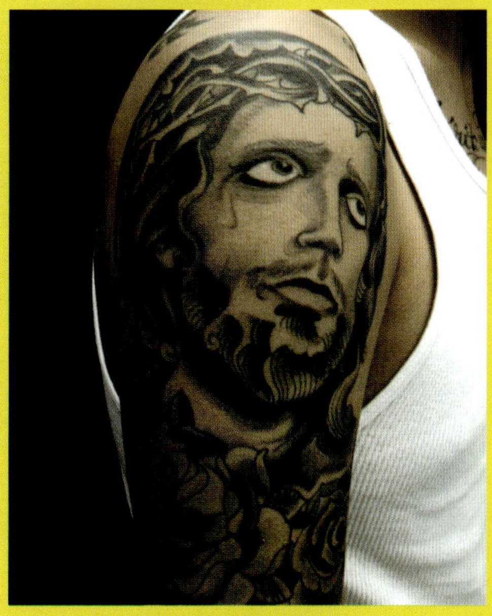

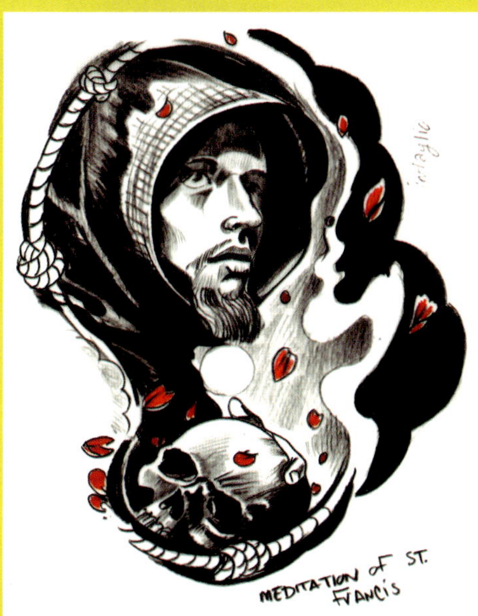

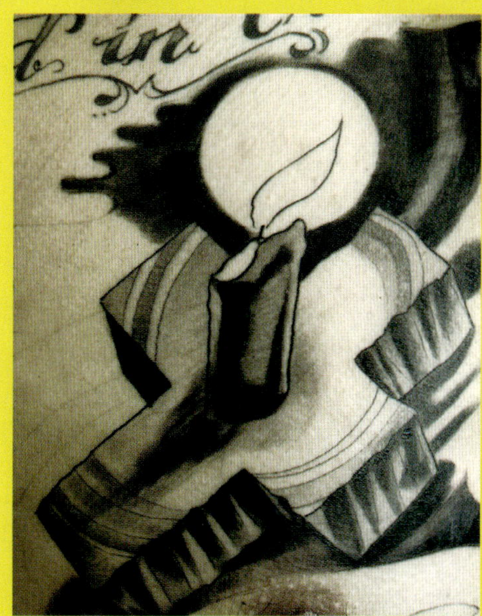

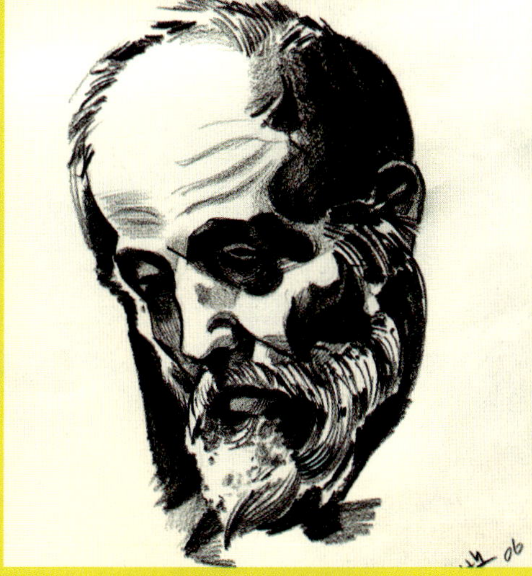

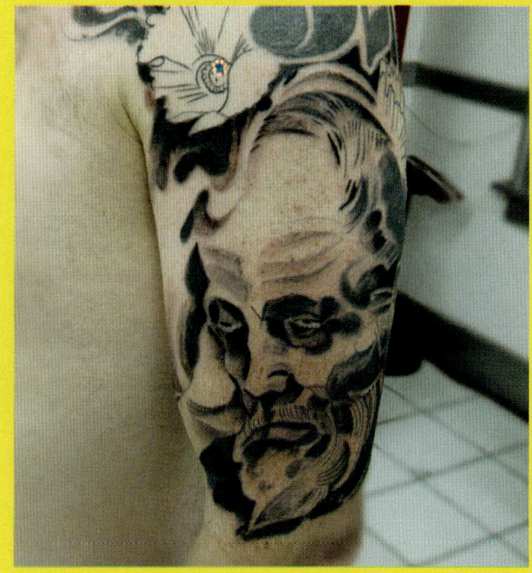

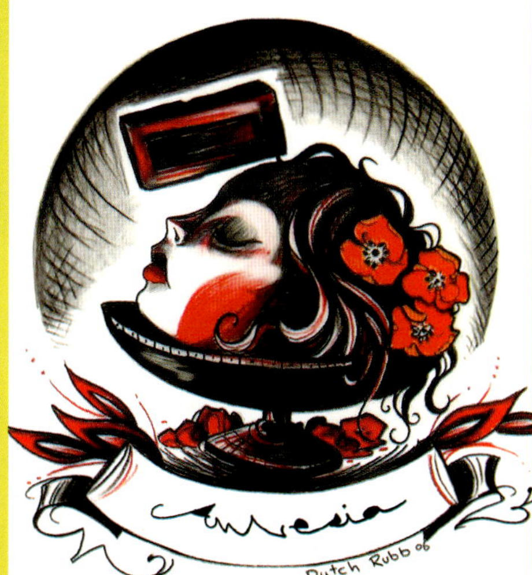

All designs on these pages by Adam Forman.

TOMAS-TOMAS

UK

1. I signed a pact with the tattoo gods.

2. At best, a tattoo is a worship or a practice connecting the individual with the divine and the magic within, or alternatively simply an insertion of pigments in the skin with the help of needles.

3. Tattoos are the representation of the time and place that people live in. London's environment is mysterious, dark, urban, overcrowded, multi-ethnic, multi-faith and technologically advanced. This is what I try to convey in my work.

4. Find the teacher within.

5. Into-you Tattoo London, www.into-you.co.uk on the web.
   www.siddhamrastu.co.uk
   www.myspace.com/frenchthomas
   or the beaches of India.

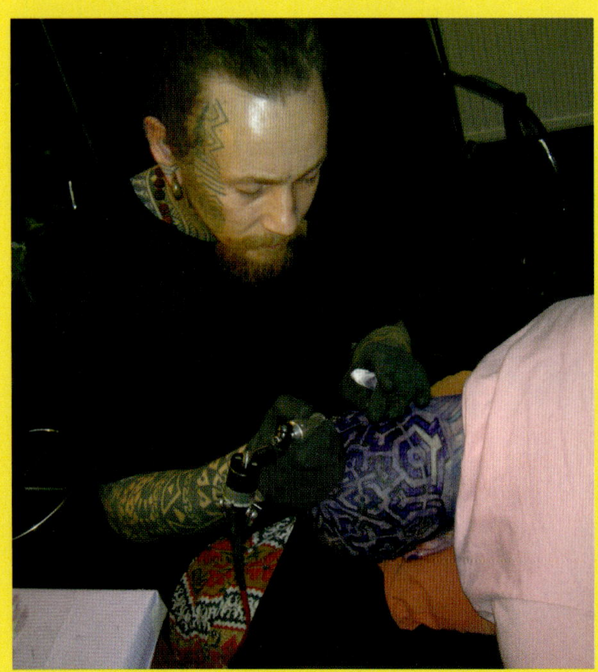

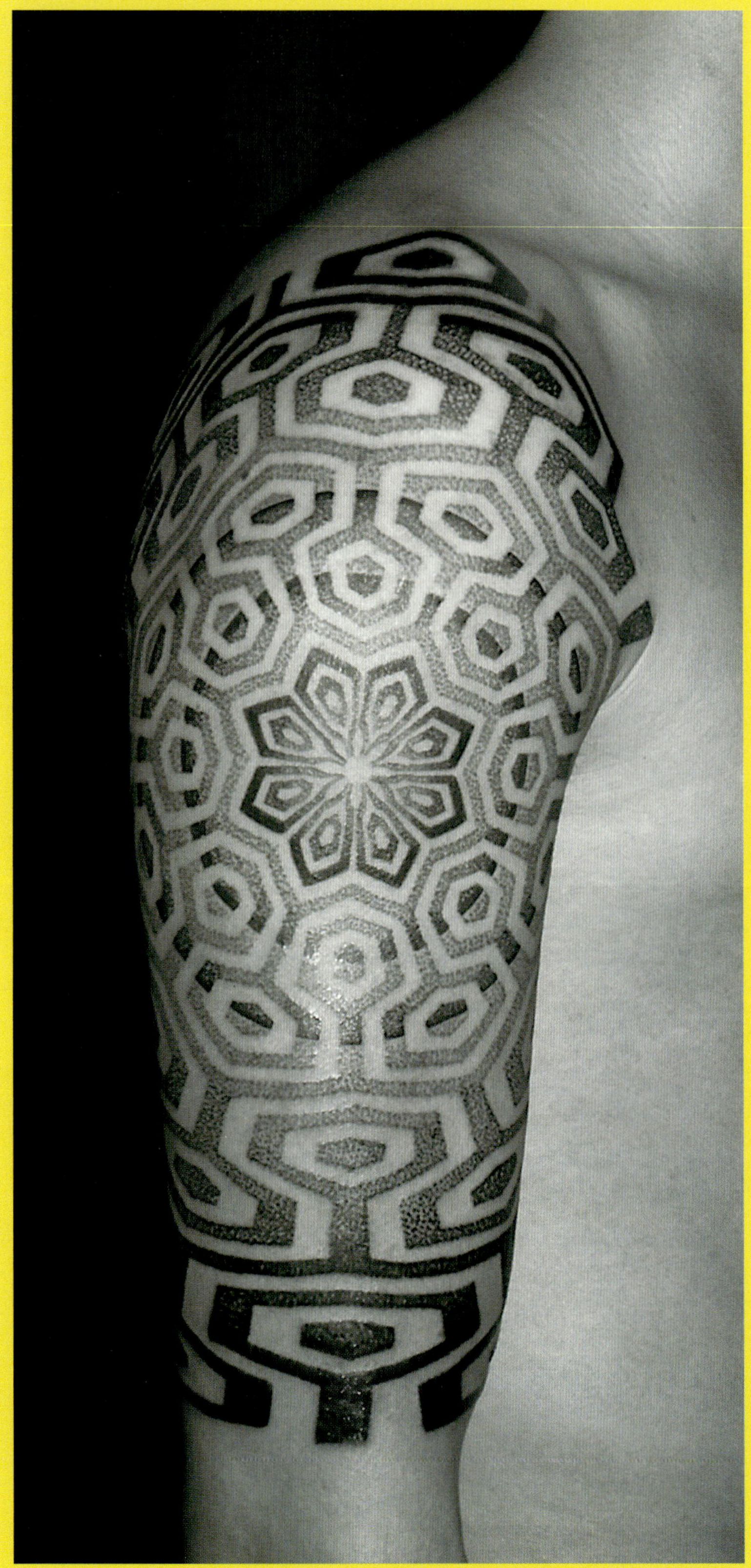

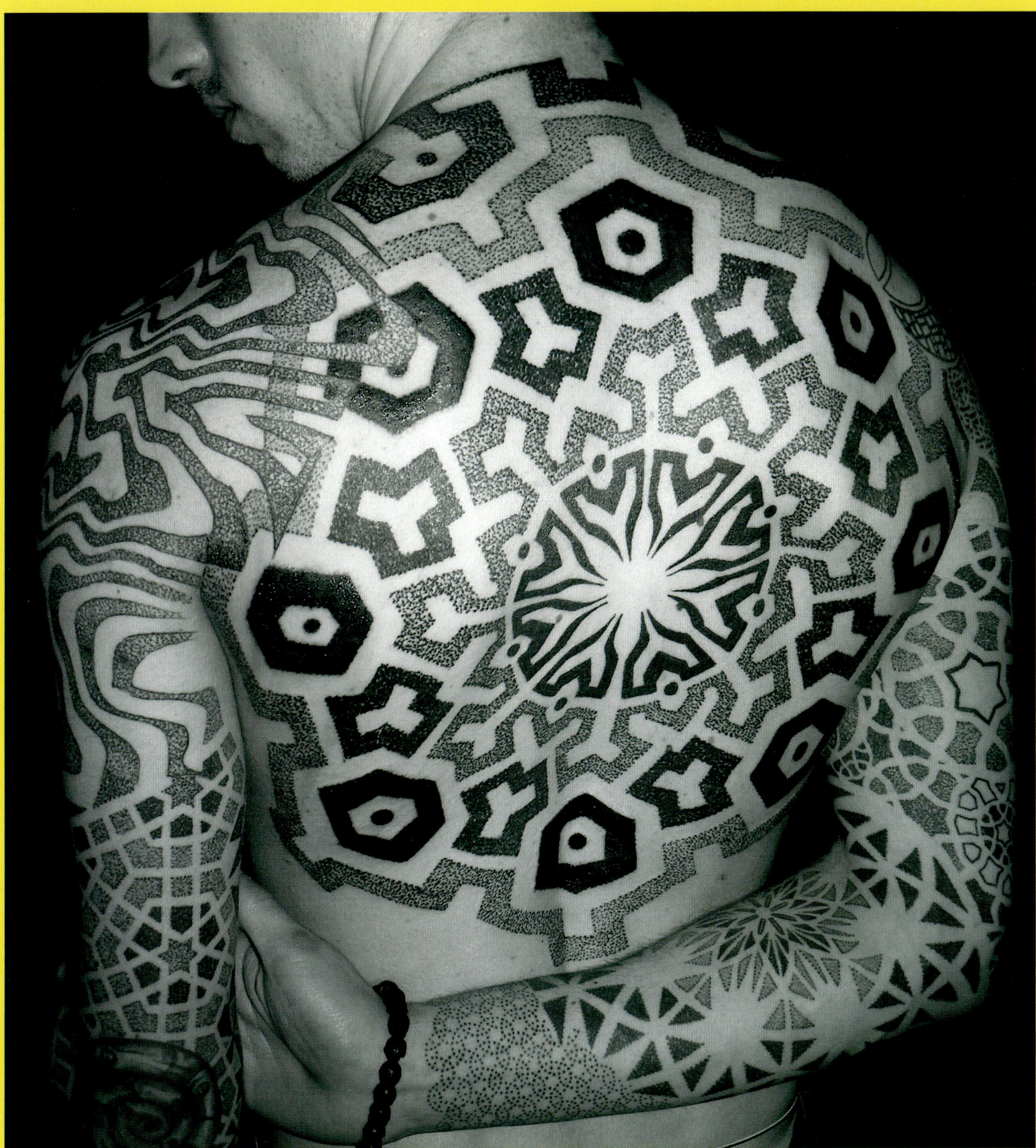

All designs on these pages by Tomas-Tomas.

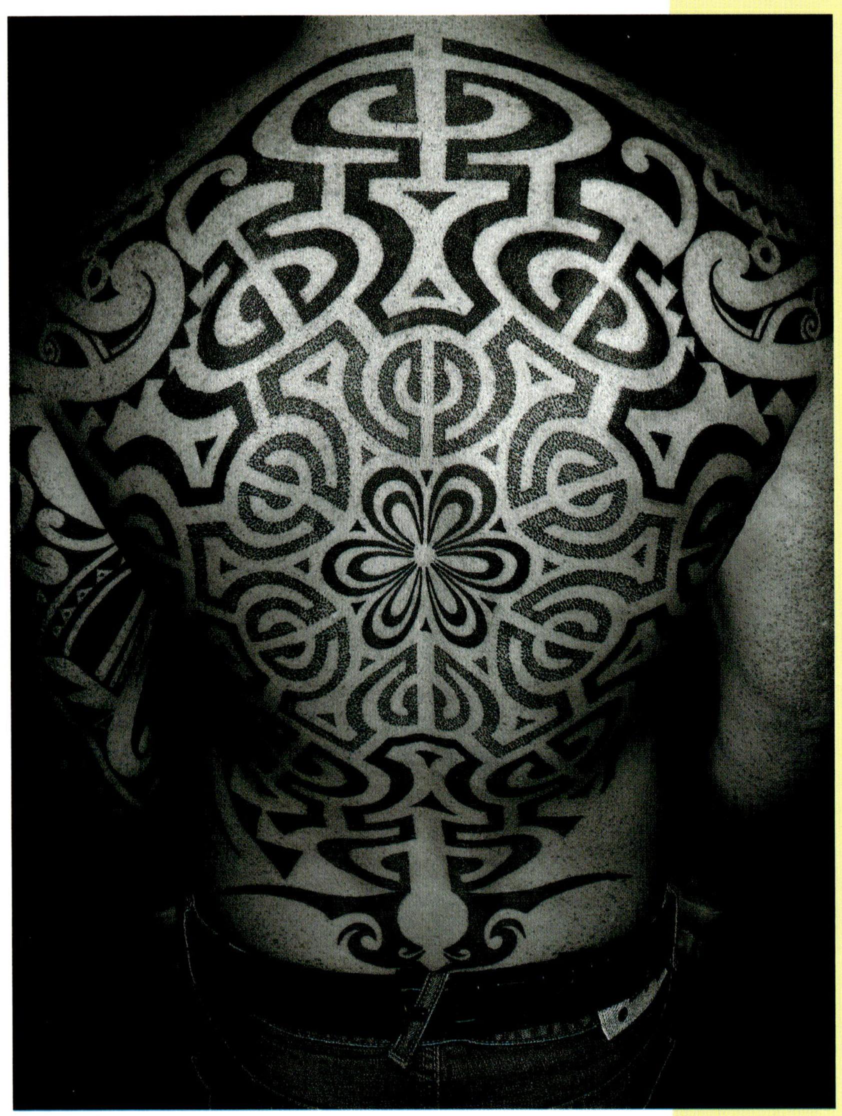

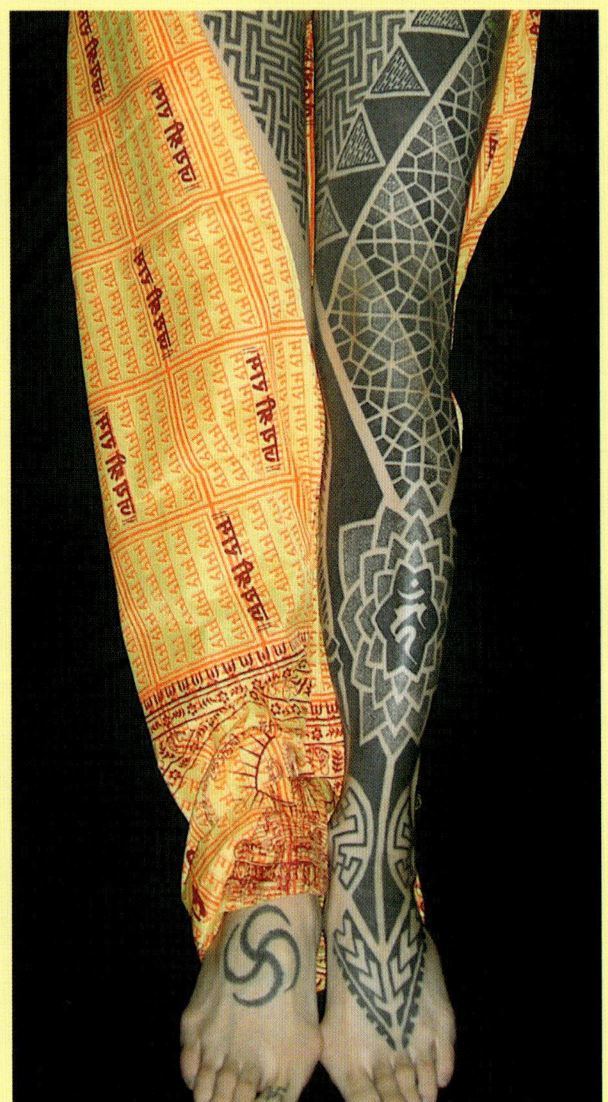

All artwork by Tomas-Tomas.

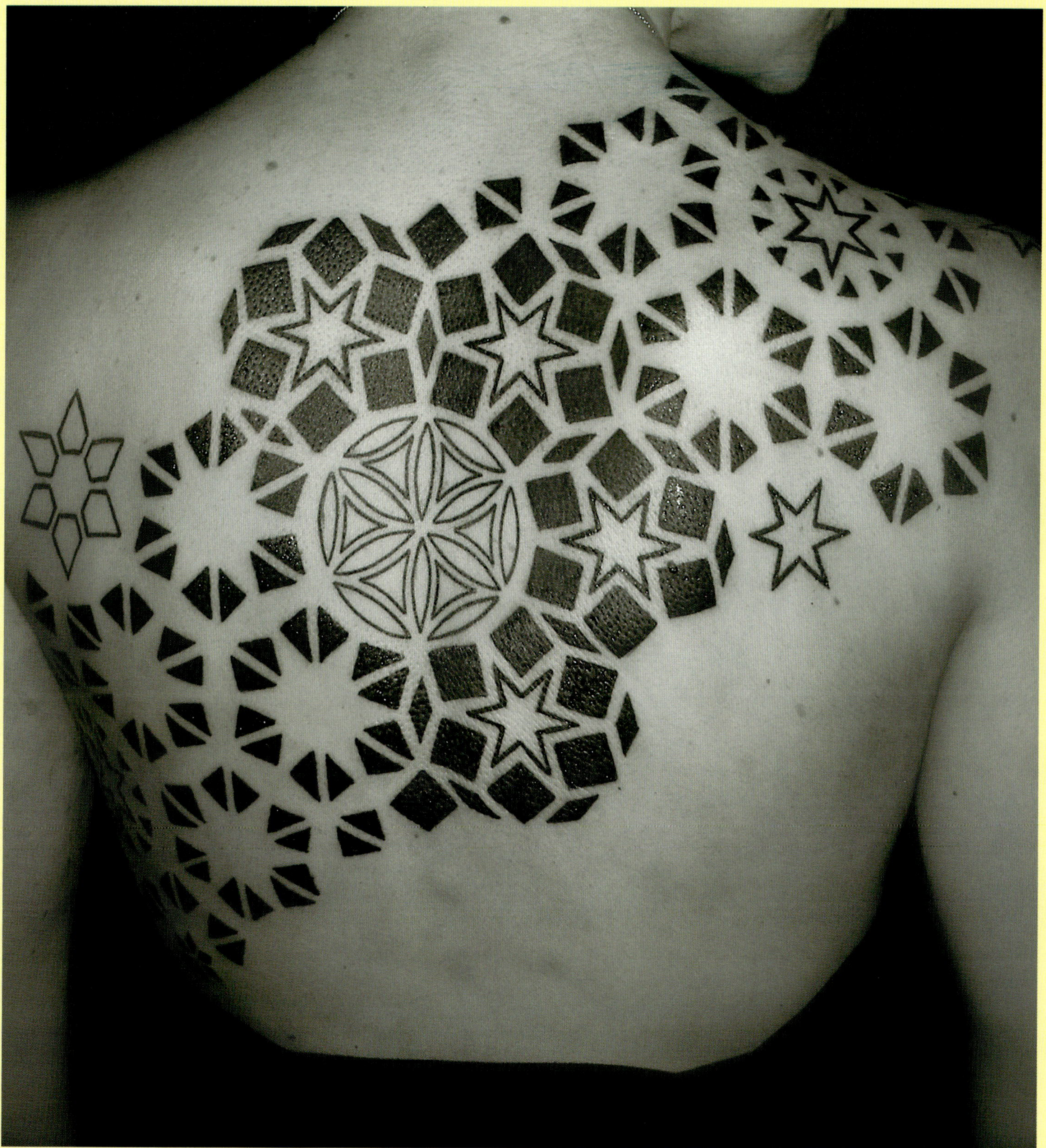

TOMAS-TOMAS

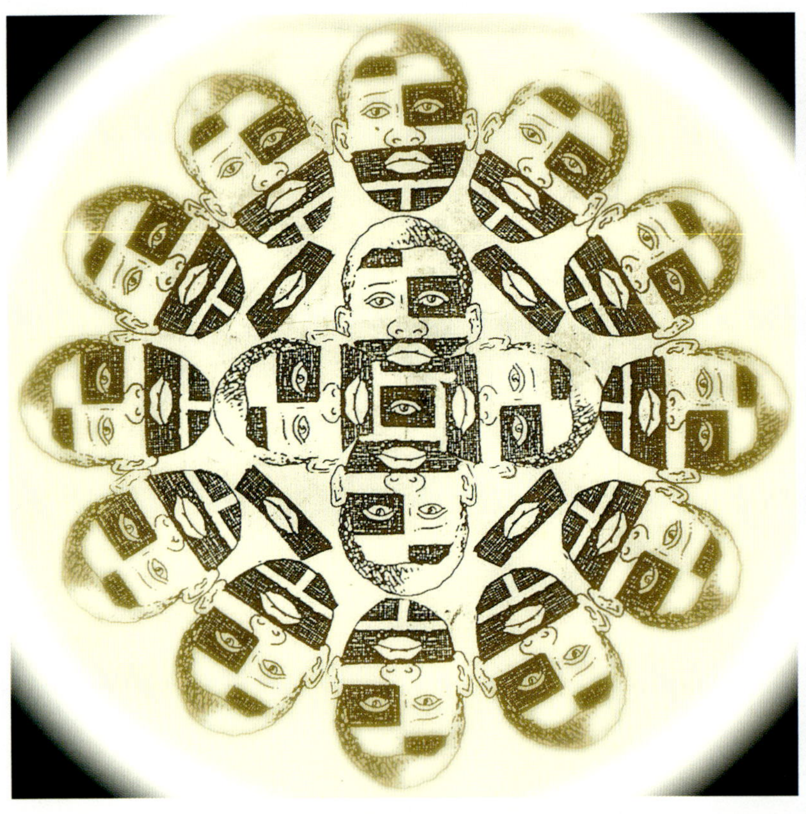

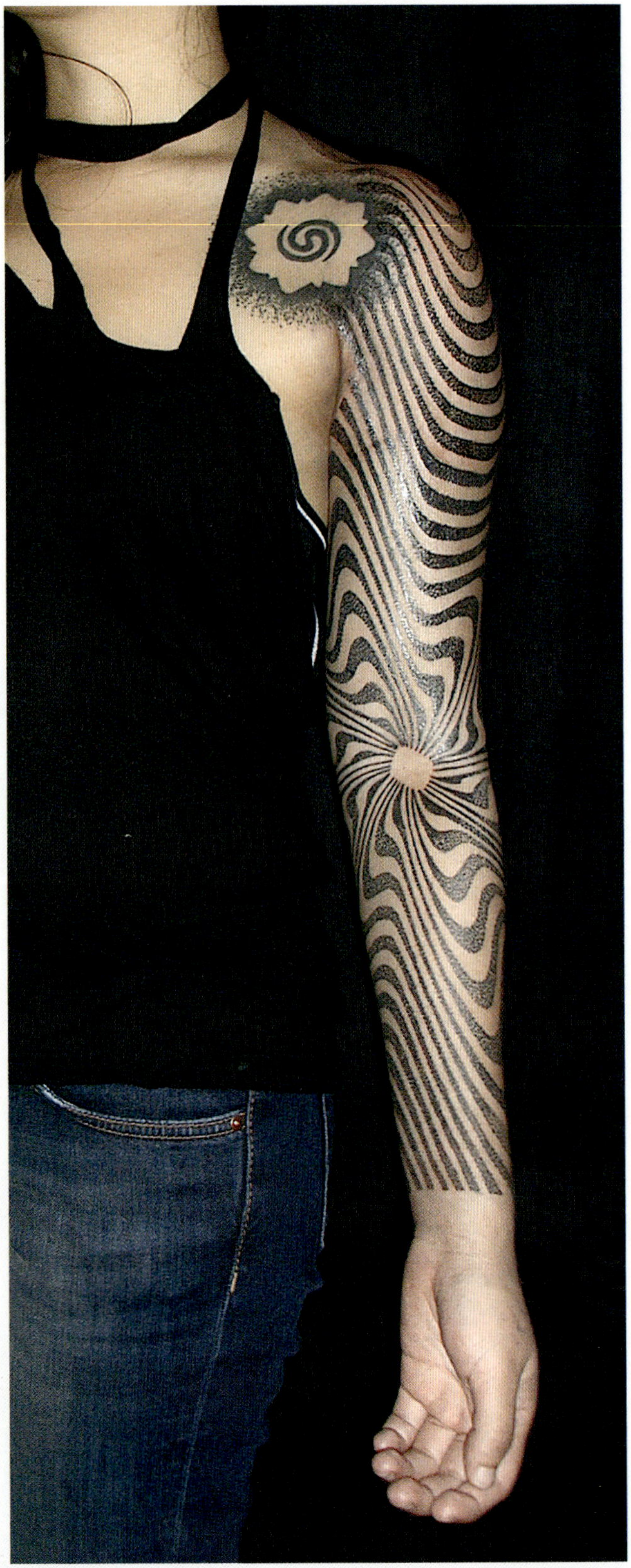

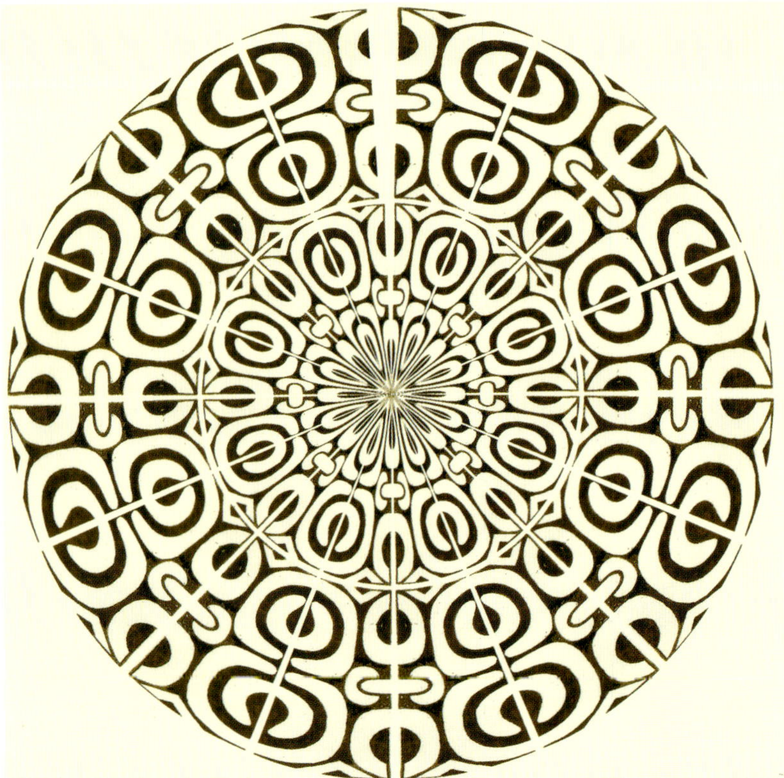

Images courtesy of Tomas-Tomas.

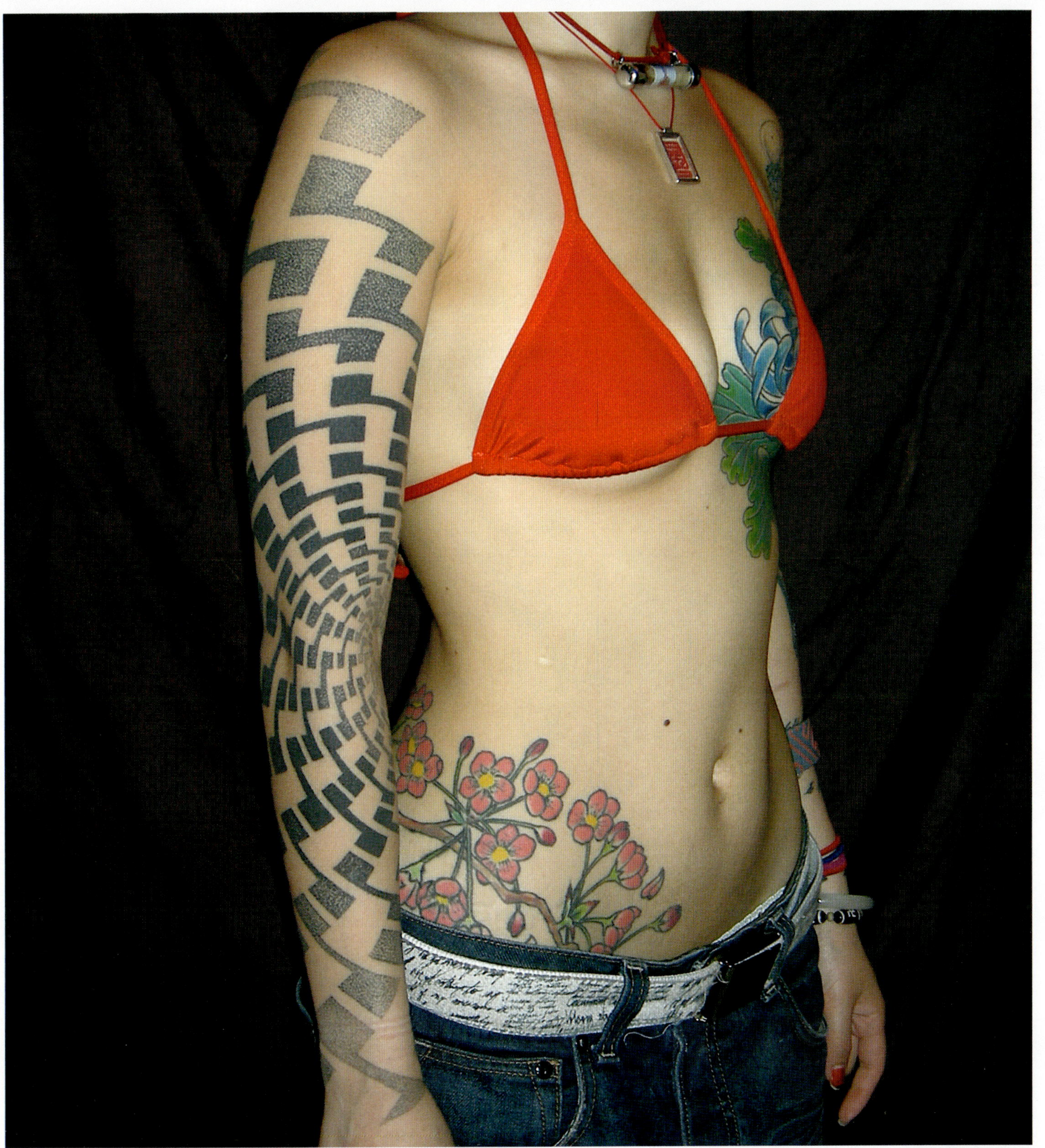

TOMAS-TOMAS

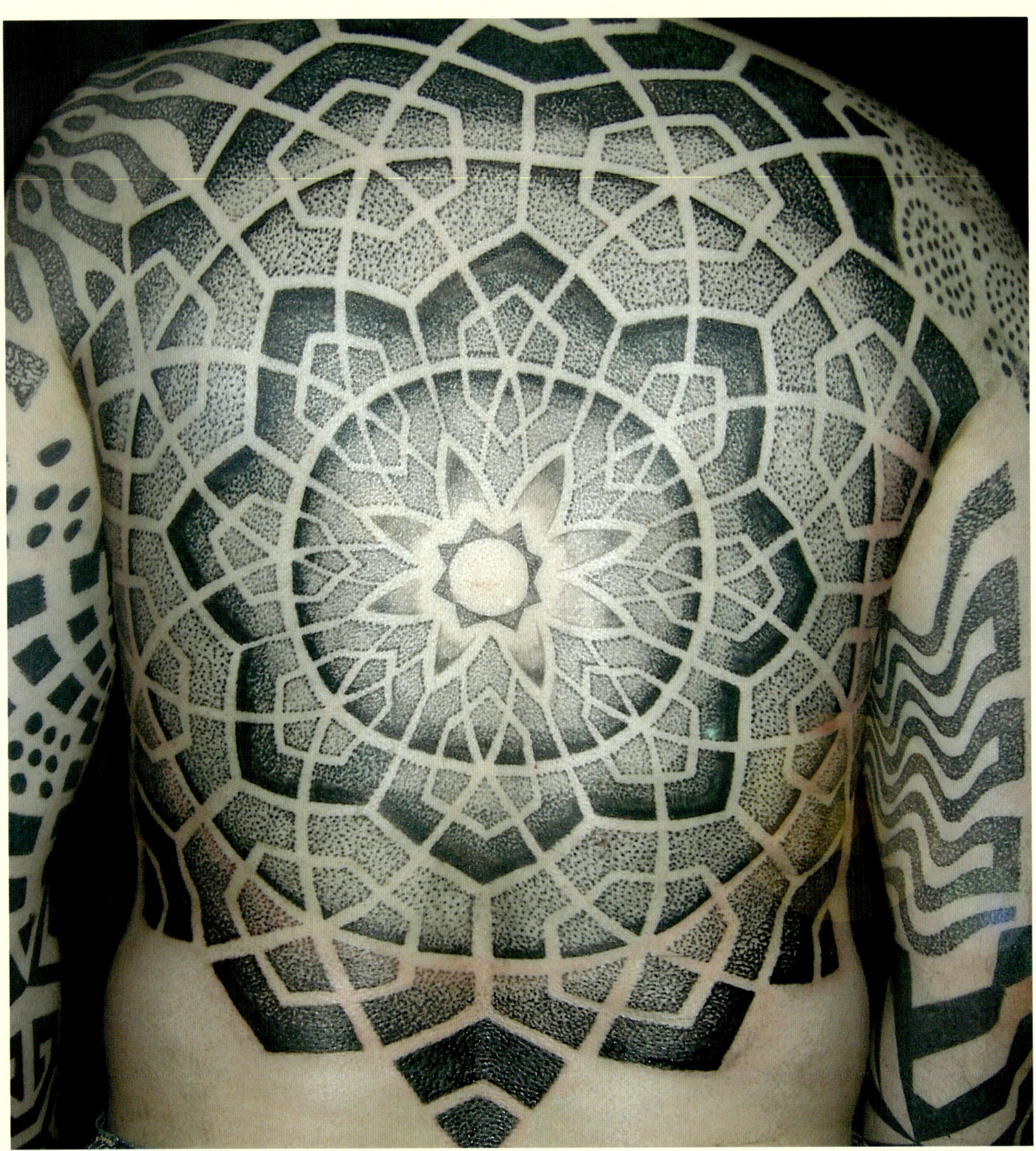

Step by step of a tattoo design by Tomas-Tomas.

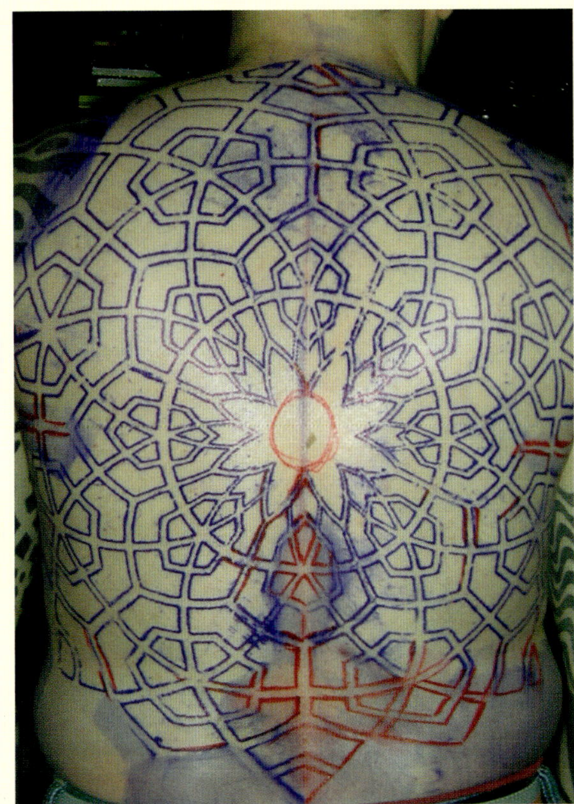

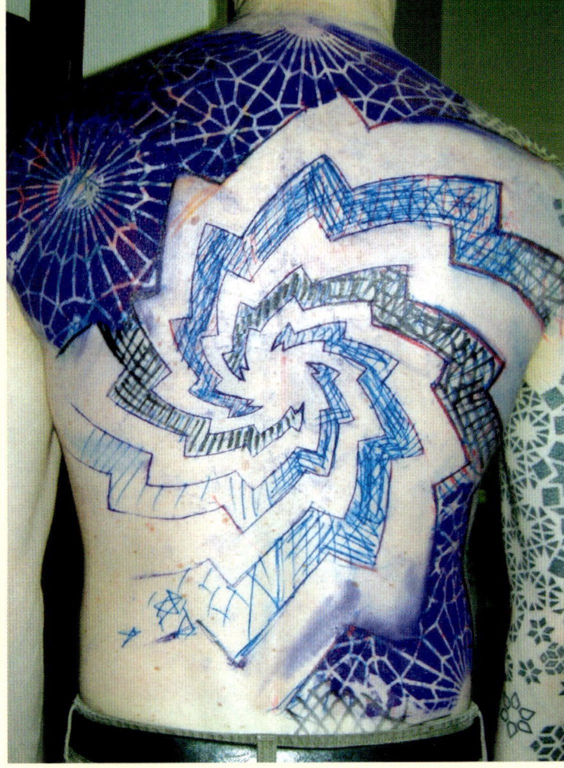

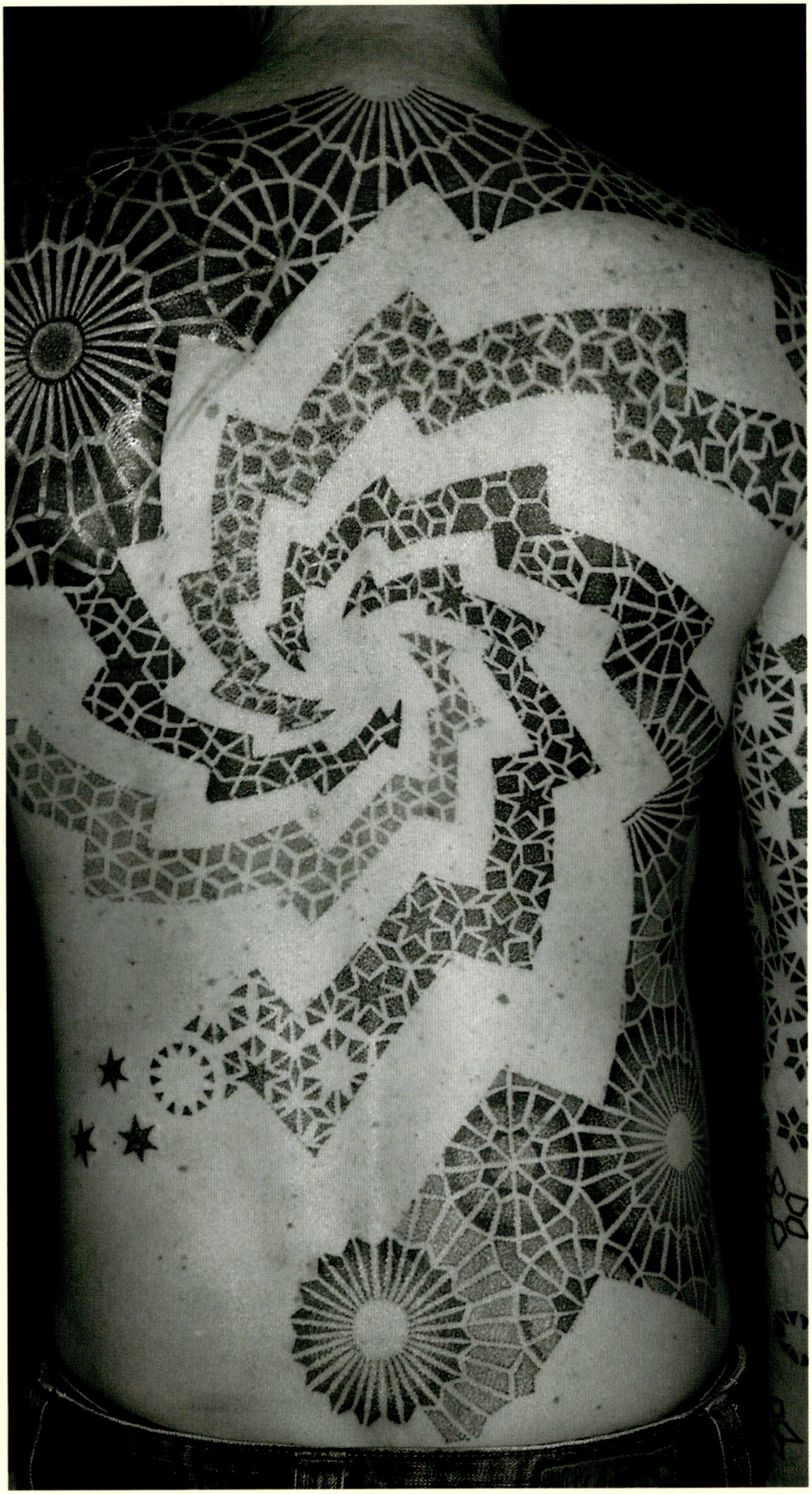

TOMAS-TOMAS

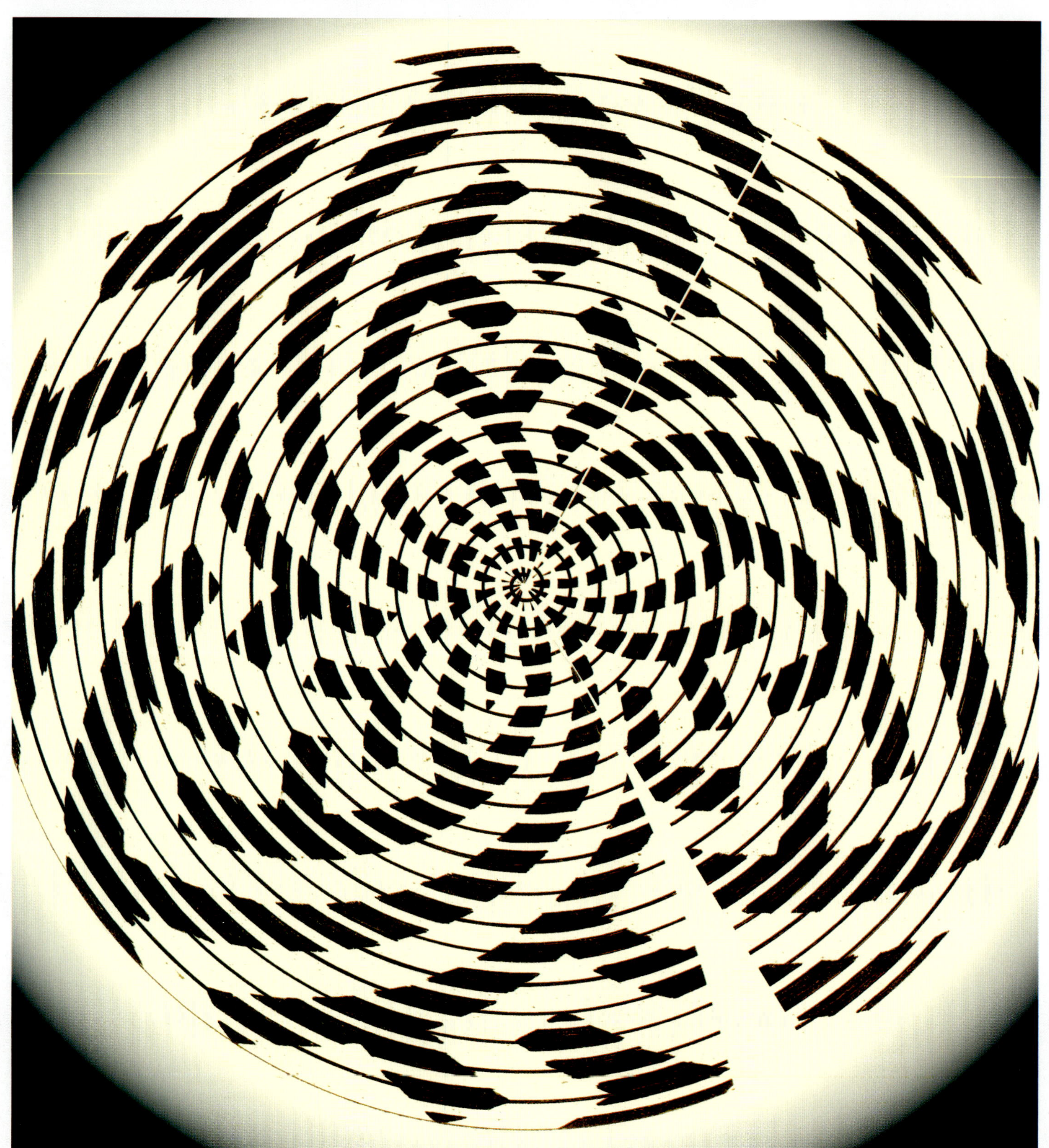

All images courtesy of Tomas-Tomas.

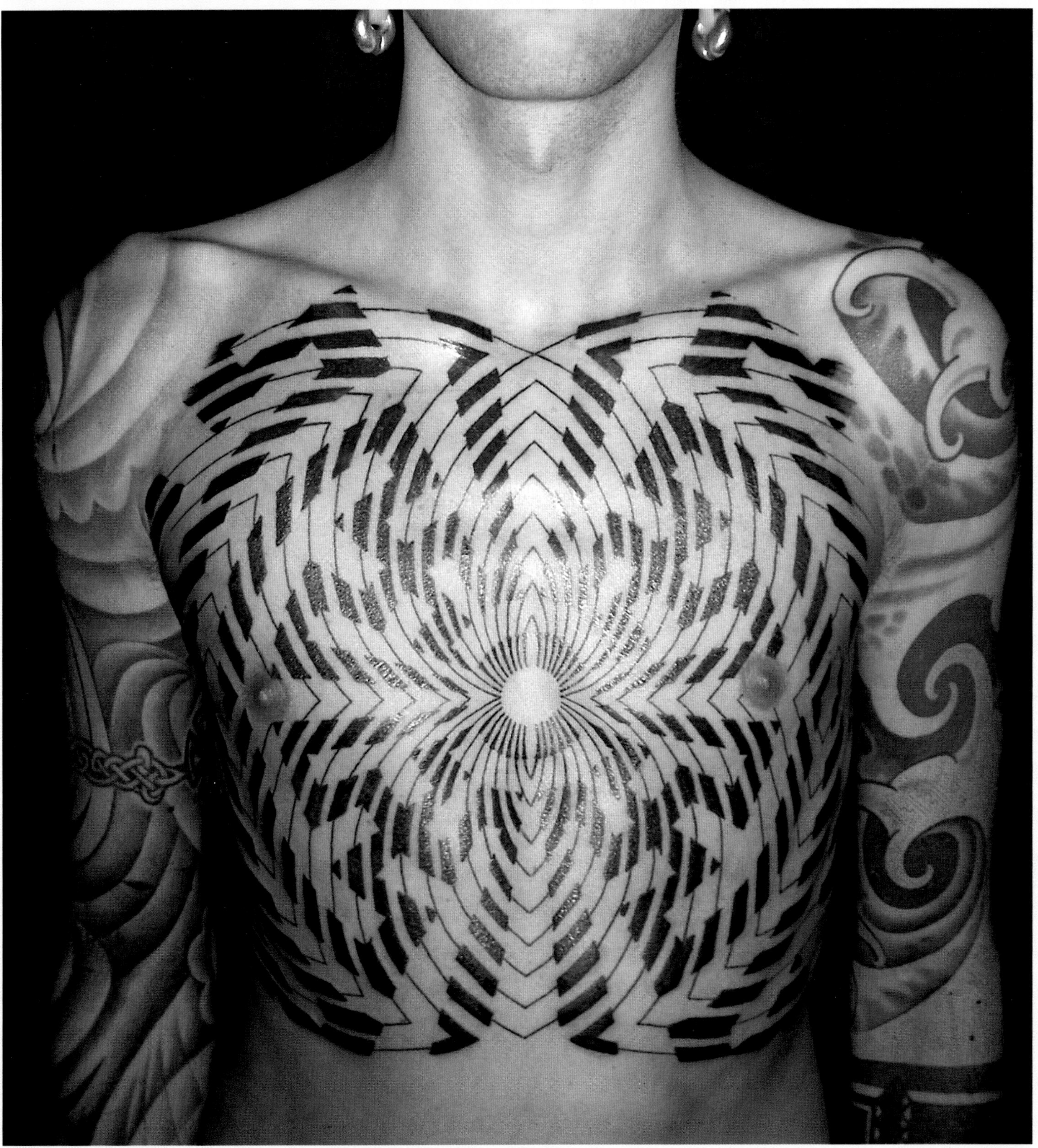

TOMAS-TOMAS

HARAI TATTOO

BELGIUM

1. I fell in love with tattoos when I was 16 years old! Some years later, after getting some nice tats, I decided to start to learn tattooing. But the road was so hard, and nobody wanted to help me out. I still have a long way to go, but I love every step of the way!

2. A good tattoo is created when the client trusts you and lets you do your thing. There must be a good understanding between the client and the artist.

3. I only tattoo Oriental stuff, mainly Japanese and a little Tibetan. I stopped doing anything else because it takes a lot of time to master and understand a certain style. You cannot be good in everything, so I think it's better to specialize.

4. If you're not sure, don't start with tattoos! And if you start, remember: it's going to be a long and painful journey.

5. You can find me at Harai Tattoo in Ghent, Belgium. The address is ST-Kwintensberg 14, 9000 Ghent, Belgium.
   You can visit my site at www.haraitattoo.com

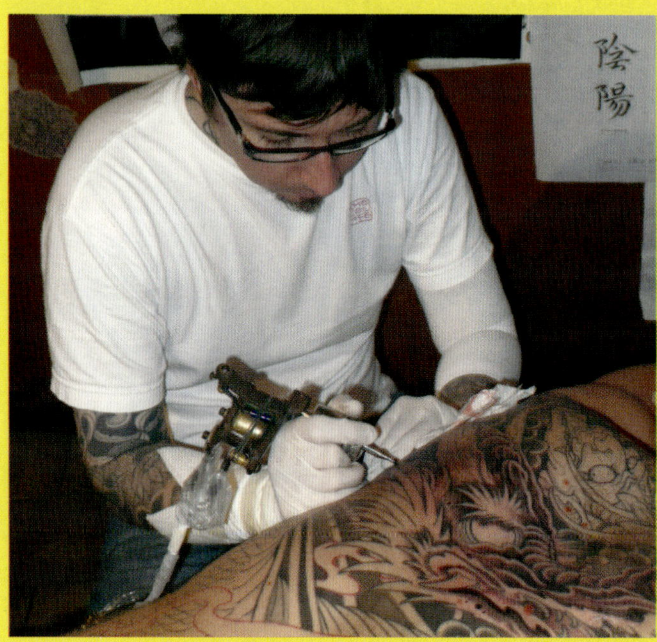

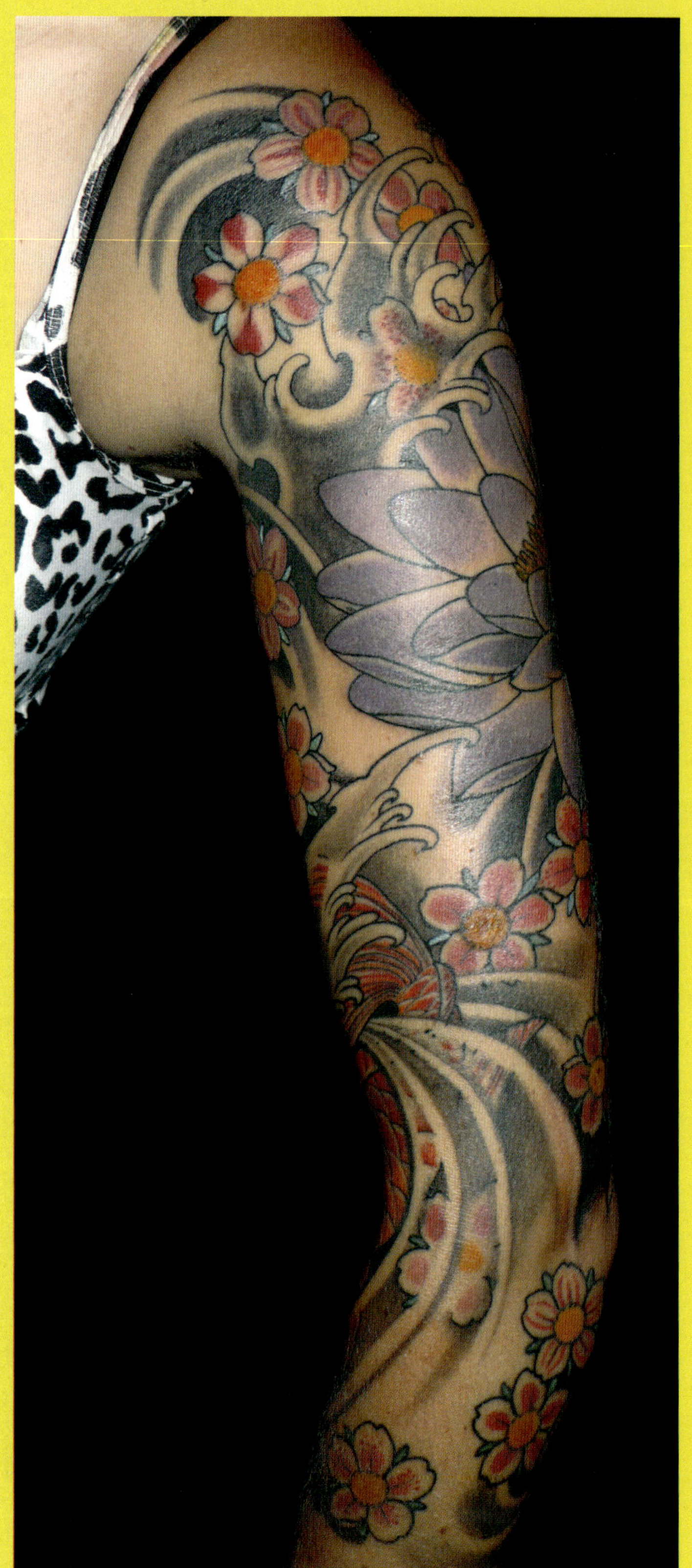

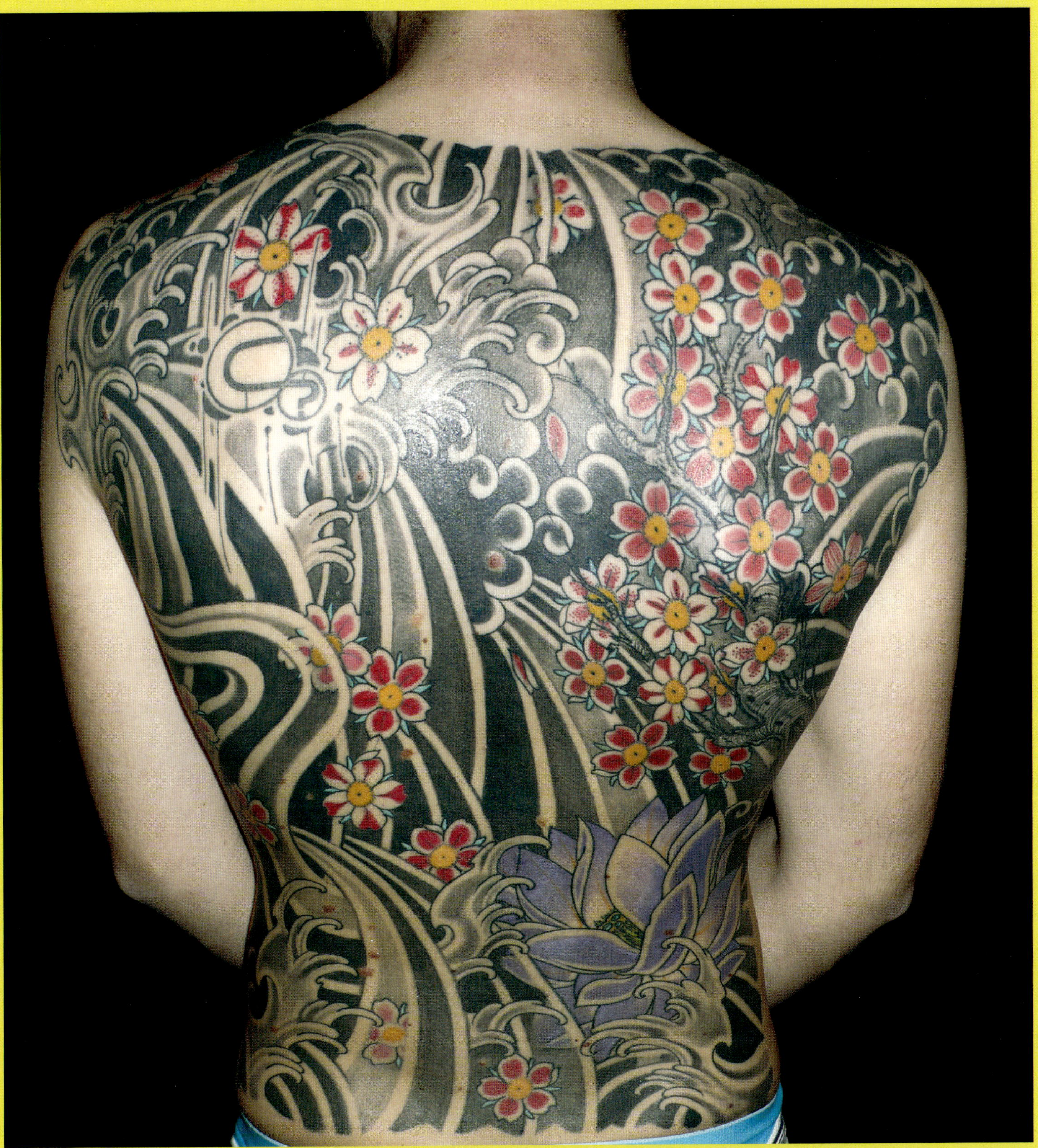

All images courtesy of Harai Tattoo.

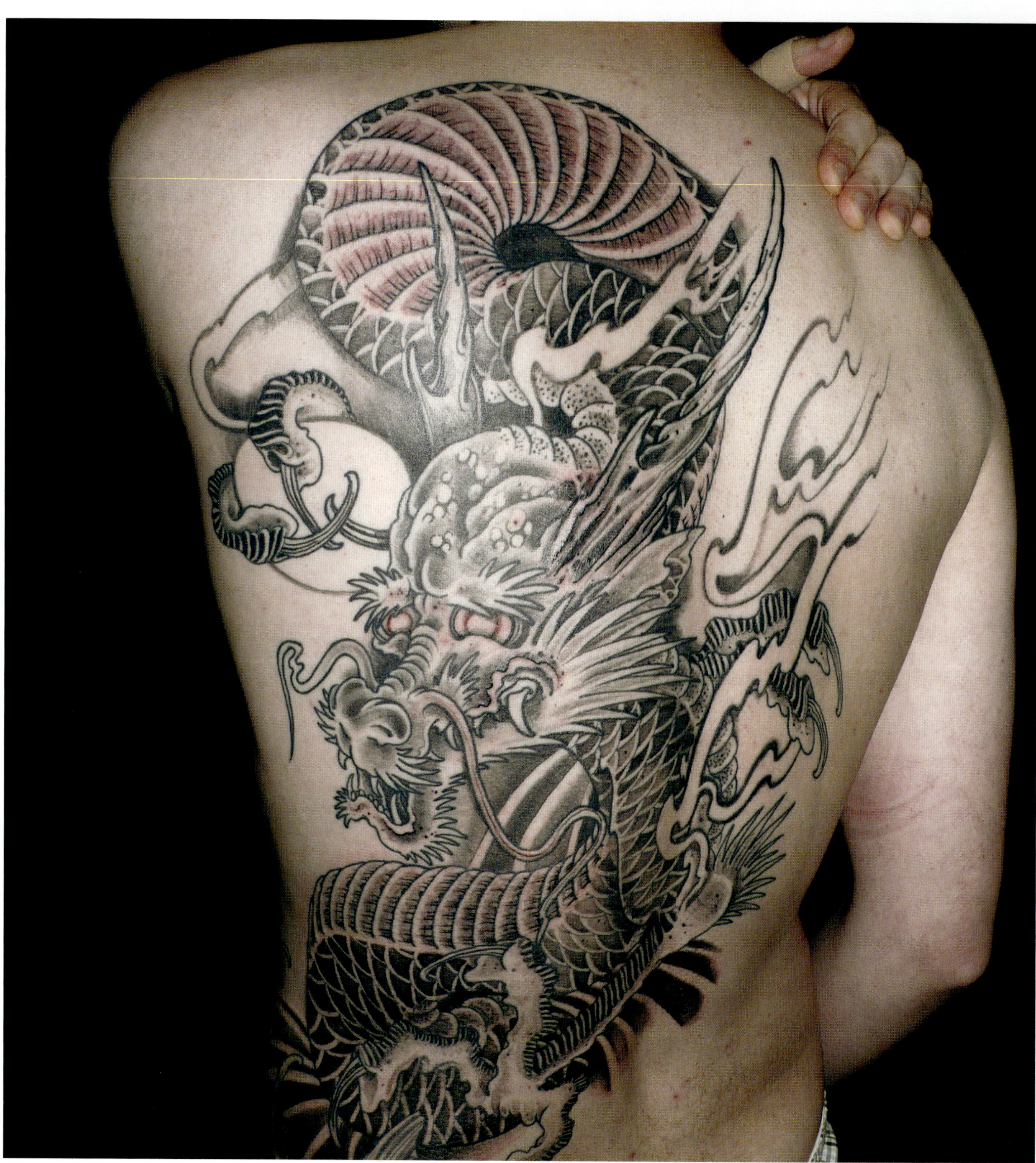

All designs on these pages by Harai Tattoo.

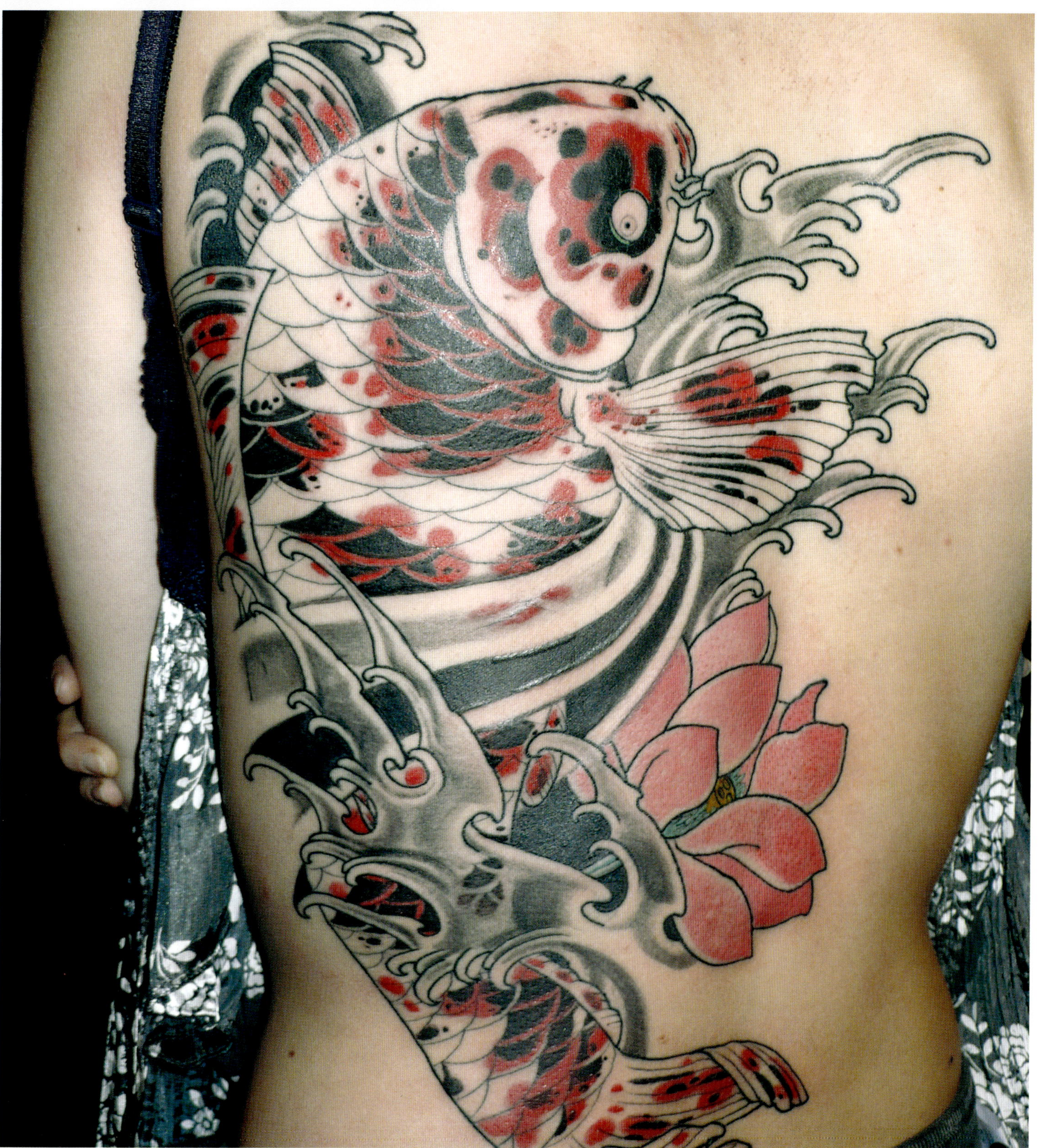

HARAI TATTOO

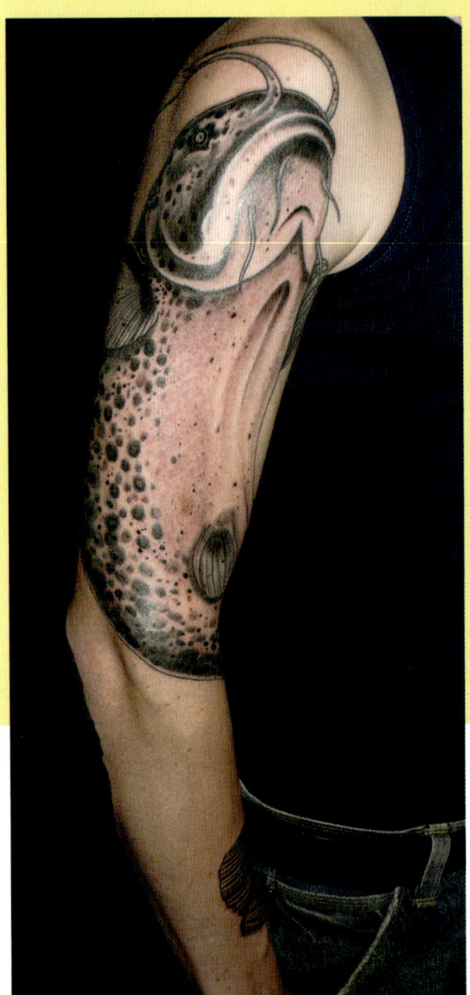

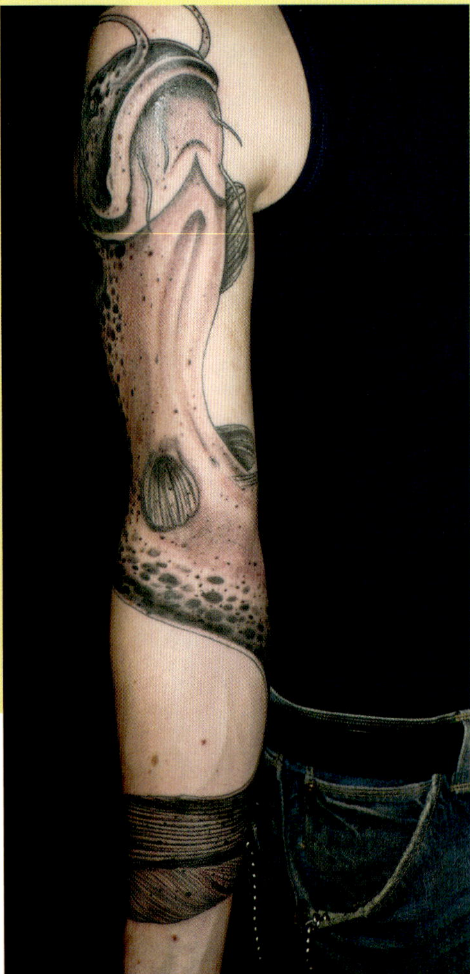

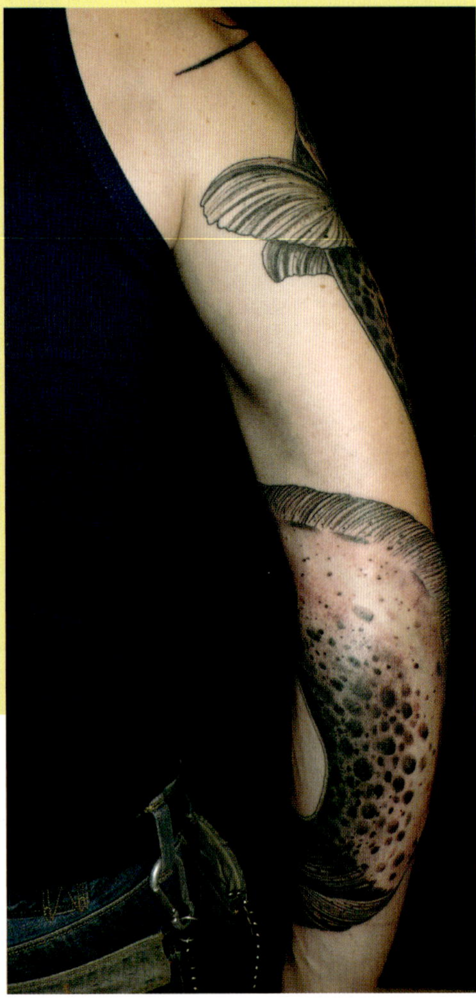

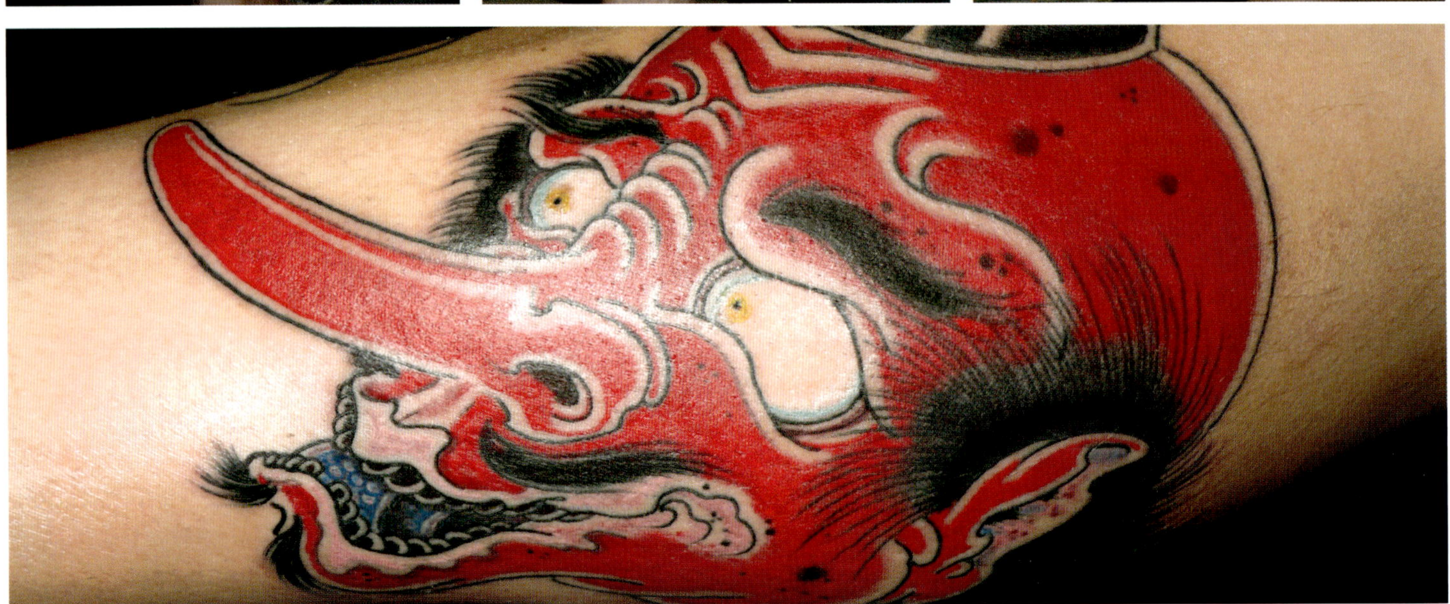

All artwork by Harai Tattoo.

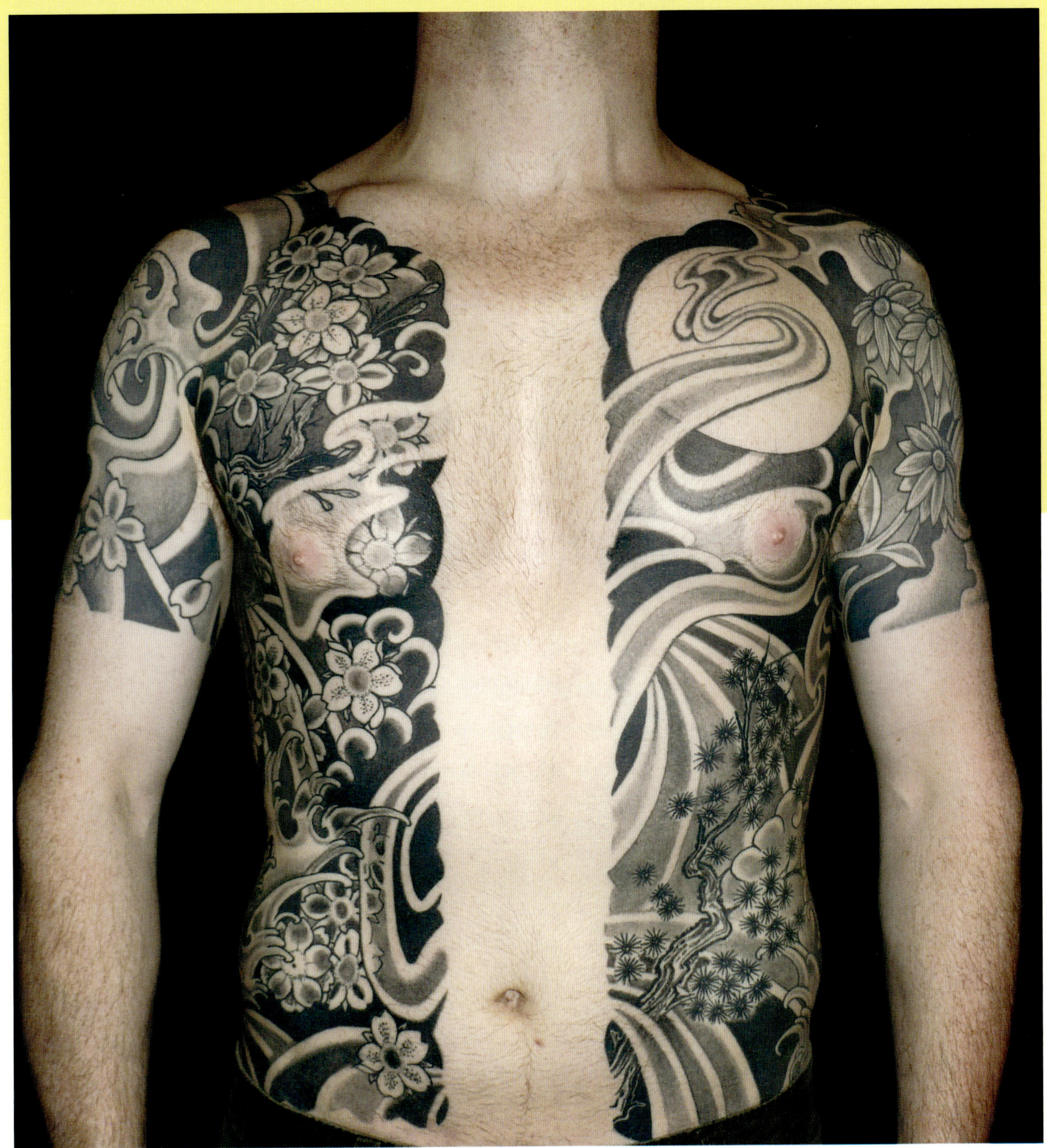

HARAI TATTOO

BOB TYRRELL

USA

1. I started tattooing in 1997, when I was 34 years old. Better late than never! I was getting heavily tattooed and finally decided it was time to start tattooing. I got an apprenticeship at Eternal Tattoos in Detroit. Tramp, the owner of Eternal, brought me in and taught me, along with Tom Renshaw, Jay Wheeler, and everyone else in the shop. Tom took me under his wing and taught me more than anyone in the business, and I'll be forever grateful to all of them. My apprenticeship lasted three months.

2. I love tattoos. They just look cool! Tattoos can have a very special meaning to a lot of people. All the horror stuff I have tattooed on me doesn't have too much meaning, I'm just a horror fan and love creepy art. They're very special tattoos and I love them—they're a part of me! I have some of my guitar heroes tattooed on me; they do have meaning.

3. I specialize in black-and-gray, photo realism and custom horror imagery.

4. It's best to seek out a good shop and get a proper apprenticeship with good artists. The fastest way to learn things is the right way.

5. I'm a little hard to find sometimes because I'm always on the road! The easiest way is to check my myspace page; it has most of my travel schedule on there. You can e-mail me to set up appointments in Detroit or on the road.
www.bobtyrrell.com

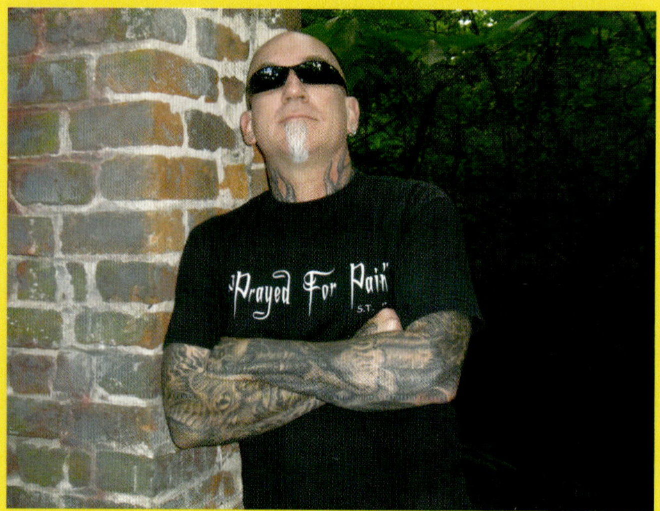

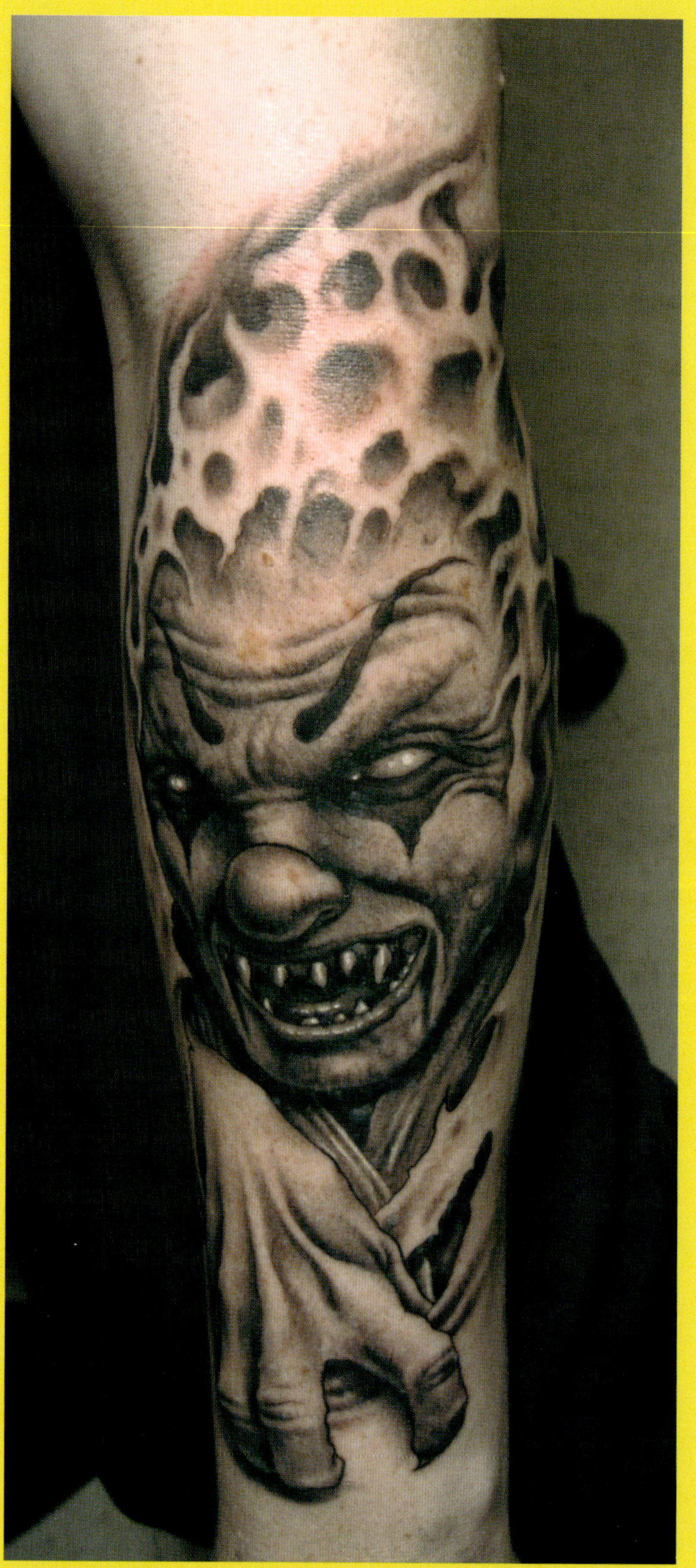

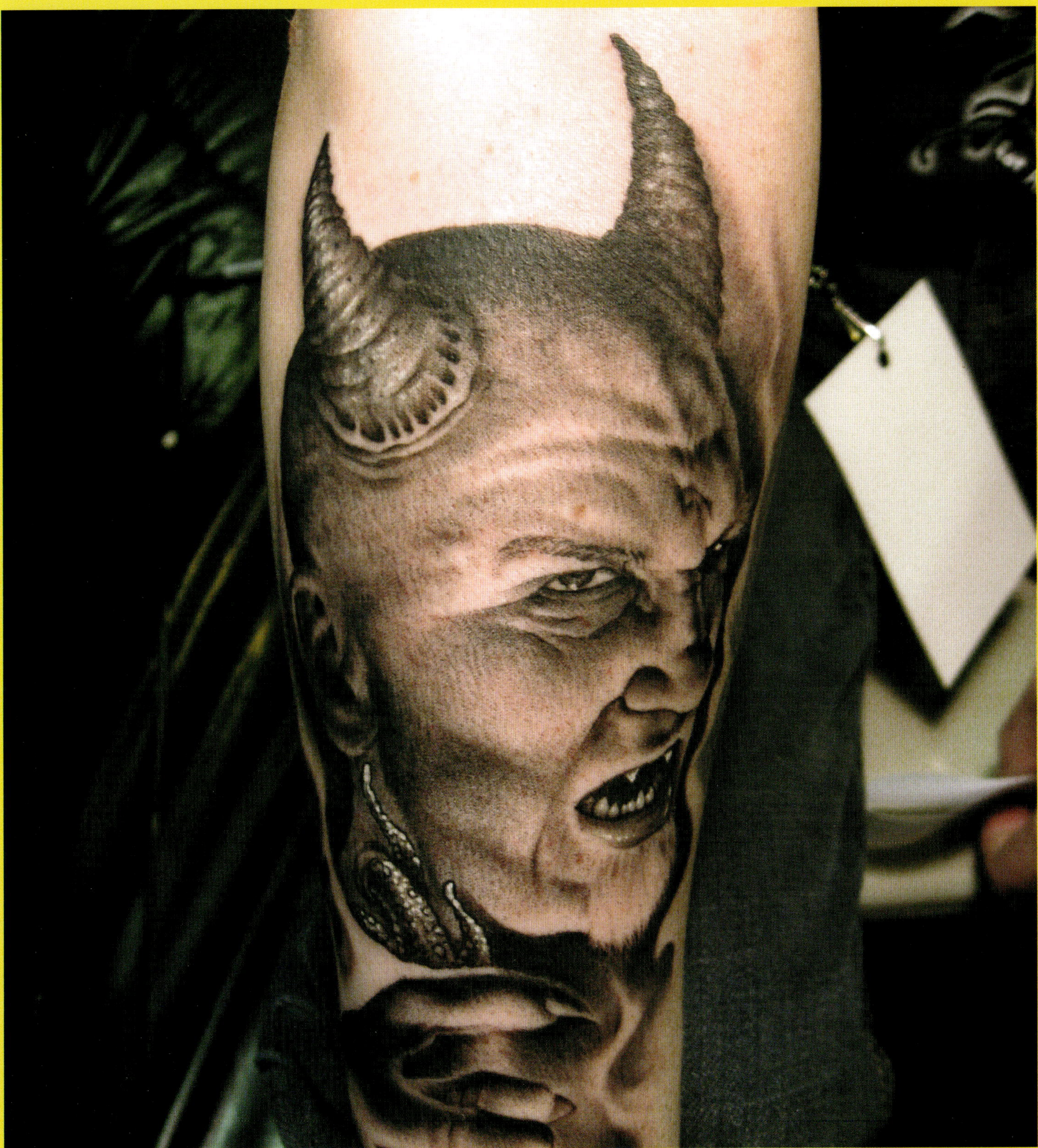

Images courtesy of Bob Tyrrell.

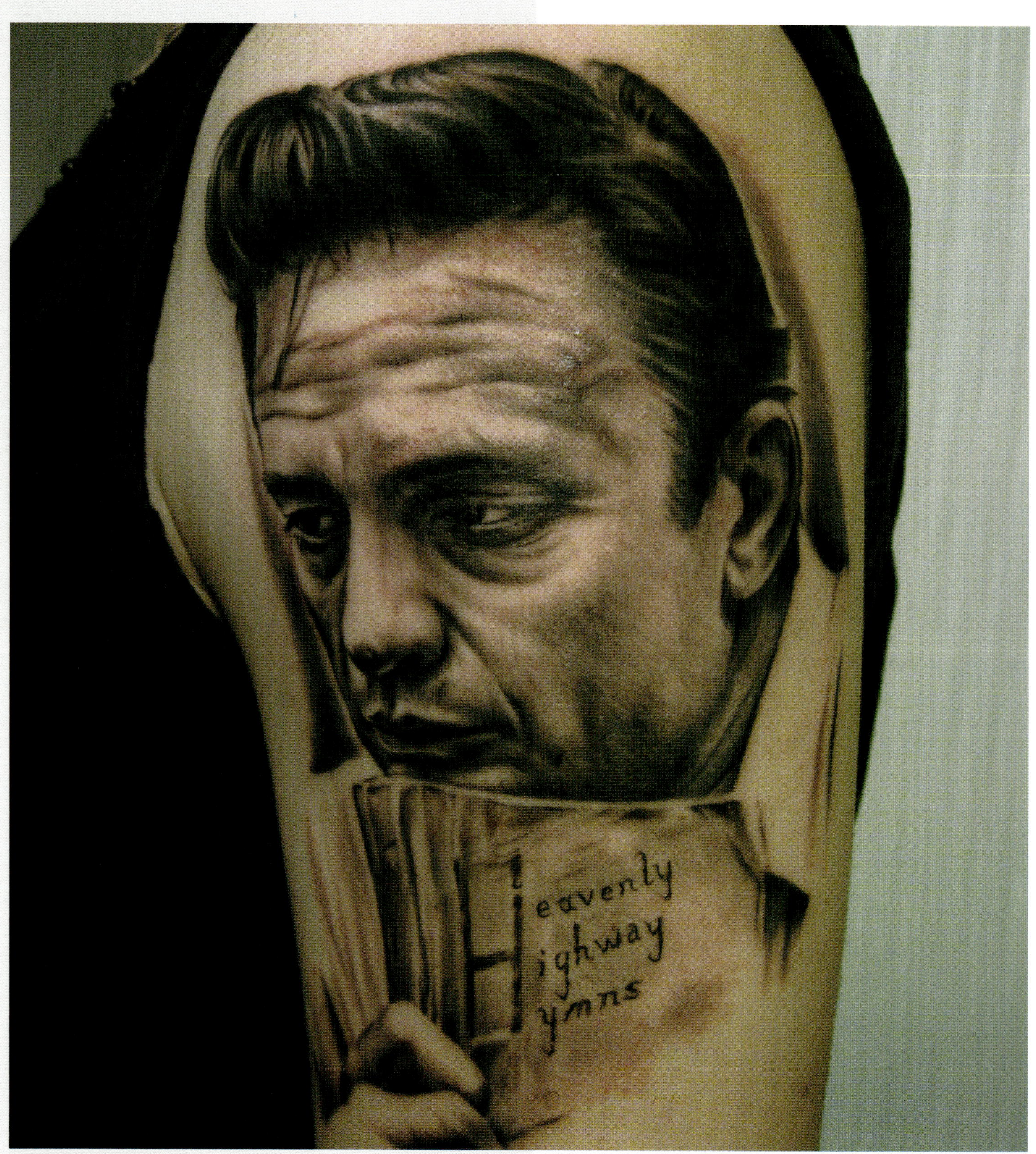

All designs on these pages by Bob Tyrrell.

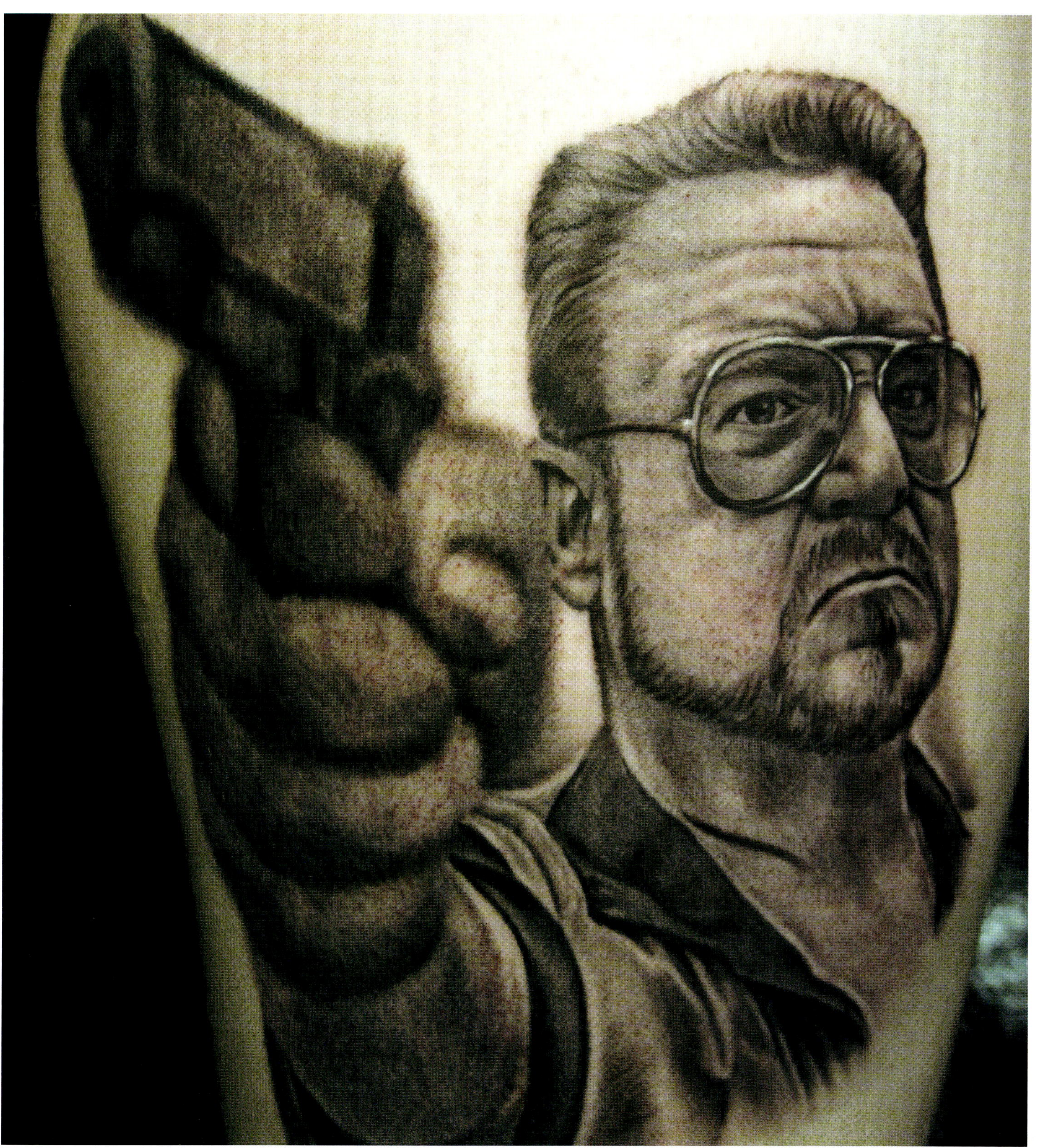

BOB TYRRELL

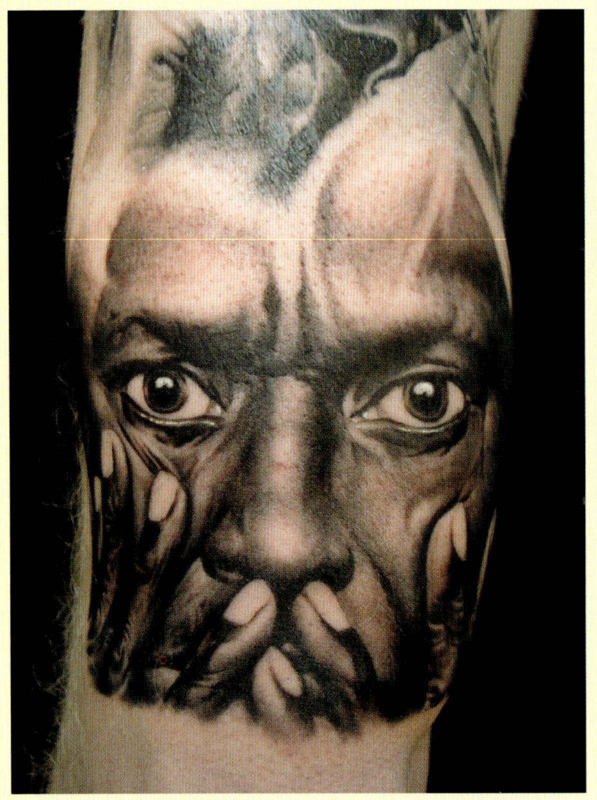
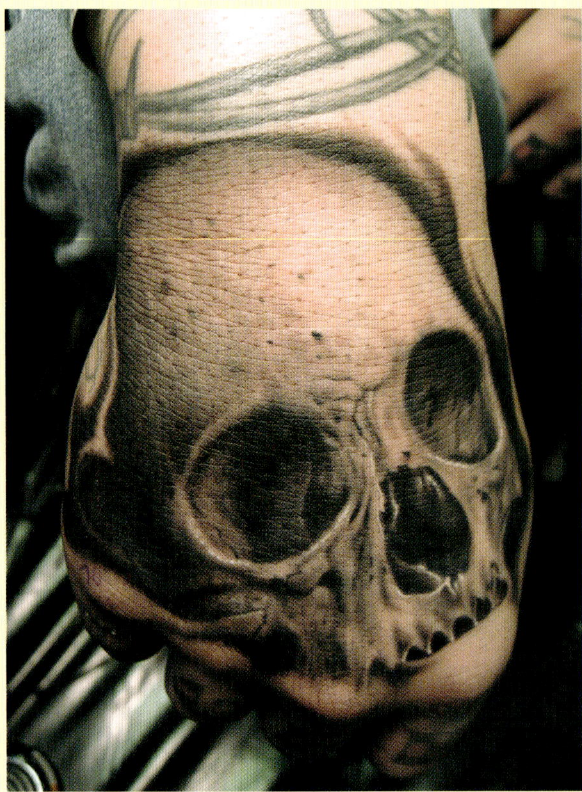
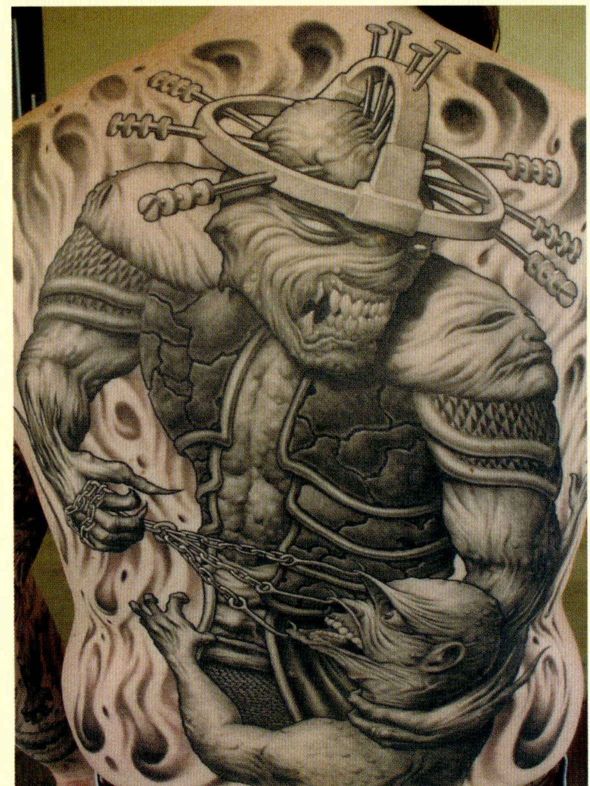
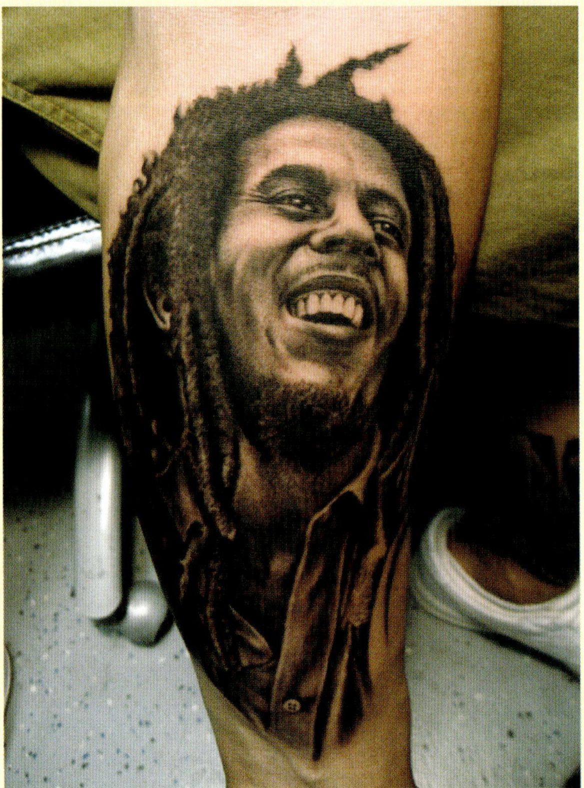

All artwork by Bob Tyrrell.

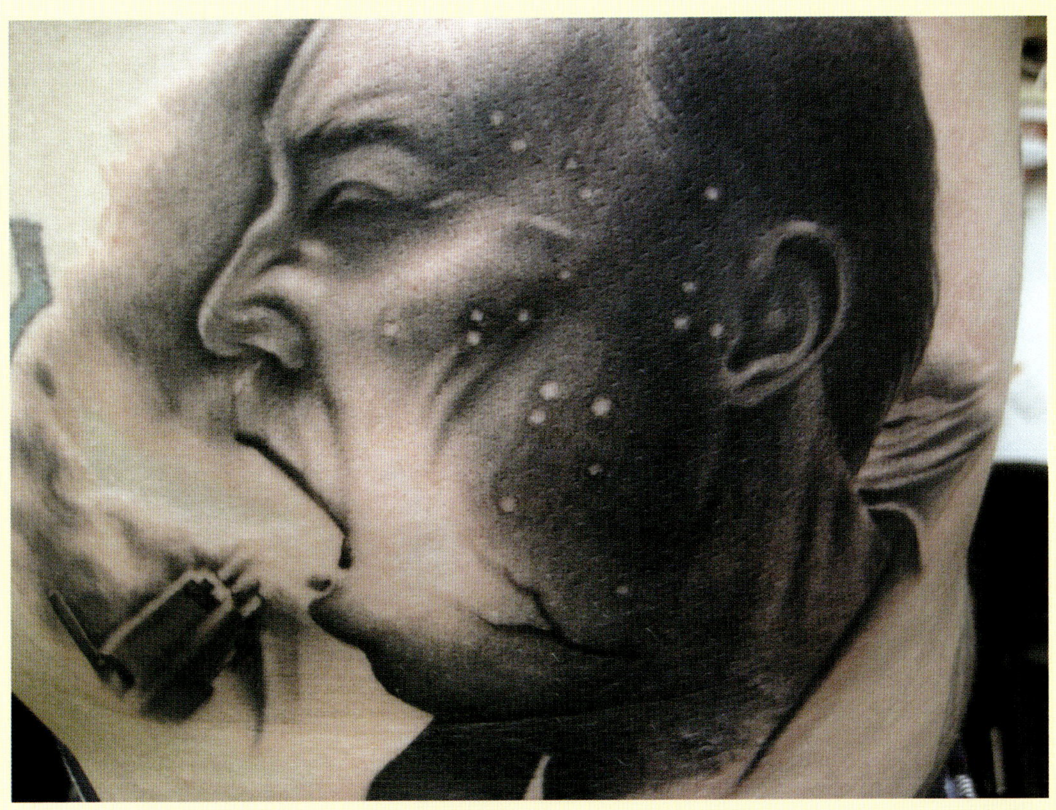

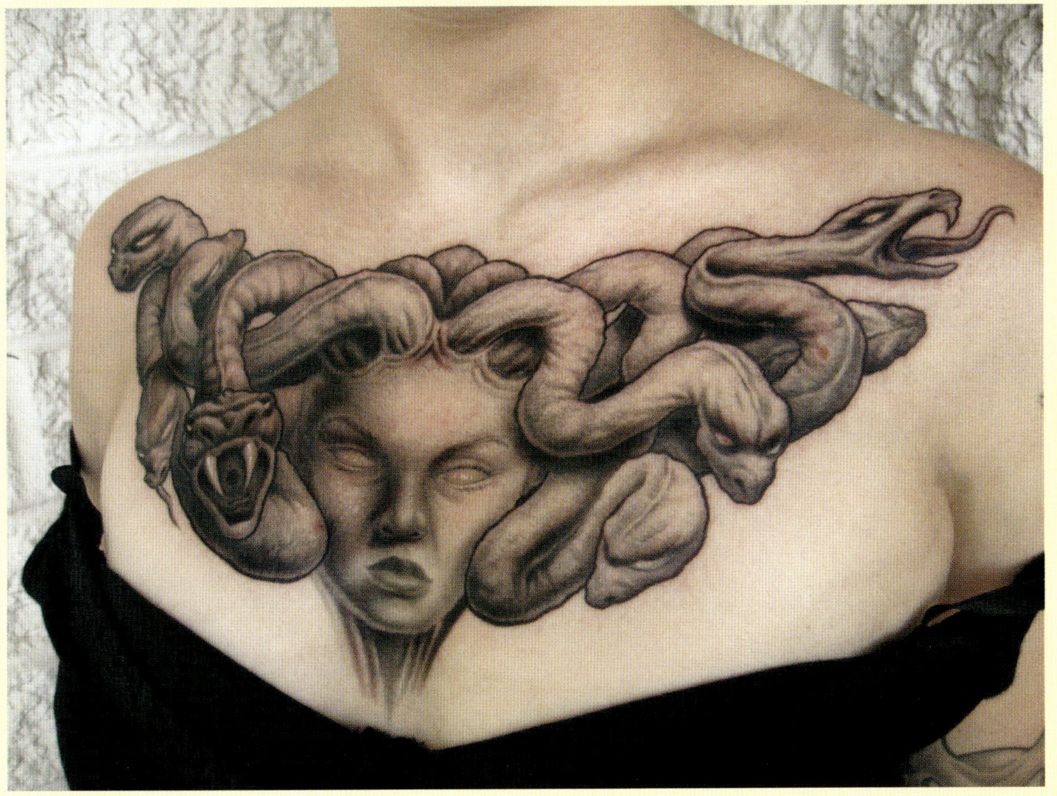

BOB TYRRELL

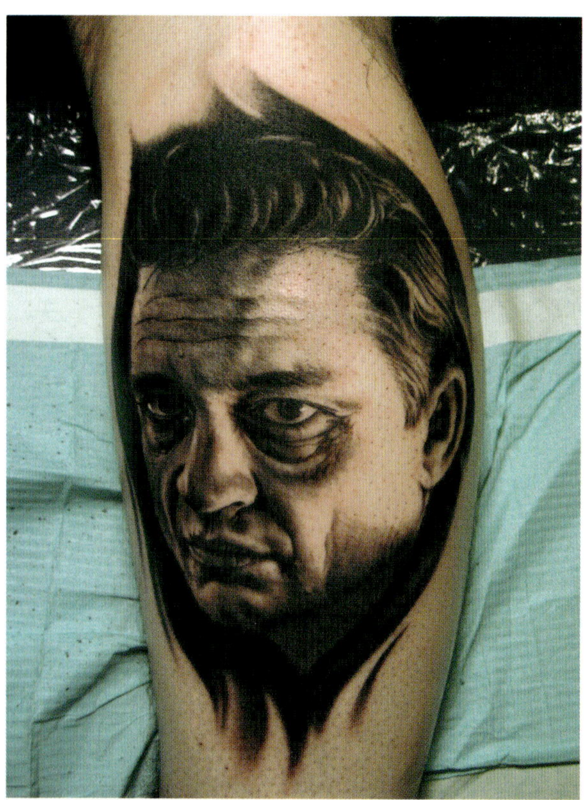

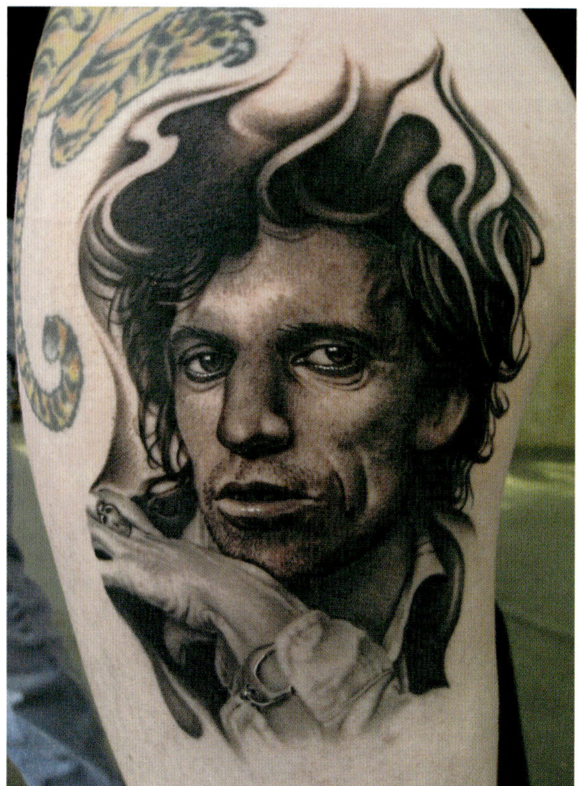

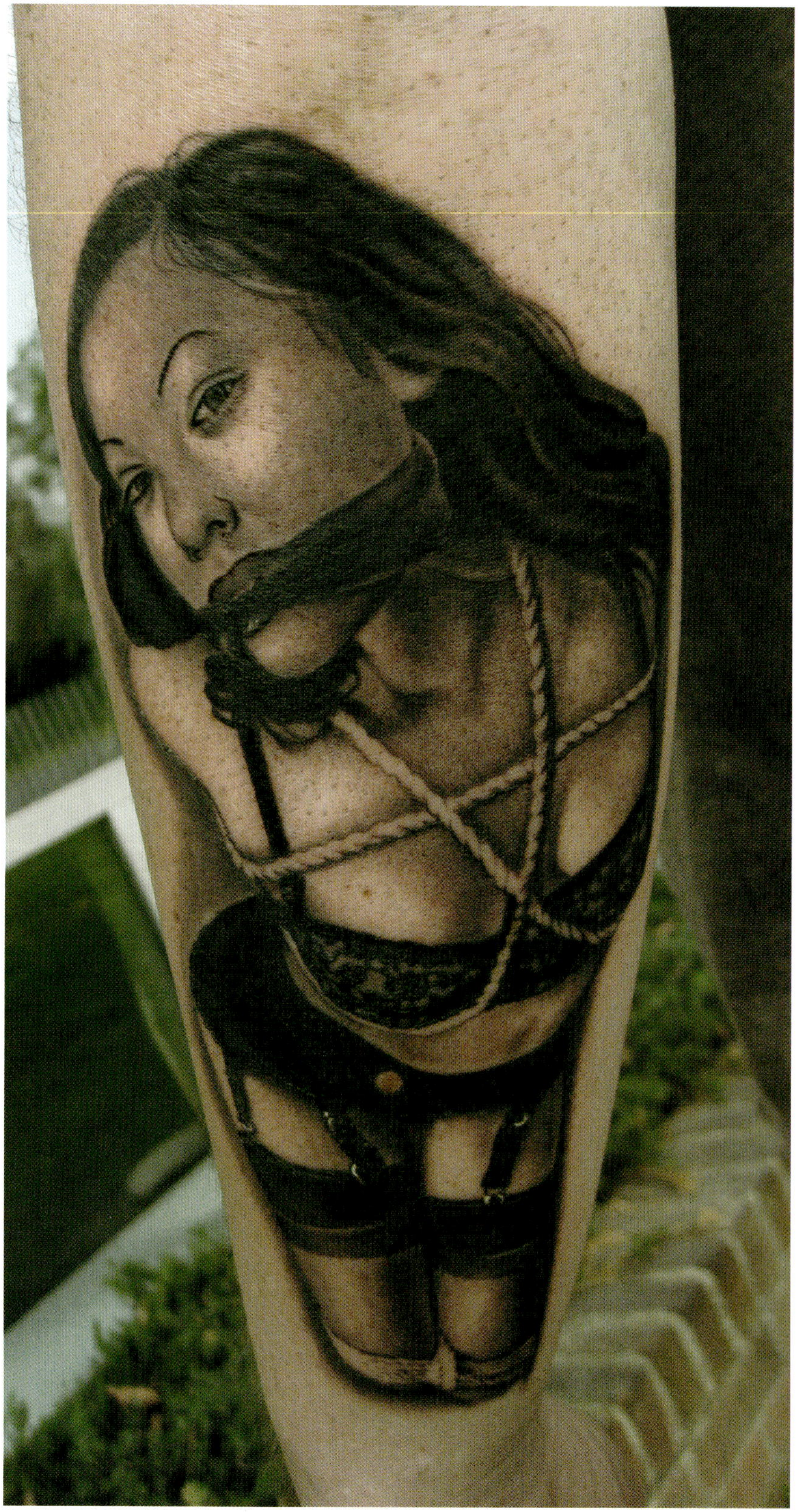

All designs on these pages by Bob Tyrrell.

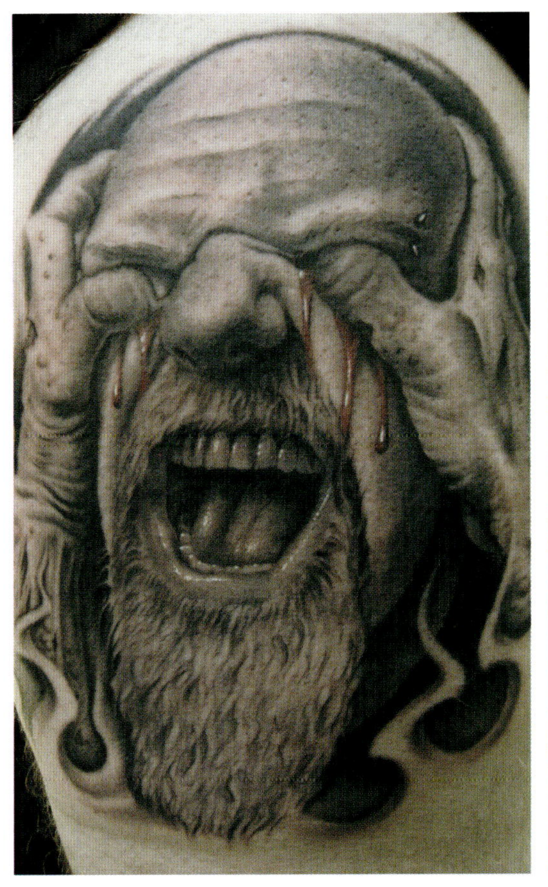

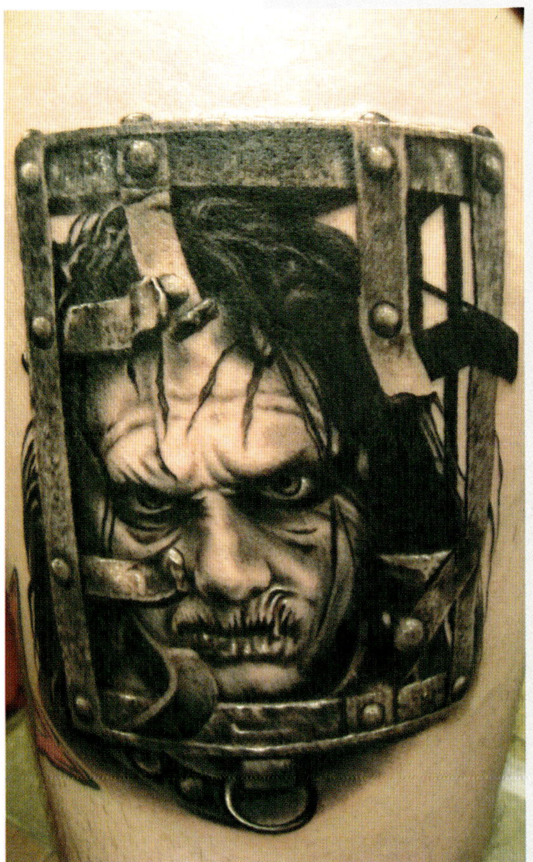

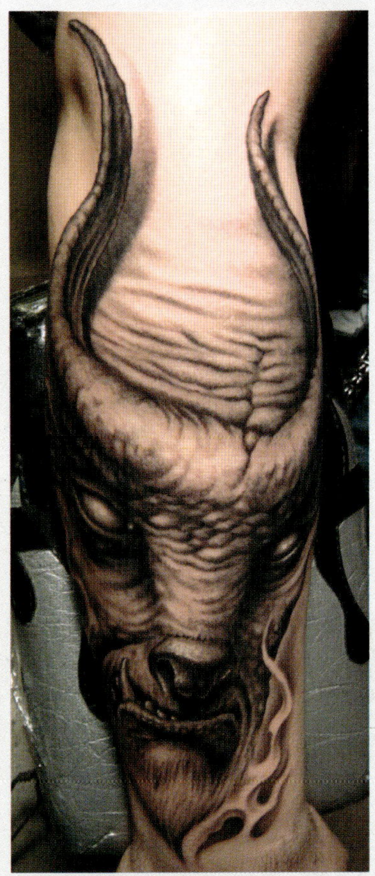

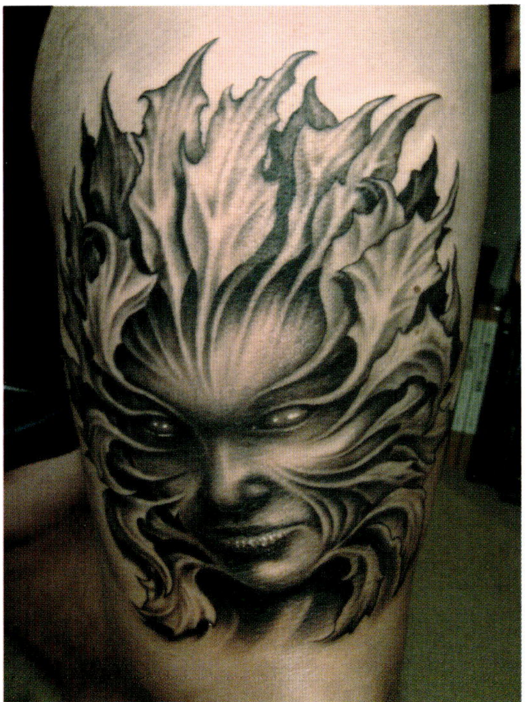

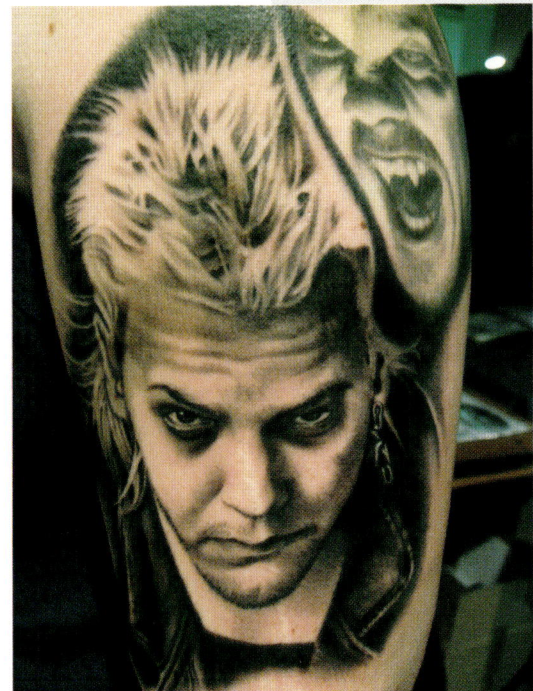

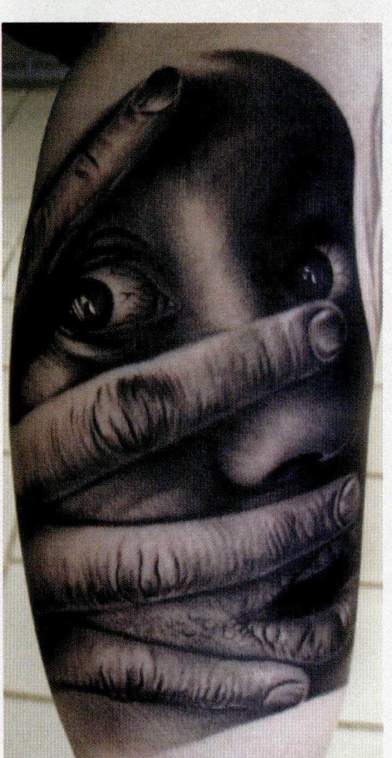

BOB TYRRELL

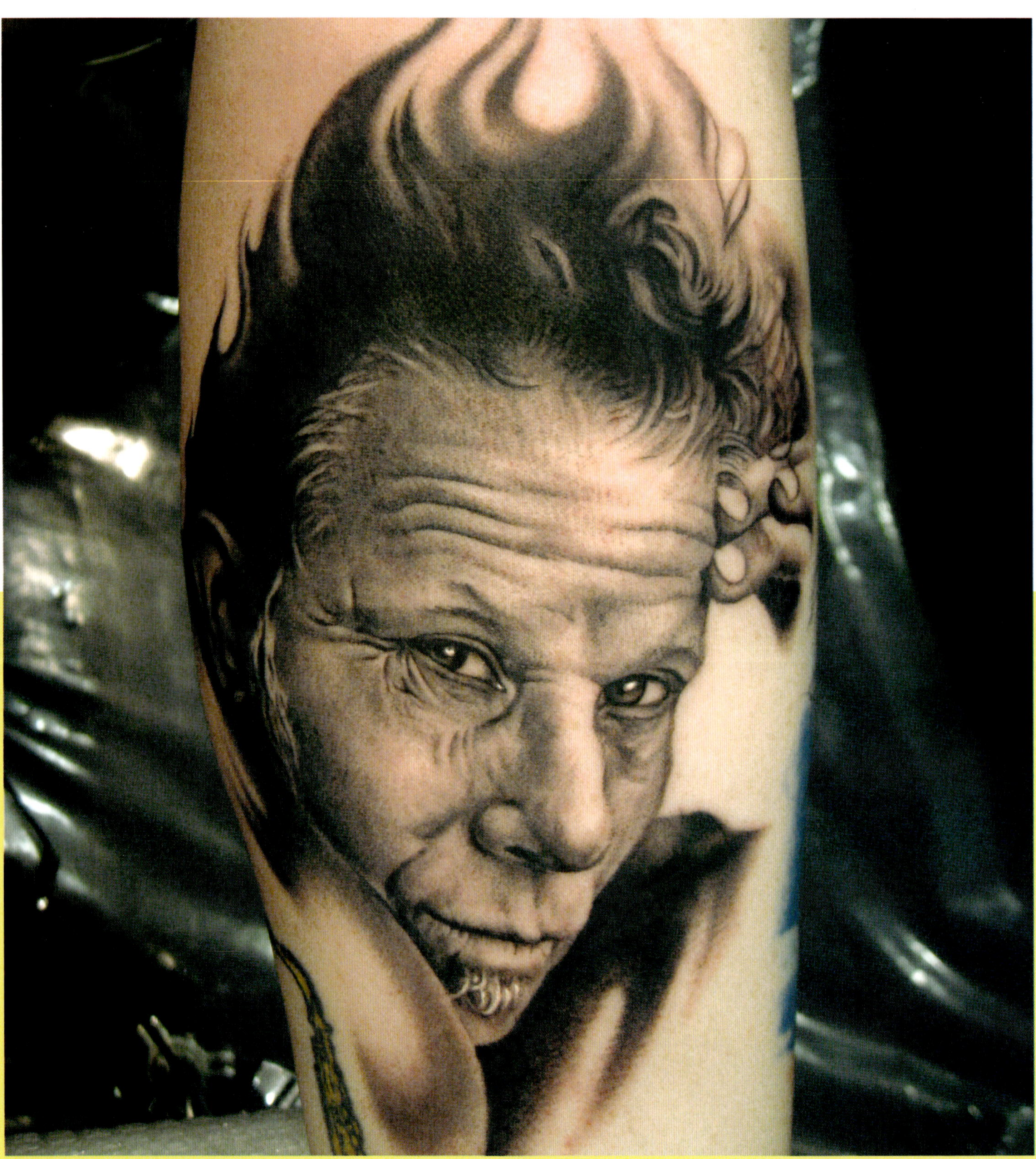

Images courtesy of Bob Tyrrell.

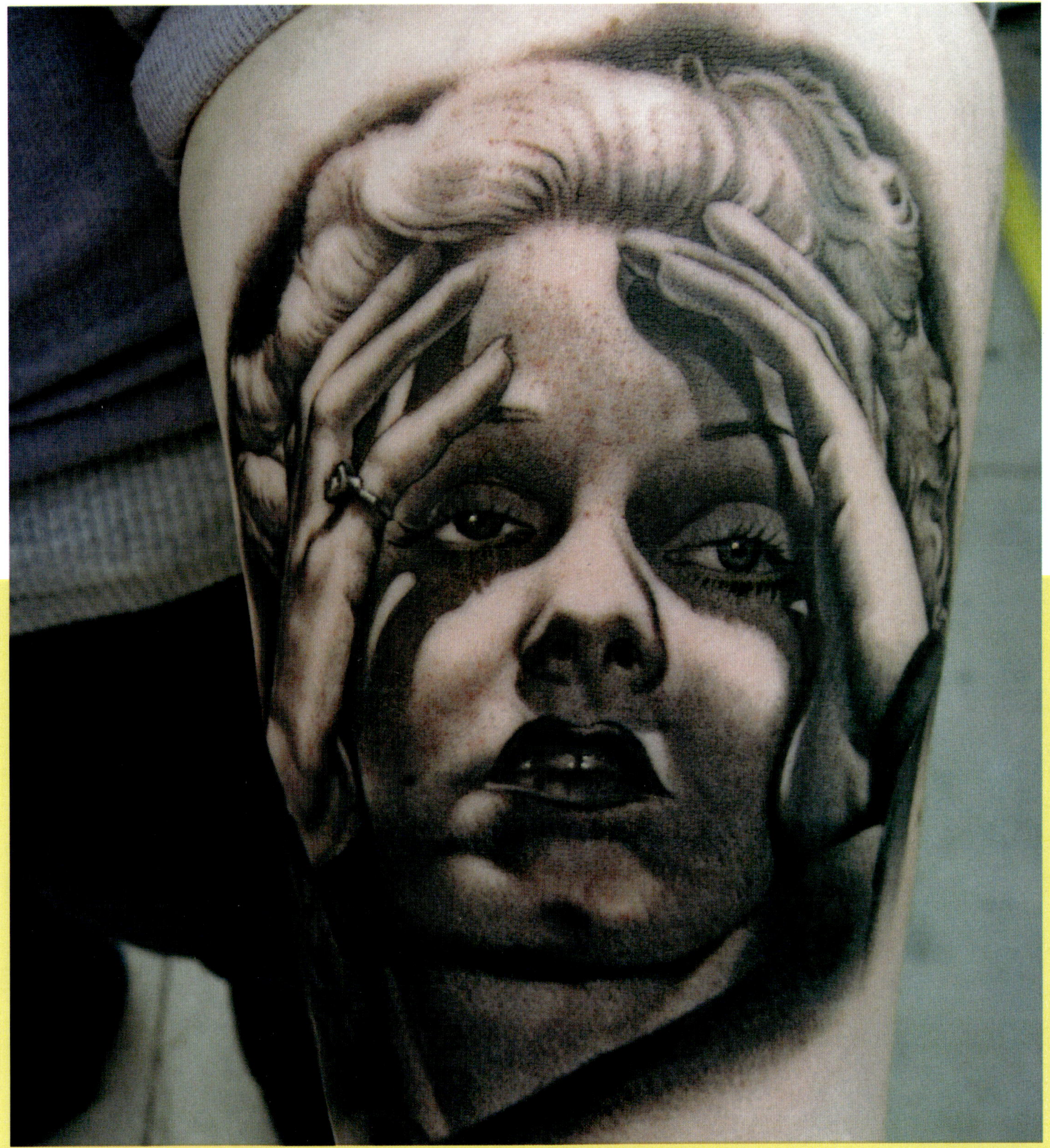

BOB TYRRELL

OUTER LIMITS

USA

1. I began tattooing at the age of 19. A friend and tattoo artist had seen some art work I had done and thought that it would transfer well to tattooing, so he said I should try it.

2. The expression of oneself.

3. I do several styles: portraits, realism, Asian, American, painterly, large body work.

4. Find something that is you. Make sure you research your artist, that he or she does that style, and that he or she has a clean work ethic.

5. I work at and own Outer Limits Tattoo and Piercing LLC, 22 Chestnut Pl., Long Beach, California, USA.
   www.outerlimitstattoo.com
   kari@outerlimitstattoo.com
   We also have studios in Orange, Anaheim and Costa Mesa, California, USA.

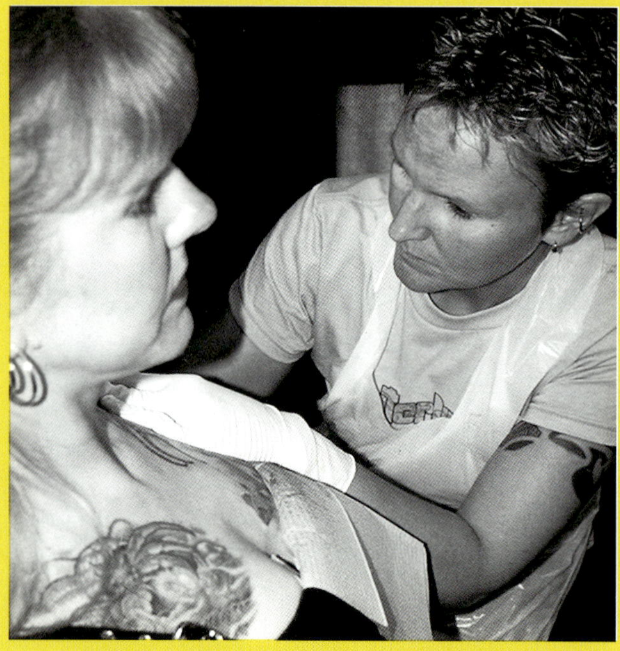

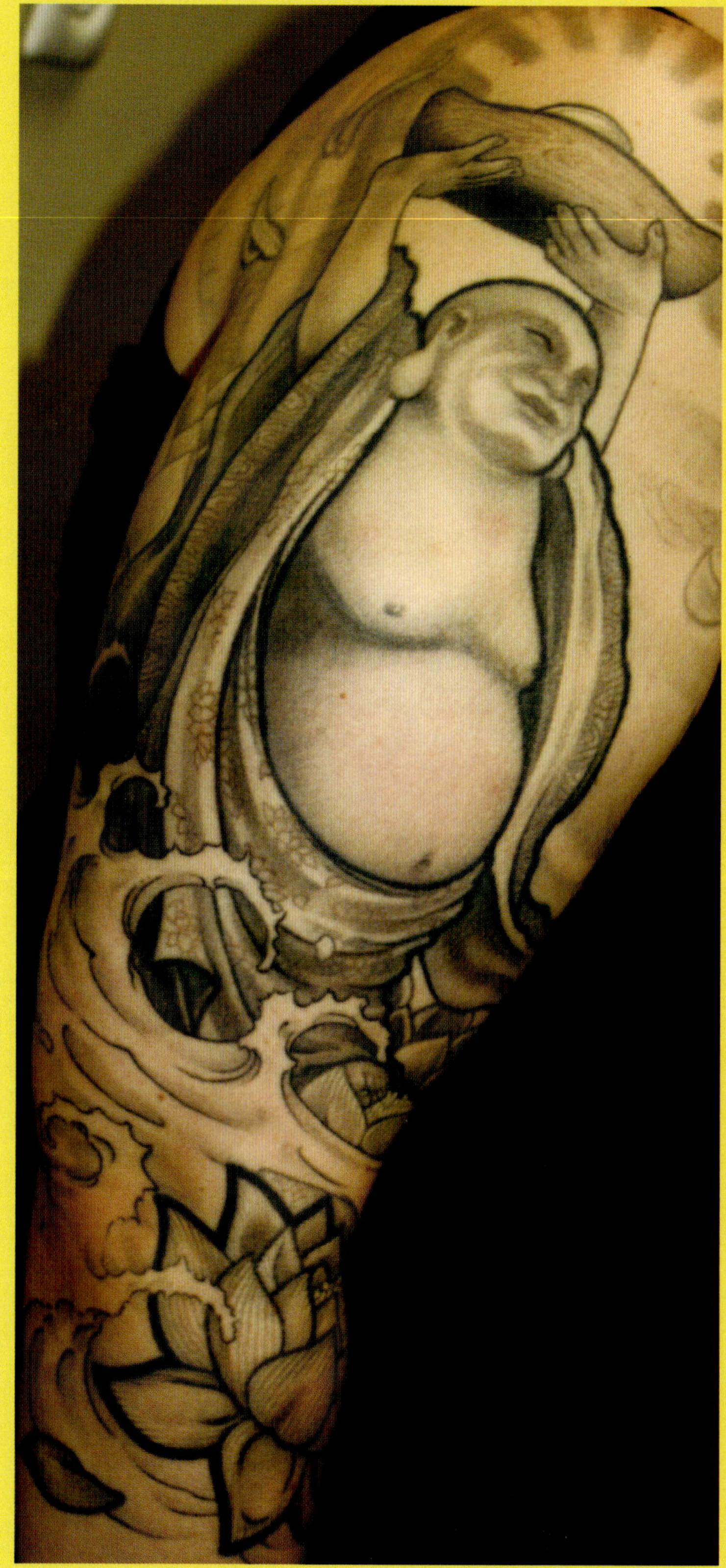

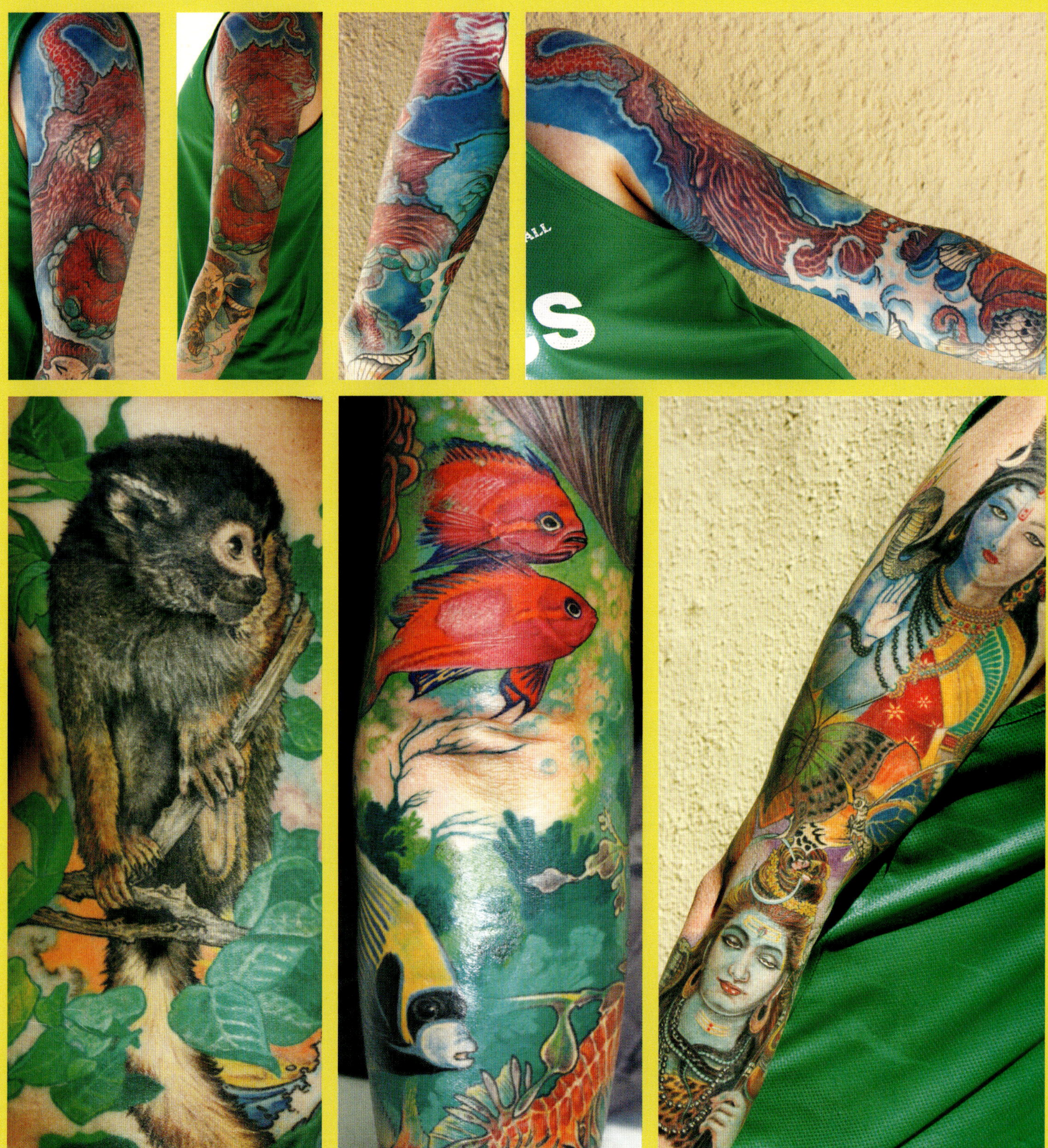

Images courtesy of Outer Limits.

XXX TATTOO

SWITZERLAND

1. I began in my house during the last year of school. I wasn't happy with what I was studying and found tattooing fascinating. Without any information, I just bought some equipment and started teaching myself.

2. Tattoos are self-expression, the right of ownership of your body, and decoration. They symbolize changes in your life and important moments.

3. I tattoo in an illustrative style mixing American, bio-mech and horror tattoos. I also do Japanese and Balinese tattoo designs.

4. Tattooing is a very difficult discipline. There are many more things to learn than it may seem from a book or magazine. Draw, travel, draw, draw and draw some more.

5. Rob Koss, XXX Tattoo, Zürichstrasse 42, 6004 Lucerne, Switzerland.
   www.xxxtattoo.com

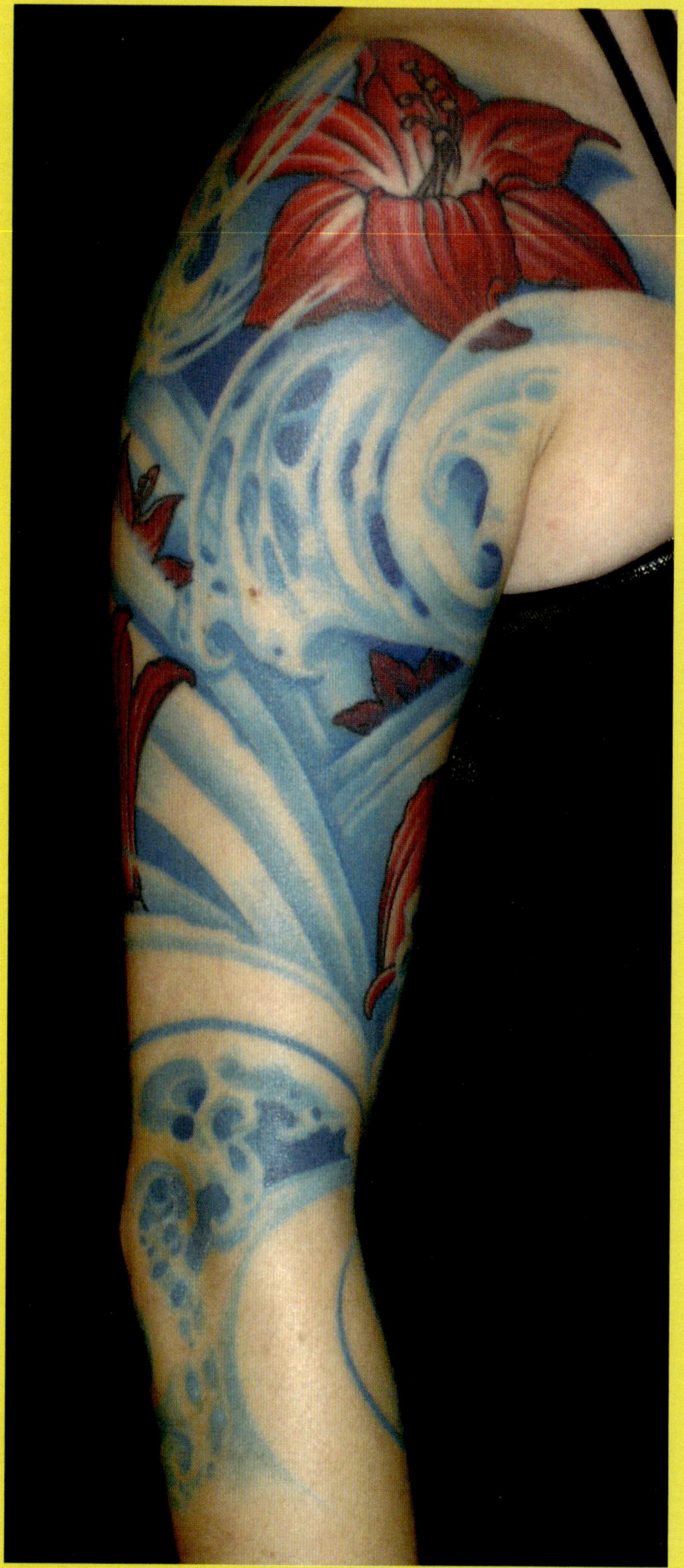

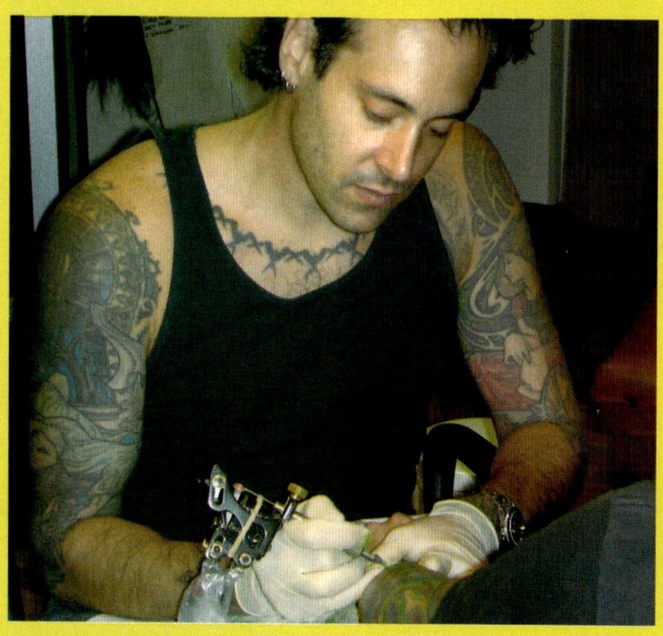

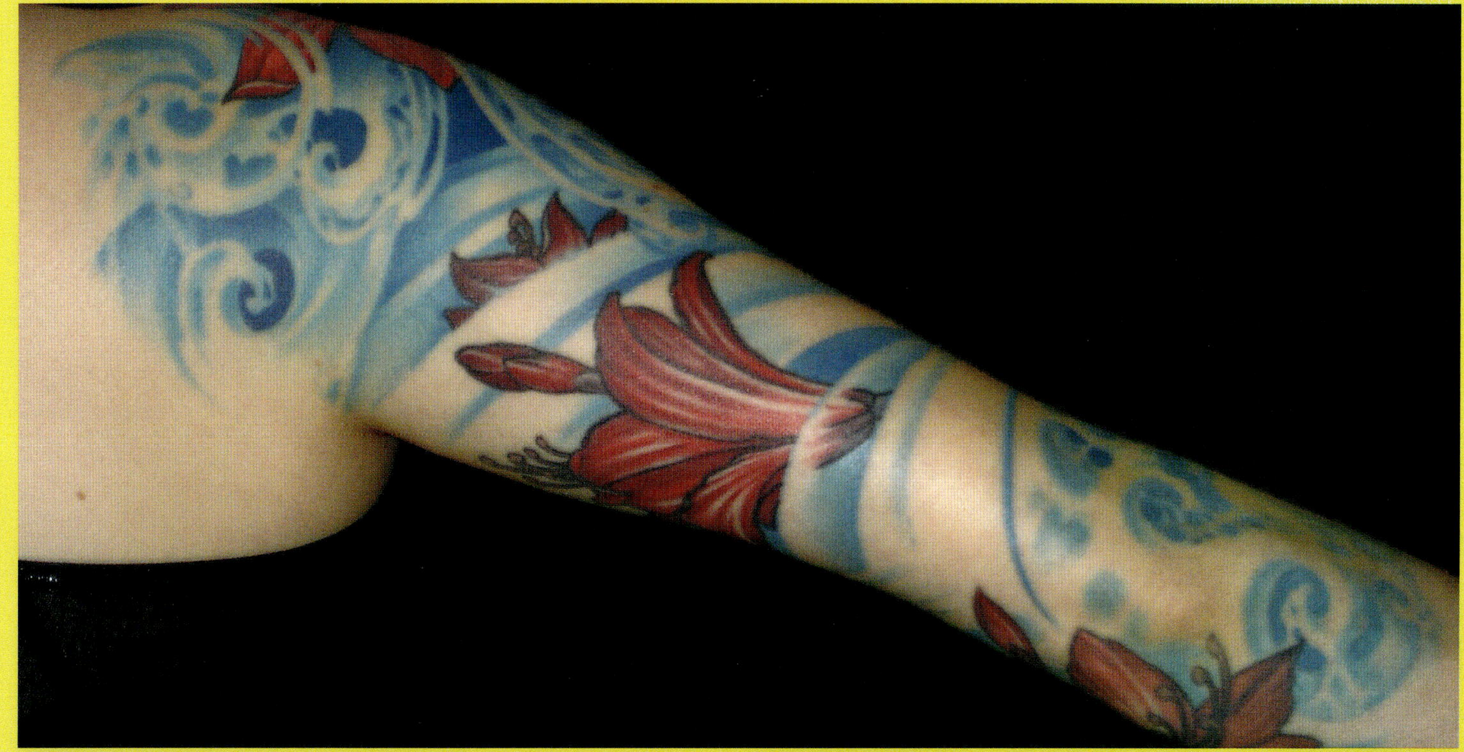

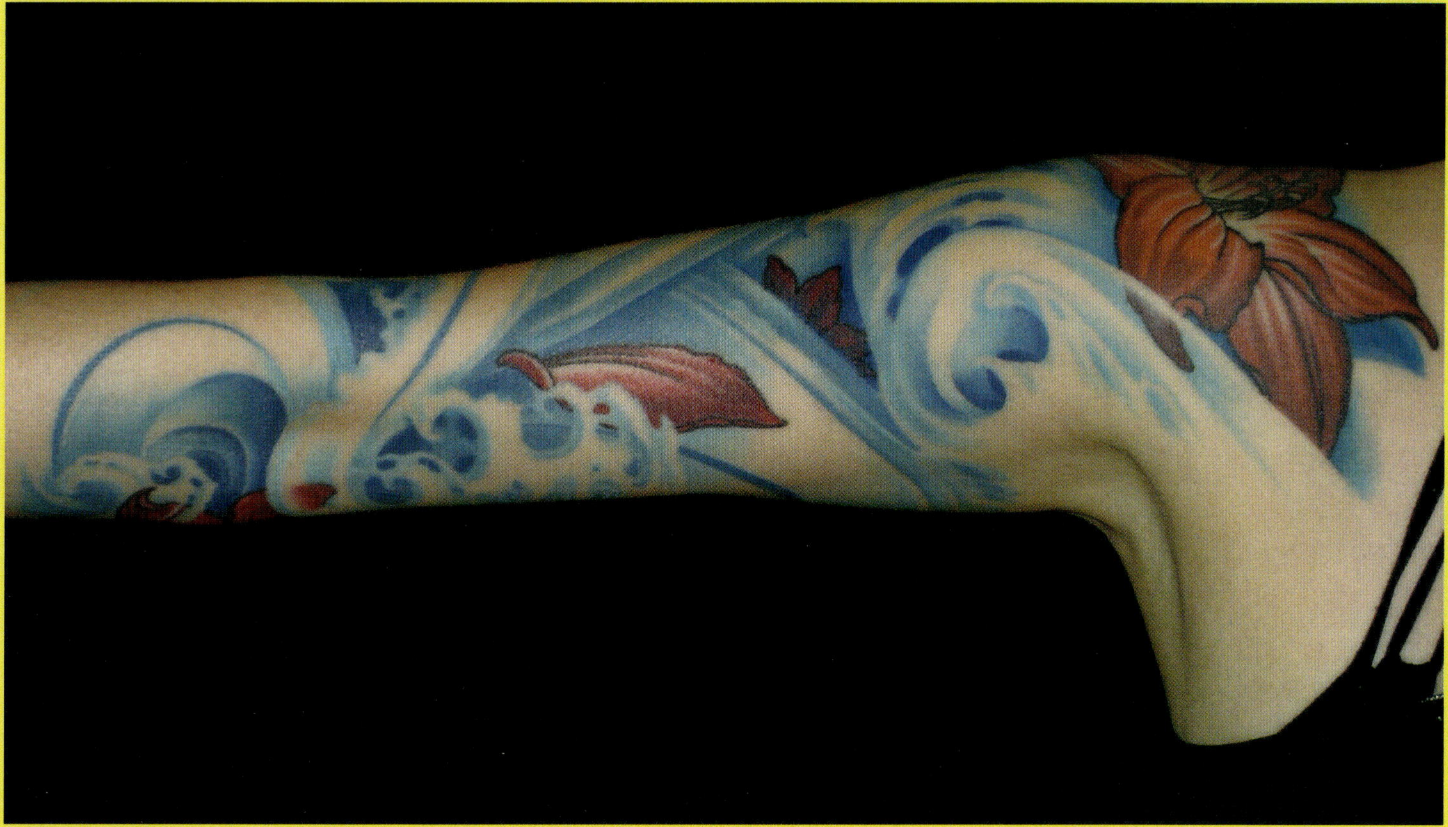

All artwork by XXX Tattoo.

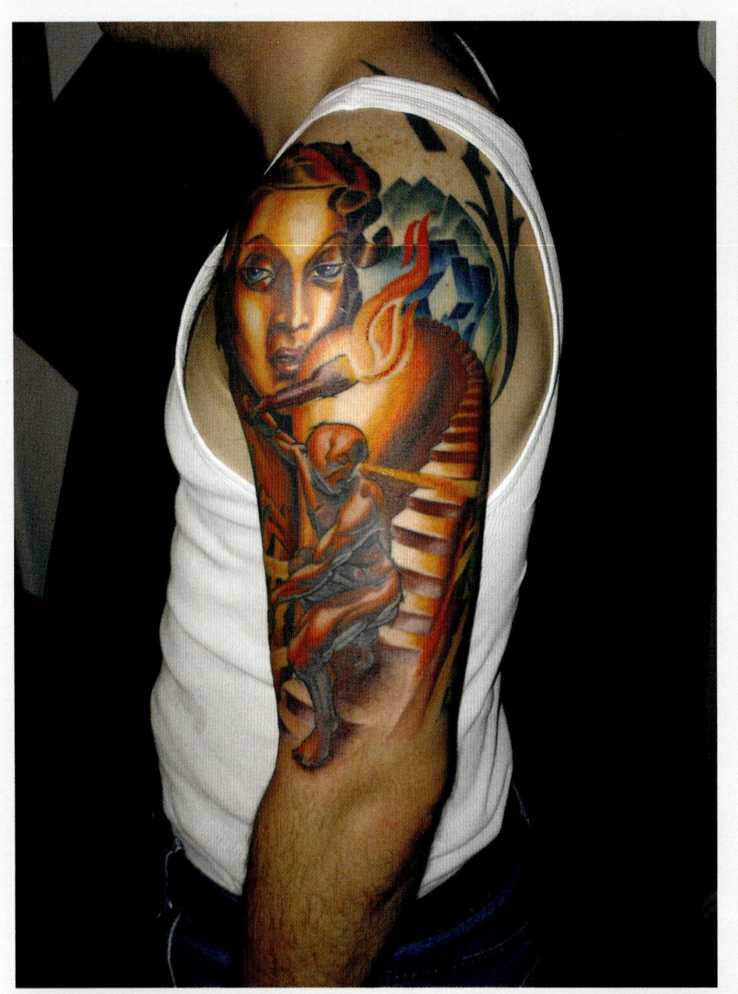

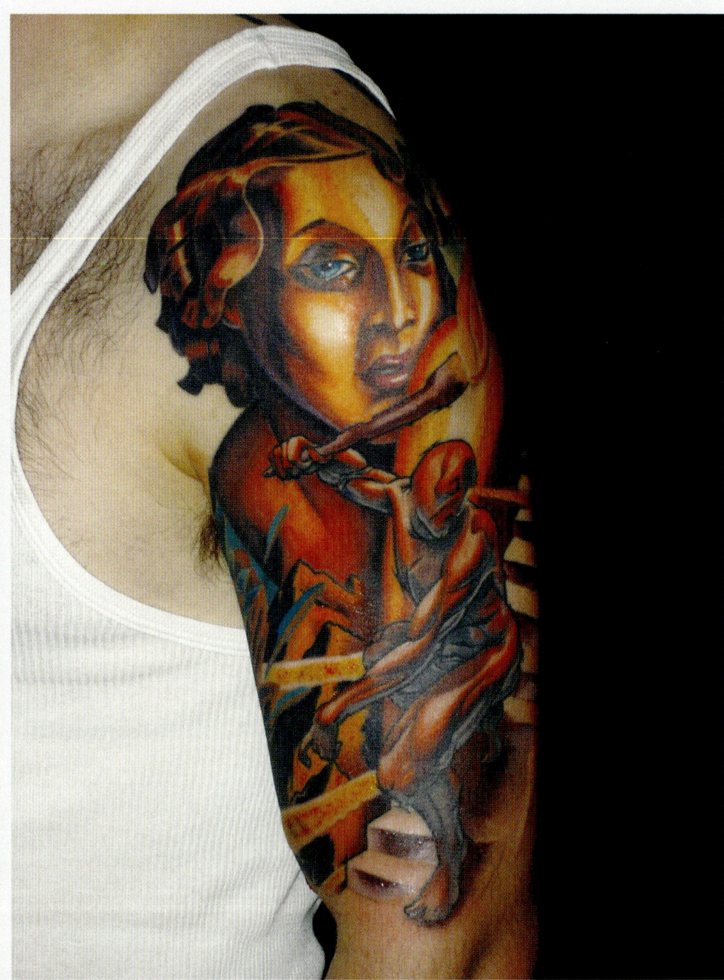

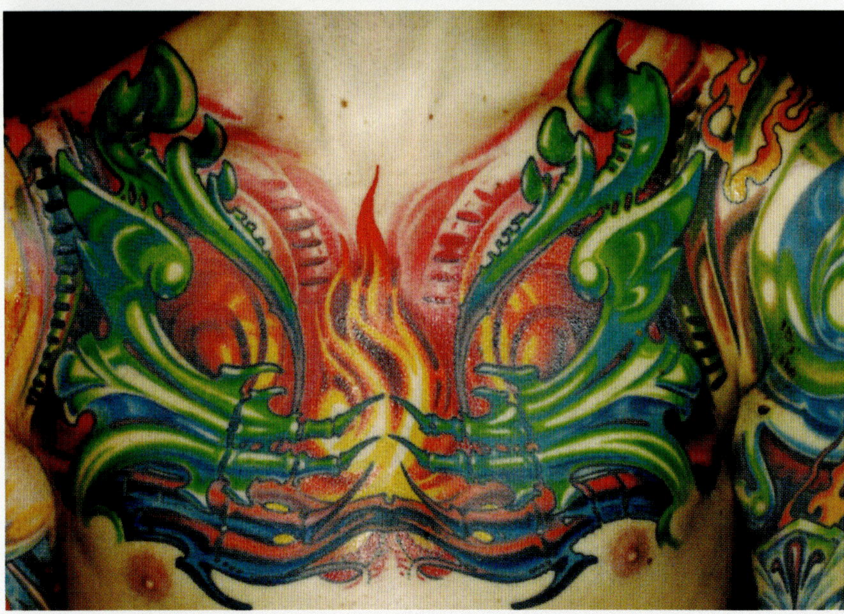

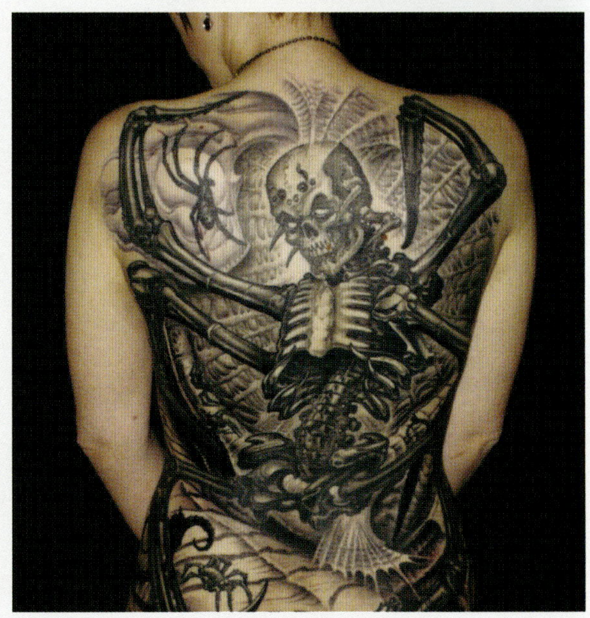

Images courtesy of XXX Tattoo.

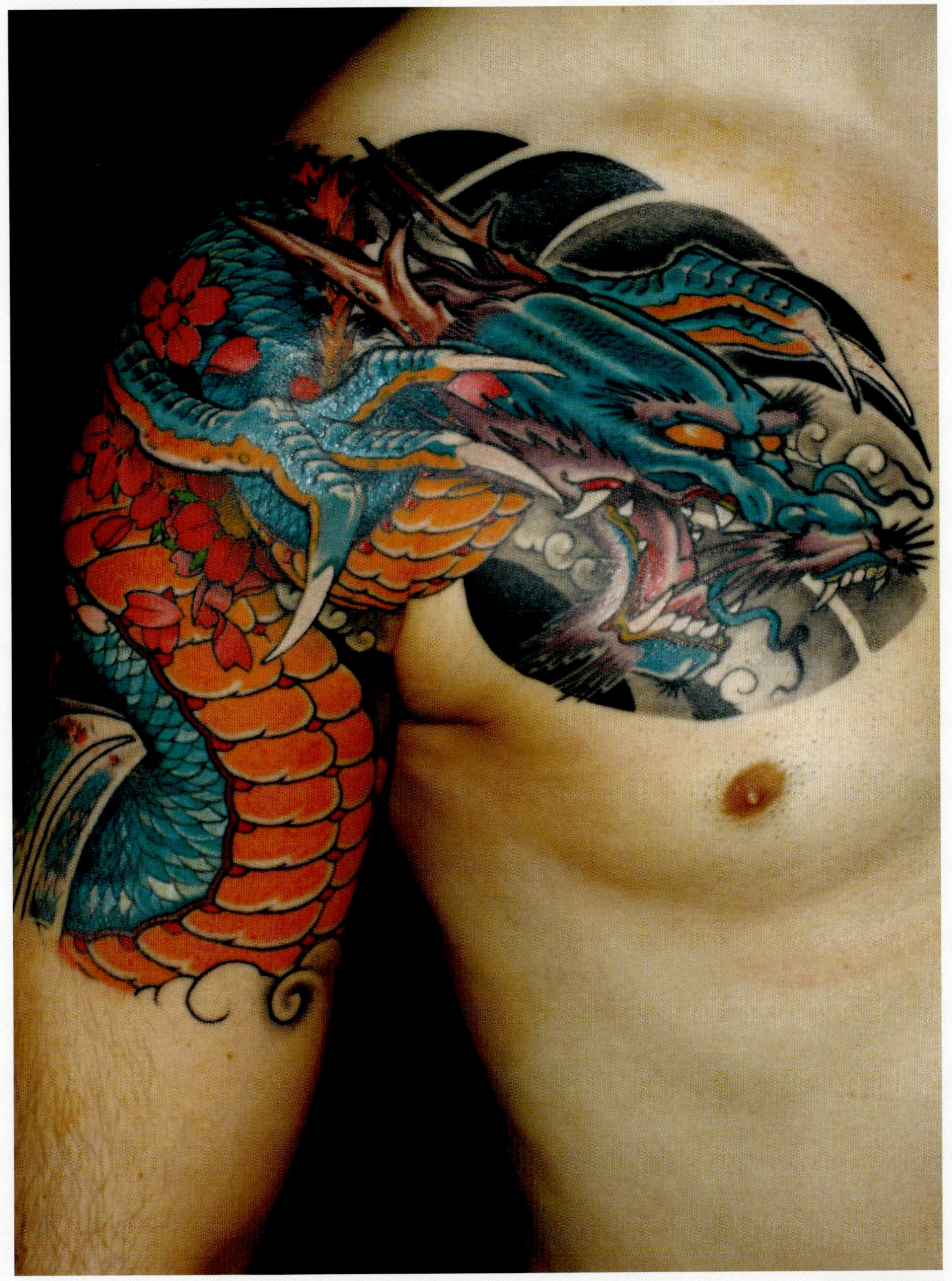

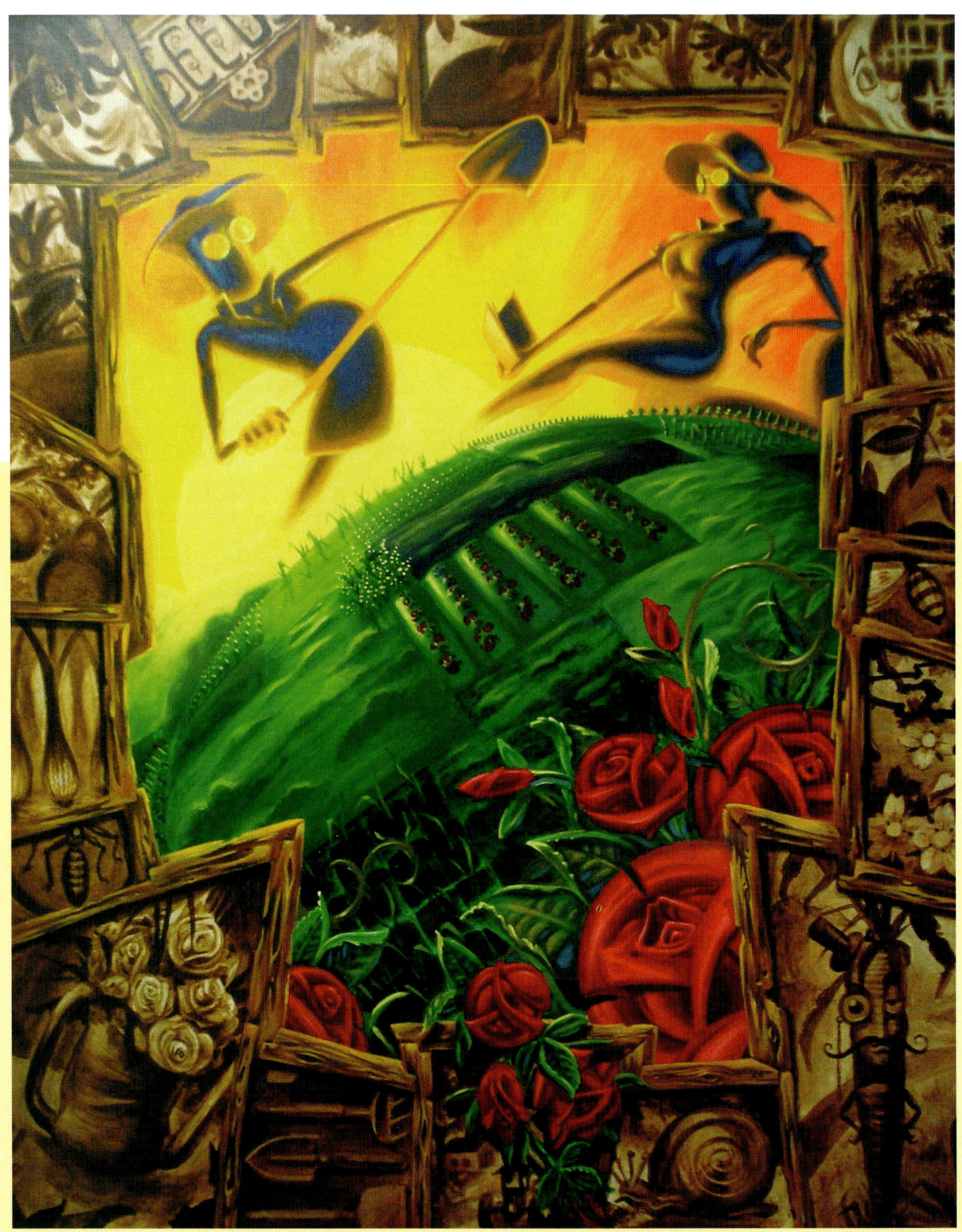

Illustration above and designs at right by XXX Tattoo.

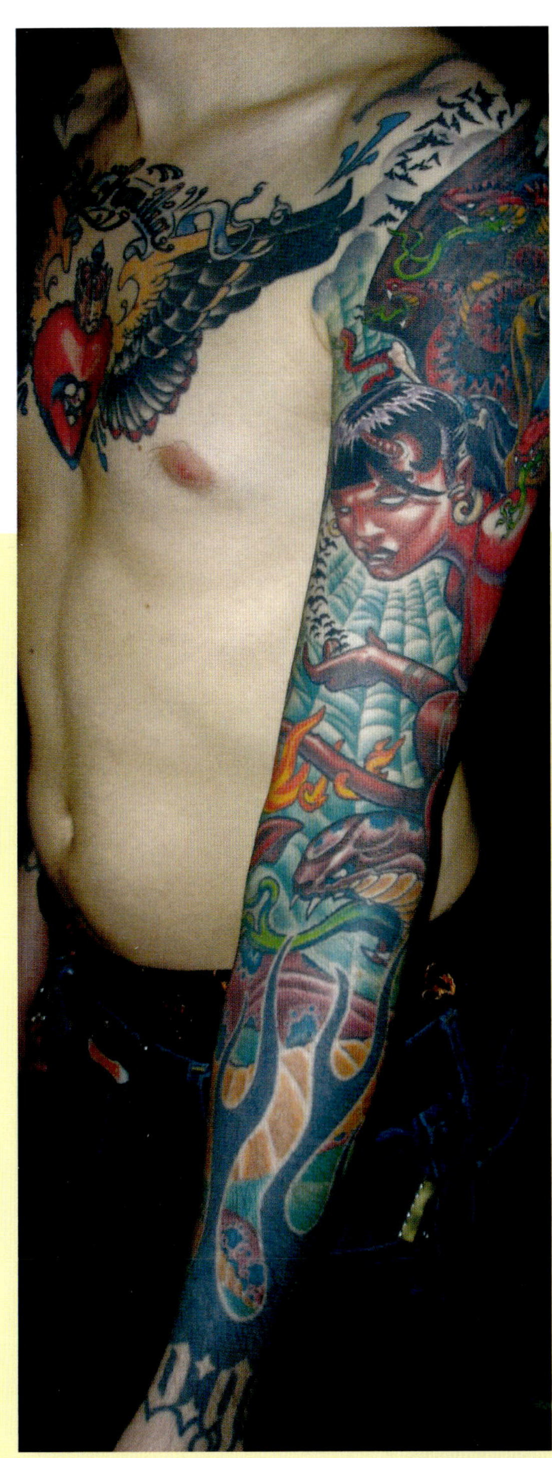

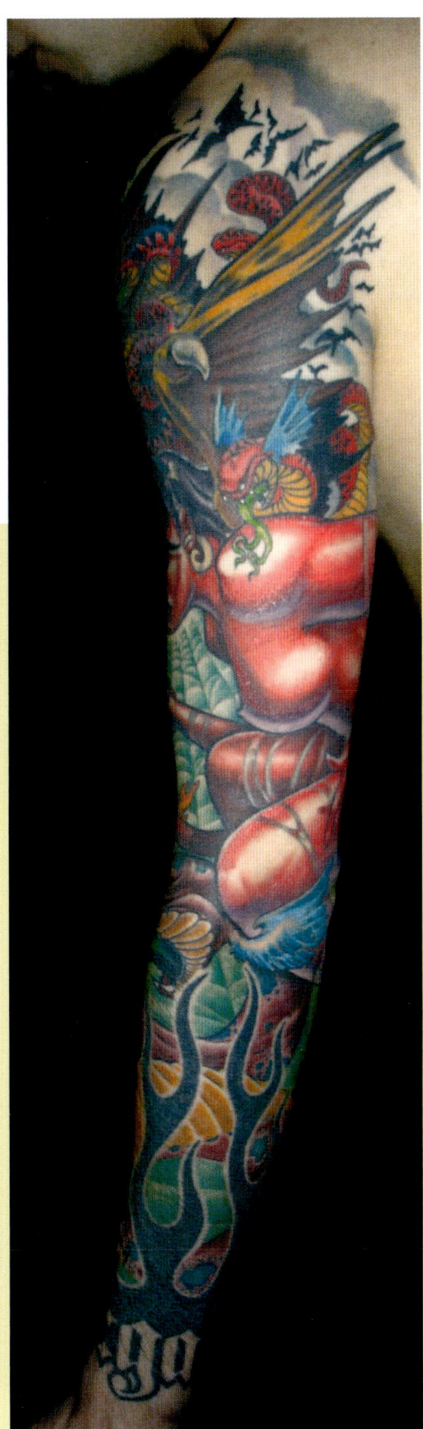

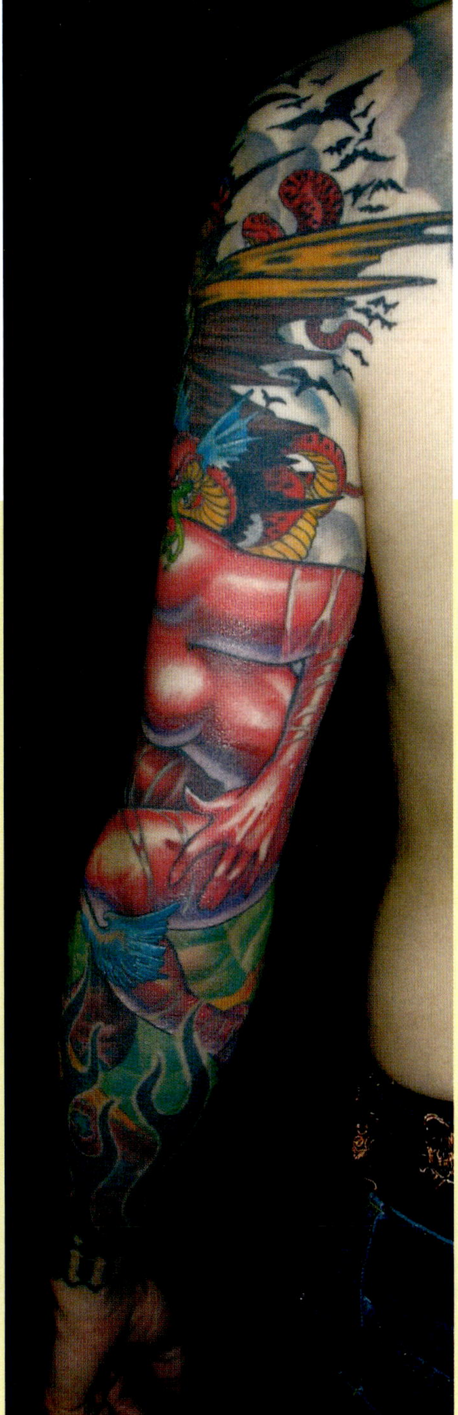

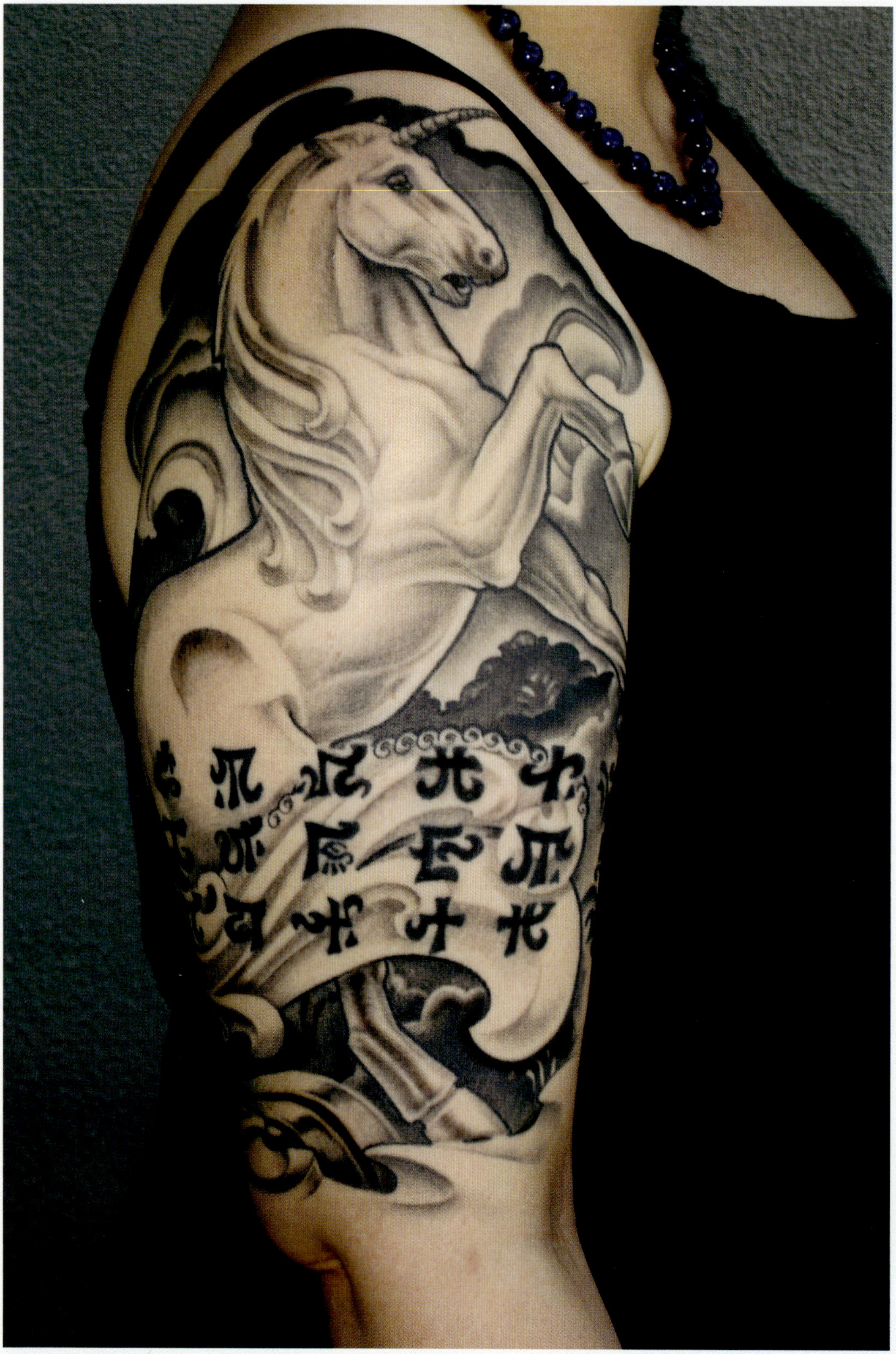

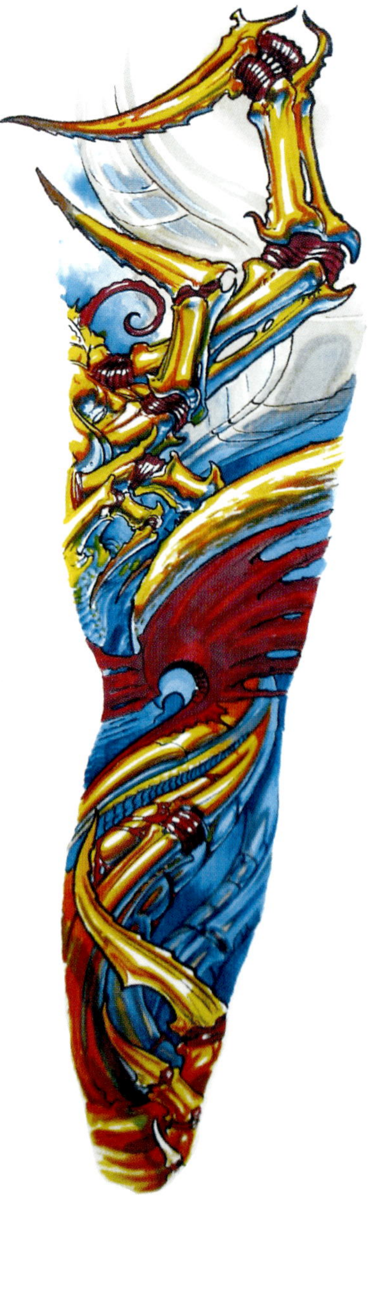

All designs on these pages by XXX Tattoo.

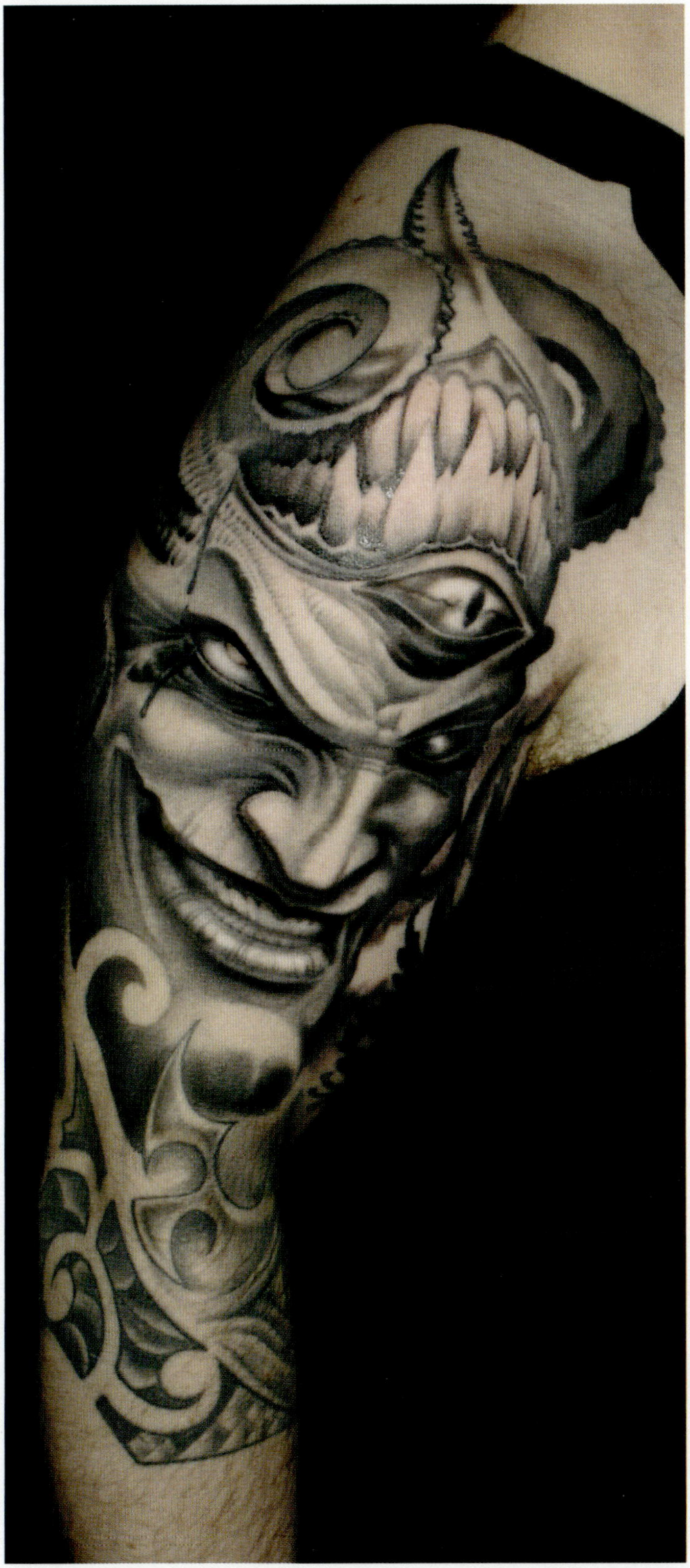

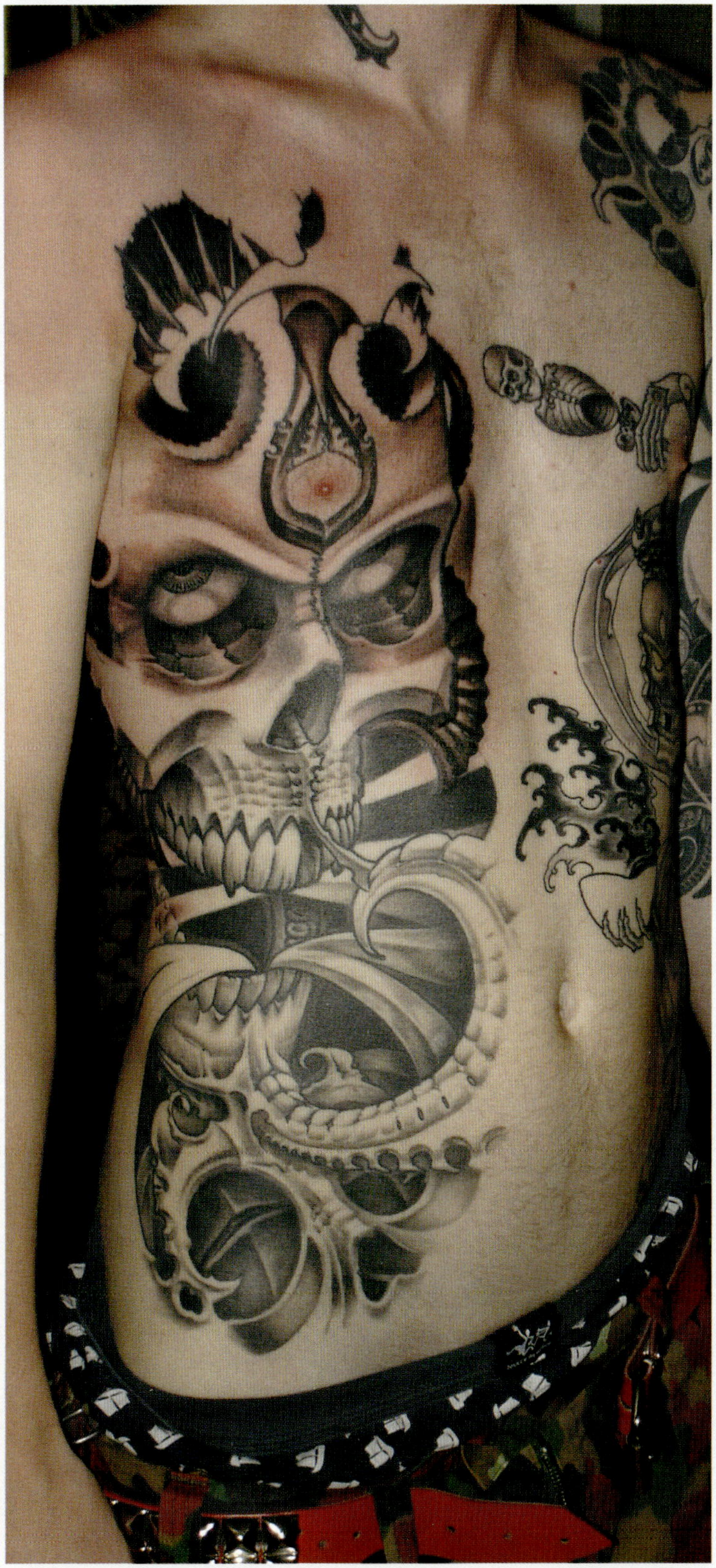

COOPER

GURU TATTOO

USA

1. I tried to teach myself, but when that was taking too long I got an old-fashioned apprenticeship. Two years longer than most by today's standards, but definitely worth it.
2. My obsession, my vice, and my service.
3. I have a very illustrative style. I am a bit of a character artist. I enjoy anything with faces or personality. I like trying to break the molds of traditional genres while still paying respect to the fundamentals.
4. Don't do it. But if you must, come see me.
5. Skid Row-San Diego!
   www.redleaftattoo.com
   www.gurutattoo.com

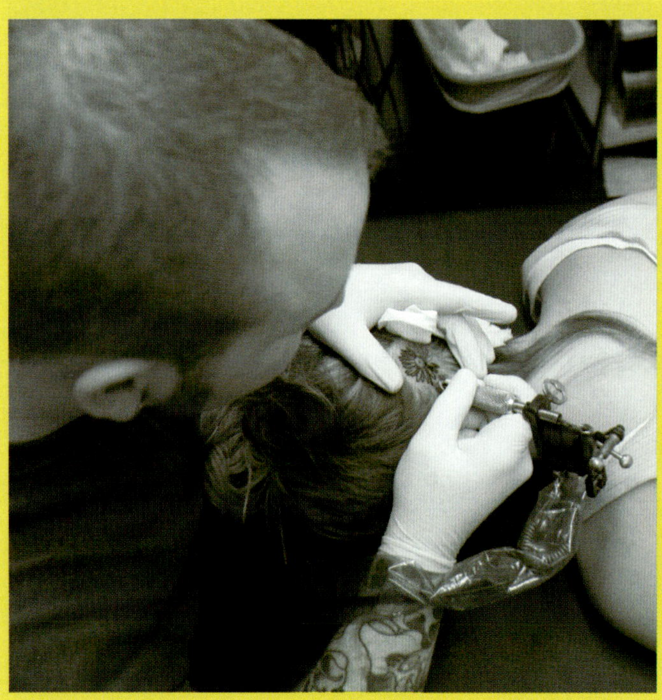

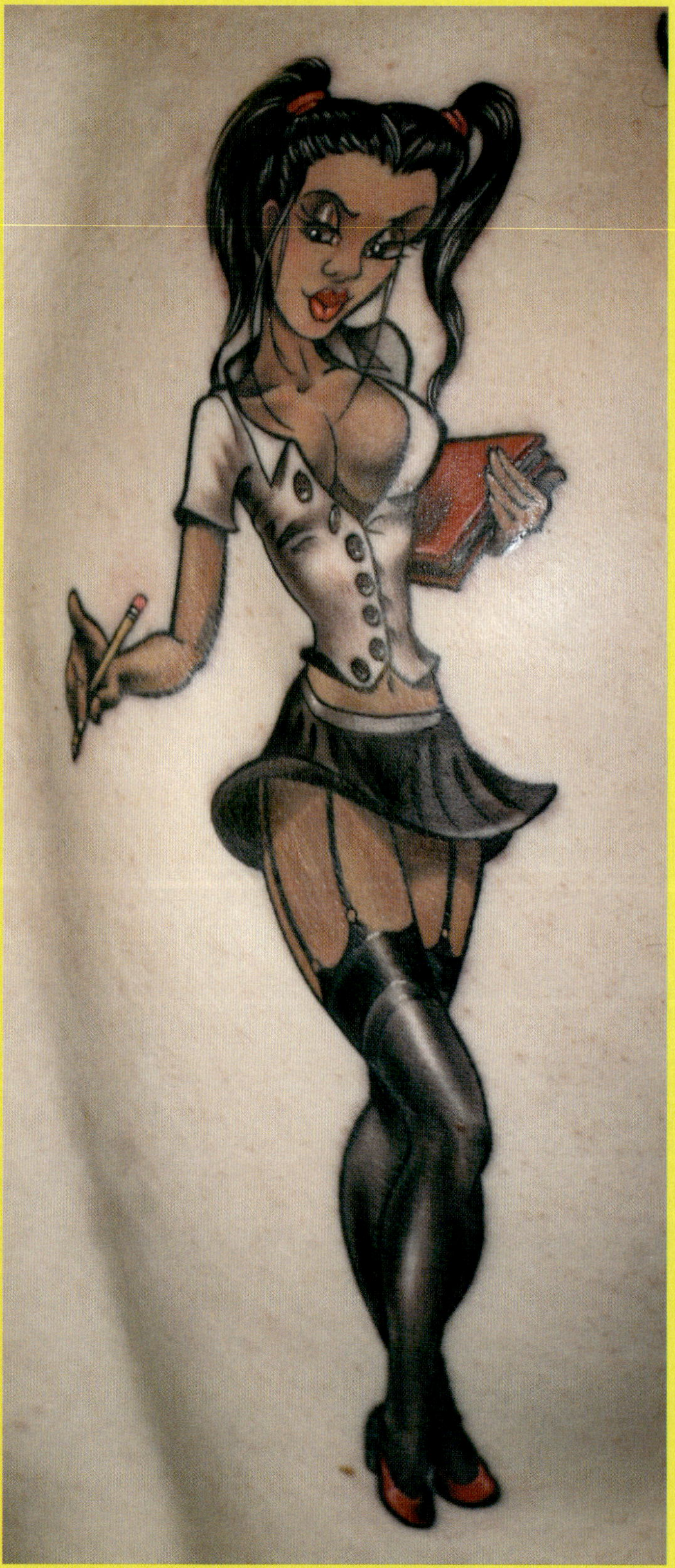

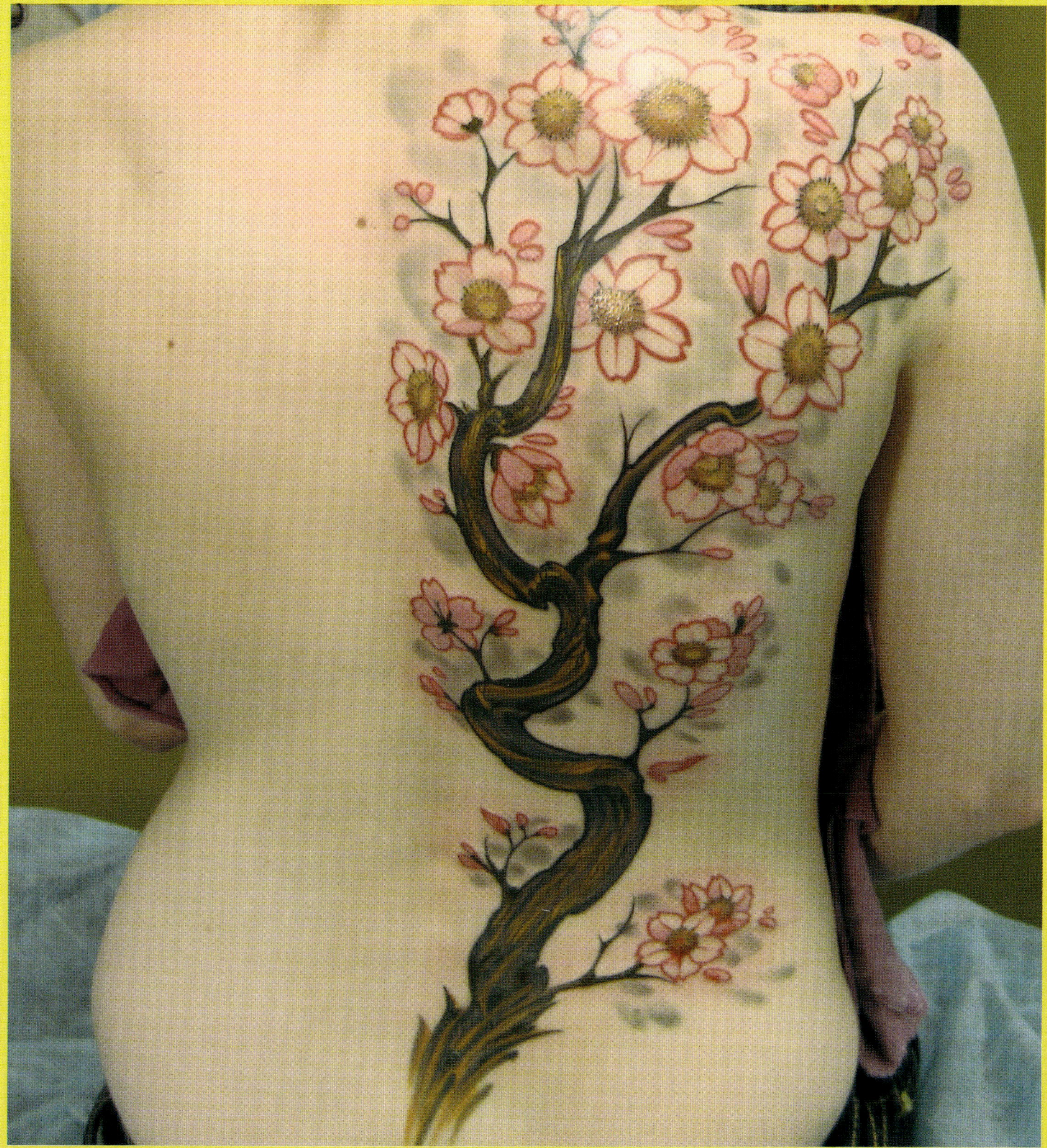

All images courtesy of Cooper.

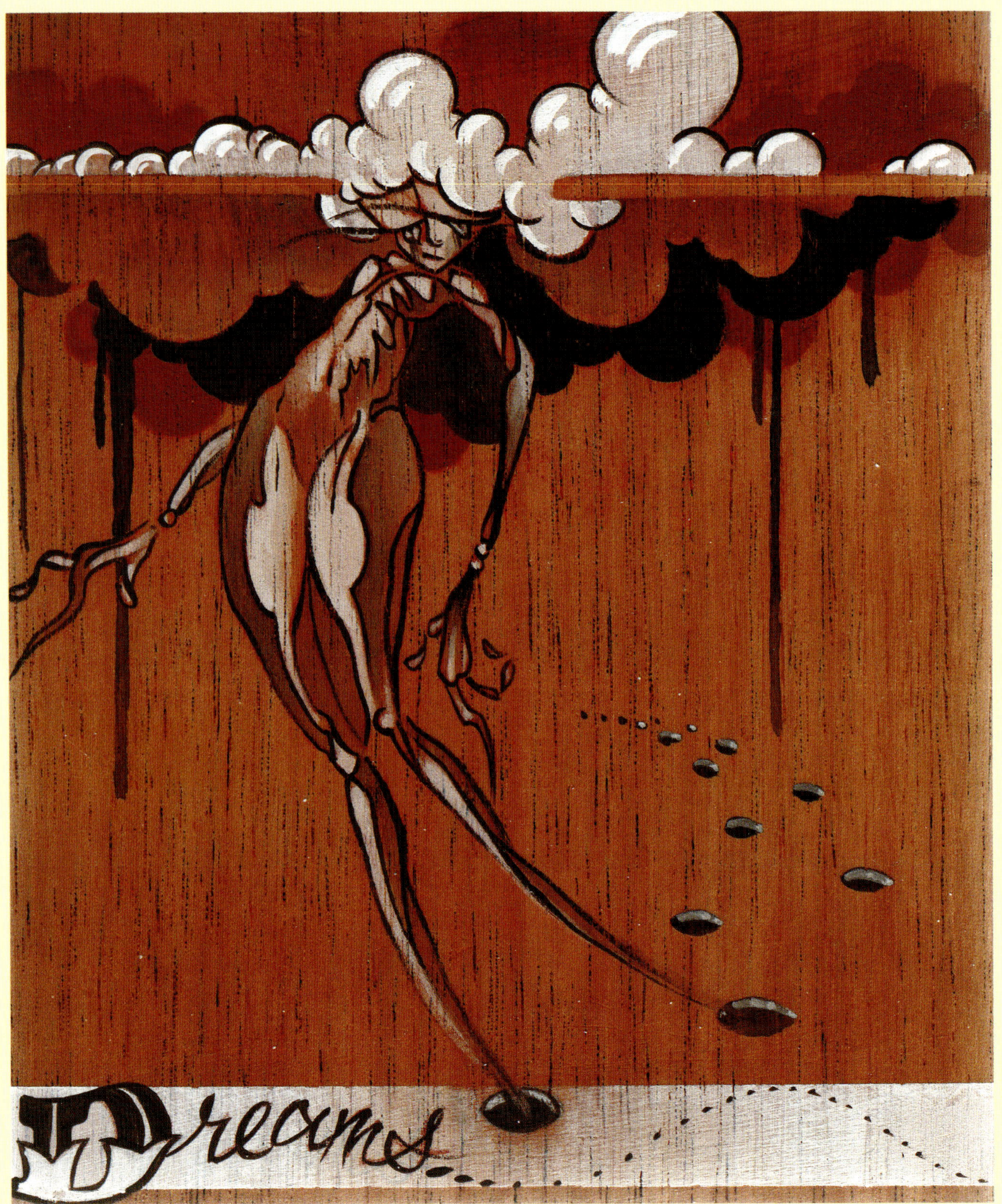

All designs and illustrations on these pages made by Cooper.

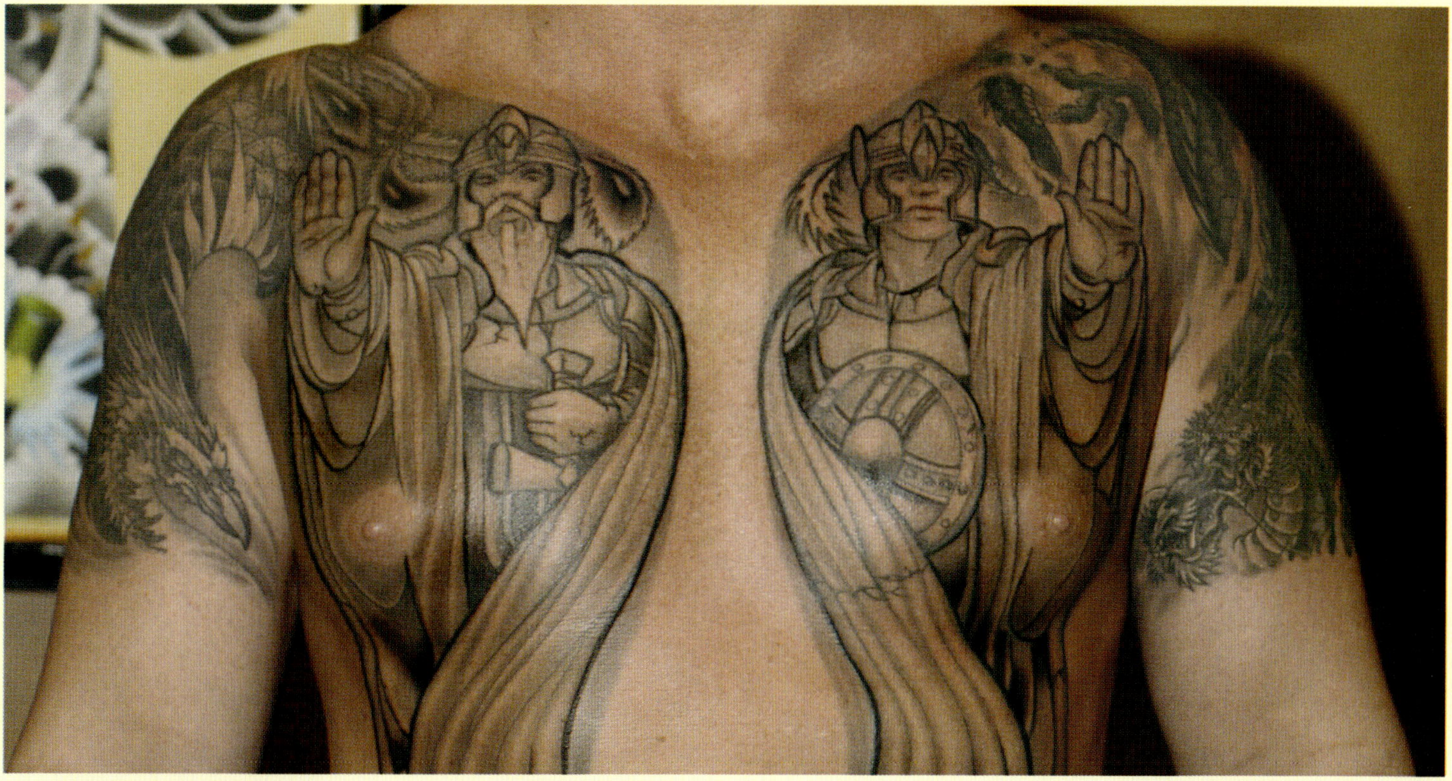

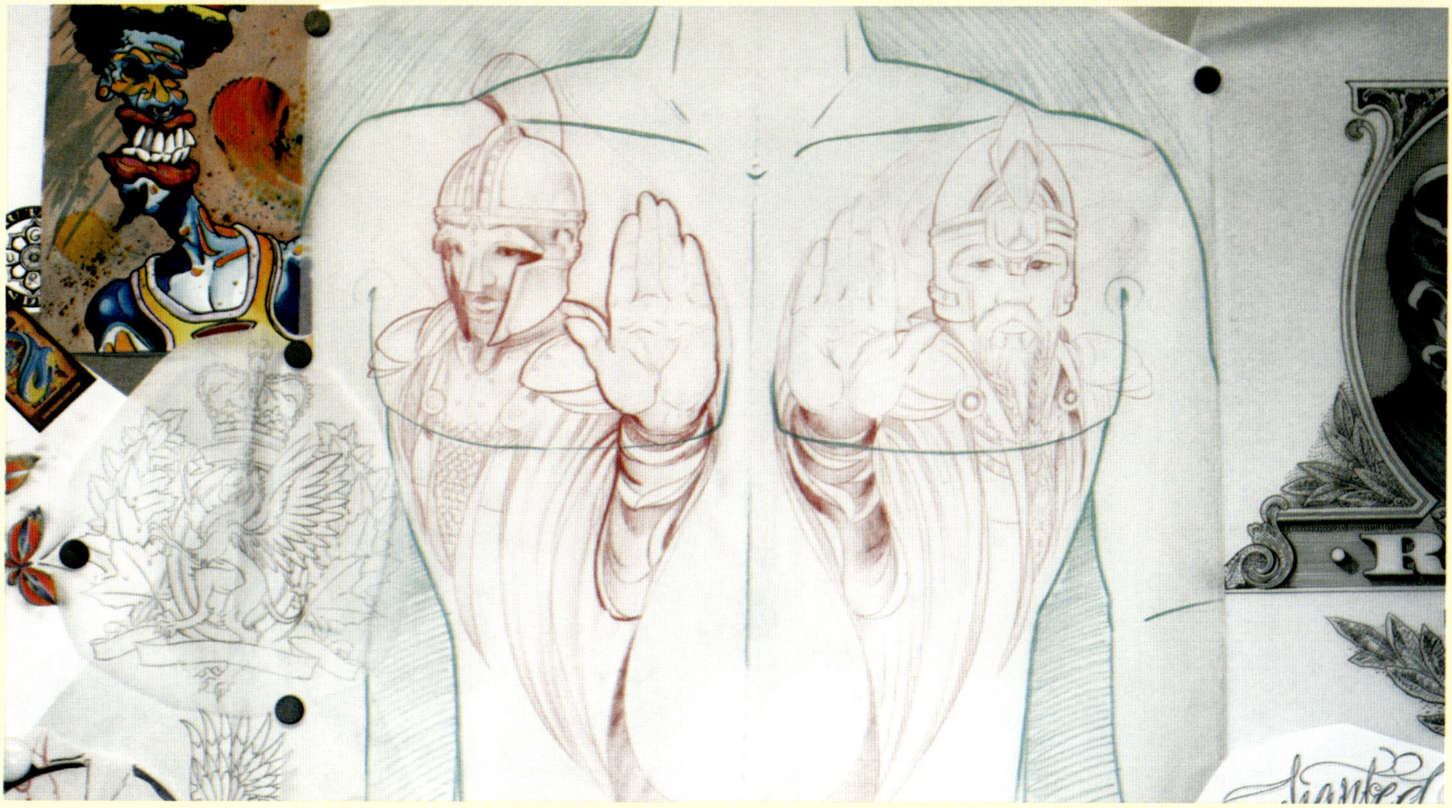

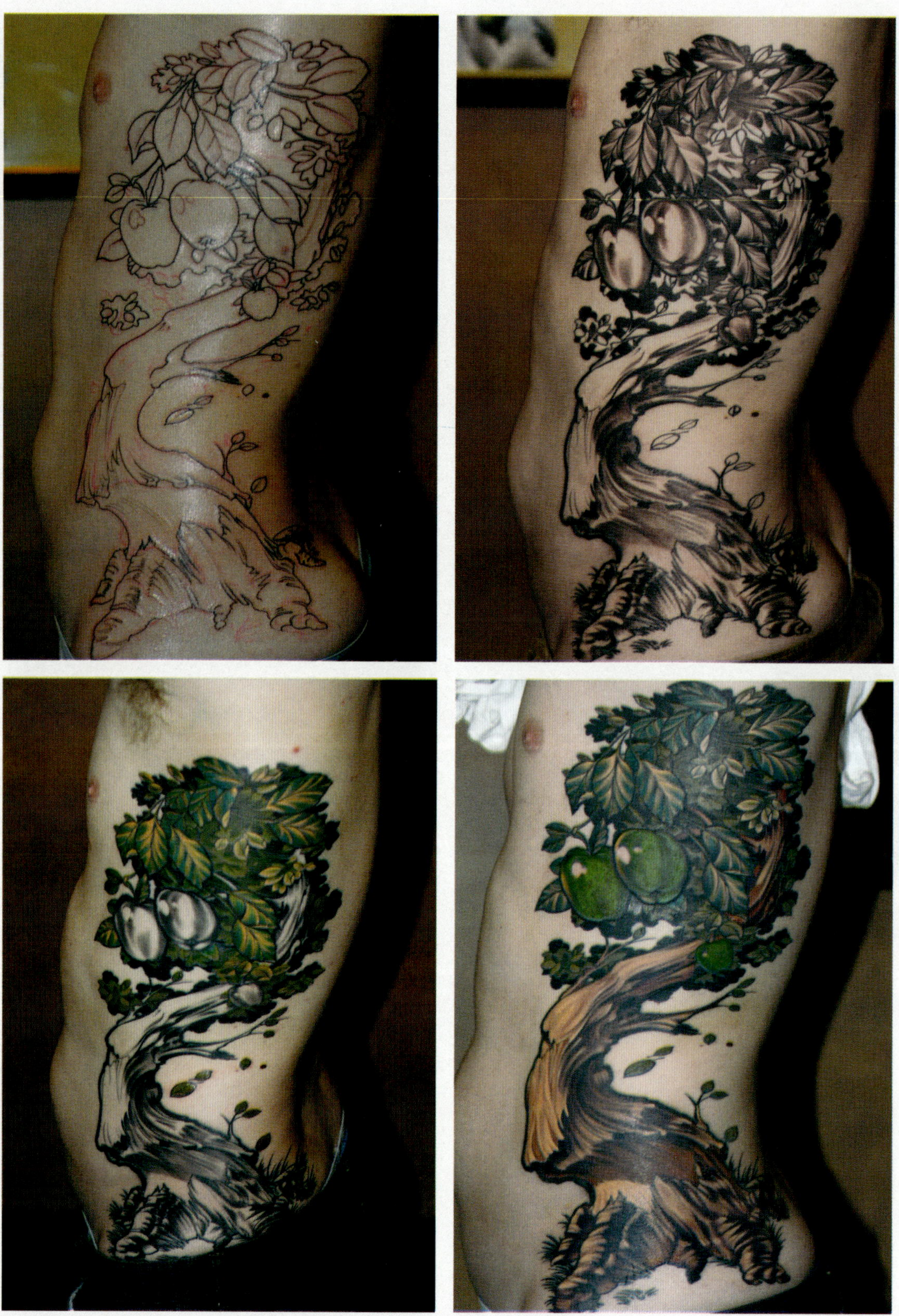

Step by step of a tattoo design by Cooper.

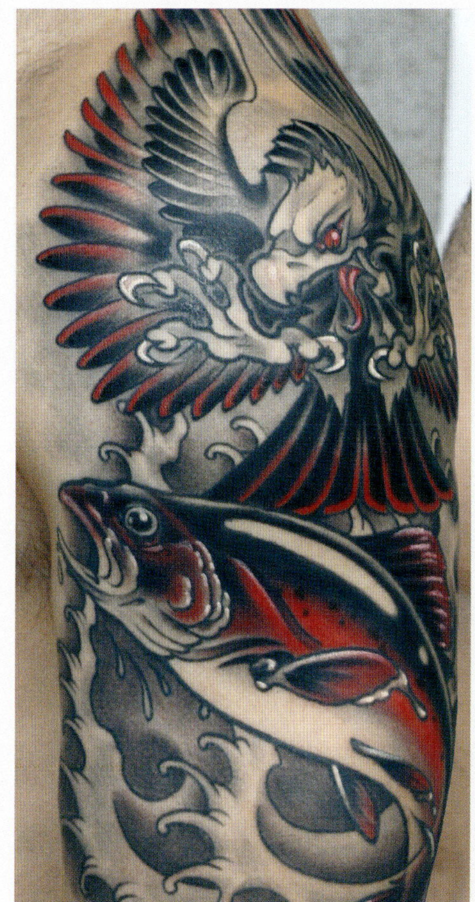

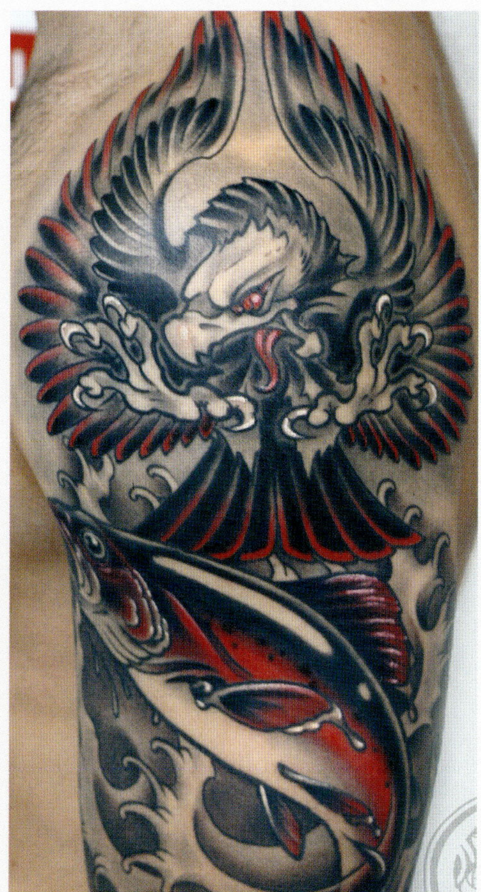

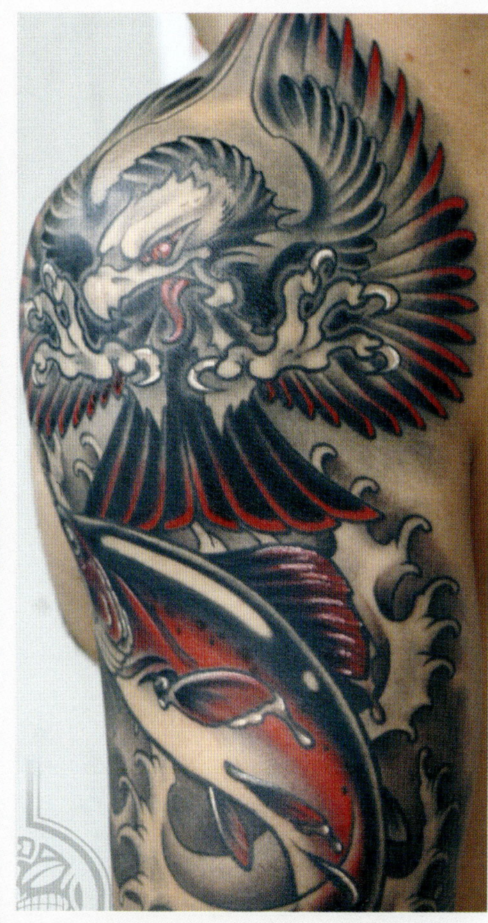

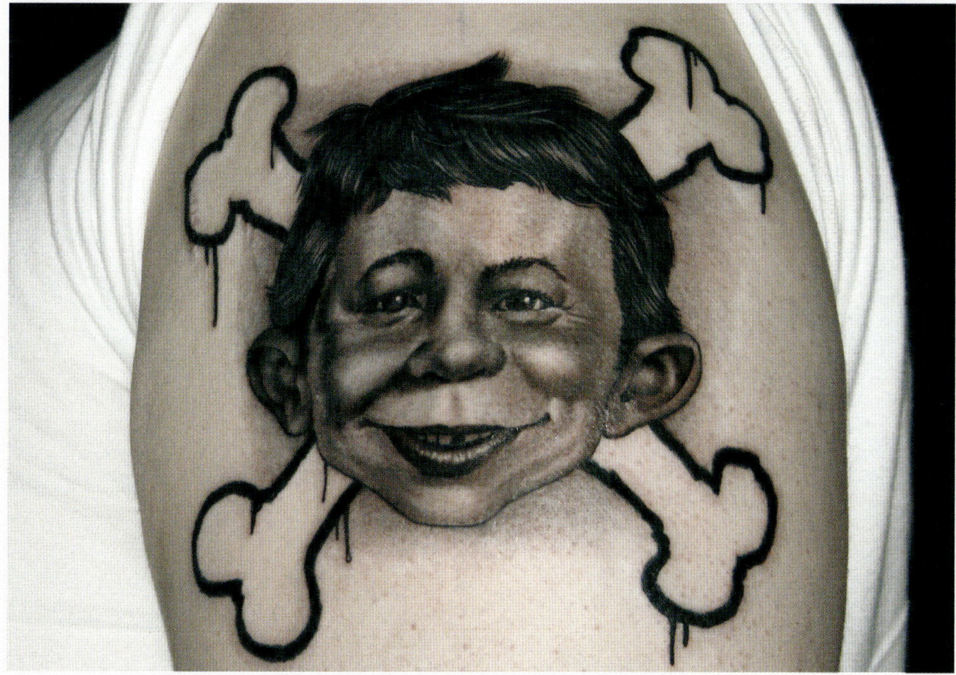

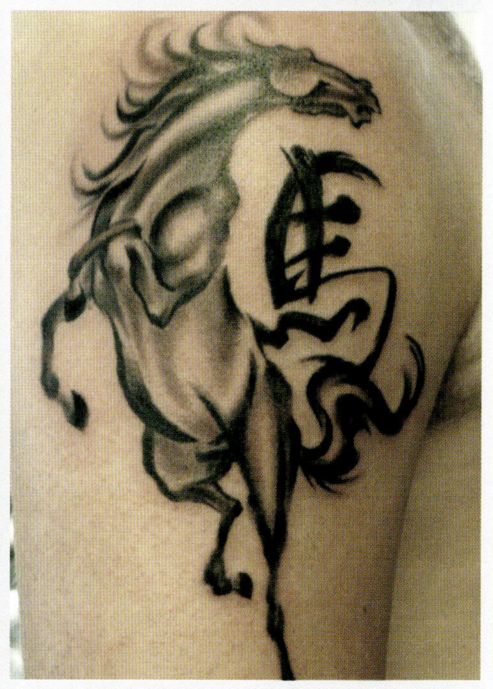

All artwork by Cooper.

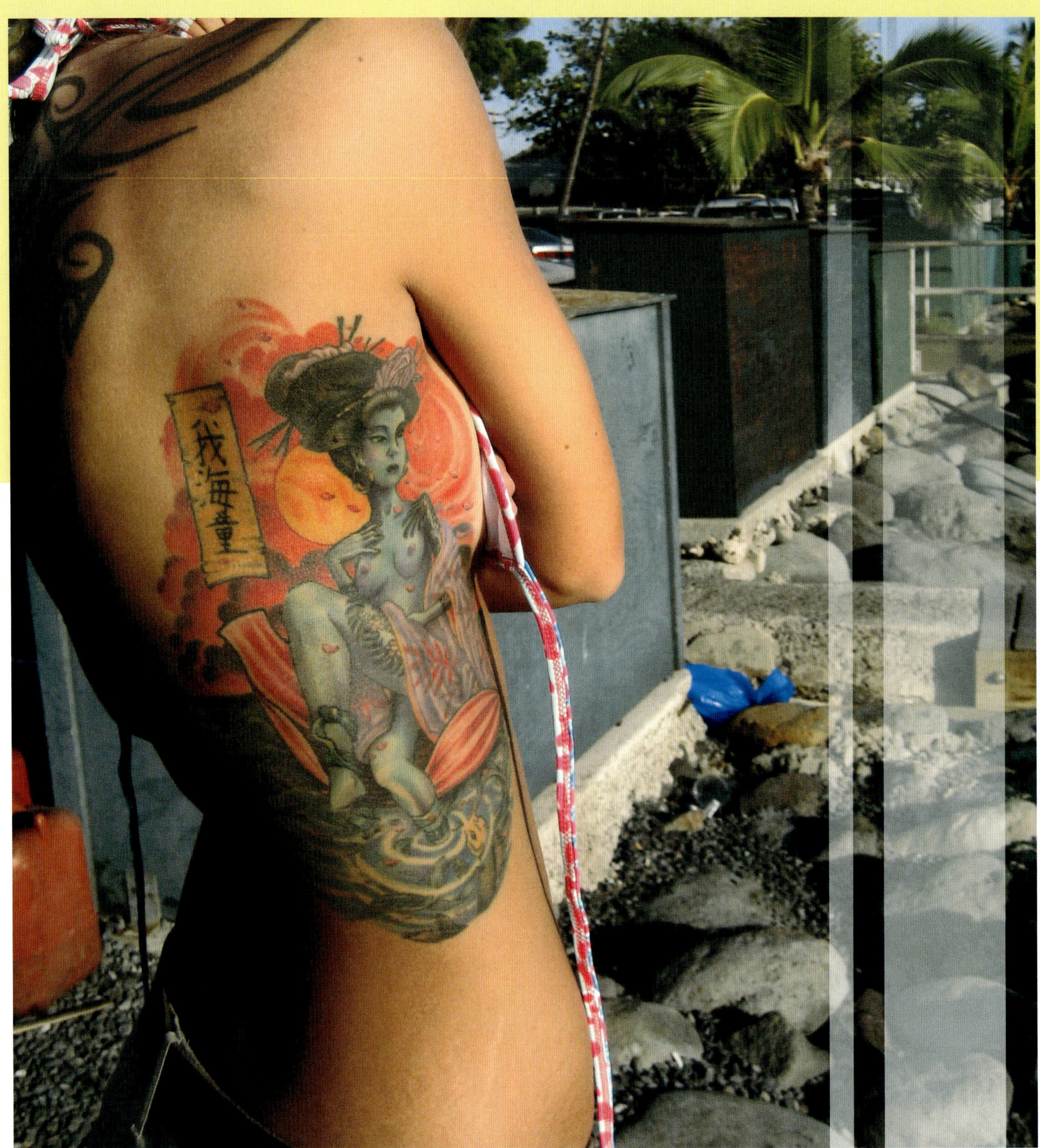

All images courtesy of Cooper.

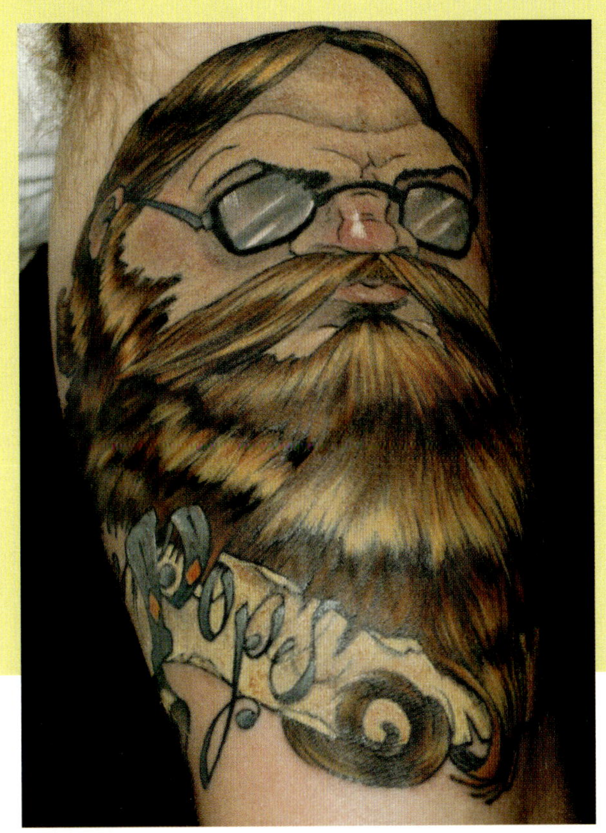

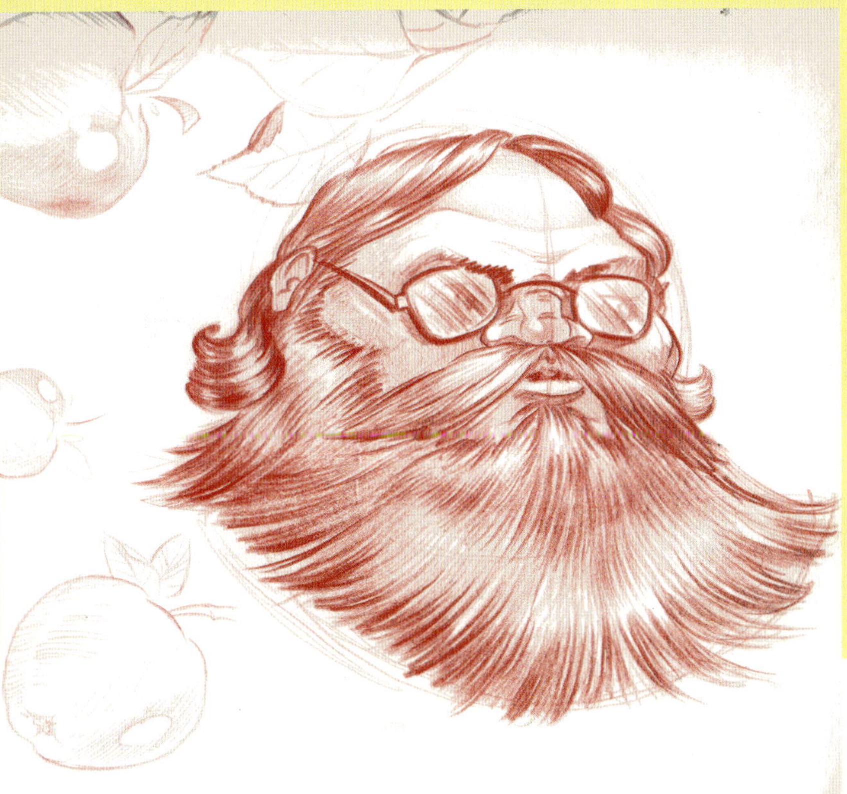

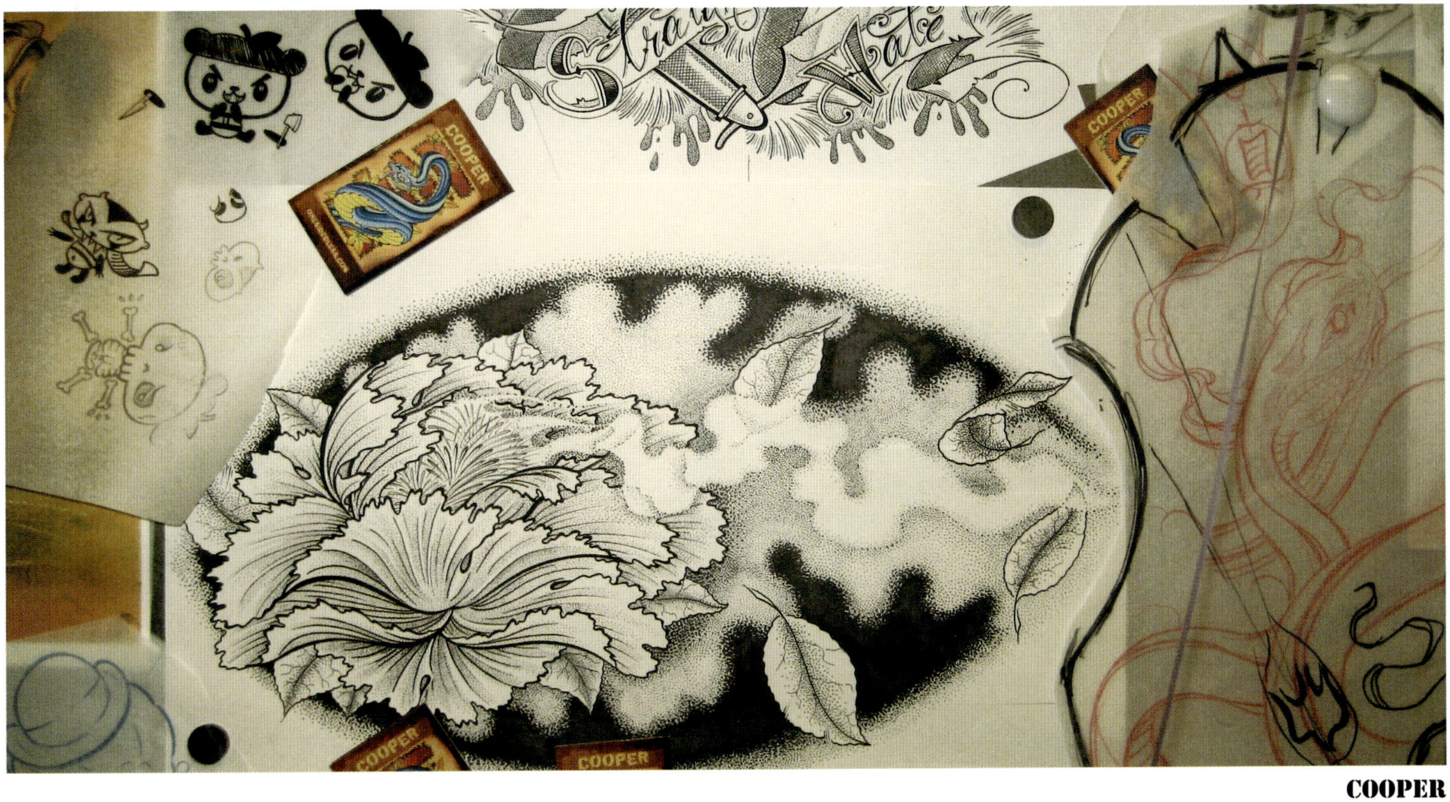

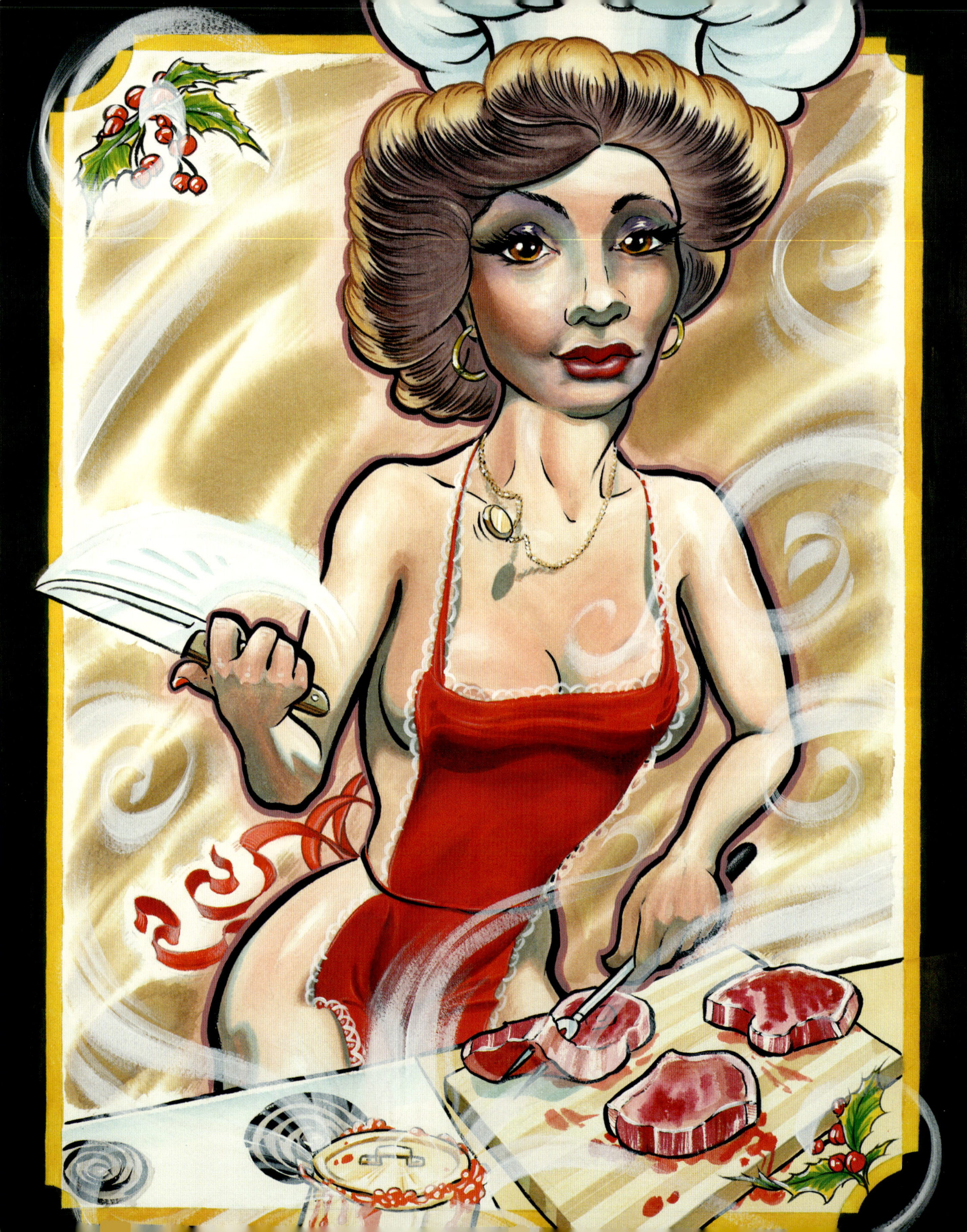

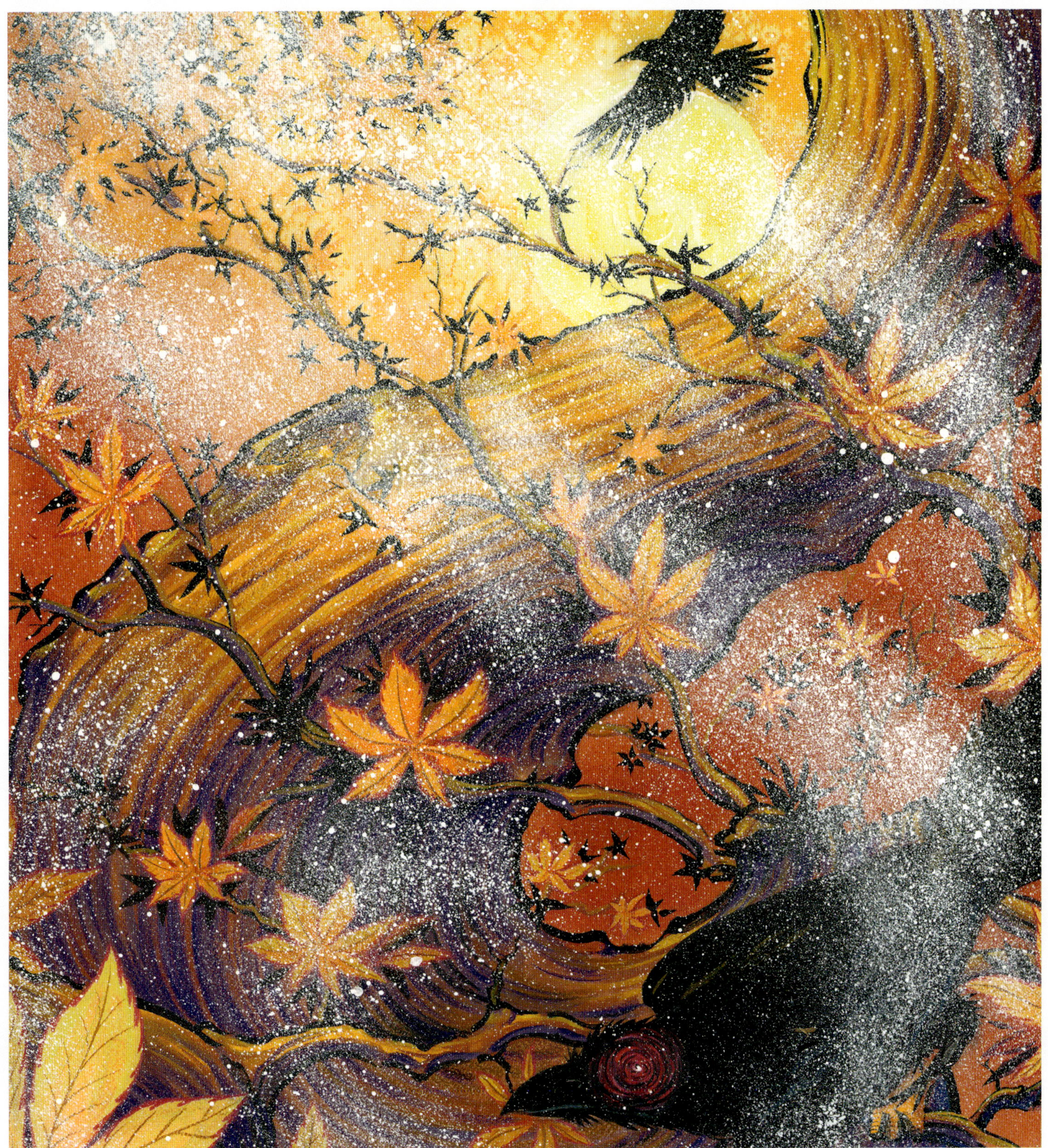

Acrylic illustrations on these pages made by Cooper.

HORI-SHIGE 7TH-TATTOO

JAPAN

1. In Japan during the Edo period, firefighters had their entire bodies tattooed with symbols of luck. I became very interested in this culture when I moved away from Japan. When I returned, I started to learn more about traditional Japanese tattooing.

2. I think tattooing is my way of expressing my art and my culture. The customer and I both gain satisfaction. The body is a living and dying canvas. It's also a moving canvas and takes many shapes.

3. My style is definitely traditional Japanese. I do a lot of manual work without a machine, body suits and so on. But I came under a lot of influence from European and American artists, like Mick Tattoo, Luke Atkinson, the Leu family, Jet and Brad Fink.

4. Think before ink! I always want my client to be sure of what they want. They should take my advice and criticism.

5. 560-52 Sakurai Kisarazu Chiba 292-0822 Japan.
   www.7thtattoo-studio.com

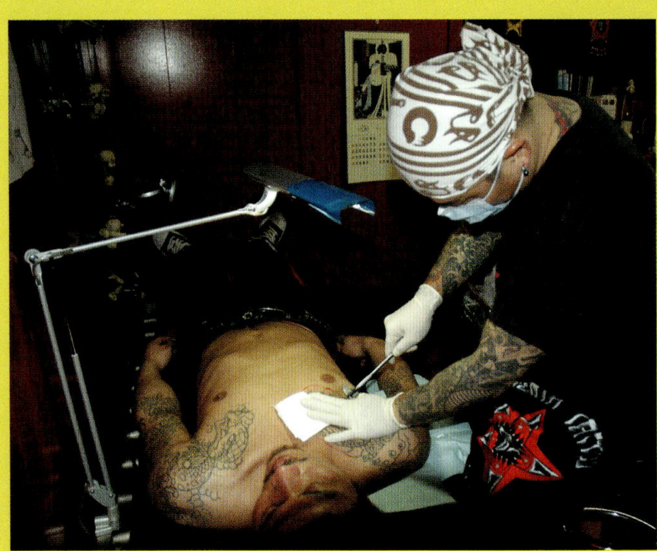

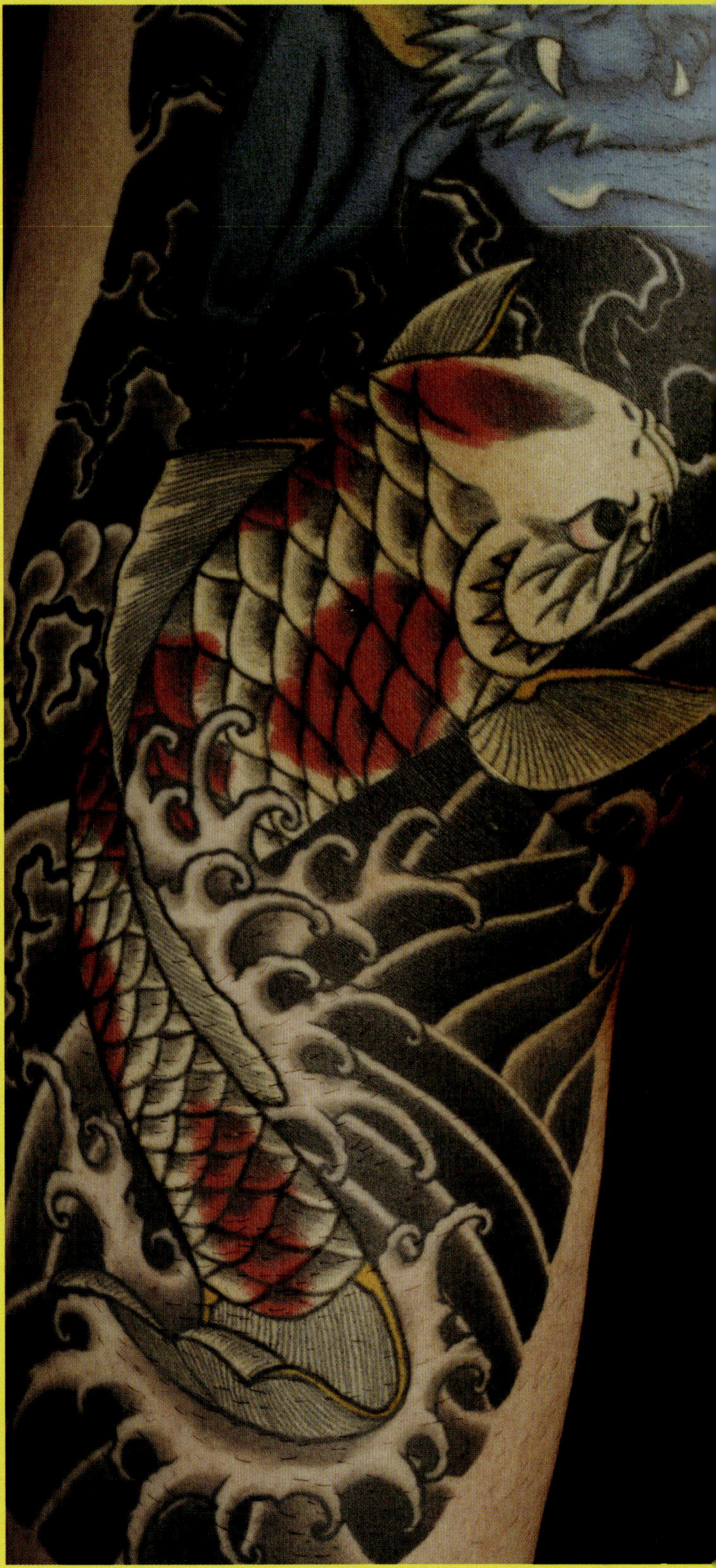

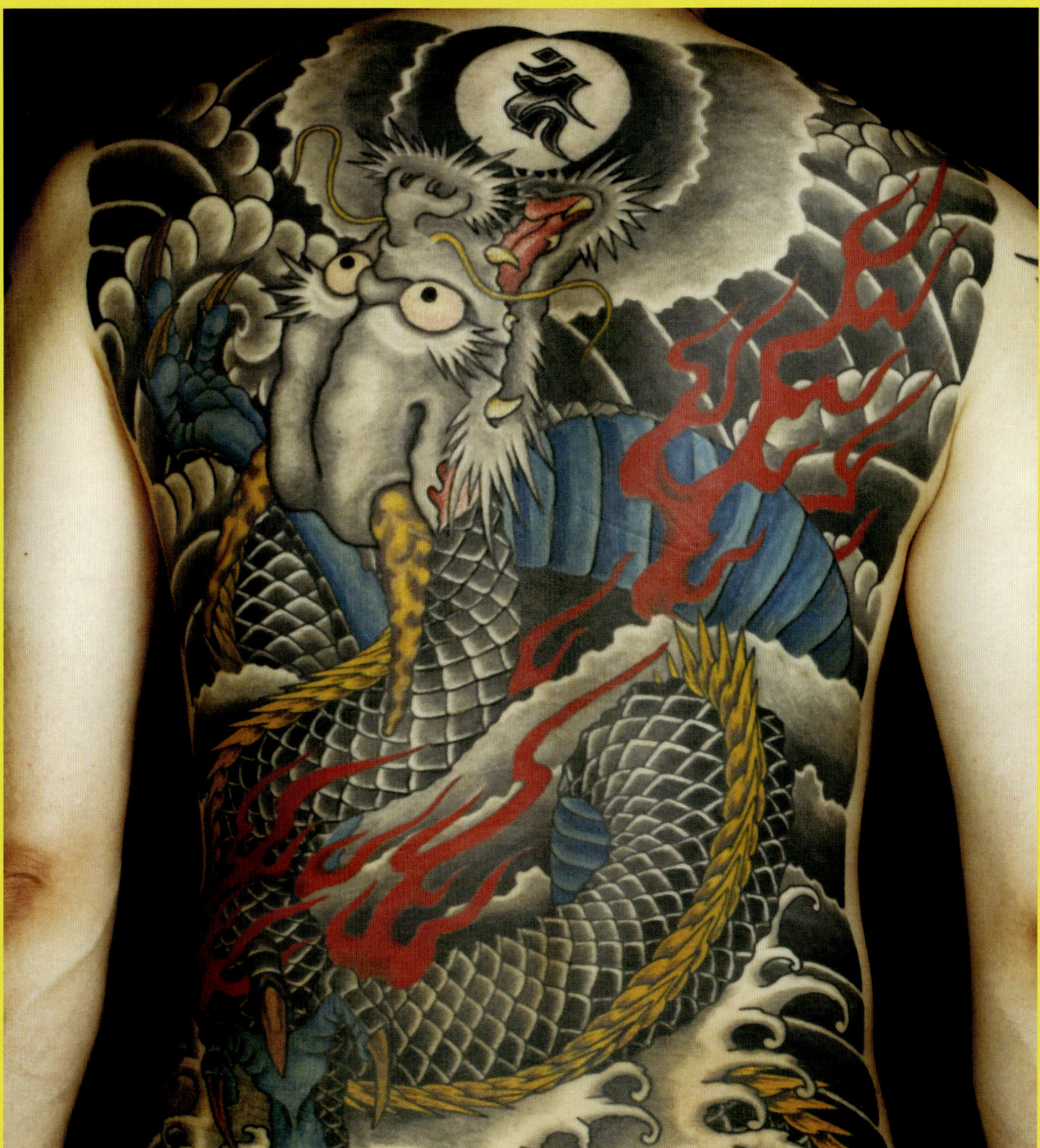

All photographs by Sogi Kanta.

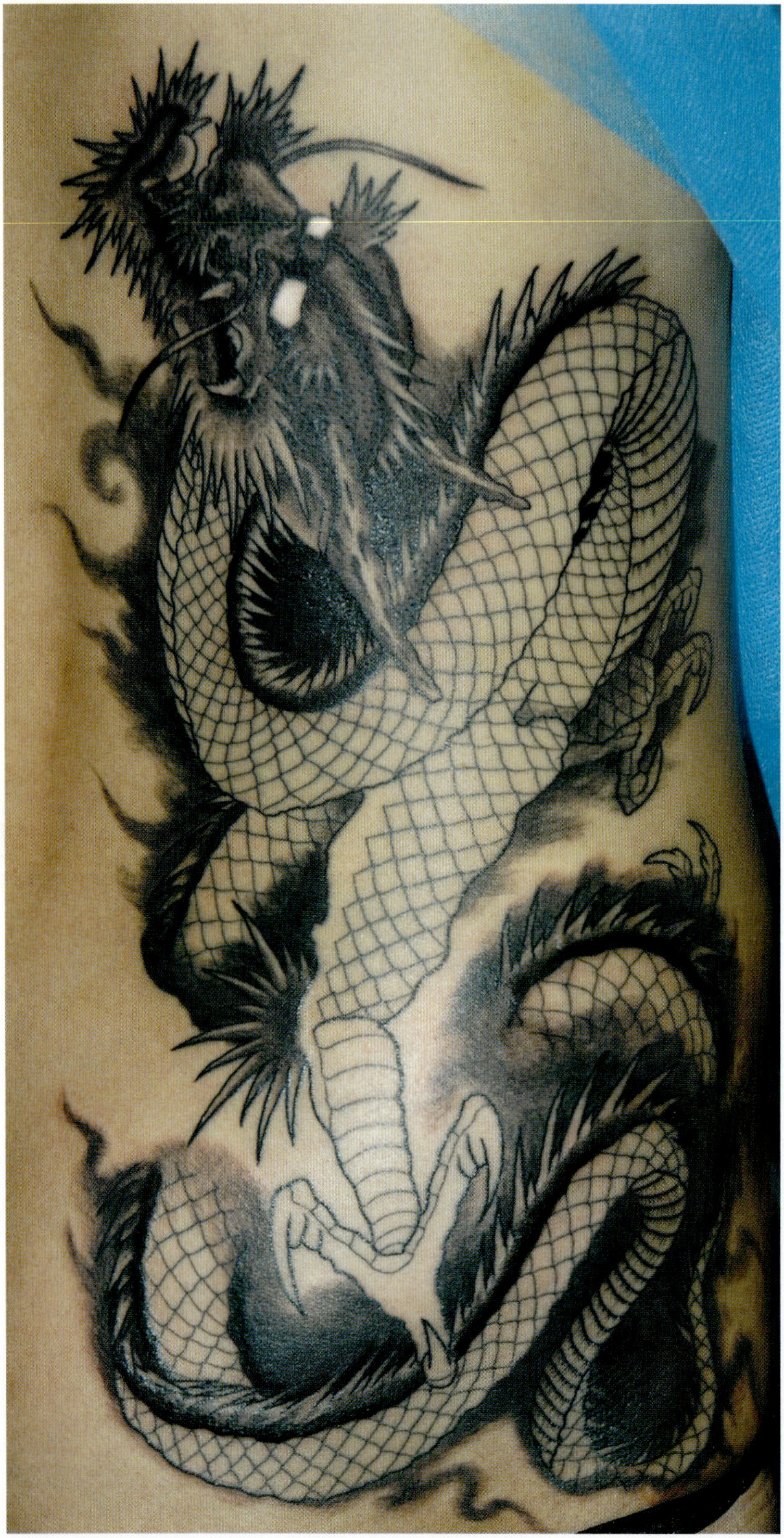

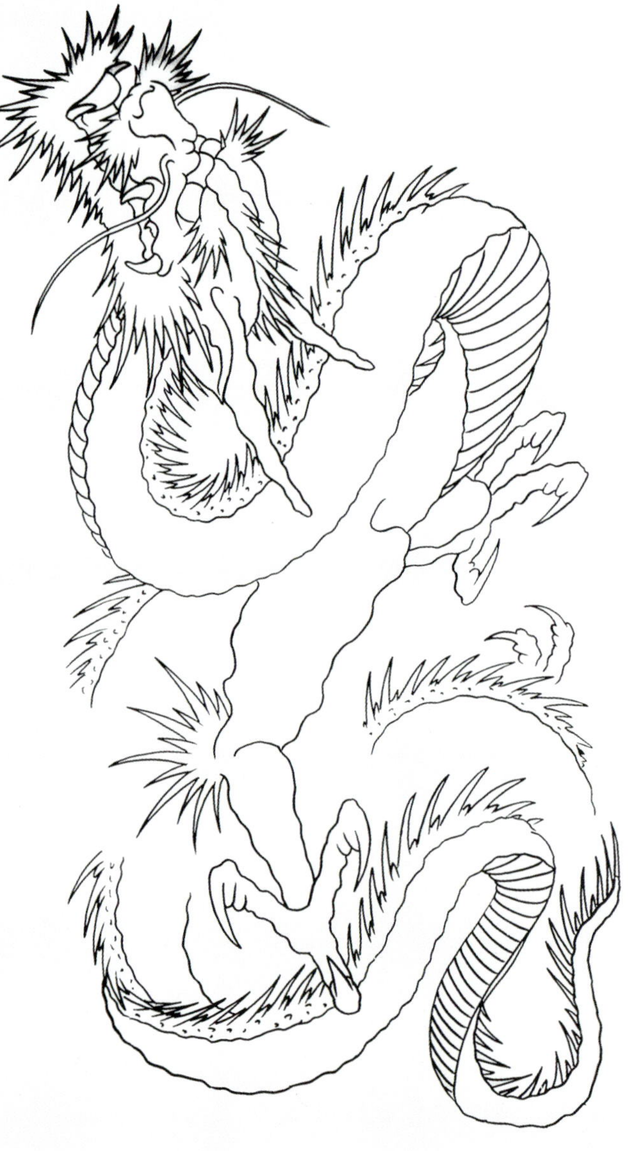

All artwork by Hori-Shige.

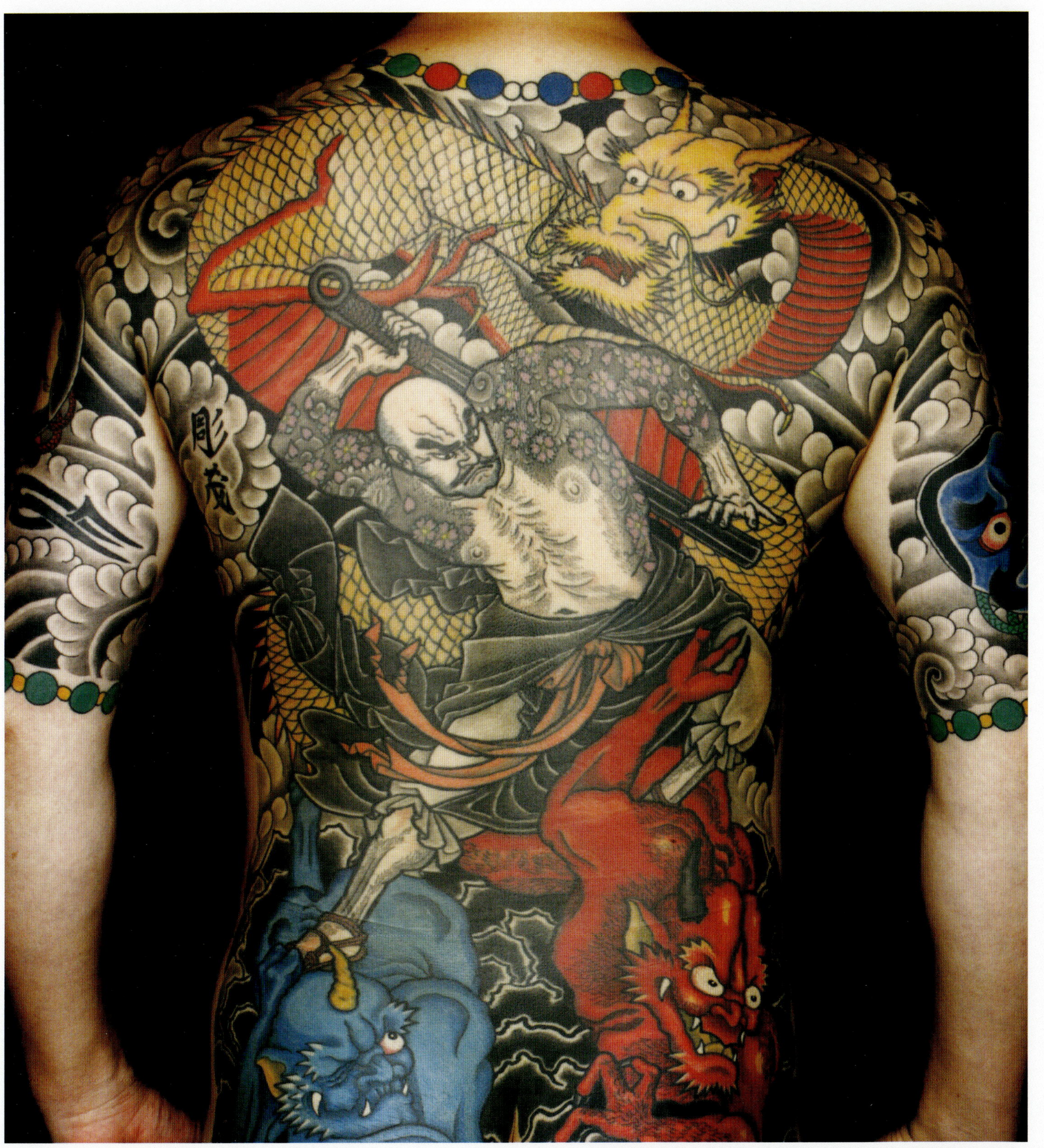

HORI-SHIGE

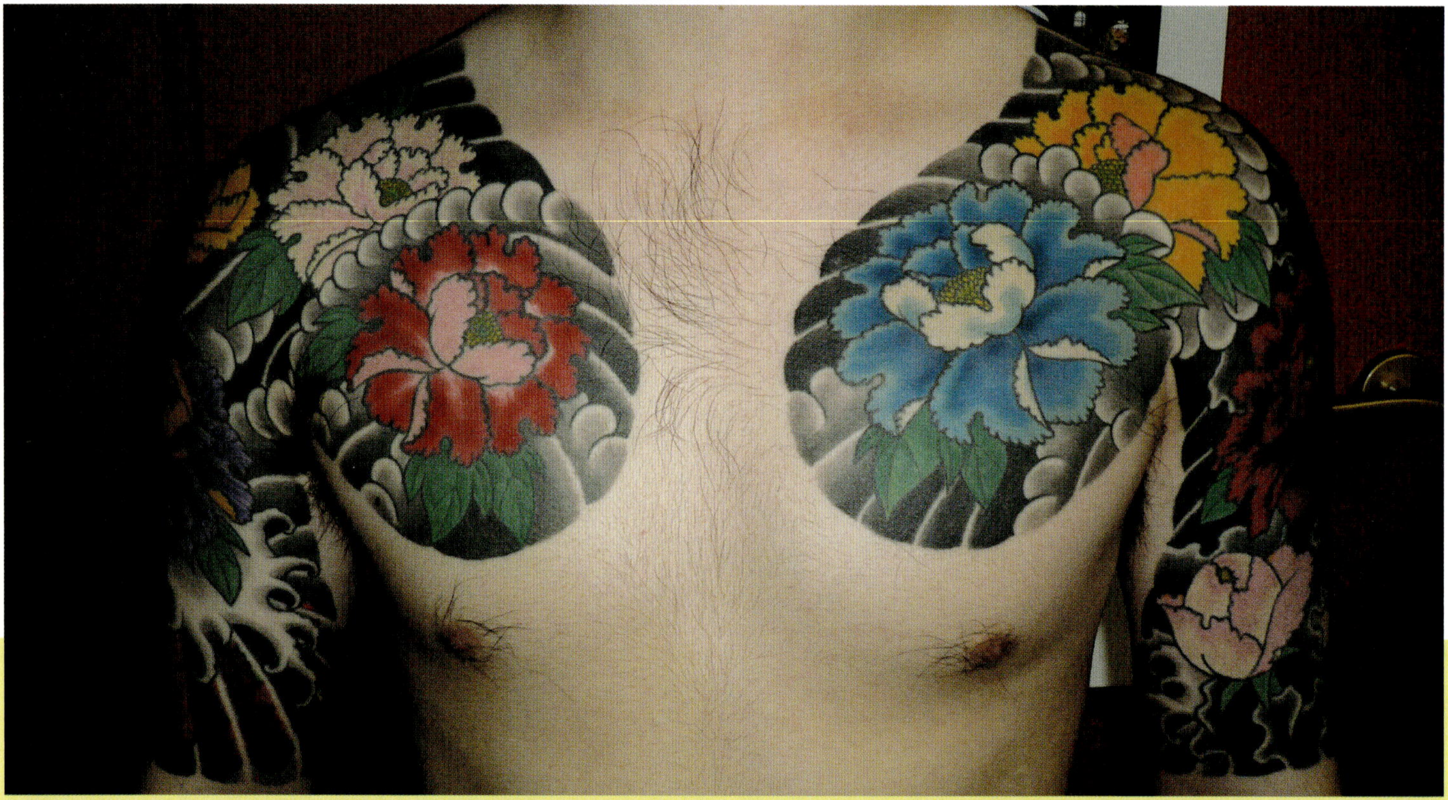

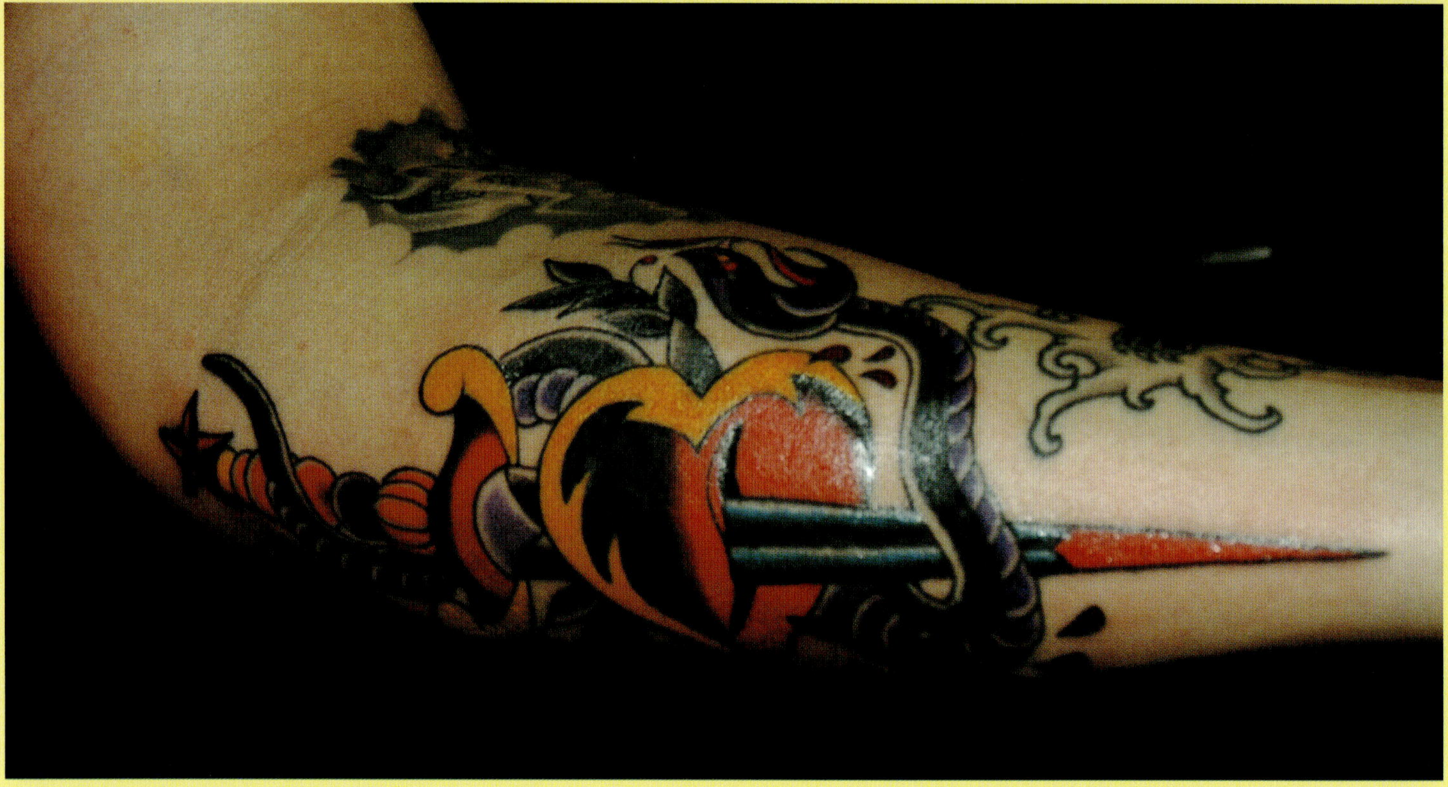

Images courtesy of Hori-Shige.

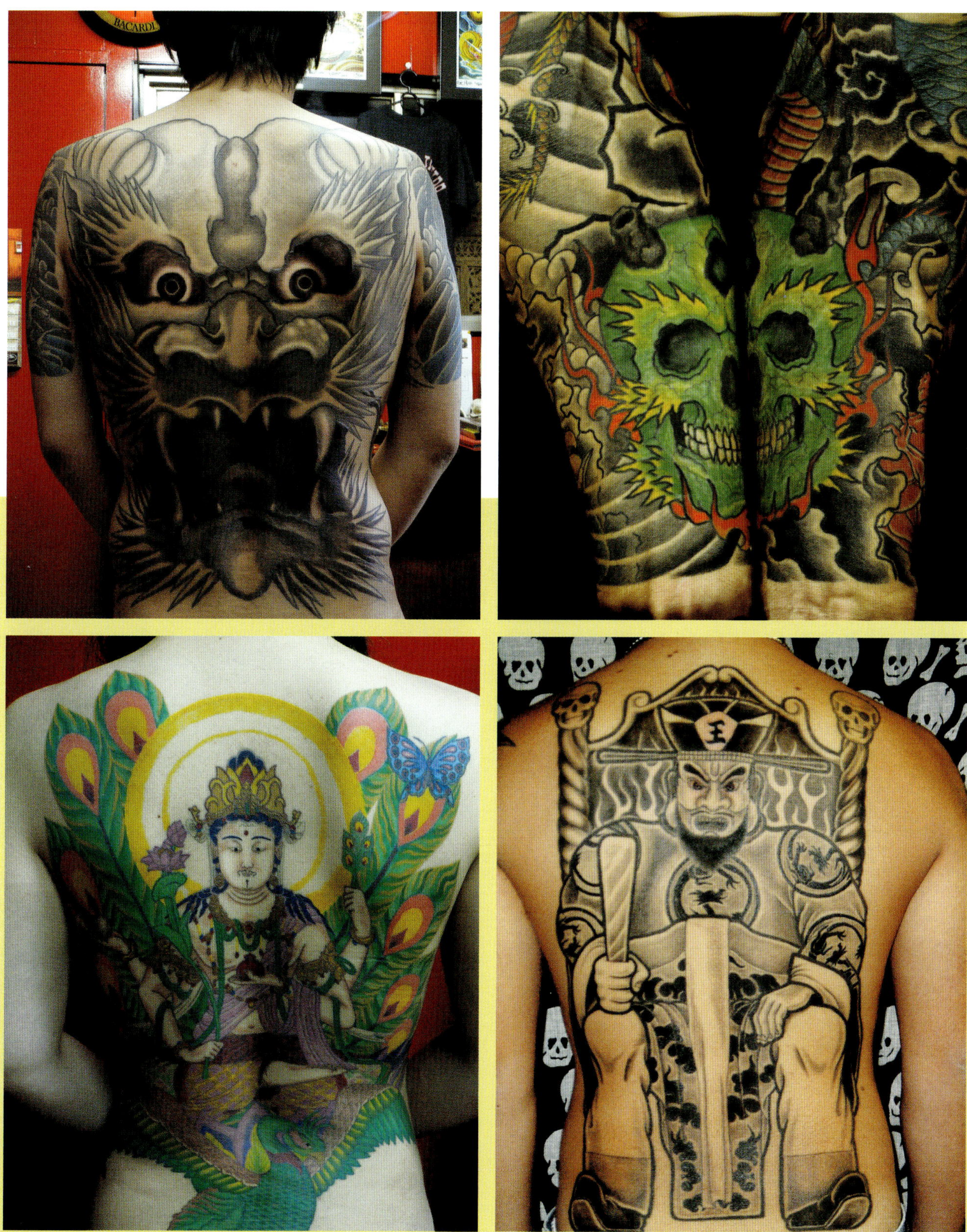

HORI-SHIGE

YONI ZILBER

USA

1. I started tattooing in Israel ten years ago. I've been drawing since I was a little kid, bought my first tattoo magazine when I was 12, and after that I dreamt about getting a tattoo. When I got older, I was lucky enough to be an apprentice under Avi Vanunu at Psycho Tattoo. I learned to tattoo in the old-school way: 18 hours a day, seven days a week of hard work.

2. Tattoos for me are my life; they're what I do, and they represent where I've been. But I think tattoos are individual to each person and mean different things to everyone.

3. My style is mostly Asian-influenced, Tibetan and Thai.

4. My advice for people who are about to get tattooed is to think about what you are getting and where you are getting it done. Do some homework, like searching for the right place. Look at the work and see if it fits the style you are looking for, and be patient: if you need to wait to get it right, then wait.

5. I'm working at New York Adorned and traveling around the world doing guest spots and conventions. My website is a good place to contact me.
   www.yoniztattoo.com
   yoni@yoniztattoo.com
   New York Adorned, #47 2nd Ave, NYC, NY 10003.

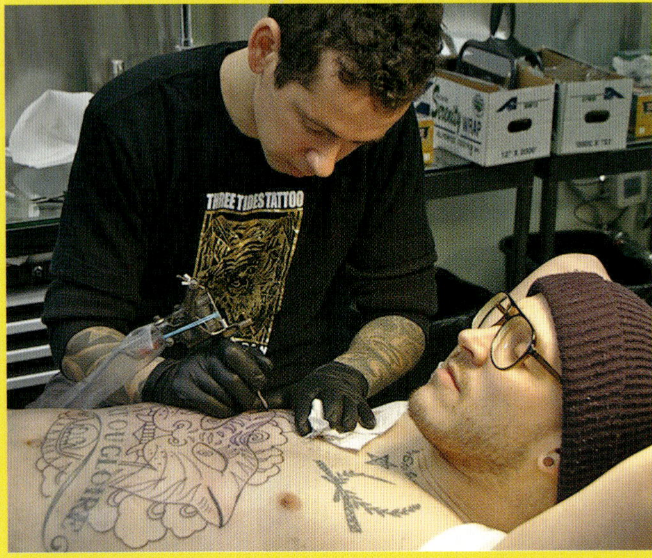

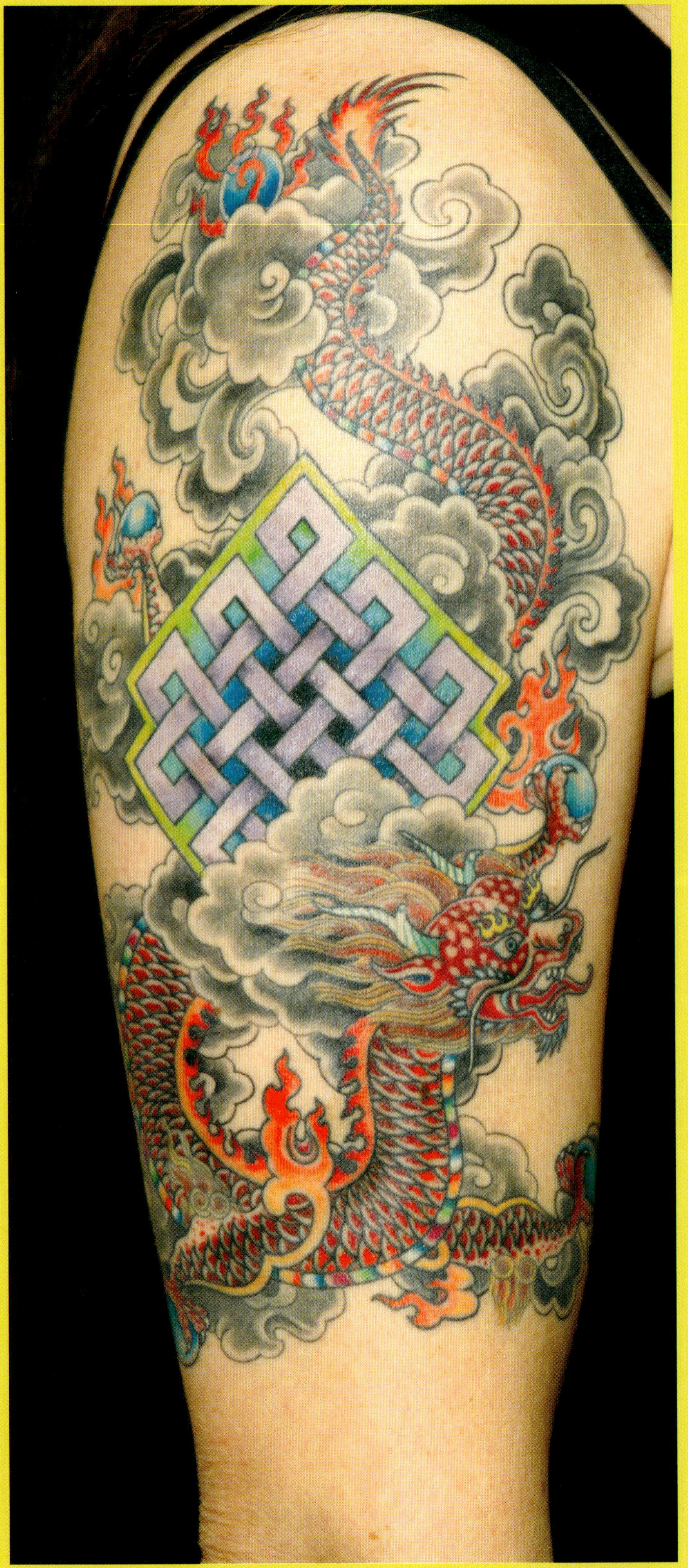

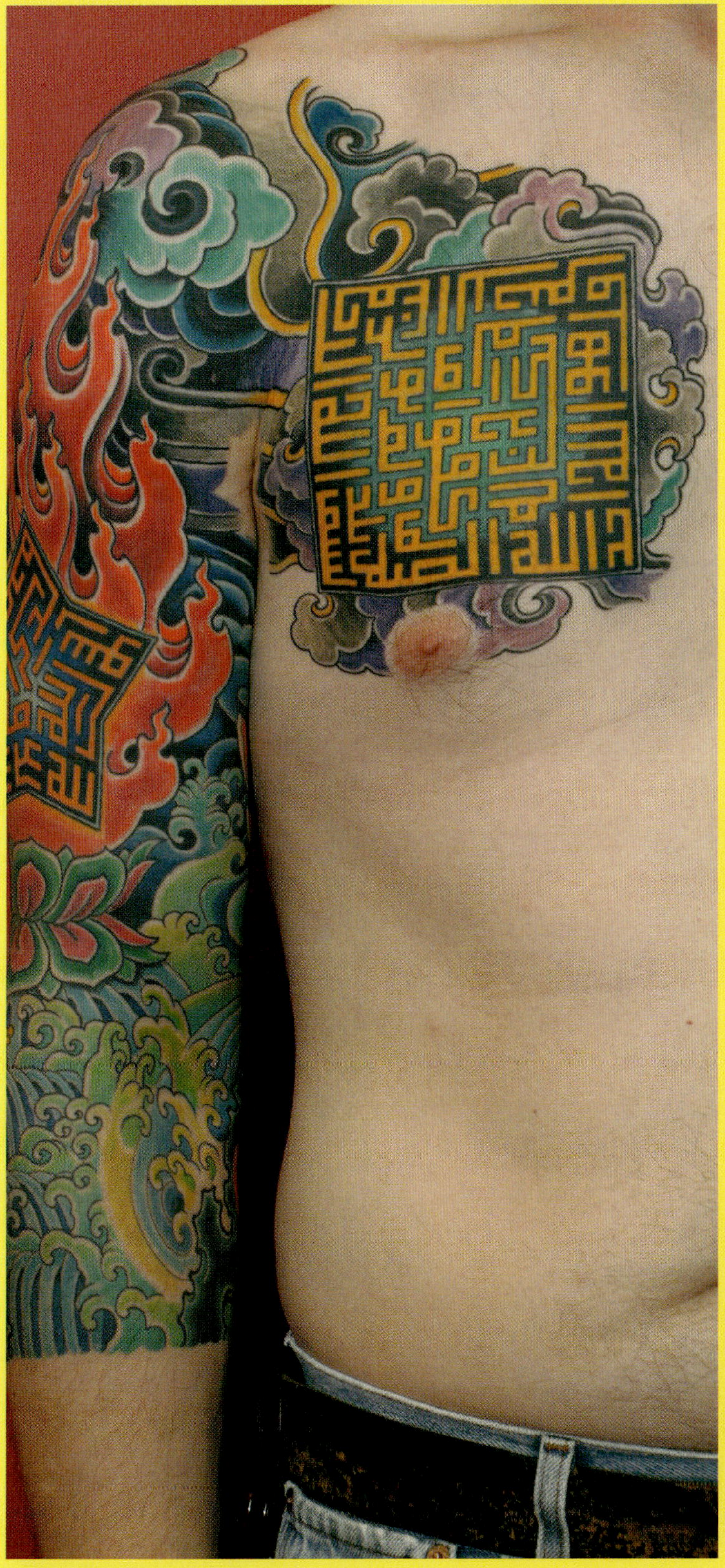

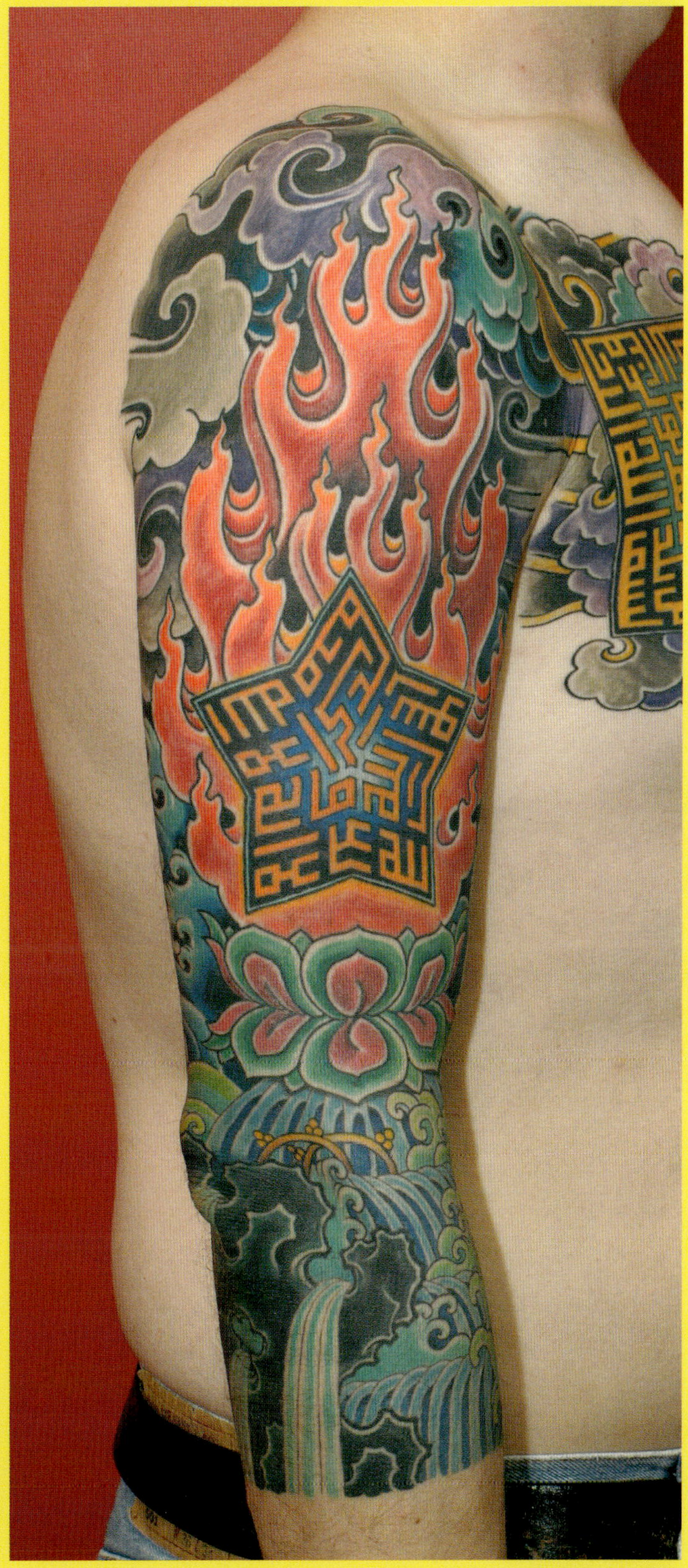

Images courtesy of Yoni Zilber.

YONI ZILBER

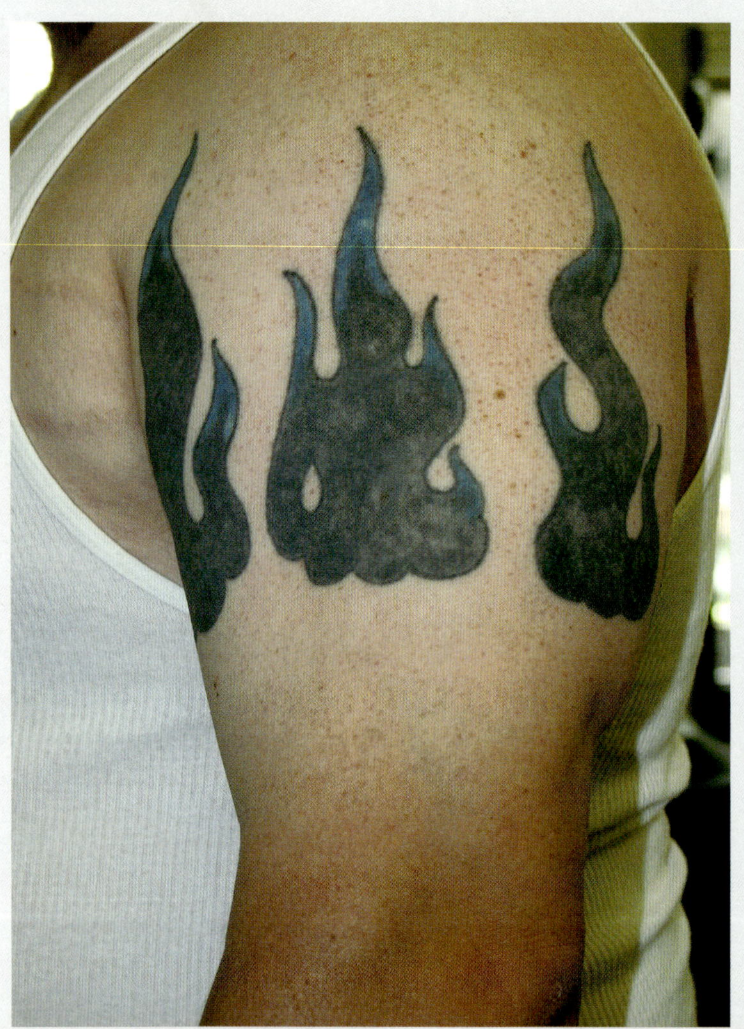
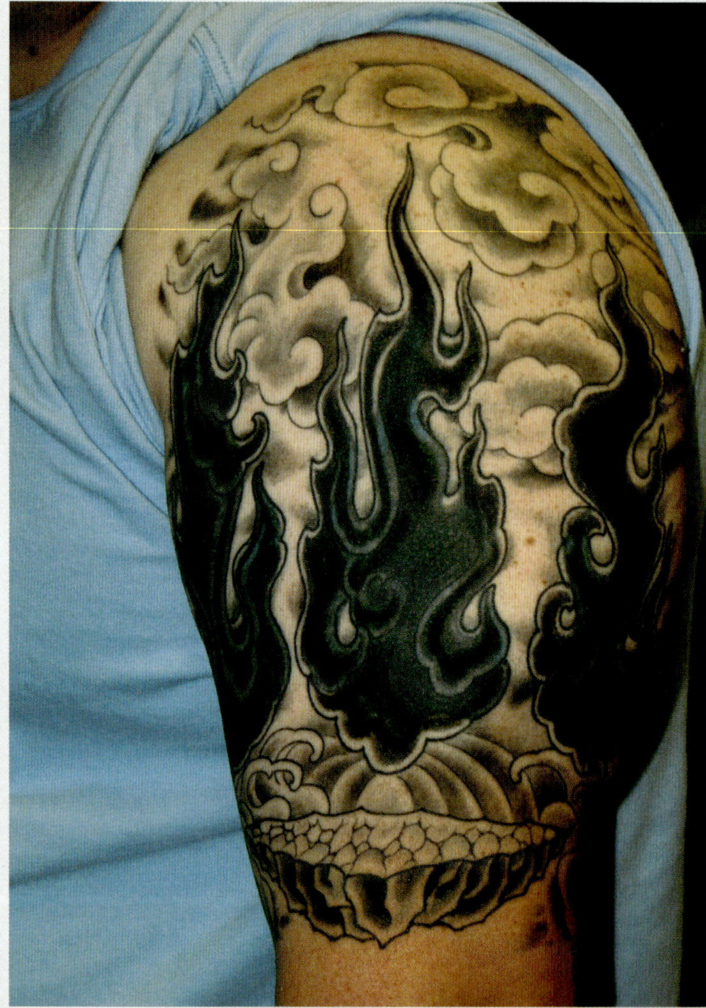
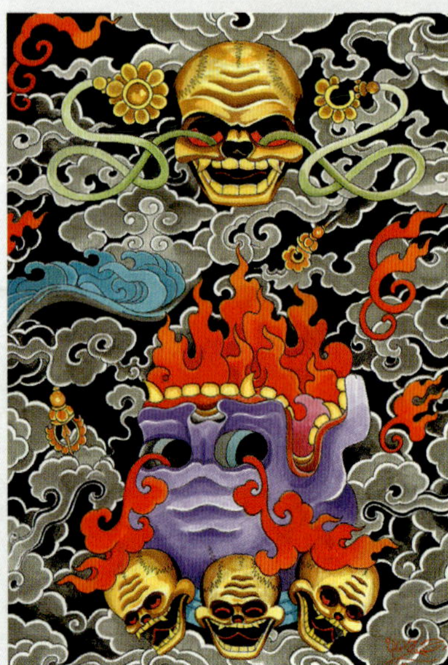
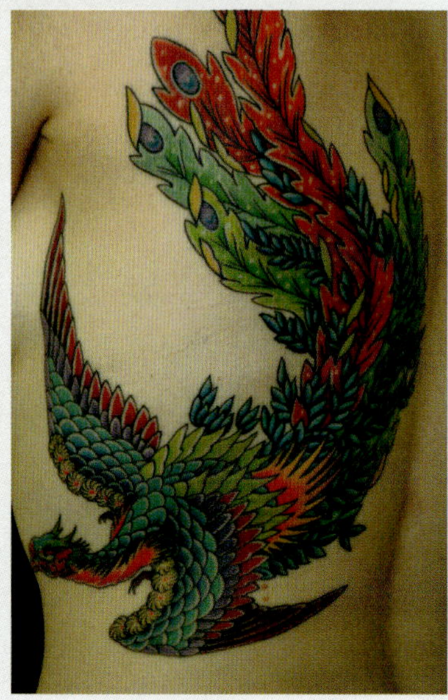
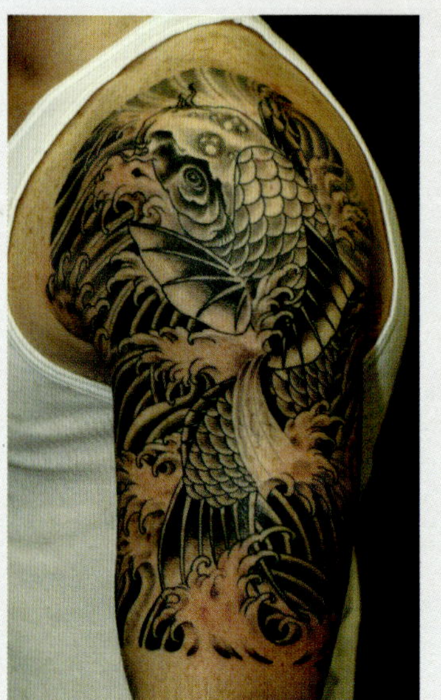
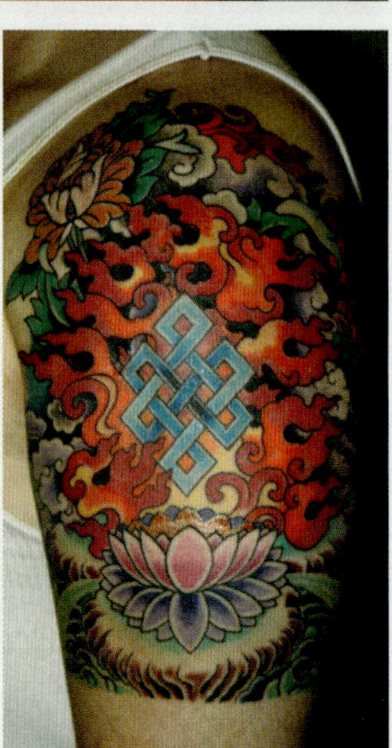
All artwork by Yoni Zilber. Top left image: cover up by Yoni Zilber.

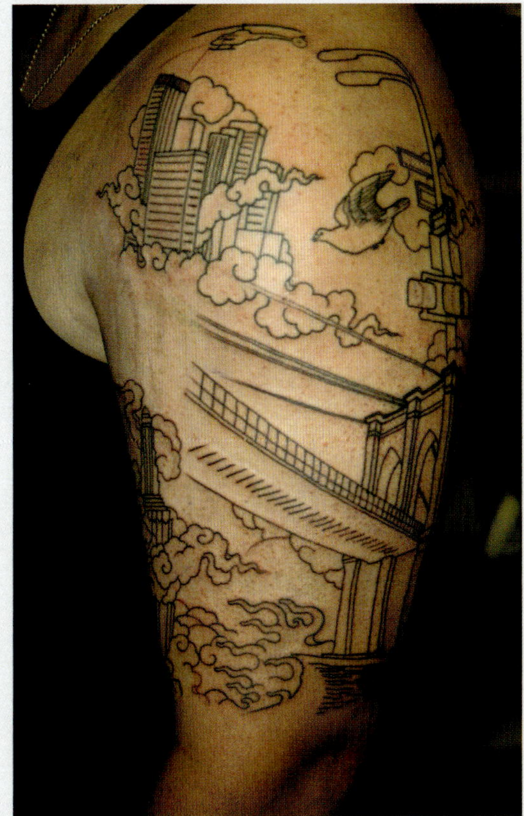

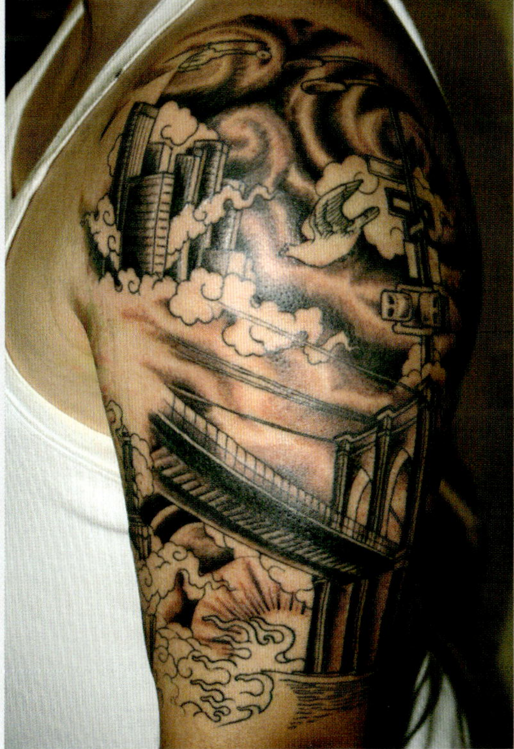

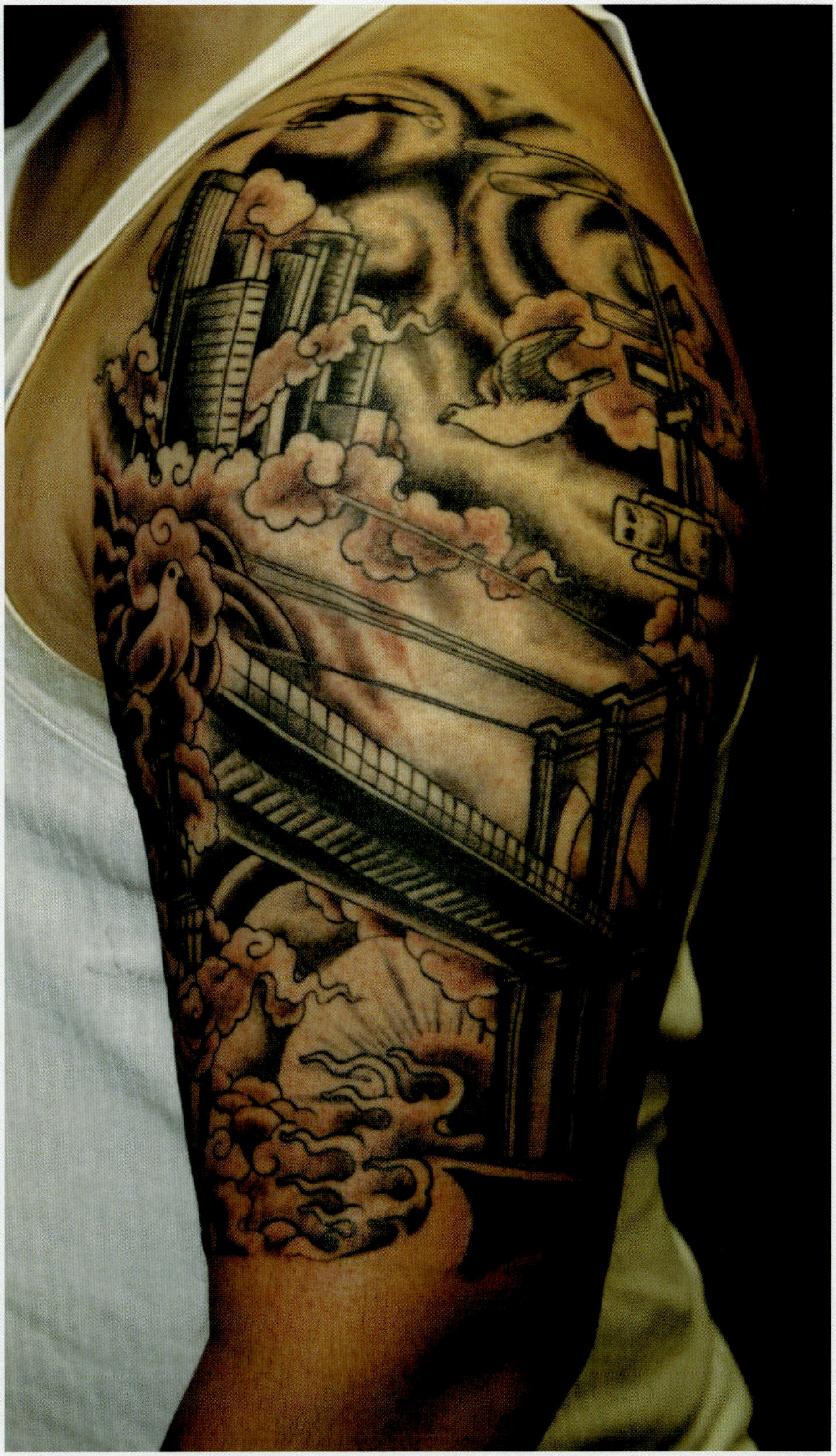

Step by step of a tattoo design by Yoni Zilber.

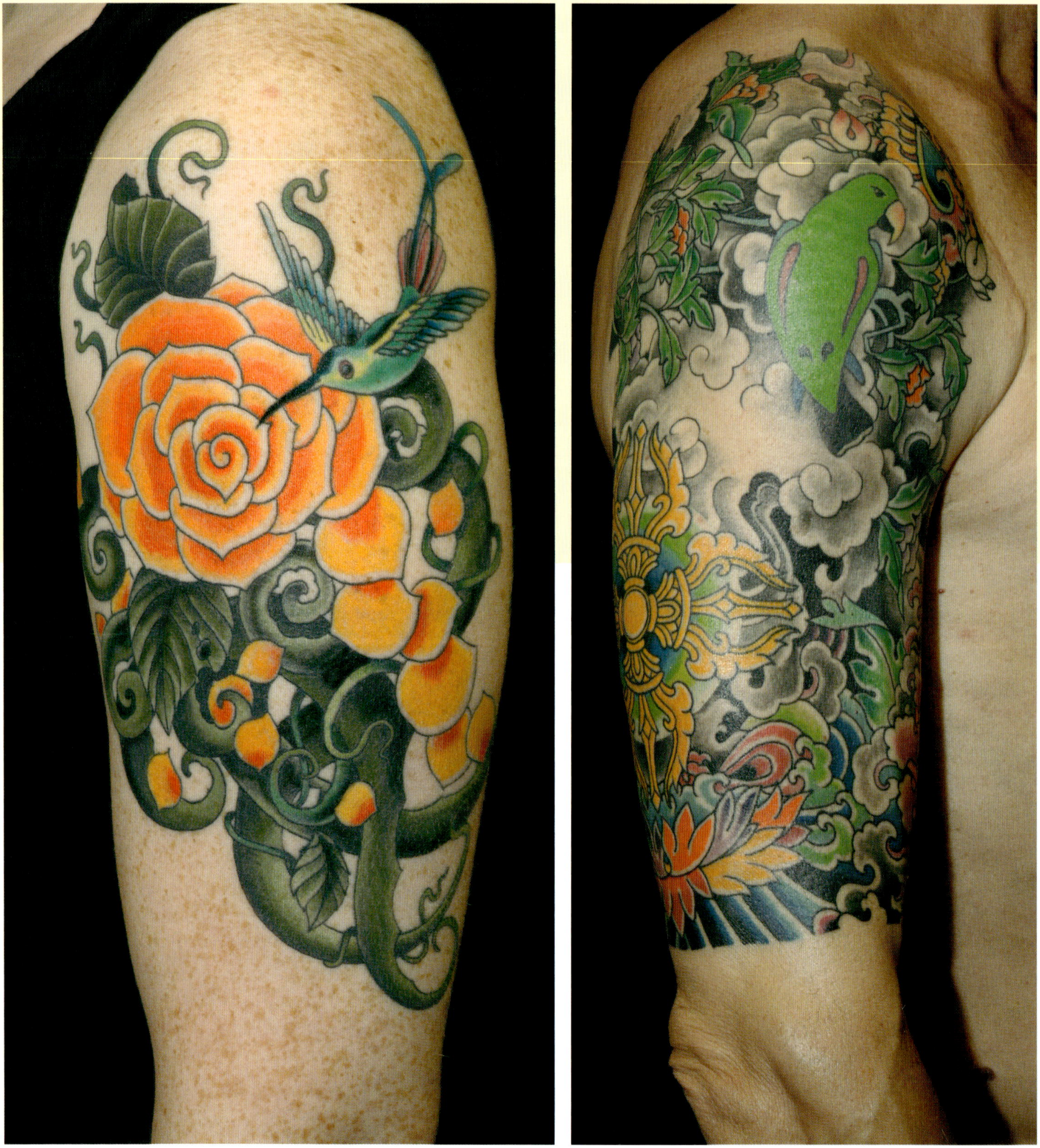

Images courtesy of Yoni Zilber.

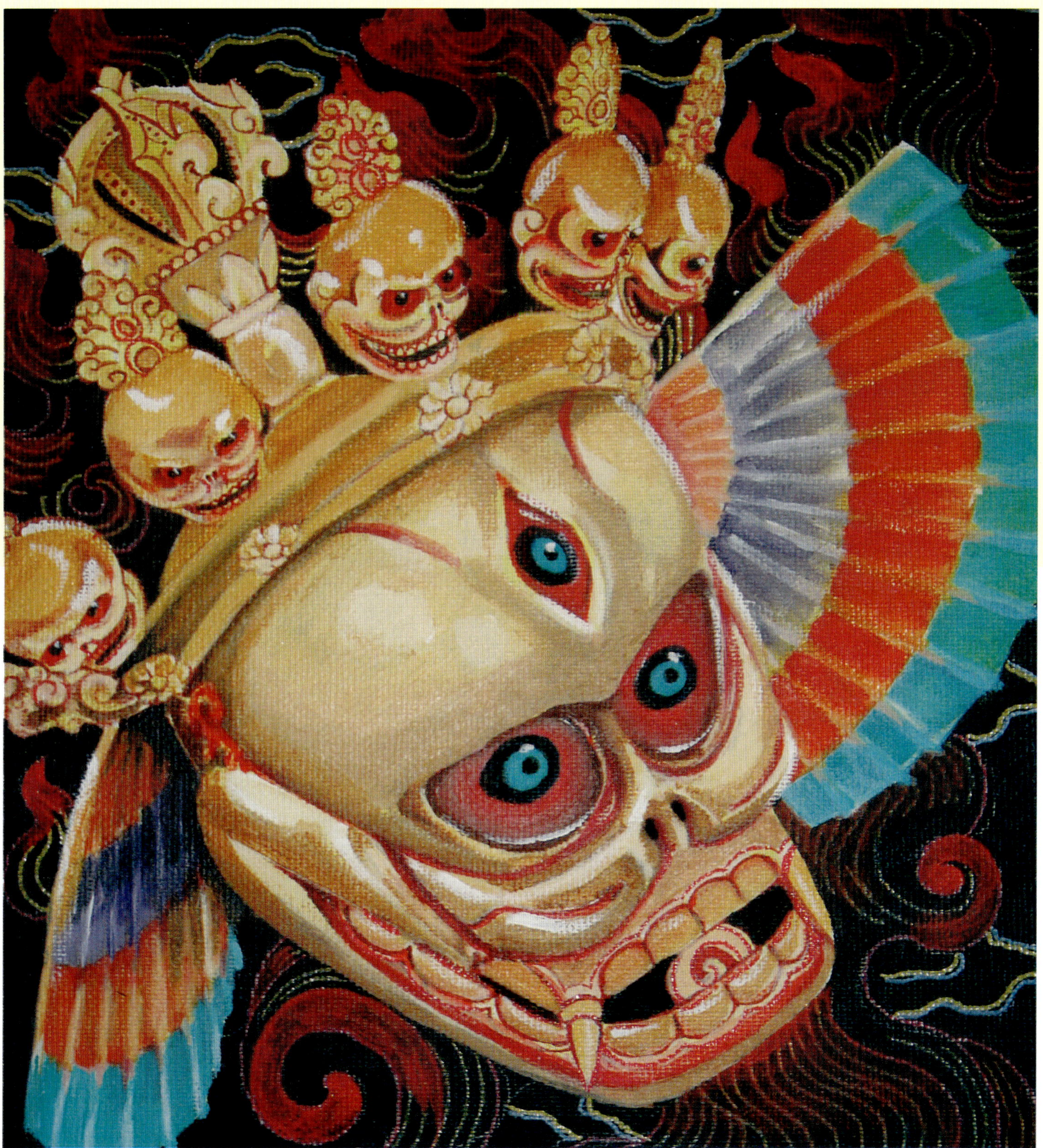

Illustration courtesy of Yoni Zilber.

YONI ZILBER

CÁMARA TATTOO

SPAIN

1. I have enjoyed drawing ever since I was a child, and I always felt attracted to the art of decorating the body. I got my start as a professional tattooist seven years ago, and I work in my own studio.

2. It is a very complex art that commands my respect. I work with the idea that my client brings me, but I personalize it to achieve a good result. This is my form of artistic expression.

3. I don't close myself off from any style; I like to experiment and try the variations that tattooing can afford me. I feel very comfortable with the tattoos I've done. Really, there is no one style with which I identify a hundred percent.

4. Hygiene and the client's comfort are necessary conditions. You should always be sure about the design you have chosen and educate the client about the healing process.

5. My tattoo and piercing studio is located in Esplugues de Llobregat, Barcelona. I look forward to your visit.

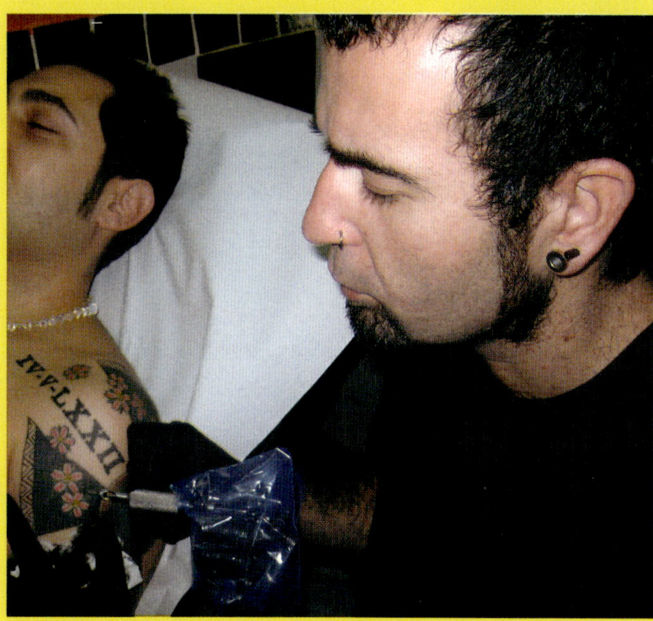

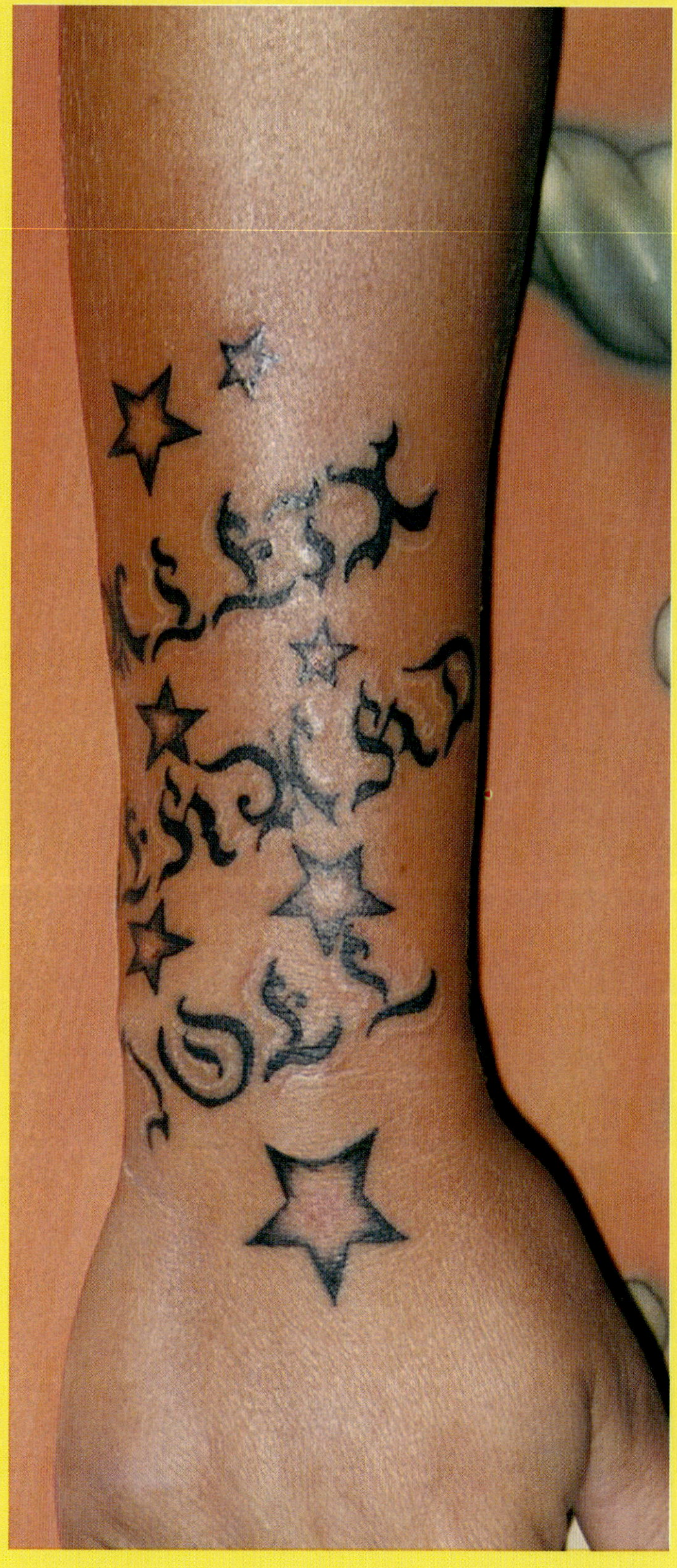

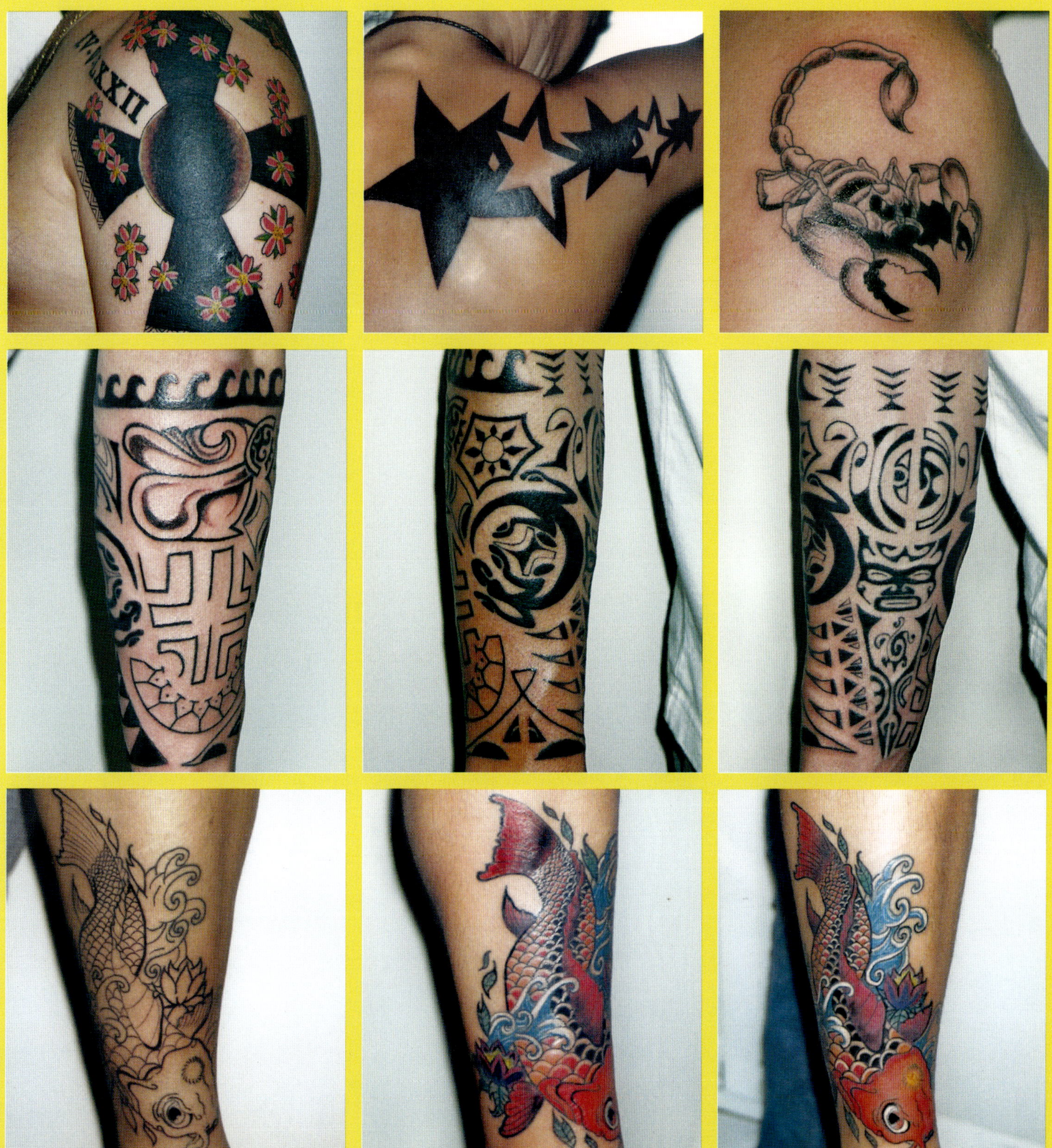

All images courtesy of Cámara Tattoo.

JOEL D. LONG

USA

1. I started tattooing in Atlanta, Georgia with the help of my good friend Bruce Chung. After working in Atlanta for about three years, I moved to Miami Beach, Florida to work for Ken Cameron at South Beach Tattoo. I worked there for about seven years. Now I work at Bolder Ink in Boulder, Colorado and have been there for about five years.

2. I do Japanese and American traditional and maybe a little weirdo art in between. But sticking with tradition and going from there is definitely a strong foundation; from there you can figure it out.

3. I tend to specialize in larger scale Japanese tattooing, as my main goal is to do traditional Japanese body suits. I also enjoy doing American traditional and tattoos of eagles, sharks, skulls, roses and daggers.

4. Well, if you really want to make tattoos, you kind of need to be able to talk to people, not get tired of drawing, not be afraid of blood, and be ready to sacrifice some other things you like doing in order to be a better tattooist.

5. I can be found in Boulder, Colorado or at www.joeldlong.com

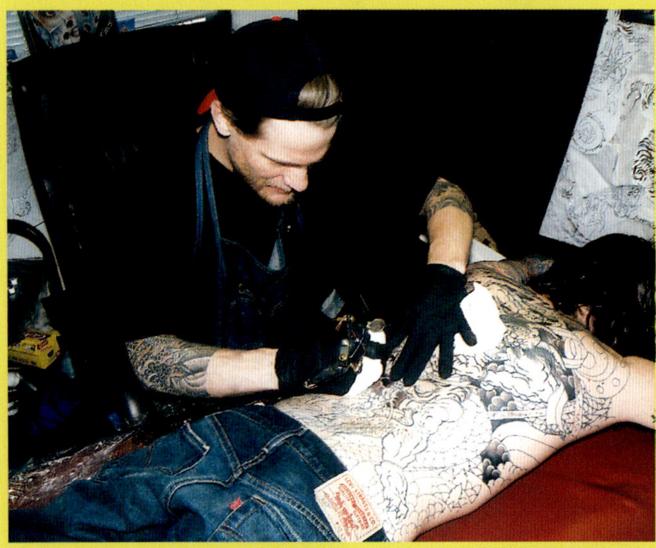

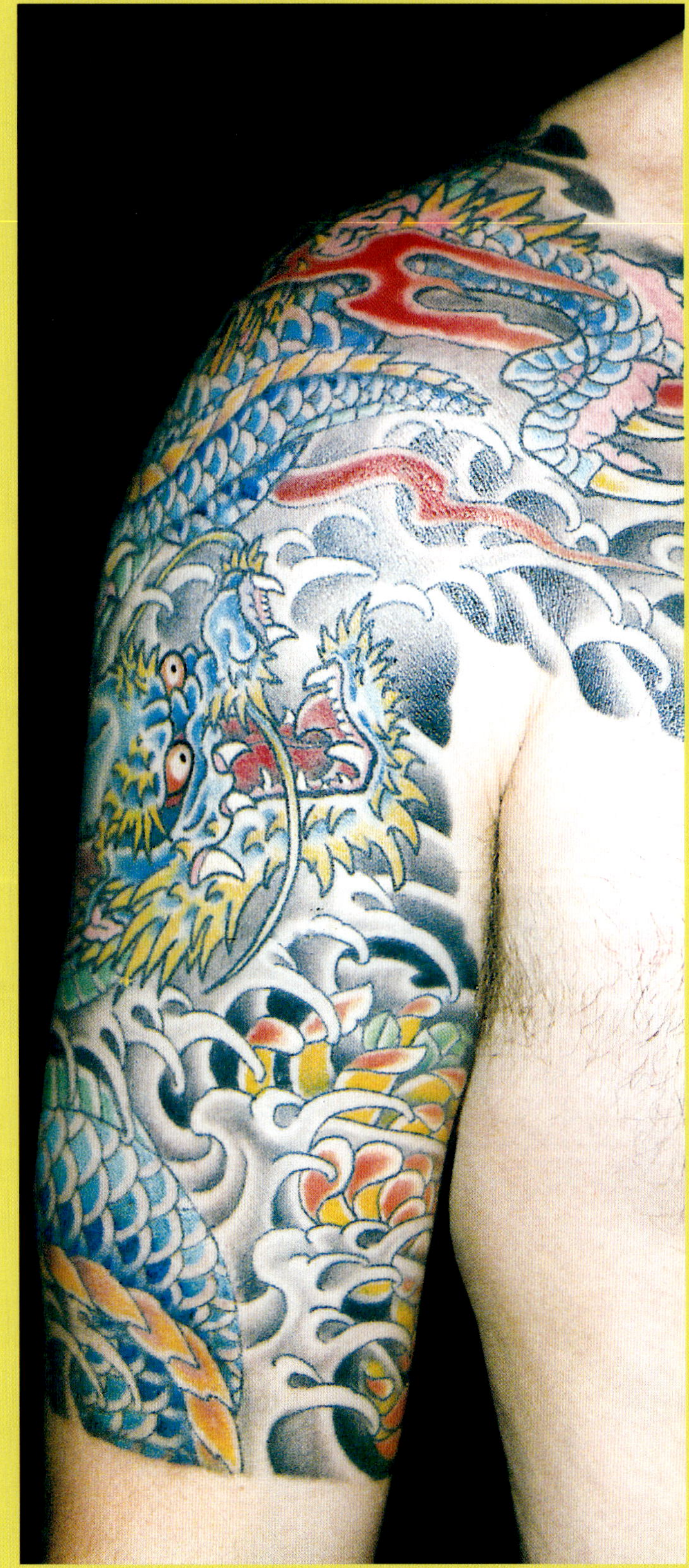

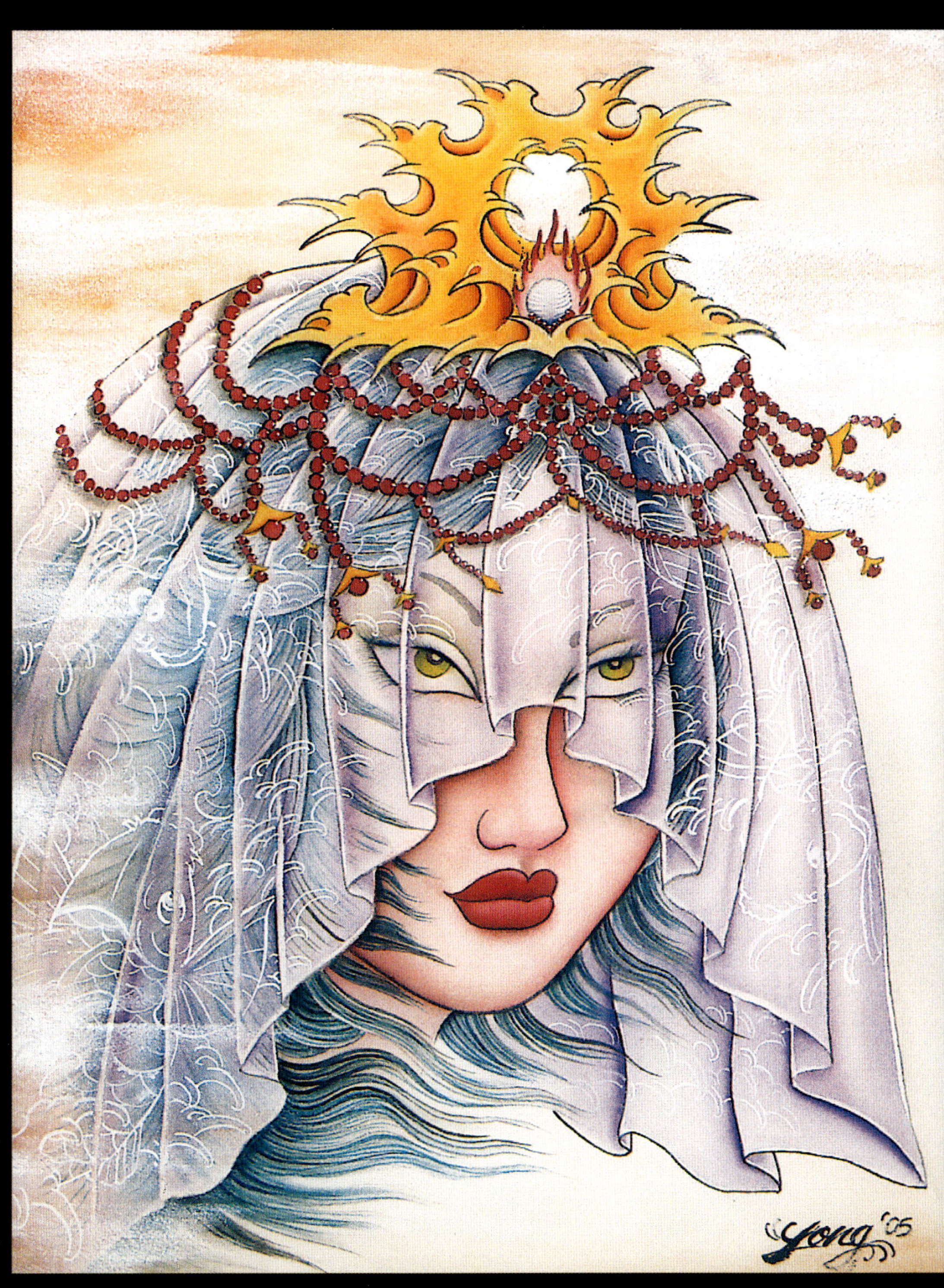

All designs on these pages by Joel D. Long.

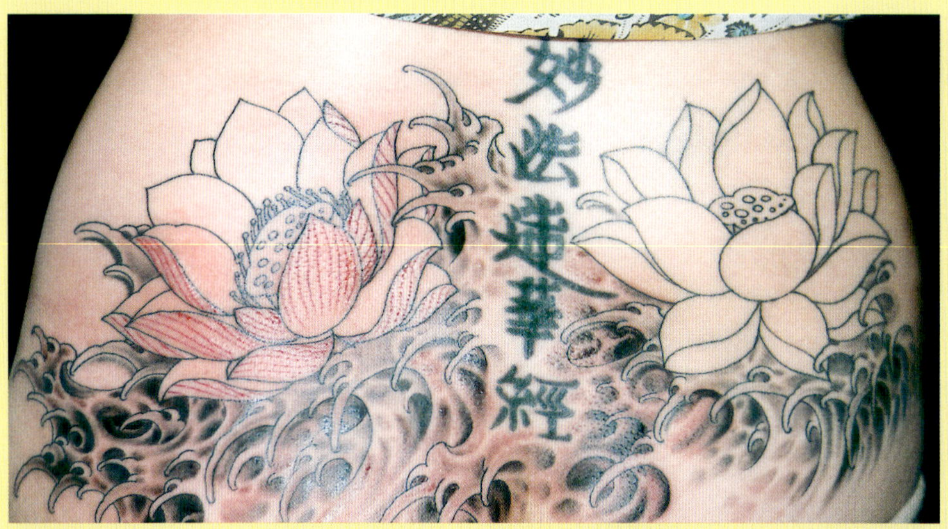

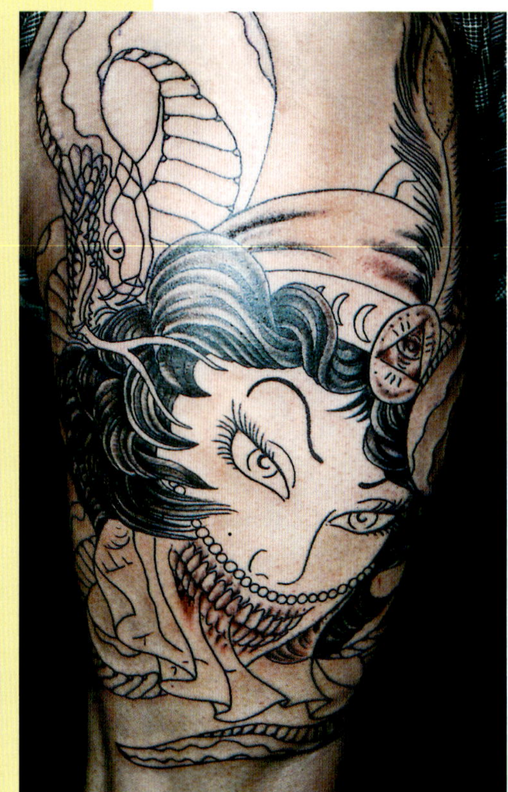

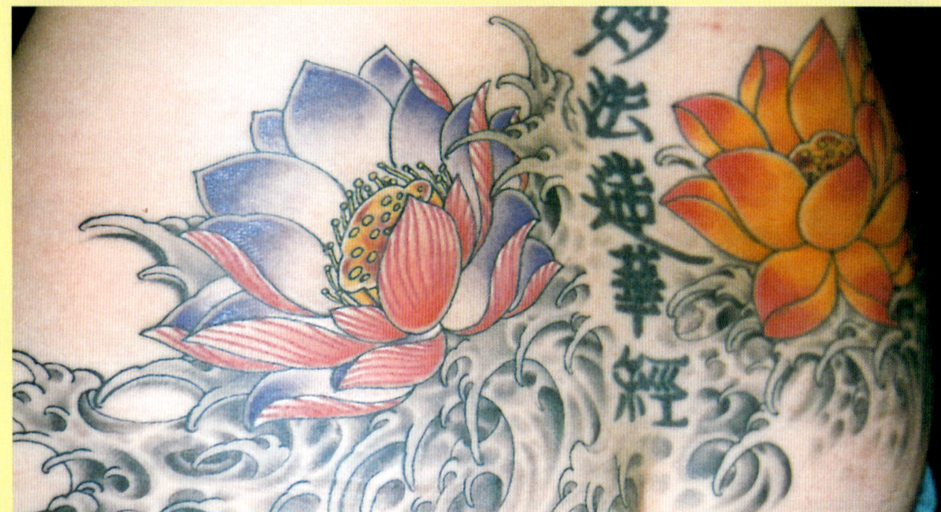

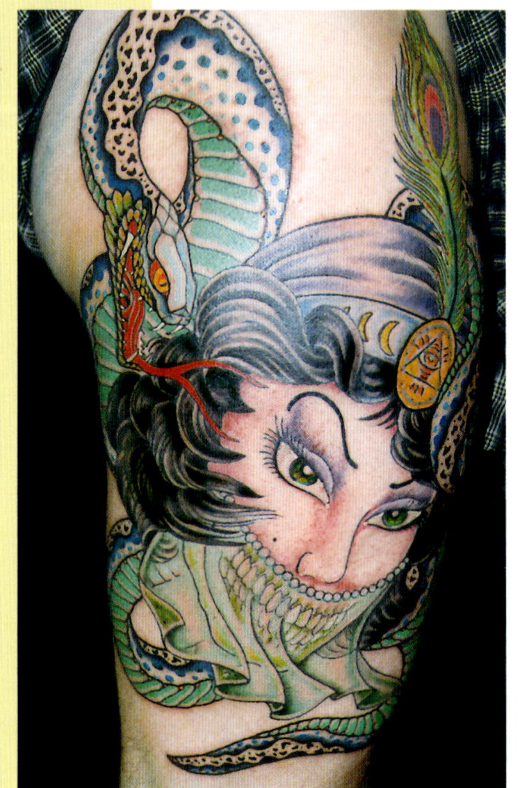

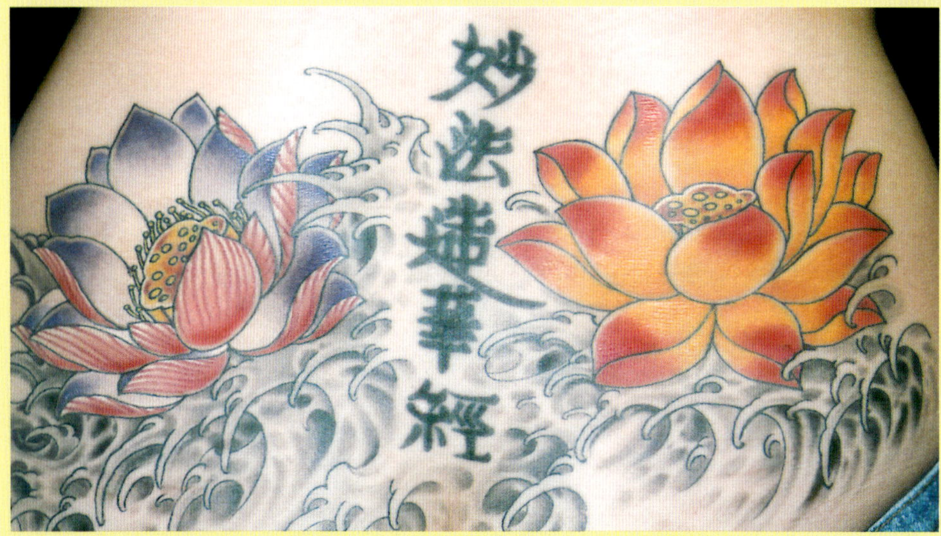

All artwork courtesy of Joel D. Long.

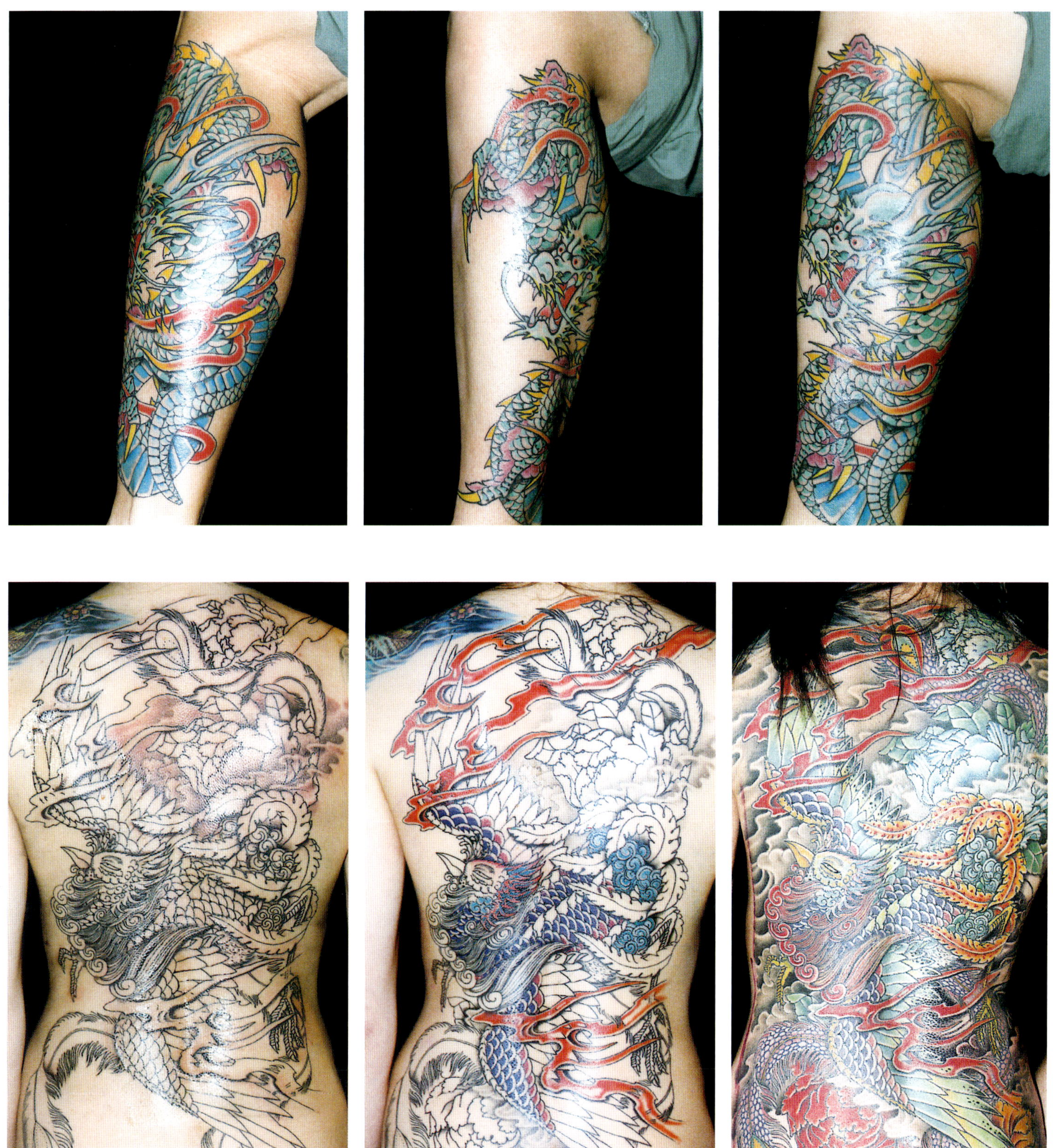

Step by step of a tattoo design by Joel D. Long.

JOEL D. LONG

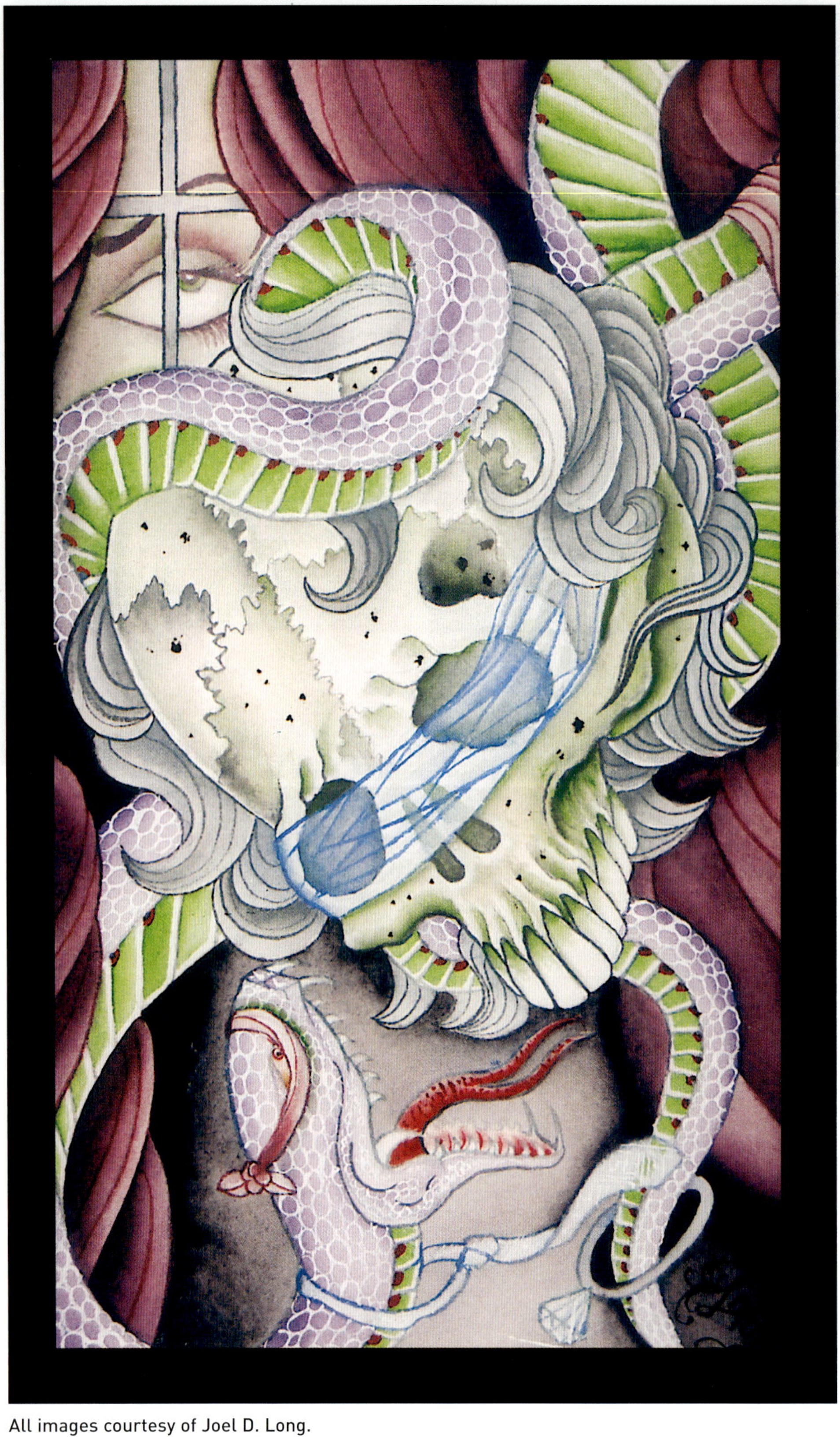

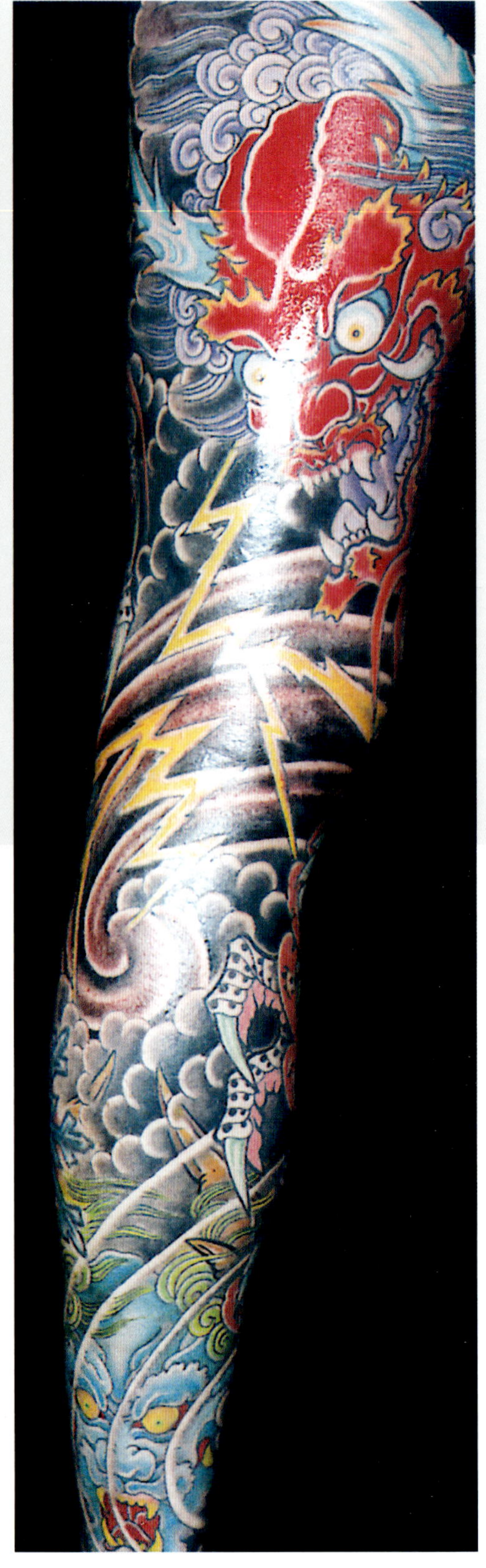

All images courtesy of Joel D. Long.

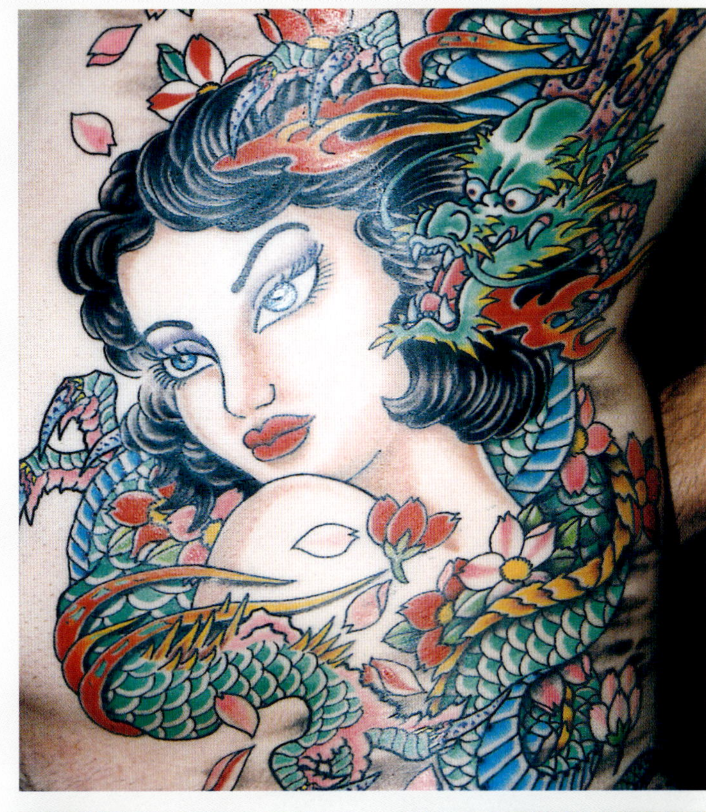

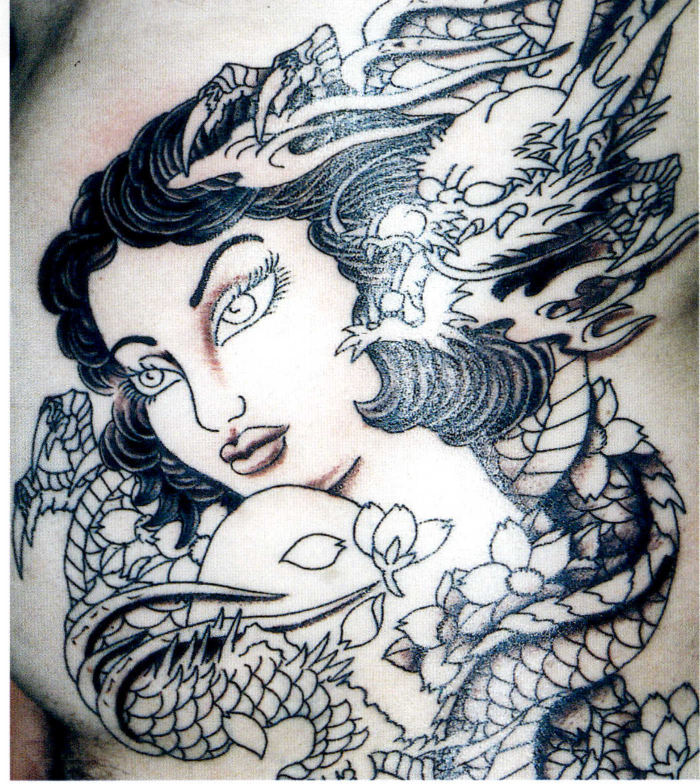

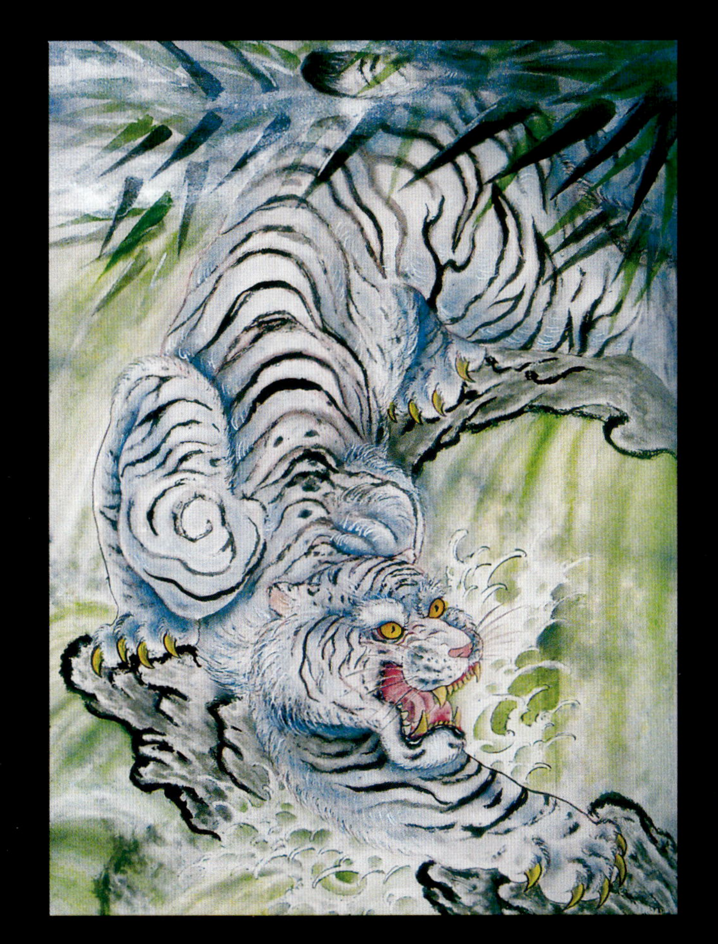

JOEL D. LONG

JOAO PAULO RODRIGUES

BRAZIL

1. I was fascinated by my dad's tattoo. After a couple years, I was in a band and was getting tattooed by my friend, and he offered to teach me how to tattoo in Brazil. Then I moved to New York City to continue learning in the biggest city in the world.

2. Tattooing can be seen from any different point of view. For me, it is a memento of a time in your life and a connection between friends or clients that is impossible to break.

3. My preference is Japanese because the highest challenge a tattooist can face is a body suit, which is well-suited for the Japanese style. I am also very fascinated by traditional American and tribal, both of which are very difficult to tailor a body suit to.

4. I think people should research a lot before getting tattooed, not just the subject matter but the personality, character and sympathy with the tattooist. You will be carrying the tattoo for the rest of your life.

5. Since moving from Rio de Janeiro seven years ago, I have been working at Rising Dragon Tattoos in New York City.
   My personal website is www.jprodrigues.com

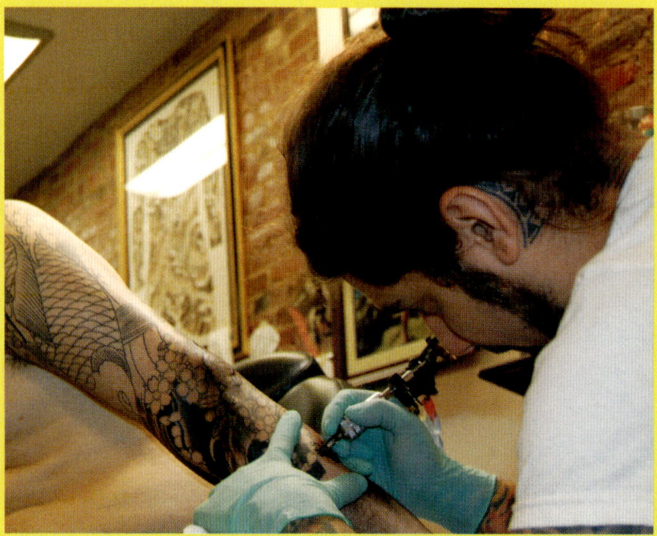

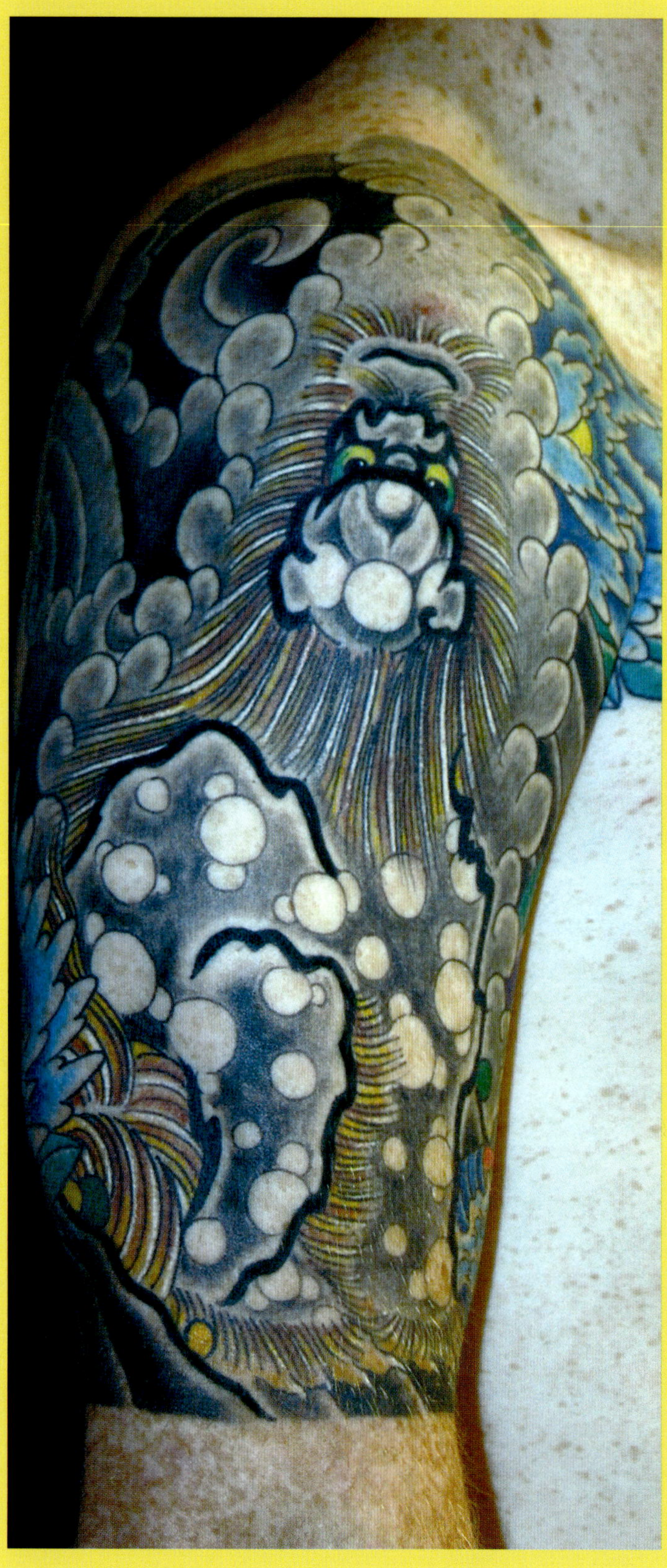

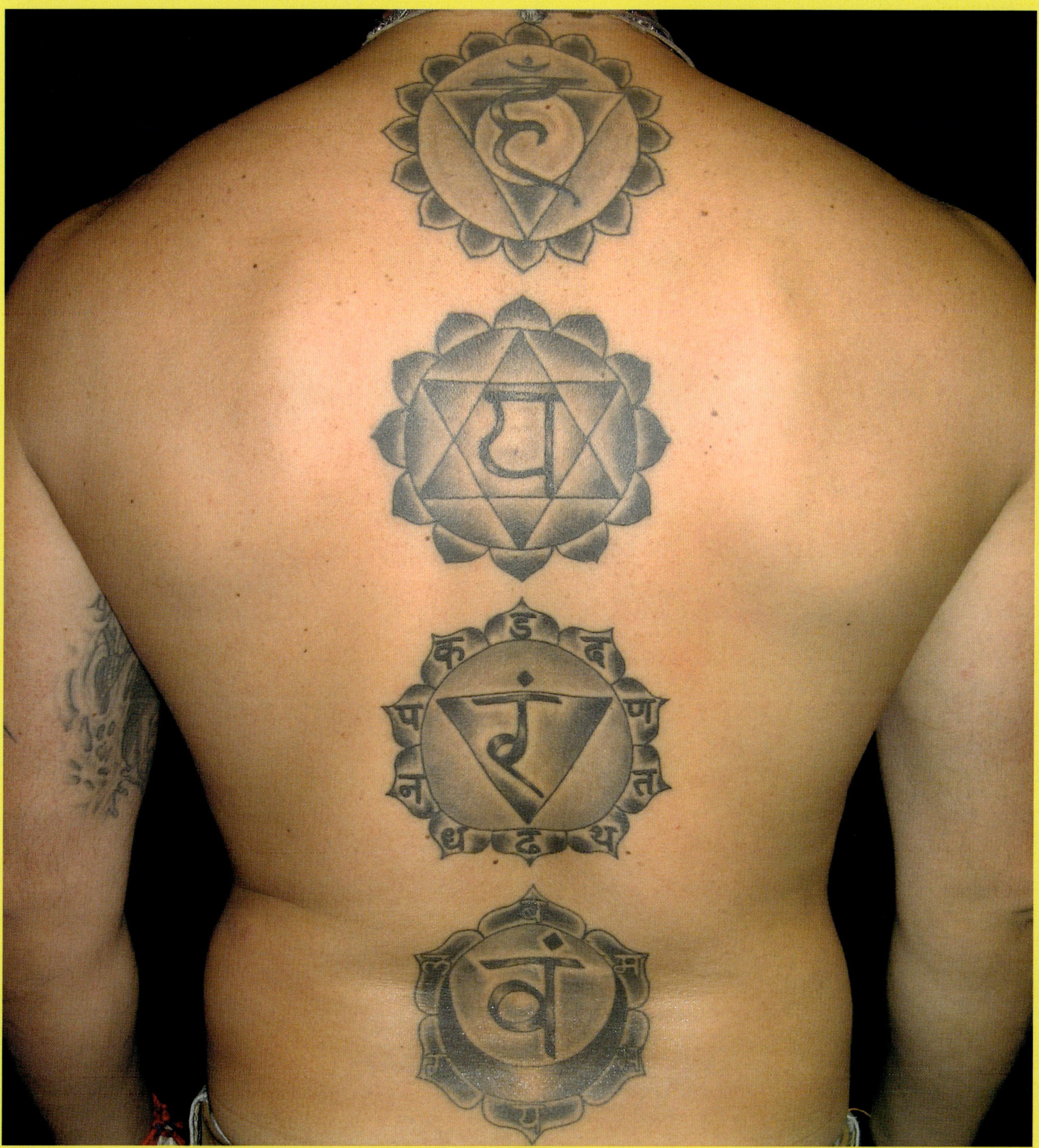

Images courtesy of Joao Paulo Rodrigues.

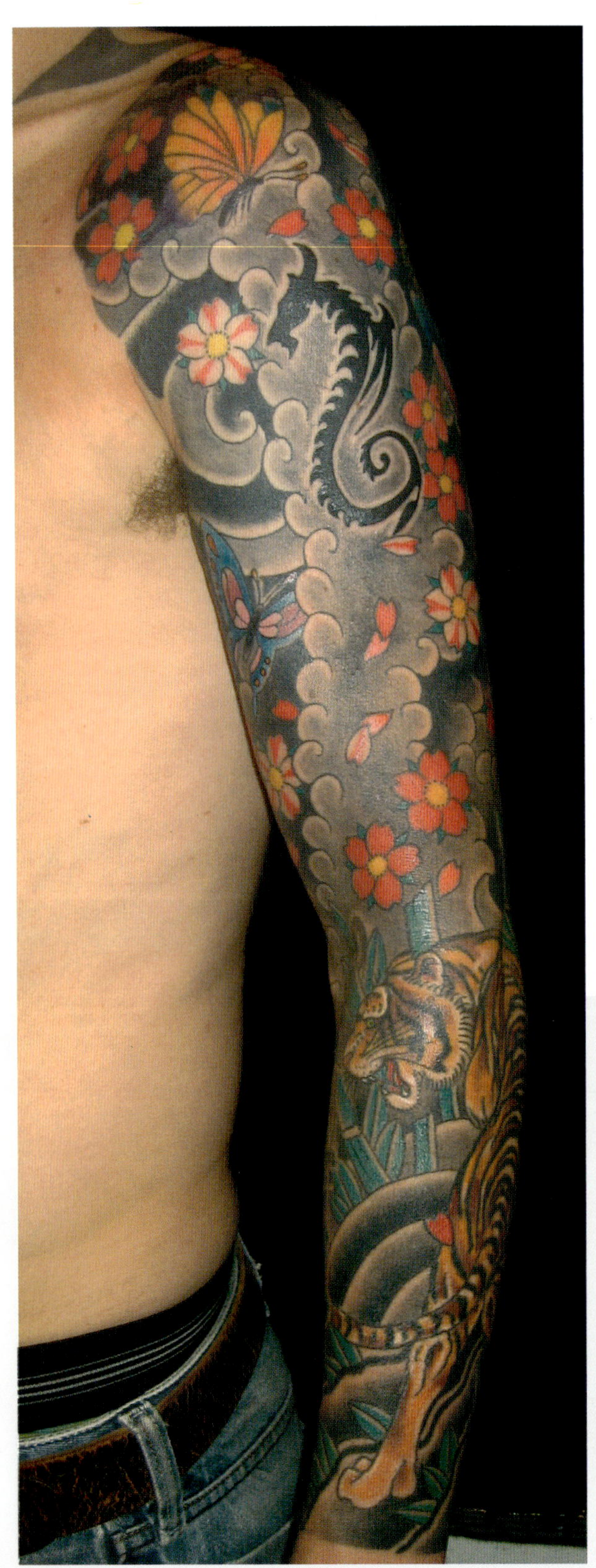

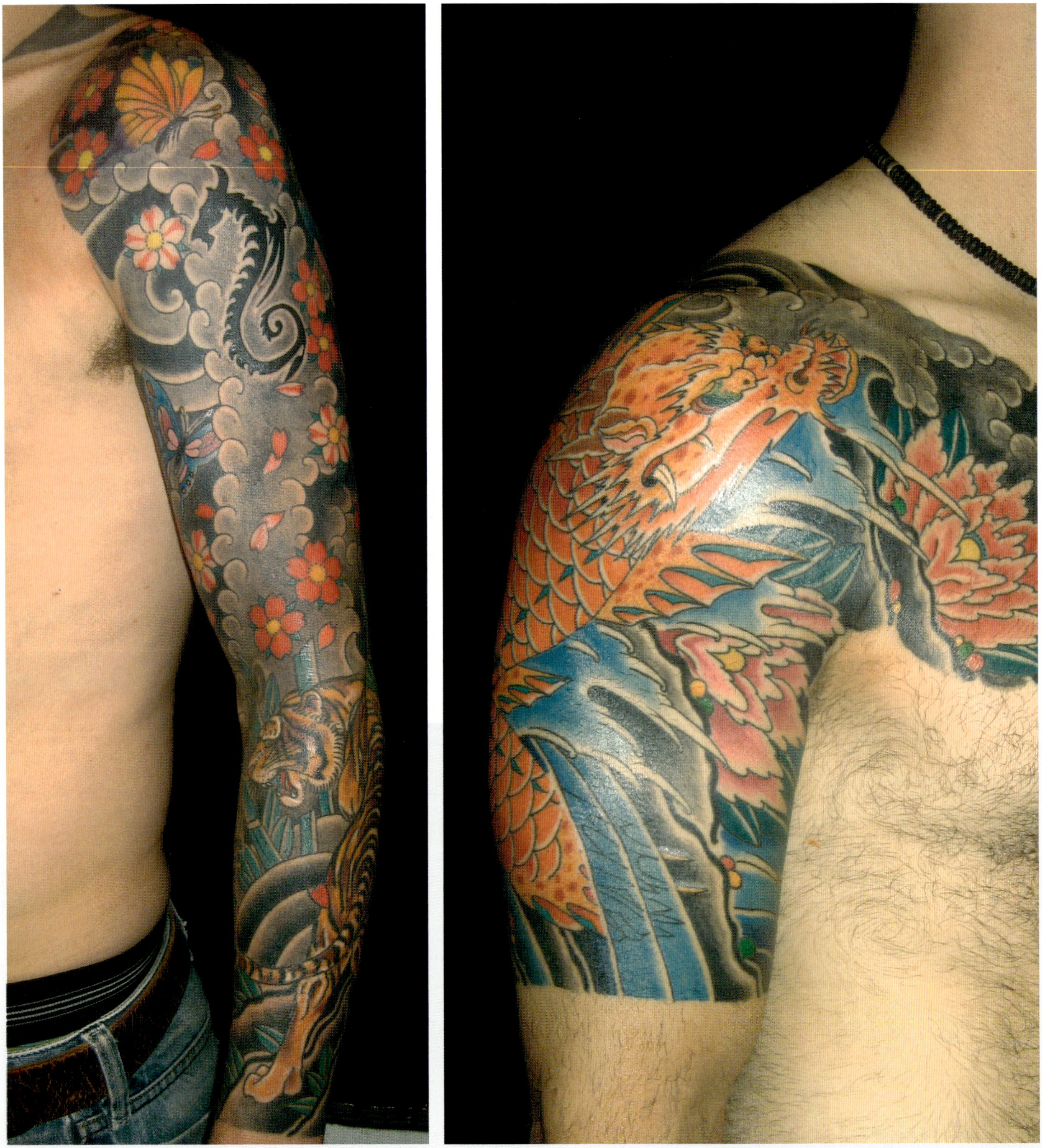

All designs on these pages by Joao Paulo Rodrigues.

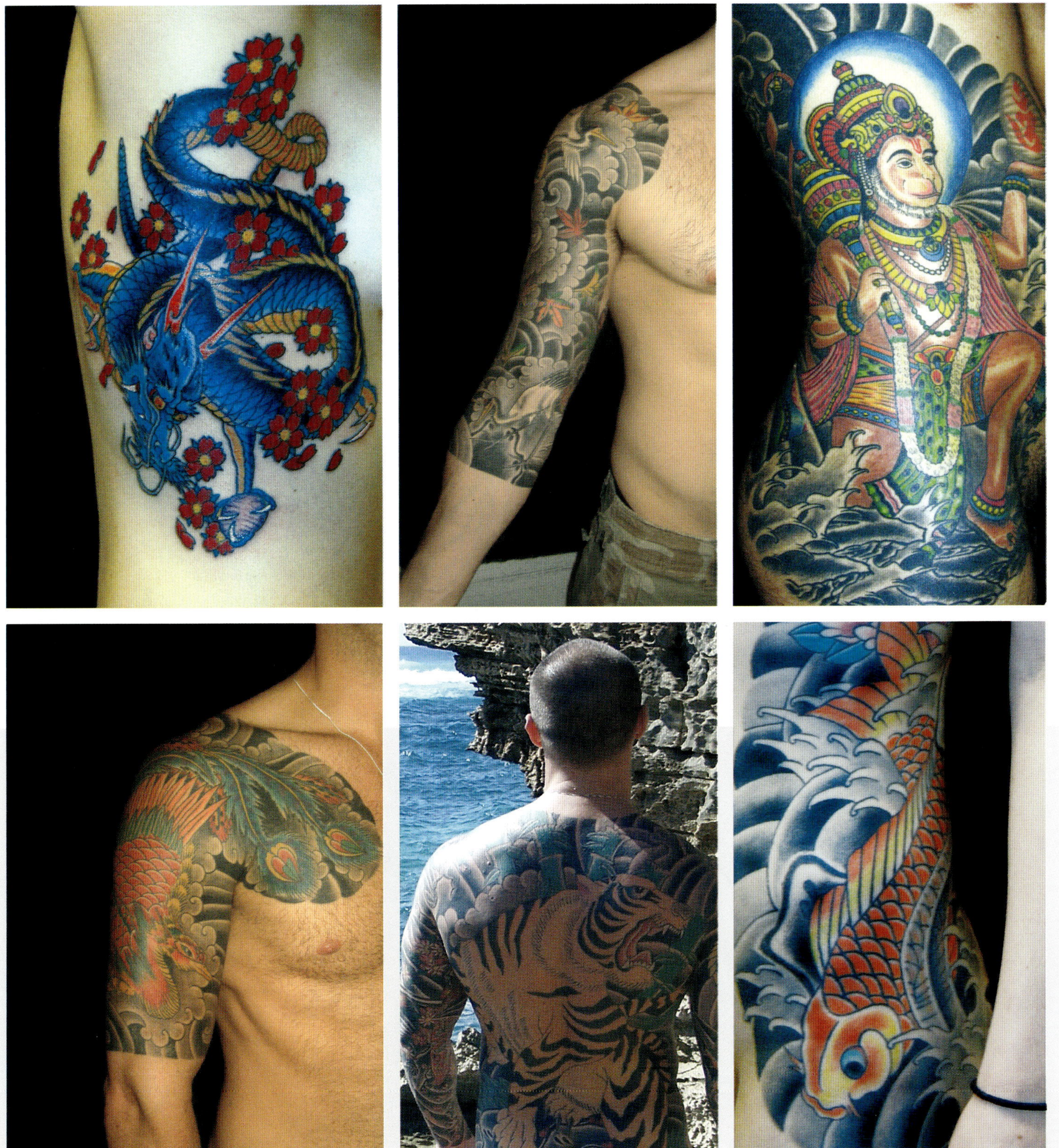

JOAO PAULO RODRIGUES

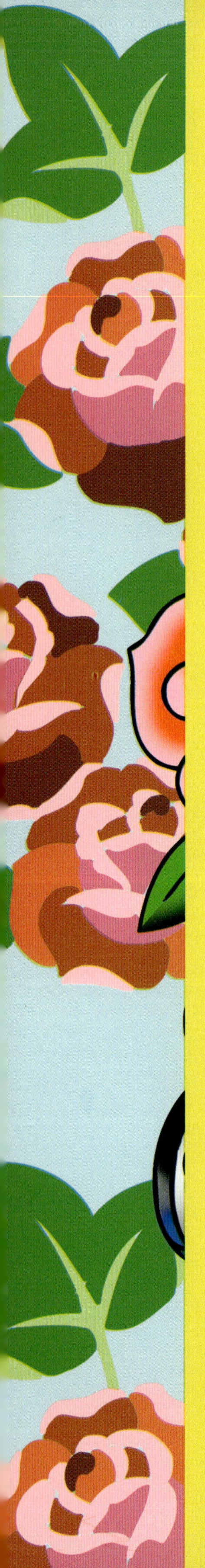
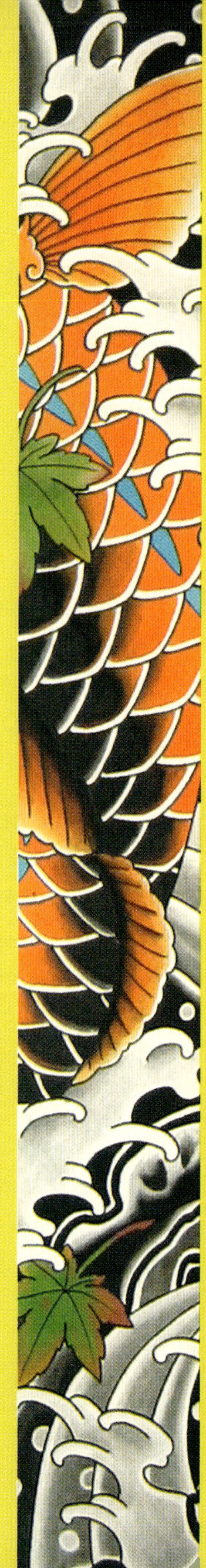
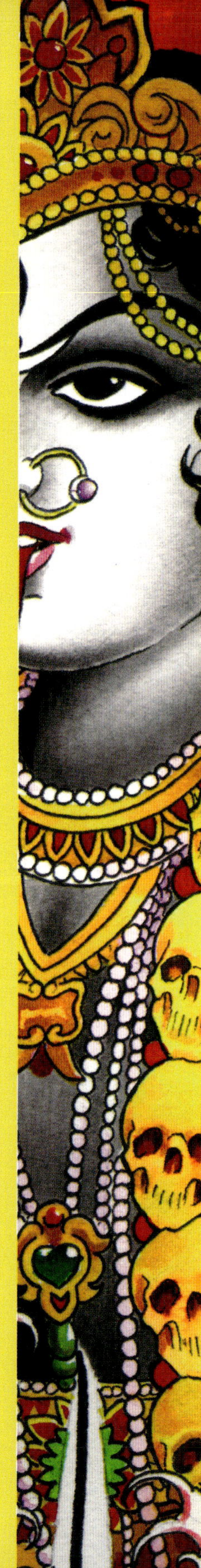
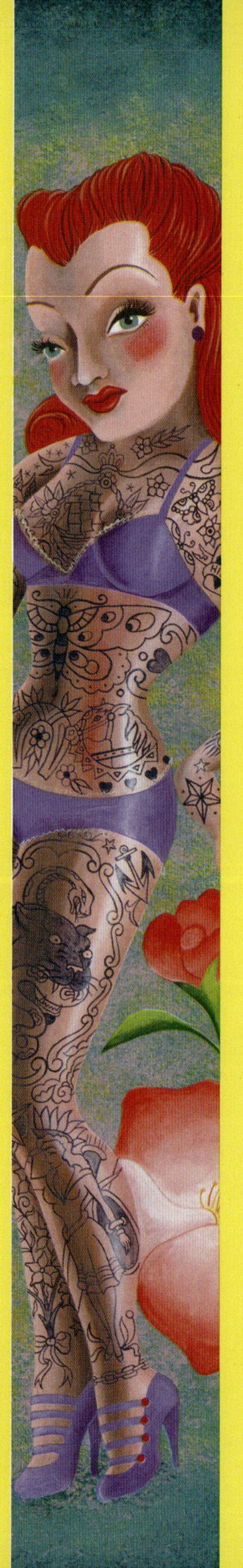

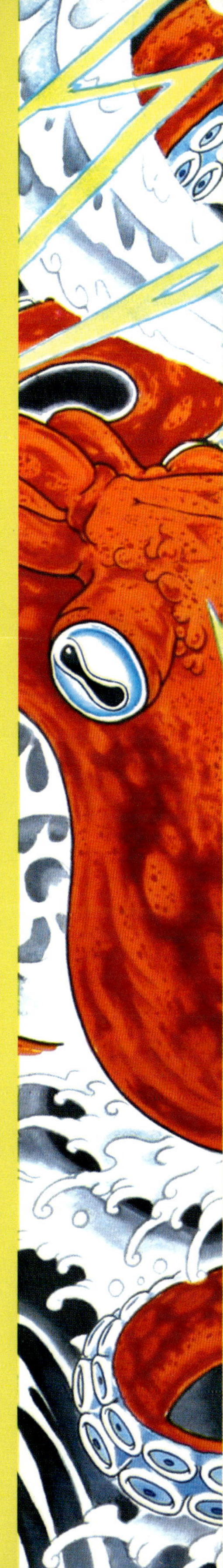
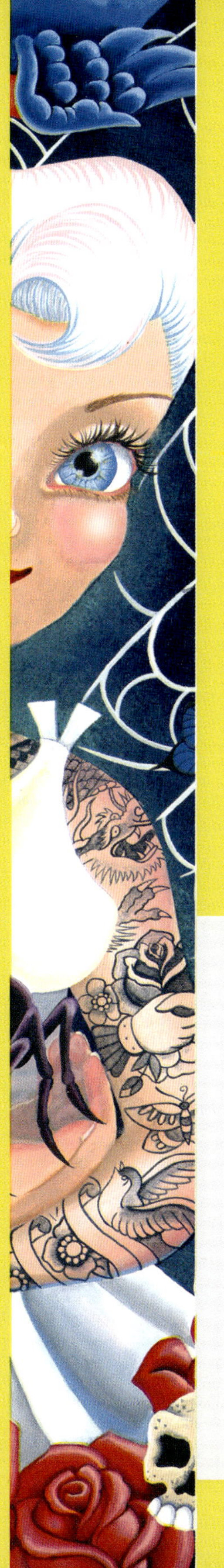
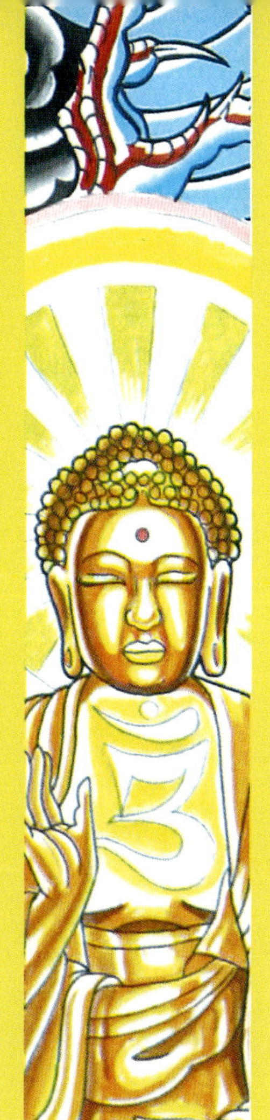
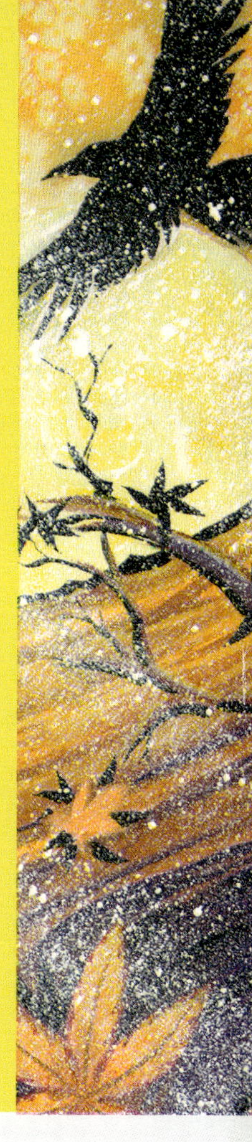

THANKS

I would like to thank to all the tattooers for their collaboration and big help, and to all the people involved, one way or another, in this book who have been indispensable in the making of this amazing project. Thank you!

Eva Minguet

Page 192 tattoo by Aaron Della Vedova of Guru Tattoo.

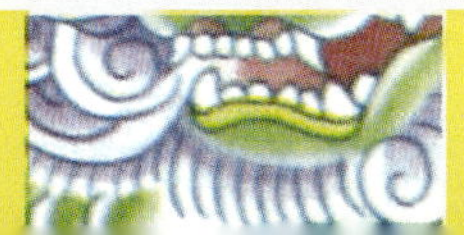
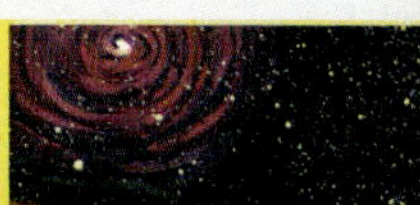

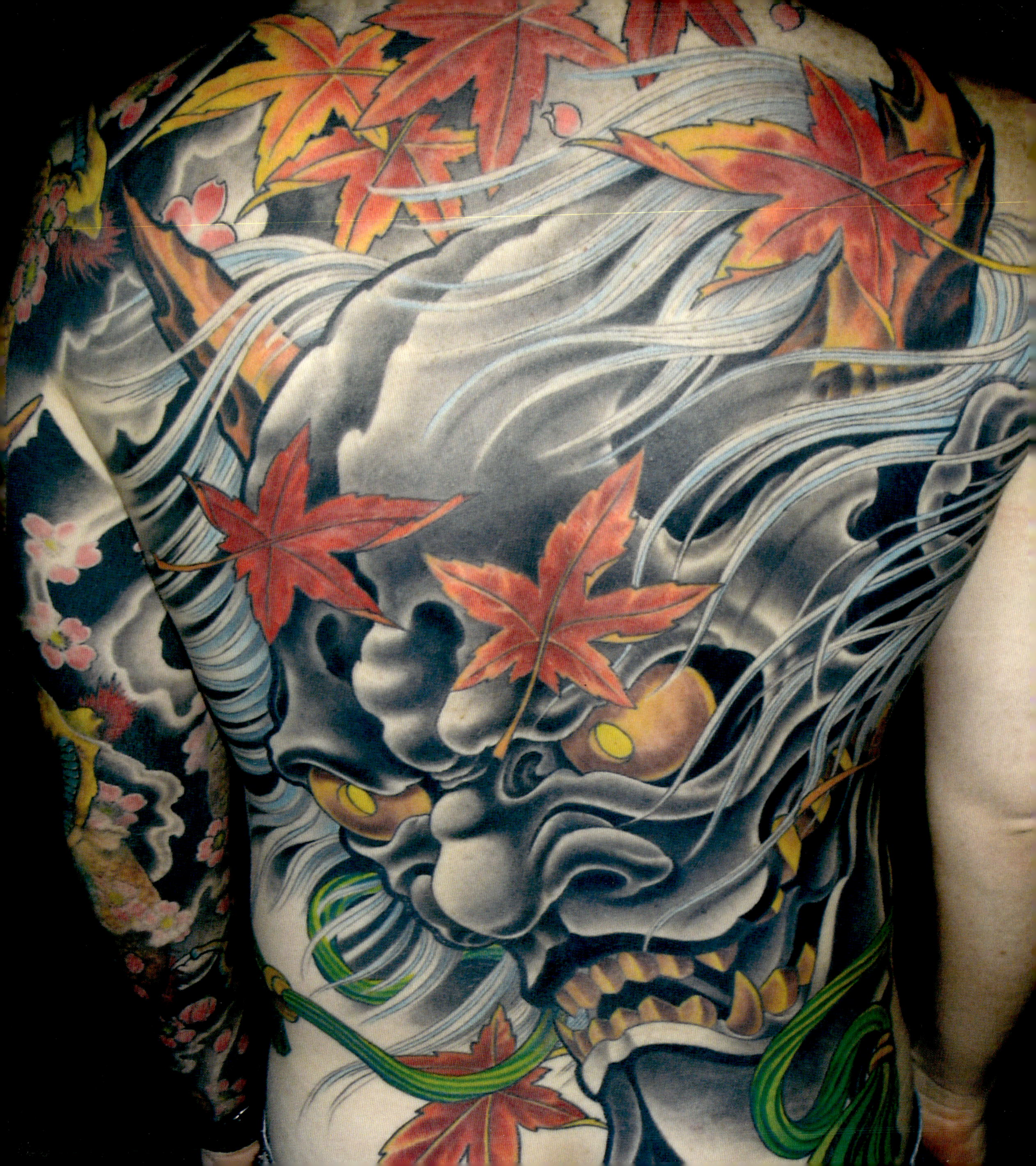